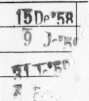

THE
LOOM
OF
HISTORY

Books by Herbert J. Muller

THE SPIRIT OF TRAGEDY

THE USES OF THE PAST

THOMAS WOLFE

SCIENCE AND CRITICISM

MODERN FICTION

THE
LOOM
OF
HISTORY

───────

by

HERBERT J. MULLER

ILLUSTRATED

HARPER & BROTHERS

Publishers • New York

The Historic Theme of East an

A NOTE FROM
HERBERT J. MULLER

THIS BOOK DEVELOPS the historic theme of East and West. This is a much-abused theme, commonly over-simplified by the prejudices of the West; the earnest talk about One World is still clouded by the notion that never the twain shall meet, or always the West shall win. Nevertheless it remains a basic theme, of major importance: one that the chronicler cannot escape, nor the philosopher afford to ignore. It provides, I believe, the most illuminating approach to the history of our civilization, and to all conjecture about the progress of the human spirit.

For this purpose Asia Minor is an ideal subject. Throughout history it has been the great bridge between East and West, and repeatedly the battleground. Here, not in mainland Greece, the Greeks first developed their brilliant civilization, and the Greek spirit gave rise to the West. As an ancient land swarming with diverse peoples, Asia Minor stimulated the adventurous Greeks and contributed much to their culture. It continued to attract other peoples from Europe and from the East, notably the Persians. It became the scene of the first great campaign of Alexander the Great, as he set out to overthrow the Persian Empire and to Hellenize the East. Later it became the richest province of the Roman Empire, then the heart of the Ottoman Empire. It witnessed the rise of Christianity, and then of Islam. Hittites, Phrygians, Ioanians, Assyrians, Lydians, Persians, Armenians, Gauls, Romans, Goths, Arabs, Seljuks, Frankish Crusaders, Ottoman Turks—these and many lesser peoples have settled in it or swept over it, all leaving their mark.

The story of Asia Minor is fascinating simply as drama, and deserves to be told for its own sake. No other region of the world has known a more richly varied, continuously dramatic history. Everywhere are the remains of magical cities—Troy and Tarsus, Pergamum and Ephesus, Nicaea

Contents

Appendix   373

Illustrations

---

xi

The harbor of Bodrum

Site of the Byzantine Hippodrome

Gate of the Seljuk Mosque of Ince Minare in Konya

Seljuk khan at Caesarea

Kiz Kalesi ("Maiden's Castle"), off the Cilician coast

Panaya Kapulu, the home of the Virgin Mary in Ephesus

Yerebatan Saray ("Cistern Basilica") in Istanbul

The Bosphorus from Rumeli Hisar, the castle built by Mohammed the Conqueror

Hagia Sophia, interior

Except where otherwise indicated with the illustrations, the photographs were provided by courtesy of the Turkish Government, through its Embassy in London, its Information Office in New York, and its Tourist Bureau in Istanbul.

Preface

THIS BOOK is an outgrowth of a previous work, *The Uses of the Past*, illustrating these uses by studies in the history of Asia Minor. In general, it develops the same "tragic view" of history, stressing the inevitable ambiguities and incongruities in the same spirit of reverence and of irony, deliberately complicating the major issues in order to deepen and toughen the same humanistic faith. In particular, it develops the historic theme of East and West. This is a much-abused theme, commonly oversimplified by the prejudices of the West; the earnest talk about One World is still clouded by the notion that never the twain shall meet, or always the West must win. Nevertheless it remains a basic theme, of major importance: one that the chronicler cannot escape, nor the philosopher afford to ignore. It provides, I believe, the most illuminating approach to the history of our civilization, and to all conjecture about the progress of the human spirit.

For this purpose Asia Minor is an ideal subject. Throughout history it has been the great bridge between East and West, and repeatedly the battleground. Here, not in mainland Greece, the Greeks first developed their brilliant civilization, and the Greek spirit gave rise to the West. As an ancient land swarming with diverse peoples, Asia Minor stimulated the adventurous Greeks and contributed much to their culture. It continued to attract other peoples from Europe and from the East, notably the Persians. It became the scene of the first great campaign of Alexander the Great, as he set out to overthrow the Persian Empire and to Hellenize the East. Later it became the richest province of the Roman Empire, then the heart of the Byzantine Empire, then the heart of the Ottoman Empire. It witnessed the rise of Christianity, and then of Islam. Hittites, Phrygians, Ionians, Assyrians, Lydians, Persians, Armenians, Gauls, Romans, Goths, Arabs, Seljuks, Frankish Crusaders, Ottoman Turks—these and many lesser peoples have settled in it or swept over it, all leaving their mark. Today, as the Turkey of Kemal Ataturk, it is the scene of an experiment as revolutionary as any in history. Resolved to Westernize the country, Ataturk set about making over its entire culture overnight.

In reviewing this history, I have chosen to concentrate on certain cities, as symbols of the major periods or cultures. This is a somewhat arbitrary design, and I have freely departed from it, using each city only as a focus or starting point of a wide-ranging discussion. Still, history is always made primarily in and by the city; it is the main scene of the commerce and industry that make civilization possible, and of the cultural activity that makes it manifest. In the form of the *polis,* it was especially characteristic of Greco-Roman civilization, which for my purposes is the most significant period in the history of Asia Minor. The many famous cities of this civilization were the conspicuous sign of its real glory and grandeur; and their death—the many sites once splendid but now desolate, with timeless shepherds grazing their flocks among ruins overgrown by thistles and blood-red poppies—is the most apparent reason for a tragic view of history. Even the arbitrary element in my scheme is appropriate in that it emphasizes a deliberate personal note. For this work is not a formal history of Asia Minor, much less a complete one. Although it is designed to inform the general reader about this history, it dwells only on the developments that to me seem most interesting and important, it is concerned more with reflection about fact than the fact itself, and it points to conclusions that I must believe are sound, but do not offer as the final or whole truth.

Or perhaps the real reason for my design is simply that I am fascinated by these cities. I have run the not too closely calculated risk of introducing considerable detail that may be more enchanting to me than to the reader. Yet the story of Asia Minor is fascinating simply as drama, and deserves to be told for its own sake. No other region in the world has known a more richly varied, continuously dramatic history. The land is dotted with mounds containing layers of towns that reach back to the Early Bronze Age. Everywhere are the remains of magical cities—Troy and Tarsus, Pergamum and Ephesus, Nicaea and Trebizond—haunted by memories of great doings and undoings, the ghosts of famous men. The modern railways still follow the routes of the royal roads of antiquity, the main trade routes to the East; so on any journey the traveler may be following in the footsteps of Xenophon and the Ten Thousand or Alexander the Great, of Pompey or St. Paul, of Harun al-Rashid or Frederick Barbarossa. And everywhere ancient marbles are embedded in the walls of village cottages or stables, memorials of long-vanished men who once strutted and fretted even as we. For me Asia Minor gives the most vivid, poignant sense of the "meaning" of human history, the ultimate theme of historian, philosopher, and poet alike—in the words of T. S. Eliot, "the boredom, and the horror, and the glory."

On all counts, I have concentrated on the western half of Asia Minor.

To the cities and peoples of the eastern regions I have given relatively little space—perhaps too little. An incidental excuse is that I have a limited first-hand knowledge of these regions, in which travel has been officially restricted for some years; foreigners have been prohibited from large areas designated as military defense zones, and discouraged from visiting other areas inhabited by the still surly Kurds. But in any case the west is historically much more interesting and important. It was here that the Greeks settled and built, and it remained the main stage of historic adventure and achievement—the horror and the glory—and the site of almost all the greater cities. Except for brief periods and some scattered cities, the east has been backward and relatively uncivilized, in some regions almost unexplored; throughout most of recorded history it served chiefly as a buffer or as a haven for nomads and mountain tribes. In recent years Turkish engineers prospecting for oil were amazed to find here some people who were still living in caves, and who were unacquainted with the wheel.

In an Appendix I have added short historical sketches of a number of important cities and peoples that I refer to only in passing in my main chapters. I recommend that those who are interested turn to these sketches upon finishing the chapter in which they are referred to in footnotes. Each illustrates and amplifies one or more of the themes developed in such chapters.

A note, lastly, on the spelling of foreign names. Usage in this matter is wayward and varied, and with little-known names I may have fallen into some inconsistency. In general, however, I have followed the most common American usage, as indicated by Webster. This means an Anglicized form of Greek names (Socrates instead of Sokrates), and for cities a Latinized form (Pergamum instead of Pergamos or Pergamon). With Arabic and Turkish names one has a wide choice, such as Koran or Qūran; Mohammed, Muhammad, or Mahomet; or with the conqueror of Constantinople, Mohammed, Mehmet, or Mehmed. Again I have tried to adhere to the most common naturalized form, dropping the apostrophes and diacritical marks used in Arabic. With modern Turkish, which is almost perfectly phonetic, I have taken some liberties, transcribing *c* as *j*, *ç* as *ch*, and *ş* as *sh*, in order to indicate the proper sound of Turkish names for English-speaking readers.

H. J. M.

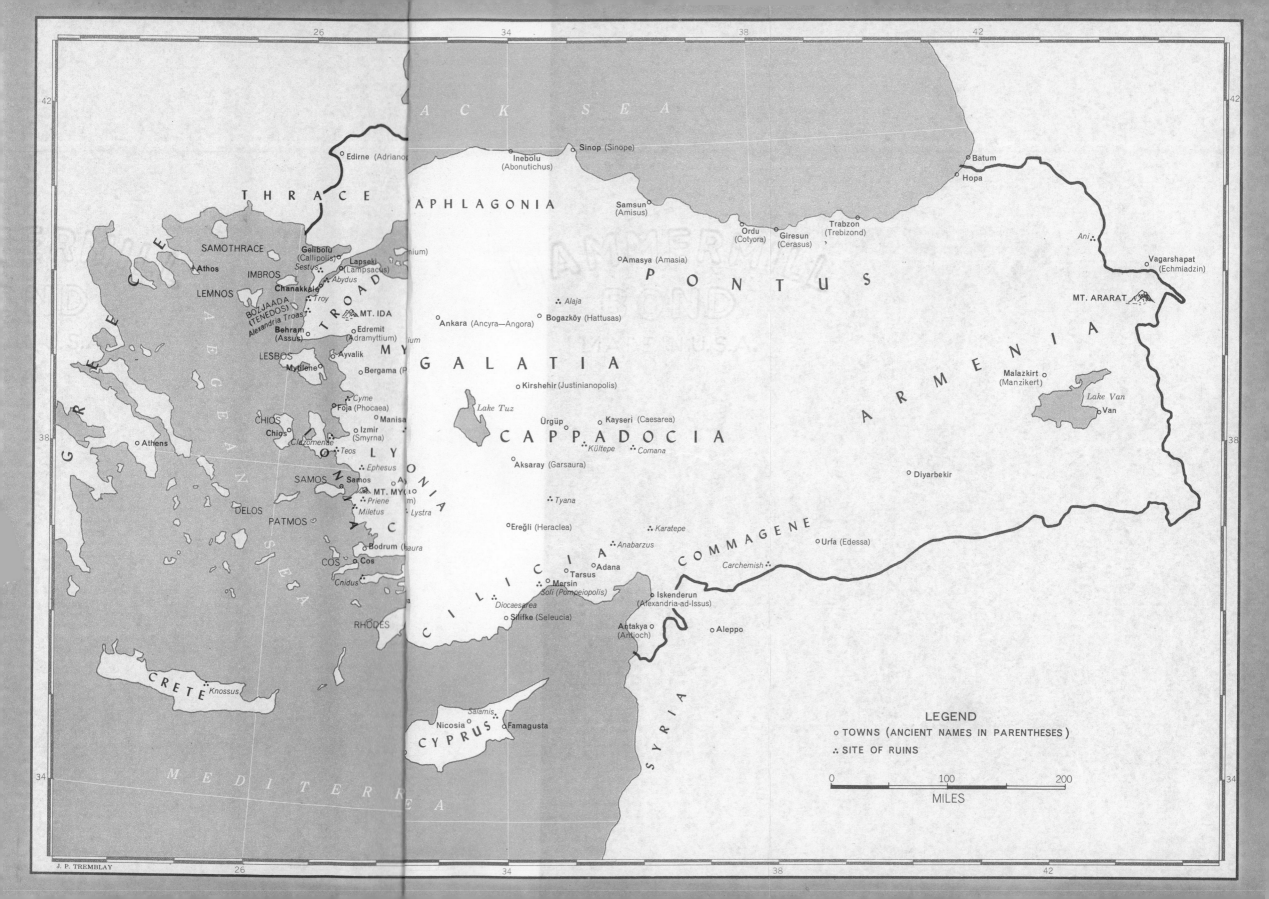

THE
LOOM
OF
HISTORY

CHAPTER I

Celaenae-Apamea: East and West

1. MARSYAS AND APOLLO

IN THE HILLS about the ancient Phrygian city of Celaenae, now the
Turkish town of Dinar, a number of streams issue more or less mysteriously from underground sources, to unite and form the classical
Maeander River. The most celebrated of these streams was the Marsyas,
or Cataract. It burst out of a grotto at the foot of the acropolis, to pour
headlong through the city. The ancients believed, however, that the ultimate source of both the Marsyas and the Maeander was a lake behind the
ridge—the Aulocrene, or "fountain of flutes." Here, according to Maximus
of Tyre, the Phrygians offered sacrifices, "some to both rivers, some to the
Marsyas singly, and some to the Maeander; and they cast the things of the
victims into the springs, uttering over them the name of the river to which
they offer them; and the offerings, borne away towards the mountain and
sinking with the water, are found not to rise in the Marsyas if given to the
Maeander, nor in the Maeander if given to the Marsyas; and if they be
offered to both, the rivers divide the gift." The courtesy of the rivers was
in keeping with their generosity, for the unfailing supply of water they
provided was a precious gift in arid Asia Minor. They still make an oasis
of the green valley in which Dinar lies.

Such a site was a natural haunt of divinities, and so became hallowed by
legend. Here Marsyas, the river god of Celaenae, invented the Phrygian
flute. According to one report he played it for Cybele, the Great Mother,
trying to console her for the death of her lover-son Attis. Later the goddess
Athena played it on the banks of Aulocrene and was charmed by its
music; but when she saw her distorted face in the mirror of the lake, she
threw the flute away, put a curse on it, and struck Marsyas for picking it
up—a scene commemorated by a statue in the Acropolis of Athens. The
hapless inventor then challenged Apollo to a contest, some say in music
(Apollo was a harp player), others say in wisdom. For his rashness Apollo

1

had him flayed to death, and his skin hung up as an example. Herodotus
reported that in his time the skin was on view in the market place of
Celaenae, but Xenophon said it was hung up in the grotto from which the
river of Marsyas issued. (The ancients were careless about such details.)
In any case, Marsyas was partially vindicated by his son Olympus, who
naturalized the Phrygian mode of music among the Greeks. The Phrygian
King Midas—he of the golden touch—also sought more harmonious relations by presenting his royal throne to Apollo's oracle at Delphi; though
his piety may have been touched by fear. He had attended the musical
contest between Apollo and Marsyas, and dissented from the verdict that
gave Apollo the victory, whereupon the god had endowed him with a
pair of ass's ears. And another visitor to Celaenae had been the mighty
Heracles. Heracles slew Lityerses, a bastard son of Midas, who as
guardian of the fields hospitably received all passing strangers but killed
them if they failed to do their share of work in the harvest, or sometimes
simply killed them anyway as a routine harvest ritual—wrapping the
stranger in a sheaf of corn and cutting off his head with a sickle. Now he
had his own head cut off by Heracles, who threw his trunk into the
Maeander. In earlier Phrygian song Lityerses had died more poetically,
slain by the sickles of his reapers, dying, as the grain must, to assure another harvest.

Once upon a time, when scholars were just beginning to grow very
scientific, such myths and legends were regarded as a species of fairy
tale, or something to be "exploded." It is now more sophisticated to dwell
on their imaginative truth, as symbolic representations of ideas about
man's life. Such ideas may be meaningful and credible whether or not
they are strictly true, just as are the ideas in all poetry—or for that matter
in religion. The myth of King Midas and his golden touch expresses a
simple moral wisdom that few will question. The myths about Lityerses
make less sense offhand because they are more profoundly suggestive. In
his Phrygian manifestation as a harvest god he symbolized the timeless
truth of the annual seasons, the cycle of life and death and rebirth; he was
a rustic counterpart of Attis (or Adonis, or Osiris), the dying god who is
resurrected. Hence he foreshadowed the ideal conception of the Christ,
the god of love who deliberately dies in order to save man, and whose
resurrection is a promise of life eternal. Christ offered an honorable
epitaph for the yokel Lityerses: "Except a corn of wheat fall into the
ground and die, it abideth alone; but if it die, it bringeth forth much
fruit."

Literary men have made a dubious fashion of glorifying the myth, as a
means of putting science in its place and insinuating the "higher truths" of

poetry and religion. But these fables are significant even for the scientific historian. To begin with, many have a factual core. There actually was a King Midas, or rather a series of kings by that name—it was probably a title, like Pharaoh of Egypt and Minos of Crete. Herodotus himself saw the gift of Midas to Apollo, which he declares was the first offering made at holy Delphi by a "barbarian." Similarly, there was an actual musician behind the mythical son of Marsyas: Olympus composed an impassioned strain to which a choral ode of Euripides was set. Other stories of local gods may dimly reflect historic events, give clues to the remote past. It is possible, for example, that the flaying of Marsyas harks back to the flaying alive of a local hero by the cruel Assyrians, whose records tell of wars with Mita of the "Mushki," seemingly the Phrygians. Greek legend in particular has proved to be a more reliable guide than was at first believed, for archaeology has revealed a historical basis for such traditional stories as those of King Minos of Crete, the Trojan War, and even the Amazons.

More important, the myths and legends are "true history" as the records of the mind of ancient peoples. They yield insights into prehistoric custom and belief, the growth of more civilized aspirations, and finally the realization of conscious ideals. Thus the story of Marsyas and Apollo, originally a story about the rivalry between the flute and the harp, came to signify the triumph of the Greek over the Phrygian spirit; Apollo developed into the most radiant symbol of Hellenism. Even the feats of Heracles, the rude strong man, took on an ideal significance. In slaying ancient monsters, he helped to deliver the Greeks from dark and deadly obsessions, the blind fears that hounded other peoples. And in slaying Lityerses, who had such a hard way with strangers, he symbolized the abolition of human sacrifice, as well as the growth of civilized intercourse, the idea of a wider hospitality that at length developed into the idea of Humanity.

Hence the mythical history of Celaenae leads us, ultimately, to a major theme of recorded history—the rise of Hellenism, and the conflict between East and West. In Asia Minor the Greeks had been stimulated by entering a new world that was a very old world, and that had much to teach the bright youngsters. Here their genius first flowered and the great "fathers" were born: Homer in literature, Thales in philosophy, Pythagoras in mathematics, Herodotus in history, Hippocrates in medicine. Hellenism was therefore not virginally conceived, nor sprung full-grown, like Athena, from the head of Zeus; but it was miraculous enough. Somehow the Greeks developed a unique way of life, much freer and fuller, more reasonable and humane—above all, more *conscious* than any man had yet known. Through Homer they grew keenly aware of their difference from all the peoples around them, and of their common ideals as Hellenes. They came to regard the Trojan War as the beginning of their conflict with Asia. Broadly speaking (as one has to speak at the outset), the Greek spirit defines the West, in the modern as in the ancient world. For us the story of its triumph is as momentous as any historic drama. We are rightly proud of the Greeks, and may rightly begin by reviewing this story in its ideal aspect.

Even at the outset, however, we must keep in mind that it was not simply a success story. The Greeks themselves were too intelligent to dote on this type of fable, the favorite American myth; they had character-istically a tragic sense of life, which was fed by plenty of tragic experi-ence. They were also too civilized to entertain notions of racial and religious purity, or to set up an ideal of 100 per cent Hellenism. Apollo himself most probably came from Asia Minor, not Greece; and another of the "fathers" was Aesop, a Phrygian slave. As for Marsyas, it turned out that he was not killed by Apollo after all. He continued to charm men with his flute, to preside over his river, to protect his city from enemies. In time the Greeks themselves offered sacrifices to him. Probably he outlived Apollo, as other ancient deities of Asia Minor certainly did; and what finally killed them both was new gods from the East. Meanwhile the rustic Lityerses lived on, as the hero of the timeless peasant who survives the rise and fall of civilizations. To this century the peasants of "Phrygia" have sung of him as a mighty reaper.

2. THE TRIUMPH OF THE WEST

"In the richness of its soil, in the variety of its products, in the extent of its pastures, and in the number of its exports," wrote Cicero of Asia Minor, "it surpasses all other lands." Today it hardly looks like a rich land, by American standards. Although fertile river valleys run down to the coasts from the central Anatolian plateau, the great plateau itself, almost treeless, is parched and sere through the long hot summer, and the mountains that rim it and roll to the coasts are mostly gaunt with rock and shrub. A traveler is impressed chiefly by the austere grandeur of the scenery, to which the Greeks seemed indifferent—their poets never rhapso-dized about it. Yet the ancients made this a rich, thriving land, and they invested it with a grand poetry by their deeds. The fabled land of the Argonauts and the Amazons, of King Priam, King Midas, and King Croesus, it is as fabulous for the history that was made in it.

According to the Greeks, the Phrygians were the oldest of living peoples, speaking the oldest of languages. We know, of course, that they were parvenus. Archaeologists have pushed the beginning of our story far back to the age of the neolithic barbarians who made the all-important discovery of agriculture, learning to produce instead of gather food, and in villages laying the foundations of institutionalized society. The mound of Troy is only the most publicized of the countless *hüyüks* in Asia Minor, mounds containing layers of settlements that go back to the Early Bronze Age. By the middle of the third millennium—the period of the second city of Troy—the chieftains of these nameless peoples commanded the services of highly skilled artisans, to build strong-walled fortresses, to make exquisite gold ornaments, and to maintain the pattern for all civilization before the Greeks, in which the increasing wealth produced by the community went chiefly into luxury goods for the gods and the privileged few, and was guarded from other plunderers in strongholds that finally never held. But these peoples remained nameless; of their history we know little except that their towns were periodically destroyed by enemies or earthquakes. Our story really begins with the Hatti, a people unknown to the Greeks and now better known as the Hittites.

By the beginning of the second millennium before Christ the Hittites were establishing themselves on the Anatolian plateau. They owed much to the older civilizations of Mesopotamia, whose merchants left large numbers of their cuneiform records in the region, but in time they built up an independent empire mighty enough to sack Babylon, conquer Syria, and hold its own against Egypt. From their capital at Hattusas, now Bogazköy, their monarchs claimed dominion over most of Asia Minor. Although their rule was often nominal, their influence extended to the western coast, as indicated by traces of a royal highway that led through Sardis, and by monuments in the vicinity of Smyrna (Izmir). A Hittite goddess carved on Mt. Sipylus was mistaken by the Greeks for Niobe.

Asia Minor was already a welter of diverse peoples, however. The Hittites had trouble especially with the Arzawa, a related people whose territory included the region of Celaenae, and who repeatedly defied the great king; Celaenae was possibly the Arzawa stronghold of Buranda. And even as the Hittite empire reached the peak of its power, more peoples were moving in from Europe. "The Isles were restless," the Egyptian scribes recorded, "and no land stood before them, beginning with Kheta" (Hatti). The Trojan War was an incident in a much larger movement. Excavations have shown that about 1200 B.C., the time Troy fell, cities were burned down all over Asia Minor. It was probably the Phrygians—according to Homer, allies of the Trojans—who destroyed Hattusas and overthrew the Hittite empire. At least the Phrygians became the next great power on the Anatolian plateau, where they established a kingdom that ruled most of the interior.

Although as yet not much is known about this kingdom, its monuments indicate that the Phrygians took over a good deal of Hittite culture. Notably they adopted the great Mother Goddess of Anatolia, whom the Hittites knew as Kubaba, among other names, and the Phrygians called Cybele. With her came such symbols as the sculptured lions of the Hittites, and her lover-son Attis. The Phrygians worshiped her wholeheartedly, in ecstasy and in orgy, as befitted a fertility goddess who was the mother of all life; though on the Day of the Blood, commemorating the death of her son, the frenzied mourning often culminated in self-castration —a seemingly illogical mode of assuring fertility. Still, such self-abandonment has a sublime aspect, and points to gentler and grander ideas represented by the Great Mother. While she preferred to reside on a mountain, she graciously accommodated herself to all localities; at Celaenae she naturally became identified with the waters, and so acted as a healing goddess of health. Above all, her endless, boundless fertility symbolized the triumph of life over death—the hope of life everlasting. Phrygian tombs were sculptured to represent doors, often with her symbolic lion above them; the door was the entrance to the other world, where man returned to her. We shall hear much more of Cybele in the centuries to follow.

Unhappily, she failed the Phrygians in this life. Although they managed to hold their own against the powerful Assyrians, who now ruled southern Asia Minor, they were less successful against new invaders from Europe, the Cimmerians. An inscription at Nineveh records that one Mita, or Midas, sought the help of the Assyrians; he or another Midas, defeated everywhere by the Cimmerians, appears to have committed suicide in 676 B.C.; and with his death the Phrygian kingdom came to an end. It was succeeded by the kingdom of the Lydians, who, after a desperate struggle, drove out the Cimmerians. Ruling from Sardis, near the western coast, the Lydian kings became celebrated for their wealth. But the wealthiest of them, the fabulous Croesus, was also the last. In the sixth century the Lydians in turn went down before the rising power of the Persians, who were building the greatest empire yet known to history.

Meanwhile still other peoples had moved into Asia Minor. Bithynians from Thrace crossed the Dardanelles and established themselves along the northern coast. Mysians and Carians, of unknown origin, gave their name to middle regions. Lycians, Pamphylians, and Cilicians took over the southwest; although some of their cities later claimed heroes of the Trojan War as their founders, their origins too are obscure. Most important, the Greeks themselves had arrived. Within a century or so after the fall of Troy, colonies of Aeolians and Ionians were settling in islands and scattered cities along the western coast. They were to make famous such names as Lesbos, Samos, and Chios, Miletus, Ephesus, and Smyrna. In time their cities came under the domination of the Lydians and then the Persians, but they retained their Greek identity and their conviction of superiority over their "barbarian" overlords. Their kinsmen in Greece came to their aid when they sought to regain their freedom. The outcome was the Persian War, the most momentous of the wars between East and West.

Now, this war was not the grand climax of the history I have been outlining. "The Isles were restless"—but not with the stirrings of new ideals, or any notion of a conflict between East and West. The peoples on the march were impelled by hunger, hopes of plunder, or the pressure of other peoples behind them. The Hittites, who built a kingdom on the ancient Oriental model, spoke an Indo-European tongue; although it is still uncertain who they were and where they came from, they were presumably "Aryans" and might have come from Europe. The Phrygians who conquered them may have been a race of heroes, as Greek tradition held, but certainly were not conscious crusaders from the West. In toppling a superior civilization they helped to inaugurate a Dark Age for Asia Minor; it took some centuries for the new peoples to regain the level that men had reached in the second millennium. Civilization was then threatened by the Cimmerians, barbarians from Europe, and rescued by the Lydians, an Asiatic people. The Persians who marched in from the East to create still another Oriental empire were again Aryans. Our theme is bloody—but the key to it is not blood or race.

Neither is it geography or climate. In the subcontinent that was not yet known as Europe there were scattered cultures, mostly primitive, which represented a diffusion—or a devolution—of Asiatic culture. If there is anything peculiarly stimulating in the air of Europe, its magic had not yet taken effect. In the vast, more civilized continent of Asia there was a greater medley of ancient peoples and cultures, but no definite entity known to them as "Asia"; the name came later from the Greeks, who were ignorant of most of the continent and its early history. (Possibly it was derived from "Assuwa," the Hittite name for a land that has not been placed with certainty, but probably was on the west coast of Asia Minor.) Not until recent years did the peoples of the East develop a common consciousness, and begin to talk of "Asia for the Asiatics."

This consciousness, however, was due to Western influence; so it recalls us to an actual historic conflict. While our theme involves physical clashes, it is fundamentally ideological. With the Greeks a new spirit entered history, in ways difficult to explain but easier to recognize and define. Beneath the many diverse Easts—Egyptian, Sumerian, Babylonian,

Hittite, Assyrian, Chaldean, Persian—we can make out common tendencies that make it possible to speak of an "Oriental" spirit. For the time being we must still speak broadly, disregarding the inevitable complications in order to get at the essential differences, but we can see these clearly enough by considering two major interests—religion and government.

"Miracle, mystery, and authority"—these are the basic needs of man, said Dostoyevsky's Grand Inquisitor. "Man seeks not so much God as the miraculous." Freedom appalls him, added Santayana; "he is afraid of a universe that leaves him alone." Certainly man in the East was a slave to such needs and such fears. His whole culture was based on religion. His religion was not very spiritual, to be sure, any more than popular religion is today; typically he was as materialistic as the conventional American. What he sought from the gods was not holiness, but good crops, children, health, victory in war, and a prodigiously long life. The difference was that he depended on the gods to produce these worldly goods. He was always subject to the tyranny of supernatural powers that could be propitiated only by priestly magic. Obedience to arbitrary authority was likewise the ruling principle in his social and political life. The characteristic form of government in all the great Eastern societies was absolute monarchy, divinely ordained; the Great King was the agent of the gods when not himself a god. The science, learning, and art of these societies were alike devoted to the service of the gods and god-kings. The chief use of thought was not to analyze, inquire, or create but to conserve, to sanctify the *status quo.*

Against this background the Greeks appear extraordinarily open-minded and clear-eyed. Somehow they had developed a faith in Mind as the distinctive essence of man; they enthroned the power of reason by which man might hope to dispel mystery and order his own life. While this faith by no means excluded the supernatural, it enlisted even the gods in the service of a reasonable way of life. The Olympians demanded ritual attentions, but otherwise left their worshipers pretty much alone. In this relative freedom from priestcraft the Greeks were able to cultivate their many interests, introducing science, philosophy, and history as we know them. Basic to all these was their free, curious, critical spirit. "The unexamined life is not worth living," Socrates was to say simply—so simply that it is hard to realize how profoundly revolutionary this credo was (and still is). In political life the Greeks accordingly refused to deify their rulers and sought to rationalize authority. They developed their characteristic *polis,* a republican city-state. Although they might be misgoverned by oligarchs or tyrants, they always had some voice in their government, and some recognized liberties. They were citizens, not subjects. Their primary duty was obedience to law, not subservience to authority.

We may now return to Celaenae, to follow a historic struggle that was much more than another clash of military powers. With the coming of the Persians, Celaenae enters recorded history as a royal administrative center. Xerxes stopped over here with his huge army, en route to Greece; and Herodotus tells of a suggestive incident during his stay. The Great King was sumptuously entertained by one Pythius, a Lydian merchant, who not only provided for the whole Persian host but offered the king his entire fortune, consisting principally of some 3,993,000 gold staters. Charmed by such munificence, Xerxes made Pythius his sworn friend, and instead of accepting the gift presented him with 7,000 staters, to make his fortune a good round sum of four million. Persian monarchs were often much more gracious than the Assyrians before them. But the aftermath was less charming. In Sardis, the next stop, the Persian host encountered an eclipse of the sun. Pythius, who had come along with his five sons, was alarmed by so fearful a portent and asked a favor of his sworn friend: would the Great King have compassion on his years and permit his eldest son to remain behind, to be his prop and stay? Angered by this craven impudence, Xerxes commanded instead that the eldest son be cut in two and the halves placed on either side of the line of march. "Then the king's orders were obeyed; and the army marched out between the two halves of the body."

So the most arbitrary orders of the Great King were automatically obeyed. His word was the law, above all question of right or reason; the noblest Persian was a slave to the royal whim. In his history of the Persian Wars Herodotus consequently made liberty the main issue. "A slave's life you understand," a Greek tells a friendly Persian who has advised submission to the Great King, "but never having tasted liberty, you cannot tell whether it be sweet or no. Had you known what freedom is, you would have bidden us fight for it." And so the Western world has rejoiced that the Greeks succeeded in retaining their liberty. After destroying the city of Athens, Xerxes was defeated at the crucial battle of Salamis, in 480 B.C., primarily because of the steadfastness of the Athenians; and at Athens the Greek spirit thereupon flowered gloriously.

After Xerxes' defeat, we gather from Xenophon, he put in a longer stay at Celaenae, refortifying its acropolis and building a palace at the springs of the Marsyas. Later in the fifth century the Persians again dominated the Greek cities in Asia Minor, as Athens became embroiled with Sparta in the fatal Peloponnesian War. At the close of the century, following the victory of Sparta, the Athenian Xenophon spent a month in Celaenae, where he had come to join the glamorous Cyrus the Younger. Cyrus, who was building up an army to seize the Persian throne from his brother, relied especially on his Greek recruits. After holding a proud review of them he marched through Asia Minor and Syria into Babylonia, where he met the army of his brother. The Greeks routed the Persians facing them, but elsewhere on the battlefield Cyrus was killed. Then followed one of the most celebrated adventures in history—the March of the Ten Thousand, recorded by Xenophon. Stranded in the heart of the Persian Empire, the relatively small band of Greeks fought their way back through Mesopotamia and Asia Minor to the Black Sea coast, and thence to Byzantium. This was not only a romantic feat of valor but an event of consequence, for it made the Greek world aware of the internal weakness of the mighty Persian Empire. The rottenness at its core—an old story with Oriental sacred monarchies—was also exposed by the fate of Tissaphernes, the ablest of the Persian satraps. Upon recovering Celaenae and other cities for his royal master, Tissaphernes fell victim to court intrigues of eunuchs and ladies of the harem; and at Celaenae he was beheaded.

Hence mainland Greece began to call for a crusade to liberate the Greek cities in Asia Minor. The response finally came with Alexander the Great of Macedon. Although he and his father, King Philip, began by subduing Greece itself, they conceived themselves as true Hellenes, claiming descent from Heracles. Alexander in particular was a self-conscious crusader, pleased to consider himself "the liberator of Hellas." As he conquered Asia Minor he proclaimed the freedom of the Greek cities, and ordered the expulsion of the tyrants and the oligarchs imposed or supported by the Persians, on the grounds that democracy was the normal form of government for Greeks. As he marched eastward he founded new cities, to radiate Greek culture. And even as he burned down the palaces of the Great Kings at Persepolis, ostensibly to avenge the destruction of Athens by Xerxes, he was conceiving a still loftier idea of his mission, which anticipated the ultimate ideal of Greek rationalism. Alexander laid the groundwork for a wholly new kind of empire—a commonwealth in which the conquered peoples were to be partners rather than subjects. He went out of his way to appoint Persians and other Asiatics to high positions, treating them as kinsmen; he encouraged his Macedonian and Greek followers to take Asiatic wives; and when they protested against his partiality for "barbarians," he sought to make peace by holding a great banquet at which representatives of all the different peoples drank from a mixing bowl, and he himself offered a prayer for *homonoia*, "a union of hearts." His prayer, W. W. Tarn observes, marked a revolution in human thought. Alexander, several centuries before Christ, was the first known man in the Western world to have had this vision of brotherhood.

Neither Greeks nor Asiatics were ready for it, of course. When Alexander died shortly afterward, in 323 B.C.—an old young man of thirty-two —his empire at once began to break up. The history of Celaenae was typical of the confused aftermath. Not a Greek city, it had been one of the few to resist the liberation, surrendering only when he offered generous terms; he made it his headquarters while his forces converged for the drive into the Persian Empire. Thereafter it became the capital of Anatolia, as the seat of his deputy Antigonus. When war broke out among his generals, it passed into the hands of Lysimachus and finally of Seleucus, the founder of the Seleucid kingdom. Nevertheless the generals continued Alexander's program of Hellenizing the East, if only to strengthen their hold on it. Antiochus I, the son of Seleucus, built a new city at Celaenae, which he renamed Apamea after his mother Apame, an Asiatic princess. In time it became a representative Greek *polis*, tributary to the kings but governed by its own council, and providing richly for both the spiritual and the material needs of its citizens.

As a Hellenistic city, Celaenae-Apamea continued to witness a parade of famous men and fateful events. Here, in 193 B.C., Antiochus the Great negotiated with the envoy of Rome, which was supporting the brilliant new kingdom of Pergamum in its struggle with the Seleucid kings for the dominion of western Asia Minor; from here he marched out with a great army, to meet disaster at the decisive battle of Magnesia in 189; and here he then signed the peace terms dictated by Rome. As an immediate result, Pergamum took over most of his domain in Asia Minor, including Apamea. But the far-reaching consequence of his defeat was the ascendance of Rome, whose ultimate rule was now virtually inevitable. Pergamum expanded only by the grace of Rome, its ally. In 133 B.C. the last of its kings recognized the facts of life by bequeathing his kingdom to the Roman people. A new era had begun for Asia Minor.

The Romans in turn were not ready for it. They were building an empire almost unwittingly, bent chiefly on exploiting their new possessions. Apamea suffered like the rest of Asia Minor from the rapacity of Roman publicans, or tax collectors. In the last century before Christ it welcomed Mithridates the Great, the brilliant barbarian who led the last desperate, unsuccessful struggle to drive out the Romans, anticipating the modern slogan of Asia for the Asiatics; he earned the favor of the city by a generous donation when it was severely damaged by an earthquake. Shortly thereafter, however, Apamea enjoyed an augury of the better days to come. Cicero, an honest, conscientious consul, spent three days in the city listening to complaints. Although the Greek cities suffered still more from the civil wars that finally destroyed the Roman Republic, paying most of the costs of these wars, they quickly recovered when the great Augustus restored peace and order.

Under the Pax Romana, Apamea prospered mightily. "You take precedence of Phrygia, and Lydia, and further of Caria," Dio Chrysostom told its citizens in an oration; "and other populous nations dwell around you, Cappadocians, and Pamphylians, and Pisidians; and to them all you make your city a market and meeting place." Strabo noted more soberly that it ranked next to Ephesus as a commercial center in the province of Asia. So happy was its state that aside from another devastating earthquake we hardly hear of it during these two or three centuries—"history" is made chiefly by conflict and disaster. One testimonial is that its acropolis today is strewn with Hellenistic potsherds, but no Roman ones: the city no longer had need of a citadel, and was building only in the valley. But most important was the ideal of commonwealth in which it shared. The Roman Empire had to a large extent realized the dream of Alexander the Great. Phrygians, Lydians, Cappadocians, Pisidians, Greeks, Romans —all were citizens of an empire that ideally conceived itself as a cosmopolis, "one single commonwealth of gods and men." As far as it went, it was something like One World.

A curious incidental illustration of this cosmopolitan spirit appears on an imperial coin minted at Apamea. It shows a man and woman seated in an ark, above which hovers a dove; it bears the inscription "Noe." The city had a large Jewish community, which had enriched its legendary history with the notion that the hill behind it was Mt. Ararat. Apparently Noah had landed here long before the coming of Athena and Apollo, or even of Marsyas. The Seleucid kings had valued Jews as colonists for the new cities they founded, granting them land, often equality as citizens, and special privileges connected with the requirements of their peculiar religion. Their prosperity was evidenced when the early Roman rulers outlawed their practice of sending annual contributions to Jerusalem; one hundred pounds of gold was seized at Apamea. Nevertheless, they continued to flourish under Roman rule, even after the bloody rebellion of Jerusalem of A.D. 70 cost them their peculiar privileges before Roman law. The emperors Vespasian and Titus presently confirmed their rights as citizens. And at Apamea they evidently became good citizens of the commonwealth. Sir William Ramsay, a leading authority on Phrygia, found only one Jewish epitaph among the many inscriptions he examined at Dinar and the vicinity. Their assimilation is confirmed by the Talmud, which mentions the Ten Tribes who had been separated from their brethren by the baths and wines of Phrygia.

Presumably this means that they became Christians. The inscriptions studied by Ramsay indicate that Apamea, like the rest of Phrygia, had a relatively large Christian community well before Constantine the Great made their heresy the imperial religion; and such Hellenized Jews were susceptible to this heresy. The triumph of Christianity, at any rate, brings our immediate story to an ideal close. Marsyas and Lityerses, Apollo and Heracles, all went into the shades, probably not unlamented, but certainly unneeded. At its best, the new religion offered all that they had offered, and much more. The Christian God, derived from the pure monotheism of Judaism, represented the divine unity that the greater poets and philosophers of the pagan world had for centuries been aspiring to. At the same time, Jesus was both fully human and fully divine. His gospel of love added warmth to the abstract Greco-Roman ideal of universal community, making it an ideal of true brotherhood. His teaching included a principle of spiritual equality, with at least an implication of spiritual freedom, which gave the individual even more dignity and worth than the Greeks had given him. In its simplest form, as recorded in the Synoptic Gospels, it could not satisfy the whole man, for Jesus seemed indifferent to philosophy, the arts, and the distinctive values of civilization; but as Christianity spread in the Greco-Roman world, it was reinterpreted and amplified in the light of Greek thought and culture. Altogether, it was potentially an ideal synthesis of East and West—of Oriental religious fervor, Greek rationalism, and Roman discipline.

3. THE TRIUMPH OF THE EAST

What Christianity actually became was rather different. The subsequent history of Celaenae-Apamea gives us pause: under its new god it dwindled, decayed, finally disappeared from sight. Allah now presides over the once great city, now a small town called Dinar. Its Turkish natives know nothing of Marsyas or Apollo, Xerxes or Xenophon. Here, one might say, is further evidence for the case against the backward, benighted East. Nevertheless the fact remains that the East did triumph, presumably for good reasons. Its triumph even looks like a "spiritual" victory, which had been won long before the Turks sealed it by military power. Historians now trace a spiritual resurgence that began even as Alexander the Great was conquering the East, and that by the time of the Christian era had largely reconquered the Greek world. "There is no more interesting process in history," wrote Sir William Ramsay, "than this which was completed by the conquest of Constantinople in 1453." It is time to complicate our theme, and dwell on the ambiguities that underlie all great historic processes.

To begin with, the conflict was never a purely spiritual one, over purely ideal issues. A major factor in this, as in all historic processes, was economic—or what an idealist is likely to call greed. The religiosity of the East seldom interfered with its commerce; while its peoples characteristically attributed all good fortune to the gods, they made their fortunes by commerce, or by plunder of wealth got from commerce. Thus it was not the gods of Celaenae that made the city flourish. It was rather its excellent location as a natural caravan station on a great trade route to the East and a natural market place for the fertile plains radiating from it. The immense fortune that the Lydian Pythius was able to offer Xerxes testified to its thriving commerce, which had been greatly facilitated by the Lydian invention of coinage. (A book could be written on the immense influence of "small change.") As Apamea, the city grew in size and importance because the Hellenistic age was the greatest age of commerce and industry the world had yet known. In the Roman period its chief business remained business. "Further, the assizes are held among you in alternate years," Dio Chrysostom needlessly reminded the complacent citizenry, "and there is brought together an endless crowd of peoples, litigants, judges, lawyers, governors, under-officials, slaves, pimps, muleteers, traders, hetaerae, and artisans; so that those who have wares sell them at the highest prices, and nothing in the city lies idle, whether two-horse carriages, or houses, or women. Now this makes for prosperity in no small degree. For where the greatest crowd meets together, there the most money necessarily results. . . ." Another Roman coin shows Marsyas in his sacred grotto surrounded by packing chests. The god was now busy supervising trade, for Apamea had become a junction where caravan goods from the East were packed for forwarding to the seaports.

The Hellenistic Age, of course, is commonly regarded as a vulgar aftermath of the glorious classical age, and the Roman era as a still grosser one. Nevertheless the classical age also throve on business. If mere businessmen could never have built the Parthenon, it could never have been built without the wealth and leisure they provided. Like it or not, the beauty-loving, freedom-loving Greeks rose on commerce and industry. Like most civilized peoples they came to profess a low opinion of business, but they were obviously good at it, able to hold their own with the Phoenicians, who were frankly devoted to it. And in many ways it was good for them too, even aside from the qualities of enterprise and resourcefulness it developed. Commerce promotes civilized intercourse, the exchange of spiritual as well as material goods; the Greeks profited immeasurably from peaceful trade with the East. For such reasons their genius first came to fruition in the busy ports and marts of Asia Minor.

The Greeks also displayed, however, the less attractive qualities of the business spirit. A Greek market, observed the Persian Emperor Cyrus, was "a place set apart for people to go and cheat each other on oath." The aristocratic Persians always found it easy to employ Greeks, and to corrupt them. Many fought on the side of the Great King Xerxes even during the crucial war for liberty. The victory of Athens was partly lost because some of the Greek heroes, including the Athenian Themistocles, went over to the Persians; for more than a century Persian money maintained in Asia Minor the power of a rotting empire. As we admire the valor of Xenophon and the Ten Thousand we may forget that they were mercenaries, fighting not for any ideal cause but for money, in the ranks of the chief enemy of Greek freedom. Other Greek mercenaries manned the citadel of Celaenae when it resisted Alexander, the liberator of the Greek cities. In general, the brilliant Greeks were often stupid enough to be "smart," like many hard-headed Americans. A major reason for their ultimate failure was simple greed.

Meanwhile the spiritual trade with the East was having as mixed results. As the Greeks adopted the Phrygian flute, so they adopted the Phoenician alphabet, Lydian coinage, Egyptian arts, Babylonian learning. Their genius lay not merely in their originality but in their adaptability and readiness to learn; their free, curious spirit led them to borrow more copiously than any people before them. Hellenism was so rich precisely because it was not pure and homogeneous but many-sided, embracing diverse or even contrary tendencies. Plato is the conspicuous example. As a severe classicist, he proscribed the use of the flute in his ideal Republic, and with it the soft, relaxed Ionian and Lydian modes of music—thereby revealing their actual popularity, the unclassical tendencies to which the versatile, volatile Greeks were always prone. At the same time, Plato's own thought was so fertile because it was not a classically ordered system but an exploration of various possibilities, a sensitive response to various influences, including Oriental thought. Its historic influence has stemmed chiefly from his inclination to a transcendental idealism, an other-worldly kind of spirituality that is more typical of India than of Greece in its heyday. Yet such spirituality was not simply an enrichment of Hellenism. It throve on the worldly failures of the Greeks. It brings us to some questionable consequences of their traffic with the East.

In keeping with the triumph of Apollo over Marsyas, early Greeks had expressed a sophisticated contempt for Phrygian rites and customs. Hipponax of Ephesus, for example, ridiculed the high priest of Cybele as mercenary and "more lascivious than a dog." But the Great Mother was impervious to mere logic or sophistication. Three centuries after Hipponax, King Eumenes of Pergamum went to Apamea to conclude an alliance with Priest Attis of Pessinus, the seat of the great temple of Cybele; lascivious or no, her high priest was still an important ruler in Anatolia. Meanwhile she had won other victories in disguise, assuming the name of Greek goddesses, such as Artemis of Ephesus. In her own person she had gone to Athens itself, where her cult was established soon after the Persian War. She inspired lyrics by Pindar and Euripides. If Greeks of the old school still condemned her, or rather the excesses of her worshipers, they rarely denied her existence or her power. "Before her," wrote Apollonius of Rhodes in his *Argonautica*, "Zeus himself . . . doth somewhat yield, when from her mountains she ascendeth to the wide heaven. And the other blessed gods do reverence to this dread goddess." It was under Greek aegis that Cybele rose to be not merely the Mother of Earth, but the Mother of the Gods.

Now this story is in part a matter of simple superstition, to which the masses of men have always been liable. Since it is fashionable to extol the imaginative value of the myth, it seems necessary to remark the obvious naïveté of most fables. Taken symbolically, as the great Greek poets and philosophers took it, the myth may be high poetry and religion. Taken literally, as ordinary Greeks took it, it represents a failure of mind. We are likely to forget the degree of gross superstition in the mentality of the precocious Greeks. Even Xenophon, the eminently clearheaded, resourceful, resolute leader of the Ten Thousand, regularly consulted the soothsayers and examined the entrails of birds before making important decisions, and at least once invited disaster by refusing for some days to lead the army out of a desperate situation because the omens remained stubbornly unfavorable. The mass of Greeks never outgrew such primitive irrationality. So the citizens of Apamea gave thanks to Marsyas for saving their city from the dreaded Gauls, a feat he had somehow performed by his flute or his waters. Among the old Greek gods they favored Poseidon, the Earthshaker, because the city suffered from recurrent earthquakes; though on the face of it their worship was futile, as the earthquakes continued to recur.

Ultimately, the issue here is the need of "miracle, mystery, and authority." It is open to question whether men today, despite the enormous increase in their knowledge, wealth, and power, can yet endure a universe that leaves them alone, or can manage to live in freedom. It is no wonder that the Greeks ran into trouble in the first historic effort to do so. They were fledglings, spirited and proud of their spirit, but naturally awed by the magic and mystery of the venerable East, and never secure from foreign domination. Asia Minor in particular should remind us how precarious the Greek adventure was. Here their scattered cities were outposts, little islands of Hellenism in an Oriental sea. When Alexander the Great created more islands, he stirred up the sea.

Hence the end result of his conquest was paradoxical, but scarcely surprising. Orientals never adopted the gods of their conquerors. The radiant Apollo was not a good god for the needy, the oppressed, the poor in spirit; he had nothing new to offer them except a freedom they could not use, or even understand. The uprooted Greeks, however, were more susceptible to the ancient gods of the enduring East. In Greece itself the most popular god had long been Dionysus, a dying god who helped men to lose themselves in ecstasy rather than to know themselves. As the Greeks lost their independence they turned increasingly to the gods of the mystery religions. At best they intellectualized and spiritualized these mysteries, purifying them of their grosser rites, supplementing their merely sacramental or magical means of salvation; the mysteries could then induce a spiritual regeneration in this life. Still, this was a miraculous regeneration that men could not achieve by their own efforts. In Hellenizing the religious life of the East the Greeks were also succumbing to the age-old religious tradition.

In political life the story was much the same. The objections to absolute monarchy now seem so obvious that we may forget that it is the simplest, most intelligible form of government, corresponding to the rule of the father, the chief, or the god; until recent times the overwhelming majority of men have agreed with King James I that it is "the true pattern of divinity." The Greeks were again extraordinary in their rejection of this pattern. And again universal tradition proved too much for them. The arrival of Xenophon in Celaenae was prophetic. Although a real Athenian, proud of his Greek heritage, he was disillusioned with Athenian democracy, which had failed in the war against Sparta. Now he drew his inspiration from a Persian, Cyrus the Younger. He pictured Cyrus as the ideal type of ruler, glorifying his kingly virtues. But it was Alexander the Great, the liberator of Hellas, who opened a new era that eventually doomed the old Hellenic spirit. Alexander became a god-king.

Given his dream of uniting East and West, we may assume that it was not mere megalomania but high statesmanship that induced him to proclaim his divinity, as the son of Zeus-Amon. In this guise he could hope to command the loyalty of his Oriental subjects, who were not accustomed to the rule of mere men. At any rate, his generals followed suit. They set up dynastic kingdoms, granting more or less autonomy to the

Greek cities, but expecting them to acknowledge the royal dominion. Their sons had them deified, and themselves assumed such titles as Soter, or Savior. If the Greeks did not really believe in their divinity, they were pleased to confer such honors when the kings protected their city, as the local gods no longer could. By the time the Romans took over, they were quite used to the Oriental custom of making gods of men.

The Romans themselves at first frowned on it. The Emperor Augustus submitted to deification only for his non-Italian subjects, and most of his early successors did not take their divinity seriously. ("Alas," said the dying Vespasian, "I am about to become a god.") But most of their subjects welcomed the cult of the emperor—and none more enthusiastically than the Greek cities in Asia Minor. Having suffered grievously during the civil wars, they were especially grateful to Augustus for the restoration of peace, and in official decrees hailed him as "Savior of all mankind" and "Founder of the whole Universe." As they continued to prosper they competed in lavishing grandiloquent titles upon even the most vicious of his successors. The ancient city of Assus, where Aristotle had first set up school, commemorated the reign of the unspeakable Caligula as the beginning of a blessed new epoch "when the Universe found unmeasured joy, and every city and every nation has striven to behold the God." The loss of the old Greek spirit was more conspicuous because in their complacence the cities were now making a cult of the past, beholding their legendary founders as well. Thus Apamea seems for a time to have resumed its old name of Celaenae, while its Phrygian heroes and deities reappear on its coins. No great men came out of the city while it did honor to its mythical past.

The grave, practical Romans in turn had long since begun to succumb to the religiosity of the Orient. This conquest may be dated from as early as 205 B.C., when Cybele went from Pessinus to Rome on a state invitation. The city was in mortal danger from the army of Hannibal, and the invitation was a tacit acknowledgment that the national gods were not up to their job. Greeted by the highest dignitaries, and installed on the Palatine hill in the heart of aristocratic Rome, Cybele had immediately obliged by performing miracles, providing a magnificent harvest and then inducing the fearsome Hannibal to leave Italy for good. Although her wanton inclinations were at first curbed, and Roman citizens were forbidden to participate in her festivals, she was popular from the beginning. Under the emperors she became the acknowledged Mother of Rome; the bans were removed. Virgil, who represented her as the constant protector of Aeneas, the founder of Rome, introduced one of her miracles with a prophetic eulogy: "Here first a new light flashed before men's eyes, and a great cloud . . . seemed to cross the heavens from the East." The cloud spread over the whole Roman world, in which the cult of Cybele became immensely popular. It was rivaled only by the cults of the Persian Mithra and the Egyptian Isis (another Mother). And when the Empire at length began to crumble, even the most cultivated pagans turned to pure magic. Greek philosophy and religion alike ended in a riot of Oriental superstition.

Meanwhile the brighter star that had appeared in the East had also become clouded. For the same reason that Christianity was potentially a higher synthesis of the religious thought and feeling of East and West, it was liable to profound confusion and corruption, the more so in a world infested with Saviors and Founders. The religion that was to become the faith of the dynamic West grew up as an end-of-the-world religion in a sick empire. For the masses of simple men, the familiar hope of salvation through a resurrected god remained the hope of life eternal in another world, not life abundant in this world, and it called for the familiar Oriental virtues of patience, obedience, resignation. It had a selfish aspect in its concern with private salvation; Christianity weakened the civic spirit that had created the Greek *polis* and the Roman commonwealth. When it became the imperial religion it entered politics, but then it reverted to ancient Oriental type. Constantine the Great and his successors, who imposed it on the empire, were also imposing a full-fledged Oriental monarchy; the Church became allied with this monarchy, crowning the emperors with haloes. And it was now a hierarchical Church, with a powerful priesthood that was alien to the old Greek world and hostile to the free Greek spirit. To the miracle and mystery of Cybele the Church added an authority on which she had not insisted, and it thereby triumphed over her, closing down her temples by imperial decree. Thereby, too, it denied the principles of spiritual freedom and equality implicit in the teaching of its founder.

Toward pagan magic, on the other hand, the Church was more tolerant. Saints and archangels replaced the local demigods, such as Marsyas, to work the same miracles as patrons and healers. A marvelous profusion of holy relics helped to combat the prehistoric host of demons, which had been swelled by the addition of the pagan gods. Superstition flourished in the highest circles because Christian culture suffered from the decline of the Greco-Roman world. A Bishop Elias of Phrygia who attended the Council of Constantinople in 448, to help make the subtle verbal distinctions in dogma that had become necessary for eternal salvation, was unable to sign his name.

In political life, the new order had as ambiguous consequences. Constantine's adoption of Christianity was one of the desperate measures by which he attempted to preserve the Roman Empire, which had been disintegrating during the civil wars of the third century; but by transferring his capital from Rome to Constantinople, this strong man from the West succeeded only in founding the Byzantine Empire. The ancient East survived the fall of Rome, the "Eternal City," which did not shake the world. With its greater wealth and more deeply rooted culture, it had more staying power than the parvenu West. This Byzantine Empire displayed a remarkable vitality, which kept it going for another thousand years, and it learned to revere its Greek heritage. Yet it had little of the essential Greek spirit. Its emperors were sacred Autokrators, or "divine despots"; among the casualties of their imperial rule was the Greek *polis*. Its Church was an ultraconservative institution that took the appropriate name of Orthodox and was devoted especially to ritual and cultus—the magical and mysterious rather than the ethical and rational elements of Christianity. It boasted truly that it never altered its dogma, which is to say that it kept a closed mind.

The basic weakness of the Byzantine Empire was illustrated by the subsequent history of Apamea, which was inglorious and obscure. The city lost some of its natural advantages when Constantine shifted his capital, for thereafter the main trade routes led to Constantinople instead of Ephesus, the port for Rome. Apamea remained a natural site for an important city, however, being only a few miles off a main road to Constantinople, and it still had its waters and its market for the fertile region roundabout. An energetic, resourceful citizenry could have kept it prosperous. As it was, the Apameans evidently lacked enterprise; denied both religious and political freedom, they were poor in spirit. Their city dwindled into a third-rate town, which remained a bishopric for some centuries only by virtue of its past. In the eighth century it no doubt suffered from the raids of the Arabs, who pillaged other cities in the region. In the eleventh century it fell to the Seljuk Turks, who poured in from the East and overran the whole region. The Apameans succumbed so quickly and completely that we hear nothing more of them. Ibn-Batuta, the famous Moslem traveler of the fourteenth century, did not mention their town, although his route led through or near it. As Christians they simply disappear—as did their fellows all over Anatolia. As they were neither massacred nor persecuted by the Seljuks, we must assume that they became good Moslems.

Hence there was both poetic justice and historic logic in the triumph of Mohammedanism, a purely Eastern religion. This too was an ambiguous triumph, to be sure. In insisting on a pure monotheism and a direct relation between man and the One God, Mohammed rejected much Christian practice and belief dear to the East, such as the monkery and priestcraft, the worship of images, the cult of saints, and the pagan ideas of a Son and a Mother of God. Yet the spirit of the Prophet was not at all Greek. He also rejected the claims of reason, never arguing the existence of Allah but simply asserting it and demanding an arbitrary act of faith. Islam means literally "surrender to the will of God." And Allah was an Oriental despot, inscrutable, in some moods implacable, before whom men had no rights; they could be saved only by his grace. With the illogic that seems natural to believers in predestination (like the Communists today), Mohammed's followers became militant crusaders. In a generation they conquered most of the East. Although they were thrown back at Constantinople, only Asia Minor was left to the Byzantine Empire in Asia. Finally the Ottoman Turkish converts to Islam overthrew the remnant of this empire, the last vestige of Greco-Roman rule in Asia, thereby completing the "interesting process" that was already under way when Alexander the Great was Hellenizing the East.

4. THE NEW HISTORY

The process was not really completed, of course—nothing in history ever is. The Ottoman Empire in turn decayed, to become known, curiously, as "the Sick Man of Europe." It was kept alive chiefly by Western powers, in particular England; they had become more fearful of Russia, a nominally European power that had fallen heir to the Byzantine sacred autocracy, and had designs on Constantinople. In World War I Turkey was still fighting Russia, but now England was on the other side. After this confused struggle, in which both Turkey and Russia were defeated, the Greeks invaded Asia Minor to recover their ancient homeland. The Turks thereupon astonished the world by coming to life under an extraordinary new leader, Kemal Ataturk. He not only drove out the hated Greeks but forced the Western powers to recognize the independence of Turkey. Having revived the heroic past of the Ottomans, Ataturk proceeded to write a new chapter, which comes down to an ironic variant on the old story. The victor over the Western infidels at once set about to Westernize Turkey and repudiate the Ottoman tradition. Among his first victims was the Sultan, the Caliph of Islam.

Ataturk's policy was a tribute to the revolutionary history that the West had been making, leading to its domination of the entire world. We may skip over this story for the time being; our wondrous achievements, and their fearful consequences, have been sufficiently publicized. But much less has been made of a quiet, incidental undertaking of the West, which is also wondrous in its way—the historical research of the last hundred years. While science and technology have been revolutionizing everyday life, a molelike scholarship has been revolutionizing the past as well. Asia Minor too has come back to life, after centuries of oblivion; and this interesting process may have some bearing on the history we are making, or hope to make.

Although Europe was agitated by the fall of Constantinople, the Pope calling for another crusade to recover this ancient capital of Christendom from the infidels, there was little fervor for the holy cause. After all, the Orthodox Greeks were heretics—a species still viler than infidels. The Italians, devoted to commerce, soon discovered that they could continue to do good business with Constantinople, while the princes of Europe were more concerned about their struggles with one another, which they were free to pursue because the Ottoman Turks were also busy conquering their fellow Moslems. Later on, the merchants and the princes had to contend with Ottoman imperialism, which twice penetrated as far as Vienna, in the heart of Europe; but by this time there was no thought of restoring Byzantium. The land of Asia Minor, with its once splendid Greco-Roman cities and its great Christian churches, faded from Western memory. When at length it was rediscovered it had merged with the mysterious, exotic East; it was among the lands visited by agents of Louis XIV in search of Oriental ornaments for his palace at Versailles. In the eighteenth century travelers began to report on its wealth of exciting antiquities. Many more came in the next century, and in their wake followed classical scholars and archaeologists, notably Sir William Ramsay. We may pick up our story again with his two-volume study *The Cities and Bishoprics of Phrygia* (1895–97), which includes a long chapter on Celaenae-Apamea.

A thorough scholar and a pugnacious Scot, Ramsay began by settling the problem of the famous rivers. Hirschfeld, a German scholar, had identified the Maeander River with the modern Dinar Su and the Marsyas with a quiet stream near the town, even though ancient writers had described the Marsyas as a headlong cataract rushing through Celaenae. By careful exploration Ramsay proved conclusively what earlier travelers had assumed, that the Marsyas must be the Dinar Su; the Maeander he traced to another pool, where he thought he recognized the Laugher and Weeper springs mentioned by Pliny. He drew up a detailed map of the vicinity, identifying all five streams that combined to form the Maeander, though he was somewhat troubled because Roman coins issued by Apamea indicated only four river gods.

To such purposes Ramsay devoted a long lifetime of intensive work. In his *Historical Geography of Asia Minor,* the standard work on the subject, he located the sites of a hundred or so ancient cities, and speculated or worried about the possible location of as many more. "Nearly four hundred pages," remarked one of his friends, "are spent in discussing a set of names none of which anybody has ever heard of before." And often he discussed them with considerable heat, because of the "hardly comprehensible" perversities of his fellow scholars. "I cannot accept M. Radet's suggestion, thrown out without any personal exploration and without any corroboration from remains discovered there, that Otrous was situated at Kusura," he would write in his milder moments, adding in a footnote that M. Radet "was driven in a wagon rapidly across the valley, prostrate from fever, a situation deserving sympathy, but not conducive to effective exploration." With Hirschfeld he repeatedly disagreed in a much sharper tone. The German had accused him of gross plagiarism as well as faulty scholarship (no doubt ignorant of the wheeze that if you copy from one writer it's plagiarism, if you copy from a dozen it's scholarship).

At Dinar the Turks have made this academic tempest seem sillier by breaking the teapot. When I visited the town a few years ago, I found as many as five little streams rushing headlong where I expected to find the Marsyas, and was informed by the natives that they were all the Dinar Su. The Turks had built a dam at the site of the once-sacred grotto and had diverted the river into parallel or crisscross channels at different levels to supply power for some small mills. When I inquired about the Maeander (Turkish Menderez), the natives surprisingly pointed to the same streams. A young British archaeologist on the spot not only agreed with them but found my puzzlement incomprehensible. Obviously this was the Maeander River—anybody could see for himself by following it to the plain below. It appeared, however, that he had never heard of the Marsyas-Maeander problem. His specialty was the Bronze Age, or more particularly the Arzawa, who had maintained themselves hereabouts long before Marsyas came. He was exploring the region for *hüyüks,* the artificial mounds built up by successive settlements; they would provide the clues to where to look for Arzawa settlements. Although he condescended to show me around and climb up the acropolis of Apamea with me, he expressed his disgust with all the Hellenistic "muck," not to mention the unspeakable Roman remains. Everywhere in Asia Minor one ran into a thick layer of the stuff, to a depth of some yards, covering up what he was interested in getting at.

Even so he threw some light on Ramsay's interests. In a recent cut the natives had made into the slope of the acropolis, to carry water pipes over it, he pointed out a litter of Phrygian and Hellenistic potsherds, as well as a few from the Early Bronze Age. This chance cut also revealed a clear stratification that included a charred layer—another burned city. Ramsay had decided that as a market town Celaenae must have been located on the plain, and that Antiochus had moved his new city up into the hills. Now it appears that the acropolis of Apamea was on the site of the old Phrygian town, which in turn had been preceded by earlier towns. (Mycenaean vases have been found in the vicinity, dating from before the Trojan War.) Ramsay might have discovered this for himself had he dug around for potsherds instead of merely speculating, and wrangling with Hirschfeld.

And so we should pause, for humanity's sake. The layman has a right to smile at these scholars—especially because they have developed an almost morbid fear of pleasing him, or being "popular." Like all specialists today, they write chiefly for one another, in a learned jargon; it appears that the badge of intellectual integrity is a complete absence of style. Industriously they make mountains of molehills, or molehills of mountains. Particularly in America the German tradition of scholarship has bred a suspicion of not only aesthetic but philosophical concerns. Some years ago, when the Oriental Institute of Chicago began reporting its explorations in Hittite Asia Minor, it announced with some fanfare the blazing of a new trail: it was going to stress the "human side" of research in an endeavor to "place historical science on a sound human basis." A layman might wonder on what other basis the study of human history could be conducted, but a well-bred scholar might take alarm: "human" implies values and value judgments. "It is not the function of the historian to pass judgments," reads the ordinary Preface. The historian then proceeds to judge men, motives, and actions on almost every page, as inevitably he must. From beginning to end his work is based on assumptions—mostly unconscious, and all debatable—about what is natural for man, important for man, good for man. And because scholars are trained primarily as fact-finders, their judgment in matters of cultural value is often questionable.[1]

Yet the layman *ought* to smile as he remarks such occupational blindness—in the other fellow's occupation. Every profession is greater than

[1] A study of Greek romances led to this edifying conclusion: "There is a clear morality in the opposition of good and bad characters and in the final victory of the good. Hero and heroine captivate by their extraordinary beauty and maintain their chastity against terrific odds. . . . The Greek romance was lifted out of the ranks of the trivial and the second-rate by its great central theme: that there is such a thing as true love; that weighed in the balance against it all the world is nothing; and that it outlives time and even death." Hence the reader leaves it "vastly improved"— the more so, one might add, as he realizes that the glorious Greeks even anticipated the glory of Hollywood.

most of its practitioners; outsiders may better appreciate its value for the whole life of man. No profession—not even the study or the practice of the arts—is automatically broadening; literary men can also be humorless, illiberal, inhuman. As for Ramsay, he was by no means a mere pedant, but a cultivated man of broad interests. His oversight at Celaenae was pardonable, since at the time of his exploration archaeologists were only beginning to establish the importance of potsherds. More to the point, he would have welcomed this knowledge. In spite of his pugnacity and his parental fondness for his theories, he was always ready to modify or discard them in the light of new evidence. For he had the scientific spirit. In this spirit he made contributions to knowledge that were no less positive because his conclusions were often questionable. So did the perverse Hirschfeld, as Ramsay repeatedly acknowledged in the course of their endless feud. Out of all the ludicrous controversy over piddling detail there has grown up an impressive body of knowledge. A great deal of the vanished life of Asia Minor has been recovered. Only the most striking example is the Hittite Empire, the mere existence of which was unknown as late as 1880.

This whole enterprise is distinctively Western, and again a product of the Greek spirit. The old Eastern societies typically wrote no history. Although they usually took great pains to preserve their annals, these were only the raw materials of history. The Egyptians awed the Greeks by the memorials of their vast antiquity, and the Hittites even made a surprising effort to keep the record straight, noting the setbacks as well as the triumphs of their kings; yet none of the scribes of the Orient made a real effort to inquire, to digest, to understand their history. They were concerned merely with royal doings, merely for the sake of the royal record. *History* is a Greek word, meaning a search for true knowledge, and as such it began with the Greeks. "I write what I deem true," said Hecataeus of Miletus, "for the stories of the Greeks are manifold and seem to me ridiculous." Herodotus was as inquisitive about the manifold stories of other peoples, traveling all over the ancient world to satisfy his curiosity.

The father of history was still a child, however. If we can scarcely exaggerate our debt to the early Greeks, we also owe it to them to appreciate the singular advance that systematic research has made in historical inquiry over the last century. The highly intelligent Herodotus often seems credulous and naïve because he had no reliable means of ascertaining fact, no clear criteria for distinguishing fact from fable. When later inquirers, such as Strabo, grew more critical of the traditional myths and legends, they still had no means of replacing them by reliable knowledge. Now historians can check the manifold stories of the Greeks against positive evidence from other sources, such as archaeology, philology, and anthropology. More important, they constantly check on one another. While the individual scholar is always fallible and partial, his work is always subject to criticism and supplement by the community of scholars, in the publicity of the scientific method. Hence we have a steadily increasing body of factual knowledge that survives all disagreement over final interpretation. Even this disagreement—the endless dispute over causes and consequences that may confuse the simple-minded and distress the single-minded—makes for a better understanding, through a clearer awareness of the multiplicity, diversity, complexity, and fluidity that are the essence of historical reality.

Consequently we not only know much more than the Greeks knew but are much more historical-minded. We have a deeper, fuller sense of the many different pasts, and of their ever-living, ever-changing influence on the present. And we have at least begun to discount the ethnocentrism that prejudices all historical judgments. Formerly most written history was national history, when not simply nationalistic. While the nation remains a natural unit of study, historians have come to realize that its history can never be understood adequately except in relation to a civilization, the greater society to which it belongs. This has led to the study of whole civilizations, then of the whole drama of civilization. Spengler, and Toynbee after him, attacked the "Ptolemaic concept" of history—the assumption that Western civilization is the center or the supreme object of world history, with all other societies revolving about us or leading to us. Both sought to make objective surveys of all the known civilizations, as essentially comparable in dignity and importance. Although they arrived at different conclusions (and in my view alike dubious ones), they greatly enlarged and enriched our outlook. Given this approach, and such related disciplines as archaeology and anthropology, we now have, for the first time, the means of writing universal history.

Here we are led to a crowning paradox. Although the ancients typically had a deep reverence for the past, and an inveterate tendency to look back to it instead of hopefully to the future, they displayed surprisingly little interest in exploring it. Even the Greeks were generally content with vague, conflicting, or preposterous legends. Thus Celaenae-Apamea, like other inland cities of Asia Minor, dreamed up stories to give it a Greek origin, while at the same time it revived its legendary Phrygian founder. It was therefore left to the moderns to recover the Greek past—the notoriously irreverent moderns, who have been so proud of their modernity, so insistent upon keeping up to date, until recently so confident that the future will be better than the past. Similarly the interest of the ancients was largely confined to their own history. Herodotus had no followers to deepen and widen his investigations of other peoples. It was again the moderns who began the close study of all other civilizations, and of prehistoric and primitive peoples as well. Only the West—the conceited, irreligious West—has made this pious effort to know all cultures and recover the whole past of mankind.

One may still smile, then, at the controversy over the rivers of Celaenae. Scholars will be scholars. But having put them in their place, in a footnote, one might marvel at the unique piety of such dusty, methodical research, which has resurrected these dead societies in the thought and feeling of living men.

5. THE OLD QUESTIONS

Now the inescapable question arises: What of it? What is the use of all this knowledge? What difference does it make? Offhand, there is no resounding answer. For all practical purposes such knowledge seems to make no difference to speak of. As Hegel said, what we learn from history is that men have never learned from it. Over and over they rehearse the same follies, the same evils—just as we do today. So it may appear that the only fruit of our study is a sad wisdom: "Vanity of vanities, saith the Preacher, all is vanity." Of the once splendid city of Apamea there remains only some debris in the back alleys of Dinar; fragments of Corinthian columns are imbedded in the walls of stables; the sculptured inscription of some ancient dignitary serves as the base of a town pump. For the rest, the earth has swallowed up its marbled monuments, as its men. Nor has it lived on in the memory of mankind, except for some scholars and their bored students. Dinar is a ramshackle little town, unlovely and untouristed; it was not even listed in Murray's *Handbook for Travelers*, the standard guide to Ottoman Turkey. In my dictionary I find Apamama, a small island in the Pacific, which I assume took on some fleeting importance for military purposes in the last war. I find no Apamea.

But I am not dismayed. The fuss over the rivers of Celaenae illustrates the plainest reason for the study of history, which is simply to satisfy natural curiosity—to give the pleasure that all men know in finding out about something, whether birds or batting averages, the workings of an engine or of a universe. This elemental satisfaction may be obscured by the triumph of science, the most remarkable outgrowth of natural curiosity. The scientific spirit is sometimes described as a holy passion for Truth in the disinterested service of mankind; sometimes as an utterly cold impersonality, a monstrous indifference to all human values and faiths; sometimes as a form of pure materialism. It may indeed become any of these things. But first of all the scientist is a man doing work he likes, because he likes it. Ramsay and his fellows were engrossed in a study that was its own reward, regardless of possible fame, fortune, or life beyond the grave; and their kind of study gives strong intimations of mortality.

The practical necessity of some knowledge of history becomes as plain if one tries to imagine a society completely ignorant of its past, or an individual without memory. From the past come all our customs and institutions, our skills and arts, our rights and duties, our faiths—all the ideas we live by, all the basic ingredients even of our prized individuality. We draw upon it, however unconsciously, whenever we make up our minds about any matter of importance; we refer to it more directly whenever we consider social and political problems. In particular we get from it our common sense, our notions about what is natural, proper, and good for man. And what we might learn from history—what at the moment we most need to learn—is the limitations of ordinary common sense. The practical man is given to saying that "history shows" something or other: it shows that he has the right ideas, and that the other fellow is a crackpot. In fact it shows nothing of the kind. He shows a superficial, confused, distorted notion of history, which is far more dangerous than ignorance of it.

On a national scale, this becomes the kind of prejudice and conceit that led Paul Valéry to call history the most dangerous product ever concocted by the chemistry of the brain. "It causes dreams," he wrote, "it makes nations drunk, it saddles them with false memories, it exaggerates their reflexes, it keeps their old sores running, it torments them when they are at rest, and it induces in them megalomania and the mania of persecution. It makes them bitter, arrogant, unbearable, and full of vanity." Herbert Butterfield, himself a distinguished historian, has echoed this charge. The national history taught in schools has tended to encourage the most general and terrifying of existing evils, "human presumption and particularly intellectual arrogance," or in other words self-righteousness. "Wrong history," he declares, "is being taught in all countries, all the time, unavoidably"; and he concludes that while we have great need of history, our first need is to *unlearn* most of what we have been taught.

We can hope to unlearn only in a longer, wider historical perspective. As has been said, one who knows only his own time and place cannot even know that. For the object is not only a better understanding of other peoples, humane and valuable though that is. It is finally a better understanding of ourselves: of who we are, and where we are, and how we got this way; of both our achievements and our failures, our strength and our weakness. In a broad view we may get a deeper, fuller, more vivid sense of the continuities of man's history, the sources of our common humanity; and also of the fundamental differences between Western and other civilizations, or between the revolutionary modern world and all previous ages.

One might argue, indeed, that history is properly the frame and the crown of human knowledge. It has become an inclusive, more democratic study, no longer confined primarily to political and military doings, or history in "fancy dress," but concerned with the whole society, from its everyday life to its loftiest cultural achievements. Historians now draw on many other fields of knowledge, such as geography, geology, economics, philology, anthropology, and psychology; while their own studies in turn are useful to students in all other fields. One cannot rightly understand art, literature, philosophy, religion, or science itself without some knowledge of their history. "A great part of the mysticism and superstition of educated men," Benjamin Farrington remarked, "consists of knowledge which has broken loose from its historical moorings"—from the particular questions it was designed to answer, under particular conditions, for particular purposes. In another sense history is the most fundamental of subjects as the study of the whole process by which man came to realize his humanity, the potentialities that distinguish him from all other animals, and make him alone capable of having a history. For such reasons R. G. Collingwood believed that "we might very well be standing on the threshold of an age in which history would be as important for the world as natural science had been between 1600 and 1900."

At least it is clearly important for the major enterprise of our time. The spirit that led Ramsay to spend years in Turkey identifying the sites of forgotten cities, or M. Radet to make scholarly notes while lying prostrate from fever in a crude Turkish wagon, has also led to the extraordinary experiment of the United Nations, where East and West are seeking to realize Alexander's dream of One World. Upon the success of this experiment depends the fate of our civilization, possibly of the human race. Its success can never be guaranteed by the most perfect knowledge of history (even, alas, the history of Asia Minor); but neither can it be hoped for without some such knowledge, and the understanding it induces. Our chances would be better if men had a deeper sense of the past —the past that is never dead and done with, since it has created the present and conditioned the possibilities of the future.

In this view we might take another look at the small town of Dinar. When I visited it in the summer of 1952, it was especially unprepossessing because the main street had been torn up to lay water pipes. The natives had no imposing monuments to boast of, but they were proud of their dam, their water power, their electricity—and no doubt their garish new buildings. Dinar is now a boom town. It symbolizes the new Turkey of Ataturk. Thereby it points to a far greater historic drama—the resurgence of the entire East. This has led Arnold Toynbee to speculate that the East may, by a religious counteroffensive, once more take captive its Western conquerors. So far, however, what is happening is a very different story. The Greeks never really Hellenized the East; it clung to its ancient ways, beneath a veneer of Greek culture, and its anonymous peasant masses were hardly affected by the change in masters. Today the East is astir as never before, but with Western ideas. In self-defense against the overwhelmingly superior power of the West it is taking to Western science and technology, and Western nationalism. With these have come Western notions of freedom and self-determination, Western hopes of progress. Even its peasant masses are getting the idea that they have been underprivileged. In time its growing self-consciousness may produce a revival of its ancient religious spirit; the Near East in particular is also astir with religious fanaticism. But the driving spirit—in China, India, and Egypt, as in Turkey—is still a secular spirit.

We cannot predict the outcome with any assurance. If history does repeat itself, it gives no precedent for this drama. The most we can say is that the drama is a logical consequence of our history, and might still be an ideal one. Civilization itself began with a pooling of effort and skill, a more extensive co-operation than man had achieved in the village. In the long view its history has been a widening stream, as societies drew on the achievements of their predecessors and their neighbors. One reason for the brilliant achievement of the Greeks, again, is that they borrowed and adapted more freely than the peoples before them. Perhaps the best argument for the usually naïve, conceited assumption that Western history is the main stream of history, and a progress, is that our civilization has been by far the most inclusive, building upon the achievements of Greece, Rome, and Palestine, drawing as well from Islam and in time India and China, and lately studying the cultures of all other peoples, appreciating the art even of primitives. It has laid the intellectual as well as the material foundations for One World.

And so, at the end, we might well drop the invidious comparisons between East and West, which are met in the United Nations, and dwell rather on the simplicities, the first and last things, that unite them in fact, in the common adventure of civilization. For both alike the Preacher of Ecclesiastes must first have his say. There is no escaping him in Asia Minor, where proud cities lie buried everywhere, usually in the most desolate sites. Nature is quick to swallow them up, covering them with the scrubbiest, thorniest kind of vegetation to accentuate their desolation, and to discourage piety. Nature does not approve the civilized works of man, whatever his faith; Hittite palaces, Greek temples, Christian churches, and Seljuk mosques alike crumble, and in decay recall "the boredom, and the horror." Nature would have it that all is vanity. As far as our positive knowledge goes, there is literally no use on earth for any of the works of man. None make any difference to the universe.

Yet they make all the difference to man, so long as he keeps striving— as he does, and must. These ruins are magical even in their desolation. They may still give a lively idea of how gloriously man can build. Above all, they stir a sense of his enduring glory—the spirit that keeps him building, in defiance of his mortality. "The amateur of history is always hankering after permanence," writes R. W. Moore. The pious student knows that all the great societies have died, but that all live on in the great heritage of arts, skills, ideas, and ideals on which men still build. He knows that even Marsyas and Apollo did not die in vain, as long as men continue to cherish and to aspire. He knows what the simple worshipers of Lityerses knew, that all living things must die, but that out of death comes new life.

CHAPTER II

The Beginnings

1. THE DEBT TO MESOPOTAMIA

IT HAS LONG been thought that the pot, the plow, the bow and arrow, and other such artifacts found in prehistoric and primitive cultures all over the world were invented independently in different regions. "Necessity is the mother of invention"; so progressive creatures like men, having the same basic needs and the same basic power of intelligence, would naturally work out similar solutions. The specialists, however, now think otherwise. Generally they assume that the key ideas were transmitted from one people to another, gradually working their way around the world—just as the Greek customs of offering meat sacrifices to the gods and divining through entrails traveled all the way to Borneo. Every excavation yields more evidence of such diffusion. We cannot know just how or when men made the basic discoveries, and some may well have been made independently by different peoples; but it seems clear that the common stock in tool and practice is due primarily to a slow spread.

This is indeed what we might expect. If the bow and arrow seems old and simple to us, it appears relatively late in man's history, and on second thought is a pretty complicated affair. That primitive men could everywhere have worked out the same combination all by themselves is hard to imagine. On the face of his long history, moreover, man is not so naturally progressive a creature, least of all among primitives; he is intensely conservative. Nor is invention mothered by necessity. If it were, we should expect to find a marked inventiveness among the innumerable poor peoples whose life is a constant struggle for a bare subsistence. By our standards, God knows, they need plenty. And our standards have obscured another elementary truth. The key inventions are not actual necessities; men got along without them for untold thousands of years, just as some primitives still do. The truth is, as Lord Raglan observed, that we have learned to "do with" what men have naturally done without. The

32

inventions were all luxuries, due ultimately to the enterprise of a few gifted individuals. "The most civilized people are those who regard as necessities the largest number of luxuries."

They may be wrong; but at least few men want to return to the cave. The rest of us must honor the prehistoric peoples who lived in southwest Asia, in or about Mesopotamia. For it was apparently here, some eight thousand years ago, that occurred the first great revolution in man's life— the "neolithic revolution," or discovery of agriculture, which transformed him from a food hunter or food gatherer into a food producer, and centered his life in the village. "Revolution" has been criticized as a misleading term, implying a more sudden, violent, and purposeful change than actually took place; yet this was a radical change, it had revolutionary consequences, and the term might be worth keeping if only to remind us how much we owe to the "unchanging East." In this prehistoric age men learned to cultivate all the major food plants and to domesticate all the major animals used today. The fourth millennium B.C. in particular was one of the great creative periods in human history. Men now invented the wheel, the plow, the loom, the potter's wheel, the brick, the sail; and they learned to work metals. From the region of Mesopotamia the new tools and skills spread to the west and north, and with them went the new customs and beliefs that had developed in the village. Eventually this culture reached Europe, in diluted or degraded form.

Two major religious figures stem from this early period—the Mother Goddess and her dying son. The Mother is the oldest known deity. Even the prehistoric cave men knew her, for where they left their superb animal drawings they also left female figurines with exaggerated breasts and wombs, or symbolic vulvae.[1] As they grew no crops, the figurines presumably represented human fertility; a Freudian might see in the cave a symbol of the womb, especially because in historic times the Mother continued to display a preference for caves. But with the rise of agriculture the goddess naturally became an Earth Mother, assuring the annual crops. Figurines of her are found in the earliest prehistoric villages. In time she came to wear cow horns, as the domestication of animals strengthened totemic bonds. Like nature, however, the Mother had a potentially ferocious aspect, perhaps symbolized by the lions that became her attendants. In the civilizations of America, where Asiatic-looking figurines are found

[1] These animal drawings, which were once viewed as works of pure art, had a religious rather than an aesthetic function. They do not adorn the entrances of the caves, where the people lived, but usually are found so far back in dark recesses that it may take an hour or two of climbing and crawling to reach them. Here some kind of ceremony was held, perhaps to assure power over the animals, perhaps to participate in their splendor. It would seem to be the origin of totemism.

on the lowest levels of excavation, she soon lost whatever motherly qualities she might have had and became simply ferocious. The Aztecs knew her only as the Eagle-Woman. (Gertrude Levy suggests that one reason for her ferocity may have been that she was not needed to promote fertility in Central America, where men had to contend against too exuberant vegetation, and also that they could not know of her cowlike gentleness because they never learned to domesticate animals.) We are clearly not dealing here with one of Jung's "archetypal patterns" or "primordial images," the supposedly universal images embedded in the structure of the brain, which have grown popular with devotees of the timeless truth of myth.

Later there appeared on the scene a young male god who was credited with the introduction of agriculture, and who annually died and was reborn, to assure the birth of the new year. His inevitable association with the Mother in the fertility rites led to their seemingly incongruous relation. Although a virgin, as the first cause of life, she became both the mother and the lover of the young god. Nevertheless he too was an authentic immortal. He survived when the sun gods made their appearance, with the realization of man's dependence on the life-giving sun. Later on the kings commonly acted for him in the New Year's festival, a ritual drama designed to secure the welfare of the community. The dramas took different forms as they spread and developed all over the Near East, under changing conditions; but the suffering, death, and resurrection of the god remained a basic theme. Out of this ritual pattern, it is now widely believed, Greek drama developed; and the survival of the pattern is plain in Christianity. But again the dying, resurrected god is not a universal image of Jung's type. He was unknown in America; he at least failed to take hold in the Far East; and Israel and Islam would have nothing to do with him. Although one might expect him to be universal, given the cycle of life and death, in fact his image is embedded chiefly in our Western heritage.

Both East and West, however, owe their being to another achievement of the fourth millennium—the so-called urban revolution that created civilization. This too was no revolution in the sense of an abrupt, marked change. The birth of civilization cannot be dated—it was a gradual change, and there is no agreement upon just how elaborate a culture has to become in order to be dignified as a civilization. The basic fact remains that the villages in Mesopotamia grew into towns of some size, and then into full-fledged cities with such characteristic institutions as the market, the temple, and the palace, served by the new invention of writing—perhaps the clearest index to the emergence of civilization. The immediate means to this development was the organization of an irrigation and drainage system in the Tigris-Euphrates river valley.

Some historians, such as Gordon Childe, make technological and economic advance the key to the rise of civilization. Others, such as Robert J. Braidwood, believe that the essential change was cultural, a new way of thinking that made possible large-scale irrigation. As we cannot actually separate these material and spiritual factors, or assign positive priorities, I assume that it is enough to recognize that the rise of civilization logically required, as it historically involved, both technological and cultural development. The "essence" of the matter, if we must have one, might be the pooling of effort and skill that was common to both. Objectively, this meant a more complex, highly organized society, with increasing specialization and division of labor among farmers, artisans, merchants, supervisors, and priests. Subjectively, it meant a new kind of life for the individual, who was no longer self-sufficient, and who was aware of a much greater world than the homogeneous, self-contained village; for if he continued to live in a village, it now served the city.

The authors of this whole development were the Sumerians, a brown people of unknown origin, speaking a language unrelated to any other known language. We who cherish the pioneering spirit should be the first to celebrate their astounding creativity, for they worked out all the novel institutions required by civilization. They succeeded in establishing large-scale government, a formal state with formal laws. In building great public works they developed monumental architecture, and with it a decorative art that for refinement and technical skill was surpassed by few later peoples in antiquity.[2] They systematized large-scale business by standard weights and measures, timekeeping, and the institution of credit. They made the all-important invention of writing. With this they laid the foundations of systematic learning, notably in mathematics and astronomy, and introduced formal education. They created literature, ranging from the tale and the proverb to the epic—a form once believed to be the creation of Indo-European peoples. Samuel Kramer, a leading authority in the translation of their literature, has listed twenty-five "firsts" of the extraordinary Sumerians.

[2] Leonard Woolley, who excavated the ziggurat at the city of Ur, reported his amazement at finding that there was not a single straight line in the vast building. Outlines were all slightly curved, walls sloped inward and had slightly convex surfaces—everything was nicely calculated to counteract the appearance of bending or sloping that would be given by actually straight lines, and so to create the optical illusion of perfect squareness and symmetry. Two thousand years before the Greeks, the Sumerians had discovered the secret by which the builders of the Parthenon were to amaze the world.

In retrospect, all this may look like a wholly natural development, as one thing logically led to another. Historians are wont to say that it was "bound" to come, once men had learned to produce food. Yet it was an astonishing development, by no means preordained. Countless peoples have remained primitive down to our time, failing to take any of the logical steps. Of the many others who have acquired civilization, almost none—if any—created it independently, starting from scratch; directly or indirectly, they built on the achievements of the Sumerians. It took European peoples about two thousand years to catch up with them. Still older civilizations may yet be found, it is true. The Sumerian archives reveal that their kings imported gold- and silverworkers from the region of Iran, suggesting the existence of a contemporaneous civilization that might have been as high as their own and possibly older. But meanwhile all the evidence indicates that Mesopotamia was the main center from which radiated the influences that stimulated other societies to embark on similar adventures.

The basic forms of Sumerian civilization were retained by the later peoples who ruled the land of Mesopotamia—the Semitic Akkadians, "Babylonians," Assyrians, Chaldeans. Some of their most famous works, such as the law code of Hammurabi and the Epic of Gilgamesh, grew out of Sumerian originals. To the east, Sumerian influence stimulated the rise of civilization in the Indus valley. Some thousand years later the impulse reached China and the Far East, which almost certainly contributed something to the civilizations in pre-Columbian America. The Egyptians developed a highly original culture of their own, but in their beginnings they too were indebted to the Sumerians; through some unknown intermediary they borrowed cylinder seals, learned to make bricks, and apparently got the idea of writing. (There is no evidence of a reciprocal Egyptian influence on Sumer.) Westward the influence spread to Syria and northward to Anatolia, where the Hittites also took over the basic forms of Sumer. Through Syria it reached the brilliant Minoan civilization, originally stimulated by Egypt. The excavations of Woolley at Alalakh, near Antioch, have shown that the great palace of Minos at Knossos owed to Asia its frescoes and the best of its architecture.[3]

In general, research has steadily magnified the historical importance of the Sumerians. It becomes ever more apparent how much they contributed to the art and thought of their successors, and through them to the

[3] As this book went to press, the news appeared that the earliest written script of the Minoans ("Linear A") has at last been deciphered. It turns out that their language was derived from the Akkadian. One may now wonder about Homer's Achaeans: could their name also have come from the land of Sumer?

Hebrews, Phoenicians, and Greeks. When Abraham left "Ur of the Chaldees" to become the father of the Hebrews, and later of the Moslems, he perhaps brought with him such memories as the Flood—a tremendous inundation that buried lower Mesopotamia under eight feet of sediment, as the excavations at Ur revealed; but he left behind a level of civilization that it would take his people more than a thousand years to recover, with the aid of other peoples who owed as much to an Ur they knew only by hearsay, if at all.

But the Flood provokes less exhilarating thoughts. If the civilization achieved by the Sumerians was a natural fulfillment of human potentialities, it was still an artificial creation, in defiance of nature. The city that made life more abundant, comfortable, and secure also made life more difficult and precarious. It promoted the exchange of diseases as well as goods; it loosened the bonds of kin and disrupted the moral order that held together the simple village community; it created the problem of maintaining law and order; it invited the attack of rude barbarians from the mountains. In times of natural calamity its citizens were more helpless than prehistoric villagers, who could pick up and move to higher grounds or more fertile pastures. The city was a triumph of man's self-assertion— and a forceful reminder of his dependence on greater powers. Its natural fate was desolation, by slow decay when not by sudden destruction. It helps to explain the less agreeable elements in the Sumerian legacy to ancient man.

The early city was owned and ruled by a god. His temple was the seat of its administration and his service the object of its enterprise; writing was invented for the practical purpose of keeping the god's accounts. The ziggurat, or "Mountain of God," remained the heart and soul of Sumerian culture. A huge artificial mound, built of brick, from which terraces rose to the temple of the god, it later became known as the Tower of Babel; but this was an arrogant Hebrew idea. So far from symbolizing the pride and presumption of man, the Tower symbolized his slavish dependence upon the god. Sumerian theology taught that man had been created merely to be the slave of the gods, to do their dirty work; as Marduk later announced in the Epic of Creation, "Let him be burdened with the toil of the gods that they may freely breathe." Nor were the gods grateful for his toil. For reasons always unfathomable they might send floods or droughts, or let their own city be destroyed by an enemy. It was certain that everything depended upon them—and as certain that they could not really be depended upon. They themselves were insecure, in a world that they had not created, but that had been wrenched out of chaos by heavenly violence and in heavenly confusion.

None was omnipotent or free from care. Sumerian mythology reveals a deep, constant anxiety that could not be allayed by the most meticulous attention to omens.

In time the cities were ruled by kings, who acted as the god's agent. The Sumerians believed that kingship "had descended from heaven" after the Flood, as the essential means to an ordered society and a proper service of the god. But that it was not a pure heavenly boon was tacitly acknowledged by the Sumerian myths of a Golden Age before the Flood —the oldest known version of the Eden theme: "In those days there was no snake, there was no scorpion, there was no hyena. . . . There was no fear, no terror; Man had no rival." Although it is uncertain just how the king was chosen by the god, his power over his subjects was virtually absolute. The most conspicuous of his own agents was the tax collector. Eventually some of the kings were deified, or at least claimed divinity, but this elevation brought no more assurance that their subjects would thrive. It created another gulf between the Sumerian commoner and the powers that be.

In every chapter, down to the Ottoman Turks of our own time, we shall keep returning to this seemingly unholy institution of the divine kingship. It was adopted or developed by almost all other societies in the Near East. But for this reason—as well as in justice to the pioneering Sumerians —we need to understand that it was a natural institution, and not caused simply by greed or lust for power. As the Sumerian cities prospered and grew, under their gods, a strong central power became necessary to protect them against ambitious rivals, to safeguard their extensive trade routes, and to defend against invaders an exposed land that had no natural boundaries. Successful kings would naturally seem godlike. As statesmen they might then take an enlarged view of the strategical requirements of self-defense. About 2300 B.C. the first empire in history was established by Sargon, the first great conqueror, whose dominions extended to the Mediterranean. Other Sumerian kings were statesmen by higher standards. They were the world's first lawgivers, promulgating, centuries before Hammurabi, codes that included more humane provisions than the Biblical law of an eye for an eye and a tooth for a tooth. They made the first known efforts at international law, or abitration instead of war; we hear of an early king called in to settle a boundary dispute between two other kings. Another, one Urukagina of Lagash, was the first known social reformer. A scribe told gratefully how he rid the city of the plague of tax collectors.

This scribe did not complain of the god of Lagash, who within less than ten years allowed Urukagina and his city to be overwhelmed by a king from another city. Characteristically he took for granted that the ways of the god were inscrutable. But he thereby points to a further reason for honoring the Sumerians, who accomplished so much in the name of the gods, and actually in spite of them. Their religion is likely to seem more irrational than it was because their means of keeping the gods on the job were purely magical (though as far as that goes, men have not yet found a better means of getting the god to end a drought—modern New Yorkers have prayed for rain *en masse*). In Mesopotamia men were at the mercy of fitful floods and droughts, and more regularly of scorching winds and dust storms; so the Sumerians at least were realistic enough not to pretend that the gods were wholly benevolent and just. They pleaded with them, bargained with them, sometimes remonstrated with them. They knew that the gods exercised rather doubtful judgment, especially when angry. They even suggest a possibly humorous toleration of such shortcomings, as in their myths about how the gods cut up when they had too much beer.[4] Sumerian art occasionally exhibits an unmistakable humor. And all such assertions of the human spirit seem at once more pathetic and more dignified because the Sumerians entertained no heavenly hopes or illusions. The furnishings in their graves include no figurines of the gods or clearly religious symbols of any kind. Their myths, hymns, and wisdom literature likewise indicate that except possibly for the deified kings, men did not dream of enjoying everlasting bliss. They had to make the best of their uncertain life on earth.[5]

The historic reward of the Sumerians for their extraordinary pioneering achievement was not fame, but oblivion. Their much less original successors, the Babylonians and Assyrians, were remembered ever after, but the men of Ur were completely forgotten for over two thousand years. They had to wait for archaeologists to bring them and their gods back to life. So it was, too, with the Hittites, who because of their achievement

---

[4] Some scholars believe that beer, one of the many minor blessings bequeathed us by our prehistoric ancestors, may have been the source of all the major ones. It was perhaps the desire for alcohol rather than for bread that inspired men to cultivate grain instead of gathering it.

[5] Although almost all ancient peoples buried some possessions of the dead, this custom does not prove a belief in immortality. The possessions might betoken simple sentiment, rather than the idea of use in an afterlife. Today man's behavior is still an uncertain guide to his belief. Archaeologists excavating our graves a thousand years hence, and finding evidence that the dead were arrayed in their finery, might conclude that we expected to enter the afterworld all dressed up; and then they might speculate why some of us preferred to be cremated, as if spurning this afterlife. We know from myths and legends that many peoples have had only a vague idea of the afterlife, and no idea of a heavenly one. Some apparently feared the spirits of the dead, putting heavy slabs on their graves to keep them in their place. We cannot rightly speak of an innate, universal belief in immortality.

were able to inaugurate the recorded history of Asia Minor, who probably knew less about the Sumerians than we now know, and who like them went into oblivion.

2. GORDIUM: INTERLUDE ON ARCHAEOLOGY

In the heart of Anatolia, near a little huddle of Turkish farmhouses known as Yassihüyük, lies a mound that was once the city of Gordium. A shaft sunk to the bottom of the mound reveals a series of cities, neatly stratified, dating from the Early Bronze Age; to peer into this hole in the ground is to look down a vista of some five thousand years of human history. One of these cities was a Phrygian capital, of King Gordius and King Midas. Beneath it is a city of the Hittites. Above it are successive settlements under later rulers of the region—Lydian, Persian, Greek, Roman. On this site Alexander the Great cut with his sword the Gordian knot that symbolized the secret to the rule of Asia. He went on to conquer Asia and so immortalized the city, in a proverbial locution.

Even so Gordium cannot be considered one of the great symbolic cities of Asia Minor. Many other mounds in Anatolia contain a similar series of settlements, reaching as far back. The Phrygians were historically much less important than the Hittites, whose capital was farther east. Under its later rulers Gordium was never again a major center. The Hellenistic town was prosperous but quite undistinguished; by Roman times—as Strabo recorded and excavations have confirmed—it had dwindled into a hamlet; and thereafter it disappeared from sight. Probably it would have disappeared from human memory as well had not Alexander cut its knot, for no other event of consequence is known in its history. At that, as we shall see, Alexander apparently missed the point of the secret. I am pausing at Gordium for a personal reason. Here I first watched archaeologists at work, as a guest of the University of Pennsylvania expedition that was excavating the site.

In his popular *Gods, Graves, and Scholars,* C. W. Ceram dramatizes the glamorous discoveries of archaeologists, such as Homer's Troy, the Tower of Babel, and the tomb of Tutankhamen. His favorite story is that of an adventurer who follows a wild gleam, undaunted by the heavy odds against him, and in the end is rewarded by a sensational find, preferably of golden treasures. These are the stories that periodically get archaeology into the newspapers. The golden treasures help to incite the sponsors of expeditions, and serve the practical needs of museums. They correspond to the popular idea of ruins: picturesque or spectacular remains, such as those of Pompeii and the Acropolis of Athens. The story of the Gordium expedition is much less glamorous, and much more typical. It illustrates a more important drama, which finally is romantic enough.

It may begin with a patient young student of archaeology whom I shall call Miss X. While the main body of the expedition was engaged on the big city mound of Gordium, she was alone with a few Turkish workmen on a nearby tumulus, digging up skeletons; and she was pretty depressed. Weeks before, she had stumbled upon a Hittite graveyard, beneath Phrygian graves that had yielded some gold jewelry. The Hittites were buried in large urns but apparently had been common people; she was finding no jewelry in the urns, only fragments of very ordinary pottery. Day after day she returned to headquarters with nothing to report except more bones. And every skeleton meant hours of painstaking work. It had to be laid bare with little sticks and brushes, the earth removed pinch by pinch so as not to break or disturb a single bone; then it had to be photographed and catalogued, with notations about its exact position in the mound; finally it had to be packed up and shipped to a museum. The work was more tedious because Miss X knew little about skeletons. Some specialist would study them in the museum, and in time write a scholarly article that a few other specialists would read. As a reward for her pains, Miss X might be embalmed in a footnote.

A layman might be as depressed by the ruins unearthed on the city mound. There were no temples, theaters, forums, statues, columns, or any marble to speak of; at first sight there was only a meaningless sprawl and tumble of foundation walls, with here and there a pile of dreary potsherds. Although the main objective of the expedition was the Phrygian city, the archaeologists were digging in the modern scientific manner, doing a thorough job on each of the layers above it. On the highest part of the mound they had cleared a section of the Roman village. They were still working on the undistinguished Hellenistic town lower down; about the best thing they had to show here was a commonplace mosaic floor. Elsewhere they were clearing a section of an older city, dating from 500 or 600 B.C., which appeared to have been prosperous, but as ordinary as Middletown; most of the objects they had found in it might have come from an ancient dime store. The architect of the expedition was disgusted with its people—they had been such slovenly, stupid builders. There were no signs of stirring event in any of these towns. If a city wants to win immortal fame through archaeology, it should contrive a catastrophe—get itself destroyed by an earthquake or burned down by an enemy; then treasures will be found in the ruins, preserved by the sudden destruction. We know that Gordium was once looted by the Romans, but otherwise the unheroic towns here had simply decayed. Their people got poorer, and gradually picked up and left—leaving very little behind them. They left so little, indeed, that after two seasons of work the expedition could still not be certain that it was Gordium they were excavating, for they had found no inscriptions that positively identified it.

So it often goes for the archaeologist. Patient, thorough, methodical— these are the good words for the routine of a dig. Another word for it is drudgery. Tons of earth must be excavated by hand, and every shovelful sifted; countless little objects must be counted, and cleaned, and catalogued; and for weeks on end there may be no exciting finds. Most excavation, moreover, ends in destruction. The foundations of a building are carefully laid bare and all the debris cleared away, so that its plan may be studied and its masonry examined; then like as not the walls must be knocked down, to get at whatever may lie beneath them. At Gordium all this routine seemed drearier because the October weather had suddenly turned cold and gray on the bleak Anatolian plateau. If the expedition at last hit upon a buried treasure—say in the huge nearby tumulus that looks like a royal tomb—we might read of the breathless moment when the tomb was opened and the dazzling hoard of King Midas leaped to the eye. Meanwhile I have a vivid memory of archaeologists who were breathing hard, dressed in corduroys, clodhoppers, and mittens, scattered in cold trenches and whipped by a raw wind, as they worked over their stones and bones.[6]

Still this was not simple drudgery. As a layman I was fascinated when Miss X's workmen hit upon two more burial urns, even though they uncovered only the invariable bones. After all, these were the bones of Hittites—people who had dreamed their dreams, said their yeas and nays, more than three thousand years ago. As I watched Miss X work on them, ever so gently dusting off each bone, I wondered whether these poor devils had ever known in their lifetime such gentle care as they were now getting. The more obvious rewards of the routine, such as the gold jewelry from the Phrygian grave, stirred some further reflections about gods, graves, and scholars. Most of the objects in our museums came from graves. If they were intended for the use of the dead in the afterlife, there

---

[6] I am pleased to add that since these lines were written, the expedition has got down to the Phrygian city. It is a much more imposing city than the ones above it; even a layman might be awed by its massive gateway. And in the summer of 1957 the expedition did uncover a royal tomb in the huge tumulus, after digging a passageway more than two hundred feet long into the base of the mound. Although the tomb contained no golden treasure—only some rich bronze utensils and ornaments— it was remarkably well preserved, behind thick walls of cedar, juniper, and pine still intact after 2,700 years. The surprising absence of weapons suggests that its royal occupant may have been revered as a statesman rather than a warrior. One would like to imagine that he was the wise Gordius who tied the legendary knot.

is some question whether these dead found them very useful, or even enjoyed an afterlife. Their gods were false gods, I am told, and certainly are dead ones; it is hard to imagine the heaven or hell they may be occupying. Nevertheless archaeologists have given these people a kind of afterlife. From the objects recovered from their graves we now know something about how they lived and thought and felt. In the absence of any sensational finds at Gordium, I came to appreciate more fully not only the patience and skill but the poetry and the piety of this methodical effort to restore a vanished life.

Even the routine finds may quicken the spirit. The temporary museum of the expedition contained many touching mementos of the nameless people who had lived and died here—pins and beads and dice, cosmetic appliances, a child's drinking pot, a jar patched by some thrifty housewife, a hoard of coins found in a pot behind the proverbial loose brick in a wall. The gold jewelry from the Phrygian grave spoke as touchingly of the unchanging ways of womankind through the ages. Another tumulus gave evidence that these obscure people too had made "history," of the familiar kind. It contained the charred remains of a two-story building, with fragments of Lydian pottery among the arrowheads and bones littering the floor; apparently a Lydian garrison had been overwhelmed here, perhaps by the Persians. The thick layer of clay piled up over the ruins to form a burial mound implied that among the slain was a notable chieftain.

But more important for the archaeologist are many remains without evident interest for the layman. Gold is of no value to him—unless it is finely wrought or given some unusual design; and even so a hoard of fine jewelry may be a less valuable find than a crude clay figurine. Although Miss X was young enough to be disappointed by her failure to find more jewelry, the monotonous bones may prove a richer haul. She was unearthing more Hittite skeletons than had yet been found elsewhere. Whatever went on in their heads, the shape of their skulls is significant as a primary index of racial type. The skulls may help to clear up the mystery of who these Hittites were, whence they came, and what other peoples they were related to. Similarly with the jumble of stones on the city mound. The architect brought to life one of the meaningless piles in the stupid archaic city—a "gem" she called this building. It was a fairly large building that had tumbled neatly, as if pushed over, in serried courses of stone mingled with remains of some beams; so she was able to reconstruct its main outlines with assurance. It had had wooden pillars at its entrance and rafters for binding in its stone walls. It thus illustrated the historic transition from wood to stone in architecture, and the apparent evolution of the Greek column from wooden pillars. With the steady accumulation of such knowledge, archaeologists are able to conjure up a great temple from a mere scatter of stone.

Still more useful to the historian is the dreary potsherd. Potsherds are really immortal: bones, wood, and metal may return to dust, but baked clay never does. They are also blessed by having no intrinsic value; while royal tombs have everywhere been looted, potsherds are left alone. Every mound is littered with them, and large mounds contain millions—giving the impression that the ancients spent most of their time making and breaking pots. By jigsaw-puzzle methods, archaeologists have put together many handsome vases from the piles of fragments, recovering much vanished art, but even the plainest pots may tell an important story. Every culture had its characteristic style of pottery, with characteristic changes as it developed. Specialists can now identify and date the shards with something like scientific certainty; by this means alone they can chart the chronological course of history. Because the pottery at most larger sites includes imported ware, historians have learned a great deal about the technology and commerce as well as the cultural development of antiquity.

In general, the most trivial objects may have weighty significance. The appearance of the bronze or copper needle marks a major development in culture. The safety pin helps to distinguish Mycenaean from Minoan culture. Seashells found in Anatolian mounds are one sign of the surprisingly extensive commerce in the Early Bronze Age. Objects made of amber, which came from the Baltic region, indicate how far-flung this commerce was. By piecing together the countless fragments of such knowledge, historians have been able to write the economic, social, and cultural histories that the ancients themselves neglected to write. And if archaeologists now concentrate on materials and techniques, rather than on the less tangible imaginative or "spiritual" expressions of culture, they provide the indispensable data for all studies of ancient culture. They have told us all we know about many preliterate peoples.

Young Miss X may have been further depressed by the knowledge that the Hittite skeletons she was so painstakingly unearthing would end up in the storeroom of a museum, or in effect be reburied. But this brings up another singular fact. The familiar museums of art and history that dot the modern world are historically unique. No other society in the past made such collections of the art and antiquities of other peoples. None had the means of studying the universal commonwealth of gods and men that a few, in their loftiest thought, conceived of.

3. THE HITTITES

The reputation of King David suffered very little from his crime in doing away with Uriah the Hittite, the husband of the Bathsheba he lusted after. The reputation of Uriah's people suffered much more. This and other Biblical references to the Hittites implied that they were a small tribe in Palestine, serving no better purpose than as mercenaries in the armies of the Hebrew kings. Orthodox scholars of the last century were simply mystified by the scattered monuments and stones with strange hieroglyphic inscriptions that travelers began running across in Syria and Asia Minor. When A. H. Sayce announced, in 1880, his very bold theory that they were the work of the Hittites, a nation centered in Asia Minor, he was ridiculed as the "inventor" of this people. They did not come into their own until 1906, when their capital was excavated at Bogazköy. A hoard of royal tablets, some written in an Akkadian cuneiform script that could be read, proved beyond all doubt that they had been a great power, ranking with the contemporary powers of Egypt and Babylon. Then came the still more startling discovery that their own language was Indo-European, of the western group that includes Greek, Latin, and Germanic. It appeared that a European people had entered Asia as early as some two thousand years before Christ.

This invasion, writes the Hittitologist Albrecht Goetze, marks "the first historical conflict between East and West." It also marks the beginning of confusion and paradox in this conflict. As an "Aryan" people, the Hittites were presumably illiterates interested chiefly in war and the breeding of livestock, but we do not know how they entered or what they brought with them. Their very name is a misnomer. They got it from the land of the "Hatti," whom they conquered; there is no telling what they originally called themselves. Their first known king, Anittas, boasted that he had stormed and destroyed Hattusas, a fortress town of the Hatti, sowing weeds where it had been. "Whosoever becomes king after me and again settles Hattusas," he proclaimed, "may the Weather God of Heaven strike him!" Later kings were proud to trace their ancestry to him but disregarded his curse, building their capital at Hattusas. The provincial authors of the Old Testament naturally would not know that the Hittites in Palestine were among the survivors of an empire that for seven centuries the Weather God of Heaven had neglected to strike down.

It is certain that the Hittites entered a level of culture considerably higher than their own. Trade had brought into Asia Minor the influence of Sumerian civilization. At Alalakh (Atchana), in the southern region on which the Sumerians drew for the timber they needed, there had been about fifteen successive towns or cities over a period of almost two thousand years, before the brash Hittites conquered it in the fourteenth century B.C.[7] The extortions of its merchants provoked the great Sargon to conquer and annex it. Anatolia proper was occupied by independent little kingdoms that presumably flourished on trade for the mineral wealth of the region, especially copper. Royal tombs at Alaja, near Bogazköy, have revealed the exquisite art developed in the third millenium. There were also scattered colonies of literate Assyrian merchants, as at Kanesh (Kültepe), near modern Kayseri. The Hittites must have learned a good deal from these peoples. They were further influenced by the Hurrians, an Asiatic people who, under another Aryan dynasty, became the powerful kingdom of Mitanni to the south. Even the names of their kings and their gods are not Indo-European. Arnold Toynbee has said that the cultural heritage of Anatolia remained predominantly Hittite down to Ottoman times, and unquestionably they put their stamp on it; but it is hard to say just what they contributed and how much lasting difference it made.

The immediate contribution of the Hittites was chiefly political. As they conquered, they did not simply slaughter or enslave, but showed some genius for organization and administration. They established a feudal empire that seemingly enlisted the loyalty of most of its diverse subjects by respecting their customs and according them some equity; the tablets found at Bogazköy contain traces of at least eight different languages. Their capital, in relatively barren uplands, was well chosen for defensive purposes and was strongly fortified; its massive walls made a circuit of five miles. From it they built a radiating system of roads, paving the way for the later Persians and Romans. By such means they built up a power that by 1600 enabled them to conquer Babylon and supersede it as the greatest power in the Near East. Although their empire then fell on bad times, it was strong enough to recover. It reached its peak in the fourteenth century under the greatest of its kings, Suppiluliumas I (1375–35), who broke the dangerous power of Mitanni and extended his rule as far as Lebanon. The widow of Tutankhamen asked for one of his sons to share her throne in Egypt. In 1296 a Hittite king fought the famous Ramses II to a standstill in the battle of Kadesh in Syria—a battle that the Pharaoh described for posterity as a glorious victory, won almost singlehanded, but that looks more like a defeat, as he retreated immediately afterward.

German scholars have hailed the political achievement of the Hittites

---

[7] It is incidentally a striking example of religious conservatism. During its long history its temple was rebuilt fifteen times, by different peoples, in different styles, to different gods—but always on the site sanctified by its first shrine.

as the first manifestation of Indo-Germanic genius, and of its superiority over the spirit of the East. At least the Hittite kings compare favorably with the Oriental monarchs before and after them. They were not so boastful as the Pharaohs, so cruel as the Assyrians, so despotic as Oriental rulers in general. They were not divine or divinely appointed, but ruled as something like constitutional monarchs. In the early empire they shared their authority with the *pankus,* a council of nobles and warriors that supposedly represented the whole community; the *pankus* could sentence to death a king who had murdered a relative. They also shared their prestige, strangely, with the queen and queen mother. More strangely, they issued some statements to explain or defend their deeds, instead of merely boasting about them. They even tried to justify their foreign policy, taking pains to communicate their grievances to insubordinate rulers before attacking them, and then referring the dispute to the judgment of heaven. "Up, then!" wrote Mursilis II to the King of Arzawa. "Let us fight, and let the Storm God, my lord, decide our case!" Perhaps the most striking testimony to the relative dignity, modesty, and good sense of the Hittite rulers is the treaty of peace they concluded with Ramses II after the battle of Kadesh—the first major political treaty known to history. Agreeing to discontinue all offensive operations, the "Great and Mighty" monarchs signed a "good treaty of peace and brotherhood that shall create peace between them for all time." As a result the Near East knew peace for seventy years, a long enough time as history goes in such matters. The vainglorious records left by Ramses make one doubt that he had the wisdom to think up such a settlement by himself.

Yet the political wisdom of the Hittites remains strictly relative. They could not solve the inveterate problem of monarchy, the problem of succession. In the early empire the king chose his successor, with the familiar result of palace intrigue and struggle, like as not ending in assassination.[8]

---

[8] One of the most moving Hittite documents is the testament of the dying Hattusilis I (c. 1650–20), who had returned from battle to find himself betrayed by a nephew he had brought up as his own son, raised above all others, and chosen as his heir:

To the words of the king he has never hearkened. But to the words of his mother, the serpent, he hearkened.
Brothers and sisters brought evil counsels to him again and again.
To their counsels he hearkened. I learned of this, I, the king.
So be it: Force shall be answered with force!
But enough! He is my son no longer! Then his mother bellowed like a cow. . . .
Always I raised him up before others; always I was concerned for his welfare. But he has never
Lovingly obeyed the king's wishes. How then could he,

In the later empire succession was made hereditary. While this arbitrary method worked better, it induced the kings to act more like Oriental sacred monarchs. Nothing is heard of the *pankus* in the last centuries. The Great King took on superhuman powers, with titles to match. He was called "Hero, beloved of the god"; upon his death it was regularly said that he "became a god." Suppiluliumas referred to himself as "My Sunship." Even so his name and his exploits were forgotten by the later peoples who ruled Asia Minor, and it may be presumed that with them disappeared any memories of the earlier Hittite forms of constitutional monarchy. What the enduring peasants thought of their new masters is not known, of course, but neither do we have any evidence that the masters were conscious of a unique political legacy. The most that can be safely said is that possibly, by indirection, the Hittite example had something to do with the humane policies of the Persian conquerors.

To religion the Hittites made no significant contribution. Their most characteristic god was Teshub, the Weather God, befitting the rigorous climate of Anatolia; they borrowed him from the Hurrians. With Teshub they took over an immense medley of native gods, the "thousand gods of Hatti," whom they organized in some kind of pantheon that remains unintelligible. The state cult seems to be represented in the two mysterious processions of deities carved on the cliffs of Yazilikaya, the "Narrow Gorge" above Bogazköy, but these processions, which started the speculation that led to the discovery of the Hittites, are still a puzzle to scholars. Perhaps the best guess is that they represent a sacred marriage. The leading goddess in one procession is a queen, Hurrian by name, who had the exalted role of "Queen of Heaven and Earth, mistress of the kings and queens of the Land of Hatti." She was akin to Inanna, the Sumerian queen of heaven, who became Ishtar, but no doubt she sprang directly from the ancient Mother Goddess of Anatolia, whom the Hittites worshiped under various names; Ma is probably as old as any. Her son, however, was not prominent. Although a god of agriculture who appears in the "Myth of the Missing God" suggests the dying god, the Weather God and Sun God were also responsible for the rebirth of life in the spring.[9]

With these familiar figures the Hittites had the usual magical accessories: lavish sacrifices, rites of purification, temple prostitutes, oracles,

---

If all went according to his wish,
Love Hattusas? (Translation from C. W. Ceram, *The Secret of the Hittites*.)

[9] The Sumerian Inanna was as unorthodox in this respect. It now appears that in her celebrated "Descent to the Netherworld" she was not bent on rescuing from death her husband Dumuzi, better known as Tammuz. As the incomplete myth breaks off, she is handing him over in anger to the netherworld demons.

scapegoats, ritual combats (including the timeless myth of the Slaying of the Dragon), and divination. But with all this supernatural help they did not escape the anxiety that haunted the Mesopotamian peoples. They took excellent care of the god in his temple, providing a highly disciplined staff to feed him, wash him, dress him in fine garments, entertain him with music and dance, flatter him with constant reminders that he was their lord and master; and even so they could not count on his wisdom or justice. While the Hittites acknowledged that their misfortunes might be due to their sins or the sins of their fathers, they knew that the god could be simply careless or absent-minded. A horde of demons was always lying in wait, eager to work evil when he was asleep, off on a trip, or wrapped up in his own pleasures; but when he was on the job he might still make bad mistakes, which they had frankly to point out to him. He also had to be reminded that when he let in plagues his own service would suffer.

Fragments of this religious patchwork survived the disappearance of the Hittite empire. The Weather God Teshub became Jupiter Dolichenus, whom the Roman army carried all over their empire; in his reincarnation he carried the emblems of lightning and the Hittite double ax, and had a lion goddess as a consort. Under the name of Tarhund he gave rise to Tarchon of the Etruscans, who migrated to Italy from Asia Minor. Apulunas, a god of the gates, may possibly be the original of Apollo. Probably Hesiod drew some of his cosmogony from Hittite-Hurrian sources, notably the ghastly myth about the emasculation of Uranus by his son Cronus, father of Zeus. The Amazons may derive from the armed priestesses depicted in Hittite sculpture, for wherever they appear in Greek legend Hittites had been in the vicinity, and in Greek art their regular weapon is the double ax. The double ax that Heracles wrested from the Amazon queen Hippolyte became the emblem of the Lydian kings, and later of Zeus Labrandeus in Caria. But the only real immortal to come through was the Mother Goddess, in particular as Cybele and as Ma. The major religious legacy of the Hittites was not Hittite, but ancient Anatolian.

For the rest, they did not develop so rich a culture as the other major peoples of the ancient East. Their architecture, centered on the walled citadel, is impressive chiefly for its massiveness and solidity. They had no real literature. Their myths and legends were mostly Hurrian or Babylonian, retold in a bald prose; they left no epic of their own, no poetry of any sort. The personal statements of their kings are sometimes moving simply because they are straightforward and free from conscious literary effect. In the decorative arts we have little but pottery from the early empire, but there seems to have been no major development, much less a brilliant flowering. Their art displays less variety and animation, refinement and elegance, than that of the natives before them (as at Alaja), and is far inferior to the Sumerian. "Exquisite" is never the word for it.

The most distinctive artistic achievement of the Hittites was in sculpture, which appeared in the late empire. Its forms were mainly derivative, including the double eagle from Sumer and the human-headed sphinx from Egypt, and its style is neither highly original nor well defined; it is most readily recognized by such characteristic details of dress as the short belted tunic, the conical headdress, and shoes with uptilted toe. But it is distinctive enough to have mystified the travelers and scholars of the last century, and to give a fairly vivid impression of the people who created it. Its most characteristic figures are its vigorous lions; the Hittites did better by them than by their gods. At best it has a rude solemnity that in the monumental figures approaches grandeur. Always it is heavy, coarse, somewhat barbarous. If by their art ye shall know them, one might gather that the Hittites were more gross and brutal than their historic record indicates they actually were; so perhaps they were livelier than their sculpture suggests. In general they seem to have been a vigorous people who were not given to humor or fancy, and at their peak had not developed a gracious, urbane way of life. They were fit only to rule, not to civilize. Although one may admire them, it is hard to feel warm toward them.

Nevertheless their sculpture remained a proof of their vitality. The Hittites survived when their empire was smashed and their main cities were burned to the ground. While some found refuge in Syria and Palestine, others maintained city-states in southern Asia Minor that were strong enough to give trouble to the kings of Assyria, and to endure for five more centuries. In these states their culture enjoyed an afterglow. The wealth of more polished, humanized sculpture found at Carchemish and Zinjirli shows a strong Assyrian influence but is unmistakably Hittite. When these cities in turn were destroyed by the Assyrians, Hittite art did not suddenly disappear from this region, as was once supposed, but survived under Greek forms. One example is the monumental tomb of Antiochus I, King of Commagene, built on a mountain top (Nimrud Dagh) shortly before the Christian era. Its colossal statues, draped in classical costumes, have pointed Anatolian headdresses and are essentially in the Anatolian tradition.

Today one may still feel the presence of the Hittites in Anatolia, in ways less definable but more pervasive. Although a traveler to their cliff shrine at Yazilikaya may be disappointed by the smallness and crudeness of the sculptured deities in the processions, the shrine is awesome enough in its silence, and it looks out on the same austere landscape that the Hittites knew. The only sound that may break in comes from the village of Bogazköy below, occupied by Turkish peasants who may still have some Hittite blood in them. The sound is likely to be the whine and screech of a wagon with solid wooden wheels, drawn by oxen or water buffaloes—such a wagon as was used in Hittite times. Reverie may then take an ironic turn and lead one to Karatepe, in the hills of southwestern Asia Minor. Here, about 700 B.C., a little king built himself a palace, and unconsciously left the most valuable testimony to the strength of Hittite tradition.

He had the two main entrances to his palace lined with sculptured reliefs interspersed with inscriptions in Phoenician and hieroglyphic Hittite. It was the discovery of these bilingual texts, only a few years ago, that finally enabled scholars to decipher the hieroglyphs, the native script of the Hittites. They were a work of artless piety, for by this time Hittite had become a "classical" language, which the king and his artists evidently did not understand. While the Phoenician inscriptions were set up in natural sequence, the Hittite equivalents were scattered about in no apparent order of any sort; they can be read consecutively only by backtracking and crisscrossing. Their contents have no connection, either, with the sculptured reliefs, which represent a jumble of gods, men, children, and animals, in worship and in revelry. These reliefs have none of the solemnity of Hittite imperial art. But they still bear the stamp of Hittite tradition, and as artlessly confirm its persistence. One represents Teshub standing on his bull. Another, of as unprepossessing a god, awed a Circassian peasant who visited Karatepe, because the god bore a dagger just like his own. He came back with his whole village to view their "ancestor."

Other peasants in southern Turkey might be as struck by Hittite sculptures. Some still wear similar dress, with conical caps, short-sleeved tunics, and upturned boots; more have a striking resemblance in feature. The modern Turk, indeed, claims the Hittites for his ancestors. And if his belief is scientifically wrong, it is poetically right. In the countryside he is much like them in his rude strength, his virility, his somberness, his want of style. In his modern city of Ankara he has revived one of their political traditions. For the first time since their empire, Asia Minor is again ruled from a capital in the heart of Anatolia.

4. THE PHRYGIANS

Potentially the most important contribution of the Hittites to civilization was made as heralds of the Iron Age. Their early subjects included an Anatolian people who seem to have been the first to learn how to work iron. This discovery was revolutionary because it made possible cheap tools and weapons, and thereby strengthened rising classes or peoples; the Great Kings could more easily control the supply of the relatively expensive bronze. Under the Hittites, however, iron was still a rare metal, much more precious than gold, and in effect a royal monopoly. Their kings turned down requests of the Pharaohs for presents of the rich stuff. The Iron Age came later. Indeed, the new metal may have contributed to the downfall of the Hittites, for it was reputedly used by the "Sea Peoples," whose migrations disrupted the Near East.

Among these "men of iron" were the Phrygians, an Indo-European people who came from Thrace. Their settlements were the first to reappear on the sites of the Hittite cities in Anatolia that were burned down about 1200 B.C. How much they had to do with this catastrophe is uncertain, for very little is known of the centuries immediately following it. Although they have generally been identified with the "Mushki" whose King Mita is mentioned in Assyrian records, these are Anatolian names. Possibly the Mushki were natives who joined the Phrygians, rebelling against their Hittite masters. The one certainty is that this was a period of confusion, and a setback for civilization; the first settlements to reappear are all much smaller and poorer than the Hittite. But by 900 B.C. civilization was on the rise again. In eastern Asia Minor there appeared the kingdom of Urartu (Biblical Ararat), with its capital on Lake Van. It was a native kingdom that worshiped Hurrian gods, including Teshup, and spoke a language akin to Hurrian; its people were excellent builders and workers in metal, who on a Hittite foundation developed a more brilliant culture than this region has ever known since except for a short-lived Armenian kingdom in the Middle Ages. Somewhat later a Phrygian kingdom emerged in the homeland of the Hittites. Its capital of Gordium was considerably to the west of Hattusas, and still farther west it had a second, perhaps independent center, the "Midas city," in the region of modern Afyonkarahisar. Greek tradition was uncertain whether Gordius or Midas was the first king.

This shift to the west befitted a people racially akin to the Greeks, a people who figured so prominently in Greek tradition. From their land came Pelops, the legendary father of the Peloponnesus. In numbering them among the allies of the Trojans, Homer suggested that Queen Hecuba was a Phrygian and had King Priam fighting with them against the Amazons. Later poets identified them with the Trojans. It appears that they brought with them the Greek type of megaron in domestic architecture and geometric ornamental design. Their pottery and metalcraft indicate that they were a much sprightlier people than the Hittites, with more sense of style. Greek tradition, which made them the inventors of music, also suggests that they were an original as well as a warlike people. Their grave furnishings at Gordium testify to the sophisticated culture they were developing until the city was destroyed by the Cimmerians.

But these also indicate that they were trading primarily with the East. What little else we know about the Phrygians, who left few inscriptions, suggests an Anatolian rather than a Greek spirit. They stayed inland, while the Greeks grew up on the Ionian coast and later planted colonies on the Black Sea. They retained the ancient institution of kingship, which the Greeks in their coastal cities began to outgrow. Gordium, like Hattusas, was more a strong fortress than a center of civilization. Essentially the Phrygians repeated the story of the Hittites, on a smaller scale and for a shorter period. Another Indo-European people, they invaded a world of superior culture, conquered it, and eventually reorganized it, establishing a kingdom atop a mixture of native peoples and tongues. In the process they became civilized, learning much from their subject peoples. In the end the native spirit proved strongest. Anatolia conquered its conquerors.

Hence the most enduring contribution of the Phrygians, aside from the flute, was their epiphany of the Mother Goddess—Cybele. Unlike the Hittites, they did not absorb and retain the host of native deities. They gave their devotion to Cybele, who became their national deity. The Phrygian Yazilikaya—a hall of columns near the "Midas city"—contained only her statue. Although they had brought with them a male god or gods, who survived in local cults, the chief god became her lover-son Attis, the type of dying god of whom the Hittites had made little. (One legend had it that she discovered him as an infant on the reedy banks of a river, where, like Moses, he had been exposed to die.) In the western reaches of the kingdom she might take the name of Leto, with a son Sabazios, who became identified with Dionysus. To the east she was likely to retain a prehistoric form, such as the Black Stone at the major shrine of Pessinus; in this form she later went to Rome. Whatever her guise, she and her son inspired essentially the same nature religion. In her native haunts she was not the Mother of the Gods she became for the Greeks and Romans, but an Earth Mother, a symbol of the union of man, nature, and deity in a single divine life that triumphed over death. For this reason her rites were at once gross and sublime, inducing obscene ecstasies and holy frenzies, of self-abandonment or self-sacrifice. Her temple prostitutes included women of high families whose husbands were forbidden to have relations with them during the holy period of their dedication to her service. The eunuch priests of Attis were embryonic Christs who had sacrificed their manhood for his sake.

Cybele offered no moral teaching or example to her Phrygian worshipers. The later philosophers who tried to spiritualize her could never overcome her earthy amorality, which is the essence of the life of nature; it is not virtue that brings new life in the spring, nor sin that makes the crops fail. Instead she intimated to the Phrygians an idea unknown to most of the earlier peoples of the Near East—the hope of in some manner joining her after death. At Gordium the dead were buried in artificial tumuli, of which there are almost a hundred in the immediate vicinity; perhaps the tumulus symbolized a mountain, her favorite dwelling place. (In Sumerian cities the name of the Mother Goddess meant Lady of the Mountain.) In any case, the invocations to Cybele resembled Christian prayers for the dead. It is therefore regrettable that these high hopes failed to bring peace of mind. The Phrygians were given to a vehement mourning that seemed undignified to the Greeks and Romans; apparently they no more rejoiced at the thought of joining the Great Mother than ordinary Christians rejoice at the thought of joining their Father in heaven. They also suffered from the fear that some unprivileged person might be buried in their tomb, and thus share or usurp their position in the afterlife. The deceased sought to protect themselves against such hitchhikers to heaven by dreadful curses, and by bequests of money to the authorities to assure punishment. Tomb inscriptions reveal that this anxiety became widespread among the natives of Asia Minor.

Nevertheless the Greek cities took to Cybele. Indirectly her cult was as influential because of its affinities with other mystery religions. She had something to do with the rise of Orphism, which spread the idea of an immortal soul among the Greeks; Midas is associated with Orpheus in some myths. She had more obvious connections with the immensely popular cult of Dionysus, which gave rise to Greek drama. In *The Bacchae* Euripides represents the god as a newcomer from Lydia and Phrygia, and has his chorus of maidens sing "with Phrygian clamor," to the tune of Phrygian pipes, the praises of "Our Mother" Cybele. Her train of Corybantes, who danced to wild music by torchlight, were likewise associated with the Curetes of the Cretan Zeus, a god much closer to Dionysus than to Homer's Zeus. Strabo devoted some pages to speculation about the common origin of these orgies, a subject he considered "not alien to the contemplation of the philosopher." Nor were the ways of Cybele's worshipers wholly alien to many early Christians, even before Mary won her title of Mother of God. Polycrates, Bishop of Ephesus, defined a good bishop as a "eunuch saint." Phrygia was the home of the Montanist heresy, a form of worship at once ascetic and ecstatic, which proclaimed that men could still be filled with the Spirit as St. Paul had been, and that prophets could be trusted as well as bishops. Its founder, Montanus, had been a priest of Cybele. His chief lieutenants were the prophetesses Maximilla and Priscilla—"two females," a contemporary recorded, who corrupted Christianity by novelties "in the form of fasts and feasts." Ramsay noted the high position of women in Anatolian tradition, which may be traced back through Cybele to the Queen of Hatti.

Long before this, however, Cybele's own people had gone the way of their predecessors. Early in the seventh century new peoples poured in from the north and east, led by the barbarous Cimmerians, whom even the cruel Assyrians called "creatures of hell." After inflicting terrible losses on the Kingdom of Urartu, the Cimmerians turned on the Phrygians and crushed the last King Midas. After them came the Scythians, who finished off Urartu; it disappeared from history by the end of the century. When order was restored by the Lydians, the Phrygians became docile subjects and remained so under their later rulers. Cybele had lost the martial qualities of Inanna, Ma, and the Hittite goddesses. The race of great warriors known to early Greek tradition was known to later Greeks chiefly as flute players, authors of the elegy, and a source of slaves. Although Aesop was one of these Phrygian slaves, it was the Greeks who made his name and preserved his fables. Still later the Emperor Julian the Apostate complained bitterly of the supine high priest of Cybele at Pessinus, who had surrendered the blessed Dame to the Christians. The Phrygians grew fierce again only as Christian heretics. They clung to Montanism in spite of severe persecution by the Church, whose bishops could not tolerate its threat to their authority. As late as the eighth century A.D. we hear of many Montanists who burned themselves to death in their churches rather than recant at the order of the Byzantine emperor.

But it was the docile Phrygians who endured. After the bloody Cimmerian interlude, life went on in Gordium and other Phrygian cities. Some, like Celaenae, became considerable cities under Greek and Roman rule. Others, like Pessinus, became famous as holy cities.[10] Most of the

[10] The best preserved of these is Hierapolis, the birthplace of Epictetus. Situated on a cliff in the valley of the Lycus River, a tributary of the Maeander, it is strewn with Roman ruins, especially of baths and sarcophagi. Besides Mother Leto it had a healing god who made it a popular health resort. From a warm mineral spring issues a little stream that calcifies as it trickles down the cliff, forming a frozen cascade—a gleaming white Niagara that has given the site its Turkish name of Pamukkale, "Cotton Castle." One may still bathe in this spring, at the bottom of which lie ancient columns. A few miles off in the valley below are the ruins of Laodicea, a

Phrygians lived in villages, where eventually they lost their identity, merging with the Anatolian peasantry. Under all its later rulers Anatolia remained essentially a village world. Lacking any navigable rivers, it is not a land for great cities.

Its subsequent history may therefore be outlined briefly. At Gordium, Alexander the Great claimed sovereignty over the whole region, but he did not bother to subdue it. From the Persian satraps or nobles who had been ruling it emerged royal families that retained their independence while the Hellenistic kings fought among themselves for the possession of western Asia Minor. The most vigorous of these dynasties, the kings of Pontus, established their capitals in the old Greek cities on the Black Sea coast. When the Romans took over, they split up Anatolia into the provinces of Galatia, Cappadocia, and Pontus, and conscientiously founded or refounded some cities, but all this had little effect on the village world. It was never really Hellenized. Throughout the whole period many of the villages belonged to temple estates ruled by priests in the service of some deity, usually a form of the Mother Goddess; typically they allied themselves with royal or imperial interests and formed another bulwark against any tendencies to emancipate or educate the peasantry. Thereafter Anatolia supplied grain, livestock, and battle fodder to the Byzantine Empire, the Seljuk Empire, and the Ottoman Empire—all ruling from western Asia Minor. It learned to speak Greek and then Turkish, to pray to Christ and then to Allah. Christianity served as a bridge from the worship of Cybele to the worship of the exclusively masculine Allah.

This history was not actually, of course, so tame or monotonous as I imply. Some great men came out of Anatolia and the regions to the east, some important work was done, some historic events took place, some horror and some glory relieved the boredom; and I shall refer to them in due course. One chapter of particular interest is the rise of the Kingdom Pontus under Mithridates the Great, who made the last great effort to throw off the Roman dominion and recover "Asia for the Asiatics." Another is the much longer story of the Armenians, who aided him in this effort; during a brief period of independence in the early Middle Ages, they created a brilliant art that influenced Byzantium and the West. But I have relegated these stories to the Appendix because they are incidental or tangential to the main drama of Asia Minor.[11] After the fall of the Phrygian kingdom, the history of the central and eastern regions was always

___

rich Hellenistic city that St. John of Revelation immortalized for its lukewarm Christianity.

[11] See Appendix, Sections 1 (Amasia: The Kingdom of Pontus) and 2 (The Armenians).

overshadowed, when not determined, by the history being made in the west. The rest of our story, until this century, is focused on the west.

5. EPILOGUE: THE SYMBOLISM OF THE GORDIAN KNOT

The village of Yassihüyük, which served as headquarters of the Gordium expedition, is a "modern" one, built in this century, and more prosperous than most villages in Turkey. At the time of my visit it already had a tractor or two. But it had no school, no mosque, no townhouse, no main street, no store, no doctor—not to mention such luxuries as electricity and plumbing. At night the only signs of life in the village were a few dimly lighted panes, which gave a feeling of loneliness rather than coziness. Its life was a simple round of the age-old routines: tending the flocks, pounding the grain, making the bread. It recalled the knot tied by King Gordius, enshrined on an altar, representing the secret to the rule of Asia. Apparently the knot fastened a pole to a yoke on a wagon with solid wooden wheels, drawn by oxen; the secret was the conquest of the land by the peasant. It was this point that Alexander missed when he cut the knot with his sword. For the empire he won by conquest has long since gone, and in Turkey today one still sees that same crude wagon, the same oxen—and the same peasant.

It was curious to see these peasants serving as workmen for the expedition. They knew nothing about Gordium, of course, but they had learned to be more or less careful about the rubble that interested their employers. They seemed pleased to indulge the odd fancies of the wealthy Americans, since they were earning almost a dollar a day, and are naturally friendly, polite, and respectful of learning. The person they respected most was the architect, and what they respected was her magic as a medicine woman. She made up a potion of brandy, sugar, and paregoric that always cured their cramps or stomach aches; they had complete faith in it because she made a ceremony of adding the paregoric with an eyedropper. It was the old mumbo jumbo—much older than Gordium. So were these peasants, aside from the possibility that they may still have some Hittite blood. They represent the timeless peasant, who has come right through history without having a real history: surviving the rise and fall of civilizations that gave different names to his gods and demons, set up different authorities to rule and tax him, taught him to speak different tongues, but made little change in his prehistoric mind or soul. Hittite, Phrygian, Roman, or Turk, he remained, like his oxen, passive in obedience and endurance. And he was a universal type. His life was what life meant for the great majority of mankind—until our time.

He should remind us that there *are* new things under the sun. In the

Western world the common man has at last entered history; for the first time he has a real voice in making it, as well as suffering it. Though we have heard too much about the tractor as a symbol of progress, the one or two tractors in Yassihüyük are in fact profoundly significant. They represent a momentous change that is coming over not only Turkey but agriculture, the ancient life of the village. The Industrial Revolution has made the most radical difference in man's life since the discovery of agriculture that created the peasant. In America the common man is now a man on a street, working in an office or a factory; or if he chooses to live in the country he is a farmer—not a peasant—who can buy all the things made in factories.

Since we are no longer so proud of our material progress, we are more often depressed by the look, sound, and feel of our industrialized world. Yassihüyük has the charm of age-old simplicities. Grassless, treeless, wind-swept, it had looked simply dreary and God-forsaken when I arrived on a cold evening; but by day it took on rhythm and color. Women in pan-taloons carried their pitchers to the village spring with ritual stateliness, and sometimes sang as they took turns pounding grain in the village mortar post; children played in the barnyards or waddled about with the geese. Flocks of sheep softened the austere landscape, which toward eve-ning became almost idyllic as peasants and livestock streamed slowly back to the village, while the setting sun painted the surrounding hills and mountains in shades of russet, gray-green, and purple-gray. The peaceful-ness of the scene awakened the inevitable thoughts about the vulgarities and the horrors of modern life.

When the Turkish peasants watched in awe as the architect added paregoric with the eyedropper, I was reminded of the ordinary American. He too stands in awe of the scientist of the advertisements—the man with the test tube, who guarantees the magic of the latest pill. It is still mumbo jumbo. The man on the street has only a vague idea of science, and a vaguer one of history. He too knows nothing about Gordium, and next to nothing about Asia Minor. The kind of natural piety I have been cele-brating runs thin and shallow in modern America. We spend an in-finitesimal fraction of our wealth on historical research. Archaeologists are finding it harder every year to get support for their expeditions; for lack of money the Gordium expedition had to stop work on the city mound for two years just as it was approaching its main objective, the Phrygian city. Congressmen and businessmen are generally indifferent to research unless it has practical, useful objectives, such as colored tele-vision and hydrogen bombs. Given those bombs, the Phrygian city may remain buried. The timeless Anatolian peasant may survive still another civilization; he is better equipped to endure than the Western man on the street. In ages to come, archaeologists may unearth the stupid archaic city of Middletown, and be disgusted by its shoddy remains. Or so I reflected as I watched Miss X clean a skeleton found near the top of her tumulus. The pains she took with this fellow were touching, for she had no high hopes of him at all. She had an awful suspicion that he was "modern."

Yet who would return to the life of Yassihüyük? The simplicity of the age-old village has not been blessed. The peasant could endure because he had always had to endure a great deal; he could be content with very little because he had as little chance of getting more, or knowing better. He was as poor in spiritual as in material goods. At that, his spiritual life was not even simple. It was always hedged by taboos, haunted by evil spirits, complicated by fears due to ignorance and superstition. I take for my text *A Village in Anatolia* by Mahmut Makal, a sensitive young Turkish schoolteacher who was born and brought up in such a village, and after ten years of schooling went back to teach in it. His is the first book to come out of the prehistoric peasant world, picture it as it is seen and felt from the inside. (Its Turkish title is *Bizim Köy*—"Our Village.") His story is sometimes charming, or what comfortable readers call quaint; but chiefly it is an appalling story of poverty, disease, brute suffering, stupid cruelty, superstitious anxiety—of physical, mental, spiritual starvation that seems worse because of the peasants' fatalistic acceptance of it as the will of Allah, who will reward them in Paradise.

It seems no better for the introduction of a British social scientist, who points out that Makal gives too black an impression because he writes of an especially poor village, in a year of famine, and judges it by "rationalist and liberal" standards. When Makal tells of the many children who died at birth or in early infancy, the scientist observes in a footnote that "the proportion of live births is, in fact, well over half." Still more depressing is his summary. The young schoolteacher "does not seem to realise that most of the world's population lives in conditions very similar or, by his standards, a lot worse, and that these rural communities may well be stable and adjusted to their environment, with a moral and social order of their own." *Stable* and *adjusted!*—the magic words of the social scientist. But adjusted to what kind of life? Order at what cost?

"Progress" is a debatable concept, and in popular discourse a very dubious one. It has inspired a naïve, uncritical faith, in America a shameless boasting about a high standard of low living. Still, the many critics who are now scornful of our material progress might reconsider the life of an Anatolian village, or of "most of the world's population." They can be more scornful because they take for granted the material well-being they enjoy; they testify by their practice that it is still possible to lead the good life in a comfortable house, with plumbing and central heating. So too with critics of "rationalist and liberal" standards. The concept of progress logically requires some criterion of the good life—the value judgments that men are notoriously unable to agree upon, and that social scientists shy away from on principle. Nevertheless these same scientists, and virtually all thoughtful men, are committed to a faith in the value of knowledge. Our knowledge entitles us to declare flatly that many beliefs of the past represent ignorance and superstition. And because our historical knowledge forces on us the inescapable relativity of judgment in the high concerns of truth, goodness, and beauty, we may forget the general agreement that these are high concerns, and the judgment of the human race that recognizes and preserves the relatively high achievements. One who knows anything about these matters can declare as flatly that Shakespeare is a greater writer than Mickey Spillane, Socrates a wiser man than Sokolsky.

We cannot absolutely prove the value of civilization, or of life itself. A civilized man may or may not be happier, more virtuous, or holier than a primitive or a peasant. But we can say objectively that civilization has enabled man to realize more fully his distinctive potentialities, and that if these plainly include potentialities of misery, evil, and folly, they are as plainly the source of his happiness, virtue, and whatever divinity may be in him. It has meant a cumulative growth in knowledge, arts, skills—in goods that men everywhere recognize as positive goods once they have known them, and hang on to, and do not willingly give up except for the sake of still "higher" goods. It may be summarized as a growth of consciousness. Call it brain, mind, spirit, or soul, consciousness is the source of all the distinctive powers and possibilities of man. The various criteria of civilization that have been proposed—the combination of diversity and order, the enthronement of reason, the growth of freedom, the spread of sweetness and light, the approach to the One True God—all involve an extension and refinement of consciousness. In this view the human race has been growing up through its long history. Civilized men may still behave very badly, as adults do, or they may pine for their lost innocence, as adults sometimes get sentimental about their happy, carefree childhood days; but they do not really wish to return to the life of the primitive village, they would not lose their minds. If history is not a clear progress, it has at least involved some irreversible tendencies.

Let us consider an early Sumerian custom. Beside a royal tomb in Ur was found a "death pit" containing the bones of almost a hundred members of the royal court, chiefly women, who had gone to the grave with their king and queen. They had been gaily dressed in crimson robes, and richly ornamented; the ladies wore elaborate gold headdresses. How they met their death is uncertain, but the composure of the bodies and the good order of the headdresses indicate that they had not been felled. It appears that they had lain down quietly, perhaps drugged. We may assume that they were willing victims, possibly even proud of their sacrifice, or happy in the privilege of accompanying their royal masters to the Beyond. Yet it is a gruesome thing. The Sumerians outgrew this practice, as other peoples have outgrown the custom of offering human sacrifices to the gods or the custom of burning witches. Once outgrown, such superstitions are invariably regarded with shame or disgust. We may honor primitive piety, or pity primitive fear; but we are repelled by the obscenities and the horrors it sanctified, and have a clear right to condemn it.

And so with the growth and spread of freedom, the precious rights to have a mind, a faith, and a life of one's own. Although men who have known freedom have often lost it to other men seeking power, or promising security, they have never deliberately reverted to serfdom and slavery. Slavery, once universally accepted, is now universally condemned in theory—it has to be called something else. Communism has to promise "real" freedom. The very fear that our mass civilization by its nature tends to crush individuality, and to breed authoritarianism, testifies that men who have really known personal liberty know how precious it is. When, in disillusionment or despair, they attack the faith in progress, they attack it in the name of ideals that have been realized in the historic process, or of higher expectations than men had in the past. If we are in danger of relapsing into barbarism, as other societies have, we at least call it barbarism.

"Progress" remains an open question. But all who value the Greek heritage will keep it open.

CHAPTER III

Troy: The Bible of Greece

---

1. THE HISTORIC TROY

"I BEGIN the real history of Greece," said Grote in the Preface to his monumental history, "with their first recorded Olympiad, or 776 B.C." For earlier times, he explained, there was only the testimony of such legends as the Trojan War, and "in the eyes of modern enquiry" it would be "essentially unphilosophical" to confound these legends with real history. He wrote this in 1846, when scholars were generally agreed that Homer's fabled Troy was only a fable. And they had good reason for their distrust of legends. The Trojan War as pictured in the *Iliad* was, after all, a preposterous affair, even apart from the constant intrusion of childish gods —heavenly playboys—and from the great battles in which armies served as a kind of chorus for combats between a few boastful heroes. The Persians pointed out to Herodotus the absurdity of all this fuss over "a single Spartan girl." He himself doubted that Helen could have been in Troy; the Trojans would surely have had the sense to give her up rather than endure all the hardships of a war that lasted for ten years.

Yet the Greeks never doubted the historic actuality of Troy or of this war; and by now scholars have come around to agreeing with them. Today anyone may see the site for himself. A philosophical historian may then appreciate a further irony about the place of legends in "real history." The truth is that the imaginative—or even imaginary—Troy of Homer is historically much more important than the real one.

We owe the real one to the fabulous exploits of Heinrich Schliemann, one of the great pioneers of archaeology in the last century. Schliemann's own story has become a popular legend: how he was inspired by a schoolboy passion for Homer (since once upon a time schoolboys used to read Homer); how when only eight years old he resolved to find the great walls of Troy, or Ilios, which he was sure must still exist; how he devoted his remarkable abilities to making a fortune in business, in the cause of proving Homer's veracity; and how he retired, about 1870, to begin his search for the "golden city." Scholars who were still inclined to believe in Troy generally agreed that its probable location was a place called Bunar Bashi, on a high cliff—the most picturesque spot in the region. Schliemann, sticking to the clues in the *Iliad*, settled on a commonplace hillock by the Turkish village of Hisarlik, a few miles inland from the entrance to the Dardanelles. Here, sure enough, he found his golden city. He found, indeed, a series of Troys in layers—nine of them, by a later count; but in one near the bottom, a settlement that had been destroyed by a great conflagration, he was thrilled to hit upon a hoard of thousands of gold objects that he identified as King Priam's treasure. Schliemann then had the same fantastic success when he excavated Mycenae in Greece, the capital of King Agamemnon. Here again he was seeking to vindicate Homer, who had described Mycenae as "a well-built city, abounding in gold"; and again he hit upon just such a city, with another hoard of golden treasures.

Since then the story has grown more fantastic. We now know that the golden city Schliemann found at Troy was more than a thousand years older than Homer's Troy; he unwittingly dug right through the city he was looking for. Likewise at Mycenae he went through Homer's city, finding his treasure in a much older settlement. Eventually realizing his mistake, Schliemann returned to the search for the great walls of Homer's Troy. He never had the satisfaction of contemplating them himself, but shortly after his death they were found by his assistant Dörpfeld, who identified them as Troy VI (the sixth city up from the bottom). Then, in the 1930's, an American expedition led by Carl Blegen spent seven more seasons on this mound, excavating systematically in the modern manner, layer by layer. They broke down the nine cities into a finer series of sublevels, marking distinct periods of resettlement or rebuilding within each of the nine major periods. They made out forty-six successive Troys, going back to about the year 3000 B.C. Homer's city is now known as Troy VIIa.

Hence a pilgrim at the site may return in good conscience to the world of romance. He may stare at the celebrated walls, with the remains of their gates and towers. On the mound he may dream over the landscape described by Homer: the windy plains of Troy stretching to the Hellespont, now called the Dardanelles; the Scamander River running through the plain, and the Simois River meandering toward it; off the coast the island of Tenedos, where the Greeks supposedly hid after sending the wooden horse to Troy; in the blue distance the islands of Imbros and Samothrace; far inland Mt. Ida, snow-capped most of the year, and majestic enough to stir memories of Zeus, the father of the blessed gods, who chose it for a celestial grandstand and nuptial couch; and here and there tumuli standing out on the horizon, recalling the barrows that were raised over the graves of the Homeric heroes. If the pilgrim believes that these heroes actually lived, as he may on the authority of some scholars, he may brood at the very spot where Achilles slew Hector, after chasing him three times around the walls of Troy: according to Homer, the spot by the "two fountains," where the Trojan women used to wash their linen in peacetime, and where today a wagon track still passes a spring.

My own reflections on the spot, I must add, were disturbed by a Turkish peasant chasing a miserable, balky horse. As usual, we cannot take our romance straight. But Homer himself was not a romanticist, for that matter; so we do him no injustice by returning to "reality."

To begin with, an uninitiated pilgrim will be disappointed by the ruins of Troy. They are not at all spectacular, consisting of the usual jumble of foundations and litter of stone, and including no monuments from Homer's city. Most imposing are the remains of the fortification wall of Troy II, with a ramp leading to it, and the exceptionally well-built walls of Troy VI, but it takes a specialist to appreciate these. And none of the historic Troys was so splendid as the Troy that Homer built. His had broad avenues, temples to Athena and Apollo, and royal palaces with sixty chambers or more; it was defended by a "thousand tribes" of warriors. The actual Troy was a five-acre lot, it had no such temples or great palaces, and it was hardly a real city at all—it was a fortress, which at most could hold a few thousand men. The fabled landscape is on the same small scale, like so much in the classical world. The Scamander River is a mud creek, the Simois a mere trickle of a brook. The "vast Hellespont" under the dominion of King Priam is an ordinary channel some forty miles long.

Neither is Schliemann's story simply romantic. Archaeologists themselves are rather unhappy about their great pioneer. When I visited Troy, one pointed wryly to the Great Trench, an ugly gash in the mound—that was where Schliemann went. In his eagerness to find Homer's golden city he did not excavate layer by layer, but barged through the mound, destroying as he went. The profession still salutes him, but with a perfunctory air, and repeated asides about the irreparable damage he did. In working over what was left of the mound, Blegen and his associates included a few areas where "Schliemann had spared a small amount of deposit." In their report they made a point of announcing that they were under "no compulsion to recover objects of startling or sensational character with high publicity value." Their only compulsion was to account for every stone, pin, and potsherd.

A layman might comment as wryly on the series of ponderous volumes that constitutes their report. For Schliemann archaeology was a "high and noble" study. Although his book on his findings at "Sacred Ilios" has been outmoded by later research, it remains highly readable because of his imagination and enthusiasm. He concluded with the fervent hope that scholars would now take to "research with the pick-axe and the spade," and so "augment the universal love for the noble study of the beautiful Greek classics, and particularly of Homer, that brilliant sun of all literature!" The American archaeologists have undertaken that research, but in their report have managed to avoid any remark that might suggest or evoke a love for Homer, the classics, or archaeology itself. Their ardor appears only in the tireless catalogue of detail, such as the 10,118 carloads of earth they removed in the sixth campaign, or the 1,471 gold beads they found scattered in Troy IIg. Now and then they risk a few pages of meager, cautious generalization about the possible significance of their findings; but then they scurry back to counting and tabulating for another hundred pages. For the layman, the forty-six Troys have been reburied.

Nevertheless he may still make his sentimental pilgrimage to Troy, find romance enough in its actual history, and feel grateful to the scholars who have reconstructed this history. In spite of his blunders Schliemann remains a great pioneer, who opened up a new world for historians as well as for lovers of Homer. In spite of his almost morbid fear of all "conjectures, theories, and speculations," Blegen commits himself to the statement that this was certainly the citadel glorified by Homer, and the painstaking work of his expedition enables us to follow its history for over three thousand years. We know considerably more about Homer's Troy than the Greeks did, or than he himself did. Again we might marvel at the singular piety that is obscured by the conventions of modern scientific research.

The Greeks themselves made no such effort to unearth the monuments of their revered ancestors. They too were uncertain about the location of Troy; Strabo, among others, rejected the site of Hisarlik where the Romans had rebuilt Novum Ilium (Troy IX). But while they speculated, it apparently never occurred to them to dig up the site, or Mycenae either. Meanwhile they had used the walls and buildings of Troy as stone quarries, just as Turkish peasants were to use their own temples. The still more pious Romans, who believed that the Trojan hero Aeneas was the father of their race, were still more incurious. They neither speculated

nor dug; or when they had to dig, to lay the foundations of their buildings, they paid no attention to the ancient walls they ran across. One reason why Schliemann missed Homer's Troy was that he naturally concentrated on the central part of the mound, and this part had been
leveled by the Greeks and Romans to build their temples to Athena, the
patron goddess of Troy. They unwittingly destroyed most of the city
they were commemorating by their temples.

Of the earlier Troys they knew nothing, of course, nor did Homer.
Although he would scarcely have been interested in most of them, their
history was in some respects appropriate. Troy I was a royal stronghold,
setting the pattern. Troy II, where Schliemann found his treasures, was
by far the strongest and wealthiest of the early settlements; its artisans
did astonishingly fine work for their royal master, considering its remoteness from the centers of civilization. (More or less contemporary were the
royal tombs of pre-Hittite Alaja.) After it was destroyed by fire, toward
the end of the third millennium, the site was occupied by relatively poor,
undistinguished villages. The inhabitants of Troy III in particular were a
remarkably dirty, stupid people, who left their refuse and garbage on the
floors of their homes until the stench became unbearable, or locomotion
difficult; then they covered the filth with a new earth floor, and so in
time were forced to raise the roof. But in general life remained much the
same in the first five Troys over a period of a thousand years. Although
Blegen has made out some thirty phases, he stresses their essential continuity, noting gradual developments in architecture, pottery, and other
artifacts, but no major innovations or importations. Rich or poor, the
peoples of Troy all lived in a small world facing the Aegean; their commercial and cultural relations were chiefly with Aegean rather than
Anatolian peoples. They knew nothing about any conflict of East and
West. The fertility goddess they worshiped could have come from anywhere, or nowhere.[1]

[1] Among Schliemann's finds in Troy II was a crude leaden figurine that he recognized as the "Asiatic Venus." It is especially interesting because its huge triangular
vulva contains the symbol of the swastika—a very ancient, mysterious symbol that
Schliemann found all over Troy, and that has since been found all over the world,
on Mayan and African as on old Teutonic and Greek pottery, in China and India
as in the catacombs of Rome. It raises the problem of the nature and significance
of symbols, the nonverbal "meanings" that to Suzanne Langer have suggested a
"philosophy in a new key." Whether the swastika was hit upon independently by
scattered cultures or—more likely—spread gradually from some unknown prehistoric
source, its universal popularity indicates some kind of "natural" significance. Or
rather suggestiveness, as like all symbols it has taken on many different meanings.
Among its elemental suggestions is a wheel in motion; hence it has served as a
symbol of the sun. Buddhists managed to see in it the footprints of Buddha. The
word itself comes from Sanskrit and means "it is well." Apparently all was well when

With Troy VI, however, came a sharp break. Early in the second millennium a new people moved in, bringing a wholly different culture. Among other things they introduced the horse—the famous horses of Troy that were coveted by Homer's Achaeans. Since there are no signs of devastation in Troy V, and some local artifacts continued in use, Blegen permits the speculation that the simple inhabitants were so overawed by the "terrifying exotic steeds" of the invaders that they submitted tamely, and were allowed to remain as serfs or servants. In any event, the newcomers settled down and soon grew rich. Fine builders, they made over the site into an exceptionally strong, handsome citadel. Troy VI flourished behind its great walls for some five hundred years, until destroyed by an earthquake shortly after 1300 B.C. Its culture persisted through the early phases of Troy VII, the city of Homer's Trojans; they used its walls, which had stood up under the earthquake. Historically, Troy VI was the greatest of them all.

Presumably Homer knew nothing about it either. He may have preserved a dim memory of it in the legend that Heracles had sacked it when refused the horses promised by Laomedon, father of King Priam, but he was certainly not well acquainted with its culture. Although he gave King Priam an Oriental cast by endowing him with a harem, he represented the Trojans as worshiping the same gods and having substantially the same culture as the Greeks, whereas the excavations show that they had different cults and customs. Nevertheless with Troy VI we definitely enter the Greek world. The pottery of its founders indicates that they were related to the early Greeks, who entered Greece at about the same time (possibly by way of the Dardanelles). While the Trojans went on to develop a distinctive culture in Asia Minor, they maintained the local tradition of trading chiefly with the Aegean area rather than with central Anatolia, now dominated by the Hittites. No unmistakably Hittite artifacts have been found on the site. In particular the Trojans imported a great deal of Mycenaean pottery. And these Mycenaeans were Homer's Achaeans.

The Mycenaeans take us to the brilliant, gay, gracious Minoan civilization of Crete. (One trouble with the history of Asia Minor is that it is always leading back, in all directions.) In the *Odyssey* Homer speaks of King Minos, who ruled from the "great city" of Knossos. This king, who with his sea empire, his labyrinth, and his Minotaur was always a his-

---

the direction of the gamma was to the right (卐); things were bad when the direction was to the left (卍). To me this somehow feels appropriate, but why I could not say. The ancient Trojans may have felt differently, for although both types were common in Troy II, the swastika on the idol of the fertility goddess pointed left.

torical figure to the Greeks, was to modern scholars another purely
mythical figure—until Sir Arthur Evans paralleled the feats of Schliemann
by excavating the magnificent Palace of Knossos, and recovering still another lost civilization. We now know that Homer's Achaeans owed much
of their culture to this civilization, and probably were responsible for its
fall; the gaiety of the Minoans ceased about 1400, when all their great
cities were destroyed.[2] The Achaeans then succeeded to their sea empire,
spreading over the Aegean world and developing a far-flung commerce;
their mass-produced pottery has been found all over the Near East. They
remained warriors, however, living in strongly fortified cities like
Mycenae, and given to plundering expeditions. The "Akaiwasha" were
among the "Sea Peoples" who raided Egypt shortly before 1200—"fighting
to fill their bellies daily," according to the Egyptian scribes. This was
just the time that Greek tradition dated the expedition of the Argonauts
up the Black Sea and the raids by Heracles on the Amazons and on Troy.

That the Achaeans penetrated Asia Minor is certain, for a Mycenaean
settlement has been excavated at Miletus. The Hittite royal archives
also contain references to the "Ahhiyawa," a powerful seafaring people,
whom scholars generally identify as the Achaeans. One document indicates friendly, intimate relations: a Hittite king hoping to be cured of his
illness sent for the god of Ahhiyawa and the god of Lazpa (Lesbos?).
Later documents imply that the King of Ahhiyawa was equal in rank to
the kings of Hatti, Egypt, Babylon, and Assyria, and that he came to be a
nuisance to the Hittites. One Attarissiyas raided their territory with a
hundred chariots; it is tempting to identify him with Atreus, the father of
Homer's Agamemnon. In Mycenae, on the other hand, a Hittite seal was
found near the Lion Gate, which is itself reminiscent of Hittite art.

More doubtful are the contemporary references to the Trojans. Although the "Derden" whom the Egyptian scribes list among the Hittite
allies at the battle of Kadesh seem to be Homer's Dardanians, scholars
are still debating a Hittite reference to a king Alaksandus of Wilusa, during the reign of Muwatallis (c. 1300). He sounds like Alexander of Ilios—
another name the Greeks had for Paris—and the possibility is strengthened by the report of Stephanus of Byzantium that one Motylos "received

---

[2] The Throne Room in the Palace of Knossos gave a graphic idea of the final catastrophe. "It was found in a state of complete confusion," wrote John Pendlebury, an
assistant of Evans. "A great oil jar lay overturned in one corner, ritual vessels were
in the act of being used when the disaster came. It looks as if the King had been
hurried there to undergo, too late, some last ceremony in the hopes of saving the
people. Theseus and the Minotaur! Dare we believe that he wore the mask of the
bull?" Whatever he wore, Herodotus was not far wrong when he said that King
Minos was killed three generations before the Trojan War.

Helen and Paris." But if he is our man, he lived in Troy VI a full century before the Trojan War, usually dated 1194. And as we approach this war —still in the realm of conjecture—we come to a more significant puzzle. Whence the wealth and power of Troy? This famous site was only a hillock—it was not a natural stronghold commanding the Troad. Neither was it a port, or a road center, or a natural site for a city. It became an important center just twice in its long history—the periods of Troy II and Troy VI (including the early phase of VII). Why then?

Scholars have answered, unromantically, that Troy was a "robber city" preying on the commerce of the Dardanelles. Ships entering from the Aegean would be forced to tarry here by the strong currents and winds that regularly come down from the Black Sea; the Trojans could then exact tribute from them, as well as payment for water and supplies. Walter Leaf developed an elaborate thesis that Troy also held an annual market fair, where traders from the Aegean met the Black Sea fleet, and that the Trojan War was a commercial war over the domination of the lucrative Black Sea trade; unable to storm or even besiege the stronghold, as other peoples of Asia Minor kept coming to its aid, the Achaeans fought a ten-year guerrilla war, shutting off its trade and gradually bleeding it to death. Other scholars have shot holes in this thesis. But at least it seems clear that Troy VI exploited its command of the entrance to the Dardanelles, whether for plunder or for trade.

In any case, there almost certainly was a Trojan War. We know for a fact that Troy was a rich enough prize, and that it was destroyed at about the time Greek tradition dated the war. If the war was purely mythical, Homer's placing it here would be a strange coincidence, for in his own day Troy was an insignificant village again. And the indulgence of all this conjecture and sentiment may be justified by the historic aftermath. Shortly after the fall of Troy, Mycenaean civilization went into a rapid and apparently ignominious decline as a ruder people, the Dorians, came flooding in from the north. These barbarians were able to sack Mycenae even though it was a much greater natural stronghold than the hillock of Troy. Homer never mentions the Dorians, but his epics presage the end of the Achaeans: few of their heroes returned safely from the Trojan War. It would seem that their victory was a costly one, or possibly no real victory at all. As a result of all this turmoil, however, other Greeks began leaving their homeland and settling along the coast of Asia Minor. The future belonged to these refugees. The supreme historic importance of the Trojan War is the meaning it had for them, and in time for the whole Greek world.

The *Iliad* was not merely a great poem for them. It was a record of their first great national adventure, comparable to the War of Independence in America. While it revealed the internal dissension that was to plague them throughout their history, it symbolized their spiritual unity in an all-Greek crusade. "It is clear," Leaf wrote, "that the Greeks saw in the capture of the Hellespont the critical point of national expansion, the step which brought Greece out of the limits of little local tribes into the atmosphere of the large human world, and opened the career of colonization which made them the creators of modern Europe." By the time of Herodotus they saw in the Trojan War the beginning of the conflict between Asia and Europe, or East and West. Herodotus states that the Persians traced their enmity to the Greeks to this wanton invasion of Asia over the abduction of a mere woman. When Xerxes invaded Greece—with an army that incidentally included contingents of Phrygians, Mysians, Paphlagonians, Lydians (Maeonians), and other peoples listed by Homer as Trojan "allies"—he visited Ilium, before crossing the Hellespont, to pay his respects to the Trojan heroes, and to sacrifice a thousand oxen to the Trojan Athena. Alexander the Great was pleased to agree with the Persians as he toppled their empire, inspired by the belief that he was completing the mission of Homer's Achaeans; he carried with him a copy of the *Iliad*, corrected by Aristotle. He too went straight to the shrine of Ilium after crossing the Hellespont to invade Asia. Plutarch described how he "anointed the pillar on Achilles' tomb with oil and ran around it with his friends, naked, according to the custom, after which he put a crown upon it."

What inspired Alexander was a pure fiction. If we do not know just why the Achaeans attacked Troy, we can be confident that they were not crusaders from the West, carrying the torch for Europe. Homer himself gives no suggestion of a clash of ideals; his Trojans have the same ideals as the Achaeans. Nevertheless he did so inspire Alexander, who was a conscious crusader. He at least had prophetic historical sense when he chose for his scene the Hellespont, to which his Dardanians gave the Dardanelles its name. It became so great a highway between East and West that it has been called the most important channel in the world. Today more monuments along its shores, commemorating the soldiers who died in the Gallipoli campaign during World War I, are a reminder that it was again fought over in our own time.

2. THE GREATNESS OF HOMER

The fascination of archaeology has its dangers. The patient, loving study of potsherds, spindle whorls, beads, pins, and skulls has brought back to life many forgotten peoples, and even given us some idea of what went on in their skulls; yet the intrinsic interest of their life is severely limited. They have little to tell us until they reach the stage where they can speak for themselves and record their thoughts. So too with anthropology. It is engrossing to study primitive religion, the many varieties of totem and taboo, magic rite and fetish; but it may also be depressing. The variety comes down to endless variation on a few rudimentary ideas, a monotony that reveals an essential poverty of imagination, a dearth of spirit, a pitiful but degrading fear. Jane Harrison, a particularly acute, indefatigable student of primitive Greek religion, concluded an Introduction with a sudden burst of feeling: "Savages, save for their reverent totemistic attitudes toward animals, weary and disgust me, though perforce I spend long hours in reading of their tedious doings. My good moments are when, through the study of things primitive, I come to the better understanding of some song of a Greek poet or some saying of a Greek philosopher." The dangers are implicit in the scientific term *culture*, which applies to all societies. It may blur the all-important distinctions, the source of high values, by its implication that all cultures are equivalent.

With the appearance of a Homer, the student's heart should leap up. If what he tells us about the past is historically unreliable, and at best does not lend itself to scientific classification or measurement, it has far greater intrinsic value than the artifacts of preliterate peoples. He represents the uniqueness of Greek culture, in the civilized sense of the word. As Werner Jaeger emphasizes, the Greeks were the first people to set up a conscious ideal of culture, as the cultivation of human nature: "The greatest work of art they had to create was Man." Confucius later did a similar work for China, no doubt more consciously than Homer, but Homer was no less a creator in this deeper sense. The first great writer of the Western world, he was the first to shape the Greek ideal.

Then we must add at once that we know nothing whatever about this man and his life. The only positive fact is that seven cities in Asia Minor disputed the honor of being his birthplace. Smyrna had possibly the strongest claim; Homer was frequently called Melesigenes because of his supposed birth on the Meles canal, a short stream flowing into the city. The pilgrim may visit this stream today, but before he indulges in imaginative transports he has to digest a story told by Aristotle. According to the great empiricist of the Greeks, the mother of Homer, Critheis, was made pregnant by a deity in the retinue of the Muses, and later married in Smyrna a Lydian king who, like Joseph, obligingly reared her child. Out of such ignorance developed a romantic conception of a genius who suddenly, miraculously, emerged from a literary void, to compose for an illiterate audience poems that would take a twenty-four-hour day to recite, and that were somehow preserved just as he recited them. In the reaction against this romance, many scholars have denied that there ever was a Homer.

The famous "Homeric question" arose in the seventeenth century, when the Abbé d'Aubignac suggested that different men wrote the *Iliad* and the *Odyssey*. By the end of the last century the obvious inconsistencies within and between the epics had convinced most scholars that both were patchworks by many authors, and that "Homer" was at most a mere redactor. Today scholars seem inclined to agree with the Greeks that there was a great poet, whom we might as well call Homer, but they are still split over the question whether he wrote both of the epics. For my purposes, fortunately, this question makes little difference. It is enough that we have these great poems and that they remained a major inspiration to the Greeks, who never questioned the reality of their Homer or suspected that he was two.[3]

More pertinent for the historian is the problem of dating him. The Greeks were so vague about his life that Hellanicus, an early Ionian writer, placed him in the twelfth century, making him practically a contemporary of his heroes. Today scholars place Homer, or the flock of little Homers, anywhere from the eleventh to the seventh century. The recent tendency has been to bring him closer to the classical period— thereby deepening the mystery of why the Ionians and classical Greeks knew so little about him. This question brings us back to the historical element in the *Iliad,* and to considerable more confusion. Thus the armies advance into battle in great lines, suggesting the later Greek phalanx; but the real fighting always settles down into individual combats between heroes, presumably in the Mycenaean fashion. What period, then, is Homer describing? And how accurately?

Some details are unmistakably Mycenaean. The heroes regularly fight with bronze rather than iron weapons, and they carry big shields reaching from head to toe, such as are pictured in Mycenaean art. Homer pictures

---

[3] Like them, I feel the same spirit and qualities of greatness in the two epics, despite the differences in style and content. As an outsider unqualified to pronounce an authoritative judgment, I can only repeat the observation I made in *The Spirit of Tragedy:* "By the kind of scholarly arguments used on Homer one could prove conclusively that there never was a Shakespeare, since plays so full of inconsistencies could only be a patchwork by many hands; or that there must have been two Shakespeares, since it is unthinkable that the same man could have written *A Comedy of Errors* and *King Lear;* or that the alleged Shakespeare must have lived more than a century before his supposed Elizabethan age, since he never once mentions printing, which dates from 1454." In this book I again propose, if only for the sake of convenience, to speak of Homer instead of "Homer."

Mycenae as a great capital, even though in his own time—whether 900 or 700 B.C.—it was a decaying town of no political importance. In general, he gives an accurate picture of the political geography of thirteenth-century Greece. But he does not give a true picture of Mycenaean culture. His Achaeans burn their dead like the later Greeks, and never refer to the great beehive tombs of Mycenae. They are apparently illiterate, never writing home during the ten-year war, whereas Mycenaean tablets have been dug up. Their most prized articles of luxury and works of art come from Phoenicia; Homer was apparently ignorant of the advanced art of Mycenae. Moreover, many details are plainly Ionian, from the caldrons, tripods, women's veils, and stained ivory to the temples with cult statues. Homer's Troy is more like a Greek *polis* than was either Troy VI or Mycenae. As a result of this confusion, one school holds that the *Iliad* is essentially a reflection of early Ionian culture, explaining away the Mycenaean details as irrelevant survivals. Another school holds that it is essentially Mycenaean, explaining the Ionian details as irrelevant accretions. Both are embarrassed by the undeniable presence of elements from widely separated periods.

All this to-do illustrates again the silly side of research. So the embattled scholars have raised a famous question: Why did the heroes of the *Iliad* never eat fish? Because, they answered triumphantly, it is a true Mycenaean story; this alone proves that Homer was not writing about Ionian times, when fish were a staple of the Greek diet. Their opponents never flinched; obviously fish lack grandeur and are unfit for a heroic diet. In their thoroughness the scholars overlook nothing but the elementary and the obvious—beginning with the fact that Homer was a poet, not a historian, and that he was not writing for a modern audience. Yet all the pedantry and the futile controversy have again yielded substantial gains. We know much more about Homer's poems. In wrangling over the nature and proportion of their ingredients, the scholars have at least specified these ingredients more precisely and more fully. And they are at least agreed that the epics are traditional poems. Homer did not blaze out of nowhere, but drew on a large body of familiar poetry that had been handed down for generations by minstrels. In retelling the traditional stories, the minstrels naturally kept dressing them up, rehandling them in current terms. Happily the specialists may continue to argue over what is old and what is new, what historical fact and what fiction. For the general reader it is enough to know that the epics are not the inventions of an isolated genius, or works of art for art's sake, but national poems, reflecting memories of the heroic age of Mycenae, and also reflecting a new culture that was to become the classical Greece of our own tradition.

Now the fascination of Homer—as of this Greece—has its dangers too. In piety let us remember that we are dealing with a man speaking out of a particular culture, not the voice of Nature speaking timeless truth. As traditional poems, full of stock epithets, the epics contain topical materials that we may find trivial or tedious. (And as at that we are dealing with only the greatest Greek poetry, while our printing presses flood us with trash that perishes quickly but never quickly enough, let us always remember that the Greeks too no doubt wrote a great deal of bad poetry, which we cannot read because it has long since perished utterly.) Gilbert Murray himself once confessed that the *Iliad* has a second-rate subject in "the wrath of Achilles," a "bitter rancor" occasioned by the loss of a captive girl who had been his share of the spoils of war. The greatest hero of the Greeks sulks in his tent during most of the epic, which grows monotonous with repetition as the tide of battle swings to and fro. This classic is no model of classical symmetry and proportion. There is no artistic justification for the presence of Diomedes, a hero almost as great as Achilles, who performs similar deeds but has no relations with him. The *Odyssey* is a still more episodic affair. The much-praised simplicity of both epics is at times a naïve simplicity, in the celebration of a heroic age when men were twice as strong and brave as they were in the poet's own age.

It was in some respects a still primitive age. The heroes of the *Iliad* are war lords whose main goals in life are fame and plunder; the chief means to both is killing. One can hardly imagine Achilles living anywhere but on the battlefield. The nobler Hector is shown at home, but in a tender domestic scene he prays to heaven that his son may grow up to be as notable as he himself is: "May he kill his enemy and bring home the blood-stained spoils, and give joy to his mother's heart!" [4] Her joy will be heightened by the knowledge that if he loses, his enemy may make her a slave. And even a devotee of the comic strips might weary of the endless battles and catalogues of the slain in the *Iliad*. Variety is chiefly in the gruesome detail: "Ajax drove the great spear crashing through his helmet, and the brains ran out along the socket. . . . The blade pierced the corselet-plate and his bowels gushed out. . . . A sword sliced off his head and sent it flying helmet and all, he lay with the marrow spurting out of the spine." The best that can be said for such detail is that it was forced on Homer by the tastes of his audience.

Yet Homer was unmistakably superior to the world of the *Iliad*, and far from primitive himself. Even in this celebration of the greatest mili-

[4] This and subsequent quotations are taken from the colloquial prose translation of W. H. D. Rouse.

tary exploit of the Greeks he does not merely glorify war; at times his heroes express their hatred of this "lamentable war." He reveals his embarrassment over some of their traditional behavior, which was evidently too well known to be suppressed, passing hurriedly over the "shameful outrage" of Achilles in dragging the body of royal Hector around the walls of Troy, and then his "vile outrage" in stretching the body in the dirt to be devoured by dogs. We see Homer himself most clearly in "untraditional" scenes, such as the tender one between Hector and his wife and child, which appear to be the poet's own invention. Hector too—the most sympathetic character in the *Iliad,* even though the champion of the "enemy"—may have been Homer's creation, for he kills no Greek leader except Patroclus, and a traditional hero would normally have a number of eminent victims. In general, the reason why most readers still believe in one Homer is that throughout the *Iliad,* as in the *Odyssey,* is felt the presence of a thoroughly civilized spirit, marked by qualities of humor, compassion, tolerance, breadth, mellowness, and sanity which are rarely found in heroic epics.

The astonishing thing about the first poet to emerge in the Grecian world is his imaginative and intellectual command of his materials. If the *Iliad* is no marvel of artistic form, it will seem marvelous enough to one who has come from the sprawl of the Babylonian Epic of Gilgamesh —a comparable traditional poem, and the product of some thousand years of thought and imagination.[5] We may still echo Aristotle's praise of Homer's skill in mingling narrative and dramatic art, his tact in unifying his poem by concentrating on the wrath of Achilles instead of on the obvious subject of the conquest of Troy. But we can appreciate more than Aristotle could his freedom from Oriental bombast and extravagance. The great hero Gilgamesh proves himself in conflict with monsters in a fabulous world, still primitive in its supernaturalism. Homer's heroes have to contend with the gods but they live and die in a real world, and prove their heroism in facing the sorrows, terrors, and horrors that men actually have to deal with. Essentially there is little nonsense in this celebration of the heroic age of Greece.

The heroic ideal itself is not so naïve and vainglorious as may appear on the surface. In his passion for fame through glorious deeds, the Homeric hero had an ideal of integrity and honor above material comfort or success. If his conception of the good life was not lofty, he was at least "spiritual" in his living faith that the good life mattered more than the long life. In courting death he was more admirable because he had

[5] In what follows I amplify but often substantially repeat my discussion of Homer in *The Spirit of Tragedy.*

a natural zest for life, and with it nerves. W. H. Auden has said that he "cannot be called brave in our sense because he never feels fear," but actually he often feels it, to the point of panic or despair. Hector was so afraid of Achilles that he ignominiously took to his heels, fleeing three times around the walls of Troy in full sight of his fellow Trojans. Then he met the test of bravery in any sense. He turned to face the dread Achilles, gaining heart as he took his stand; and when his doom was upon him, he stood up to it too. "Now then, death is near me, there can be no delay, there is no escape. . . . Yet I pray that I may die not without a blow, not inglorious."

A more striking proof of Homer's mature artistry is what he was able to make of the traditionally fierce Achilles, and his "second-rate" subject. Achilles is not at all attractive as he sulks while his fellow Greeks are being slaughtered, and he becomes positively repellent in his fury when aroused by the death of his lover-friend Patroclus. We are reminded, however, that he is crazed by grief and long fasting. He knows, too, that he himself is doomed. His goddess-mother had told him that he would live a long, prosperous, comfortable life if he returned to his native land, but was fated to certain death if he stayed to fight at Troy; and he had spurned the life of ease to win his brief glory. Finally he makes amends for his outrages on the body of Hector, in the sublimely simple scene when old King Priam comes to beg him for the body. He is reminded of his own father: "God gave him evil too, because he got no family of royal princes in his palace, but only one son, to die before his time. And now he is growing old, and I cannot care for him; for I am here in Troy, far from my country, troubling you and your children." Still, Achilles remains in character—the scene does not fade out in sweetness and light. He makes no pretense of remorse for the slaying of Hector, instead asking forgiveness of the shade of Patroclus. There is no profit in sorrowing either: man must endure. And meanwhile man must sup: "Well then, venerable prince, let us two also think of something to eat. After that, you may weep for your son again when you have brought him back to Ilios. Many tears he will cost you!" Thereupon follow the heartrending lamentations of the Trojans. The epic ends simply: "That was the funeral of Hector."

There is nothing naïve in such simplicity. It is the work of a humane poet who knew and respected his heroes, but also knew and respected much more than they did. For Achilles, Homer provided a tutor, Phoenix, to teach him the arts of speech and try to warn him against the evils of stubbornness, hardheartedness, and violence of temper. Other warriors, such as wise old Nestor, often recall the values of peace and civility, which receive more stress in the mellower *Odyssey*. These naturally include the arts—even Achilles plays a lyre—and in particular poetry, since Homer was a proud minstrel. Altogether, the ideal expressed in the epic as a whole is not simple glory through valor, but *arete,* a word for which there is no equivalent in English but which is usually translated as "excellence." It covers all forms of human excellence—physical, intellectual, artistic, moral; it implies the ideal of wholeness and harmony. Odysseus is the supreme example of *arete:* a mighty warrior, with the valor and "unconquerable soul" of the hero; an athlete who excels at running, boxing, wrestling, and throwing the discus; a practical man who can skin an ox, plow a straight furrow, and build his own boats; a civil man, of fine tact and courtesy; a lover of song, unashamed to be moved to tears; a ready speaker and a crafty schemer, never at a loss for words or wiles; a genuinely wise man too, famous for his "understanding mind"—in short, a master of all the arts of peace and war, equal to any civilized occasion.

These values are more convincing because Homer wrested them from an unflinching pessimism about man's destiny, the powers beyond his control. The final proof of his sovereign spirit is his tragic sense of life. As Dio of Prusa noted, he "praised almost everything," from the fruits of the good earth to horses and men; his narrative is constantly vivified by his intense interest in all that man can see, do, and enjoy on earth; but this very zest for life deepened his sense of mortality, of the living truth in the commonplaces about the generations of men that pass like the leaves and forever cease to enjoy. He offered no easy consolations about a life to come. All the heroes end in Hades, a ghostly underworld in which there is nothing to see, do, or enjoy, nothing but shadow, and which to them was dreadful even though it was not yet lit with hellfire. On earth meanwhile there was always sorrow, with no clear justice. The immortal gods dispensed good and evil fortune with a sovereign unconcern for propriety. It did not help that they too were subject to Moira, a mysterious, impersonal, inexorable Necessity. Moira made Zeus himself forgo his humane impulses. It put the seal of the cosmos on the tragic reality, that no man can escape his fate.

Greek literature is notorious for such "fatalism." Yet the upshot in Homer is not fatalistic resignation, much less despair. While his heroes often talk like fatalists, they seldom act so. Their talk is conventional piety, or sensible recognition that men are indeed at the mercy of greater powers. Their action is a dauntless assertion of their own power, by which they will win glory and demand full credit for it. When they know they are doomed, they are still free in spirit. Like Hector, they will meet death with a final assertion of their unconquerable soul: "First may I do

some notable thing that shall be remembered in generations to come!"
Such defiance of death is quite irrational, since fame will do the hero no
good in his grave, and it may still seem unspiritual to those who look
forward to an eternal reward in heaven. In Homer it nevertheless
amounts to a historic declaration of spiritual independence, from "miracle,
mystery, and authority."

Magic, myth, and religion are literally matters of life and death—
especially death. Primitive religion generally does not recognize death as
natural or normal. Myths often attribute it to some accident, when they
do not explain it away or simply deny it. The Babylonian Epic of Gilgamesh still refuses to accept it as an inalterable necessity of man's being.
Its hero finds the thought of death intolerable; his quest of life everlasting
is narrated with an often moving rendition of "the pathos of mortality";
but the epic ends in mere pathos, unheroically, trivially, with the great
hero weeping because a snake has crawled off with a magical means of
rejuvenation he had at last found. Like primitive myths, it implies that
death is the result of a mere accident, a miscarriage of magic. Later religion would more positively deny the reality of death, while philosophy
would conjure up elaborate proofs that man is immortal. Homer faced up
to the stark reality. He does not explain why men must die: "Do not try
to explain death to me," Achilles says to Odysseus in Hades. Homer
simply says that death is the law of man's being, that he must learn to
accept it—and that he can learn. He teaches the art that is the final lesson
of philosophy: how to live well and how to die well.

The heroic personality, not myth or religion, was the inspiration of his
work. In a historical view, nothing is more astonishing than the freedom
with which Homer treated the myth. Although we cannot be sure how
seriously or literally he took the traditional myths, it is at least clear that
unlike the Eastern peoples before him and around him he possessed
them—he was no longer possessed by them. He took them in his stride,
using them unaffectedly for his poetic purposes much as he used the
similes he was so fond of. He felt free to introduce humor into the scenes
on Mt. Olympus. By discrimination he introduced a measure of rhyme
and reason. He purified or ignored the more barbarous myths that have
come down to us from other sources. He ignored as well the most ancient
and common ritual patterns in the world around him, such as the Year
Daemon who annually dies and is reborn, and the semidivine Hero whose
birth and death are alike mysterious or miraculous. He ignored even the
Mother Goddess, who had been worshiped by both the Minoans and the
Mycenaeans.

Freedom is much more than Engels' "consciousness of necessity." The lamentations of Eastern peoples record a keen consciousness of painful necessities. Some end in despair, some in resignation, some in pious acceptance; but all state or imply the utter dependence of man upon the gods. None give dignified expression to a dignified way of life that man can maintain by his own efforts, in defiance of his mortality. Homer was the first to demonstrate the independent power of the human spirit. He alone showed that by facing his inescapable destiny, man might escape his bondage to it.

3. HOMER AS THE "EDUCATOR OF HELLAS"

When Plato grew hostile to poetry, as a mere imitation of mere appearances and an inducement to emotions unbecoming a philosopher, he centered his attack on Homer. Why, he asked rhetorically, had Homer's pupils not handed down to posterity a Homeric way of life? But already he had implied the answer: they had done so. He himself was attacking this way of life. As he went on to say, he wanted to give his own pupils an answer to all the eulogists who declared that Homer was the "educator of Hellas," and that he was "profitable for education." Xenophanes, another who deplored Homer's influence, likewise testified to it. "All men's thoughts have been shaped by Homer from the beginning," he wrote.

Today some literary critics would shudder at such talk of Homer as an educator. While they have an exalted idea of the importance of poetry, and a dismal idea of a society like ours that fails to honor it, they want to keep it pure and autonomous, judge it simply as poetry, and avoid like a plague the traditional concern about its usefulness for moral, political, or social purposes. Homer himself might well have been surprised, or amused, by his later reputation. It seems safe to assume that his primary aim as a minstrel was entertainment, not education. Yet he would also have been surprised at the idea of pure poetry, composed simply for art's sake or the poet's own sake. As traditional poems composed for traditional purposes, his epics were expressions of national ideals. As a proud minstrel he evidently took for granted that poetry was absolutely good, but also that it was always good for something else. It made life better and men better.

At any rate, Homer unquestionably did become an educator for Hellas. In the classical period his epics were recited by relays of minstrels at the major national festivals. They were a basic course in formal education; we hear of Athenians who knew all of Homer by heart. He was studied more intensively than ever in the later Hellenistic period, when scholars edited his texts and finally, about 150 B.C., gave them their canonical form.[6] Meanwhile his stamp was all over the culture of Hellas. Among his early pupils was Pindar, who consciously sought to educate. A perfect example of Homer's *arete*, he wrote odes to victorious athletes celebrating their godlike excellence, and passing naturally to thoughts of the dignity and frailty of man, a race akin to the gods, but also apart:

> Thing of a day! such is man; a shadow in a dream.
> Yet when God-given splendor visits him
> A bright radiance plays over him, and how sweet is life! [7]

Another famous pupil was Herodotus, whose history is a prose epic about the heroic war to preserve Greek independence; he too was fond of praising the deeds of great men, despite his melancholy refrain that the gods seem bent on destroying them merely because they are great. Still other pupils were the tragic poets. Aeschylus described his own plays as "slices from the great banquet of Homer"; Sophocles was called the closest disciple of Homer. Both made tragic drama the heir of the high epic tradition, a means of expressing the national ideals of Athens.

These were somewhat different from Homer's ideals, however, and they bid us pause again over the limitations of his curriculum. His civics was old-fashioned. The heroes are kings and nobles, loosely united in a semifeudal organization under the great King Agamemnon, a feudal overlord. We hear several times that the great king gets his right from the gods; he consults with the lesser chieftains on affairs of state much as Zeus calls a council of the gods on Mt. Olympus. A shadowy popular assembly also makes an appearance on important occasions, but acts merely as a sounding board. "No man of the people is allowed to disagree by any means in council or in war," a Trojan prince remarks. As a courtly poet celebrating the great old days when heroes could hurl stones "such as two men could not lift as men are now," Homer naturally showed little interest in the common people or, for that matter, in political affairs. The Greeks hardly consulted him as they developed their republican *polis* and drew up constitutions. But they never quite outgrew the cult of the hero, the great leader. Later on, Alexander the Great, Homer's star pupil, would restore the kingship that the less cultivated Macedonians had preserved from Homeric times.

At his best Homer had the defects of his virtues, in particular of his

---

[6] Hence we do not have "pure" Homer, whether he was one or many; quite a few fragments of his work quoted by Greek writers do not appear in our text. Classical scholars have the problem of spotting the later accretions or expurgations and trying to get closer to the original Homer. But what the Greeks made of him is no less important to the historian concerned with his influence.

[7] Translation by H. D. F. Kitto.

distinctive clarity and sureness. As Erich Auerbach pointed out in *Mimesis*, nothing is left unrealized or unexpressed, veiled or shadowed; there are no fleeting glimpses or haunting suggestions. Everything is set in the foreground, bathed in full light, with little sense of perspective either in time or in space. The inner world is as self-contained and free from shadow or lacuna. Character is clearly defined; emotion and motive are simple and completely expressed, with no suggestion of unplumbed depths. Neither does character grow or change; after twenty years of adventure Odysseus returns to Ithaca the same man he left it, just as Helen retains her ageless beauty. In general, the world of Homer is like the beautifully drawn world of Keats' Grecian urn, two-dimensional, unwavering, fixed for all time. It may lead one to brood over why things should be as they are, but what and where and how they are is perfectly clear. No great poet is less hospitable to the hunter of secrets or underlying meanings.

Hence the later Greeks wasted their piety and ingenuity when they tried to find allegory in Homer, in order to explain away his "lies" about the gods. That they made this hopeless effort revealed how much to heart they had taken their great educator. They could not see him in his time and place because they had as little historical perspective as he had, as little sense of genesis and development. In this respect the world of Homer remained essentially the world of classical art and thought. It became more varied and more complex; it remained Euclidean, static, fully illuminated, without shadow or perspective—the world of frieze and vase. And this ideal classical world was rather different from the world of Greek experience, especially in the East. It represents a brilliant triumph over experience. It also helps to explain, perhaps, why the Greeks were finally unable to cope with the complexities, ambiguities, and incongruities of the actual world of flux.

Yet the triumph remains most remarkable and significant—the triumph over extravagance, confusion, anxiety, fear. No people before the Greeks had so reasonable, clear-eyed, and sane an educator as Homer. Just how he or his contemporaries had won to this command we cannot know. The extraordinary fact of it is our sufficient concern.

We must therefore qualify the obvious criticism of Homer's politics, or lack of politics. What state, asked Plato in the *Republic*, was ever better governed by his help? The stooge in the dialogue answers truly enough that not even the Homerids pretended that he was a legislator. But at least a people brought up on Homer would not accept the despotism natural to the East, or Plato's own ideal of an anthill state. The epics incidentally contain the seeds of democratic government, as in the popular assembly. The nobles are not aloof from the common life and have no fancy gentility; in war they lead their men in a common action, in peace join them in manual labor. As W. P. Ker observed, Sir Lancelot was horribly distressed when he had to ride in a cart, but in a similar situation Odysseus was not at all embarrassed—he had no doubt built a cart with his own hands. All the leaders owe their prestige to their exploits, not to noble birth or blood. Most important, the kings are not absolute monarchs, nor their subjects slaves. They are expected to govern responsibly, in accordance with "Themis" or law, not by arbitrary command or private whim. Nor are they gods. If in theory they rule by divine right, they do not actually talk or act as if they were divine agents, and are never regarded as themselves divine. Given the political history of mankind, Homer had uncommon good sense in recognizing that the greatest king or hero was not a god. He might have appreciated Bury's comment on the legendary Lycurgus of Sparta: "He was not a man: only a god."

In general, the breadth and sanity of Homer's spirit allowed the Greeks to develop freely, and to continue to revere him as an educator even when they were learning quite different lessons in new schools. Poets and artists were most directly indebted to him, and for much more than specific themes or slices. By his freedom he made the traditional mythology a treasury instead of an intellectual nuisance. For philosophers it became something of a nuisance, while for ordinary Greeks it remained a source of confusion; they were always prone to mistake fable for fact. The great tragic poets wrote as if they knew better. Like Homer, they handled the traditional myths with imaginative independence, to suit their different poetic purposes and express their different religious thought. After denouncing the poets, Plato himself felt free to introduce new myths of his own, in essentially the same spirit as Homer.

Even Greek philosophy was indebted to Homer, as were all branches of inquiry. If he was not speculative himself, he left ample room for speculation by his essential rationality and his freedom from superstitious awe. He also offered some leads. Moira, the impersonal Necessity governing both gods and men, could become the universal lawfulness that makes possible philosophy and science. The respect for wise old Nestor could develop into a love of wisdom. In particular, Homer implicitly asserted an idea that was to rule Greek ethical philosophy until the end: the idea that while man is subject to some kind of universal law and order, he is nevertheless free, responsible, and ideally self-sufficient.

When on trial for his life, Socrates appealed to the authority of

Homer. In the *Apology* he declared that he would hold to his way of life even if it meant death, because he believed, like Achilles, that disgrace was worse than death and that what man should value most is not life, but a good life. Socrates may seem Christlike in his martyrdom; yet the ideal he died for was the pursuit of wisdom and righteousness on earth, not the service of God or life immortal, and an ideal that man could attain by his own efforts, without the grace of God. The issue raised by this new version of the pride of the Homeric hero was forced by Aristotle. The great man, he said, is neither vain nor humble, but proud. He thinks himself worthy of great things and makes as great claims on others as demands on himself; he seeks the highest good that men render the gods—honor. Pride is the "crown of the virtues," for it makes all the other virtues greater and is "concerned with honor on the grand scale." The unduly humble man, by contrast, "robs himself of what he deserves, and seems to have something bad about him from the fact that he does not think himself worthy of good things, and seems also not to know himself; else he would have desired the things he was worthy of, since these were good." Such humility, Aristotle adds, is "both commoner and worse" than vanity.

It was to become still commoner in the Christian era of Greece. Aristotle's pride would be branded the deadliest of sins. As always, the issue is complicated by the ambiguity of these terms. In their humility the Christians performed great deeds of martyrdom, and thought themselves worthy of such great things as joining their Lord in heaven. In their pride the Greeks counseled the wisdom of moderation, "nothing to excess," and hoped for no greater thing than fame on earth. Still, there is a plain difference in spirit. Odysseus was the all-around man— except that he had in him nothing of the saint. Greece in its heyday produced no saints. Until it lost its freedom, it was frankly devoted to Homer's ideal. Even then its Stoic and Epicurean philosophers still taught, in the spirit of Homer, that man could be master of his own soul, by his own reason and will, without need of special revelation or divine grace. St. Paul taught something very different.

4. THE OLYMPIAN GODS

Another common name for the Homeric epics is "the Bible of the Greeks." As Herodotus said, Homer was the first to name the Olympian gods and put them in their place, giving them their forms and their functions. Although he did not create them out of nothing, since he was not himself a god, he was in a real sense their author. The glorious inspiration of Greek art, the Olympians were created by it. And also ruined by it, one might add; for we come at once on an anomaly. While the blessed gods became revered all over the Greek world, Homer himself showed less respect for them than he did for his heroes. Often he made fun of them; they are the chief source of comedy in the *Iliad,* and the comedy is sometimes farcical. Hence there is considerable difference of opinion about the glory of Homer's handiwork. Gilbert Murray himself veered between the extremes. In an early work he lamented the incalculable "injury done to the human race" by the invasion of this blasé, mocking spirit into the greatest of poems and highest of concerns. In a later work he concluded that Olympianism was one of the great religious reforms in history, marking the triumph of Hellenism over barbarism.

To find a possible way between these extremes, we must consider what lay behind Homer. Strabo noted a difficulty in all discussion respecting the gods in that the ancients had expressed themselves "enigmatically," and always mixed fable with their discoveries about the nature of things. "It is not easy therefore to solve these enigmas exactly," he observed; "but if we lay before the reader a multitude of fabulous tales, some consistent with each other, others contradictory, we may with less difficulty form conjectures about the truth." Compounding confusion might seem a strange way of simplifying and arriving at truth; among the ancients it generally had the more likely effect of increasing confusion. But the multitude of fabulous tales has been a boon to modern scholars. With the aid of contemporary materials from primitive peoples, they have been able to explain many of the enigmas, in terms of prehistoric origins unknown to Strabo and the ancients. The fables reflect the older worship of nature deities: of mountains, rivers, springs, caves, trees, stones, and of snakes, bulls, and other animals representing fertility daemons. Many are outgrowths of magical rites whose original significance had been forgotten.[8]

Homer's Olympians were originally mountain gods of the invaders from the north (thus the twenty-odd Mount Olympuses over the Greek world).

[8] The Greeks were troubled, for instance, by their custom of offering sacrifices to the gods, in which the gods got the poor portions of the animal while men feasted on the choice portions. It appeared that the gods not only were open to bribery but were not very bright. Hence a myth told how Prometheus had tricked Zeus into choosing the worse share of the gift. Etymologically, however, *sacrifice* did not mean gift: it meant simply a holy doing or making, suggesting a communal feast shared by men and the god. Earlier it had probably meant what it still means to some primitives: the animal was the god himself, and men were eating him in order to get some of his magical power. In later times Cicero would exclaim rhetorically, "Where would one find a man insane enough to believe that he drinks and eats a god!"—and some still later Christians would be embarrassed.

As conquerors, they mostly lost what interest in agriculture they may have had, becoming more concerned with fighting and feasting. Zeus, the "Cloud Gatherer," had started as a sky god and was always given to boasting and hurling thunderbolts. The family he collected had more obscure, mixed origins, like the Greeks themselves. Hera, who became his second wife, had been an earth mother; whether she is of Hellenic descent is uncertain. The names of the other goddesses, including the ultra-Greek Athena, are not Greek. That Athena began life as a nature deity may be inferred from the symbols she kept to the end of her life —her owl and her olive branch. Aphrodite and Artemis plainly were sprung from fertility goddesses, and were always especially susceptible to Oriental influences. As for the gods, Poseidon and Apollo are probably Indo-European by name but certainly of mongrel ancestry. Poseidon, the sea god who was somehow the "Earthshaker," had been a river god and apparently also a horse. Apollo was an earth god, not Greek in origin, who came to have some connection with the sun, though not until after Homer's time did he become the glorious Phoebus Apollo. The chances are that he came from Asia Minor, where he might have picked up the priestesses who delivered his oracles.

The antecedents of the Olympians were further confused by their historic careers. Polytheistic gods naturally tend to keep breeding, as one myth leads to another, but as they take on new functions they are practically obliged to. The native gods might be abhorrent to the Greek invaders, or might have to be destroyed for political reasons, giving rise to such myths as the war between the Olympians and the older Titans and the triumph of Zeus over Cronus. (It is unfortunate that Zeus had to be the son of Cronus, but no other father was available for him.) Since it is ordinarily both impious and impolitic to kill gods, however, many were brought into the family as offspring or distant relations. Zeus in particular became a kind of heavenly bull. He seems so lecherous because he had to sire so many deities, and if there was no suitable local nymph or goddess he could bed only with a mortal woman.[9] While there are no signs that Zeus was embarrassed by these duties, he could not well display reluctance without seeming ungracious and imperiling the cause of international good will which he

[9] The goddesses usually did not associate with men, but one exception that had historic consequences was the affair of Aphrodite with Anchises on the slopes of Mt. Ida, resulting in the birth of the Trojan hero Aeneas. The story is most likely a relic of the Idaean Mother, one of the manifestations of the Great Mother, and her lover-son. Scholars assume that the early Greeks, not yet familiar with her ways, failed to understand that her lover was also her son, and therefore split him into two men. Aeneas could then go on to found Rome.

was serving. To this cause he even sacrificed his own domestic peace. A Homeric Hymn indicates that Hera was not at all happy about the marriage forced on her; her injured pride inflamed her jealousy and caused constant quarrels. In spite of his regal authority Zeus might have envied his son Apollo, who likewise had innumerable affairs, but was never bedeviled by a nagging wife.

Although Homer was probably unfamiliar with most of this whole story, he reflects some of the confusion. The Asiatic connections of Poseidon and Apollo are suggested by the myth that they built the walls of Troy; but whereas Poseidon is bent on destroying the city, Apollo—the chief god of the Ionians—is a champion of the Trojans and the slayer of Achilles. Athena, the most ardent champion of the Achaeans, is nevertheless the patron goddess of Troy. The Scamander is now a river, now a god; when Achilles starts to wade the river he has to fight the raging god. Yet in so doing he expresses his contempt for this god—and here we are led to Homer's handiwork. Homer brought order out of the confusion. He eliminated the fertility daemons, the mother goddesses, and all but the traces of primitive nature worship. He refused admission to Olympus even to Dionysus, though he knows him as "the darling of the world." He reduced the countless gods to a definite family, with a definite home. Zeus has emerged as the leader of this family, with sovereign powers that the others may resent, but never deny. Apollo and Athena have lost their Asiatic traits and acquired much of the dignity and the radiance that were to make them the most Hellenic of the gods. All the Olympians have clear personalities and clear functions.

Much too clear, indeed; so we are struck at once by their glaring limitations. They are not spiritual gods, but only glorified human beings. Even for mere supermen their behavior is often shockingly undignified, quite apart from all their philandering. They bicker and scold, and then complain that their breakfast has been spoiled; they tell clumsy lies and are caught in them; they fight with men and bawl when they get wounded. They call their father a "hard-hearted tyrant"; call one another fools and bitches. Zeus, who "laughs with glee" when they fight among themselves, "knocks them all over the place" when he gets mad at them. He has to keep thumping his chest and reminding himself that he is all-powerful, which in fact he isn't. The father of the blessed gods falls like an adolescent for the Hollywood charms of Hera when she seduces him in order to distract him from his intentions of aiding the Trojans.

Lovers of Homer, such as Werner Jaeger, like to find a "deeply religious conception" in his majestic councils of the gods, and especially in his approach to the idea of a supreme god. Actually, Zeus was in this respect not at all in advance of the times. Some such idea was implicit in Marduk and Amon long before his time, and was furthered as much by military conquest as by religious aspiration; the main god of conquerors naturally tends to become supreme. Zeus was essentially no more than a feudal overlord, reflecting the aristocratic society of Homer's time. Hence he was both tyrannical and limited in the exercise of his authority over the other gods; like the Greek chieftains, they could disobey or connive against their leader, as well as quarrel among themselves. In their relations with men the Olympians were often as arbitrary as feudal lords dealing with their underlings. While they were generally expected to deal justly, they played favorites and might act on caprice when not out of pique or spite; men were often dismayed but never surprised by their capricious or cruel behavior. And the gods displayed no gratitude for Homer's doing so handsomely by them in enabling them to live like lords and "dwell at ease" forever. They performed little service in return for the attentions they demanded of their worshipers. They assumed no responsibility for the life of nature or the fate of man.

In fact they couldn't. They had not made this world, they could not explain it—they could not answer the first questions put to them by a religious thinker. When the later Greeks groped toward the conception of one god, Zeus might lend his name but could hardly play the role. The pious Aeschylus appealed to "Zeus, whoe'er he be"; the noncommittal Sophocles referred to a "God of many names." Xenophanes gave him up—Zeus would never do for the purely spiritual god he had in mind. Even had the lord of Olympus been able to live down his lusty past and grow disposed to cease dwelling at ease, he was incapable of assuming such universal responsibilities as the Greeks wished to charge him with. It is again a token of the real progress of the human spirit that no sane man today would dream of worshiping Homer's Olympians.

Yet they too represented a clear religious progress. It was something that the gods feasted, laughed, and went to sleep at night, for men did not have to live in constant fear, and might even go abroad in the dark. (It is a sorry tribute to Deity, incidentally, that men today would think it unseemly of him to laugh, but still think it proper for him to get angry.) Homer's world is almost entirely free from black magic, fetish and taboo, demon and monster. The traces of barbarous practice, such as human sacrifice, that survive in his myths only accentuate his emancipation from the heritage of primeval anxiety. His creation of the Olympians in man's own image was actually no degradation of the supernatural, or loss of spirituality. It meant first of all that the gods were no longer brutish or material, no longer identified with snakes or stones. Men could now distinguish between the human and the non-human, and so might realize their humanity—without which there can be no true spirituality. Likewise the shift of the gods from the earth to the heavens meant that men were no longer obsessed with food and phallus, and might cultivate finer possibilities of life.

To such purposes the easygoing Olympians were quite amenable. However capricious, they were often genial and gracious, never simply hostile, never so savage as Yahweh sometimes is in the early books of the Old Testament. Men could hope to get along with them reasonably well, much as they could with other men. The very limitations of the gods were an advantage, for in demanding only ceremonial attention they left men free to cultivate *arete*. And as glorified human beings they too could be educated. In Homer they are already working toward standards of honor and justice. Among them is Themis, who convenes the assemblies and represents the power of law or collective conscience in human affairs. Although Zeus is disposed to play the tyrant, because of his pride in his newly won power, he often listens to reason, even from Hera, and the heroes take for granted that he will punish all who break their oaths or give "unrighteous judgments." In the *Odyssey* he is becoming more sensitive, complaining that men blame the gods for the consequences of their own wicked deeds. More surprising, the old buccaneer has moods in which he frowns on war. "I hate you more than any other god alive," he tells his son Ares. "All you care for is discord and battle and fighting." He speaks here for Homer, who makes plain his own dislike of the incorrigible god of war and "enemy of mankind." Homer shows little respect either for Aphrodite, who is fit for nothing but the arts of sensual love. The only gods whom he treats with invariable respect are Athena and Apollo—and these were to become the great patrons of Greek culture.

Meanwhile the family as such had humane uses. Individually biased, they were relatively impartial as a group; they were the gods of the Trojans too. In this respect they had a quality of "universality" lacking in the tribal Yahweh of Moses, who was concerned only with his chosen people. Their mongrel ancestry also kept them free from vulgar race prejudice. Polytheism itself is more profoundly humane than we are likely to realize. It may seem simply irrational, given the mysterious passion of the human mind to reduce the many to One; yet it corresponds to the plain diversity of the world of experience. It provides appropriate gods and rites for all occasions; symbolizes the manifold possibilities of ideal value. The very favoritism of the gods and the conflicts between them are as intelligible as unseemly. To conceive an almighty god of perfect goodness takes a very lofty thinker—lofty enough to lose touch with the realities of every day life. As it is, the imperfections of the Olympians seem more pronounced because they had no Devil to take the blame for the manifest imperfections of the creation.

Ultimately these so-human Olympians lead us to the sublime mysteries, or the apparent incongruities, of all religion. As "high" gods, they represent a universal tendency to conceive God as high up, in the sky. Edwyn Bevan observed that the religious vocabulary of all languages includes such words as *superior, lofty,* and *heavenly,* which imply that spiritual worth is in proportion to distance from the earth. One might conclude that the Olympians were not lofty enough to satisfy the religious spirit. They lived on a terrestrial mountain, in human form; they were never really transcendent, out of this world. Yet one might as fairly say that they were too lofty and remote. To understand religious experience one must also look down, to the earth, to the underworld. Here dwell the chthonian gods, who insure fertility and are likely to have some connection with the souls of the dead. Some are wholly of the earth; others acquire a kind of dual nature—like the heavenly-earthy Mother Goddess, who might live on a mountain or in a cave. And these too represent a universal tendency.

The Olympians never had it all their own way in the Greek world, even aside from Moira. Peasants clung to the fertility gods, as well as to prehistoric magic. (Blessed is he, wrote Hesiod, who is "knowing in Birds and not overstepping taboos.") The man in the street honored all the Olympians, but more fervently he worshiped the mystery gods, such as Dionysus, who became increasingly popular even though Homer had banned them from Olympus. Zeus himself was confused with the Cretan Zeus, a mystery god who dwelt in a cave. These earth gods all had a dark, unholy aspect; typically their rites involved the sacrifice of black animals and were celebrated in the evening or the dead of night, whereas the Olympians were honored by the offering of white animals in the morning. Nevertheless the earth gods were more "spiritual" than the heavenly gods in that they enabled communion, an ecstatic transport out of the world and the self.

Jane Harrison accordingly argued that the inadequacy of the Olympians was due not so much to their human shortcomings as to their idealization. Because they were a product of reflection and differentiation, they could not inspire the fervor that comes from a sense of the unity of man, nature, and deity. As they were idealized and transported to their heaven on Olympus they were freed from the woes of mortality—suffering, failure, death—and by the same token were separated from mankind by an impassable gulf. At worst they bred the notion that any effort to bridge this gulf was *hubris*, seeming pitiless in their jealousy of human fame. At best their worshipers could never really commune with them, be at one with them in this life or the next. "It is only a step further," Jane Harrison wrote, "to the conscious philosophy which will deny to God any human frailties, any emotions, any wrath or jealousy, and ultimately any character whatever except dead, unmeaning perfection, incapable of movement or change"—the chill Absolute of Aristotle. But short of this, the Olympians were doomed by the very completeness of their victory over the earth-born daemons, as reflected in the myth of the Gigantomachia; for thereafter they simply lived like lords. "The god like the man who substitutes privilege for function, for duty done, is self-doomed and goes to his own place. 'If any will not work, neither let him eat.'" Although the Olympians were long given enough to eat, out of sentiment or mere habit, real worship went to the hard-working fertility daemons and mystery gods, who did not dwell at ease but kept on the job, serving their people, even dying for them.[10]

At least there is no question that the Olympians eventually were lost in the blue. They were not killed in turn—they simply vanished; and though they had been great breeders they left no descendants. Their only apparent contribution to subsequent religious thought and feeling was their survival in the form of Christian demons. And so we might more fairly assess Homer's handiwork, I believe, if we grant his severest critics their contention that Olympianism was not "truly" religious at all. The *Iliad* has no word either for "god-fearing" or for "love of God"; Homer would certainly have agreed with the observation in the *Magna Moralia* that "it would be eccentric for anyone to claim that he loved Zeus." But for the

[10] An interesting example is the enduring popularity of Heracles—a hero god who never quite made the grade as an Olympian, having been adopted by the gods but not admitted into the family. In the *Iliad* he is spoken of as a man; Achilles points out that even so great a hero, dear to Zeus, could not escape the common fate of death. In the *Odyssey* he is referred to as a god, and Hesiod tells how he was admitted to Olympus as a reward for his heroic labors. Herodotus was puzzled by his dual nature, but concluded that the Greeks were wise in hanging on to him. Jane Harrison suggests that the reason for his popularity was his deep, ancient connection with yearly death and resurrection, as a fertility daemon; doomed to Labors, he was beloved of working people. Another apparent reason was the new hope of immortality: here was one man who did get to Olympus. In later Hellenistic times, when this hope became a faith, the image of Heracles appears on grave reliefs.

same reason the Olympians helped to make possible the unique glory of Greece. Their all-important contribution was to Greek culture: directly as an inspiration of art, indirectly through the freedom they permitted— freedom from the "miracle, mystery, and authority" that dominated thought throughout the ancient East.

The Olympians never authorized a church or a powerful priesthood, a class set above the citizenry. Neither did they authorize scriptures, or any rigid dogmas to impede the advance of thought; "the Bible of the Greeks" was in the Christian sense no Bible at all. Though like all gods the Olympians tended to be conservative in matters of ritual, demanding the proper ceremonial respect, they tolerated critical inquiry and accommodated themselves to new ideals. By such reasonableness they encouraged the effort to live in accordance with reason. Most of all, they encouraged the life of the distinctive Greek *polis*. They were essentially neither earth gods nor sky gods but community gods—champions *against* the forces of nature—who presided over major civic occasions, enjoined civic duties, promoted the civic welfare; instead of private salvation they offered a rich communal life. As gods who were accepted all over the Greek world, the Olympians helped to unite this world in a common consciousness of Hellenism, but they deepened fellow feeling especially by their devotion to the *polis* that every Greek was devoted to. On these secular grounds, and for those who cherish the Greek ideal, W. R. Halliday's final verdict on Olympianism is fair enough: "Its influence upon the development of civilization had been profound, beneficent, and sane. From Homeric times it had stood consistently for progress; it had fostered the arts of painting, sculpture, music, poetry, and drama; it had promoted the ideals of justice, law, and order and had guided the development of political life."

In this view the subsequent career of the Olympians is neither so incongruous nor so pathetic as may at first appear. On the surface it is simply a matter for irony. After Homer had brought order out of chaos, illustrating the reputed Greek genius for simplicity and harmony, the Greeks reverted to chaos—retaining many ancient deities, adopting many foreign ones, foisting more bastards on the Olympians. They never mastered the first lesson of their great educator, to distinguish clearly between heavenly and chthonian gods. In Homer's own alleged birthplace of Smyrna the cults later included Zeus in several of his sixty-odd forms, Asclepius, Dionysus-Briseus, the Sipylene Mother, the Ephesian Artemis, the Syrian Atargatis, Nemesis, Tyche, Hestia, Isis, "Lady-Moon," Semele, the river Hermes (though Homer had ridiculed river gods), and Homer himself. The Olympians seem absurdly ineffectual, lost in the crowd—unless we keep in mind that hospitality was one of their chief virtues, and civic patriotism one of their chief concerns. Since this patriotism may be called the living religion of classical Greece, they were of real account while the *polis* was flourishing. When the *polis* lost its independence and self-sufficiency, they lost their vital function. They displayed some resentment at the intrusion of foreign gods, but eventually they retired with becoming dignity, content to dwell at ease again while holding purely honorary positions. The proof of their virtue is that they did not have to be killed.

In taking farewell of them, we might note in piety the light they throw on the genius of Christianity. Like the older mystery religions they succumbed to, Christianity offered not only the promise of life to come but sacramental communion with the god in this life. Unlike the others, it insisted on both the full divinity and the full humanity of the dying god, while also asserting that his death was a deliberate sacrifice for man. In practice it emphasized the human aspect of the divinity; the most vital figures in popular Christianity have been the Son and the Mother, not to mention all the saints and martyrs. Thus, too, it managed to retain the practical uses of polytheism under a nominal monotheism. For the more thoughtful or truly spiritual it provided the Holy Ghost, to make possible constant spiritual relations with the transcendent Godhead. And though God the Father always tends to become more remote and abstract than the Olympians—to attain the "dead, unmeaning perfection" deplored by Jane Harrison—he too has a human aspect, a heritage of Yahweh of Israel. Theoretically endowed with absolute perfection and self-sufficiency, he is also endowed with personality, including such human frailties as jealousy and anger.

But the Olympians may also suggest certain disagreeable analogies. Among the masses of Christians, ritual has become as mechanical as the sacrifices once offered to the gods; sacramental communion may give little real sense of union, especially to city men lacking any deep sense of nature. Thoughtful Christians are troubled, as the Greeks were, by traditional practices and beliefs that they wish to honor, in respect for venerable tradition, but cannot really believe in, because of new knowledge and changing ideals. "One reason why it is so hard to please the gods," Jane Harrison noted, "is that it is so hard to know beforehand at what moment they will have outgrown the sort of things which used to please them." One way of easing this difficulty is by remembering that historically the morality of the gods has seldom been in advance of that of their worshipers. Loftier moral, social ideals have generally been the cause rather than the result of loftier conceptions of deity. So Aeschylus taught Zeus to be just. And so Homer had given the Olympians their first lessons in *arete*.

5. HOMER AND TROY THROUGH THE AGES

In an age when educated men no longer read Greek, it is hardly profitable to discuss Homer's poetry as poetry. Both sound and sense come out differently in every translation; one who goes from the *Iliad* of Alexander Pope to the *Iliad* of W. H. D. Rouse might not realize that he was reading the same poem. Nevertheless, it must always be remembered that the great man was proud to be a poet, achieved his greatness as a poet, and as such made his lasting impression on Greek culture. The fact remains that Homer's Troy—the literary, largely fictitious Troy—has had incalculably more influence on history than the actual one. Except for the *Iliad,* the nine or the forty-six Troys would be as unknown as the thousands of anonymous settlements buried in the mounds of Asia Minor. The story of what Homer did for Ilium, the actual town, is as fabulous as any he wrote.

Following the Trojan War, Ilium sank into wretched obscurity. When the Greeks began settling in the Troad, such important cities as Abydus and Lampsacus grew up on the always important Hellespont, but Ilium remained a mere village. It commanded nothing now that the Greeks controlled the whole region about the Hellespont. In the sixth century Athens and Mitylene fought over the possession of nearby Sigeum, reputedly built out of the stones of Homer's Troy, but they did not bother about the real Troy. The village took on more importance when Alexander the Great piously made it a *polis* free from tribute, and his successor Lysimachus built a new wall around it; Troy VIII became the honorary capital of a little federation of towns in the Troad. But on the coast to the south Lysimachus built up a new city, Alexandria Troas, which soon dwarfed it. Troy remained a small town, so poor, reported Demetrius of Scepsis, that it lacked even tile roofs. Demetrius subjected it to further indignity by denying that it was the site of Homer's Troy, dismissing its claims as mere pride. Its pride might have suffered when the Gauls who crossed from Europe took a look at it but found it not worth sacking. It suffered materially as well during the Mithridatic wars, when it managed to catch the attention of one Fimbrias, a Roman traitor; he took it after a short siege, sacked it, slaughtered its inhabitants, and thereupon boasted that he had done in ten days what it had taken the old heroes ten years to do. A survivor could only reply that they had no Hector to defend the city.

Yet they still had Homer. Through all its misfortunes the town lived chiefly on its temple to the Trojan Athena, a shrine for pilgrims because it supposedly contained the arms of some of the old heroes. In other words, the town lived off Homer—there had actually been no Trojan Athena or temple. Once, to be sure, Athena did her part by performing a miracle, recorded on a local monument; but her shrine was not a wonder-working center. The pilgrims came in a purer piety, under the spell of Homer. One would like to think that it was the spirit of Homer that caused Xerxes, after his visit to the shrine, to burst into tears as he sat on a marble throne on a hill overlooking the Hellespont and contemplated his vast, shining host. He felt a sudden pity, he told his uncle, at the thought that not a man in this host would be alive a hundred years later. "And yet there are sadder things in life than that," replied the uncle, according to Herodotus:

Short as our time is, there is no man . . . who is so happy as not to have felt the wish—I will not say once, but full many a time—that he were dead rather than alive. Calamities fall upon us, sicknesses vex and harass us, and make life, short though it be, to appear long. So death, through the wretchedness of our life, is a most sweet refuge to our race: and god, who gives us the tastes that we enjoy of pleasant times, is seen, in his very gift, to be envious.

For Troy, however, the god had one more gift—the greatest in its history, and the most impressive, ironic tribute to the power of Homer. Rome, the mistress of the world, became the daughter of his Troy. As the Romans conquered the Greek world they were won by the myth that the Trojan hero Aeneas was the father of their race. This seems to be a pure myth, inasmuch as there is no historic evidence whatever to support it (though scholars have speculated that the vanished Trojans might possibly be the mysterious Etruscans). One reason why the Romans were ready to believe it was that they had started building their empire, and the myth enabled them to pose as the natural heirs of Asia Minor. They were encouraged by some Greeks, likewise for political reasons; the scholars of Pergamum worked industriously to fill out the details of the story at a time when their King Attalus wished to cement his alliance with Rome. By the end of the third century, at any rate, the myth was widely accepted. Homer had managed to prepare for it by arranging to have more gods intervene to save the life of Aeneas than that of any other hero, Trojan or Achaean, and by indicating that he was to succeed Priam as king of the Trojans. Finally it was immortalized by Virgil, whose Aeneid told the whole story of how Aeneas survived the fall of Troy and went on to found Rome. Virgil's epic was a conscious effort to do for the Romans what Homer had done for the Greeks.

The new era for Ilium began with the coming of Julius Caesar, after his defeat of Pompey. An ardent admirer of Homer and Alexander,

Caesar traced his descent to Iulus, the alleged son of Aeneas. He guaranteed the freedom of Ilium, exempted it from taxation, and even considered making it the capital of the empire. At last it became a real city—Troy IX—if still a small one. Then the Emperor Augustus honored it by rebuilding on a grand scale the temple of Athena. Later emperors who visited the holy city ranged from the benevolent Hadrian to the vicious Caracalla, who on starting a campaign in the East imitated Alexander by offering sacrifices at Ilium. Shortly thereafter it was plundered by the Goths, but it recovered to witness still another striking proof of the power of poetry, or of sentiment. Constantine the Great actually started to build his new capital here before settling on the far more advantageous site of Constantinople.[11]

Sentiment touched even the hearts of some early Christians, the fierce enemies of Homer's paganism. Among the last recorded scenes in the history of Ilium was a visit by the Emperor Julian the Apostate, who was shown around by Bishop Pegasius, the local shepherd, and was pleased to find the old altars still burning with sacrifices to Hector. The good bishop explained that it was natural for the inhabitants to venerate their great hero, just as it was for Christians to venerate their martyrs. Most Christians, however, were not so tolerant of pagan piety, or by now were simply ignorant of Homer. The city lost the holy past that alone had kept it alive, and sank into obscurity again. When the Turks took over, they naturally ignored a site that had no natural advantages; they built their forts farther up the Dardanelles at Chanakkale, a little below the site where Xerxes had built his bridge. In the Troad they were interested chiefly in the ruins of Alexandria Troas, from which they carted so much stone to build in Istanbul that the site is known as Eski (Old) Istanbul. The much smaller city of Ilium served the humbler purposes of neighboring villagers, and in time became simply a hillock, a pasturage for sheep and goats. Homer could do nothing more for it until he inspired a passion in Heinrich Schliemann.

Meanwhile an ironic kind of continuity was provided by venerable Mt. Ida, which through the ages has dominated the landscape. It was here that Zeus was seduced by Hera, who encouraged him by remarking how shameless it was to make love in so conspicuous a place; their nuptial couch was a bed of clover, crocus, and hyacinth, which still bloom on the

[11] Had he not changed his mind, history might have been profoundly different. Only the natural strength of its fortress-capital enabled the Byzantine Empire to survive some attacks that threatened to topple it, particularly the first great surge of the Arabs that threatened all Christendom; whereas the great city of Alexandria Troas was deserted as early as the eleventh century, unable to withstand the raids of pirates.

slopes in the spring. Here too Aphrodite and Anchises made love, to give
birth to Aeneas. Both couples were no doubt drawn to the mountain unconsciously by the presence of the Great Mother, who had dwelt there
since long before their time. Helen of Troy was related to her, for among
the Dorians she was worshiped as a vegetation deity. Hence Ida remained
a holy mountain even under Turkish rule. In this century the Greeks of
the vicinity still went to it to celebrate an annual festival on August 15,
the ancient day of the Great Mother, though they now called her the
Virgin Mary. The mountain was sacred as well to Moslem nomads, possibly in the name of some Moslem saint, but actually because of the nameless sanctity that has attached to "high places," as to caverns, since
prehistoric times. This kind of sanctity Homer had outgrown.

But all this while the literary Troy lived on. Homer's heroes, who had
such a passion for fame, have won a more glorious and enduring fame
than they ever dreamed of, in a far greater world than they knew. Even
in Hades they might take some comfort in the thought that few monarchs
of great empires are better known than they are, and that perhaps no
woman except Mary is so well known as Helen of Troy, the "single
Spartan girl" over whom they so absurdly fought.

CHAPTER IV

Miletus: The Birth of the Modern World

---

1. THE ANCIENT EAST

THE MODERN Western world, it is often said, was born in the Greek cities of Ionia toward the close of the eighth century B.C. Its proud children should therefore take note that this blessed event occurred in what is known as the "Oriental" period of Greek culture. Geographically, Greece faces East, and as it emerged from the dark age following the fall of Mycenae, it drew extensively on the cultural capital of the East. The Greeks in Asia Minor were stimulated by closer association with older peoples, who began educating them long before Homer, teaching them new arts and skills. They owed most of all, directly and indirectly, to the art and learning of Egypt and Mesopotamia.

Now, our incalculable debt to the ancient peoples of the Near East gives reason for some embarrassment as well as humility. I do not believe that we can do full justice to these peoples. To the Greeks they were all "barbarians"—not savages, but aliens, men who might have admirable qualities, yet were strangely content to live without freedom and to believe without reason. To us, as spiritual descendants of the Greeks, they inevitably seem as alien, and more remote. When we are fascinated by them it is usually because of their exotic quality, their strange differences from us, or now and then surprise at the discovery that they could be very human after all. We cannot really share their distinctive thought and feeling about the cosmos and the gods. While specialists puzzle over the precise meaning of their key terms, the most sympathetic students of their great societies, such as Henri Frankfort, are likely to combat Western prejudice by insisting that their values are incommensurate with our own; but if so, I again conclude that we cannot know them intimately. We can no more shed our values than shed our skins. Or if I am exaggerating these difficulties, at least it is well to stress them at the outset. Simply because we have grown more historical-minded, more objective, capable

97

of a more sympathetic understanding of other cultures, we should realize that we are creatures of our own history, and can never achieve complete objectivity or perfect understanding.

Yet we must still try to understand, of course. We owe this effort to ourselves for the sake of self-knowledge, as well as to dead peoples for humanity's sake. The historical and anthropological research of our time has made it both a special privilege and an intellectual duty. For at least we can now go far toward a better understanding.

To a Western eye there is a depressing sameness in the outcome of the Eastern adventures in civilization; so let us first remark the diversity and spontaneity of these early adventures. By 2500 B.C. there were three independent civilizations, in Sumer, Egypt, and India. All rested on the same basic discoveries and inventions; all flourished in great river valleys by means of irrigation and drainage systems; all were connected in a trade network. But each was pursuing an original course, developing its own culture. Already the "static East" was a welter of activity—as it would remain down to our own time, in almost every century one or more of its diverse peoples being on the move, embarked on commercial, military, or religious adventure.

The Egyptians in particular developed a unique civilization, quickly adapting to their distinctive purposes whatever skills they learned from Sumer. Whereas Sumerian civilization arose in independent cities, ruled by gods, which later formed temporary kingdoms but never became a real nation, the Egyptians dated their history from the unification of the land in a royal, largely rural domain, by a king (or series of kings) known as Menes; and they always remained a nation. They were united in the belief that their welfare depended wholly upon Pharaoh. Their earliest writing appears in legends on royal monuments or on seals identifying royal officials; their early monumental architecture was not the temple but the pyramid, the royal tomb, built grandly in stone instead of the brick that the Sumerians had taught them to make; their art had chiefly royal or historical rather than religious themes. They had much more confidence in man's powers than the Sumerians had. For nature was much kinder to the Egyptians. They lived in a sheltered land of perpetual sunshine, with no dangerous enemies on their borders, and with the munificent Nile that could be counted on to bring the life-giving waters every year on schedule. In this favored, unchanging land the Egyptians conceived their ideal of an immutable society completely ordered and permanently maintained by divine power in the person of Pharaoh, himself divine. "It was an ideal," wrote Henri Frankfort, "which ought to thrill a Western historian by its novelty, for it falls entirely outside the experience of Greek or Roman or Modern Man. . . . It represents a harmony between man and the divine which is beyond our boldest dreams." It is perhaps not really so novel or thrilling, in view of the Byzantine Empire and the ideal of the medieval Papacy; but the Egyptians more nearly realized it, and clung to it for over two thousand years.

Hence the rule of Pharaoh was not the simple despotism that it may seem to us. Nothing in Egyptian tradition suggests that this order was imposed by violence, and certainly it remained government by popular consent—the masses never rose up against Pharaoh. If they complained, as men often do, of the dispensations of Providence, they did not dream of kicking out Providence. During the Old Kingdom, which established the basic, enduring forms of their civilization, the Egyptians appear to have been supremely confident of their destiny under Pharaoh. The wealth they squandered on their tombs has suggested a morbid obsession with death that lovers of Greece are wont to contrast with the Greek zest for life, but in fact there was nothing sad in their elaborate preparations for death. They had the happy belief that they *could* take it with them—all of it—as they followed Pharaoh into the Beyond. Historians now picture the early Egyptians as bustling extraverts, pragmatic, optimistic, thoroughly devoted to the goods of this world; and though we may suspect a degree of exaggeration in this corrected portrait, the art of their tombs expresses an unmistakable delight in nature and life. For the upper classes, at least, the Old Kingdom seems to have been a golden age. It was at once exuberantly creative and delicately appreciative, enjoying a way of life that was no doubt too complacent, and not very spiritual, but was refined, gracious, genial, lit by humor as well as splendor. And they knew it would go on forever. The Pharaohs to come would be the same as the Pharaohs that had been, and there would be no new thing under the sun because Pharaoh in effect was the sun.

It was accordingly a terrific shock when the Old Kingdom collapsed, about 2200 B.C., and a period of anarchy ensued. We have no trouble understanding the response of the Egyptians. In despair, some took to the later religious view of death as a release from this life. Others began to doubt the afterlife, and drew the familiar conclusion: "Behold, no one who goes over there can come back again!"—so "make holiday," and "let thy desire flourish." But still others groped for higher, more enduring values. There were glimmerings of ideals of righteousness and social justice, anticipating the prophets of Israel, just as Ikhnaton, the first religious reformer known to history, was later to anticipate the idea of One God. In the Coffin Text, a god announced that he had created all men equal, made the Nile to overflow for the benefit of rich and poor alike, and given all access to the kingdom of the dead. The afterlife was in fact made more democratic. Nobles freely claimed special privileges of admission that had once been reserved for Pharaoh, and there is some evidence that even the lower classes shared in the new hopes. At the same time the idea of a judgment of the dead entered religious history: paradise had to be earned by good conduct. Osiris now embarked on the career that was to make him, with his consort Isis, the most popular of the Egyptian gods, and the most spiritual of the dying gods before Christ.

Apparently he had been in Egypt from the beginning. Like the other dying gods, Osiris began life as a fertility god, and as such he inspired the usual phallic simplicities. Some portraits of him, Frazer observed, "indicate in the plainest way that even in death his generative virtue was not extinct but only suspended, ready to prove a source of life and fertility to the world when the opportunity should offer." But in time he became more Christlike than the other dying gods. He dominated his sister-wife Isis, who was not a Great Mother. He defeated death once and for all; the Egyptians made much less of his suffering and death than of his role as king of the dead. Most important, he became a judge who ceased promising resurrection by merely ritual or sacramental means. Recorded professions made by the dead at his judgment bar reveal that he tried to hold them up to a morality as lofty as that of the Ten Commandments (though it is not clear what fate he imposed on the wicked). And like Christ, he may have been a real man. While Egyptian traditions gave diverse accounts of his career, they all agreed that he had been a great and good king on earth, who not only taught his people how to cultivate grain but gave them laws.[1] On all counts, Osiris inspired a more fervent and prolonged devotion than any other pagan deity except the Great Mother. In the fourth century after Christ, St. Athanasius was horrified to see Egyptians still mourning his ritual death.

By this time such devotion was pathetic. Egypt had long since lost the spirit that created the forms of its civilization, and was preserving only the forms, the dead letter, in the slavish piety that has made it a byword for petrified life in death, its fellah the symbol of the silent, viewless, hopeless peasant. Yet this tenacity also calls for some respect, or even awe, such as the Greeks felt for venerable Egypt. The fixed forms of its culture had long represented a reasonable pride in an achieved stability. They had permitted the development of the richest art before the Greeks,

[1] Another sign of his humanity is that shrines owned parts of his body, which had been dismembered and scattered before he was revived by the sun god Ra. The Egyptians were not troubled by the fact that both Abydos and Memphis had his head, and many other shrines a leg—any more than medieval Christians were troubled by all the heads of John the Baptist owned by different churches.

an art marked by energy and vigor as well as exceptional refinement and grace. As we contemplate its most conventional expressions—the massive solidity of its pyramids, the unblinking stare of its rigid statues, the stereotyped figures in regular rows—we may feel something of the Egyptian sense of the immortal and immutable, or of superiority over the passing show of history. History finally caught up with Egypt; but only China can rival it for longevity, and China was much like it in its patience, industry, and stubborn devotion to its own tradition. By contrast America has lived a brief, noisy hour.

The later societies of the Near East were much less original than either the Sumerian or the Egyptian, but they have some claim upon our sympathy even apart from their abstract "contributions." (And let us never forget that the most sympathetic historian can never do justice to the drama of millions of human beings—very human beings to whom life meant something rather different from what appears in our histories, and always meant much more.) Hammurabi of Babylon declared a high responsibility in the preamble to his law code: the gods had sent "me, Hammurabi, the obedient, god-fearing prince, to cause righteousness to appear in the land, to destroy the evil and the wicked, that the strong harm not the weak." In this spirit the gods themselves were showing some concern for righteousness. Enlil, the leading god of the Sumerians, had become fatherly and beneficent, seeming unhappy when he had to send the tempests and fires decreed by the assembly of the gods. Marduk of Babylon, who replaced Enlil by right of military conquest, nevertheless took on some ethical responsibilities as the supreme god of a state with a code of law. The Babylonians may still appeal to the religious conscience by their painful efforts to hold the gods to the higher standards of justice they had developed. So the author of "Ludlul Bel Nemeqi" wrestled with the insoluble problem of evil, a thousand years before Job. The hero is a righteous man who is afflicted, and like Job finally reconciled and rewarded—but only after acknowledging more plainly that divine standards are incomprehensible to man:

> What to one's heart seems bad is good before one's god.
> Who may comprehend the mind of gods in heaven's depth?
> The thoughts of a god are like deep waters, who could fathom them? [2]

In their efforts to fathom them, the later priests of Babylon became the most famous astronomers of antiquity, and made its most enduring contribution to posterity. Without instruments, they built up a remarkable body of exact knowledge, arriving at some estimates more accurate than

[2] Translation by Mrs. H. A. Frankfort.

those of Ptolemy, or even of Copernicus. The Greeks were the first to acknowledge their indebtedness to these wise men, whose lore was to guide the three Magi to Christ.

It is harder to feel sympathy for the arrogant Assyrians who overthrew Babylon and became famous for their cruelty; but a cold-blooded historian must pay them some tribute too. The first people to dream of world empire, they were also the first to organize and administer one over a large area. They likewise anticipated the Romans by carefully preserving the culture of the Babylonians, much as the Romans took over the Greek. To Ashurbanipal, the last of their great rulers, we are indebted for the two great libraries that he collected at Nineveh, as well as for the superb reliefs in his palace, the finest examples of Assyrian art. The "Age of Ashurbanipal" (669–626) is among the notable epochs in the history of culture. And the monarch himself, so forbidding in his sculptured majesty, suddenly comes to life as an unhappy old man, lamenting the strange evil that befalls even holy kings. "I did well unto god and man, to dead and living. Why have sickness, ill-health, misery, and misfortune befallen me? I cannot do away with the strife in my country and the dissensions in my family. Disturbing scandals oppress me always. Misery of mind and of flesh bow me down; with cries of woe I bring my days to an end." Within a few years all Assyria was to cry out as its empire crashed and Nineveh was sacked by the Scythians and the Persians.

These Persians, who finally lead us to the Greeks, first wrote a glorious enough chapter of their own. They silenced the ghost of Ashurbanipal by creating not only the greatest but the most civilized empire yet known to history. Their early kings were remarkable rulers, with an eye to economics. While organizing their empire in provinces under satraps, they unified and strengthened it by such measures as standardizing weights, issuing an imperial coinage, and building imperial highways lined with caravanserai, including the "Royal Road" from Sardis to Susa traveled by Herodotus. Herodotus testified to their most statesmanlike qualities— their justice and their liberality. The Persians did not enslave the peoples they conquered, nor despise them; they respected other cultures, freely adopting customs, techniques, and arts superior to their own. They were so generous to the Jews that Isaiah hailed the Emperor Cyrus as a Messiah. In particular they respected the Greeks, from whom they learned much (unfortunately including the custom of pederasty). Altogether, the Persians laid the foundations of the later Hellenistic and Roman empires, inaugurating the cosmopolitan era that was to last until the coming of the Turks.

Herodotus also admired their strenuous moral code, which was distinguished by its emphasis upon truthfulness as well as valor. Persian scriptures taught that perjury was as bad as a hundred heresies. And though in time the Persians learned an almost Christian horror of heresy, first they produced one of the greatest of religious prophets—Zoroaster. His Gospel was a pure monotheism with a lofty ethic. Ahura-Mazda, the one true God, required of man primarily not ritual service but purity of life, or righteousness and good thought. As a god of perfect goodness he was not responsible for the evil on earth, but was in constant struggle with the Evil Spirit. Man had the privilege and the duty of aiding him in this struggle, which finally would end in the triumph of righteousness and the last judgment. Salvation lay wholly in a strenuous moral life, not in escape from life or a ritual resurrection. Like all the higher religions, Zoroastrianism became radically different from the teaching of its founder; he was made divine and soon lost sight of, while the Lord of Evil acquired more power and generated a sharp dualism. But in this process Zoroastrianism deeply influenced Judaism and Christianity, where Satan at last came into his own.

Still, this noblest creation of the Persians did not endure. In a much corrupted form, Zoroastrianism succumbed to Mohammedanism; today it survives only as a minor sect, confined to some hundred thousand Parsees in India. Otherwise the Persians left little mark on the world they once owned—and least of all on Asia Minor. Their chief claim to historical importance is that they came face to face with the Greeks in the West, and eventually drew them into the East. And so they recall me to my main theme.

Now even apart from its brevity, this survey of the ancient East may be deemed unjust. While indicating the achievements stressed by the most sympathetic historians of these peoples, I have dwelt on what *we* can admire, or in effect have held them up to our standards, not their own. Yet there is no escaping such habits of judgment, and no absolute need of escaping them. They are quite natural, as we study history for our own living purposes; they are quite proper, so long as we are conscious of what we are doing and do it in a humane spirit; in the end they are essential, since it is our business as thinkers to judge. Nor must our judgments be mere cultural prejudices. Granted that our standards are finite and partial, conditioned by our culture, ultimately subjective, still they are not arbitrary, *wholly* conditioned, *simply* subjective. We know much more than these ancient peoples knew, if only because we know all of them and also the Greeks; and we must believe that knowledge counts for something. To say only that their values are incommensurate with ours, or that we should try to judge them only by their own standards, is to surrender the value of our measure of detachment, our wider perspective, our more extensive experience, our awareness of different possibilities of life—our profits from the study of history.

We may begin with fairly obvious judgments of these peoples by their own standards, which included some notions of decency and justice. In their own day the Assyrians made a name for themselves by their abominable cruelty. They accordingly earned their fate: no other great empire disappeared from history so quickly and so utterly. If they contributed something to the organization of the Persian Empire, they otherwise left scarcely a trace—except for the memory of their cruelty preserved by the Hebrews. Nineveh was not even a name to Xenophon and the Ten Thousand, who marched by the site two centuries after its destruction. Let us grant that the Assyrians no doubt had a different opinion of themselves, that all peoples have been guilty of cruelty, that atrocities are still common in our own world, that political authorities may still justify them as necessary expedients. But who mourns the fall of Nineveh? Who will openly defend cruelty on principle?

The goals of the ancient East likewise included some simple, universal goals. Its peoples wanted material and spiritual well-being; or to put it simply, they wanted to enjoy life. They prayed to their gods for what men still pray for: good crops, good health, successful ventures, children, a long life. In the light of these simplicities let us consider the issue raised by the divine Pharaoh, the heart and soul of the favored land of Egypt. It is "revealing," wrote Henri Frankfort, that "during Egypt's long history no attempts to overthrow the existing order were made." The question is: What does this reveal?

For Frankfort it was the basic contentment of the Egyptians, the general success of their ideal. The service of Pharaoh, which at first glance looks like slavery in the gratification of a monstrous conceit, unquestionably had an ideal aspect that was very real to the Egyptians. Pharaoh might have, and often did display, a high sense of responsibility in his divine role. Ordinary Egyptians might feel exalted by the assurance that a divine power was visibly in charge of their affairs, daily on the job. Although they were never really free, always liable to conscription in the service of Pharaoh, they might enjoy a psychological security, deepened by religious emotion, which Western workers evidently do not get from their social security programs.

How they actually did feel we can never know for certain—as usual, we hardly ever hear the voice of the common man. But Pharaoh had to rule through a bureaucracy, which could obviously be oppressive. While Frankfort was pleased to cite the testament of one overseer who declared,

"I did not take away a man's daughter nor his field," this clearly implies that other overseers did take away daughters and fields. The evidence from other quarters is conflicting. Although the scribes tend to emphasize the poor lot of the peasants, they may have exaggerated it to set off their own exalted position. ("Put writing in thy heart," ran their typical advice to Egyptian youth, "so that thou mayest protect thine own person from any labor and be a respected official.") Although the sculptors and painters generally portray a cheerful, light-hearted people, they may have been flattering their wealthy patrons, or making out a good case for them to present to the judge in the underworld. The chief reason for suspecting that the lot of the Egyptian masses was unenviable is the uncertainty about their prospects in the hereafter, the great white hope of Egyptian life. There is no evidence that they shared in this hope during the glorious Old Kingdom, and only slight evidence that the hereafter might have been opened to them in the Middle Kingdom. Nobody argues that they were lively or gay in the last thousand years of imperial Egypt's history.

That the Egyptians never attempted to overthrow the existing order might also reveal sheer ignorance and inertia. Their belief that their whole civilization depended on the divine Pharaoh—that he alone acted, and acted alone—was literally preposterous; and it is certain that Egypt paid a heavy price for its ideal of harmony. The proper maintenance of Pharaoh in the life to come was a huge drain on the national resources, one evident reason for the collapse of the Old Kingdom. An immense amount of labor and wealth went into the great pyramids, instead of into provision for the needs of an increasing population. The Pharaohs saddled future generations as well with their costs by exempting pyramid towns from all further service to the state, at the same time granting them perpetual endowments to take eternal care of the royal tombs. After the end of the Old Kingdom the Pharaohs were still worshiped and served lavishly —but not wholeheartedly, to judge by the many "execration texts" ceremonially cursing their enemies, and by the continual robbery of their tombs. The New Kingdom, which brought imperial grandeur under such rulers as Ramses II, brought with it a harsher authoritarianism, grosser corruption, and still grosser ostentation. The divine Pharaohs now acted like mere supermen, vain and vulgar. They plastered Egypt with inscriptions boasting of their prowess, pictures showing them defeating whole armies singlehanded, while rows of little Egyptians cleaned up the little enemies.

By this time the little Egyptians symbolize an utter absurdity: that men should consent to live and die to feed so colossal a conceit. They were also supporting an immensely rich priesthood, which had risen to power as the prestige of the Pharaohs declined, and which was a further source of corruption, apathy, and waste. The temples came to own something like one out of every five Egyptians and a still greater proportion of the land. The priests earned their keep in part by circumventing the moral requirements for admission into paradise; they sold charms and magic passports that contained verdicts of acquittal in advance. The holy men of Egypt most clearly illustrate the conclusion of John Wilson's sympathetic history: a people who had once caught a distant glimpse of the Promised Land ended by wandering for centuries in the Wilderness, resigned, devoted to an ideal of "silence," lost to all hope except magic. Wilson acknowledges that Egypt not only proved unable to realize the promise of her beginnings, but made relatively slight intellectual and spiritual contributions in view of her size, wealth, and longevity. It is fitting that her most enduring works remain the pyramids. They are monuments to the majesty of her ideal, and to its basic absurdity; to the promise of her beginnings, and to its curse. They failed even in their primary purpose as sacred houses for the dead, for they were always desecrated by robbers. They served chiefly to inspire the Egyptian masses to endure—blindly, without question, without need.

So men also endured in Mesopotamia, under all its different rulers. If we hear of occasional disorders and royal assassinations, we never hear of popular revolutions in the name of rights to life, liberty, or the pursuit of happiness. The people had no such constitutional rights. At best they had good laws, often proclaimed as measures to protect the weak from the strong, but always proclaimed by the Great King—by "me, Hammurabi." Generally the laws favored the moneyed classes, protecting the creditor more than the debtor, setting maximum rather than minimum wages. Always they were royal favors, subject to change at the royal discretion. If men complained, they did not question the royal authority. As Hammurabi said, he was sent by the gods to "light up the land"; and this was the only source of light known to Mesopotamia since the Flood, when "kingship descended from the gods." The social order was as immune to fundamental criticism as the order of nature, for both were divinely ordained.

In this respect the great Persian Empire represented no real advance. Herodotus tells a characteristic story of Cambyses, the son of its founder Cyrus. Wishing to marry his sister, Cambyses called in the royal judges to inquire whether there was a law permitting this practice; the wise judges answered that they could find no such law, but they did find one "that the king of the Persians might do whatever he pleased." The Great King Darius vouched for the essential truth of the story in one of his royal inscriptions: "This land Parsa, which Ahura-Mazda has granted me . . . by the favor of Ahura-Mazda and of me, Darius the king, it has no fear of an enemy." His successors all dwelt on the theme of me and God, in boastful inscriptions that somewhat belie the Persian reputation for truthtelling. They also fixed the pattern of the Oriental monarchy that was to recur down through the Ottoman Empire: a period of military expansion, under vigorous kings; a much longer period of degeneration, under feeble, corrupt, or vicious kings who rose or fell by the intrigues of eunuchs and the ladies of the harem; and at all times a barbaric splendor at the court, where all prostrated themselves before the purpled autocrat. In particular the later kings of Persia anticipated the Ottoman idea of how to make a throne secure, murdering all their brothers as they ascended it. After the opening chapters, the history of the Persian Empire makes dismal reading even in the account of A. T. Olmstead—an "objective" historian who tries to build up the Persians by disparaging the Greeks and the Hebrews. Meanwhile Zoroastrianism was taken over by the Magi, who reverted to polytheism and ritual magic, grew fanatical in their insistence on ceremonial and doctrinal purity, and became symbols of Oriental wisdom.

The basic issue here is not merely the shortcomings of Oriental law or the abuses of Oriental monarchy—such failings are common to all societies. It is an essential failing, due to an essential irrationality. Obedience to the gods and the Great King remained the ruling principle of all the societies of the ancient East. It bred the virtues of patience and fortitude, it might appear as fervent devotion, in time it could lead to the wisdom of resignation or the holiness of renunciation; yet it always looks slavish because it was not a free choice but an unreasoned obedience, to an arbitrary authority. The rare spirits who adventured never proclaimed an ideal of free choice or adventure. Priests, scribes, astronomers—all the holy and the learned men continued to serve the gods or the god-kings, not the community. None led any popular movement toward enlightenment, freedom, or social reform.

It is hard for us, once more, actually to feel all the sympathy that intellectually we may extend to these peoples. Their most wonderful achievements do not seem wonderful because they have become part of our heritage, and are taken for granted. Their limitations are glaring, and likely to seem shocking. In humanity we should not judge too harshly their irrationalities and barbarities, which were authorized by age-old, universal tradition—and which persist in the twentieth century. Yet in humanity we must judge, declare the irrational and barbarous—if only because they still persist. And in any case, on any grounds, we must realize the great difference that was made in man's life by the rise of the Greeks. Only by contrast with the ancient East can we fully appreciate their singular achievement, which has also been obscured by familiarity.

2. THE RISE OF IONIA

On the coast south of the Troad the Aeolians founded Cyme, according to Strabo the "largest and best" of their cities. Although one legend made it the birthplace of Homer, few Greeks believed this; to them "Cymean" was a synonym for stupidity. Strabo reports that it took the Cymeans three hundred years to get the idea of levying tolls for the use of their harbor, during which time the city received no revenue of any kind. "It was late before they perceived that they inhabited a city lying on the sea." Hesiod's father was among the dull-witted, for he migrated from Cyme to Boeotia, another agricultural region that became proverbial for stupidity. In *Works and Days* Hesiod suggested that he himself lacked wit and spirit. While describing the wretched life of the farm, with its thankless toil, he pictured it as the "natural" life for man, warning against the foolishness of going to sea and trading; and as a primitivist he mistook the dawn of Greece for a twilight, calling his era the Iron Age—the last stage in degeneration from the Golden Age. Centuries later, Cyme had a livelier son in the historian Ephorus, author of a book on inventions, but the city had yet to perform any exploits worth commemorating. Wishing at least to mention his countrymen in his history, Ephorus could find no better way of slipping them in than by remarking, "At this time the Cymeans were at peace."

No doubt the Ionian Greeks were much amused by his embarrassment. They had known from the beginning what it meant to have a city lying on the sea, and we may be confident that they charged high enough tolls. No one ever accused them of dullness. All their cities afforded plenty of material for historians; they included such celebrated ones as Miletus, Ephesus, Samos, Chios, and Smyrna—the latter taken away from the Aeolians.[3] It was in these cities that life as we know it began. A new kind of splendor now enters history, not regal and pompous, but bright and buoyant. It glows in works of art inspired by an evident joy in creation and a zest for life amounting to a holy passion. It appears in vivid personalities, of individualists expressing their own thought and feeling instead of recording or adorning the monotonous annals of Great Kings. It envelops the free, full, many-sided life of the *polis*—the first "open society." How much came out of this *polis* is indicated by the many basic

[3] The rest of the original twelve Ionian cities were Priene, Myus, Lebedus, Teos, Clazomenae, Erythrae, Phocaea, and Colophon—the only one that lay inland.

terms of Greek origin, such as philosophy, theology, ethics, politics, physics, aesthetics, comedy, tragedy, and history itself. But the essential fact is that the Greeks became fully conscious, and self-conscious. Although man in the East had made himself, he did not see himself as a maker. Now man realized the wonderful potentialities of the human spirit for knowing, feeling, and striving, pursuing truth, beauty, and goodness.

This spirit naturally got the Ionians into trouble. They became conscious of problems that do not bother peoples who live simply by custom, in obedience, on faith; in choosing their own ends, they discovered the hazards of free choice. At times they might have envied the sluggish Cymeans, for they were seldom at peace. They themselves acquired an even worse reputation in the Greek world for the sins of wealth and ease. They could indeed be very foolish in their cleverness. And although we, their heirs, must first marvel at their achievement, we may be further embarrassed as we try to understand it. Little is known of their early history. The cities to which we owe our being are still buried; excavations at these sites have usually stopped at the Hellenistic-Roman level, to preserve its more spectacular remains. Homer has practically nothing to say about the Ionians. They had no Heroic Age, and their arrival in Asia Minor was not "historic."

From the beginning they were a mongrel people of uncertain origins. Although they appear in the Bible as the sons of "Yavan," the Greek Ion, they had no common ancestor. They liked to believe that they came from Athens, as some of them almost certainly did, but they did not speak the same language; Herodotus noted four different dialects in Ionia. There is little doubt that they were pushed out of Greece, by either the invading Dorians or the dispossessed Achaeans, and came to Asia Minor as émigrés, not as conquerors. Their legends indicate that they met some resistance but do not tell of a glorious conquest. They had the good fortune to arrive at a time when there was no imperial power in the Aegean region. The Hittite Empire was no more; Egypt had withdrawn within its borders, to devote to a pious archaism what spirit it had left; the Assyrian Empire expanded chiefly to the south, impinging on the Greek world only in Cilicia in southern Asia Minor; and the Phrygian kingdom was apparently content to hold its own in the interior. At that it took the Ionians a long time to establish themselves securely among the small nations or tribes that occupied the coastal region. Nor did they ever establish a nation. They were held together by pride in their common name, and celebrated an annual festival at the Pan-Ionium, a temple on the promontory of Mt. Mycale; but "Ionia" remained a congeries of scattered cities. No vestige remains of their Pan-Ionium.

Nevertheless their settlement in Asia Minor was a real adventure, somewhat like that of the American frontier. If they did not have to clear forests or deal with savages, they were boldly starting life over again, in a land of opportunity that also called for enterprise, resourcefulness, and courage. Their cities were outposts, which they had to hold without the support of a powerful mother country. As they prospered they lived on an advancing frontier, founding new colonies in which enterprising spirits again started afresh. And all along, in the very absence of "historic" events, they were making a much more significant history than Heroic Ages have ever made. "The circumstances which have most influence on the happiness of mankind," wrote Macaulay, "the changes of manners and morals, the transition of communities from poverty to wealth, from ignorance to knowledge, from ferocity to humanity—these are, for the most part, noiseless revolutions." We may now get some light on the revolution that took place in Ionia by following the history of Miletus— the greatest of its cities, the only one mentioned by Homer, and the first to enter recorded history, as the Millawanda or Milawata mentioned in Hittite archives.

When the Milesians arrived, they found the region occupied by Carians, and their first acts should dispel the idea that Ionian blood was the secret of their brilliant success. Herodotus reports that although they came from Athens and considered themselves the purest Ionians of all, they brought no wives and therefore married Carian girls, whose menfolk they had slain. The women avenged their fathers and husbands by taking an oath, which they handed down to their daughters, that "none should ever sit at meat with her husband, or call him by his name"; but they were not so patriotic or unwomanly as to refuse to bear him children. The Milesians preserved the custom of communal meals for men, which Plato thought made for civil strife instead of unity.[4] The Carians remained on the scene, however, and point to further confusions. While they asserted that they were aboriginal inhabitants of Asia Minor, Greek tradition represented them as an Aegean people who had maintained a thalassocracy until suppressed by King Minos of Crete. But *thalassa*, the Greek word for sea—the sea that was all-important to them throughout their history—is not an Indo-European word. Like Parnassus and Athens itself, it was borrowed from some older people.

Probably the Ionians owed considerable to the brilliant Minoans of

---

[4] It has been remarked that the Greeks had shrines everywhere to the Companion, but none to the Wife. Women may therefore be pleased by the thought that from Miletus later came Aspasia, the brilliant mistress and companion of Pericles of Athens, who amazed Plutarch by loving her so much that he kissed her whenever he went in or out of the house.

Crete, though how much is uncertain. These Minoans are believed to have come from Anatolia, bringing their Mother Goddess with her double ax and attendant lions, and they are known to have learned much from the Egyptians; but they developed a civilization strikingly different from all the Eastern civilizations. They had no ziggurats or pyramids, no great temples or tombs, no colossal statues of kings—none of the Oriental monumental forms that are so imposing, and finally so oppressive. They had only palaces, airy, well-drained, exuberant with color, as livable as they were splendid. Instead of celebrating royal triumphs, the awful majesty of gods or kings, the frescoes in these palaces portrayed the Minoan delight in nature, sport, art, and civilized intercourse. They include scenes of court ladies, lively and lovely "Parisiennes": not rows of robots, but groups of animated human beings carrying on so expressive a conversation that one may almost overhear the gossip and chitchat. Toynbee has doomed these gay, spirited people because in dying they failed to hand down a Universal Church—for him the only justification for the existence of a civilization. Others may forgive the Minoans because they died so abruptly, or may even rejoice that they did not encumber the Ionians with such a legacy, since Universal Churches tend to be set in their ways.

As it was, the outnumbered Ionians typically sought the protection of the local god, in piety or in prudence. The Milesians took over an ancient oracle at nearby Branchidae, where eventually they moved in Apollo. It became the most famous of the nineteen oracles of Apollo in Asia Minor, second only to Delphi. The temple later built on the site (now called Didyma) is the grandest ruin of Ionic architecture in Asia Minor. But it is significant that the Milesians never quite completed this temple. Their minds were more on the natural advantages of Ionia.

The land and climate seemed to them (or to Herodotus) "the most beautiful in the whole world." If there is some question about the climate, which can be oppressively hot in the summer, it is certainly a beautiful region, with green valleys under bright blue skies, and much more hospitable than the bleak Anatolian plateau. Here the Ionians could count on an abundance of their few necessities—olives, corn, wine, fish, fruit, cheese. In particular they enjoyed an excellent location for purposes of trade. Most important for all their purposes were the river valleys running down to their ports. Fertile in themselves, they were also highways to the interior and the farther East; down them came the commerce that further stimulated and enriched the sons of Yavan. Miletus, at the mouth of the Maeander River, became a great terminal for caravans from the East.

Now such advantages were only opportune conditions—they were not the "cause" of the Ionian achievement. Earlier peoples who had enjoyed the same advantages achieved nothing like it, nor did the later Turks.[5] Ultimately we can no more explain the originality of the Ionians than we can explain genius. The vulgar truth remains, however, that they throve on business. Like most of the brilliant cities in history, from Athens to Florence, their major cities were commercial cities. Each developed specialized industries; Miletus became known for its fine wool and purple fabrics. The Ionians also built merchant fleets—keeping to the sea in spite of Hesiod—to compete with the energetic Phoenicians for the eastern Mediterranean market. Their victory in this trade war was signaled early in the seventh century when Egypt granted them the trade center of Naucratis in the Nile delta. Miletus, which took the lead in establishing and maintaining this center, was also the first Greek city to issue coinage, and the first to produce maps and writings on navigation. Until the fifth century B.C. it was the richest city in the Greek world.

One sign of Ionian prosperity was the vigorous colonizing movement that began toward the year 700 and went on for two centuries. Miletus alone was said to have founded more than seventy colonies along the northern coast, from the Hellespont to the end of the Black Sea, including such important cities as Abydus, Lampsacus, Cyzicus, and Sinope. Other Ionians went west as far as France and Spain, and south to Libya. And by the seventh century this was a recognizably Greek culture, centered in the *polis*. Homer had done his great work. Art had turned from geometric to naturalistic, humanistic motives. The temple was making its appearance, typically on an eminence where it could gleam in the sunlight; unlike Oriental gods, who dwelt in dark inner sanctums accessible only to priests or only on special occasions, the Greek deities were always visible and available. For the first time poets, such as Sappho, Archilochus, Terpander, and Anacreon, were freely expressing their personal thought and feeling in lyrics. In Miletus philosophy, science, and history had been born.

To these supremely important achievements we shall return. Meanwhile, for the sake of the record, we have to note that with their success

---

[5] The Greeks themselves were fond of explaining basic differences in character by differences in physical environment. Hippocrates, for example, wrote that Asiatics were "more gentle and affectionate" than Europeans, but also more torpid and cowardly because of their relatively mild, equable climate and fertile soil. This is at least a more sensible and humane theory than the racial theories popular in the modern world, environment being a definite, constant factor. But that it is only a conditioning factor, not the key to culture, is made clear by the many diverse cultures that have occupied Asia Minor. In any case, the Ionians were neither gentle nor torpid.

the Ionians had run into serious trouble. In the seventh century rose the new kingdom of Lydia, centered in the Hermus River valley that runs down to the coast a little above Smyrna. It began making inroads on the Ionian cities, concentrating on wealthy Miletus. The Milesians were able to withstand repeated and prolonged sieges because of their mastery of the sea (what later saved Athens from the Persians), but in the sixth century they at last succumbed to King Croesus. Croesus became master of all the Greek cities in Asia Minor. The Ionians had lost their freedom, which except for brief periods they never completely recovered.

At the time this was not simply a catastrophe. The Lydians were a civilized people, whose capital at Sardis became one of the most brilliant cities of Asia Minor.[6] Their reputed invention of coinage—their major contribution to civilization—was a special boon to the Greeks. As Gordon Childe points out, small change not only facilitated trade, but stimulated industry by making the manufacture of cheap goods profitable; small producers could convert their goods readily into pots and pins, or save their coins for substantial purchases, while a workman no longer had to "eat his wages." Like the later Romans, moreover, the Lydians paid the highest tribute to their Greek tributaries by adopting most of their culture. Croesus was a particular admirer of the Greeks, making fabulously rich offerings to all their major oracles. Sardis under him became known as the resort of "all the wise men of Hellas."

Unhappily, Croesus misinterpreted the Delphic oracle when he consulted it to decide whether he should make war on the rising Persians. Although Apollo answered truly enough that if he did so he would destroy a mighty empire, the wise men in Sardis evidently neglected to inform him that Apollo was prone to ambiguity, and that his own empire was meant. It fell to the Emperor Cyrus in 547–46. The Ionian cities, which had honored the liberal rule of Croesus by rejecting the Persian invitation to rebel against him, were easily overcome by the Persians. Within a few years Cyrus was master of all Asia Minor. The rule of the Persians was also generally mild, if only because they had the wit to see that trade with and through the Greek cities was mutually profitable; but the creativity of the Ionians declined. They produced few famous names during the fifth and fourth centuries.

On the whole this is an ignominious chapter in their history, to which we shall also return. For the time being we should note, in fairness, that

---

[6] Herodotus incidentally remarked, however, that its houses were mostly built of reeds. We are always likely to forget such details of the common life as we contemplate the marbled ruins of ancient cities. For further details about Sardis and the culture of the Lydians, see the Appendix, Section 3.

the Ionians were almost always fighting against odds, and that they wrote some heroic pages. The citizens of Teos distinguished themselves by taking ship, one and all, and sailing away to find a new home rather than submit to the Persians. Miletus, still independent in spirit, led a revolt against them at the end of the sixth century. It was completely destroyed, after a desperate resistance; but this resistance helped to save Athens, giving the Athenians more time to build up their strength, and also inflaming their spirit. When the Milesians rebuilt their city, they made it still handsomer by one of the earliest experiments in city planning. It remained the most important city in Ionia down to the time of Alexander the Great.

All in all, Miletus was a worthy example of the most typical and fundamental of Greek institutions—the *polis*. The emergence of the *polis* marked the dawn of Greek civilization; its decay and death marked the end. It was a unique institution, and one not easy to do full justice to. We do not even have a word for it: "city-state," the usual translation, has misleading connotations. So we must now go back to the beginning, to take a closer look at its development.

3. THE GREEK POLIS

Walls, said Aristotle, were built so that man might live. Nature does not love a wall, Robert Frost has added, intimating that it resents these barriers between men; but one may suspect Nature of a more jealous motive. Walls created a world of man's own. From first to last the city has been the main center of all the distinctive activities that mark civilization. Primitive societies may hold to the sanctities, such as religious belief, patriotism, chastity, and private property, by which moralists are prone to distinguish civility from barbarity. Primitive societies never have the city —the always sinful city. It nurtured the finer, richer consciousness that made possible the realization of its wickedness, and then of the supposedly blessed simplicities of rural life. It changed the village too by creating the type of the peasant, who unlike the prehistoric villager is not preliterate but illiterate, conscious of the writing he does not know, and conscious of a greater world to which he is subject.

The early Sumerian cities appear to have enjoyed considerable political and economic freedom. They had a word for freedom, a theory of equality, and a popular assembly. When kings descended from heaven there was still considerable free private enterprise; independent merchants organized the trade that in Egypt was conducted by the officials of Pharaoh. But the self-ruling city disappeared, and with it all real political life. As A. E. Zimmern remarked, there were no politics in the great Eastern societies because there were no public affairs; government was the affair only of the rulers. Although the king had to contend with other kings and would-be kings, and sometimes with the aristocracy or the clergy, such conflicts took place within the ruling class and involved no open recognition of the common or public interest. The Greeks were the first to maintain steadily that there was such a thing.

As latecomers, they had reversed the development in Sumer. The early Ionians, like the Achaeans, were ruled by kings; we hear of such rulers as late as the seventh century. Once the Ionians were securely established, however, and busy in commerce and industry, they had little need of a king, who had served chiefly as a war leader. An oligarchy rose to power. With prosperity came the familiar by-product of class conflict, in Miletus between parties known as the "Wealthy" and the "Handworkers." One apparent motive of the colonizing movement was to relieve this conflict; the poor and the malcontents sailed off to make a better life for themselves—and upon success, to rehearse the same story. The conflict continued until the bitter end of ancient Greek history. Yet out of it had come the *polis*. The Greeks believed that this had been founded deliberately in order to establish justice, and ranked with their greatest national heroes the Solons who had given them good laws and constitutions. At least the *polis* grew out of a conscious struggle for justice.

An early phase in its development—and the beginning of possible misunderstanding—was the rule of the "tyrant," who first appeared in Ionia. For the Greeks the word did not have all the evil connotations that it has today, and at first carried no stigma at all. If the tyrants were virtual dictators, they usually won their power as champions of the common people, and might even be elected by them—as was Pittacus of Mytilene, an honest democrat who ruled for ten years. They never claimed divine rights, and in theory were always responsible to the public interest. Generally they represented a transition between aristocracy and democracy. The early tyrants were the first known politicians, and at their best exemplified what "politician" once meant—a professional public servant, or statesman. It was as a great statesman that Thrasybulus of Miletus made his reputation: arbitrating a war between Athens and Mytilene, successfully defending Miletus against the prolonged campaigns of King Alyattes of Lydia, finally concluding a treaty with him, and corresponding with other monarchs. The tyrants inaugurated programs of public works, at once to give jobs to the poor and to beautify the city. They were patrons of culture, much like the Renaissance Medici, entertaining poets and seeking out the most celebrated artists to build or adorn the local temples. Two of them—Periander of Corinth and Pittacus of Mytilene—were numbered among the traditional Seven Wise Men of Hellas.

As one-man rulers, these men nevertheless had the makings of tyrants in the worst sense, and for the Greeks were no solution of the political problem. Most of them were eventually expelled. Then, more often than not, came renewed strife between the oligarchy and the common people, and another tyrant might rise to power. But the essence of the *polis* was not a particular form of government. It knew every form, short of the Oriental sacred monarchy. As Aristotle said, "Even tyranny is reckoned by us to be a form of government"—though "there is not much to be said about it." The essential idea was rule by law, in the public interest, by public consent.

Or more fundamental, perhaps, was the idea expressed by the poet Simonides: "The city is the teacher of the man." For this reason "city-state" is an imprecise translation of *polis*. It was incidentally more than a city, as it included the surrounding territory. Many or even most of its citizens were farmers, who appreciated the world within its walls but were not cut off from the natural world; there was not the sharp division between city and country that has given us the familiar types of the hayseed or yokel, the city slicker, the man about town, the man on the asphalt street. Above all, the *polis* was much more than a "state" as we know it. For us the State is a limited province of society, which must be carefully walled off from other provinces. We are at pains to separate it from the Church, to keep it out of Business, to maintain our freedoms against it—in general to protect "the people" from it. For the Greeks the *polis* in effect *was* "the people." It was virtually coextensive with society, embracing their religious, moral, cultural, and social as well as their political interests. It had its own gods, whose festivals were the major civic occasions and amounted to a fusion of Christmas, Mardi Gras, and the Fourth of July; it built the temples, the gymnasiums, the theater, the market place; it staged the annual dramas and games; its open-air centers were the center of social life, the home of the Greeks. In a real sense the *polis* was one big family. It was happy or unhappy, in the manner of families; its members quarreled often enough. But they took for granted that they were quarreling with one another, not with the State. Death itself was hardly a more dreadful fate than exile.

At the same time, the *polis* was by no means a totalitarian state. Sparta was—and for this reason was unique. The rest of the Greeks were essentially free men, from whom the *polis* in its heyday demanded a great deal, but got it freely, because it also gave them a great deal. In private life there was generally less state interference than Americans submit to, with their laws restricting everything from gambling and drinking to sexual behavior and suicide; Greeks lived and died more nearly as they pleased.

If many doubtless felt like the aging Plato, who wanted strictly to regulate art, morality, and religion, the very pains he took in drawing up his *Laws* make clear that his depressing ideal was not the living ideal of Greece. Most important, the Greeks were not slaves to the totalitarian mentality. In the Eastern empires men accepted the State as they accepted the weather; it was all they knew, and there was nothing they could do about it. The Greeks accepted the *polis* because they had thought about it, grown fully conscious of it, and believed that it was the essential means not only to security but to justice, freedom, the good life—to being a Hellene instead of a "barbarian." It was precisely in and through the *polis* that they developed their distinctive individualism.

This is still distinctive by modern standards. The Greeks did not conceive the individual as set apart from the state, as in our democratic world he is both in fact and in theory. Their lexicon contained no equivalents for such words as the "individual," the "self," the "ego." They were self-seeking, of course, but at their most egotistical they sought fame, which was the praise of their fellow citizens. So, too, the highest good they could achieve was in the service of the *polis*. Conscience was public, not private; the Greek lexicon included no equivalent of "conscience" either. They had no double standard of morality, no sharp distinction between the ethical and the political, no gulf between the things that are Caesar's and the things that are God's. In a well-governed *polis*, said Aristotle, the virtue of a good man and of a citizen is the same. And when he defined man as a "political animal" he did not mean an animal whose distinctive function is to vote, be a member of a political party, or conscientiously take an "intelligent interest" in current political affairs. He meant an animal who participated naturally, freely, and fully in the life of the *polis*, which was the means to his peculiar excellence. The Greek word for a man so devoted to his private business that he lacked such public interest was our word *idiot*.

Now we must add—and not merely in fairness to our go-getting businessmen—that all this represents the *polis* at its best, and that even at its best it cannot possibly serve as a model for us. It was a very small affair. A visitor to the sites of the "great cities" of the classical world may be startled by their smallness; even Miletus, as replanned in 480 B.C., covered only some 220 acres, of which a quarter was in parks and gardens. Add its surrounding territory, and the *polis* was still a tiny state. Moreover, it had to be small to realize its unique ideal. Its citizens could lead their full political life only because all were within hailing distance; all could attend the popular assemblies. They had so deep and vivid a sense of community because all participated in the civic festivals, went to the same temples, theater, and agora, and knew most of their fellow citizens at least by sight. For them it was always the time for all good men to come to the aid of their country because the country and the home town were one, and its issues were immediate. Duty was plain common sense, not abstract idealism. They never had to wonder why they were fighting in Korea.

Hence their political philosophers took for granted the necessity of smallness. "It is difficult, if not impossible, to govern properly a very numerous body of men," wrote Aristotle, and to indicate the extremes he declared that a body of a hundred thousand citizens would be as absurd as a body of only ten. Plato was more specific. He decided that the ideal *polis* would have 5,040 citizens—the extra forty for administrative convenience, to make a total that could be divided by all the numbers from one to ten; then he worried over the problem of how to maintain exactly that number, how to prevent the growth that is the boast of every American town. Add women, children, slaves, and resident foreigners, and this makes a community of about 50,000, which was probably not much smaller than the average Greek *polis* before the Hellenistic period. Even in that period Priene, an independent neighbor of Miletus, was a town of but 5,000.

If the experience of the Greeks, or the counsel of Plato and Aristotle, might be pertinent for Middletown, it hardly provides a political manual for America. But even for Middletown it needs to be severely qualified. We "added" women and slaves to make up our average *polis*, whose adult citizens represented only 10 per cent of the population. Although some scholars now argue that the low status of women in classical Greece has been exaggerated, it is certain that women had no voice in political life and could enter no professions except the oldest ones of priestess or prostitute. We must assume that their emancipation has made some difference (especially as we recall the Cretan legislator who introduced the love of boys in order to lessen the danger of connections with women). And there is no question about the great difference made by the slaves, who did most of the hard, dirty work of the *polis*. Serfdom or slavery was indispensable to its rich civic life: its citizens had to have considerable leisure to discharge their public duties and cultivate their varied interests. Many came to believe, like Plato and Aristotle, that it was unbecoming a citizen to engage in trade or the mechanic arts. The Greek ideal of excellence cannot be realized by the workers of Middletown.

Even the ideal unity of the *polis* involved an essential limitation. It is well to set the individual above the state, and to maintain a distinction between public and private morality. Only the individual can perceive that what is lawful and established may not be right or good. Politics can never maintain a lofty ethic; nations always fall short of the decency, honesty, and good will that we can more or less count on in private life. The loyal citizen who completely identified himself with his *polis* might be committed to a shabby treatment of the poor and needy, a disgraceful treatment of fellow Greeks in other cities—and often he was. At best the moral code of the *polis* was sharply limited. Its highest ideal of public duty did not encourage ideals of altruism and love, and positively excluded the loftier ideal of humanity. Sparta is the conspicuous example of its narrow patriotism, but every Greek *polis* in its heyday was a stranger to such notions as "the interests of mankind."

The natural result was the jealous particularism that fatally weakened the *polis*. As greater powers grew up in the hinterland, its smallness was a plain handicap; only in union could the Greeks hope to defend their common interests and maintain their independence. Yet they never achieved a real federation, much less a United Greek States.[7] Among the first recorded events in the history of Ionia was a dispute between Priene and Samos, about the year 700; and it set the pattern of strife that endured as long as the Greeks were free to determine their foreign policy. None of the Ionian cities except Chios came to the aid of Miletus during its long wars with the Lydians. The Ionians again failed to unite against the Persians, rejecting the advice of Thales of Miletus; they fought separately, and fell quickly. Their Pan-Ionium suggests the most the Greeks achieved by way of political union—alliances or leagues, which separated them from other Greeks, and typically fought with other cities or leagues. The strongest of them, the Athenian Confederacy formed after the defeat of Persia, was soon dominated by Athens, held together only by its compulsion, and directed against Sparta and its allies. Miletus, a member of it, rebelled against its parent city toward the end of the Peloponnesian War, and had to defend itself against an Athenian attack—which it held off with Persian help.

In this view, the dazzling Greek world is a fantastic spectacle: hundreds of little city-states carefully walling themselves off from all the rest, continually fighting with one another, and in the presence of a common enemy proudly cutting their own throats. The most miraculous thing about them would seem to be that they lasted as long as they did. Why, then, did so ingenious, resourceful, enterprising a people stick to so senseless a political system, fail to take so obvious a step as confederation? The common explanation is geographical and economic. The city-states of

[7] One striking exception was a related people in Asia Minor, the Lycians. For their history see the Appendix, Section 4 (Xanthus).

Greece were more or less isolated by mountains, in a country that was not an economic unit; others were scattered all over the Mediterranean world, too widely separated to form anything like a nation. But the Ionians had no such excuse. Their country was a natural unit, communications were easy along their coast, and they did in fact gather at their Pan-Ionium. They suggest that the reasons for Greek disunity lie deeper, in the character and mentality formed by the *polis*. This made them independent, proud, and provincial.

Since the Greeks knew intimately the great advantages of the *polis*, their failure is as understandable in terms that do them more credit. Kitto points out that they also knew of a vast, powerful State—the Persian Empire—and naturally they wanted none of it. It was fit only for "barbarians." "Better a small city perched upon a rock," the poet Phocylides of Miletus had written earlier, "than all the dizzy splendor of Nineveh." As for a possible federation with a parliament, they did not want to be "represented" by anybody; they were used to governing themselves. And they might still have felt this way had they visited New York, or attended a session of the United States Congress. What price size and numbers? At the end, we have reason to feel wistful as we contemplate the Greek *polis*. It could not possibly endure; but it was wonderful while it lasted. Given all the sharp divisions in our life—the separations of religion, business, government, art, science, entertainment—we must envy the unity and community it knew, amid a rich diversity of interest that was never a miscellany or a mere multiplicity. We could set no better goal than to recover, as far as possible, its ideal of the full, rounded, harmonious development of the individual who is yet one with the community. That we can never hope to recover it completely, under the radically different conditions of our mass civilization, only makes the effort more necessary. One reason why modern art and thought are so often eccentric, precious, extravagant, or trivial is that they are not rooted in a rich communal life.[8]

[8] An example is Clive Bell's *Civilization*, a lively study that begins in something like a Greek spirit. Bell locates the distinctive essence of civilization in self-consciousness, or more specifically a "Sense of Values" and the "Enthronement of Reason," and defines its proper end as "good states of mind." The important thing is not so much that a society be creative ("savages create furiously") as that it be appreciative. By this standard he declares Periclean Athens the first clearly civilized society and concludes that modern democracy can never be civilized unless it deliberately maintains a class of connoisseurs. It must endow them with an income large enough to assure complete civility, and must exempt them from all work, for after a day's work it is impossible "to savor the subtler manifestations of the spirit." We may pass over this civil proposal, which is made with some humor. But Bell's wit and appreciativeness both suffer from a painfully self-conscious aestheticism. Puritanically antipuritan, he dismisses as mere cant all talk about rights, duties, and sanctities; he

All sentiment aside, the final verdict on the *polis* seems plain. Its smallness was both its strength and its weakness, its pride both its virtue and its
vice. It constituted the vital religion of the Greeks: a religion, as Gilbert
Murray said, that was rooted "in knowledge and real human need, not in
ignorance and terror," and that existed to serve man instead of imaginary
deities. This was also a parochial religion, inadequate for their needs in
the greater world they ventured into, or created by their own efforts.
Without the *polis* the Greeks could not have achieved their uniquely free,
rich way of life. With it, they were doomed to lose their freedom.

4. THE BEGINNING OF PHILOSOPHY AND SCIENCE

Although the Western calendar is dated (somewhat inaccurately) from
the birth of Christ, perhaps as important a turning point in our history is
the simple, erroneous statement made by Thales of Miletus six centuries
earlier: "All things are made of water." His statement was less naïve than
it now seems, inasmuch as water can be solid and gaseous as well as
liquid, and is essential to life. But had his conjecture been truer it would
not have been more significant, or more astounding. It represented an
effort by pure reason, without benefit of oracle and in defiance of all
tradition and common sense, to explain the universe in its given natural
terms. It symbolized the birth of rational inquiry—the emancipation of
mind that Renan called "the only miracle in history." It heralded the beginning of natural philosophy and science, the revolution in thought that
eventually, for better or worse, was to transform man's life on earth more
profoundly than the teachings of Christ have transformed it.

Again the singular originality and audacity of the Greeks can be appreciated only by contrast with the ancient East. There had been plenty of
nonmythical thought in the East, as evidenced by all the empirical knowledge it had accumulated in agriculture, metallurgy, medicine, mathematics, and astronomy. Its learned men did not have the Hebrew belief
that all man's woes began when he ate the forbidden fruit of knowledge,
or the medieval belief that to pry into the secrets of nature was to play
the Devil's game. They were very practical men who wanted to know all
the secrets in order to predict or control the course of nature. Often they
exhibited a tireless industry in the collection and organization of data. In
Mesopotamia particularly they built up elaborate systems of divination,

---

asserts that a serious interest in political affairs is vulgar and absurd, and a concern
with social justice fatal to civility ("Only the Esquimaux and their like enjoy the
blessings of social justice"); he insists that all action has "nothing to do with civilization," which is wholly a matter of choice states of mind; etc. One may enjoy a
choice enough state of mind by trying to picture Clive Bell in the agora or gymnasium of a Greek *polis*.

astrology, dream interpretation, and demonology. Yet all this industry only underlines the failure of the East to develop philosophy and science. Its learning simply fortified its essential irrationality. From the beginning its thinkers were on the wrong track, and they never suspected it, never discovered a means of getting on another track. Magic remained their premise, myth their conclusion.

The miracle that took place in Ionia was the realization that natural events are not miracles. Oriental thought explained all natural phenomena in supernatural terms—the gods had made everything so. Thales and his followers left the gods out; they began with "the things that exist." Later the gods could be put back, if need be, but meanwhile the Milesian philosophers assumed that the universe was a lawful order intelligible in terms of natural causes. None of their own works having survived, their approach is best illustrated by the Hippocratic writings. "It seems to me," said a writer on epilepsy, "that the disease is no more divine than any other. It has a natural cause, just as other diseases have. Men think it divine merely because they do not understand it. But if they called everything divine which they do not understand, why, there would be no end of divine things." In this spirit the Milesians laid the philosophical foundations of science. Thales became famous by foretelling a total eclipse of the sun (on a day now fixed as May 28, 585 B.C.)—an event that had always filled men with religious fear. Later another Ionian, Anaxagoras, stated clearly the natural cause of eclipses, and also ventured the very bold opinion that the sun was not a god but an incandescent stone, quite possibly as big as Greece.

Another primary discovery of the Greeks was deductive reasoning, the means to systematic thought. Oriental thinkers failed to generalize either their working principles or the truths they discovered. In geometry, for example, they apparently had a rule-of-thumb knowledge of the property of right-angled triangles stated in the famous theorem of Pythagoras, who quite likely picked up the idea when he visited Egypt; the difference was that he made it a *theorem*, a proposition that applied to *any* such triangle and made possible the discovery of further properties, the development of further propositions. Similarly Oriental cosmologies, however elaborate, remained mythological or strictly unreasoned; for if a myth may be refined, deepened, imaginatively enriched, it cannot be analyzed or refuted by other mythmakers—on its own ground it is immune to fundamental criticism. The Milesian cosmologists looked for a first principle, a logical instead of an imaginary chronological beginning, and their reasoning invited analysis, which could demonstrate its weaknesses and lead to other possibilities. Thus Anaximander, the immediate successor of Thales in

Miletus, concluded that all things were made not of water but of some indeterminate substance, the "Boundless"; Anaximenes then substituted mist, arguing that it was condensed into water and earth or rarefied into fire; Heraclitus of Ephesus settled for "everliving" fire; Leucippus of Miletus, the teacher of Democritus, set him on the track of his atomic theory. Later thinkers disagreed with all of them, and with one another. But the very disagreement emphasizes the lasting importance of the Greek pioneers. They were not only thinking for themselves instead of consulting the gods, but thinking in a way that made possible criticism, and presently thinking about thinking.

Now, as might be expected, the Milesian philosophers did not make a complete break with the past. Their "logical" explanations of the universe contained mythological elements; the gods they left out had some say after all. It is not surprising that Thales made water the essential reality, for Homer had remarked that Oceanus was the source of the gods and all things, and other myths associated the primal water with the womb of life. For Thales, moreover, water was not dead matter in the modern sense. The All was alive, he declared; "all things are full of gods." The Boundless of Anaximander was likewise implicit with life and potentialities of divinity, while the air or mist of Anaximenes was also the soul of man. Aristotle observed that none of the Ionian philosophers made earth the primary substance. All looked to something more mobile, fluent, akin to the "spiritual." We cannot be sure precisely what they meant by their key terms because they made no clear distinction between the material and the spiritual.

Yet their essential naturalism is clear enough. Although Thales and his followers seem more indifferent than hostile to the gods, their philosophy came to be known as "atheistical" to the Greeks. They prepared the way for the philosophical materialism that has almost always been unpopular but has never ceased to haunt the mind of Western man, and in so doing they inaugurated the historic conflict of science and religion, or more broadly of reason and faith. At the same time, their critical, rational spirit led other thinkers to introduce other permanent possibilities of thought, including loftier religious possibilities. Among the most remarkable figures in the Ionian Enlightenment were Xenophanes of Colophon and Pythagoras of Samos.

Best known for his epigram that if donkeys could speak they would describe God as a superdonkey, Xenophanes was another "atheist," but only in that he attacked the anthropomorphic gods. Himself a poet, he denounced Homer and Hesiod for the disgraceful behavior they ascribed to the gods, and went up and down the land preaching a higher religion.

He seems to have believed that the supreme god, if not the only god, was infinite and incorporeal, "not like mortals either in form or in thought, swaying all things without toil by the thought of his mind, and abiding ever in the selfsame place, not moving at all." Xenophanes even rejected divination—almost the only classical Greek known to have done so. Werner Jaeger has said that with him began the "dogmatic pathos," or impatience with the erroneous religious opinions of one's fellow men; yet he was humble as well as ardent, far from the bigotry of later Christianity. "The gods have not revealed all things to men from the beginning," he wrote, "but by seeking, men find in time what is better." Meanwhile he could present his findings modestly: "Let these be taken as fancies, something like the truth." And as an old man, worn by good works, and by the knowledge that his countrymen had not fully appreciated them, he was still a good Ionian, who knew the simple joys that may engender both piety and civility:

Now is the floor clean, and the hands and cups of all; one sets twisted garlands on our heads, another hands us fragrant ointments on a salver. The mixing bowl stands ready, full of gladness, and there is more wine at hand . . . soft and smelling of flowers in the jars! . . . Brown loaves are set before us and a lordly table laden with cheese and rich honey. The altar in the midst is clustered round with flowers. . . . Then after libation and prayer made that we may have strength to do right—for that is in truth the first thing to do—no sin is it to drink as much as a man can take and get home without an attendant, so he be not stricken in years. And of all men is he to be praised who after drinking gives goodly proof of himself in the trial of skill, as memory will serve him. Let him not sing of Titans and Giants—those fictions of the men of old—nor of turbulent civil broils in which is no good at all; but to give heedful reverence to the gods is ever good.

Pythagoras was a much more influential thinker, if a less attractive one. At first the "materialism" of the Milesian philosophers inspired him to become a scientist, conducting experiments in acoustics that in Greek tradition were considered the beginning of experimental science. His major discovery of invariant mathematical relations in spatial properties led him to conclude that number was the key to the universe—an idea that was to have a spectacular career in modern science. But it set Pythagoras on a course that led away from the Milesians. The Greeks traced to him the rival tradition of philosophical idealism, which culminated in Plato and later helped to determine the nature and destiny of the Christian soul. Numbers have an ideal quality, as brain children that are at home in the "real" world, yet are immaterial and immutable; so Plato went on to conceive of a purely spiritual reality, a suprasensible world of Ideas that can be apprehended only by the mind. Pythagoras himself arrived at a belief in the immortality of the soul, specifically in transmigration, and thereupon founded a religious brotherhood that devoted itself to the study of mathematics primarily as a means of purifying the soul. It also took up the practice of asceticism as a further means of escaping from the wheel of mortal life and joining the divine. With such unworldly ideals were mixed some primitive taboos, such as a ban on beans.

This semi-Oriental religious philosophy looks strange in busy, worldly Ionia—which, in fact, Pythagoras left for Italy. Probably he was influenced by Indian thought, coming through Persia, for it is hard to believe that he independently hit on so novel an idea as transmigration. He points to the possibility of still deeper, wider connections. Ionian philosophy may have been a response to a profound stir in the civilized world in the seventh and sixth centuries, manifested by the almost simultaneous appearance of the greatest religious pioneers before Christ: Buddha in India, Zoroaster in Persia, Confucius and Lao-tse in China, the major prophets in Israel. Conceivably some underlying current of diffusion, or ground swell, carried over the known world. But if so, the Greek response was no less unique. It forces the question of how and why the Milesian philosophers got started on their extraordinary speculations.

As usual, we cannot give a positive answer. We can only make out certain conditions that explain why philosophy *could* have developed, not why it *must* have. These conditions are worth considering, however, for the light they throw on Greek thought and the issues it raises.

By now we know better than Burnet, who in his *Early Greek Philosophy* wrote that Ionia was "a country without a past"—"there was no traditional background there at all." An immediate stimulus was the cosmopolitan life of Ionia, behind which lay the whole background of the ancient East. The Milesian philosophers were men of the world, less provincial than the mainlanders. Thales himself was half-Phoenician and like other pioneers —Pythagoras, Herodotus, Democritus—was reputed to have visited Egypt or Babylonia; all drew on the learning of the East. This helps to explain why Thales seems more original and significant to us than he evidently did to the Greeks. He appears as only an incidental character in the history of Herodotus, nobody spoke of him as the Educator of Hellas, and Aristotle could even write that "true philosophy" began with the Magi and the Chaldeans.

Another apparent stimulus, the commercial interests of the Ionians, was long neglected because of later Greek tradition. Classical scholars have given the impression that the Greek genius suddenly took to metaphysics for no practical reason whatever. The Greeks themselves had a story of how Thales fell down a well while gazing at the stars. Aristophanes, who reflected the attitude of the common man, habitually satirized philosophers as ludicrously impractical fellows, quite harmless except for their radical ideas about morality and religion—in other words, eggheads. (Those who are unhappy about democratic culture might remember that the ordinary Greek was not altogether different from the ordinary American.) The later Greek philosophers tended to confirm these popular notions by their contempt of utility, the "base mechanic arts," the vulgar activities of doing and making—a contempt that might seem healthier if their society had not rested on the labor of slaves, and if their thought about ideal essences and eternal verities had not reflected their unideal temporal order.

Recent historians, such as Gordon Childe and Benjamin Farrington, have accordingly dwelt on the practical, social motives that induced the Milesians to speculate. According to them, Milesian philosophy was based upon observation and experiment, guided by economic and technological interests. For early Greek tradition was not so supercilious about practical interests. The hero Odysseus had built ships and wagons; the poet Hesiod had written a farmer's manual, versifying all he knew about scientific agriculture; the lawmaker Solon had invested the crafts with honor. "At that time," writes Plutarch, "work was no disgrace, nor did the possession of a trade imply social inferiority." All the other stories that the Greeks had about Thales, the stargazer, indicate that he was indeed a practical man. Herodotus tells of how he enabled the army of King Croesus to cross the Halys River by partly diverting the river into a new channel; Aristotle tells (perhaps in a not purely disinterested spirit) how he refuted the critics of his idle pursuits by getting a monopoly on the olive crop of Lesbos and making a fortune in oil; other sources report that he made practical applications of geometry and contributions to the art of navigation. It would seem no accident that natural philosophy and science were born in busy Ionia, specifically in its leading commercial city. One reason why the early philosophers were able to ignore the supernatural was that the Ionians were so successfully engrossed in the business of the natural world. And in a broad sense all the early philosophers were practical men, as active members of a *polis*. Even Pythagoras, the mystical mathematician, was a statesman and a city planner.

Nevertheless it seems too much to say, with Farrington, that the techniques of the age provided the inspiration and the positive content of Milesian thought. If so, the Greeks might have been expected to develop physics and especially chemistry, as chemical practice had been far advanced by the basic industry of metallurgy; whereas in fact, as he himself emphasizes, they contributed relatively little to physics and nothing to the theory of chemistry. Neither did they distinguish themselves by technological discoveries and inventions until the time of Archimedes, centuries later. In view of Farrington's thesis one must emphasize still more that the practical Ionians failed to develop the two habits that have made science a force in the modern world—the habits of systematically applying their knowledge, and of consistently checking their thought against experience. They never got hold of the experimental method of verification. Their speculations included brilliant anticipations of modern scientific theories, such as the evolutionary theory of Anaximander and the atomic theory of Democritus; but these remained philosophical speculations, not scientific theories, because they had no pragmatic means of choosing between alternative theories.

The broader economic interpretation of Gordon Childe is no less inadequate, and may be more misleading. He explains natural philosophy as a product of the Iron Age, a new conceptual tool for dealing with reality, corresponding to the iron tools that had created a new social reality. He does not explain why, then, this age failed to call out philosophy in Egypt, Assyria, Babylonia, Persia, and above all Phoenicia. The very practical Phoenicians were even more frankly and fully devoted to commerce than the Ionians; yet they never developed philosophy or science. There was in fact nothing inevitable about the pioneering achievement of the Ionians, nothing predetermined by Marxist "iron laws" of history. We are again led back to misty, immaterial factors.

In spite of its debt to tradition, natural philosophy was not primarily the product of "society" or "history." First of all it was the creation of exceptional individuals. Under common social and economic conditions the Ionian philosophers gave independent, widely divergent, singularly uncommon answers to the riddle of the universe. And however practical they may have been, more important was their addiction to stargazing, or to speculation out of pure curiosity. When Thales asked himself what the world was made of, he was first of all simply curious, trying to make sense of the world for no better reason than to satisfy his mind; his answer was of no practical use to him, and would not have been even were it more correct. The later Romans, like the earlier Phoenicians, were pre-eminently practical in spirit—and if only for this reason, made no contributions whatever to science. Science begins when truth is sought for its own sake. Thales launched the disinterested kind of inquiry that can be a passionate interest, and was to become the ruling passion of Galileo, Newton, Darwin, and Einstein.

Ordinary Greeks were inquisitive but had no such passion for truth-seeking. Although Farrington represents Ionian philosophy as a "popular movement of enlightenment," there is no evidence that the oracle at Didyma did poorer business because of it. Much more conspicuous is a popular religious revival that swept Greece in the sixth century. This was a revival of more primitive faiths, in the dying gods or gods of the under-world, such as Dionysus and Orpheus; its goal was not spiritual enlighten-ment, but ritual purification or ecstatic union with the gods—what Plato called "eternal drunkenness." It makes more remarkable the originality and audacity of the philosophers. And the apparent insecurity and anxiety that it reflected accentuate the issues they raised.

The plainest social condition of the birth of philosophy was the freedom of the *polis*. In thought and behavior, the Ionians enjoyed a degree of freedom that made them a scandal to the more pious, provincial main-landers. Their lyric poets could indulge in quite un-homeric sentiments, unbecoming a citizen. Archilochus wrote blithely of how he had disgraced himself on the battlefield by throwing away his shield and taking to his heels, but had got away, thank God—"So hang the shield! I'll get another just as good." The graver philosophers were as unconventional. Although they apparently did not shock the worldly Ionians, they were too radical for classical Greece. The Athenians anticipated the silencing of Galileo, as well as the martyrdom of Socrates, by banishing Anaxagoras for his sacrilegious teaching that the sun was only a hot rock.[9] So they recall us to the hazards of freedom, and of thought itself. "Let us admit the case of the conservative," wrote John Dewey: "if we once start thinking no one can guarantee where we shall come out, except that many objects, ends, and institutions are doomed." Philosophy is typically a sign of trouble, not of tranquillity; and then it becomes a source of further trouble. It worked to disrupt the ideal unity of Greek culture.

Immediately it gave rise to the "ancient quarrel" with poetry mentioned by Plato, as its devotees discovered that poetry was full of lies. The Scylla and Charybdis of Homer were only a rock and a whirlpool. Worse, his gods were the figments of a disgraceful imagination. "Homer should

---

[9] He might have taken a grim pleasure in the thought that they were later punished for their piety by the disaster at Syracuse that practically assured their defeat in the Peloponnesian War. The Athenian armada, the greatest the city had ever assembled, was about to leave Syracuse when an eclipse of the moon occurred. Had its generals heeded Anaxagoras, they would have known that this was a wholly natural, pre-dictable event, not a dread omen. Instead they heeded their soothsayers, who declared that they must remain in Syracuse for thirty days; the army remained, to be slaugh-tered or captured almost to the last man. The conventional moral drawn from the Peloponnesian War is that the brilliant Athenians were punished for their *hubris*. It is perhaps as true—even as wholesome—to say that they lost the war through sheer ignorance and stupidity, sanctioned by piety.

be turned out of the lists and whipped," said Heraclitus, "and Archilochus likewise." Plato declared that all poetry was mere imitation of mere appearance, thrice removed from the truth. In return, the comic poets derided the philosophers and led the popular opposition to them.

The main issue in this quarrel was religious tradition. On the one hand Xenophanes, Heraclitus, and others were seeking to moralize and spiritualize the gods, a humane but ungrateful enterprise, likely to induce exasperation on both sides. On the other hand, the naturalism of the Milesians made for skepticism, which became a ferment in Periclean Athens and produced the Sophists. "In the matter of the gods," said Protagoras, "I have not been able to attain the knowledge of their existence or nonexistence, or of what form they are; for many things hinder the attainment of this knowledge, both the obscurity of the subject and the shortness of human life." Diagoras pointed out the unanswerable objection to the universal belief in the material efficacy of sacrifice or prayer: when shown some tablets erected in gratitude by survivors of shipwrecks, he remarked, "Those who were drowned did not put up tablets." Later Epicurus would teach men in so many words that there was nothing to fear in the gods or in death. Meanwhile, even before Euripides, the "god-fearing" Aeschylus and Sophocles had become infected by the spirit of philosophy. They asked the tragic question: What is man? What is his position in the universe?

For all along, of course, the philosophers settled nothing. They made for a new mode of conviction; and with it they introduced new modes of confusion and contradiction, and by their disagreement testified to a basic uncertainty. Confusion was intensified by a kind of innocent dogmatism, owing to the lack of a clear distinction between metaphysics and science, and to the Greek passion for clarity, symmetry, and order. All the early philosophers believed that there was a simple answer to cosmic questions, and all were prone to impose order on the universe instead of finding it. The Pythagoreans even defied the facts of observation, which indicated an irregular motion of the planets—a scandalous kind of behavior that had given them their Greek name of "vagabond"; they decreed that the motion of all celestial bodies must be circular and uniform, since the circle is the perfect figure. Plato then made astronomy entirely respectable, as Plutarch noted, by "subordinating natural laws to the authority of divine principles," restoring the strictly heavenly status of the heavenly bodies. Aristotle systematized this astronomy; and while as a biologist he worked scientifically by close, patient observation, he could nevertheless announce that Nature makes nothing imperfect or in vain. A passion for logical consistency carried the philosophers still farther away from the world of experience. Parmenides demonstrated that if there was One—the principle of Being that they typically sought—there could be nothing else. There is either Being or Not-Being; there can be no Becoming, which would involve some admixture of the nonexistent or Not-Being; so there can be no motion, no change, no growth, no variety. It is a logical enough argument—only it completely denies the facts of experience that philosophers are presumably trying to account for.

Yet such excesses are not surprising, or simply distressing. Once thought becomes autonomous and systematic it is always prone to depart from good sense. In seeking the essential reality behind the multifarious appearances, philosophy, science, and religion have alike tended to a kind of inhumanity, commonly neglecting to "save the appearances," to preserve a decent measure of "reality" for the world we have to live in. The all-important point remains that the Greeks set thought free, and that in so doing they provided a corrective for its excesses. However arbitrary their assertions, the philosophers kept the mind open to new possibilities. Together they explored these possibilities in the spirit of Plato's Dialogues—thoroughly civilized discussions representing different points of view, and symbolizing an ideal freedom of thought. They did not compel assent by invoking any absolute authority, human or divine. None of them was ever the authority in Greece that Aristotle became in later Europe.

Even Pythagoras, who represents the tendencies that eventually smothered Greek rationalism, bequeathed a critical spirit with his mystique. Our present story may conclude with an appalling discovery later made by his brotherhood. They found that the square root of 2, which expressed the fundamental relationship between the diagonal and the side of a square, is an "irrational" number—one that cannot be expressed by any other number, and that therefore disrupted the perfectly symmetrical mathematical universe they had constructed out of their own heads. Their shock did not really bring them to their senses, cause them to reconsider the many other appearances of irrationality in the universe. Still, the fact remains that they made the discovery and then faced up to it, honestly wrestled with the problem it raised. The learned men of the East had had no such sense of the irrational or incongruous.

5. HERODOTUS AND HISTORY

When Herodotus traveled to Egypt and Babylonia, all eyes and ears, he was properly awed by the antiquity of lands that had been making history for thousands of years. We should be as awed by his youthful spirit of inquiry; for after all those years the study of history had only now begun. While the scribes of the East carefully preserved the royal annals, they had eyes and ears only for the deeds of their kings, and no minds for critical analysis. The Great Kings had some idea that they were making history, or at least a desire to impress posterity by records of their great deeds, but their kind of eminence hardly made for perspective or historical sense.

The Egyptian conception of the world as essentially static and unchanging precluded an understanding of the changes that kept taking place. The scribes had no word for history in our sense, and apparently no idea of historical cause and effect beyond the idea that everything depended on Pharaoh. The anxious Mesopotamians had a more vivid sense of flux but no better understanding of it. With the royal annals they preserved rituals, prayers, and manuals of all that had been found "good for kingship" (in the words of Ashurbanipal); and as in spite of this accumulated wisdom kings kept coming to grief, they developed a rudimentary theory of history. The gods ruled history: a successful king had been favored by the gods, an ill-fated king had somehow offended them. The trouble with the theory was that it merely baptized the mystery. The will of the gods remained inscrutable—the king himself might never know the nature of his offense. For it was not a moral theory such as the Hebrew prophets evolved. A mighty king was always right; an ill-fated one was always wrong but not necessarily unjust or unrighteous. All were god-fearing—for good reason, and likely as not to no point.

The early Persian kings have been credited with a moral interpretation of history. The Emperor Cyrus proclaimed that he was a just and upright king, even a savior, who had delivered Babylon from its unjust and impious king. Darius similarly took pains to justify his possibly illegitimate seizure of the throne, and not only told the world of his good deeds but implied that as "an Aryan, having Aryan lineage," he had brought in a new order. One might see in these royal proclamations a "decent respect to the opinions of mankind," even an embryonic theory of progress—a belief that the venerable past could be improved upon. One might also see in them typical Oriental bombast, again belying the Persian reputation for truthtelling. At any rate, the later Persian emperors did not proceed to remake or rewrite history. They reverted to the old order of bombast, without pretence of a new equity. And no Persian wrote the history of the empire. The first connected account of it appears in Herodotus.

History too was born in Ionia. Although a Dorian from Halicarnassus, Herodotus was a spiritual child of Ionia, who wrote in Ionic. Behind him were Cadmus and Hecataeus, the first known historians—both from Miletus. Although their works have disappeared, like almost all the literature of Ionia, scattered fragments and allusions indicate that Hecataeus in particular was a typical Milesian pioneer. He was credited with the first treatise on geography (c. 520 B.C.). Probably he had a practical motive— Strabo noted that many an early colonizing expedition came to grief through ignorance of geography—but he also displayed an interest in truth for its own sake. He was a rationalist, more explicitly critical of the traditional mythology than the Milesian philosophers seem to have been. So he wrote that "the stories of the Greeks are manifold and seem to me ridiculous." None of these stories, one might add, was more ridiculous than his own reputed belief that he was descended from a god, sixteen generations back; yet the astonishing thing was his skeptical spirit.

Herodotus inherited both his skepticism and the measure of ancient superstition that the Greeks never quite outgrew. He too was critical of their manifold stories, such as that of Helen of Troy; often he tried to rationalize them and separate fact from fiction. Even when narrating with obvious relish the fabulous stories he had picked up on his travels— the kind of "Oriental tale" that continued to fascinate Westerners—he periodically warned the Greeks that he was merely repeating what he had heard, and did not feel bound to believe it all. We are obliged, however, to discount his stories much more than he apparently did. He never felt bound by the "laws of evidence," as conceived by modern historians, for the simple reason that he knew of no such laws, had no clear criterion for distinguishing fact from myth. And one of the main "laws" of history, as he saw it, suggests a gloomy rationalization of the Mesopotamian theory of god rule. He explained the recurrent tragic cycle of glory and downfall by the inveterate jealousy of the gods: "The power above us suffers none but himself to be proud." The gods appeared to resent any marked prosperity on earth and to destroy great men, proud or no, just because of their greatness. That Herodotus himself remained so cheerful was presumably due to a belief that a mere historian would not catch the eye of the gods.

But his fundamental attitude was very different from the attitude of the Mesopotamians. He did not assume the utter dependence of man on the gods or seek anxiously to divine their will, solicit their favor. As a pupil of Homer, he continued to celebrate the great deeds that men could perform in spite of the jealous gods. As a lover of the *polis*, he made his main theme the successful struggle for Greek liberty. In effect, he treated history as man-made. His cheerfulness was due as well to a measure of ironical detachment, or philosophical humor. If we cannot always be sure when he is being consciously ironical, we can be confident that he was not so naïve as he may appear on the surface. Unlike Eastern writers, including the authors of the Old Testament, he does not say all that he knows.

The most important difference, however, remains the most obvious. It is the eager curiosity and acute intelligence, coupled with breadth and openness of mind, that led Herodotus to travel "for the sake of learning, for the sake of inquiry," and to say much more than was called for by his theme of the Persian Wars. The rarest thing he learned was something that moderns have only begun to learn—an anthropological sense of the power of custom. He told a story of how Darius shocked the Greeks by asking them what would persuade them to eat the dead bodies of their fathers, and then opened their eyes by calling in some Indians, who were as shocked by his question as to what would persuade them to burn their fathers' bodies. "If one were to offer men to choose out of all the customs in the world such as seemed to them the best," Herodotus concluded, "they would examine the whole number, and end by preferring their own." He himself usually ended by preferring Greek ways; but first he examined dispassionately all the other ways he encountered, as very few men would. He was in this respect much wiser than Plato and Aristotle, who continued to generalize provincially about "barbarians" and slaves, and erected Greek customs into universal forms or laws of Nature. His exceptional freedom from prejudice made Herodotus an ideal pioneer, serving him better than a critical standard or even a scientific methodology might have served. Although innocent of the laws of evidence, he tampered with the evidence less than have some modern historians, whose more positive ideas about the laws of history or the power above are a source of more systematic distortion.[10]

Herodotus was accordingly broader and more dispassionate than Thucydides, whose famed objectivity was limited by his primary concern with the political and moral lessons of the Peloponnesian War. Yet the Athenian Thucydides reveals by contrast other limitations of Herodotus, and of the Ionians in general; and these bring us back to their bad reputation in the Greek world. The Ionians lacked his moral earnestness. They lacked as well the political energy of the Athenians, and their ardor for liberty; they never developed as strong a democratic tradition. Although Herodotus frequently noted their shortcomings, and left Ionia for Athens, he

---

[10] I cite an eminent example, Arnold Toynbee, by way of making further amends to the early Eastern societies. They have all suffered from his inexorable patterns, and suffered still more since he discarded the humane assumption he started with, that all civilizations are essentially comparable in dignity and philosophical importance. Now he asserts that the only conceivable justification for the existence of a civilization is that it may "minister to the progress of Religion" by giving birth to a Universal Church in its death throes. By this standard none of the first "litter" of civilizations—to use his pious term for them—had an excuse for their existence; so all their extraordinary pioneering achievements were mere vanity, and their "almost demonic craving for life" was mere perversity.

himself manifested relatively little interest in political history, the means and ends of the freedom he celebrated. We should be grateful for all the extraneous information about manners and customs which he crammed into his history of the Persian Wars, but we must admit that it obscures his main theme, and suspect that it reveals his primary interest. His freedom from prejudice seems to have been a matter of temperament, suggesting the worldly spirit of the Ionians more than philosophical wisdom or an ethical ideal.

This spirit was reflected in their deplorable behavior during the crucial Persian Wars. Vast numbers of Ionians, Herodotus remarks casually, flocked to Egypt with the Persian King Cambyses when he marched against it, "some, as might have been looked for, to push their trade; others, to serve in his army; others again, merely to see the land." No doubt most of them profited in their various ways. Ionians had started serving as mercenaries a century before. (One scratched his name on an Abu Simbel Colossus in Egypt.) Later they provided a contingent for King Darius when he marched against the Scythians, serving him so loyally that the Scythians branded them as "the faithfulest of slaves." When they rebelled against their Persian masters they disregarded the practical wisdom of Hecataeus, who advised them to build up their sea power; after burning down Sardis they were quickly defeated, their army melted away, and their cities were sacked, one by one. They recovered in time to contribute a hundred ships to the armada of Xerxes, to fight against their fellow Greeks at the battle of Salamis. Following his defeat they again rebelled against the Persians when the Athenians and Spartans sent a fleet to Mt. Mycale, the site of their Pan-Ionium; this time they contributed to the Greek victory that ended the Persian Wars, regaining their freedom for a while. But eventually the Persians re-established their dominion, by intrigue and bribery more than by force of arms. Throughout this period the Ionian cities were generally ruled by tyrants, who maintained their power with Persian aid.

While Herodotus does not analyze the Ionian character, as Thucydides might have done, his anecdotes speak for themselves. Most revealing is one of a council held by the fleet during the first revolt against the Persians. "Men of Ionia," said a Phocaean captain named Dionysius, "our affairs hang on the razor's edge, either to be free or to be slaves"; he therefore proposed a rigorous training to fit themselves for the coming battle. When the Ionians agreed, he proceeded to drill them from morning to night. They stood it for just one week. On the eighth day they began to confer, saying to one another, "What god have we offended to bring upon ourselves such a punishment as this?" Slavery itself could be no worse than the hardships imposed by this Phocaean braggart. Accordingly they refused to obey his orders, instead pitching their tents on an island "where they reposed under the shade all day." Their Samian allies, disheartened, sailed for home when the battle got under way; and presently most of the Ionians followed suit, leaving the Persians in command of the sea. As a result Miletus was besieged by land and sea, taken, and razed to the ground.

This story may not be literally true, since Herodotus, a Dorian, was not free from prejudice where the Ionians were concerned. The fact remains that they played an unheroic role during the most inspiring chapter of Greek history, and the story is at least in keeping with their own words and works. The worst plague for a state, said Plato, is not faction but distraction. Ionian lyric poetry was chiefly a celebration of distraction. "No man would enjoy very many delights who heeded the censure of the people," said Archilochus.

> Now is the moment, now,
> To take what happiness the gods allow

—so sang Alcaeus, another poet who once left his shield on the battlefield. Sappho sang of love for young girls, Anacreon of the pleasures of wine and beautiful boys. A single line has survived of one Pythermus: "There's nothing else that matters—only money." If the charming candor of their poets gave the Ionians a worse reputation than they deserved, all their art suggests a design for hedonistic rather than heroic living. In architecture their style is notable for grace and delicacy, not the strength and austerity of the Doric. In music the Ionian mode was known for its voluptuous rhythms. Among the many vivid personalities we catch glimpses of, there are few grand types comparable to Aeschylus and Socrates.

All this gives much to brood over, but little to puzzle about. For one thing, it is the familiar story of the corruptions of wealth. Prosperity brought Ionia plenty of both faction and distraction; money mattered a great deal to its ruling class. As familiar were the costs of its bold individualism. Its poets are important as the first known writers to assert the rights of the individual against the state, anticipating Socrates, but they lacked his strong sense of duty and reverence for law; they displayed discipline only in their poetic measures. The Ionians grew less concerned with serving the *polis* than with exploring the new world of individual consciousness, or speculating about the cosmos. At best they were interested in knowledge for its own sake, not—like Thucydides—for the sake of "right action." At worst they were blasé. Altogether, it is significant that Ionia, the land of the "fathers," did not give birth to Tragedy. Athens created this supreme synthesis of the poetry, piety, philosophy, and civic patriotism of the Greeks, with its solemn sense of the mystery of man's being and its high sense of his dignity, both deeply rooted in the life of the community. Ionia might well have produced Euripides, with whom Tragedy died. As it was, its most notable dramatist was the typically versatile Ion of Chios, a lyric poet and philosopher who wrote some forty or fifty plays, once won a third prize at the annual festival of Dionysus, and celebrated this not too notable victory by presenting every Athenian citizen with a flask of Chian wine. Herodotus was in this respect a true child of Ionia. His prose epic has sweep and stir, and now and then the somberness of tragic, heroic life; but it has nothing of the sublime.

Yet Herodotus should remind us chiefly of all that we owe to the spirit of the Ionians. We cannot simply deplore their reluctance to live and die for the *polis*, or their indifference to "the censure of the people." Most of us treasure their independent spirit, which historically was much more novel and significant than their self-indulgence. They remain attractive even in their failings. "Never shall love of thee grow old or die," Critias of Athens wrote of Anacreon, the lifelong lover of banquet, wine, and song; and it is gratifying to know that Athens set up on its Acropolis a statue of the gentle, joyous old reprobate in his cups. We may more fully appreciate the liberality and the charm of Ionia when we recall that this same Athens banished Anaxagoras for his impious teaching about the sun. He retired to Lampsacus, a colony of Miletus, where he taught freely for the rest of his life, and asked that after his death the school children be given an annual holiday to remember him by; and where, years later, the citizens still honored his memory by setting up in their market place an altar to Mind and Truth.

"How pleasant it is," comments Freya Stark, "when the fragile things, the defenceless, come through!" And how melancholy to add that so few of the beautiful things made in Ionia have come through. We know only by hearsay the works of their famous musicians, painters, sculptors, casters in bronze, workers in gold. We seldom hear their own voice. If we deplore their volatility and worldliness, we must regret still more the loss of so much of the poetry they wrote after leaving their shields on the battlefield, and of almost all the historical and philosophical treatises they wrote "for the sake of inquiry" instead of right action.

Herodotus should also remind us that the brightness of Ionia was not simple sunshine. In his insistent refrain about the jealousy of the gods and the nemesis of fame he echoed the Ionian poets, who often expressed a bitter sorrow over the futility of man's purposes. Now was the moment for happiness, now, because many evidently suffered from more dread than Homer had; they knew the deep insecurity that gave rise to the popular religious revival of the sixth century. In Ionia it reflected an actual insecurity that mitigates the political failures. The dawn that Hesiod mistook for the twilight of an Iron Age was in fact the dawn of the historical Iron Age, and the Ionians were quick to realize its new possibilities of wealth and power and freedom, and of tension and strife. Their favorable location for purposes of commerce and cultural exchange was *ipso facto* an exposed position for attack by greater powers. The river valleys down which came the caravans from the East were natural highways for invading armies of Cimmerians, Lydians, and Persians. And the rivers themselves, especially the Maeander, were piling up silt in their harbors, working to ruin most of the ports they had enriched. Miletus fought a long battle for its life but had lost its natural harbor by the Christian era. Today it is some miles inland, on a plain that had been the Latmus Gulf.

Lastly, Herodotus did a serious injustice to the Ionians by a permanent confusion in historical thought that he introduced or confirmed: he represented the Persian War as a struggle between Europe and Asia. Ever since, the valid ideological distinction between East and West has been confused by a wholly artificial geographical distinction. The identity of "Europe" is as unclear as its etymology; with Asia it forms part of a single land mass. Eventually geographers separated them by drawing an arbitrary line through the Ural Mountains—thus cutting Russia in two, and generating the widespread illusion that Russian history is part and parcel of Western European history.[11] The Greeks did not know enough geography to draw a clear line, but the mainlanders were no less pleased to obscure the natural unity of the eastern Mediterranean world by flaunting the fiction of "Europe." The Athenians in particular looked down on the Greeks in "Asia," and branded the superior sophistication of the Ionians as mere decadence. "What a disgrace it is," said Isocrates, "to sit idly by and see Asia flourishing more than Europe." How the Ionians felt about this we can only imagine, but certainly they had good practical reasons for not tying themselves to mainland Greece. They suffered enough from the imperial ambitions of both Athens and Sparta.

In any case, the proud Athenians failed Hellas, by notorious folly and infamy. Their great age ended in military disaster, social and political chaos. They recovered from the Peloponnesian War only to repeat their folly, with less dignity; they displayed neither wit nor heroism in their belated, halfhearted effort to resist the Macedonians under Philip and

[11] In Volume VIII of *A Study of History* Toynbee has dwelt on this and other confusions resulting from the arbitrary distinction.

Alexander the Great. And now the despised Ionians proved that they were less decadent than the Athenians. Submission to rule by the Persian Empire, which was something less than a sheer disgrace, had not killed their spirit. They and their fellow Greeks in "Asia" took the lead again in the Hellenistic Age following the conquests of Alexander, and they held it to the end of the Greek world. When the Emperor Justinian signaled the Byzantine era by building the great cathedral of Hagia Sophia, about a thousand years later, his architects were Isidor of Miletus and Anthemius of nearby Tralles, up the Maeander River. Meanwhile the history of Ionia had become still more mixed and ambiguous, but for us it is still more pertinent. The Hellenistic Age has had much more influence on Western civilization than has the much more celebrated Periclean Age of Athens.

CHAPTER V

*Ephesus: The Hellenistic Age**

---

1. DIANA OF THE EPHESIANS

"GREAT IS DIANA of the Ephesians!" According to Acts, so cried the mob that had gathered in the theater of Ephesus, angered by the report that an upstart Jew named Paul had insulted their magnificent goddess, saying that gods made by human hands were not gods at all. They had been stirred up by the local silversmiths, who made images of her; Paul's teaching was also bad for business. They cried out for two hours "with one voice," for they knew that "all Asia and the world" worshiped their Diana. Finally they were quieted when the town clerk reminded them that the whole world did in fact know that their city was the guardian of her temple, and nobody could really deny her greatness. And so their cry has come ringing down through the ages, as a text for sermons on vanity. Today no one in the whole world worships Diana. All that remains of her great temple—one of the Seven Wonders of the World—is the base of a column or so and a few fragments of marble lying beneath the surface of a swamp. There is no love among these dismal ruins, but only the croak of frogs to recall that she had been a goddess of fertility, worshiped in ecstasy and abandon. Nothing seems deader than a dead religion.

Yet Diana was indeed great. She had inspired, after all, a Seventh Wonder, which many ancients regarded as the most wonderful of them all. She had presided over Ephesus for a thousand years, and made it one of the greatest cities in Asia Minor. Her fame had spread all over the Greek world. She had gone as far west as Massilia (Marseilles), where the Phocaeans brought her on the advice of the Delphic Apollo, and whence merchants later brought her to Rome; she had received tribute from the heart of Asia, as Xenophon and the Ten Thousand dedicated a tenth of their spoils to Apollo and her. Her fame was such that exorcists,

* This chapter is a considerably revised and expanded version of my article "Homage to Diana" in the *Virginia Quarterly Review*, Winter, 1954.

prophets, and miracle workers of all kinds were drawn to her city, to give it perhaps the most luxuriant religious life of the ancient world. It is no accident that St. Paul spent three years teaching in Ephesus—the longest stay in his missionary career—and felt called to work "special miracles" in cures. St. John paid similar tribute by spending his last years here, preaching and writing his Gospel, with its promise of life abundant: a genial idea more familiar to the worshipers of Diana than to those of the Hebrew Yahweh. And at that Diana was greater than they knew, or even than the Ephesians knew. The sermons deriding her worshipers are also a matter for irony. She is not really dead.

For Diana was not her real name. Neither was Artemis, the Greek name by which her worshipers called her. The truly Greek Artemis was a chaste huntress, sister of Apollo, who had asked of her father Zeus the gift of eternal virginity. The Artemis of the Ephesians was a many-breasted Asiatic goddess whose principal emblems included the date palm and the queen bee, symbols of fertility.[1] Although her antecedents are obscure, she was clearly another manifestation of the Great Mother, or in other words a child of Cybele. The Greeks characteristically tempered her worship, eliminating much of the frenzy that was inspired by the earthier Cybele; Diana was more like her supposed mother, the "ever sweet and kind" Leto (known in Palestine as Lat). Like Cybele, however, she managed to retain the aspects of both a virgin and a mother of life. And in her own nature, as well as through her divine connections, she enjoyed a kind of resurrection. She had much to do with the rise of another Oriental virgin-mother, from Palestine.

Early Christian writings, like Scripture itself, contain few references to Mary. St. Paul never mentions her. Theologians were properly wary of such pagan ideas as a mother of God, and some simple Christians apparently prayed for her rather than to her. But the Ephesians would naturally have known better. They might have had some memory of Mary, for there is a tradition that she accompanied St. John to Ephesus. In any case they had the first known church to be dedicated to her. It was in this church, in the year 431, that an Ecumenical Council overrode the purists and finally made official her title as Mother of God. The feast of her Assumption was assigned to August 15, the date of an annual festival to Diana. No doubt Diana was jealous of her chaste rival, who had been

---

[1] Some scholars believe that her many breasts were actually ova. Later Greeks, including Aristotle, mistook the queen bee for a male, calling it the king bee; but the old Ephesians presumably knew better. Other scholars say that her supposed breasts were large golden dates, which the Libyans were wont to hang on the statue of their fertility goddess.

relieved of all earthly functions as a fertility goddess; but we may imagine that she was also feminine enough to be consoled by the knowledge that a man's world could not do without the Mother. We may say that she has been forgotten, like her relatives, only because she was reincarnated in purer form.

At least Diana symbolizes fundamental religious continuities, as well as religious changes. She was intimately involved in the greater drama, of the triumph of the West and the resurgence of the East, which gives the Hellenistic Age a special significance for us. Her city was in the main stream of this most "interesting process" that culminated in the fall of Constantinople to the Turks. Ephesus was the least Hellenic of the Ionian cities, and became the greatest of them during the Hellenistic Age. Diana makes plain that the interesting process was well under way before this age.

The first historic mention of the name Asia is "the Asian mead by Caystrios' stream," in Homer. Greek legend had it that Ephesus, a son of the river Caÿster, helped to found the city at its mouth, and that the Amazons had founded Diana's sanctuary during their campaign against Theseus of Athens. There is little question that here as elsewhere the Ionians moved into an older settlement and that Diana was already there, probably in a Hittite guise. She had become merged with Artemis by the time of the oldest temple excavated at the site (about 700 B.C.), but her Oriental nature is conspicuous in a treasure of votive offerings found beneath her altar. The destruction of this temple by the Cimmerians led to an impressive, if somewhat feminine, demonstration of her queenly ways. Herodotus reports that when besieged by King Croesus, the Ephesians offered the entire city to Diana by stretching a rope from its walls to her temple, a mile away. Their faith in her magic was seemingly vain, since Croesus took the city; and it was nevertheless vindicated, since they profited from his conquest. The Lydian king held Diana in such veneration that he helped to build her a much more splendid temple, which Herodotus thought a wonder worthy of comparison with the Pyramids of Egypt. Henceforth Lydians were ranked first among the five tribes of Ephesus, even holding the priesthood of the temple. The city was ever to have more of the opulence of Lydia than the radiance of Ionia.

The poet Hipponax, who lived in Ephesus toward the end of the sixth century, gives a few insights into its everyday life. Fragments of his scurrilous satires tell of the peoples of the interior coming down to the coast with their products, bargaining in "pidgin lingo," a mixture of Phrygian, Lydian, and Greek. It was Hipponax, a spokesman of the skeptical Ionian spirit, who ridiculed the high priest of Cybele as mer-

cenary and "more lascivious than a dog"; and no doubt he put a finger on
one reason for her spreading popularity—her orgiastic rites were a good
paying business. What he thought of Diana herself is less clear, but a
celebrated remark indicates that he had no high regard for her sex. The
two happiest days of a woman's life, he said, were the days of her marriage and her death. Possibly the goddess had something to do with his
ultimate banishment from her city.

At about this time Ephesus gave birth to Heraclitus, its best-known son,
who spent his entire life in the city and indirectly gives a deeper insight
into its history. The most profound, subtle, and enigmatic of the Ionian
philosophers, Heraclitus stood apart from all of them. Like them, he reduced the world of shifting appearances to an essential reality, which he
called Fire.[2] But whereas the others typically sought a principle of Being,
in terms of a basic stuff or immutable essence, he conceived a perpetual
flux in which nothing ever remains the same. Change is the essence:
"One cannot step into the same river twice." Being is endless becoming,
like the ever-living, ever-dying fire; permanence lies only in the order and
regularity of process. "It rests by changing." Likewise the life of man is
perpetual tension and strife. "It is the opposite which is good for us";
harmony comes only from "an attunement of opposite tensions, like that
of the bow and the lyre." "It is sickness that makes health pleasant; evil,
good; hunger, plenty; weariness, rest." This oracular mode of utterance
illustrated his saying that "nature loves to hide," but it also sprang from
his concept of the *Logos*—the Word that was to serve as the beginning in
the Gospel according to St. John. "It is wise to hearken not to me but to
my word," wrote Heraclitus. Through him spoke the eternal Word, which
is "both willing and unwilling to be called by the name of Zeus," and in
accordance with which "all things come to pass."

Now we cannot be certain just what Heraclitus meant by this Word, or
by many other words in the hundred-odd sayings of his that have come
down to us from the book he deposited in Diana's temple. Philosophers
have pieced together and interpreted these sayings in various ways; they
have made him out as an empiricist and an idealist, a materialist and a
pantheist, a pessimist and an optimist. In any view, however, his thought
is scarcely "classical." Of all the Greek philosophers he was the least
concerned with lucidity and logic, and the only one to reject flatly the
wisdom of moderation or "limit." For him strife, not limit, was the way to

[2] He suggests, incidentally, that the invention of coinage is one clue to the monism
of the philosophers, and in particular to the atomic theory. "All things may be reduced to fire, and fire to all things," he wrote, "just as all goods may be turned into
gold and gold into all things."

harmony and justice. Often he sounds like a lonely prophet, anticipating St. Paul's scorn for the foolishness of the Greeks. He not only attacked Homer and Hesiod but dismissed Hecataeus, Xenophanes, and Pythagoras alike as men who had learned many things without attaining understanding. Yet neither was the philosophy of Heraclitus typically "Oriental." He was still a rationalist, not a mere oracle. If the Word was hard to put into words, it was nevertheless lawful and intelligible—*Logos*, not *Mythos*. "The mysteries practiced among men are unholy mysteries," he declared. He ridiculed in particular the cult of images and the rage for ritual purification, and he was the first known man to explain dreams realistically, as a retreat into a world of one's own. Altogether, his thought was perhaps the truest reflection of Greek experience in the East—the actual, ceaseless tension, strife, and change that stimulated them, and that eventually wearied them, induced them to seek repose in the mystery religions.

What Heraclitus made of Diana is uncertain, but her worshipers evidently could make little of him. They failed to heed his plainest advice, that "the people must fight for its law as for its walls." The Ephesians were not resolute fighters. Long before, their poet Callinus (c. 700) had complained bitterly of their shameless devotion to pleasure and ease, at a time when the Cimmerians were threatening their life as well as their liberty. Once we hear of their inviting Aristarchus from Athens to act the part of Solon for five years and help them set up a limited democracy. Otherwise we hear chiefly of their tyrants, who were so numerous that one Baton wrote a history of the Tyrants of Ephesus. During the Persian wars their most dramatic contribution was a sorry epilogue to the Ionian revolt. The Chians, who had performed prodigies of valor in a naval battle but were forced to flee when deserted by the other Ionians, had to cross the territory of Ephesus by night; the Ephesians, who were busy celebrating a festival, mistook them for bandits and slew them all. Judging by the account of Herodotus, the Ephesians were again busy with other things during the battle of Mycale that restored the freedom of Ionia, for he does not mention their presence. They then joined the Athenian Confederacy, but pulled out at the first opportunity. Once the Persian Tissaphernes helped them defend Diana's temple against an Athenian attack.

She was good for both Greeks and barbarians, as Tissaphernes kindly put it in offering her a sacrifice; but it must be granted that like Cybele, Diana was not a goddess to inspire the martial virtues, or a passion for liberty. While her worshipers tried to maintain the independence of their *polis*, and succeeded in preserving more or less autonomy when under foreign domination, they never made a name for themselves by heroic resistance to their conquerors, usually opening their gates without a struggle. Croesus inaugurated a parade of famous monarchs down the Sacred Way that led to Diana's temple. Nevertheless she continued to protect her city in her fashion. She awed all but the rudest conquerors, as she had awed Croesus. Xerxes spared her temple at a time when he was destroying other Greek temples in a fit of royal wrath. In 356 B.C. it was burned down by one Herostratus, who set fire to it merely in order to have his name go down in history, but she might have smiled at this simpleton. As her worshipers set about building a still more magnificent temple, foreign kings contributed columns sculptured by the greatest artists of the age. Alexander the Great offered to defray the entire cost of the new sanctuary, provided only that his name be inscribed on it as the dedicator. (According to one legend, the temple had burned down on the day he was born because Diana was away bringing him into the world.) The Ephesians could afford to spurn his proposal, which the goddess doubtless regarded as an impertinence.

This new temple, which straightway was ranked among the wonders of the world, also became known as a "common treasury for all Asia." Diana's worshipers were not indifferent to the immense wealth that poured in on her. Like the other Ionians, they were devoted to business; Ephesus was a great port and industrial center, noted for its metalwork, perfumes, and wines. Like most Oriental peoples (and many Americans), they knew that it was possible to serve both God and mammon. For Diana herself smiled on business. Not only did her annual festivals attract thousands of pilgrims, who spent freely in their piety and gaiety, but she explicitly encouraged business enterprise. She owned considerable land in her own name, she held mortgages in Sardis and other cities, and she welcomed deposits of wealth, charging a percentage for taking care of them. Her temple became the greatest bank in the province of Asia. If such interests seem unbecoming a goddess, we must remember that she was a goddess of fertility and increase. Unlike the Christian monasteries that went into the banking business in the Middle Ages, she at least made no bones about it.

Hence her city throve mightily during the Hellenistic Age, in which business became more extensive than ever before in history. Now that Miletus, its chief rival, was losing its battle against the silt of the Maeander River, Ephesus became the chief port for the trade route leading down the Maeander valley. Although it was fighting a similar battle against the smaller Caÿster River, it would be able to maintain its port for some centuries yet, with the help of gifts to Diana. From 300 B.C. on, it was the greatest of the Ionian cities. In its prosperity it never rivaled the brilliant cultural achievement of Miletus in its prime, or attained anything like the eminence that Athens had, but its lesser historic importance was characteristic of the new age: one in which the Greeks moved out onto a world stage, and the *polis* was overshadowed by the rise of kingdoms and the growth of a cosmopolitan culture. If the famous men of the age might still be identified by their native city, they rarely spent their lives in it and never confined their interests to it; typically they traveled, to build or conquer, learn or teach. The great city of Ephesus is memorable for all the history it saw rather than the history it made.

2.   THE HELLENISTIC ACHIEVEMENT

With an army of no more than thirty or forty thousand men, Alexander the Great crossed the Dardanelles into Asia, defeated the huge hosts of King Darius in three crucial battles, destroyed the Persian Empire, conquered the known world from Egypt to India, and died in Babylon, in 323 B.C., not yet thirty-three years of age. So extraordinary a career naturally made him a mythical figure. "It is allowed as certain," wrote the sober Plutarch, "that Alexander was a descendant of Heracles." The eastern world he conquered reincarnated him in more exotic or exalted forms. The Alexander Romance, which began to take form soon after his death, eventually proliferated into some eighty versions in twenty-four languages, including Persian, Arabic, Ethiopic, Hebrew, and Turkish. In Egypt he became the son of the last Pharaoh, in Ethiopia a Christian saint, in Central Asia a god known as Iskander. He appears in the Koran as Dulcarnain, Lord of the Two Horns; Moslem poets had him praying at Mecca, as the Jews had him praying at Jerusalem. In medieval Europe he became a gallant knight devoted to his lady, the beautiful Persian princess Roxane. As late as the seventeenth century Racine pictured him as more interested in winning the love of his mistress than in winning a world.

Since then historians have been trying to recover the actual man, but we still have our choice of Alexanders. There is the tyrant known to many Greeks, the son of the Macedonian King Philip who had won dominion over Greece in the battle of Chaeronea, who himself murdered his friends in drunken rages, leveled Thebes to the ground, and sealed the loss of Greek independence. There is the ardent Hellenist, the pupil of Aristotle and lover of Homer, whose avowed mission in overthrowing the Persian Empire was to serve as the liberator of Hellas. There is the vainglorious conqueror who took to wearing the purple, the megalomaniac who had himself proclaimed a god, the son of Zeus-Amon. There is the idealist whose maxim, wrote Plutarch, was that "God is the common father of men, but more particularly of the good and virtuous," and whose dream of world unity, an empire bound by brotherhood, marked a revolution in human thought. "Alexander's goal was a new and better world," concludes Charles A. Robinson, Jr., his latest champion, "and beside his success in winning it little else really matters."

Few would deny that his conquests resulted in a new world. The important question remains: Was it a better one? Here again we have a wide choice of answers. Classical scholars have generally pictured the Hellenistic Age as a period of decline, as in Athens and mainland Greece it plainly was. For them the Age of Pericles is the apex of the conventional historic curve; by classical standards Hellenistic culture looks degenerate. Historians of Rome have likewise dwelt on the "failure" of the Hellenistic kingdoms in order to justify the Roman absorption of them or magnify the Roman achievement of bringing law and order. In these views the "new world" turns out to be either an unhappy aftermath or a chaotic prelude. Recent historians, such as Tarn and Rostovtzeff, have therefore tried to see it as its own people did, and not to prejudge it by what came before or after. They stress that it was a remarkably vigorous, adventurous, creative period—in Asia. Although we know too little about the mentality of its early leaders, not to mention their followers, their enterprise strongly suggests a belief that they were living at the beginning rather than the end of an era, and were improving their life. Many Greeks seem to have been proud of their "modernity"; some even began dreaming of Utopias. Certainly their outlook was widened, in a world much greater than Plato's little Republic, a society in some important respects more "open" than Periclean Athens. By now there is at least little question that it was Hellenistic culture—as Robinson says, "the only Greek culture the world ever really knew, until modern scholarship resurrected that of Periclean Athens"—that educated Rome, enabled her to create a world state, and enabled Christianity to conquer that state.

Yet for just this reason we must look more closely at the means and ends of Hellenistic enterprise, the value of its creations, the quality of its culture. The "new world" was indeed much more like our own; only now we are in a mood to have misgivings about some of its likenesses. Among the "modern" types it developed in increasing numbers were the bourgeois and the city proletarian, the one complacent in his prosperity, the other sullen in his failure to share in this prosperity; the half-educated man on the street, now cut off from the country but still prey to crass superstition; the unpolitical man or "idiot," primarily concerned with his business, his private life, or his personal salvation; and in all fields of activity the specialist—the professional bureaucrat, technician, propagandist, scholar, entertainer, athlete. The Hellenistic Age also resembled our own in its increasingly violent contrasts, of wealth and poverty, learning and ignorance, splendor and squalor; and in its profound contradictions, of freedom in thought and atavism in behavior, a deepening consciousness of Greek solidarity and more bitter strife, a growing ideal of humanity and more brutal inhumanity. In general, Hellenistic Greeks seemed as proud as we of what they had wrought, and often as dismayed or appalled. They were as free to roam in their cosmopolitan world, and as liable to feel lost. Their exciting adventures may illustrate depressing morals. As always, the final verdict on their achievement will remain debatable; but we may at least hope to approach an impartial one by keeping an eye on the complexities and the incongruities of the age, as of Alexander himself.

Its political history is obviously lamentable, if less disgraceful than at first appears. The generals who succeeded to Alexander's empire were worthy of him in energy, daring, and ambition, and their own successors were more original than they may seem to us as they built up administrative systems for their sizable kingdoms—a feat of government that the classical Greeks had never attempted, and that Aristotle had declared impossible. But they lacked the vision of Alexander, and seemed more determined to prove the moral of Plutarch, what an "unsociable, solitary thing is power." The generals at once began fighting among themselves, initiating the almost continuous warfare that marked the Hellenistic period. Antigonus, the first of the Successors, boasted that he was not afraid to have his son Demetrius stand beside him with a weapon in his hand. The later kings could not be so sure of their sons, still less of their brothers and wives (who were sometimes their sisters), and could never trust one another. Antigonus lost his Asiatic empire and his life at the battle of Ipsus, where he and Demetrius were defeated by the combined forces of Lysimachus and Seleucus. Seleucus in turn defeated and killed Lysimachus, and then was murdered himself. Ptolemy, who took over Egypt, was the only Successor to die in bed.

Thereafter the house of Seleucus claimed dominion over Asia Minor but exercised only partial, wavering control over it, periodically losing coastal regions to the Ptolemies. Its power was also disputed by new kingdoms that rose in the confusion, such as the kingdoms of Bithynia and Pontus in the north. Nicomedes of Bithynia added to the confusion by bringing in some tribes of Gauls to help him against the Seleucids, and then turning them loose on Asia Minor. For years the Gauls ravaged and blackmailed the Greek cities, until they were finally subdued by the kings of Pergamum and settled down in the Phrygian interior, in the province that consequently became known as Galatia. Pergamum was now the strongest power in Asia Minor, but to maintain its ascendance felt obliged to lean on Rome.[3]

The rich city of Ephesus, which had welcomed Alexander as a liberator, was naturally a focal point of this disorder. Loyal to Antigonus, it submitted to Lysimachus after the battle of Ipsus, later was retaken by Demetrius, and then fell to Lysimachus again. Over the protests of the Ephesians he moved the city to a more defensible site, where he strongly fortified it and swelled its population by moving in the inhabitants of the old Ionian cities of Lebedus and Colophon. Here the Ephesians were to stay put for a thousand years, but for the next century or so their new city remained a pawn in the royal struggles. After a brief spell of freedom it came under the domain of the Ptolemies. Antiochus II recovered it for the Seleucids and made it a royal residence, only to be poisoned in it by his wife Laodice; when she started another war by having her son proclaimed king in Ephesus, it fell to the Ptolemies again. Reconquered by Antiochus III, it became the headquarters for his campaign against Rome. Hannibal, the most feared enemy of Rome, now came to Ephesus to offer the king his services. When Antiochus was nevertheless defeated in the battle of Magnesia that ended Seleucid rule in Asia Minor, the hapless Ephesians opened their gates to the Roman general Manlius. The Romans decreed that the city should be tributary to Pergamum, their faithful ally. Thereafter it was never really independent.

Yet Ephesus prospered in spite of its repeated humiliations. Diana remained an unfailing source of wealth, and continued to awe the parade of conquerors. Thus when Demetrius fled to the city after the battle of Ipsus it was feared that he might seize the treasures in her temple, but instead he at once set sail for Athens, to prevent his soldiers from looting it.[4] The main reason for the growing prosperity, however, was an immense expansion of commerce. Alexander had directly fostered trade by

[3] See the Appendix, Section 5, for the brief but brilliant history of the Kingdom of Pergamum.

[4] In Athens Demetrius showed much less respect for the virgin Athena, entertaining licentious women in the back temple of the Parthenon that the Athenians had given him as a lodging in gratitude for his aid. He is perhaps the most striking example of the vigor, enterprise, and waste of the early Hellenistic period. A brilliant adventurer, Demetrius won the name of Poliorcetes, "the taker of cities," by his daring campaigns, eventually met disaster again in Asia Minor, and ended his life in dissipation, as a prisoner of Seleucus. His most enduring achievement was a statue that he had made to commemorate a naval victory over the Ptolemies at Cyprus, and that is represented on one of his coins. It is possibly, though doubtfully, the original of the Winged Victory of Samothrace.

instituting an international coinage and putting into circulation the hoards of gold and silver he captured. (So the moneychanger made his appearance in the temples, to the greater glory of their divine occupants.) Indirectly Alexander promoted a boom by opening up the East to the Greeks, providing an outlet for surplus population, a greater market for Greek goods, and a further incentive for Greek enterprise. The Seleucids in particular continued his policy of founding new cities on the trade routes, and also moved Greek colonies into older foundations, as at Celaenae-Apamea; they built scores of Seleucias, Apameas, Antiochs, Laodiceas. In their greater world the Greeks now became builders, on a large scale, of roads, aqueducts, and harbors.

More important, the spirit of the *polis* was still alive. At Ephesus Alexander had proclaimed that henceforth all Greek cities were to be free and independent, and he had a democratic constitution drawn up for the Ephesians. As he liberated other cities he removed the oligarchies and tyrannies that had been supported by the Persians. Their freedom was somewhat nominal, to be sure. Alexander himself had *ordered* them to be democratic, his successors might give them different orders, and like him they usually called for contributions in return for the royal favors. Nevertheless the Hellenistic kings paid at least lip service to the ancient ideal of "the autonomy of the Hellenes," if only to enlist the aid of the cities in their incessant wars on one another. Some of the cities— notably Rhodes—were actually independent, and real powers. And democracy remained the rule in the Greek cities throughout the period, ultimate authority residing in the popular assembly. The Greek was still a political animal, or enough so to remain an energetic, enterprising animal. Thought everywhere was freer than it had been in Athens, even more diverse than it had been in Ionia. In this respect the Hellenistic *polis* was a wide-open society.

Civic spirit also maintained a high level of culture. While the Hellenistic Greeks were engrossed in business and increasingly devoted to material comforts—high living and plain thinking—they were by no means mere Philistines. The kings were typically patrons of culture. The wealthy bourgeois as typically took pride in adorning their cities, staging their festivals, maintaining their cultural traditions; the cities vied with one another in the splendor of their works. The Greeks who moved into the interior as piously preserved their great heritage, to make themselves feel at home. Old or new, every city of any consequence had its marbled temples, its statuary, its gymnasium, its theater—the more imposing as we keep in mind that most of them were small towns, with smaller material resources than ordinary American towns. And art now moved into the home as well, to adorn courtyards with statuettes. All in all, the Hellenistic Greeks cultivated a highly civilized mode of life, in cities planned for both comfort and beauty.

Their spirit was essentially different, however, from that of the old *polis*. It was not so much devotion to the city-state as pride in the home town, and expressed itself less in political than in social activity. No longer really independent, self-sufficient, in control of its destiny, the *polis* could neither give nor demand of its citizens, body and soul, what it once had. If still patriotic, its citizens were generally more concerned with private affairs, which could be conducted as well elsewhere; exile was no longer a dreadful fate. One sign of the changing spirit was the host of wandering teachers, mountebanks, prophets, exorcists, jacks-of-all-trades. A related sign was the rise of the professional, or mercenary; soldiers, athletes, actors, engineers, artists, and rhetoricians were alike for hire. Still another sign was the growth of nonpolitical clubs or associations that served something like the purpose of the Elks, if on a higher cultural plane. The most attractive consequences of the new spirit was a higher status for women and a deeper interest in the home and family life; the family had been the principal victim of the classical *polis*, and the limited home life one reason for the volatility and disorder as well as the richness of its public life. Less attractive was the very splendor of the Hellenistic cities, displayed in their public buildings and their festivals. It was too much a display, theatrical and rhetorical. In its showiness it too often showed a complacence without high seriousness or real composure. It emphasized that Ephesus was a good place to live, but hardly represented an ideal worth fighting and dying for. In general, there is no mistaking the bourgeois spirit that to lovers of classical Greece makes Hellenistic culture seem decadent.

But the issues of this culture remain complex, and cannot be dismissed by such brand names. Culture involves much more than fine art. Although lovers of art are naturally disposed to agree with Shelley that it is the best index to the quality of a civilization, and that the great periods of poetry are periods of improvement in manners and morals, the golden ages do not in fact clearly mark the zeniths of societies; nor are they generally distinguished for their manners and morals. Great achievement in art and literature commonly precedes the highest development in not only wealth and power but freedom, knowledge, sophistication, and civility—as Homer did in Ionia, Dante in Italy, Shakespeare in England. The very limitations of Hellenistic culture, moreover, made it more serviceable for posterity. By its professional, relatively commonplace quality, it preserved the Greek heritage in forms better suited to peoples lacking the genius of the Athenians; neither Rome nor early Renaissance Italy was capable of building Parthenons or producing Sophoclean drama, but both could learn readily from the art and thought of the Hellenistic Greeks. In any case, these Greeks could not have gone on creating indefinitely in the mode of their glorious forefathers, even had these forefathers not failed Hellas. As it was, they made over their heritage in ways that connoisseurs of culture may deplore but students of history may appreciate. The new modes in art and thought were a logical, organic outgrowth of new conditions of life—and for better or worse a positive growth, not a mere decay.

Least impressive is the Hellenistic achievement in literature. Some writers attempted ambitious performances, such as the *Argonautica* of Apollonius of Rhodes: a highly polished epic, elegant, and essentially commonplace, the more so because its author took infinite pains to avoid the commonplace. Most writers in effect heeded the advice of Callimachus, who recommended that they avoid the well-traveled highways of literature and follow instead some little bypath of their own. The bypaths flowered with such new forms as the epigram, the diatribe, the pastoral, the erotic "Milesian tale," and the romance, with the new theme of romantic love. Especially characteristic of the age was New Comedy, a bourgeois comedy of manners. In all these forms there was little real seriousness, and as little magic. Lacking vital public issues or national ideals, writers cultivated the rhetoric of sentiment and passion, in keeping with the growing rage for oratory. They refined the traditional myths into pretty tales or reduced them to poetic ornaments, for the benefit of minor poets ever after. When they took themselves most seriously they were likely to be "educators" in an unimaginative, pedantic sense. A typical figure of the period was Alexander of Ephesus, an orator surnamed the Lamp, who impressed Strabo by his poems describing heavenly phenomena and the geography of the continents.

For the rest the Hellenistic Greeks pored over their great literary heritage, to the harm of their own reputation. They had something like Matthew Arnold's conception of culture, as the best that has been thought and said; and it had all been said by their forefathers. In their piety they created the new types of the literary scholar, editor, grammarian. They studied Homer line by line, purifying and annotating the traditional texts, reading a world of allegorical meaning into them; they read the tragic poets as reverently, setting up the Attic dialect as the standard for literary Greek. They inaugurated the "classical" tradition that Europe inherited, with its emphasis on imitation, propriety, obedience to authority—an academic spirit utterly different from the spirit that created the masterpieces. They did their work so well that the great bulk of creative Hellenistic literature has disappeared, just as the works of Shakespeare might have been lost had classical scholars ruled the roost in Elizabethan England; for most contemporary literature was naturally written in the living language, which was "impure." (In this language the New Testament was to be written.) But at least they preserved the masterpieces for posterity, and with them passed on the tradition of scholarship that may enliven and illumine as well as deaden the masterpieces. We also owe to the Hellenistic Greeks the first public libraries, beginning with the famous Museum set up by the Ptolemies in Alexandria.

Their achievement in science was comparable but much more significant. Here the Hellenistic Greeks unquestionably outdid their forefathers —and showed up the mainlanders who looked down their noses at "Asia." Athens saw a remarkable physicist in Strato, a foreigner from Lampsacus on the Hellespont, who from 287 to 269 served as head of Aristotle's Lyceum, and who appears to have developed and applied the experimental method; but his successors turned the school to ethics and rhetoric, and thereafter Athens neither produced nor attracted any scientists or natural philosophers of consequence.[5] The great names in Hellenistic science are almost all Asiatic or Alexandrian Greeks. From Asia Minor came more "fathers": in anatomy Herophilus of Chalcedon, in physiology Erasistratus of Chios. As original was the astronomer Aristarchus of Samos, a pupil of Strato, who was the first to offer a heliocentric or "Copernican" theory of the universe. Another astronomer, Hipparchus of Nicaea, invented trigonometry for the sake of his extraordinarily accurate calculations. In mathematics the Hellenistic classic is the *Elements* of Euclid, but as brilliant a pioneer was Apollonius of Perge. A still greater mathematician, Archimedes of Syracuse, was also the greatest engineer and inventor of antiquity, laying the foundations of the science of mechanics.

An immediate stimulus to this extensive scientific activity—much too extensive and technically advanced to be catalogued here—was the con-

[5] Cicero gives a glimpse of the lively Ionian mentality of this physicist:
"Strato of Lampsacus gives god a dispensation from his arduous task, opining that if the priests of the gods get holidays it is only fair that the gods should have them too. He says he does not use the help of the gods to make the world. Everything that exists, he says, is the work of nature, but adds that he does not mean that in the sense of the great man who said that all things are concretions of atoms, rough and smooth, hooked and barbed, with an admixture of void. These views he calls the dreams of Democritus, who could not prove them but only desired them. He himself goes through the parts of the universe one by one and proves that whatever exists or comes to be has been made or is made by purely natural forces and movements."

quest and opening up of the East. Alexander himself encouraged it by bringing scholars along with him. It was more obviously promoted, however, by the growing professional spirit of the age, which led to systematic research instead of brilliant amateur speculation. Thus the Museum of Alexandria was not only a great library but a research institute, equipped with an observatory, a zoo, a botanical garden, and dissecting rooms, and staffed by a hundred professors to train scholars, scientists, and technicians. It inaugurated what Farrington has called the Age of the Textbook—an unexciting development, but a significant stage in human progress. It represented the noiseless kind of revolution that may bring about major changes in man's life.

Only it failed to revolutionize Greek thought or life. The experimental method of Strato was not developed; the basic natural science of physics virtually ended with him. Archimedes' science of mechanics was likewise stillborn. Although Hellenistic technicians became aware of the potential power in water, steam, and air pressure, they never developed for industry a source of mechanical power to replace the manual labor of slaves; they made practical use of their knowledge chiefly in producing engines of war and elaborate gadgets for the wealthy. Science in general remained essentially an academic pursuit. For the Hellenistic Greeks clung to the traditional scorn of the "base mechanic arts." Plutarch states that Archimedes himself "looked upon the work of an engineer and everything that ministers to the needs of life as ignoble and vulgar." Farrington contrasts him with the humble Simon Stevin (1548–1620), known as the Archimedes of the Low Countries, who in offering to the public his decimal system of notation wrote, "It is not a great invention, but it is eminently useful to everyone."

Farrington explains the halt in Hellenistic science and technology by the institution of slavery. He argues that although the early Ionian thinkers were accustomed to slavery, they belonged to a business class that was still accustomed to working and still familiar with techniques, whereas by the time of Plato and Aristotle gentlemen were above working with their hands. One trouble with this plausible explanation is that the major Greek achievements in science and mechanics came in the centuries after Plato and Aristotle. As good an explanation as any may be simply that scientists, like literary scholars, were awed by their classical heritage. All we can safely say is that scientific advance did not alter the mentality of the Hellenistic Greeks, which had doubtless been influenced by the ancient institution of slavery. Their aristocratic indifference to utility might seem loftier had they not depended on slave labor, and sufficiently enjoyed material wealth and ease. As it was, theory as well as practice suffered from this indifference. Since they lacked the discipline of practical application and close attention to vulgar fact, their preferences in theory were largely determined by the traditional passion for order—logical, aesthetic, or religious—and with an almost unerring instinct the Greeks turned away from the potentially most fruitful theories, such as the evolutionary of Anaximander, the atomic of Democritus, and the heliocentric of Aristarchus.

In art the Hellenistic Greeks were truer to their own experience, and their achievement is therefore more controversial. While Athens clung to the classical style, the Asiatic Greeks developed an architecture and sculpture more in keeping with their restless, adventurous, inharmonious life. Diana's last temple was representative. It was more ornate than the Doric temple, with bands of sculpture encircling the base of its columns. It became a wonder for its imposing dimensions, which placed it among the colossal monuments of the East; visitors were awed by its 127 columns, sixty feet high, just as they were awed by the towering Pharos of Alexandria and the Colossus of Rhodes—two other wonders of the world. Although we can get little idea of its magnificence from the few mutilated chunks of column that survived, what we know of it and of Diana's worshipers suggests that her temple was more grandiose than grand. Such impressions are confirmed by the lack of restraint or repose in Hellenistic sculpture. It was often theatrical, as in the Laocoön, and rarely chaste. Its gods became more muscular and less godlike, resembling athletes or supermen; its goddesses became more exquisitely feminine, conscious of their nakedness or of the folds of their drapery. Aphrodite came into her own at her bath.

Nevertheless Hellenistic art was essentially a Greek, not an Oriental creation. Diana's temple, classical in form, was still a civic center, a dwelling for a goddess who lived with as well as off her people. It contained many masterpieces of Greek painting and sculpture, including statues and an altar by Praxiteles. Its ornateness was not simply a departure from classical tradition, which was much less chaste and serene than one gathers from the time-washed marble of the Parthenon. This leads us to forget that the classical temple was painted in gaudy colors and decorated with gold leaf, that it typically contained a colossal statue of the god, out of proportion with his dwelling, and that this statue might also be painted or overlaid with gold and ivory. Athenian vases of the classical period, designed for use instead of for posterity, were likewise not ultrarefined or ultrarestrained. The artists who made them employed the traditional myths and legends for decorative rather than edifying purposes, in an essentially playful spirit; their favorite themes included worldly scenes of young men and women, and Dionysus with erotic satyrs and maenads—which might remind us that the austere Aeschylus also wrote satyr plays. Their artistry is exquisite but less chaste than the art of Praxiteles, who inscribed on his nude Aphrodite of Cnidus that his statue "portrayed the love he felt." And the sensuous beauty of his art, which was still close to Attic tradition and a major influence on early Hellenistic art, points to the unmistakable continuity. Hellenistic sculpture was a logical development of the essentially naturalistic, humanistic inspiration of all Greek art. It foreshadowed the similar development from medieval art to the art of Giotto, Michelangelo, and Raphael.

The most conspicuous tendency was toward realism and individualism. Classical sculpture had achieved an idealization of the human form; it represented gods who were all young or in their prime, all glorious, all 100 per cent Greek. Hellenistic sculptors represented different races, classes, ages, and types of men and women, in many different moods—a Dying Gaul, an Old Market Woman, a Running Negro, a Drunken Woman, a Shepherd Boy, a Boy Strangling a Goose. Similarly they developed the art of portraiture, to which we owe the busts of classical Greeks.[6] They discovered the interest, even the beauty, of the ugly, distorted, grotesque. They sought to express more passion and movement, developing the baroque style that reached its peak in the powerful Gigantomachia adorning the Altar of Zeus at Pergamum, representing the battle between the Olympians and the Titans. The School of Pergamum specialized in dying Gauls, Persians, Amazons, and giants, in vividly realized attitudes of pain, terror, despair, or defiance. As vividly it rendered weariness, sleepiness, and the sleep of death, and by contrast the gay, lively movement of satyrs and dancers. Elsewhere sculptors cultivated the rococo style that was to swamp posterity with nymphs, Pans, and Cupids, but that also left much graceful, playful work, especially in the studies of children, teen-agers, and old men and women.

Now, most students of art today consider the Hellenistic style—realistic, baroque, or rococo—inferior to the idealized style of classical Greece Connoisseurs are wont to prefer even the naïveté of the "archaic" period.

[6] Hellenistic coins are among the best examples of this striking art and its reflection of a changing culture. Earlier Greek coins always picture the gods and the emblems of the city, never its human heroes. Lysimachus now issued a most beautiful coin with a portrait of the deified Alexander—as noble a head as one can find in any period. Ptolemy of Egypt then put himself on his coins, and other kings followed suit. Many of the portraits are surprisingly realistic and unflattering. The life story of Antiochus I may be traced from the glorified, godlike youth of his early coins to the drawn, hollow-eyed, weary old man on his last ones. All along, however, Ephesus remained devoted to Diana: the standard emblem on its coins is her queen bee.

istory suggests, however, that such preferences are in part matters of fashion or temperament, not merely of purity of taste; and only an art snob would dismiss Hellenistic sculpture as simply decadent or vulgar. It made notable advances in technique, beyond its mastery of anatomy and elaborate drapery. To the statuesque world of frieze it added the third dimension of depth, which opened up new possibilities of more complex movement, dramatic grouping, and free-standing monuments. It expressed much more feeling for man and life than had classical sculpture, and gave the artist more freedom. In its broader humanity it could be called more truly universal. If it sacrificed serenity and harmony to passion and power, so did the mature art of Michelangelo.

In any case it was true to the life and spirit of the times. Had it been more "ideal" it would have been more sentimental, insincere, essentially un-Greek. As Tarn wrote, the Altar of Zeus at Pergamum—the "Satan's seat" of early Christians—was the epitome of the Hellenistic Age: "the whole tumult of the age, the meeting of civilization and barbarism, the conflict of good and evil, the striving with unfamiliar ways of expression, knowing no rest—all is there." Sculptors could not long maintain such intensity; but when their art became largely exhausted, as it did by the first century B.C., the clearest sign of decadence was the effort to revive classical forms and subjects.

A similar fidelity marked Hellenistic philosophy, to its glory, and finally to its ruin. As the *polis* lost its independence and self-sufficiency, philosophers became concerned primarily with private ethics, the good life as it could be lived apart from the *polis,* or under any kind of rule. Their thought accordingly looks like a retreat, if in good order, from the full life of early Ionia and Athens. The Cynics went farthest, rejecting the values not only of civic life but of civilization, ignoring their actual debt to the community—saving their souls, Tarn observed, "by living on common people who had no time to save their own." The more admirable Epicurean and Stoic schools moved in the same direction, toward a kind of individual self-sufficiency that resembled Oriental impassivity. An Oriental cast was most pronounced in Stoicism, whose founder, Zeno, was a Phoenician from Cyprus, and whose later leaders came chiefly from the more Asiatic provinces, such as Babylon, Phoenicia, Phrygia, and Cilicia. Yet Hellenistic philosophy was again an essentially Greek creation, on the whole the grandest achievement of the period, and certainly the most influential one.

In concentrating on ethics the philosophers were still being practical, seeking to make the Greeks at home in their new world. Strato of Lampsacus considered natural philosophy the most serious as well as ancient branch, connected (in the words of Farrington) "rather with the basic arts on which life itself depends than with the arts which are the adornment of a decadent civilization"; but in any kind of civilization no concern is more serious than the quest of wisdom and virtue. The Stoics and Epicureans harked back to Xenophanes and Socrates. Often they were men with a mission, having something like the fervor of the Hebrew prophets; they produced almost saintly types. More important, they were still free men in their thought—much freer than the prophets, or than the Athenians who banished Anaxagoras and sentenced Socrates to death. Among the Hellenistic schools was Skepticism, whose founder Pyrrho had gone to India with Alexander and presumably had had his eyes opened to the relativity of custom and belief. But more typical, and paradoxical in view of the fate of Hellenistic philosophy, was the initial faith in reason. Aristotle was supremely confident of the power of reason to discover ultimate truth. The Epicureans and Stoics were as confident of its superiority over circumstance or convention, its power to control man's life. On rational grounds they asserted the implicit faith of the Homeric hero, that man could achieve excellence by his own unaided efforts, and that he was equal to his fate however he conceived the universal necessity.

Thus Epicurus taught that by meditating on philosophy one could live "like a god among men," and for this purpose banished the gods: "It was fear that first made the gods." The happiness that for him was the sole and sufficient end of man's life was not, of course, the popular idea of eat, drink, and be merry. It was a rational enjoyment of the higher goods, especially friendship and the uses of mind, and it required temperance. His ideal of serene wisdom accordingly called for the rejection of the wild hopes of an afterlife that were growing popular. His disciple Lucretius had a still holier zeal for liberating men from the superstition and fear bred by religion. The Epicureans alone held out against the superstition, and cult of salvation, that in time swamped Greek philosophy. In the early Christian era an obscure, saintly Epicurean known—or almost unknown—as Diogenes of Oenoanda still sought "to give help to future generations (for they are ours, even if they are yet unborn)." He engraved in marble his testament: "Nothing to fear in God: Nothing to feel in death: Good can be attained: Evil can be endured."

Although the future generations were to shudder at this ungodly wisdom, Christian and pagan alike might conquer fear and blind desire in the different way of the Stoics. Zeno had identified reason with God. He affirmed that temples were unnecessary because the human intellect was God's temple, and he taught that it must will things to be as they were, since God in his rationality had so willed them. His successors talked variously of Reason, Nature, Zeus, Providence, Destiny, the Universe; but alike they asserted resolutely a will to accept and endure with perfect equanimity whatever the controlling Power ordained. They insisted at once on a principle of unconditional freedom and a principle of unconditional duty: freedom through absolute mastery of the will, in obedience to a rational or providential order. As Epictetus said, "You will not wish to be praetor, or prefect or consul, but to be free; and there is but one way to freedom—to despise what is not in our power." Stoicism in fact nerved countless men to live in this spirit, and to endure with fortitude a great deal of painful history. It held up the loftiest ethical principle, of virtue for its own sake. While many Stoics believed in an afterlife, most continued to insist that virtue is all that matters, whether or not it pays. The Stoic ethic was cheapened when it entered Christianity and took on promises of eternal rewards.

Much more important historically was the Stoic concept of a universal community, rationalizing Alexander's prayer for *homonoia*. Plato and Aristotle never got beyond the parochial little *polis;* with it they took for granted such institutions as slavery and war, the right of every *polis* to determine and maintain its own interests against every other one. Zeno's earliest work was a quite different *Republic,* unfortunately lost, which appears to have envisaged a *cosmopolis.* A man could not become the property of another, he said, by either conquest or purchase. His successors made explicit the ideal of "one great City of gods and men" in accordance with universal Reason or Nature. This concept entered Roman law, became the ruling ideal of the greater Roman emperors, and prepared the ground for Christianity. At Athens, St. Paul quoted the Stoic Cleanthes as saying that all men are the offspring of God, as elsewhere he echoed the idea of Zeno that God "dwelleth not in temples made with hands."

St. Paul reminds us, however, of the limitations of the Stoics. The will they exalted was not good will in the fullest sense, for it was not informed by love. Love would endanger the imperturbable calm they aspired to above all. So would compassion, or even a lively concern for justice and righteousness. "To feel pain at the misfortunes of others is a weakness unworthy of the wise man," declared Seneca, and in the same spirit the more humane Epictetus said, "It is better for your son to be wicked than for you to be miserable." The ideal was freedom from all passion—in effect apathy, not sympathy. Hence the ideal of a universal community remained an abstract concept, not a communal ideal vitalized by a spirit of brotherhood. Neither did the Stoics display any real love of Nature or God. And their heroic effort to remain passionless had a pathetically irrational aspect. There was something desperate, as well as too sententious, in their constant insistence on the rationality of the universe, the rightness of things as they are. They were never able to demonstrate this rationality and rightness, elucidate the purposes of Nature or God. The clearest thing about these purposes was that they were not clearly good; else stoical acceptance and endurance would not have required so heroic, desperate an effort of will.

Briefly, Stoicism was a response to actual uncertainty, insecurity, and fear, in an age in which things were not really going well and men might have to endure a lot, for reasons they could not really understand. It was a philosophy for the few, beyond the capacity of the many, but it sprang from the same anxiety that was leading the many to seek salvation or peace of mind in the mystery cults. It did nothing to remove the causes of such anxiety by promoting either understanding or reform. Its metaphysics was an improvisation, not the root but the wan flower of its ethical theory.[7] Its ethics of duty and endurance, social service without desire or concern, was essentially a fatalistic acquiescence in the status quo. And the more genial philosophy of Epicurus, in theory radically opposed to Stoicism, in effect had much the same upshot. Ardently he sought to suppress ardor; his ideal too was freedom from passion or concern. Neither school was devoted to critical inquiry or the discovery of new knowledge; neither made further contributions to the understanding of man or the universe. Both turned their backs on the basic social and political problems.

About 200 B.C. there set in the slow but steady decline in philosophy that eventually carried it back to the world of myth and magic from which it had arisen. It mirrored the gradual decline in energy, enterprise, and imaginativeness that marked the close of the Hellenistic Age. By the first century before the Christian era the Greeks had pretty well lost the feeling that they were building a new and better world. One sign of loss of confidence in the future was the ugly practice of infanticide, which was especially common in Greece proper. Inscriptions bear out the remark of Posidippus that "even a rich man always exposes a daughter"; families in the later Hellenistic period most commonly had a single child —a son.[8] The son was taught a reverence for the classics of the past that

---

[7] A curious example is the "hard syllogisms" that Zeno put together to give the appearance of logical system and certainty. One goes as follows: "It is reasonable to honor the gods; it would not be reasonable to honor beings that did not exist; therefore the gods exist." It is harder to understand how Zeno got by with such a plug as this.

[8] One must wonder how women felt about this practice, but one cannot know. Although they now had a higher status, including the privilege of education, and

was unlikely to inspire any conviction of a manifest national destiny. Polybius had written a characteristic "universal" history, of the rise of Rome, that reflected the growing feeling that the future belonged to Rome. Elsewhere the visions of Utopia that some early Hellenistic thinkers had entertained gave way to variations on Hesiod's theme of a golden age in the past. Stoics in particular took to this theme, or else to the cyclical theory of history—an endless recurrence of rise and fall that was again pronounced rational, because authorized by Nature or Providence, and that again was in effect meaningless.

In general, men no longer sought so much to make history as to escape it. And the obvious means of escape was religion. This involved some aspiration to a purer spirituality, some approach to universality, but chiefly it looks like a disorderly retreat, or even a flight from reason. E. R. Dodds has summarized the drama as "the return of the irrational." In other words, it was the return to "miracle, mystery, and authority."

3. THE RETURN OF THE IRRATIONAL

Of the medley of gods, demons, and magical rites that constitutes popular religion, Gilbert Murray wrote: "Anthropology seems to show that these Inherited Conglomerates have practically no chance of being true or even sensible; and, on the other hand, that no society can exist without them or even submit to any drastic correction of them without social danger." The danger was illustrated by the witch-hunts in classical Athens. Seemingly the lesson was taken to heart by the men of the Hellenistic Age, for there was little further effort at drastic correction outside the Epicurean school, and this held aloof from the common people. The major religious development was a further agglomeration.

Now in dealing with this development historians have probably exaggerated the influence of the Orient, especially of its mystery cults. The Greeks did not have to look to the East for such cults, which they had in their own tradition. Dionysus had long been popular. Herodotus wrote that even the barbarous Scythians reproved the Greeks for the frenzies he inspired, holding that no god would impel man to madness; and though a native of Thrace, Dionysus was so much like Eastern gods that Herodotus identified him with Osiris, as he identified Demeter with Isis. We cannot be certain, either, of all the apparent additions to the Conglomerate, such as the demons who seem to have come in from Persia. While one historian declares that neither the Greeks nor the Romans had known these demons before, another suggests that they may have been

---

contributed quite a few forceful queens to the Macedonian line, down to Cleopatra of Egypt, we have no record of their feelings in the matter.

there all the time, in the countryside, and merely changed their names. The truth remains that we know little of the mentality of ordinary Greeks in classical times. What we do know indicates that most of them were as far behind Thales and Heraclitus as they now were behind Epicurus and Zeno, and that they had never been emancipated from miracle and mystery.

Yet we must keep our eyes on the world stage—the *oikoumene* now known to the Greeks. This was not merely a Hellenistic concept, but in fact the scene of a cosmopolitan drama. Diana of Ephesus, once more, is a reminder that the drama began long before the Hellenistic period, from the moment the Greeks entered Asia Minor. Sappho had celebrated the Syrian Adonis. Sophocles had entertained the new god Asclepius in his own home until the stranger from Asia could be suitably housed. Herodotus noted that Greek writers before his time had borrowed from the Egyptians the doctrine of the immortality of the soul; and if he considered this doctrine an unseemly superstition, remarking that he would not mention the names of these writers, tombstone inscriptions reveal that the hope and the fear of an afterlife became widespread by the fourth century B.C. In that century Isocrates of Athens complained that the old gods were being neglected in favor of foreign gods. Such spiritual traffic with the East naturally grew much heavier after Alexander opened up the *oikoumene* to the Greeks. Now we encounter men of the type of Zeno, a wandering Semite who sounds like a prophet, anticipating St. Paul. Among the masses of Greeks, Oriental deities began flooding the religious market.

As only a nominal Olympian, Diana of Ephesus held her own during this influx, or even gained in majesty. Her mother, who was not tied down to any community, became still more popular all over Asia Minor, arousing little recorded complaint on behalf of the old gods. With Cybele flourished such goddesses as the Syrian Atargatis and the Egyptian Isis. The most striking revelation of the Hellenistic mentality, however, was the success of Serapis—a wholly synthetic deity, invented by a Ptolemy of Egypt in an effort to unify his kingdom. The new god was christened by combining the names of two local gods, Osiris and Apis; then an Athenian sculptor was hired to carve a distinctive image of him, an Athenian philosopher to compose paeans in his honor. Although Serapis was a failure in Egypt, where no Greek upstart could compete with Osiris, he proceeded to travel to the far corners of the Hellenistic world, even reaching India. A late third-century inscription from the island of Delos tells the story: how the god had been brought there by the priest's grandfather, an Egyptian, and how the god then asked the priest in a dream to build a temple, which he did after some opposition from the local authorities. Other inscriptions from Delos reveal that within a generation or so Serapis was receiving as much in alms as was Apollo, who had one of his most famous oracles on this island, while Artemis, Aphrodite, and other Olympians were living on a pittance.

More symptomatic was the popularity of Tyche, representing Fortune or Chance. Supposedly a daughter of Zeus, she seems to have been another artificial deity, invented by early philosophers, and stood apart from both the old and the new gods. While she was irresponsible in her favors, her whims were a source of hope as a possible escape from Necessity, or the severely rational Providence of the Stoics. She was an appropriate deity for a world again full of magic, in which the traditional superstitions were taking on a more morbid, neurotic quality. Exorcism, for example, became a thriving business in the hands of private traders, such as the sons of Scaeva at Ephesus, who long before the Christ of St. Mark specialized in driving out demons.

On higher levels, the most revealing development was the vogue of Chaldean astrology—a superstition of which there is hardly a trace in Greek thought before Alexander's conquest. It had a rational aspect in its implication of universal law; the fate of Hellenistic man, living in a greater cosmopolitan world, was determined not merely by local gods and kings but by cosmic forces. Hence the Stoics were especially prone to believe in the power of the stars. They helped to kill the heliocentric theory of Aristarchus, which is fatal to this belief—and which, ironically, among important astronomers was defended only by a Chaldean, Seleucus of Babylon. Astrology was firmly established by the learned Posidonius of Rhodes, the last great thinker of the Hellenistic Age. A Syrian by birth, Posidonius was still seeking knowledge in all fields, still trying to make men at home in the *oikoumene* and the cosmos; but he was basically uncritical and inconsistent. As a Stoic he accepted the cosmic order as right and good, even to the pain it ordained. "Do your worst, pain, do your worst," he wrote pathetically when in misery; "you will never compel me to acknowledge that you are an evil!" Most men, however, knew that it was an evil, and tried illogically not only to foretell but to escape the fate decreed by the stars. By the Christian era Cybele's son Attis was wearing a starry cap on the coins of Pessinus. Cybele herself was no doubt matching the offer of Isis, who announced, "Fate obeys me."

Still, all these were symptoms rather than causes of the decline of Hellenism. The Oriental mystery and magic cults did not directly attack Greek rationalism, did not create a void—they moved into a void. They force the critical question: Why did the Greeks succumb to them? The obvious answer, the failure of their worldly kingdoms, is still not a sufficient answer. If the Hellenistic kings rehearsed on a larger scale the tragedy of classical Greece, the chronic particularism that had led to incessant strife between the city-states, this was indeed an old story to the Greeks. In Asia they were prospering materially in spite of the wars. Spiritually they were rising above the particularism of the *polis* to wider visions of their interests. Their failure is plain enough; but it is not a simple story, even apart from the destructiveness that almost always results from creative energy.

For one thing, it involved external factors that are commonly neglected because they mess up the tidy logic or wholesome moral that men like to find in history. Moralists have ignored the plausible suggestion of W. H. S. Jones, made long ago, that malaria may have had much to do with the decline in vigor and intellectual courage. There is a great deal of evidence that it became widely prevalent in Greece and Asia Minor during the Hellenistic period. And malaria is a peculiarly disastrous disease, lowering vitality without causing extensive death, leaving its victims liable to nervous debility and despondency.

A more apparent factor beyond the control of the Greeks was the growing strength and ambition of Rome. At the outset of its imperial career Rome had little or no sense of the ideal mission that has induced historians to justify its conquests. It set about to weaken, humiliate, and demoralize Pergamum and Rhodes, its allies—states that were displaying great energy and held a bright promise for the Greek future. It ruthlessly pillaged most of Greece itself, destroying its one prosperous city, Corinth; it entered Asia Minor chiefly to exploit and loot. In combating Rome, moreover, the overworked Hellenistic kings were distracted not only by their wars on one another but by the problems of administering their heterogeneous kingdoms. From the beginning these kingdoms were a *tour de force:* vast states made up of miscellaneous peoples, administered by a relatively few Greeks with no previous experience. The surprising thing is not that they failed but that they accomplished as much, remained as stable, and lasted as long as they did.

Less surprising, but still not simple, was the major development in these kingdoms—the institution of the sacred monarch. The Athenians were the first to give Antigonus and Demetrius the title of kings. Plutarch remarked that "a spirit of pomp and arrogance" thereupon entered the habits of these kings, and concluded, "A single flattering voice effected a revolution in the world." Strictly, this was no revolution: kingship was a Homeric tradition, it had always been the rule in the East, and the Greeks in Asia Minor had long submitted to it. Similarly with the worship of kings, which began when Athens honored Antigonus and Demetrius as Tutelar Deities and Deliverers. The other successors of Alexander received divine honors from other cities, presently their sons had them officially deified, and in Egypt the Ptolemies became gods during their lifetime. This "revolution" too was a reversion to very ancient practice in the East, and to the old Greek cult of hero worship.

Now the Hellenistic kings can hardly be blamed for not instituting large-scale democracy in their kingdoms. Classical Greece had provided them with no parliamentary institutions for such purposes, and in any case their Asiatic subjects were wholly unprepared for self-government. Their motives were no doubt mixed, to some extent honorable as well as practical. The Asiatic idea of claiming divinity was perhaps the most feasible way of meeting the need of legitimacy that they felt as Greeks. Probably neither they nor the bulk of their Greek followers literally believed in their divinity. The educated had grown skeptical about the Olympians themselves, and were familiar with the idea of Euhemerus that the gods had once been mere men. Many common men must have had the pragmatic attitude expressed in a popular song of Athens, addressed to Demetrius: "The other gods either are not, or are far away; either they hear not, or they give no heed; but thou art here, and we can see thee, not in wood or stone, but in very truth." In fact the cities often had good reason to regard the kings as Soters, or Saviors. If the kings deprived them of their cherished freedom to make war on one another, they also protected them from other cities and from barbarians.

Nevertheless the general acceptance of the god-king signified a profound change in Greek mentality, which in the long run did amount to a revolution. Only one of the Hellenistic kings, Antigonus Gonatas, is known to have rejected this Oriental absurdity. (On hearing himself called a god he remarked, "The man who empties my chamberpot has not noticed it.") Otherwise there might be bitter opposition to the king himself, but there seems to have been little rational protest against his claims to divinity. The acquiescence denoted a want of intellectual enterprise and courage, if not of intellectual integrity. Thus one Hecataeus of Abdera was hired by the Ptolemies to write a propaganda history demonstrating that Egypt was the home of the Greek ideal of kingship; so we may recall that centuries before him another Hecataeus, of Miletus, had ridiculed the absurd fables of the Greeks. We are also recalled to the philosophers. They were now concerned primarily with the good life apart from the State; but all the leading schools took time off to justify the institution of monarchy.

Ultimately, the failure of Greek rationalism—the eventual collapse into rhetoric and superstition—was an internal breakdown. The innocent dogmatism of the philosophers, compounded of their faith in metaphysical simplicity, their habit of arbitrary assumption, and their passion for logical consistency at any cost, was fortified by their lofty indifference to practical application or utility. In this indifference they failed to establish any clear criterion of empirical truth. The Skeptics were no more helpful than the Stoics in combating the rising superstition, for in declaring that everything was uncertain they had no way of declaring that superstition was false. Stoics and Epicureans alike could teach a hopelessly unrealistic psychology, trying simply to banish passion, deny the power of the irrational that was to engulf them. And the separation of theory from practice encouraged the growing aloofness of philosophy from the community, the separation of "culture" from the common life, which left the popular mind still more at the mercy of superstition, old and new. All the schools were likely to spurn wealth and denounce the desire for material gain, but all ignored the social, political, and economic problems created by the unequal distribution of wealth. The Stoics proposed no concrete measures to realize their ideal of cosmopolis or universal brotherhood. They were on principle indifferent to poverty.

Meanwhile the disunity that made the Hellenistic kingdoms easy victims of Rome was intensified by a basic problem that the savior-kings, the cities, and the philosophers alike failed to tackle, or even to recognize —the increasing gap between rich and poor, and the cankerous growth of a hostile or apathetic working class. Although, as always, we have little direct knowledge of proletarian life, it was clearly a poor life. Slave labor kept wages miserably low. The workers naturally bore the brunt in hard times or war; they suffered as well from prosperity, which was likely to bring inflation. The rich were liberal enough to give donations to the city in emergencies, but they were not enlightened enough to organize philanthropy, still less to raise wages or institute reforms. In the free play of economic forces the rich got richer, the poor got poorer, and the middle class shrank. Hellenistic history conformed to the Marxist analysis, short of the inevitable revolution, because there was little effort at government regulation or control, and no Marx to arouse and lead the workers.[9] The Age of the Textbook produced no treatises on the economy. No important thinker attacked the moral and economic evil of slavery.

There was still less unity between city and country, or Greek and

[9] In Egypt the Ptolemies did set up a kind of planned economy that conservative historians have labeled "socialist," and that nevertheless made them the wealthiest of the Hellenistic kings; but their controls were designed to promote their own interests, not the interests of the workers and peasants.

Oriental. Upper-class natives became Hellenized to some extent, producing a number of kings, artists, and thinkers who made their mark on the age; the peasant masses were almost untouched. The many new cities founded by the kings were designed primarily to further the commercial and military interests of the Greeks, not to educate, to radiate Greek culture, or to promote fusion. The Greeks never had a missionary zeal for spreading the blessings of freedom or of Hellenism. In one aspect their policy was a becoming tolerance, which also appeared in their habit of intermarrying freely. In another aspect it was simple indifference to the lot of the peasant, or callous exploitation. Viewed either way, it brings us back to the paradoxical end result of Alexander's conquest of the East. The coming of the Greeks left a few striking traces, such as all the statues of Buddha in Asia today. These may be attributed to some anonymous Greek sculptors who, in north India, first taught his worshipers to represent him in human form instead of by symbols; the first appearance of the statues can be dated from coins. But other coins, from the kingdom of Parthia, reveal how thin was the veneer of Greek culture, and how steadily it wore off: each issue grows more Oriental-looking, with kings wearing embroidered robes and assuming grandiloquent titles, until the coinage ends in barbarous stereotypes with almost illegible inscriptions. At most Asia took over some superficial forms of Greek culture, never its spirit. Much deeper and more lasting was the influence of Asia on the uprooted Greeks, through its women and its gods.

All in all, the failure of the Hellenistic world may be summed up as a moral and intellectual failure. The "return of the irrational" points to its ultimate issues, in terms that are now all too pertinent: the fear of freedom, the escape from freedom—from the burden of responsibility, in an open society that forces choices instead of prescribing thought and behavior, and in a universe that leaves man alone. For many men this is still an intolerable burden. It remains an open question whether men at large can learn, and maintain under stress, the habits of self-reliance and responsibility that are required by an open society. The return of the irrational has been a major development of our century. It is the more alarming because this time it has led to not only a flight from reason, in fear or panic, but to a direct attack on the claims of reason, in the name of instinct or intuition, myth or faith, the voice of the blood or of authority. Worse, the voice of unreason is now enormously amplified by the media of mass communication.

But this also points to the radical differences underlying the similarities between the Hellenistic world and our own. Tarn noted the most obvious: "it was a world empty of machines and full of slaves." Some other historians have obscured the differences by attributing the Hellenistic failure to the vulgarization of culture by popular education, but the common man in fact had nothing like the opportunity he now has. Outside the *polis* there was no democracy, and within it neither universal suffrage nor universal education. Nowhere was there anything comparable to modern science and technology, our intellectual as well as material resources. We are at least aware of the power of the irrational, the folly of trying to ignore or simply banish it. We have means of combating as well as of amplifying it.

In this view we can be fairer and kinder to the Hellenistic Age. Given our knowledge of the historic outcome, its failures are likely to be more conspicuous than its creative achievements, which have become part of our unconscious heritage; yet Alexander's conquest of the East remains an extraordinary adventure, and its aftermath another striking proof of the versatility, flexibility, and originality of the Greeks. Their failure to master the *oikoumene* is as understandable as the failure of classical Athens in the first adventure in democracy. Our historical knowledge enables us to appreciate, as they could not, the truth stated by Whitehead: "The major advances in civilisation are processes which all but wreck the societies in which they occur." Then a later people, such as the Romans, may profit by the advance and restore order. The Hellenistic Greeks at least held the fort until the Romans were ready to take over; and at that they handed over no mere wreck. To the end their cities had shown their spirit in their passion for autonomy, their enthusiasm—however misguided—over potential liberators. They still had enough energy and vitality to recover from their misfortunes. They continued to educate the Romans and the early Christians, and so passed on their heritage to Byzantine and Western civilization. Other periods in history have been more brilliant; but few have had a deeper, wider, more lasting influence.

4. THE DEATH AND RESURRECTION OF DIANA

When the last king of Pergamum bequeathed his kingdom to Rome, Ephesus became the seat of the Roman governor of the province by now called Asia. It therefore continued to witness a parade of the most famous men of antiquity. From here Mithridates the Great, in his guise of liberator, ordered the wholesale massacre of the Romans in Asia Minor— an affair in which the long-suffering Ephesians co-operated enthusiastically, not even sparing the Roman suppliants at the altar of Diana. Two years later they knew him better and shut their gates against him; so his conqueror, Lucullus, honored the city with the first gladiatorial show known to have been staged in Asia Minor. Pompey, who finally destroyed

Mithridates, ended his triumphal tour of Asia Minor at Ephesus, sailing off to Rome with his immense booty. Julius Caesar, the conqueror of Pompey, sailed in to make amends to the Greek cities and to reform the tax system from which they had suffered. The grateful Ephesians set the style for the East by honoring Caesar as "a god made manifest, and the common savior of all human life"—a worthy husband for Diana, it would seem, had she not been so set against matrimony.

More symbolic as well as more dramatic was the coming of Mark Antony, victor over the assassins Brutus and Cassius. Because they had imposed terrific levies on the cities, he was hailed as another liberator, and as the incarnation of Dionysus. "When he made his entry into Ephesus," writes Plutarch, "the women met him dressed up like Bacchantes, and the men and boys like satyrs and fauns, and throughout the town nothing was to be seen but spears wreathed about with ivies, and harps, flutes, and psalteries." The festivities continued as Antony wintered here in 33–32 B.C. and prepared for his final struggle with Octavius, the Emperor Augustus to be, summoning ships and troops from all over Asia and Africa. He was joined by Cleopatra, who brought a large fleet and some millions in gold to add to the splendor of the spectacle. The city was thronged with soldiers and sailors—Romans, Egyptians, Gauls, Moors, Thracians, Armenians, Paphlagonians, Cilicians, Cappadocians— and with dancers, lute players, acrobats, comedians, and prostitutes to entertain the warriors. While Cleopatra dominated the scene, at the cost of some dissension among the Romans, the Asiatic kings vied with one another in the daily parades, shows, and banquets, in anticipation of the glorious triumph. "Merciless as usual to the conquered," wrote Ferrero, "history has stigmatized these rejoicings upon the eve of the final struggle as shameful folly; but the more attentive ear can distinguish across the centuries the agony of the death-throes in the distant echo of these festivities." For in one aspect this was a struggle of Cleopatra against Rome: a final desperate effort by the last of the Macedonian dynasties. Had her nose been shorter, or her sailors sturdier, the whole course of history might indeed have been changed.

The Ephesians missed the moral, if any. The festivities had not been gratis, for Antony too had imposed a huge levy on Asia Minor, collecting nine years' taxes in advance. In victory Octavius was much more lenient and equitable. With him began the era of peace and prosperity that was to last for over two hundred years, and to make Ephesus richer than ever. Its population rose to at least 200,000. And as it throve at the gateway to the East, its religious life grew still more luxuriant.

Diana still dominated it, in so queenly a fashion that she was known as

Ephesia in many places. The Roman jurist Ulpian mentioned her as one of the few local deities to whom it was permissible to bequeath property under Roman law. She now grew coarser, however. In the Roman era her images acquired their monstrous cluster of breasts, accentuating her primitive functions as a fertility goddess that had been decently veiled in the Hellenistic Age. The other glimpses we catch of her worshipers suggest a restless, feverish kind of piety. Specialists in incantations and magical formulas were so numerous and popular that these became known as "Ephesian writings." Among the celebrities accorded an enthusiastic reception was Apollonius of Tyana, the miracle-working sage and holy man; he ended a local plague by telling the citizens to stone a beggar who was really a demon in disguise. A later woman philosopher, Sosibia of Ephesus, got her start in life from two demons, who brought her up from childhood by disguising themselves as field workers and hiring out to her father. The Neoplatonist philosopher Maximus, who in Ephesus taught philosophy to Julian the Apostate, acquired some fame by causing the image in the local temple of Hecate to smile.

But by this time Diana was no longer reigning over her city. It had also had famous Christian visitors, beginning with St. Paul and St. John. Among them were Justin Martyr and Bishop Ignatius of Antioch, the latter en route to martyrdom at Rome; with Smyrna, Ephesus became known as the "Gateways of the Martyrs." The local tradition of miracle and mystery likewise attracted legendary visitors. The Babylonian magic number that had given the city one of the Seven Wonders of the World and Seven Churches of Asia now produced the Seven Sleepers: Christian youths who were sealed up in a local cave during a Roman persecution, and who emerged like Rip Van Winkles two centuries later, to edify the awestruck townspeople with high discourse about God until they were called to heaven in the evening. (Later they talked their way into the Koran too.) Diana might have held her own in normal times, but the prosperity of Ephesus declined sharply as the Roman Empire began to disintegrate in the third century. When the Goths sacked the city and destroyed the great temple, toward the end of the century, her worshipers were apparently too poor and disheartened to restore it. At least it was in ruins in the next century, and thereafter served only to provide marble for Christian builders.

The city of Diana, however, not only survived the fall of Rome but even regained some of its splendor as the West went into the darkness. When St. Paul's church became the imperial religion, it grew kinder to business and worldly goods. It also chose to disregard the flat Biblical injunction against graven images, thereby permitting the growth of Christian art and the survival of pagan idolatry; artisans whose forefathers in Ephesus had cried out for the blood of St. Paul were in time making new images, icons of the Mother he ignored. Pilgrims flocked with gifts to the new shrines, where the bones of saints and martyrs worked the old wonders. Ephesus became a major Christian center. Two Church councils met here in the fifth century to wrangle furiously over the new beliefs necessary for everlasting bliss.

The shade of Diana—still immortal, but now a demon—might have been mystified by these councils, especially the first. This "Robber Council" was a struggle between two ambitious bishops, Cyril of Alexandria and Nestorius of Antioch. The devout, or unscrupulous, Cyril achieved the necessary unanimity by convening the council before the chief opposition bishops arrived, and stationing guards to confine the rest of the bishops until he had forced through a condemnation of Nestorius. A rabble of Egyptian monks provided a weird contrast to the festivities that had gladdened the Ephesians in the dim past when Cleopatra and her Egyptians had come to town. "They acted in everything as if it was a war they were conducting," wrote Nestorius, "and went about in the city girt and armed with clubs, men with high necks, performing strange antics with the yells of barbarians, snorting fiercely with horrible and unwonted noises, raging with extravagant arrogance against those whom they knew to be opposed to their doings, carrying bells about the city, and lighting fires in many places and casting into them all kinds of writings." Nevertheless the Ephesians, and perhaps the shade of Diana, rejoiced in this uproar. The chief issue at stake was the insistence of Nestorius on the genuine human nature as well as the divinity of Christ— an idea ethically inspiring, but theologically monstrous in its implication of a split personality. ("May those who divide Christ be divided with the sword," proclaimed the next Christian synod that met at Ephesus, "may they be hewn in pieces, may they be burned alive!") Worse, Nestorius attacked as a pagan fable Mary's title of Mother of God, with its implication that God had worn diapers. The Ephesians championed the honor of Mary the more ardently because they believed that her body was buried within their walls. Cyril was able to rush through in a day the official proclamation of her title, and although a bloody conflict ensued when the opposition bishops arrived five days later, this proclamation was never revoked.

Thereafter the chief glory of Ephesus was the Church of St. John, built in the sixth century by the Emperor Justinian who built Hagia Sophia in Constantinople. It drew large annual revenues down to the Middle Ages. Yet the city was slowly dying. It was no longer a gateway to Rome or to the East, now that all roads led to Constantinople. Under the Byzantine emperors it lost the autonomy it had enjoyed under Diana, and with it evidently lost much of its spirit. It continued to decline even though it exchanged its name for the holy name of St. John, Hagios Theologos. In the fourteenth century it was revived for a time by the Seljuk Turks, under the corrupted name of Aya Soluk. They made it a provincial capital and adorned it with handsome buildings; the traveler ibn-Batuta found it a large town notable especially for a cathedral mosque, "formerly a church greatly venerated by the Greeks." It had just enough luster to attract history of the conventional bloody kind, falling to the Knights of St. John of Jerusalem, then to the Ottoman Turks, then to Tamerlane and his Mongols. In 1426 it came permanently under Ottoman rule, thereafter to make no more history, and to dwindle into a wretched hamlet, the resort only of camel drivers.

But the memory of Diana's temple was green enough to attract archaeologists. Although the site had long since been obliterated by a caprice of the Caÿster River, which meandered over to cover it with a layer of ooze, the Englishman Wood started looking for it in the last century. After six years of searching under a broiling sun, in a region infested with malaria, he at last found it. Early in this century Hogarth dug down to the lowest foundation—after a comparable perseverance because of the water and slime that kept oozing in—and uncovered a hoard of jewelry and ivory statuettes in the first House of Diana.[10] Later excavations uncovered much of the ancient city, as well as the Church of St. John. They helped to restore a measure of prosperity to Ephesus, which is now a bright little village known as Seljuk.

Most promising, however, is a discovery that brings back the magic of Diana's city. Early in the last century a German nun, Catherine Emmerich, had visions of the life of Mary, including a detailed one of a house in Ephesus where Mary spent her last years. At the end of the century a group of clerics set out to look for this house, and after many days of fruitless search were finally guided by Greek peasants to some remains that corresponded closely to Catherine's description. Local tradition, they learned, held that the Virgin had died on this site, known as Panaya Kapulu; the Greeks in the vicinity had long celebrated mass here on August 15, the supposed day of her death. Archaeologists lent partial

---

[10] In *The Wandering Scholar*, Hogarth left a moving account of the hardships and heartbreaks of excavation, and also of the rewards. The hoard, amounting to some three thousand objects, was a treasure of early Ionian art. It revealed that by 700 B.C. the Ionians were already highly skilled craftsmen but were still using Egyptian and Mesopotamian motifs.

confirmation by reporting that while most of the building was of Byzantine construction, part of the walls might date from the first century. And although the generally accepted Christian tradition places the death and burial of Mary in Jerusalem, this did not appear until five centuries after her death, and is supported only by apocryphal texts. An older tradition that she died in Ephesus seems more plausible because St. John records in his Gospel that the dying Jesus confided Mary to his care, and early Christian texts agree that John spent his last years here.[11] At any rate, pilgrims began visiting Panaya Kapulu; soon a number of miraculous cures were reported; the Vatican lent a favorable ear to the news. The campaign to build up the shrine was interrupted by the war between the Turks and the Greeks, but in recent years the chapel has been restored and a hostelry put up nearby. Pilgrims are coming again in increasing numbers, on August 15 in crowds. With the collaboration of the Vatican and the Turkish Tourist Bureau, Ephesus may well become a famous shrine once more.

Meanwhile an ordinary traveler might not be edified by the clay images of the Virgin, made from the holy soil, that the "Ephesus Corporation" offers for sale on the spot. He might be skeptical of the whole business. Still, Panaya Kapulu has a hallowed air. The little shrine stands humbly on a mountainside behind Ephesus; it was and is a secluded spot, facing away from the city, looking out on a magnificent view of mountains rolling to the sea. One imagines that the historic mother might well have retired here "to get away from it all." At least it is a fitting idea, poetically and historically. In the stillness one may reflect on man's continued hunger for miracle and mystery. On August 15, Diana's day, one may hear ghostly echoes of the cry that as a mother Mary might have come to understand: "Great is Diana of the Ephesians!"

[11] One serious objection to this tradition is that St. Paul failed to mention her presence in Ephesus, despite his long stay in the city. But it may be answered that Paul was apparently ignorant of the virgin birth, since he never referred to it either; and for that matter he neglected to mention the presence of St. John, or even of St. Peter in Rome.

CHAPTER VI

Tarsus: The Mission of St. Paul

1. THE EARLY HISTORY OF CILICIA

AS WE TOOK leave of the Hittites, at Karatepe, we encountered a little king who built a palace here about the year 700 B.C. He called himself King Azitawadda, and his fortress Azitawaddiya; it crowned a hill between the Pyramus River and a caravan road to the East. On the bilingual inscriptions lining the two main entrances, he narrated his royal achievements on behalf of his people, the Danuna. With the help of his god Baal and another great king, he had led them on a march of conquest from Syria into the plain of Adana (Hittite Ataniya), where he now had his capital. By his own wisdom he had brought the blessings of justice and prosperity upon his people. He concluded his narrative with the usual ceremonial curse, invoking the wrath of Baal upon any other king so bold as to try to move his statue into this city, or to undo his work. He seems modest and decent as Oriental kings go, since he boasted of his justice rather than the number of people he had slaughtered or enslaved. But even so he was vain enough to look ludicrous now.

Azitawadda was plainly an insignificant king, ruling a small kingdom only by the grace of some more powerful monarch. One may suspect that he boasted of no great victories for the simple reason that he had won none. The sculptured reliefs commemorating his piety and his pride are crude, naïve, almost childlike. And his fortress had so short a life that two of the reliefs were never finished. Probably it fell to the Assyrians, slightly swelling the number of slaughtered or enslaved recorded on their royal monuments. Whoever destroyed it seems to have looted it thoroughly, for aside from the invariable potsherds excavators found only an arrowhead and a tool; but the poor quality of its pottery and its unimposing sculpture and architecture suggest that its conquerors got little wealth for their pains. The only reason no other king moved his statue into the palace is that none thought it worth occupying. While the caravan road

173

was a well-traveled route—important enough to attract the Crusaders, who built a castle in the valley below—Azitawaddiya remained deserted to this day.

As we have seen, however, the event was to give a more humane twist to the irony. By recording his deeds in both Phoenician and "classical" Hittite, this boastful little king contributed more to posterity than he could possibly have imagined in his most vainglorious dreams. His naïve inscriptions and reliefs illumine an age of fantastic fusions, which in turn illumines the historically far more important age to follow. Apparently his Danuna had entered Syria from the sea at about the same time as the Biblical Philistines; probably they were the Dananians whom Egyptian scribes listed among the Sea Peoples. In Syria they adopted the Phoenician script and their god Baal, but also picked up ideas from more ancient civilizations. The reliefs depict Mesopotamian as well as Hittite motifs, and include a grotesque figure of an Egyptian fertility god. They even suggest Greek influence in one or two motifs, for instance, a goddess who displays the "archaic smile" as she suckles her infant. Most curious, Azitawadda claimed descent from "Mupshu"—the Greek Mopsus, hero of the Trojan War, whom other cities in the plain of Adana claimed as their founder. Hence the little king gives us an insight into the background of a much greater city on the plain, the city of Tarsus, which had been founded more than two thousand years before his time, and was to endure down to our time. Against this background we may better understand the mission of its most famous son—the Saul of Tarsus who became St. Paul, the Apostle of the Gentiles.

The whole region became known as Cilicia, though it was made up of two disparate parts. Cilicia Aspera (or Trachea) to the north is rugged mountain country falling to a rocky coast, with almost no fertile land. Cilicia Campestris, a rich plain watered by three rivers, has always been the garden spot of Asia Minor. It is hemmed in by the lofty Taurus Mountains, through which a spectacular gorge, the Cilician Gates, served as the main passage into the interior. Lying on the trade route between Syria and Anatolia, and facing west, the plain very early began preparing itself for the fusions and confusions of its later history. Its inhabitants had relations with pre-Sumerian Mesopotamia, with Egypt, with Cyprus and Crete, with Troy II, III, and V. Excavations at Yümük Tepe, a mound near Mersin, to the north of Tarsus, have laid bare sixteen main levels, going back as usual to the Early Bronze Age, and soundings beneath them indicate more than forty floors of occupation by neolithic peoples, going back to 6000 B.C., many centuries before the Anatolian plateau was inhabited. At Tarsus itself Gözlü Tepe has told a similar

The walls of Troy (p. 63)
Photograph by Halet Çambel

Eski Antalya: Village guesthouse on the sea walls
of ancient Side (p. 356). *Photograph by the author*

Bogazköy: From the procession of deities at the
Hittite shrine of Yazilikaya (p. 48)

Late Hittite sculpture, from Zinjirli
(p. 50)

Gordium: Phrygian inscription. *Courtesy The University Museum, Philadelphia*

Greek coins

Lysimachus (c. 300 B.C.): the deified Alexander; reverse, Athena holding winged victory (p. 155)

Tarsus (c. 375 B.C.): Ares; reverse, local Baal with the scepter of Zeus (p. 175)

Ephesus: the bee and the stag, symbols of Diana (p. 140)

Author's coins, photograph by American Numismatic Society

Gordium: Phrygian architectural ornaments in limestone
Courtesy The University Museum, Philadelphia

Gordium: The gate of the Phrygian city (p. 42)
Courtesy The University Museum, Philadelphia

Modern Amasya on the ancient Iris River (p. 377)

Modern Amasya, the rock tombs of the Persian kings and the citadel in
the background (p. 377)

The harbor of Antalya, with the sea walls of ancient Attaleia (p. 421)

The Sacred Way of Ephesus (p. 144)

Ephesus: The library of Celsus

Promenade in the Asclepium of Pergamum, sacred spring at the lower right (p. 396)

The great theater of Pergamum (p. 392)

In the Roman agora of Smyrna (p. 399)

The temple of Cybele at Sardis, Byzantine church in foreground (p. 386)

Floor mosaic from Antioch (p. 404)

Lycian rock tombs at Myra (Demre), bishopric of St. Nicholas (p. 389)

St. Nicholas of Myra, as reproduced on a Turkish postage stamp (p. 389)

Frescoes by the Cappadocian "troglodytes" (p. 254)

Göreme: Cappadocian rock chapel

Landscape near Ürgüp: Cappadocian rock dwellings and chapels

The "petrified valley" of Göreme, vicinity of Ürgüp,
with Cappadocian hermitage (p. 254)

The harbor of Bodrum (ancient Halicarnassus), with the castle of the
Knights of Rhodes (p. 421)

Site of the Byzantine Hippodrome in Constantinople, Hagia Sophia at the left,
Sultan Ahmed Mosque (or the Blue Mosque) at the right

Gate of the Seljuk Mosque of Inje Minare in Konya (p. 281)

Seljuk khan at Caesarea (Kayseri) (p. 416)

Kiz Kalesi ("Maiden's Castle"), off the Cilician coast (p. 320)

Panaya Kapulu: the home of the Virgin Mary in Ephesus, as restored (p. 172)

Yerebatan Saray, Byzantine cistern in Istanbul (p. 367)

The Bosphorus from Rumeli Hisar, the castle built by
Mohammed the Conqueror (p. 369)

Hagia Sophia, interior (p. 243). (For scale, note man standing at lower left.)
Courtesy Archaeological Museum, Istanbul

story. Among the diverse findings here were Minoan artifacts, Hittite seals, Mycenaean pottery, and Assyrian clay tablets.

Both Tarsus and Mersin were Hittite strongholds of some importance, well built and prosperous, in a kingdom known as Kizzuwatna. Then came a period of disturbance, during which Mycenaean ware appears— the Greeks always brought trouble to the ancient world. About 1200 B.C. Tarsus and Mersin suffered the familiar fate: a burned layer appears in both mounds. At some time thereafter Greeks settled among the older inhabitants of the region. Homer placed the "Kilikes" in the southern Troad (among them were Andromache, the wife of Hector); but wherever they came from, they brought memories of the Trojan War, which King Azitawadda picked up.

The coming of the Assyrians is of some interest because this was their only appearance in western Asia Minor, and their only known clash with the Greeks. In the eighth century Shalmaneser III recorded his conquest of "Tarzi," indicating that the name of the city was an ancient one, and recalling that the Bible lists Tarshish as one of the sons of Yavan, or Ion. Sargon, who made Cilicia an Assyrian province, boasted of catching the ships of Yavan "like fish" off the coast of Cyprus. Nevertheless Sennacherib had to put down a rebellion, in which Tarsus joined other cities. The story goes that he rebuilt the city in imitation of Babylon, and left his famous inscription on the so-called monument of Sardanapalus, at Anchiale in Cilicia Aspera: "I built Tarsus and Anchiale on the same day. But thou, stranger, eat, drink, and be merry; for all else is worthless." Aristotle commented that this inscription was fitting for the tomb of an ox, not a king, but Sennacherib was at least prophetic. Within a generation the Assyrians lost control of Cilicia, and in another generation or so their empire was no more. The legend of Sardanapalus was about the only lasting memento of their stay in Cilicia.

The land regained its independence under native kings who bore the Oriental name or title of Syennesis, and had their capital at Tarsus. They were powerful enough to serve with Nebuchadnezzar of Babylon in arranging a peace treaty between the Medes and the Lydians, and later to maintain at least a nominal independence under the Persian Empire. Xenophon tells of how Cyrus the Younger made his peace with Syennesis after some initial hostilities, and then spent several weeks in Tarsus, among other things negotiating with his balky Greek mercenaries. One of the coins struck in the city a little later epitomizes its mongrel tradition. It bears the name of a Persian satrap in Aramaic script, the language used for commerce throughout the Persian Empire, and later spoken by Christ. On one side appears the helmeted head of the Greek god Ares. On the other the local Baal, also with an Aramaic name, is represented in the form of Zeus, seated on a throne and holding a scepter. A bunch of grapes in the margin, or sometimes an ear of corn, indicates that he had been an Anatolian peasant god—a hard-working god, who in this region was therefore often identified with Heracles. He got little help from the local goddess, a minor deity of uncertain ancestry. For the Great Mother of Anatolia failed to queen it over Cilicia, perhaps because of the strong Semitic influence here. St. Paul's complete indifference to Mary becomes more understandable.

It was most probably the energy and resourcefulness of its Greek inhabitants that made Tarsus the greatest city of Cilicia, enabling St. Paul to remark proudly that he was a "citizen of no mean city." For Tarsus had no natural advantages. It lay on a small mound on an ordinary little river, the Cydnus, some miles inland from the sea. In the Roman era Dio Chrysostom made fun of its pride, dwelling on the relative inferiority of its beloved river, its climate, and its location. Adana was more advantageously situated in the center of the plain—and today is by far the greatest city in the region. But the Tarsians had early set to work with an eye to trade. They dredged the Cydnus to make it navigable, and made over into an inland harbor a swampy lake that lay between them and the sea. They cut a road through the rock of the Cilician Gates, which for centuries was the only wagon road through the Taurus Mountains. This remained one of the most important passes in history.

The critical turning point in the history of Tarsus came in 334 B.C., when Alexander the Great marched down through the Cilician Gates and liberated the city. He almost died on the spot from a chill caught bathing in the icy waters of the Cydnus; so one might ponder how much difference sheer accident can make in history. Spared by the gods, Alexander proceeded to win his decisive victory over Darius at Issus, to the south of the Cilician plain. (The Seleucids commemorated his victory by founding nearby the city of Alexandria-ad-Issum, later to be known as Alexandretta and today as Iskenderun—a major port for the entrance of American military supplies to Turkey.) Henceforth Tarsus was a real *polis*, if never a wholly independent one. The Seleucid kings moved new colonists into the city. While retaining the legend of its foundation by Sardanapalus, it invented more Greek founders and became more Hellenized.

In particular it took to philosophy. Chrysippus, the successor of Zeno, came from Tarsus, and he was in turn succeeded as head of the Stoic school by Zeno of Tarsus. The city became the main seat of Stoicism. Strabo, who ranked its schools ahead of those of Athens and Alexandria in their ardor for philosophy and encyclopedic learning, remarked on the fluency of its inhabitants in lengthy, impromptu discourse on any given subject. Meanwhile its Oriental inhabitants, notably its Jews, were maintaining their ancient traditions, and no doubt were voluble enough. For such reasons Sir William Ramsay saw "the perfection of a Divine purpose" in the choice of Tarsus as the birthplace of the Apostle of the Gentiles. God, he wrote in *The Cities of St. Paul*, chose it as the "one suitable place" because it most completely and perfectly united Hellenism and the Orient.

First, however, God arranged to have the Romans take it over; though he worked in devious ways that long tended to obscure the Divine purpose. The preliminary phase was the emergence of Cilicia Aspera, hitherto a historical backwater. Ancient temple-states controlled the mountainous, almost inaccessible interior, little affected by the few Greek towns along the coast.[1] But in the second century B.C. the people of this hinterland at last realized their historic destiny by adopting the profession of piracy, for which Cilicia Aspera was ideally suited. They could slip in and out of the many little coves along their rocky coast to prey on shipping; they could store and defend their booty in the many natural fortresses of their wild, rugged country. In time they grew so powerful that they were raiding and sacking seaports all over the eastern Mediterranean, carrying on an especially profitable traffic in slaves. The Romans, who had given them their opportunity by weakening the sea power of Rhodes, now sent expeditions to subdue them, but with humiliating results. Finally, after one complete fiasco, they called on the great Pompey, who crushed them. In the course of restoring order, Pompey introduced in Tarsus the privilege of Roman citizenship that Saul was to inherit. From here he went on to assure Rome the dominion of all Asia Minor.

Like the Greeks elsewhere, the Cilicians at first had some excuse for failing to recognize this as a heavenly boon: the tax collectors did not act like agents of a divine purpose.[2] As the capital of the province, Tarsus

[1] The most important of these towns was Soli, reputedly founded by Athenians. Their language became corrupted and so gave rise to the word *solecism*.

[2] The fate reserved for Pompey himself was more appropriate to Greek tragedy than a Christian morality play. Upon completing his victorious campaigns in the East, he returned to Rome to enjoy the most magnificent triumph on record, one that took up two full days. He retired to private life with becoming dignity, possibly to ponder the lectures on philosophy that he had attended at Rhodes; but before long he had to ponder the ingratitude of the jealous Roman Senate and the ambition of Julius Caesar. In his eventual struggle with Caesar, wrote Plutarch, he lost in one hour "all that glory and power that he had been getting in so many years and bloody battles." He fled to Asia Minor, then to Egypt. Here his fate was decided by the advisers of the young king Ptolemy, in particular a eunuch and a hired Greek rhetorician; they thought it politic to lure Pompey ashore and stab him in the back.

experienced all the vicissitudes of the new regime. Its citizens must have been grateful for the arrival of Cicero as governor. If he was not too dignified in his pursuit of fame, taking the title of Imperator after a piddling campaign against some bandits, he was a conscientious governor and maintained a relatively honest, economical administration despite the protests of influential men in Rome (especially the noble Brutus); he himself marveled that he brought home only some $100,000 from his year in Cilicia. The Tarsians were positively enthusiastic in their welcome of Caesar, even renaming their city Juliopolis. But then came Cassius, busy in another civil war; he confiscated the entire wealth of the city. And the hand of God was still not apparent in the next scene, the most famous in the history of Tarsus: Cleopatra arrived, to make the acquaintance of Mark Antony. Plutarch described the scene:

She came sailing up the river Cydnus in a barge with gilded stern and outspread sails of purple, while oars of silver beat time to the music of flutes and fifes and harps. She herself lay under a canopy of cloth of gold, dressed as Venus in a picture, and beautiful young boys, like painted Cupids, stood on each side to fan her. Her maids were dressed like sea nymphs and graces, some steering at the rudder, some working at the ropes. The perfumes diffused themselves from the vessel to the shore, which was covered with multitudes, part following the galley up the river on either bank, part running out of the city to see the sight. The market place was quite emptied, and Antony at last was left alone sitting upon the tribunal; while the word went through all the multitude that Venus was come to feast with Bacchus, for the common good of Asia.

It seemed to be for the good of Tarsus, at least. As a recompense for its sufferings at the hands of Cassius, Antony made it a "free city," governed by its own laws. Augustus confirmed its privileges. Still, the mixed multitudes that deserted Antony to gape at Venus-Cleopatra—the fateful historic scene that was staged like a Hollywood extravaganza—make a rather lurid prelude to the mission of St. Paul, one he would scarcely have appreciated. The fusion of Hellenism and the Orient in Tarsus seems not so perfect as Ramsay would have it. There was something hectic in the air. Another suggestive incident was the return of the philosopher Athenodorus, a son of Tarsus who had been the tutor of the youthful Augustus and was now his friend and counselor. Sent by the Emperor to reform its administration and deal with a clique that was plundering a gymnasium, the venerable philosopher was openly mocked in his native

---

The epilogue, however, was more becoming. When offered the head of Pompey, Caesar burst into tears and ordered the execution of his murderers; and though the rhetorician escaped, he was finally caught in Asia Minor and put to a shameful death.

city. "Action for the young, counsel for the middle-aged, discharging wind for the old," some giddy Stoics had written on the walls; and at night they committed nuisances at his door. "We may perceive the sickly condition of the city," Athenodorus told the popular assembly, "from many circumstances, but particularly from its discharges." In jest he spoke perhaps more truly than he knew. As Tarsus went on to enjoy an immense prosperity, it grew more extravagant, flaunting its pride in its mythical founders, its heroes, its imperial benefactors—but not its son Paul. Ramsay was strangely silent about the Christians in the ideal birth-place of the Apostle of the Gentiles.

One reason for all this was a deeper subtlety in the divine purpose. The followers of St. Paul were to profit more from the failures than from the grand achievements of the Roman Empire, both of which we shall consider presently. First we must take up a further complication. The Apostle might have been influenced by Athenodorus, who as a moral philosopher was highly esteemed and widely quoted. He would have found congenial, for example, this maxim of the old Stoic: "Know that you are free from all passions only when you have reached the point that you ask God for nothing except what you can ask openly." Yet Paul had gone to a different school. "I am verily a man which am a Jew," he averred, and "so worship I the God of my father, believing all things which are written in the law and in the prophets." Long before, God had contrived to introduce his chosen people into Asia Minor. The colony at Tarsus believed things that were strange alike to Hellenes and to other Orientals, and that deeply affected both the Christians and the Moslems after them. Nevertheless these beliefs did not make for a perfect fusion of East and West.

2. THE JEWS IN ASIA MINOR

"This people," wrote Strabo of the Jews, "has already made its way into every city, and it is not easy to find any place in the habitable world that has not received this nation." The Diaspora began with the fall of Jerusalem to the Babylonians in the sixth century B.C. In Asia Minor the major influx of Jews started after the conquest of Alexander. The Seleucids had a high regard for them as colonists, settling them in their new foundations at Tarsus as at Apamea and elsewhere. Although in Palestine they had been primarily an agricultural people, they now concentrated on trade and finance; and many prospered in this age of business. Generally they were not a poor, despised minority but a more or less aristocratic faction, loyal to the kings or the Roman rulers-to-be. Their success in the trade center of Tarsus is indicated by the privileges Paul enjoyed. Though a tentmaker, he was an educated man and a Roman citizen.

As all this suggests, there was considerable assimilation, preparing the way for Christianity. The Jews were not, after all, an utterly God-fearing people. One reason why their prophets so insistently denounced worldly interests and false gods was that the people were so susceptible to the worship of mammon and Baal. In Asia Minor they came to feel quite at home. Judging by inscriptions, many took Greek names or mates, and by the Roman era they often filled high municipal positions, even priest-hoods. In some cities, such as Smyrna and Philadelphia, Yahweh himself assumed the name of Zeus Hypistos, the "Most High God." Even in Palestine Hellenization went so far that three successive high priests of the second century B.C. adopted Greek names (Jesus becoming Jason), while we hear of many lesser priests who neglected their duties because of the new passion for athletics. The author of Ecclesiastes was mani-festly acquainted with Greek philosophy, and the original author of Job may have been too. In Alexandria there appeared the first Jewish philos-ophers, who aspired to a synthesis of Judaism and Hellenism. Philo de-veloped the idea that Scripture has an inner meaning, which is Greek philosophy—an idea that was to be generally accepted in Christian, Jewish, and Moslem philosophy.

The Greeks in turn showed some interest in the peculiar people and their God. According to Josephus, when Aristotle first met a Jew he recognized him as a member of a race of philosophers. (Apparently they got this reputation from their odd habit of discussing religion in their temples.) The common people considered Jewish magicians the equal of any. Yahweh, under the name of Iao, was well enough known as a god of power to appear in ancient curses. He became associated with Greek and Persian ideas in the "Hypistarii," a sect that survived for some centuries; St. Gregory of Nazianzus at first belonged to it. In Cilicia a society of Sabbatistae evidently confused him with Zeus Sabazius.

Yet Judaism had a negligible influence on the Greeks until Paul set out on his missionary journeys. They knew little of the history of Israel, and nothing of its great literature. Strabo dismissed Palestine in a single sen-tence, as a land to which Arabians brought loads of aromatics. And the more devout Jews were not merely indifferent but fiercely hostile to Hellenism. They were not actually a race of philosophers, least of all in their homeland. Here the Maccabees led a successful revolt against both Greeks and Hellenized Jews, and the later King Herod—an able monarch and a favorite of the Emperor Augustus—incurred a violent hatred by his addiction to Greek culture. Elsewhere the food laws and the jealous God

of the Jews were always likely to make them seem antisocial and
atheistical. In Alexandria outbursts of anti-Semitism occurred even before
the Christian era. In Asia Minor we hear of little disturbance except that
occasioned by the preaching of Paul and his followers; probably many or
even most of the Jews here became completely assimilated, like the lost
brethren in Phrygia lamented in the Talmud.[3] But by the same token
these lost their identity, disappeared from history. Those who made history were the many others who remained loyal to the law and the
prophets of Israel.

Granted that Judaism retained much prehistoric superstition in ritual
and taboo—the primeval touch of nature that makes the religions of the
whole world kin—it was strictly a unique religion, radically different
from all others in the East. The great prophets had made it the purest,
loftiest monotheism that the world had yet known, or would know until
the rise of Allah. Israel had no Divine Family, no Great Mother, no Dying
Son, no Divine King on earth. It had only Yahweh, who was wholly
transcendent. While its psalms and its New Year festivals contained relics
of ancient fertility cults, Yahweh was now out of this world, with no
responsibilities for bringing new life in the spring; and while he was intensely concerned about the affairs of his chosen people, there was no
thought of his suffering or dying for them. The prophets severed the
ancient bonds between man, nature, and divinity, in effect devaluating
both man and nature to confine value to God alone. They made heavier
demands upon man by declaring that God no longer welcomed seasonal
sacrifices, but was pleased only by righteousness, in complete subservience. Although he had made covenants with their forefathers, and
revealed to the later prophets that he would send or appoint a Messiah,
first they foretold that he would destroy the nation for its wickedness,
and cause to perish all but a "saving remnant."

Judaism was as unique in its exclusiveness. Yahweh had at first tacitly
acknowledged the existence of other gods, commanding only that his
people should have no others before him, but in his absolute sovereignty
he eventually refused to tolerate any rivals whatever. He grew more
relentlessly uncompromising as his people eyed the seemingly more
powerful gods of the greater nations around them, or the seemingly more
fruitful Mother Goddesses; he announced that these were all false gods.
And because he was the one and only lord of all creation, his chosen

[3] One of the few inscriptions bearing a Jewish name is notable for its pagan spirit:
"I Aurelius Moses, son of Karpus, having been everywhere often and having often
investigated the world, now lie in death no longer knowing anything—but this only:
'Be of good courage, no man is immortal.'"

people were set apart in a manner unknown to other peoples, whose tribal deities at their most ambitious never sought to annihilate all other deities. The greater prophets taught that this high privilege was an awful responsibility: the people had been chosen to lead all mankind to the knowledge of the one God, and first must themselves play the part of the "suffering servant." Still, they had a unique destiny.

Now this lofty faith had ugly as well as pathetic aspects, which were accentuated by the tragic history of Israel. Its pure monotheism has been called "spiritual totalitarianism"; its universalism was rooted in provincialism, a simple ignorance of other religions or a bigoted refusal to consider their claims; its righteousness was always prone to a dangerous self-righteousness. Only the greater prophets, in their most exalted moods, had attained a spirit of true universality; and there was little prophetic inspiration in the centuries immediately before Christ. Israel sought to preserve the purity of its faith chiefly by the formalism of the Pharisees and the fanaticism of the Zealots. The apocalyptic writings stressed a message of vengeance on the enemies rather than of hope for mankind; their hope was for the faithful among the chosen people. The Hellenized Jews could be as presumptuous. Some tried to prove that their culture was the oldest in the world, the source of all others. One Artapanus made Moses the inventor of almost everything, from weapons and ships to philosophy.

For better or worse, at any rate, Judaism was a major element in the heritage of Saul of Tarsus. He had left his ideal birthplace to go to school in Jerusalem under the Pharisees, and he entered history as a savage persecutor of the followers of Jesus. Certainly he was not a typical son of Tarsus. Then Saul had his crucial mystical experience, as the resurrected Jesus spoke to him from the heavens and he fell to the earth, blinded for three days. Thereafter he was a "new creature," the "fool for Christ's sake," living only to preach the gospel of the new life in Christ. Such religious conversion was very rare in the Greco-Roman world before the Christian era; if many men felt purified by initiation into the mysteries, we hear of none who had so intense, profound, and enduring a sense of regeneration, or who dedicated themselves so utterly to the service of the god they had seen. In the light of Judaism, however, Saul's experience is less strange. He had behind him the tradition of the prophets, out of which Jesus himself spoke—men who had been called by God to prophesy to his people, and who often supplemented or even scrapped his earlier commandments, as in teaching that he was no longer pleased by the savor of animal sacrifices. There was more than one martyr among them.

But the all-important fact remains that Saul left Palestine to carry his good news into the Greco-Roman world. He wrote the Galatians that he spent only fifteen days with Peter in Jerusalem, several years after his conversion, and that he saw no other apostle except James, the brother of Jesus. He preached instead in Damascus, in Tarsus, and in Antioch, where Christians first became known by that name.[4] Then he set out on his missionary journeys through Asia Minor and into Greece. As the Apostle of the Gentiles, he sought to become "all things to all men." So the immediate question is: What things in his preaching owed to Judaism? What to Hellenism? What to the "Orient"? The question is complicated by his passion and his genius; for we are dealing with an extraordinary creative individual, not a mere product of the age or mouthpiece of history. Nevertheless we must see him against the background of his age as we hope to do justice to his complex legacy, and to understand what his Church made of it. St. Paul still means quite different things to different men.

3. THE LEGACY OF ST. PAUL

Over the Taurus Mountains behind the Cilician plain lay the ancient city of Tyana, known to the Hittites as Tuwana. Here, a generation before Paul and possibly in the same year as Jesus, was born another famous holy man, Apollonius of Tyana. He was educated at Tarsus but soon left the city, denouncing its luxury and license; later it was nevertheless pleased to include him among its many "founders"—an honor it did not bestow on Paul. Inspired by the teachings of Pythagoras, he became an ascetic, eschewing meat, wine, and women. He taught that there was one supreme creator, that all good men had in them something of the divine essence, and that the soul of man was immortal. His disciples asserted that he was the son of Zeus. While he himself made no such claim, he at least displayed superhuman powers. He cast out demons, who "fled squeaking as ghosts do," and once brought a dead girl back to life; at Troy he summoned up the spirit of Achilles, to assure the hero that the Pythagoreans did not share the vulgar illusion that he was dead. Toward the end of his life he got into trouble with the Roman authorities, who charged him with preaching against the Emperor. Though acquitted, he chose to vanish from the courtroom, saying, "I am not fated to die!" And though stories differ about when and where he departed this earth, they agree that he died no ordinary death. One had it that he vanished again, to the sound of girlish voices singing "Come to heaven."

Several Epistles of Apollonius have been preserved, but he is known

[4] See the Appendix, Section 7, for the history of Antioch.

chiefly through the biography written in the next century by Philostratus. Later, shortly before Constantine the Great embraced Christianity, another admirer wrote a book to prove that Apollonius had been "as great a sage, as remarkable a worker of miracles, and as potent an exorcist as Jesus Christ." Contemporary Christians naturally saw a devilish purpose behind the seeming parallels in his career and Christ's. While granting that he had performed real miracles, Bishop Eusebius argued that it was only because demons had aided him. (In the seventeenth century the Catholic clergy still opposed the publishing of a translation of Philostratus.) His recorded life was so fabulous that the skeptical Gibbon was at a loss what to make of him—whether "a sage, an impostor, or a fanatic." Nevertheless Apollonius offers an illuminating, if somewhat garish, prelude to the mission of St. Paul. If a "Divine purpose" selected Tarsus as Paul's birthplace, it seems possible that the holy man of Tyana was sent to prepare the ground—and that Satan then co-operated in an ironical spirit.

Apollonius was typical of the period in his eagerness to explore religious possibilities. Philostratus records that he traveled to India, where one sage told him that in his previous existence he had been an Egyptian steersman—which he admitted. Sometimes he talked like a Brahman, or like Plato, on the relation of the soul to the natural world. He also took to heart the wisdom of the Stoics. He taught that since the gods know everything, and do not need to be told what to do, the most suitable prayer was: "O ye gods! give me what I ought to have!" His customary prayer was still humbler: "O ye gods, grant me to have little and to stand in need of nothing." At the same time, the saint in Apollonius cohabited with a good Greek of the old school. He was inquisitive about all schools of philosophy. At Olympia he discoursed on "the most useful subjects, such as wisdom, and manliness, and self-control, and every other virtue." He spent much of his later life in Ionia, where all the main oracles agreed that he shared the wisdom of Apollo himself. Teaching chiefly in the old cities of Ephesus and Smyrna, he took up such subjects as sound methods of city government; at Smyrna he emphasized the need of "discordant harmony," or rivalry in public service.[5] While constantly deploring the indolence and insolence among the Greeks, he praised them because they still loved freedom.

Yet we can never be sure that we know Apollonius, really understand his mentality. With his apparent wisdom and humility went the rankest superstition and conceit, manifested in his miracles, his conversations

[5] For the history of Smyrna, which became a great city in the Roman era, see the Appendix, Section 6.

with dead heroes, his boasts of his immortality. We recall that he ended a plague in Ephesus by telling the citizens to stone a beggar who was really a demon. He may have been an impostor after all. Doubts are forced by the fantastic venture of Alexander of Abonutichus, a pupil of one of his disciples.

Deciding to set up business as an oracle, Alexander buried at Chalcedon some bronze tablets stating that Asclepius with his father Apollo was going to migrate up the Black Sea to Abonutichus (modern Inebolu). When the tablets were found, not by accident, the townspeople of Abonutichus immediately began building a suitable temple, and Alexander began playing the prophet. He foamed at the mouth; he planted an egg in the foundations of the temple, planted a story that a small snake had emerged from it—Asclepius himself; he displayed a big snake into which it had at once grown; he announced that the god would presently begin to make prophecies through him; and then he sent men abroad to spread rumors of how true these prophecies turned out to be. He did a flourishing business from the outset, suppliants coming from everywhere with gifts for the prophet. As the oracle grew famous the god took on a new name, Glycon, and Alexander sent men all over the empire warning of imminent plagues and earthquakes that he could prevent.

This man, it would seem, was obviously a charlatan. But again we cannot be sure. Possibly he was exploiting to the hilt a prophetic gift in which he himself believed, possibly he was acting on instructions that Asclepius had given him in a dream. Certainly his contemporaries were grateful to him. Glycon survived his death, Alexander was thereafter honored as his prophet, and the oracle retained considerable fame. Much greater men than he, and men of unquestioned sincerity, acted on similar principles. Marcus Aurelius, gravest and highest-minded of emperors, thanked the gods for dream revelations that cured him of giddiness; and he had two lions thrown into the Danube at the bidding of the oracle of Abonutichus. "The tradition yields us only ruins," Wilamowitz concluded. "The more closely we test and examine them, the more clearly we see how ruinous they are; and out of ruins no whole can be built. The tradition is dead; our task is to revivify life that has passed away. We know that ghosts cannot speak until they have drunk blood; and the spirits that we evoke demand the blood of our hearts. We give it to them gladly; but if they then abide our question, something from us has entered into them."

About Saul of Tarsus, who as a "new creature" took the name of Paul, there is much less uncertainty. His tradition is not in ruins; we have his own eloquent words for it, and no one would question his entire sincerity.

Yet he too demands something of our blood. His words were not addressed to the likes of us, or intended as Scripture. Like other early Christians, Paul believed that the Second Coming was imminent, and prayed that his Lord "come quickly"; he was scarcely building a religion for our world. While he seems to have meant his words to be taken literally, they are often vehement and imprecise, sometimes obscure. When most luminous, his message still requires interpretation—and has received very diverse interpretation. It includes beliefs that few can now take as literally as he himself plainly did: for example, that the Lord would "descend from heaven with a shout," and that when the trumpet sounded, the dead would rise from their graves. Such beliefs might remind us that to those outside the Christian faith the Gospels tell a story more fabulous than the life of Apollonius of Tyana as recorded by Philostratus, and that although the Acts of the Apostles gives an essentially credible account of the career of Paul, it has him too working the routine miracles.

The plainest facts about his mission give some trouble to the orthodox. His own Epistles, written before the Gospels, show that Christianity was born in schism, the dissensions that were to multiply and keep it disunited ever after. The earliest followers of Jesus split over policy toward the Gentiles. Paul wrote the Galatians that when Peter came to Antioch "I withstood him to the face, because he was to be blamed." Obeying the order of James, the brother of Jesus, Peter had separated himself from the uncircumcised Gentiles; Paul led a faction that would exempt the Gentiles from circumcision and all other ceremonial requirements of the Hebrew law. According to Acts, it was in Asia Minor, at Antioch-in-Pisidia, that he made the momentous decision that transformed a Hebrew sect into a universal religion. "Men of Israel, and ye that fear God, give audience," he began his sermon here. When a multitude of the God-fearing came to hear him on the next Sabbath, the men of Israel grew envious and blasphemous; so Paul turned to the Gentiles, declaring that the Lord had commanded him to be a light to them and bring salvation "unto the ends of the earth." In retrospect, all Christians must applaud his decision, even if most of the earth still refuses to hearken to him. At the time it meant not only an irreparable break with Judaism but discord among Christians. To loyal Jewish Christians, the great Apostle was an apostate from the Law. They could hardly take communion with their Gentile brethren and certainly could not eat with them, since they had to eat kosher. It might be for this reason that Acts fails to mention any meeting between Peter and Paul in Rome.

As we seek to understand Paul's revolutionary decision, and his whole teaching, we must begin with his mystical experience. It is impossible to doubt the reality of this experience, however it be explained; his whole subsequent career testifies to his overwhelming conviction that Christ had spoken to him, and kept speaking through him. Repeatedly he insisted that he knew nothing by himself. The gospel he preached was "not of men, neither by man, but by Jesus Christ"; his preaching was "nothing to glory of," but a "necessity" laid upon him; and only because of this had he become "more" than other ministers of Christ—"in labors more abundant, in stripes above measure, in prisons more frequent, in deaths oft." Nevertheless Paul perforce did speak as a man, to other men. Regarded as a man, he becomes still more sublime, in the fervor and selflessness of his utter devotion to his Lord; he also becomes more tragic, in his martyrdom to no certain end; and finally he becomes more troublesome. We cannot share his mystical experience—we can only read his interpretation of it. He had not known Jesus in the flesh; he rarely referred to his human life; he never spoke of the "Son of Man," as Jesus called himself according to the Synoptic Gospels. What he knew was the resurrected Christ he had seen in the vision that blinded him. He preached the crucified Son of God, "unto the Jews a stumbling block, and unto the Greeks foolishness." More than a hundred times he wrote of the life "in Christ"; but his Christ had aspects that were indeed alien to both Hebrew and Greek tradition, and evidently unknown to the author of Acts.

God had not prepared the men of Israel for the idea that he would send his own Son to suffer and die for them. The Messiah told about in their Scriptures was variously conceived, but in his most ideal aspect, as the "man of sorrows" who would bear their griefs, he was still a man. The second Isaiah, who conceived of this "suffering servant," also entertained the notion that the Persian Emperor Cyrus had been sent as a Messiah. The idea of a suffering, dying god was a pagan idea—as pagan as that of a virgin birth or a Mother of God.[6] The pagan dying gods, on

[6] Since history seldom does justice to the defeated cause, we might pause to consider a passage in the *Toldoth Jeshu*, a Jewish life of Jesus of unknown date but ancient origin:

"And there went forth twelve wicked ones, sons of insurgents, and they transversed twelve kingdoms and proclaimed in their public places false prophecies. And some of Israel went astray after them, and these were men of repute, who strengthened the faith of Jesus, for they said they were apostles of the hanged one, and much people of the children of Israel adhered to them."

Paul, one of these men of repute, quoted the text in Deuteronomy: "Cursed is every one that hangeth on a tree." He interpreted this as meaning that Christ had deliberately suffered himself to be cursed in order to redeem men from the curse of

the other hand, were wont to die annually, cyclically, ritually. Although Christ would eventually come to do likewise in Passion plays, his death was a unique historical event, to Paul the climax of all history. Christ was as strange to the Greeks as a god who had deliberately put on mortality—not a man (like Heracles) who had achieved divinity.

Still, Paul was deeply indebted to both traditions as he interpreted his mystical experience, inevitably in terms of his knowledge and previous experience, the thought and feeling of his time and place. It was Christ Jesus who spoke to him—not Buddha, or Osiris, or Allah. His gospel included many familiar ideas, from the demons of common folk to the more spiritual concepts of the educated. "In whatsoever state I am," he wrote, "I have learned therewith to be content"; and he might have learned this from Athenodorus of Tarsus, Apollonius of Tyana, or his Pharisaic teachers in Jerusalem. Above all, his universalism was nothing new. "There is neither Jew nor Greek, there is neither bond nor free, there is neither male nor female: for ye are all one in Christ Jesus." Save for Jesus, this idea is implicit in Isaiah's loftier visions of the era of universal peace to come, when all the nations would stream to the Lord of Israel; and it was explicit in the Stoic ideal of a universal community of gods and men.

At the time, however, there was little spirit of universality in Israel. Peter and James, reared in Palestine, opposed the Apostle of the Gentiles; elsewhere the chosen people fiercely resented and persecuted him. In this respect Paul's gospel owed much more to the atmosphere he had breathed in Tarsus than to the education he had received in Jerusalem. We are brought to the question of what in his preaching may be traced to Hellenism.

Now Paul spoke and wrote in Greek, not the Aramaic of Jesus. It was a rude Greek, which his enemies called "contemptible" (II Corinthians 10:10, 11:6), but it inevitably gave his thought a Greek cast. He habitually called Jesus the *Christ,* a Greek word that translated *Messiah* and connoted the idea of a Saviour long familiar to the Greeks. He incidentally drew metaphors from athletics: "I have fought a good fight, I have finished my course." He leaned heavily on the typically Greek figures of light and freedom. "Ye are all the children of light, and the children of the day," he told his churches more than once; to serve Christ was to be the "Lord's freeman," for "where the Spirit of the Lord is, there is liberty." And as an Apostle of the Gentiles, seeking to emancipate them from bondage to the Law, the traditional letter, Paul in effect asserted the claims of mind. "I will pray with the spirit," he told the Corinthians, "and

---

the Law. The men of Israel understandably preferred to take their Scripture literally, as Christians would come to take their New Testament.

I will pray with the understanding also." He reasoned with his followers; he wrote as an educator, not merely as an inspired prophet. His Epistles are much more sophisticated in tone and content than the simple gospel of repentance and salvation preached by the other Apostles, as recorded in Acts. They bring one into a world of thought quite different from that of the Synoptic Gospels, foreshadowing the intellectual Gospel of St. John that identified Christ with the Logos. Albert Schweitzer has called Paul "the patron-saint of thought in Christianity."

Celsus, the first pagan writer known to have attacked Christianity, declared that it took a Greek to understand the real meaning and value of truths barbarians might stumble on. Paul was at least Hellenic enough in spirit to interpret in more or less philosophical terms the truths he had been granted to know by the Holy Spirit. In the Synoptic Gospels Jesus is represented as mysteriously secretive about his identity, even forbidding the disciples to announce that he was the Messiah. Paul taught unequivocally that he was the Son of God—again an idea familiar to the Greeks, not to the Hebrews. Like Jesus, he was not too clear or consistent about the new notions of an afterlife that had entered Judaism, but he made some effort to rationalize them. Concerning the strange idea of the resurrection of the dead, he explained that the dead would be raised not in the flesh but in a "spiritual body." If this suggests the Stoic conception of the soul as a fine form of matter, elsewhere Paul reflected the radical dualism of spirit and flesh that harked back to Plato and Pythagoras, and appeared in the asceticism of Apollonius of Tyana: those who live in the Spirit "have crucified the flesh." He sounded more like a Platonist when he stressed the distinction between the temporal things that are seen and the eternal things that are not seen. Later Christians therefore had some excuse for attributing to him the Epistle to the Hebrews, an effort at a philosophy of history combining Hebrew thought with the idea that temporal events are shadows of eternal verities. (Most modern scholars agree with Origen that "only God knew" who wrote this work.) Paul had started the Hellenizing of Christianity, because of which it was never to take deep root on Semitic soil.

There remains the most obvious implication of Paul's mission to the Gentiles, emphasized by Ramsay: a conviction that there was some real good in them—more good, it soon appeared, than in most of his own countrymen. Paul carried his gospel into the homeland of Greece, preaching in Athens itself; he wrote a long letter to the Church at Rome before he went to Rome. "Deliberately and consciously," Ramsay concluded, he "aimed at bringing together on the higher plane of Christian thought and life all that was true and real in the pagan world," in the hope of regenerating that world.[7]

But this language brings us up sharply. Paul never declared any respect for Greek culture, and clearly was indifferent or even hostile to much that we find "true and real" in its art and thought. "Was it conceivable," wrote T. R. Glover, "that life in Christ lacked something that life without Him gave?" The answer is yes—and most emphatically in the teaching of Paul. The Greeks had taken pleasure in man's own creative works, his natural powers for the realization of truth, goodness, and beauty on earth. How little Paul cared for such humanistic values becomes plainer when Ramsay attributes to him a passion for freedom and for education. One may argue that "true" freedom is found only in the knowledge and service of the Lord; but Paul displayed no passion whatever for freedom by Greek standards, or by our own—political and intellectual freedom, the rights to have a mind, a faith, a life of one's own. Not once did he refer to the ideal of the *polis*, in which Apollonius of Tyana still took a live interest. He displayed no passion at all for education in the traditional Greek sense. He had none of the eager curiosity that led Apollonius to travel and inquire into all available schools of thought. He warned the Colossians against such curiosity, "lest any man spoil you through philosophy"; he told the Corinthians that God had "made foolish the wisdom of this world," in particular the wisdom of the Greeks. He admitted no independent claims of reason, no spirit of free inquiry. Like the later Church, he contended against the best as well as the worst in the pagan world. Call him transfigured or call him obsessed, he was indeed, as he said, "the prisoner of the Lord," "an ambassador in bonds."

Hence the most cultivated pagans were most likely to be mystified by him. The Roman procurator Festus, who heard the Jewish charges against him in Palestine, could understand only that they involved some superstition about "one Jesus, which was dead, whom Paul affirmed to be alive"; and after listening patiently to an account of this resurrected Jesus he said: "Paul, thou art beside thyself; much learning doth make thee mad." The Apostle would have seemed as mad to Plato and Aristotle. The reason why many Gentiles could understand him was that

[7] In *The Cities of St. Paul*, Ramsay developed the thesis that this pagan world had originally had some true knowledge of God, but had degenerated into idolatry and magic; he believed that Paul too subscribed to this theory of primitivism, a variant on the ancient idea of decline from a Golden Age. Father Schmidt has since given it more weight by anthropological evidence that monotheism may have been the earliest form of religion. In the Near East, however, the evidence of archaeology and myth hardly supports any notion of a purer spirituality in earlier times. In the Greek world the plainest religious development was the resurgence of pre-Homeric religion.

the "pagan world" he preached to was now a semi-Oriental world, in which the gods of Homer had long since become lost in the crowd.

One commentator on the missionary journeys of Paul has remarked his "sure instinct for great commercial cities and highways." Actually his choice in Asiatic cities was curious, unless we assume a surer instinct for ancient religious byways. From Syrian Antioch the Holy Ghost first sent him to the island of Cyprus, which had never become Greek enough to outgrow kingship.[8] He then sailed to Perge in Asia Minor and went straight to Antioch-in-Pisidia, a minor Greco-Roman outpost in a Phrygian sea. Paul next went to Iconium, another ancient Phrygian city; it did not become important until more than a thousand years later when it became Konya, the capital of the Moslem Seljuks. When driven out of here, he sought refuge in the rude towns of Lystra and Derbe, inhabited largely by illiterate Anatolians. The Lystrians hailed a miraculous cure by mistaking him for Hermes and his companion Barnabas for Zeus; as Orientals they knew that the lesser god did all the talking. After returning to Jerusalem to defend his policy toward the Gentiles, Paul again went through the outlying provinces of Syria and Cilicia, Phrygia and Galatia. When he at last approached the more Hellenic region of Ionia, he was "forbidden of the Holy Ghost to preach the word in Asia." The Spirit also frowned on his intention of going to Bithynia, where he might have served tradition by preaching in Nicaea and crossing over to Byzantium, cities later to figure prominently in Christian history. As it was, Ephesus was the only great Greek city in Asia Minor in which the Apostle of the Gentiles settled; and this was the most Oriental of the Ionian cities.

We cannot speak positively of direct Oriental "influences" on Paul in so commingled, cosmopolitan a world. We can only point to elements in his gospel that are more suggestive of the ancient East than of classical Hellenism or prophetic Judaism. The plainest is his transformation of Christianity into a mystery religion. His gospel was centered not on God but on Jesus the Christ, and in him not on the beautiful humanity of Jesus but on the promise of the resurrected Christ. "If Christ be not risen, then is our preaching vain, and your faith is also vain." To a good Greek, moreover, his faith might seem simple credulity. "I have shewed you all things," he told the Ephesians; but he never seemed concerned about proving the crucial fact of the resurrection. He simply remarked that "he was seen," adding nothing about how or in what form. Paul seemed still

[8] At Paphos, where he changed his name to Paul, he was near the site where Aphrodite had been born of the sea foam; but the Cyprian Aphrodite was a markedly Oriental type. See the Appendix, Section 8, for the history of Cyprus.

more naïve in his belief in the resurrection of the dead, an idea that seems to have come from Persian sources. The philosophers in Athens were eager to hear him, it is said in Acts, since like all the Athenians they "spent their time in nothing else but either to tell or to hear some new thing"; but they naturally mocked so preposterous a thing as this.

Probably most of them could not yet understand either Paul's intense longing for resurrection. Both Stoics and Epicureans would consider selfish and unseemly the attitude he expressed to the Corinthians: "If after the manner of men I have fought with beasts at Ephesus, what advantageth it me, if the dead rise not?" Paul's Anatolian congregations could better understand his passion for the life to come. It betokened a despair of this life, of any values that man might realize on earth by his own efforts. "If in this life only we have hope in Christ, we are of all men most miserable."

In this spirit Paul made his fateful pronouncement to the Romans: "There is no power but of God: the powers that be are ordained of God. Whosoever therefore resisteth the power, resisteth the ordinance of God: and they that resist shall receive to themselves damnation." He did not, of course, regard kings as themselves divine. His counsel of obedience probably reflected a decent gratitude for the law and order restored by the Roman emperors; at least he seemed proud of his Roman citizenship. For the most part he was simply indifferent—like Jesus himself—to political life in temporal kingdoms, because of his consuming passion for the heavenly kingdom to come. Yet this indifference was typically Oriental, and again set Paul apart from both classical Hellenism and prophetic Judaism. Although Israel revered its David, it was strikingly different from most Eastern peoples in its refusal not only to deify its kings but even to regard them as sovereign agents of the divine will; its priests and prophets had repeatedly resisted the power of the kings in the name of a higher law, and sometimes in the interest of social justice. Now Paul in effect reverted to the ancient idea of kingship, the kind of power that God had always ordained in the East. He provided the plainest text for the sacred autocracy of the Byzantine Empire, and in later Europe for the divine right of kings. In the same spirit he accepted slavery and counseled obedience to the master. Such relations "in the flesh" were unimportant, for "in Christ" all men were one.

On earth, meanwhile, there were both male and female, as well as bond and free, Greek and Jew; and about females Paul taught a more emphatic doctrine of inequality and natural bondage. Woman had been created for man; she should be subject to her husband "in every thing"; she must keep her head covered in church to signify her subjection. Although Paul could have supported this doctrine by citing the classics of both Greece and Israel, woman had risen to a higher status in the Hellenistic world, and had acquired still more dignity as a Roman wife and mother, while in Anatolia she had long had considerable prestige as a priestess of the Great Mother. Possibly he encountered the type of prophetess who became influential in the later Phrygian heresy of Montanism. "I suffer not a woman to teach," he supposedly wrote to Timothy, "but to be in silence"; and if his authorship of this Epistle is doubtful, the saying was characteristic, and prophetic. About the only thing that Dio Chrysostom found to praise in the non-Hellenic city of Tarsus was the modest dress of its women, who were heavily veiled in the Oriental manner. Paul's Church would long keep them in their place.

But here we are led to the much more important Hebraic element in his teaching. The Great Mother was a favorite of the Gentiles in all the Asiatic cities where the Spirit sent him; and the surprising thing is that Paul made no concessions to her whatever, even no mention of her, as he made none of the Virgin Mary. He remained completely loyal to the transcendent, purely male God of his Semitic forefathers, who had created man in His own image. No more than the historic Jesus did Paul clearly intend to found a new religion. Despite his violent controversy with his fellow Jews over the Mosaic law, Judaism was always the frame and basis of his gospel.

First and last, he owed to it his Lord—an inspiration loftier than any known to Apollonius of Tyana. Paul could preach without having heard Jesus because the historic Jesus had come not to destroy but to fulfill the Law, and had brought no clearly new message. The essential teachings of the Synoptic Gospels all derive from the greater prophets of Israel. At most, Jesus deepened and sweetened their inwardness; he was more outspoken in his contempt for formalism and legalism, and he stressed more often the mercy of God, preaching a purer gospel of brotherhood and love. Paul was in these respects true to his Lord. As an Apostle of the Gentiles he was still more explicit in dispensing with the formal requirements of the Law, such as the embarrassment of circumcision. A naturally somber, fierce man, he nevertheless wrote beautifully of charity as the supreme virtue, and in ministering to his congregations displayed as beautiful a spirit of love—the spirit so conspicuously wanting in Stoicism, and not too apparent in Apollonius. And while he transformed Jesus into the Christ of a mystery religion, he was too good a Jew and too faithful to his Lord to be a mystagogue. He put little stress on baptism and communion, set up nothing like the elaborate initiation rites of the other mystery religions. While teaching a doctrine of justification by faith that might easily be abused, he emphatically required good works of the faithful, and retained the moral law of Judaism. Christianity as Paul preached it was far more ethical than all the other mystery religions of his time, never a merely sacramental or magical means to salvation.

Similarly Paul taught no new ideas about God, except that he had sent his Son. Like Jesus, he hardly conceived anything so abstruse as the later Trinity, or so irrelevant to his overriding concern of salvation. Jesus was distinct from the Father who had sent him and "highly exalted him"; it was enough that he had been sent. The Father was still the Yahweh of Israel: intolerant of all idolatry, exclusive, jealous, rather awful. There was no salvation for believers in other gods. If Paul tried to "pray with the understanding," he took for granted that the ways of God passed understanding. "We walk by faith, not by sight," he told the children of the light. Like the prophets, he had no idea of human freedom, teaching that man had no more right to question or complain than the clay had to question the potter. There was nothing in Paul of the Greek ideal of the self-sufficient wise man as still expressed by Stoics and Epicureans, by Apollonius of Tyana, and later by Plotinus in the twilight of Hellenism. "Knowledge puffeth up," Paul insisted, and "let no man glory in men."

Still Hebraic in spirit, though not in origin, was his eschatology. Paul had a very literal belief in Satan, angels and demons, the resurrection of the elect, the damnation of the wicked and the unbelieving—ideas that have become an embarrassment to many modern Christians. Most important was his belief in the imminent Second Coming. A heritage from the millennium dreamed of by the prophets, reinterpreted by Paul in the light of his mystical experience, it again made his gospel different from the Greco-Oriental mystery religions, based on the permanencies of nature. Whereas they aspired to a mystical union with the god, he worked to prepare men for another unique event. And given the intensity of his own experience, the urgency of the situation—the unique state of the temporal world—Paul went on to draw inferences of his own. He preached some ideas that, if not wholly original with him, were at least first popularized by him, and that became doctrines of a Church that was obliged to accommodate itself to an indefinite postponement of the Second Coming.

Paul's major bequest was the cornerstone of Christianity—the doctrine of the Atonement. Having been miraculously redeemed himself, he believed that Christ had suffered and died to redeem all mankind, to free man from "the law of sin and death." If this belief may be traced to the ancient rituals of the dying god and the royal scapegoat, it was nevertheless the loftiest, or the most presumptuous, conception of divine benevolence in religious history. It does not appear in Acts, nor in the teachings of Jesus himself in the Synoptic Gospels. With it Paul coupled another novel idea that became a basic doctrine—the idea of Original Sin. The sin and death from which Christ came to free man had entered the world by one man's disobedience. This idea too may be linked with an ancient belief of both Greeks and Hebrews that the sins of the father were visited upon the children, but it had never been extended to the whole human race. The prophets of Israel, the authors of the historic books, and again Jesus himself made no mention whatever of the Fall of Adam.[9]

Still another related idea of Paul's, at once humbler and harsher, was that salvation was possible only through a gift of grace. Jesus had not stressed the necessity of such a gift; he taught that men could save themselves by their own efforts, through repentance and righteousness. Paul flatly declared otherwise: "By grace are ye saved through faith; and that not of yourselves: it is the gift of God: not of works, lest any man should boast." He spoke here out of the Hebrew tradition of absolute dependence on God. He spoke with a logic that St. Augustine would appreciate; for if men could be saved by their own strength and virtue, in the Greek spirit, there was no absolute need of Christ's redemption. He spoke most movingly out of a humble gratitude: it was only by the grace of God that Christ had spoken to him from the heavens—to Saul of Tarsus, "who was before a blasphemer, and a persecutor, and injurious." But Paul's logic, and his experience, drove him to a dreadful conclusion, that grace was granted only to some, "God's elect," and that others were predestined to damnation. From the beginning his God had played favorites by singling out a "chosen people," and he had often been callously, even brutally indifferent to other peoples, as when he "hardened the heart" of Pharaoh in order to inflict more plagues on the hapless Egyptians, to make a more flamboyant display of his power. Now God was plainly denying grace to many of his chosen people; only so could Paul understand the fierce hostility he met from them. "Therefore hath he mercy on whom he will have mercy, and whom he will he hardeneth."

In retrospect the divine purpose is more intelligible. The perversity of the Jews may seem providential: it drove Christianity into the Greco-

[9] Since the doctrine of Original Sin has become the rallying cry of the neo-orthodoxy today, it seems worth repeating that the author of the Biblical myth was not acquainted with it either. In punishing Adam, the Lord God expresses no sorrow or moral indignation, but a jealous fear. "Behold the man is become as one of us, to know good and evil"; so the man is driven out of Eden lest he "take also of the tree of life, and eat, and live forever." Paul's belief that death resulted from sin was at most a divine afterthought. In the beginning the Lord God plainly did not intend his new creatures to be immortal, "as one of us."

Roman world, where the gospel could spread and flourish. Still, Paul's teaching had appalling implications, especially since he coupled it with the new ideas of heaven and hell, and since the overwhelming majority of mankind were to be eternally damned without ever having known his Redeemer. And although his Church was eventually to reject his doctrine of predestination, together with other heretical implications of his teaching, it emphasizes that the "glorious liberty" he preached in fact meant a sharp restriction of freedom of choice, of thought, of conscience. In offering the highest hope that religion had yet held out to men, he burdened them with a tyrannical need of this hope, denying them any more reasonable hopes, insisting that without faith in the resurrected Christ their condition was absolutely hopeless. At best, the gospel according to Paul represented the ultimate in both humility and pride, and was peculiarly liable to abuse. His conviction of man's unworthiness of his Redeemer led him to aspire the more passionately to the "crown of righteousness" that was laid up for him in the kingdom to come. Later too many of the elect would wear a crown of self-righteousness; and for uncounted millions of his fellow Jews it would mean another crown of thorns.

Yet Paul earned his own crown. The greatest of the Apostles, he worked with extraordinary energy, fervor, and self-abnegation in spite of his yearning to be with Christ. One may deplore much of his doctrine and still be profoundly moved by the man. One may condone his excesses in view of the peculiar urgency of the temporal situation as he saw it. He could scarcely be expected to preach a balanced, humanistic, sweetly reasonable gospel to prepare men for the imminent coming of their Lord. At that he laid foundations broad and firm enough to survive the disappointment of the hopes that fired him. He might even be called prophetic; for the Greco-Roman world was in fact coming to an end, and was already decaying at its core. Paul seems much more vital and creative, and infinitely grander, as well as narrower and harsher, when he is set beside Apollonius of Tyana.

We should discount, too, the common charge in liberal circles that Paul, not Jesus, was the author of the Christianity that conquered the world. In his alleged Epistle to Timothy he wrote that "all they which are in Asia be turned away from me"; and by the time this was written his Church was in fact turning away from much of his teaching, as from that of Jesus. Beginning with the Gospel according to St. John, Christianity became much more Hellenized; the thinkers who developed its theology largely ignored Paul. The Church transformed it into a sacramental religion, more ethical than the other mystery religions, but like them making its sacraments essential to salvation. The legalism denounced by Jesus and Paul came back in full force. With it came a ritualism derived largely from the Oriental mystery religions; the mystery of the Mass gave the old aura of eternal recurrence to the unique sacrifice of Jesus. The Mother ignored by Paul rose to be Mother of God. In its wisdom and its humanity, one might say, in a world that had turned out to be a going concern, the Church recognized that the pure monotheism and transcendent spirituality of prophetic Judaism were too lofty for humble men. Certainly the Church more nearly realized the synthesis of Hellenism and Orientalism that Ramsay believed was the divine purpose in calling out Saul of Tarsus. But Paul himself, one suspects, might have felt more at home among the Semitic followers of Mohammed than among the descendants of his Gentiles.

In any case, Peter was given the keys of the Church. Early Christian mosaics honored Paul by placing him on the right hand of his Lord enthroned in the New Jerusalem, with Peter on the left; but having won his victory and established the Church among the Gentiles, Paul was robbed to pay Peter. He faded into the background as the Church of Rome went on to convert barbarians in the name of Peter; early medieval pilgrims paid tribute at Rome by bringing "Peter's pence." In the East, Paul was overshadowed by the Mother of God and by other saints and angels, in particular the mythical Archangel Michael. The Holy Orthodox Church developed an elaborate cultus that was alien to his spirit. He did not come into his own until the rise of Luther and Calvin—and then he suffered still more from Paulinism, which generally seized on his harshest teachings; the Reformers rigidified into a basic dogma his incidental idea of predestination, and were far more severe and self-righteous in separating the elect from the damned. The Church of Peter long refused to permit Paul's Protestant disciples to worship within the walls of Rome, where he had met martyrdom with Peter. In recent times it has tried to explain away his early position on the right hand of his Lord by arguing—in the face of plain statements in the gospels of Mark and Matthew—that the left hand was then the place of honor.[10]

[10] More melancholy was the tribute paid him by Walter Lowrie in S.S. *Peter and Paul in Rome*, a work designed to reconcile the martyred saints, and published a year after the outbreak of World War II. An American minister in Rome, Dr. Lowrie went out of his way to celebrate the glorious achievement of Mussolini in effecting a moral and spiritual regeneration of Italy, rescuing it from Jewish Freemasonry, etc. The early followers of both Peter and Paul, he stressed, had "no prejudice at all" in favor of democracy, and he added that the Old Testament also gave examples of rule by "a Duce like Moses." In effect he agreed with Pope Pius XI that Mussolini was "a man sent by Divine Providence." Paul acknowledged that the ways of Providence are mysterious, but he was never so shortsighted and smug as this.

4. THE ROMAN ERA IN ASIA MINOR: FROM PAUL TO HADRIAN

For all the awe inspired by the grandeur that was Rome, it is difficult to do full justice to the blessings it brought to Asia Minor. We have seen that the Roman era had a sorry beginning, in a century of brutal exploitation and civil war. We may nod approvingly as we read how Rome then went on to its most majestic achievement, the Roman law; but only a specialist can read in this law. We know that for more than two centuries the cities of Asia Minor enjoyed unparalleled peace and prosperity, and we might well envy the contentment they knew in a comfortable, secure, cultivated way of life; but it now looks like a shallow complacence. For we know, too, that the Roman era had a dismal ending. Meanwhile there was little splendid achievement amid all the splendor of civic life. Asia Minor no longer displayed the brilliant creativity that it had for centuries under the Greeks. In science the Hellenistic tradition was still strong enough to inspire some notable work, as by Strabo of Amasia and Galen of Pergamum. In literature, art, and philosophy there were almost no great names. Chiefly, Asia Minor produced orators and historians. The one recited panegyrics on the deathless glory of a universal order that was in fact local and transient; the other wrote respectable academic studies of the past that had little feeling for the future—either the actual future that was in store or the better future that man might work for in a clearer understanding of his past failings and present problems.

The Roman ruins in Asia Minor may tell the story most graphically. Everywhere massive walls, arches, and gateways still stand; extensive remains of aqueducts, bridges, baths, stadiums, temples, and theaters testify to the power and skill of their builders, and to the richness of civic life. But these ruins grow monotonous and somber. They lack the bright charm and grace of Greek art; they do not readily enchant or take on a hallowed air. Too often they have a gross quality, reminding us of the severe limitations of the famous Roman character. We may gaze with awe, for example, at the great theater of Aspendus, near Perge (where St. Paul landed on his first missionary voyage). Substantially intact, it is the best preserved of the greater Roman buildings; until this century even the statues were still in place in the lofty marbled façade that served as a backdrop for the orchestra. And built for the ages, this majestic structure was designed immediately for vulgar, brutal spectacles, such as the infamous gladiatorial shows. Like the Colosseum, it suggests that the worst of Rome was as massive and enduring as the best.

Hence Arnold Toynbee quotes with approval the conclusion of A. Bazard that the net result of the Roman conquest was the destruction of all city-states, including Rome itself, to make way for an empire that brought nothing new. All its sentiments, habits, and ideas went back to the *polis*, which was no longer vital. "In short," wrote Bazard, "the Roman Empire in no sense constitutes a society; for, in its capacity as an empire, it has no religion, no goal, and no general practical aim whatsoever; it represents merely a vast aggregation of human beings, a shapeless congeries of the debris of societies."

But this is surely an overstatement. The Roman Empire was no mere aggregation but an order, a society unified enough to inspire a great deal of patriotism in both its emperors and its subjects. It gave vital meaning to such ideas as universal law, which the *polis* had never been devoted to in its prime; it came close enough to realizing the ideals of commonwealth and cosmopolis to make a deep impress on the religion that survived it and the civilization that succeeded it in the West. It remains one of the most impressive historic achievements of man. If we may say that all empire is doomed to fail by its nature as an arbitrary power system, the Roman Empire still haunts the imagination of Western man because it was more than such a system. Finally it succumbed to the worst in its works; but first we must try to do justice to the best, which has survived in our heritage.

So let us return to the Roman ruins in Asia Minor. They also tell a grand story, even a humane one. They reflect the character of the countless "anonymous Romans" whose realistic busts and statues adorn museums everywhere: somewhat too complacent, rarely lively or lovable, but dignified in their gravity, firmness, controlled power—iron character on a grand scale. In both art and life these Romans had style. If their favorite Corinthian order is too ornate for lovers of the Doric and Ionian, it is nevertheless a noble and graceful order, wrought delicately as well as richly. Their more vulgar works, such as the great baths, were still not the work of mere vulgarians. Roman architects might be called better humanists than the classical Greeks, who never got beyond the form of their temple. They were better builders for civic purposes, with a freer, bolder imagination, a stronger feeling for organized space and functional form.

Or let us begin by having St. Paul bear witness to the blessings of Roman rule. No doubt he took for granted the excellent Roman roads that allowed him to travel without difficulty or danger, even though they would not be equaled in Turkey until a few years ago. Probably he did not marvel either at the cosmopolitan ideal of the empire—the fact that he, a Jew of Tarsus, was a Roman citizen. But he was conscious of the advantages of his citizenship. He expressed nothing but respect for the imperial power, even describing it as "sublime." He had particular reason to be grateful for the majesty of the Roman law, which already was developing the principles of universal justice and equality before the law that were the major Roman contribution to Western idealism. At Ephesus the town clerk saved him from the mob howling for his blood by reminding them that they would be held to account; the accusers of Paul should lay their charges before a lawful assembly. In Jerusalem he suffered from the tolerance and liberality of the Romans, who permitted their subject peoples to keep and enforce their own customs so long as they honored and obeyed the emperor; but again Roman justice saved him from the Jews who clamored for his death. The governor required them to present their charges at a fair hearing, where the accused could answer them. Though mystified by the fantastic superstitions at issue, he promptly honored Paul's appeal to Caesar, and had him sent to Rome.

This Caesar was the abominable Nero, who chose to use the Christians as scapegoats for a great fire that destroyed much of Rome; so Paul met his martyrdom. Quite possibly he welcomed it. It hastened the union with his Lord that he had long yearned for, and he may have foreseen that the true faith would be strengthened by such persecution. The Romans themselves were ashamed of Nero, however. His persecution of the Christians was an act of simple barbarity; there was as yet no clear issue between them and the imperial power. Paul had some reason to believe that this power was ordained by God, for the Empire still had a great deal to contribute to Christianity, directly and indirectly. In Asia Minor its contribution is best represented by the life and work of the Emperor Hadrian, two generations after Paul.

Under Hadrian the "Golden Age" inaugurated by Augustus reached its zenith. After considerable military experience, he had been appointed Governor of Syria by the Emperor Trajan, his cousin, and took up residence at Antioch. Here, in A.D. 117, Trajan spent the last winter of his life after a brilliant campaign in the East; en route to Rome, he died on the coastal road of Cilicia, not far from Tarsus. Upon succeeding him, Hadrian promptly reverted to the Augustan policy of deliberate retrenchment, abandoning Trajan's conquests beyond the old Roman frontier of the Euphrates, and building his famous wall in Britain. He was proud to say that he won more by statesmanship than by arms, and he in fact restored peace and prosperity to an empire whose finances had been almost exhausted by the successful wars of Trajan. He reorganized the imperial civil service, giving it the essential form it was to retain for a century and a half. He paid close attention to the most minute details of provincial administration, even to laying down rules for the shoemaker and barber of a mining village. He began the codification of Roman law conceived by Julius Caesar; Julian, the jurist he selected for this long labor, initiated the classic age of Roman jurisprudence. In his own decrees Hadrian was conspicuously humane, especially to women, slaves, and the poor. He is the pre-eminent example of the efficient, just, liberal government by which the Roman Empire won the fervent gratitude of the peoples it ruled.

Hadrian is chiefly remembered, however, for the travels on which he started at the age of forty-five and spent more than half of his twenty-one-year reign. He marched on foot through every quarter of the empire. In Asia Minor alone he spent several years on two separate trips. Each time he landed at Ephesus, one of his favorite cities, and proceeded to visit almost all the other cities that have made the land famous. He paid his respects to the tomb of Ajax at Troy; he went on to Cyzicus, Nicomedia, and Nicaea to repair the destruction of a terrible earthquake; at Trapezus he built a harbor and a temple to commemorate the site where Xenophon and the Ten Thousand had hailed the sight of the sea; he honored Iconium by making it a Roman Colonia; he came bearing gifts to Pergamum, Smyrna, Sardis, Laodicea, Byzantium, Amasia, Antioch-in-Pisidia, Myra, Adana, Tarsus. He left a trail of new temples, gateways, granaries, bridges, statues, games, and festivals. In ruder regions he founded new cities—Hadriana, Hadrianea, Hadrianopolis, Hadrianotherae.[11]

One motive for all this travel was simple love of it. Hadrian was a sightseer, with an intellectual curiosity rare among Roman rulers; he alone displayed a lively interest in knowing the world that Rome had won. Another motive was administrative zeal. He traveled without pomp or regalia, bareheaded, through all kinds of weather; everywhere he inspected, conferred, regulated, reformed. But a particular inspiration was his love of Hellenism. As a youth he had acquired the passion for Greek culture that won him the nickname of "the Greekling," and made him the most cultivated and cosmopolitan of the emperors. Hence he traveled mostly in the Greek-speaking East and was most generous to the Greek cities, especially to his "beloved city" of Athens. His many works here spelled out his dream of reviving Hellas and marrying it to Rome. He completed the colossal temple of Olympian Zeus, which for centuries had been an abandoned ruin; he enlarged and ornamented the stage of the theater of Dionysus, presiding over the annual festival; he built a new quarter that doubled the size of the city; he made it the capital of the

[11] The last is now the site of Balikesir, a considerable town on the railway from Izmir to the Sea of Marmora. Hadrianopolis has survived through the centuries as the much more important city of Adrianople (Edirne) in European Turkey.

Greek world, establishing annual assemblies to which delegates came from all over; he selected Herodes Atticus, its celebrated millionaire and benefactor, to take over the administration of the "free cities" in the province of Asia. At Rome he built an Athenaeum, a library and lecture institute to serve as a center of Greek culture. He was himself a learned writer of both prose and verse, in both Greek and Latin, and he surrounded himself with poets, artists, musicians, scholars, and philosophers. As an administrator he exempted schoolteachers from local taxes. He endeavored to build up a cultivated middle class, perhaps as a bulwark against the tides of Orientalism and barbarism, certainly as a means of unifying the empire and promoting the commonwealth.

All in all, no other emperor worked so hard to realize the ideal of cosmopolis, or more fully exemplified it in his own person. In particular he symbolized the Roman mission of consolidating and preserving the Greek heritage in the East and transmitting it to the West. In government and law the Romans applied the abstract Greek ideas of justice, reason, and philanthropy, at once on a large scale and in practical detail; Hadrian proved his living faith by public works. Greek culture they transmitted in a prosaic form better suited to peoples without the high gifts of the Greeks. Hadrian represented an unoriginal, unexciting, but highly civilized type developed by the Romans: the connoisseur and man of the world, urbane, tolerant, moderate, tactful, sensible. He preserved a measure of the skepticism and irony by then lost to most Greeks except the Epicureans. His arduous imperial labors are the more admirable because he evidently had few illusions and seldom wore the purple. "Nature betrays us, fortune changes, a god beholds all things from on high"—so runs one motto he is said to have engraved on a ring. He did not believe that he was divine, or even immortal. As a good Roman he had a decent respect for the ancient pieties, and as a cosmopolitan a curiosity about the mysteries new and old, the many gods worshiped by his age; but he remained skeptical of them all. He did not commit himself to the foolishness of the Greeks, or of St. Paul.

The gods were not kind to the Emperor Hadrian. Nature betrayed him when his travels took him to Jerusalem, still a waste after its destruction by Titus in A.D. 70, when the Jews had risen in bloody rebellion. A humane impulse to restore civilization to this ancient center led him to order the founding of a new Roman Colony and the building of a temple to Jupiter Capitolinus in the desolate precincts of the local god. The result was another uprising in Palestine, the last and fiercest, led by the fanatical Simon Bar-Kochba. The rebels took and held Jerusalem for two years. Hadrian had to take to the field again, in a war that was fought savagely to the death in every town—the death of some 600,000 Jews and up to 100,000 Romans. Palestine became a desert, if at last a placid one. Hadrian contracted an incurable, wasting sickness that racked him for the last two years of his life. For months, wrote his biographer, he "died daily."

The emperor carried on in a stoical spirit he might have been taught by his contemporary Epictetus. His imperial coins, which had borne legends of the Golden Age and the Times of Happiness, were the only ones to bear the figure of Patience. On his last birthday he made his final bequest to the Empire, recommending to the Senate the benign Antoninus Pius as his successor. When he formally adopted Antoninus as his "son," he specified that the new Caesar must himself immediately adopt two sons, one of whom was the young Marcus Aurelius. In thus presenting Rome with two of its noblest emperors, Hadrian manifested the *pietas, gravitas,* and *constantia,* the high and heavy sense of responsibility, that distinguished the Romans from the more imaginative Greeks, and enabled them to give the ancient world the law and order merely dreamed of in Greek philosophy. Even so the dying emperor was jaunty enough to write his one immortal poem, beginning *"Animula vagula blandula"*:

> Soul of me, vague, debonair,
> Guest of this body and friend,
> Say whither now thou wilt fare,
> Pallid and rigid and bare,
> Little soul,
> All thy jests at an end? [12]

This touching little poem becomes moving when we look more closely into the life and work of Hadrian. His soul was not too debonair. He had had little occasion for jest; he got little manifest joy from being Emperor. He was lonely, childless, estranged from his wife, with few intimates and fewer to understand him. Most of his last years he spent at the villa near Rome that he started building early in his reign, and to the end kept crowding with souvenirs of his travels: a nook seven miles in circumference, cluttered with temples, porticoes, statues, baths, theaters, replicas of the glory of Athens—a Lyceum, an Academy, a Prytaneum. His private retreat was a world's fairgrounds, a tourist's scrapbook in marble, an imperial white elephant. It included a corner representing the Styx. What were his thoughts here? Had he a weary sense of failure? We can never know; but in retrospect we can see that there was a curse upon him. The career that ended in this bizarre sanctum has a tragic aspect, foreshadowing the prolonged death agony of the Roman Empire.

[12] Translation by Marcus S. Dimsdale.

The Greeks were properly grateful to their benefactor. They honored Hadrian not merely by the perfunctory titles of "Divine Savior of the World" and "Redeemer of the Universe," but by titles that must have been more pleasing to him, such as "Zeus Olympios" and "Zeus Panhellenius," "Restorer" and "Liberator," "Ionian and Friend of Greece." His fellow Romans, however, made only formal sacrifices to his genius. He was pursued by scandalous rumors from the beginning of his reign, when he was blamed for the execution of four of Trajan's generals, rivals for the throne; although he swore he had not ordered their execution, he was never able to live down the legend of his "cruelty." At the end of his life he did put to death his brother-in-law and nephew for conspiring against him. Conservatives always disliked and distrusted him because of his reforms, especially his favoritism to the provinces. Upon his death, Antoninus Pius had to work hard to get the Senate to accord him the routine honor of deification.

Hadrian was indeed restless and enigmatic enough to warrant a measure of distrust. "*Varius, multiplex, multiformis,*" the subtlest of the Roman emperors lacked the candor, the element of simplicity, that might have assured his reputation as a great and good emperor. We can never be certain that we know him as we know St. Paul before him, or Marcus Aurelius after him. What did he really think of the Olympian Zeus whose temple at Athens he so proudly restored? For sophisticates, like Lucian, the Olympians were by now a subject for ribald jest; and the Athenians themselves had never bothered to complete this temple, allowing it to lie in ruins for centuries. Hadrian seemed fonder of the goddesses, notably Cybele, Diana of Ephesus, and Venus; on the anniversary of Rome's birth he dedicated his temple of Venus and Rome. Was it primarily his sensuality that attracted him to these goddesses, or was it a genuine reverence for the symbol of the Heavenly Mother? And was he seeking thrills, or peace of mind, when he got himself initiated into various mysteries? At least he seems not to have been a serene skeptic. Beneath his skepticism ran a thick streak of superstition, which in the next century was to corrode the old Roman temper of reserve. It appeared in his fondness for consulting oracles and dreams, his habit of annually forecasting his life in the year to come. One cannot escape the impression of something decadent in the Emperor Hadrian.

The plainest sign is his celebrated love for Antinoüs, the beautiful Asiatic Greek youth he met in Asia Minor and made his page. Here again we cannot really share the thought and feeling of Hadrian. His love was evidently in some sense spiritual as well as sensual, in the Platonic manner, and there is no question of his bitter grief when his beloved drowned in the Nile while still in the flower of his youth. "He wept for him like a woman," wrote Hadrian's biographer. Now, however, his behavior becomes incomprehensible to us. He had Antinoüs deified, and identified his soul with a new star in the heavens. He founded in his honor a city in Egypt, named Antinoöpolis or Antinoe, while in Arcadia he established an "oracle of Antinoüs" with yearly mysteries. He listened avidly to poems and orations in praise of the divine youth, he rejoiced in the Antinoüs Games instituted at Athens and elsewhere. Everywhere the new cult inspired statues, from colossal ones resembling Egyptian gods to busts idealizing his sensuous beauty—the "Antinoüs type," which romantic critics were wont to adore but moderns regard as effete. Hadrian need not have literally believed in the divinity of his beloved: perhaps he was merely seeking to preserve his memory by conferring on him the kind of immortality his age believed in. But whatever his thought, his taste seems egregious. "You would think it would sicken him," writes Eleanor Clark, "to have thrust at him from everywhere, wrapped in every atrocious hypocrisy, the face that he had known in ecstasy and sleep, to whose risky eyes he had entrusted all that is most secret and true in himself. No; he demands it."

We are obliged to note that Hadrian's ardor for Hellenism did not conspicuously refine his sense of the beautiful. His taste ran to the romantic, the sentimental, the exotic, the extravagant, the colossal. He preferred Antimachus to Homer, Ennius to Virgil. In rhetoric he liked the "Oriental style." Of his own work almost all has been lost, including—most unfortunately—his autobiography; but except for "The Dying Emperor to His Soul," the fragments attributed to him are all mediocre. One suspects that the imperial poet was at his best in his lascivious verse. And if his own literary shortcomings are hardly significant, it is significant that no notable literature came out of his court, at which poetry was said to have become the rage. Hadrian symbolizes the decline in classical culture.

The "Silver Age" of Roman literature was fading out with Pliny and Juvenal. Epic and drama no longer had vital meaning. Cut off from them, poetry had turned to satire, lyric, and romance, but it was losing spontaneity in all forms. Later the anonymous author of "The Vigil of Venus" would abruptly abandon his theme, to lament the wintry death of song in Rome:

Ah, she sings. But we are silent. When shall *my* spring come to me?
When shall *I* grow as a swallow, and my lips at last be free?

Greek literature was in much the same state. Both suffered from the blight of rhetoric, which by now was the chief end of education. Public

speaking was a major means to fame, and as great public issues were no
longer being debated, formal eloquence, or elegance, was prized for its
own sake. A favorite subject of oratory was the panegyric; it could be
turned on in honor of any emperor, on any occasion. Among the most important personages in the cities were the "sophists," pedagogues who
doubled as orators on public occasions; these were the men to whom
Hadrian granted special favors as he tried to raise the level of education.
One of them, Polemon of Laodicea, he invited to orate at the dedication
of the temple of Olympian Zeus, the symbol of a revived Hellenism.

Architecture and sculpture continued to flourish as the cities went on
building and embellishing, but they flourished as industries, not as arts.
Their practitioners were typically anonymous and imitative. Thus the
historian Arrian, Hadrian's governor in Pontus, wrote in to order some
replacements, including "another Hermes, about five feet high," and
"also one of Philesius, four feet." In the next century the chief business
of sculptors was adorning sarcophagi to suit the florid tastes of their
customers. In the West their art deteriorated so badly that Constantine
the Great borrowed figures from earlier buildings to adorn his triumphal
arch in Rome.

So we must wonder how much good Hadrian did the Greek cities by
all the new temples, statues, festivals, and what not that he lavished on
them. It would be inhuman to deride his gifts, which no doubt heightened the felicity of the age; but at least we must note that he failed in
his ideal objective. No renaissance of Greek culture resulted from his
generous ardor. His beloved Athens, which had long since ceased to
create anything, grew only more complacent. The more energetic cities
of Asia Minor were brightened by his visits but stimulated to no more
original enterprise. And the fault was in part Hadrian's, typified again by
the temple of Olympian Zeus. He was trying to revive a dead past. He
succeeded chiefly in strengthening a traditionalism that was the chief
enemy of fresh creative effort. The cities took to a cult of the past, reviving their local gods and mythical founders. They created only more preposterous myths about their antiquity.

We must wonder, too, whether any ruler or any policy could have
awakened these cities to a sense of new possibilities, stirred them to new
experiment and adventure. It is too easy to say no out of hand. Toynbee
has made popular the view that this age was the "Indian summer" of
Greco-Roman civilization, or the downturn of the inevitable historical
cycle; and it follows that only winter can come after the autumn haze,
that nothing creative can come out of an age of degeneration. Actually,
Asia Minor was not simply moribund; it still had reserves of energy and

natural genius. We are always prone to forget that the "Roman Empire" did not fall—the Eastern half went on. With Constantine the Great a new adventure did begin. Out of Ionia came the builders of Hagia Sophia, a masterwork in a new style. Neither Constantine nor these builders started from scratch; both profited from creative effort that had been going on all the time. The domed Pantheon built by Hadrian himself was a striking example.

Yet it seems clear that in Hadrian's time only an extraordinary ruler could have struck sparks in Asia Minor, a ruler of a radically different type. For all his reforms, he was not an adventurer nor a creator. He was at best a great conserver. The keynote of his reign was not renaissance but retrenchment. In effect the Roman Empire went on the defensive all along the line, militarily, politically, economically, culturally. In giving his age a real security Hadrian also gave it a false sense of security. His self-appointed successors failed to carry on his mission of culturally unifying the empire, but essentially they sought as he did to maintain the status quo. Antoninus Pius—honest, conscientious, virtuous, noble—had no new ideas, and no reason to travel. Marcus Aurelius, the high-minded philosopher king, had no more vision. His kind of wisdom precluded creative effort; he simply did his duty as emperor, with selfless devotion, and without love, without hope. He traveled chiefly because of the foreign and civil wars in his reign which presaged the end of the Pax Romana.

Elsewhere I have taken up some of the fifty different reasons given by historians for the decline and fall of Rome.[13] Here I shall dwell on one basic reason for the lack of any live sense of possibility, any disposition to fresh adventure, in a once enterprising world. This was the loss of freedom. It was no less paralyzing—it was even more paralyzing—because the Emperor Hadrian was by no means a despot.

As Trajan had made war on his own initiative, so Hadrian had decided for peace. In either case the emperor's word was law—the people had nothing to say about it. The Roman Senate had only a nominal say. Hadrian was punctilious about displaying an outward respect for this venerable institution, but it was a purely formal respect. He himself suffered from the impotence and futility of the Senate; unable to oppose or criticize him freely, it vented its injured dignity in backbiting and scandalmongering. The Greek cities were much less jealous, because they had grown accustomed to their dependence on the emperor, and seemed unaware of anything anomalous in their proud description of themselves as "free and autonomous from the beginning by grace of the

13 *The Uses of the Past,* Chapter 7.

Augusti." The "free cities" of Asia were not yet a fiction, to be sure. They still had considerable local autonomy, passing their own laws; more than three hundred of them in Asia Minor issued their own coins; and civic pride still inspired their wealthy citizens to enterprise in maintaining the civic festivals and providing new public buildings. But they had no voice in determining federal policy, no major public isues to debate. Their range of choice and action was restricted to local affairs of no serious conse-quence. Their freedom appeared chiefly in a reckless extravagance, intens-ified by their traditional rivalry as they now competed for grandiose titles or the rank of metropolis.

Hence the positive achievements of Hadrian in strengthening the em-pire tended finally to weaken it, illustrating the thesis of John Stuart Mill that a benevolent autocracy is in the long run more fatal than a tyrannical one. In reforming the imperial civil service, Hadrian enlarged it and at-tached it more firmly to the Emperor. Sincerely devoted to the ideal of the *polis,* he nevertheless centralized power in the Emperor and further restricted the real independence of the cities. In his benevolent concern for their welfare he felt impelled to straighten out their mismanaged affairs, when not to bail them out. Trajan had sent Pliny to look into the irresponsible administration of Bithynian cities, which became a scandal when aqueducts at Nicomedia collapsed before they were completed, and following the destructive earthquake in Bithynia Hadrian took over its entire administration from the Roman Senate. The city fathers displayed little resentment over such infringements on their sovereignty; usually they were pleased to dump their problems in the imperial lap. In general, the individual might still feel free in his private life, but there was vir-tually no corporate freedom—freedom for political organizations or for associations of citizens for public purposes. There was nothing like a Roman Civil Liberties Union.

Nor a Roman Labor Party. The "cities" were grateful to Hadrian, I have said. More precisely it was their articulate ruling class, the Councils of the wealthy who alone could afford to hold public office, and for whom the popular assemblies now served as little more than rubber stamps. The voice of the proletariat is seldom heard, but when it is they were usually disturbing the peace, as by disorders in Tarsus. The indirect evidence makes it plainer that the city masses did not share in the security and felicity of the age. Although Hadrian tried to protect the poor in some of his legislation, he did little or nothing to improve their basic economic condition. As a pupil of Hellas, he was indifferent to technology and economics. Like all the other Roman emperors, he was too aristocratic or too "practical" to conceive of long-range programs for economic development. All lived fiscally from hand to mouth, meeting emergencies by special levies, with no idea of cushioning shocks or spreading costs by national loans or debts; and the poor got all the shocks. Likewise the masses hardly shared in the culture that Hadrian sought to revive, and they had little opportunity to contribute creative energy or talent. The kind of education he promoted was not for them. The practical Romans had never developed a public-school system for their own children, and in the provinces they helped chiefly to feed, manage, and above all amuse the cities—amuse them by the gladiatorial shows that most luridly exposed the insensitiveness of the grave Roman character, the pedantry of its Stoic ideal. If Hadrian had any idea of the brutalizing, degrading effect of these shows, he kept it to himself.

Hence we are led back to St. Paul, whose faith was a conceivable means to the unification and the regeneration of the empire that Hadrian failed to achieve. Hadrian was acquainted with this faith. At Athens he was said to have read with interest the work of one or two Christian apologists, and according to early Christian tradition he was even inclined to offer Christ a place in his Pantheon. He might have considered the Pauline teachings that in Ramsay's view were most pertinent: that only the Divine is real, and that "a Society, or a Nation, is progressive in so far as it hears the Divine voice: all else is degeneration." But we cannot blame Hadrian for not heeding this wisdom or banking on this faith. The Hellas he loved had created its brilliant culture in a spirit very different from Paul's. Christ would never have accepted a place in his Pantheon, the "Temple of All Gods."[14] The followers of Christ were bound to repel the tolerant emperor, in either his skeptical or his pious moods. Simply as he aspired to an ideal commonwealth he would distrust these "atheists," who expressed such contempt for all the other gods worshiped by the vast majority of his subjects. This latest mystery cult was still a negligible minority sect, far from ready to assume the responsibilities of an imperial religion.

Indirectly, however, Hadrian helped to prepare the soil for the long, slow growth that eventually would enable Christianity to take on these responsibilities. Although in later centuries, when the manufacture of legendary martyrs became a flourishing industry, he was made the author of a persecution that contributed an appropriate number of saints to the

[14] Fifteen centuries later this grandest of Hadrian's buildings served the Christian purposes of Pope Urban VIII. Although Michelangelo declared it to be of angelic rather than human design, Urban stripped off its bronze roof to make cannon. As a pious contemporary noted, "It is becoming that such noble material should keep off the enemies of the Church rather than the rain."

calendar, early Christian tradition knew nothing of such a persecution. His own records show that like all the most conscientious emperors, he felt obliged to combat a subversive sect, which refused to make the nominal patriotic obeisance to the imperial cult, but that he insisted on due process of law and took pains to guard against a popular witch-hunt. "In Heaven's name," he wrote the governor of Asia, "take the very greatest care that if a man prosecute any one of these men by way of false accusation, you visit the accuser, as his wickedness deserves, with severer penalties." Hence Christianity was to be strengthened by an occasional persecution that produced inspiring martyrs while its humbler followers enjoyed the blessings of Roman law and order, a justice such as "security risks" in modern America might envy. And Hadrian himself might have appreciated the irony of the further Roman contributions to the religion of the future. The great roads he kept in repair facilitated travel by missionaries and organizers (as later they would the barbarian invasions). The culture he cherished made possible the development of Christian theology, an intellectual distinction achieved by no other Oriental mystery cult. His ideal of *cosmopolis* prepared the way for a "catholic" church, while the Roman imperial system provided the model for a hierarchical, autocratic church that gained another advantage over its Oriental competitors by introducing Roman order and discipline into its worship.

But Hadrian would have taken no pleasure in his main personal contribution, aside from the apocryphal saints bred by the legends of his persecutions. His deification of Antinoüs was a godsend to Christian apologists, a favorite text for the absurdity and the immorality of paganism. Nor would Hadrian have relished the thought that the new religion profited still more from the failures of Rome, the inner rot that weakened the foundations of the empire. To testify to this we might call in a final witness—Apuleius, whose *Golden Ass* was one of the few immortal works to come out of Hadrian's century. Apuleius was another student of philosophy and religion who traveled widely in the Greek world, including Asia Minor. He too was acquainted with the Christians. The "wickedest woman" in his book was a baker's wife who "rejected all true religion in favor of a fantastic and blasphemous cult of an 'Only God,'" and made its absurd communion an excuse for "getting drunk quite early in the day and playing the whore at all hours." The satire of Apuleius is a blend of bawdiness and piety that might have delighted Hadrian as much as it would have horrified Paul. But he is a more positive witness than the skeptical, frustrate emperor to the high values of paganism, and also to its inadequacies, the basic reasons why it succumbed to the fantastic and blasphemous cult of Paul's Lord.

A gentler Rabelais, Apuleius was a man of lively curiosity and wide learning, humor and gusto, and withal a capacity for reverence and awe. His reward was a religious experience that evidently gave him more peace of mind than either Paul or Hadrian knew. In dreams and visions corresponding to the Christian gift of grace, the Queen of Heaven revealed to him that she was known by many names—Ceres, Cybele, Hera, Hecate, Cyprian Aphrodite, Ephesian Artemis—but that her true name was Queen Isis. She was "Nature, the universal Mother, mistress of all the elements, primordial child of time, sovereign of all things spiritual, queen of the dead, queen also of the immortals, the single manifestation of all gods and goddesses that are." Initiation into her mysteries meant a spiritual regeneration, not merely a ritual rebirth. She required "voluntary death" to the world, "perfect chastity," lifelong devotion to her service—so difficult a life that Apuleius for some time put off his initiation. He learned, however, that "her service is perfect freedom"; the greatest pleasure in life was contemplation of his loving Goddess. His prayer of gratitude suggests the Litany of the Blessed Virgin: "Holiest of the Holy, perpetual comfort of mankind, you whose bountiful grace nourishes the whole world; whose heart turns toward all those in sorrow and tribulation as a mother's to her children; you who take no rest by night, no rest by day, but are always at hand to succor the distressed by land and sea, dispersing the gales that beat upon them. . . ." Apuleius was so convincing that many Christians believed in the literal truth of the miraculous transformations of his hero into an ass and then into a man again. Even St. Augustine, who violently denounced his discourse on the *God of Socrates,* wrote uncertainly that he "either reported or invented" these transformations.

Apuleius would have been amused by such ludicrous credulity, on which Christianity throve. Yet he himself was credulous enough. Although well bred and well off, he had suffered from a deep anxiety, due not so much to a sense of guilt or unworthiness as to the power of "blind Fortune," whose cruelty was amply documented in his episodical narrative. His beloved Goddess promised deliverance from such fear. In his prayer of gratitude he went on: "Your hand alone can disentangle the hopelessly knotted skeins of fate, terminate every spell of bad weather, and restrain the stars from harmful conjunction." At that, her power seemed insufficient. Apuleius was also initiated into the mysteries of the "invincible Osiris," the "God of Good Fortune," which involved "nocturnal orgies"—apparently a less chaste manner of regeneration. Then another vision instructed him to undergo yet a third initiation, to secure the eternal blessing of the holy number three. Later he became a priest of Asclepius too. He might have played it safer by a single throw on Paul's Lord, who required no more.

And Paul's Lord was much more accessible. Although Queen Isis inspired a beautiful faith—the loftiest spirituality that the other mystery religions had to offer—it was still through "secret knowledge," which the initiate was sworn never to divulge. It was not a gospel open to all. Worse, it was quite expensive knowledge. Apuleius tells proudly how he spared no expense as he prepared for his initiation—the expense that the Goddess was careful to detail to her priests in dreams she sent them. His union with Osiris was delayed because he lacked the money to pay the initiation fee, until at length the priest of Osiris ordered him to sell the clothes off his back, pointing out that poverty was a small price to pay for so holy a sacrament; and with his independent income he could soon buy more clothes. The masses of poor devils in the empire who had much greater need of Good Fortune had no clothes to spare. Those who might go bare to enjoy the luxury of such sacraments still lacked the necessary virtue and tact, at least in the eyes of the well-bred Apuleius: his poor people are more or less abject, his slaves generally base. They were deprived of the highest spiritual as well as cultural goods of the pagan world. But Paul's Lord did not discriminate between bond and free, rich and poor. Christianity was the one missionary religion that sought out the unfortunates who most needed comfort in an age whose felicity did not go wide or deep.

5. THE RECONVERSION OF TARSUS

In the century after Paul, Tarsus hardly lived up to its Hellenic or Stoic traditions. Its chief excitement seems to have been its competition with Anabarzus, a rival city on the plain, for metropolitan honors and titles—a competition as fierce as it was childish, if bloodless. The city maintained its extravagant loyalty to the Roman emperors, repeatedly renaming itself after them: Hadriane, Antoniniane, Commodiane, Severiane. Perhaps it was proudest when it induced one emperor, Alexander Severus, to accept the post of city magistrate. A more doubtful honor was the death of five emperors in or near the city. That of the Emperor Tacitus, in A.D. 276, might have sobered the Tarsians, for he had defeated the Goths in Cilicia: the Pax Romana was no more. Shortly before this the Parthians had invaded Cilicia. Shortly afterward Tarsus was sacked by the Emperor Shapur, of the rising Sassanian Empire in Persia. Later the Emperor Julian the Apostate marked the end of an era by making the city his winter headquarters as he prepared his ill-fated invasion of Persia. During the same year, 363, the last imperial champion of Hellenism and paganism was carried back there to be buried. Thereafter Tarsus was to have a sufficiently colorful history for the next thousand years—but Oriental peoples provided most of the color.

The birthplace of St. Paul failed to live up to him in early Christian history. It was completely overshadowed by the church of Antioch, if only because it had no great church tracing its foundation to him. Although Tarsus had its inevitable martyrs, the first important figure it produced after Paul was Diodorus, who with Theodore of Mopsuestia—another Cilician city—introduced the basic teaching of the Oriental heresy of Nestorianism. They taught that Jesus had two distinct natures, human and divine, and that only the man had been born of Mary and died on the cross, a distinction smacking of Persian dualism, as well as of the absolute separation of God and man in Judaism.[15] What Paul would have thought of Nestorianism it is hard to say, but he might well have accepted the subsequent, more influential, heresy of Monophysitism, which insisted on one incarnate nature of Christ. Hebrews and Orientals generally never found very luminous the formula that eventually became orthodox: "Two natures, without confusion, without change, without division, without separation." Their aversion to subtle Hellenistic theology helps to explain why Cilicia, long subject to Semitic and Syrian influence, succumbed so quickly to Mohammedanism.

In the seventh century appeared a kind of spiritual descendant of St. Paul in Theodore of Tarsus, who went to England to become Archbishop of Canterbury and organize the English Church. But by this time the Arabs were on the surge, under the banner of Mohammed. Cilicia was among their early conquests. In 787 the Caliph Harun al-Rashid made Tarsus a Moslem stronghold, rebuilding its walls; from it the armies of Islam sallied forth year after year to ravage the Byzantine provinces behind the Taurus Mountains, marching up through the Cilician Gates that the energetic citizens of ancient Tarsus had made a passable road. The Byzantines recaptured the city toward the end of the tenth century, but did not hold it long. It was another people from the East, the Armenians, who restored Christianity, though in a Monophysite version. Fleeing from the Seljuk Turks, they found refuge in the Taurus Mountains and

[15] Mithraism, a Persian mystery religion that came through Asia Minor, picking up new ideas along the way, had early taken root in Cilicia. Plutarch cited as its first appearance the rites of the Cilician pirates. It later developed into about the strongest rival of Christianity, which it closely resembled in many of its rites and doctrines. Early Christians had some reason for their belief that it was an especially insidious invention of the Devil, for Satan himself had come from Persia.

then gradually conquered the Cilician plain. Tarsus succeeded Anabarzus as the capital of the kingdom of Little Armenia. Meanwhile it had fallen to the Crusaders, who had marched down through the Cilician Gates—to them "the Gates of Judas"—and whose leaders proceeded to fight among themselves over its possession. The Crusaders naturally looked askance at the heretic Armenians, but as they had a bond of brotherhood in their common hatred of the Orthodox Greeks and the Moslems, they patched up an agreement. In 1199 an Armenian king was crowned in Tarsus in the presence of a Papal ambassador.

Little Armenia managed to hold out against the Moslems longer than any of the Crusader kingdoms in Asia. Its pleas for aid were ignored by the Christian West, however, and in 1375 it fell to the Mamelukes of Egypt. The Armenians again found refuge in the mountains, where they maintained their form of Christianity to this century, but the Cilician plain became permanently Moslem. The Mamelukes left their mark on the homeland of St. Paul chiefly in their distinctive mosques, whose minarets are encircled by a roofed balcony. The next conquerors were other Moslems, the Ottoman Turks. On the historic date of 1492—the year 7000 after the Creation, in the belief of Eastern Christendom—Cilicia became a permanent part of Ottoman Turkey. Tarsus had no reason to celebrate this event: it faded into an unimportant provincial town. Dim memories sanctified a cave near a supposed tomb of Paul, but there were none to do honor to the Apostle.

In the new Turkey of Ataturk the rich Cilician plain has enjoyed a secular revival through modern methods of agriculture. Tarsus is now a busy town of over 30,000, again devoted to commerce, among other things boasting of its yoghurt and *baklava*—"the Best in the World." It is a poor shrine, however, for lovers of either Hellas or St. Paul. Drab and dusty, it is an overgrown village of mud brick, squatting on a site of no natural beauty except for the Taurus Mountains in the background. Excavations have yielded much of interest to specialists but no monuments to dazzle the layman, and nothing clearly associated with Paul.[16] A few scattered relics of its crowded past remain in place: near the central plaza a Roman gateway named for St. Paul, though generally attributed to Hadrian; on backlying streets some medieval buildings, including a tomb reputed to contain the bones of relatives or associates of

[16] Antioch-in-Pisidia, so important in Christian history, is also no Mecca for tourists. Now known as Yalvach, it is a forlorn site with no reminder of Paul or ruins worth speaking of. Apart from a temple of Men excavated by Ramsay—a center of the Phrygian mysteries—the chief memento of its religious history is a cave in the vicinity. Once sacred to Cybele, it is now sacred to the Virgin Mary.

Harun al-Rashid; here and there a section of ancient wall. Otherwise there is no trace of the former splendor of Tarsus. Its inland lake and harbor is a swamp. Its beloved River Cydnus is a commonplace stream, lacking the colonnades that once lined it. In place of its famous University, of which nothing remains, it has an American School. Although probably drawn here by the memory of St. Paul, this offers a wholly secular education, carefully purged of any missionary influence that might offend the Turks; the ghosts of the proud, free-thinking Tarsians might think poorly of it. They would also be unhappy in the knowledge that Adana is now the great city of the plain. Their one comfort might be the thought that their ancient rival Anabarzus is a mere ruin, grazed by the flocks of the nearby village of Anavarza.

But again the pious student of history need not be simply depressed by such thoughts, in a land again thriving, and still a historical fairyland. Returning to Adana from the palace of King Azitawadda at Karatepe, one may watch the leatherworkers in the bazaars making boots with upturned toes, like those of the Hittites. En route one passes a number of the fortresses—Byzantine, Arab, Armenian, Crusader—that stand out on eminences all over the plain of Cilicia, once a main thoroughfare for the makers of history. The most spectacular is one at Anabarzus, a mile long, on a precipice that rises abruptly out of the plain to a height of six hundred feet. From Adana to Tarsus and beyond, the plain is dotted with mounds dating from thousands of years before the time of St. Paul; so one may wonder whether the young student of the Old Testament, or the missionary to the Gentiles, ever had any curiosity about them, any inkling of the story they could tell. And as one approaches the rough country of Cilicia Aspera, he may find it easier to do more justice, finally, to the Empire that gave Paul citizenship.

A mile or so of monumental ruins along the rocky, jagged coast marks the site of Pompeiopolis—the old Greek city of Soli, which Pompey refounded and into which he moved some of the hardy, enterprising pirates he had subdued. This too was no mean city, though an ordinary one by ancient standards. Of a double colonnade that had stretched for several hundred yards, some Corinthian columns still stand, among great blocks of richly wrought frieze and cornice strewn about in the underbrush; one may better appreciate the nobility and grace of the Corinthian order in its natural setting, bathed by bright sunshine under blue skies. A valley beyond Pompeiopolis is spanned by the massive arches of an aqueduct, one of the many that made possible the luxuriant civic life of Roman Asia Minor by bringing in water—for lack of which most of the once magnificent sites are now deserted, or occupied only by villagers. And even one who is blasé about these repetitious ruins may be awed by the much better preserved remains of Diocaesarea (Uzunjaburch or "High Tower"), on a mountain top in the heart of the wilderness of Cilicia Aspera. Its main building is a great Corinthian temple to an Asianic god who had owned a temple-state, centuries before Paul, and who came to be known as Zeus Olbius. Above the temple stands a huge square tower, thought to have been a watchtower of the Cilician pirates. About it are porticoes, arched gateways, a theater—the amenities of civilization that the Romans had brought to this almost inaccessible site, still a wilderness today. One may hope that these pagans sleep well in their lovely temple-tombs, with columned porches, that lie in the quiet woods of the mountain below.

CHAPTER VII

Constantinople: The Byzantine Era

---

1. THE WORK OF CONSTANTINE THE GREAT

"WE SWEAR BY Caesar Augustus, our Savior and our God," wrote the citizens of Assus on marble, "and by the Pure Virgin, whom our fathers worshiped, that we will be faithful to Caius Caesar Augustus and all his House." They remind us again that the pagan world was ripe for a new savior. Their Pure Virgin was Athena, a defunct deity cherished only because their fathers had once worshiped her; the Caesar to whom they swore fidelity was the vicious Caligula; and even the great and good Caesars were useless for religious purposes—men never prayed to them in illness, trouble, or peril. In such soil the growth of Christianity was hardly so miraculous as it seemed to Cardinal Newman, who declared that its triumph could be explained only by the "Hand of God." It was much slower than the later growth of Mohammedanism: the Hand of Allah accomplished in a generation what took God three centuries. And the triumph of Christianity was immediately due to another Caesar, Constantine the Great—a man of the sword who was closer in spirit to Mohammed than to Jesus.

Now I have already pointed to some of the major reasons for the growth and spread of Christianity. At the outset it owed a great deal to the genius of St. Paul, whose mystical experience might seem more miraculous were it not common to worshipers of "false" gods. Thereafter it drew heavily on the classical world, becoming the most Hellenized of the mystery religions in its theology and the most Romanized in its organization and discipline, while remaining the most ethical, democratic, and humanitarian through its heritage from Judaism. It was a community to which one could belong body and soul, and which took care of both body and soul of its less fortunate members. As helpful were more questionable elements of popular appeal. It took on a heavy freight of familiar

217

superstition, exploiting in particular the fear of demons, now marshaled under the rule of Satan. It became a completely sacramental religion, adopting the familiar means to the familiar hopes inspired by the dying god. By its exclusiveness and its literalness it drastically simplified the whole problem of salvation. It gave its followers an absolute certitude that was comforting and sustaining alike to the simple-minded and to the dispirited intellectual, while intimidating the doubtful by the threat that God would punish most surely and terribly those who shopped around in the spirit of Apuleius.

Yet with all its advantages, in its promises and its threats, the triumph of Christianity was no more clearly inevitable than it has since proved in other quarters of the globe. By the time of Constantine the Great, after three hundred years, it had won only a small fraction of the imperial population—scholars estimate as small as 10 per cent. Its chief rivals, such as Mithraism, were also thriving; the adaptable mother goddesses and dying gods might have survived indefinitely in a free religious market. (When the Emperor Justinian, in the sixth century, sent out a bishop of Ephesus as a missionary to the pagans still holding out in western Asia Minor, he baptized as many as 70,000.) If sooner or later some emperor was bound to be attracted to Christianity, the conversion of any emperor at any time was not bound to be crucial. As Hadrian could not have Christianized the empire, so Constantine might not have been able to preserve it without the work of the pagan Diocletian before him; and if it had collapsed, Christianity might have disappeared with it—just as it might disappear with the destruction of Western civilization today. At any rate, the crucial event proved to be the conversion of Constantine, A.D. 312, through a vision of the Cross as he prepared to battle another Caesar.

In this conversion we may see the Hand of God; but if so, God worked in ways as mysterious as usual. Contemporary Christians regarded the embattled Constantine as the "Peer of the Apostles" and were quick to canonize him. Bishop Eusebius, who baptized him on his deathbed, wrote a kind of spiritual campaign biography of him, with an ominously fulsome introduction: "When I gaze in spirit upon this thrice-blessed soul, united with God, free from all mortal dross, in robes gleaming like lightning and in ever-radiant diadem, speech and reason stand mute, and I would willingly leave it to a better man to devise a worthy hymn of praise." Unfortunately, only the good Bishop's reason stood mute—his speech did not; and no better man appeared to write a reliable biography. Modern historians are still debating the motives of Constantine the Great, the measure of his greatness, and the consequences of his handiwork.

Chiefly they agree that the "Thirteenth Apostle" was no saint, and that his legacy included a permanent confusion of the things that are Caesar's and the things that are God's. Still, his adoption of Christianity as the imperial religion was literally epoch-making. In historical importance Constantine was indeed the Peer of the Apostles; so we must try to recover him from the pious fog in which Eusebius shrouded him.

The third century had been a period of almost continuous war, civil and foreign. The empire was ruled by generals who had little time for statesmanship. Emperors by the dozen were made and unmade by the army; few died in bed. Conspiracy and assassination were the order of the day. Political disorder created as serious economic disorder, which was intensified by plagues, famines, and the devastations of barbarian invaders. It was in the middle of this century that the idealistic Emperor Decius made the first systematic effort to eradicate Christianity. The gods were plainly angry, and one plain reason was the many "atheists" who refused to worship them. Decius ordered all his subjects to offer sacrifices to them, duly certified by the authorities.

Near the end of the century, however, the gods or the genius of Rome finally produced in the Emperor Diocletian another savior comparable to Augustus. His reputation has been clouded because he carried out the last major persecution of the Christians, and the most severe. Although his motives are uncertain, since we have none of his edicts and know only the Christian side of the story, his entire career suggests that he acted in a spirit of high-minded superstition and statesmanship. Otherwise he succeeded in bringing order out of anarchy by extensive fiscal and administrative reforms, establishing a central authority strong enough to control the army too. At the same time he created three other Caesars, to help him defend and rule an empire threatened on all fronts; he himself took command of the Greek-speaking East, setting up his capital in Bithynia at Nicomedia (Izmit). In retrospect we may deplore the heavy cost of his reforms. He attempted to freeze the entire economy by fixing wages and prices, and more successfully, by binding peasants, city workers, and officials to their jobs; he transformed the Principate into an Oriental monarchy, to strengthen the authority and secure the life of the Emperor; he introduced Oriental ceremony into his court at Nicomedia, shutting himself off from his subjects by graded ranks of palace officials and eunuchs, and requiring prostration before the royal person, now a demigod called Dominus, "Lord." Nevertheless this rigid, atavistic order may well have been the only kind that could have saved an empire so far gone in anarchy. Diocletian at least succeeded in mastering a desperate crisis and in restoring peace to Asia Minor. He proved his devotion, and perhaps his weariness with playing the Oriental monarch, by voluntarily abdicating in the year 305 after reigning for a fixed period of twenty years, and by retiring to plant vegetables and die as a private citizen. No Roman emperor had more thoroughly earned the pagan honor of deification, which he was the last to receive.

Diocletian's careful arrangements for his successors were disrupted by their personal ambition, which soon inspired struggles among them. Constantine the Great, son of one of the two Caesars appointed to rule the West, had not been born to the purple; his mother, Helena, was a Bithynian concubine. There is no question that he was a great general as he fought his way to the top, in bold, brilliant campaigns. Served well enough by his early patrons—Mars, Hercules, Jupiter, and especially the "Unconquered Sun"—he became unconquerable when he shifted to Christ, before a battle fought outside Rome. After winning the West he waited while Licinius, a Caesar in the East, disposed of the remaining Caesar. In the final struggle with Licinius, Constantine was clearly the aggressor, but by this time he could justify his attack as a crusade, since Licinius had grown hostile to the Christians. Fighting in the name of the old gods, and with superior forces, Licinius was defeated at Hadrianople in Europe and then crushed at Chrysopolis (Scutari), across the Bosphorus from Byzantium. Constantine became master of the whole Roman world that Diocletian thought too big and complicated to be ruled by one man. To maintain the large standing army he created, he was obliged to recruit more extensively among German tribes, who later would control the army and then sack Rome. (The "barbarian" Alaric was a Roman officer leading a Gothic tribe subsidized by the imperial treasury.) But this army preserved the East, and it at least held the West long enough to make possible the conversion of the German barbarians to Christianity.

Constantine's "greatness" as emperor and statesman is more debatable. He completed the transformation of the state begun by Diocletian, cementing the absolute authority of the emperor and binding the great mass of his subjects to their jobs or their land. His clearest success was in stabilizing the imperial currency; he issued a gold coin that remained standard throughout the commercial world for many centuries. Otherwise he did not distinguish himself either as administrator or as reformer. While he showed some concern for social justice, and more indignation at the corruption of the civil service, he was neither firm nor clear-sighted enough to do anything effectual about restoring equity and honesty. If anything, the poor were worse off for his rule because of his lavish, indiscriminate spending and the special privileges he created for his crowds

of friends or flatterers. He was always an authoritarian, sometimes violent
in temper, habitually bombastic in style. Having united the empire at the
cost of so much bloodshed, he could think of nothing better than to divide
it up again, among three sons and a nephew. Upon his death the nephew
was soon assassinated, together with Constantine's brother; the sons, an
unscrupulous lot, proceeded to fight among themselves; and the survivor
died without issue as another civil war was about to break out. The
dynasty of Constantine ended with his brilliant, tragic young nephew
Julian, whose brief reign won him only the title of Apostate.

But Julian's failure to revive paganism brings us back to Constantine's
enduring achievement, the establishment of Christianity. Bold as it was,
this was not clearly an act of deliberate statesmanship. Although some
historians have regarded his conversion as a mere pretense, due either to
cynical expediency or to farsightedness, this seems unlikely in view of the
universal superstition that by now prevailed. Free thought or disbelief
called for greater powers of mind than Constantine ever displayed; he
was a half-educated man, and seems to have been an essentially simple
one.[1] For the same reason, it is hard to believe that Constantine was per-
spicacious enough to recognize in Christianity the one force that could re-
vitalize his decadent empire. The small minority sect had made least
progress in the ruling class to which he belonged and among the soldiery
on whom he depended; nor did he seem aware that his empire was decadent. I can see no good reason to doubt the actuality of his conversion.
His vision of the Cross was, after all, a common kind of experience: the
gods habitually gave men cues in dreams and visions; and his vision had
proved a true omen—he had won the battle. Thereafter his edicts and his
official behavior testified to his gratitude. The whole issue of his motives
has been confused by the needless assumption that his conversion was a
spiritual experience comparable to St. Paul's, and that it meant a complete
change of mind and heart.

There was always something of the pagan in Constantine. As a good
Roman and a conscientious emperor, he would not simply scrap and
scorn the faiths of his fathers; as an unsophisticated soldier he would
naturally tend to confuse the "Unconquered Sun" with his new God, and
have difficulty grasping the nice theological distinctions about the nature

---

[1] Diocletian, a wiser and more original statesman, was slavishly devoted to oracles
and omens, even in the matter of proper names; he ordered his co-Caesar Galerius
to take the more magical name of Maximianus. The Christian mentality of the period
is as foreign to us. Thus the eminent Lactantius acknowledged that the demons residing in pagan temples could perform real miracles, but added that Christians need
not fear them: "they must flee at the mention of the name of God, and a pious man
can even force them to reveal their own names."

of the Godhead. For he had not been instructed and converted by a missionary—God himself had given him a sufficient sign, without at once telling him that he was a jealous God who would resent any appearance of respect for the gods. Hence it is easy to point out lapses in the Christian emperor. He retained the title of Pontifex Maximus; he continued to issue coins in honor of his former patrons, especially Sol Invictus; in a decree making Sunday a day of rest he referred to it as "the venerable day of the Sun" instead of the Lord's day; etc. It is still easier to demolish his claims to sainthood. He shocked his contemporaries by putting Licinius to death after accepting his surrender and promising to spare his life. He embarrassed even his Christian eulogists by arranging for the murder of his wife Fausta and his son Crispus; though they were presumably guilty of some sin or crime, Eusebius was careful to delete all mention of them in the last edition of his *Church History*. The most that can be said for Constantine's character is that he was basically an earnest, well-intentioned man, on the whole a pretty good one by the lights of his time.

Nevertheless he sufficiently proved himself as a Christian emperor. He prohibited the erection of his own statue in any pagan temple and removed the pagan gods from his later coins. He was especially lavish in his favors to Christian communities, allocating public funds to provide them a regular income and to repair or enlarge their churches, while he himself built magnificent churches in the major cities. He even set himself to an earnest study of Christian scripture and theology. The Arian controversy that shook all Christendom he had at first considered an "extremely trifling" matter, writing Arius and his major opponent, "You ought not to have raised such questions at all, and if they were raised, you ought not to have answered." His later letters reveal an informed, if somewhat unhappy, interest in such questions. And on his deathbed he was baptized. Though it is no doubt unfortunate that Constantine should have been hailed as the Thirteenth Apostle before he had taken the indispensable sacrament, deathbed baptism was still not uncommon; and as an emperor who had been vouchsafed the Sign by God himself, he may well have regarded the sacrament as a mere formality, or his election to the company of the Apostles as an honor to them.[2] Certainly he had a royal idea of his Christian mission.

The all-important matter for the historian is the nature of Constantine's

[2] There were also good reasons for preferring deathbed baptism, apart from the early belief that mortal sins committed after baptism meant certain damnation. Tertullian and others argued, soundly enough, that infant baptism would become a mere formality or magical routine, exciting nothing like the awe or feeling of rebirth afforded by initiation into the pagan mysteries.

faith. While we know very little of his personal religion, any private worries he might have had about his salvation, his letters and edicts make his official position perfectly clear. For him Christianity was a success religion. The God he habitually appealed to was a God of power—the "Mighty One," the "Greatest God"—who promised his faithful servants victory on earth. Bishop Eusebius, who took a similar view, records a "prayer" Constantine made his soldiers learn by heart: all about the Emperor and victory, with nothing about humility, love, brotherhood, or moral duty. Constantine had proper things to say about purity of heart and loving-kindness, and naturally assumed rewards and punishments in the next world too, but his stress was on the worldly success that he had himself enjoyed. "It is not vainglorious," he wrote, "to acknowledge and boast of the beneficence of the Supreme Power." It may seem vainglorious only because the imperial convert took for granted that he was God's deputy. Thus he worried over the contentions within the Church, lest God "may perhaps be moved to wrath, not only against the human race, but also against me myself, to whose care He has, by His celestial will, committed the government of all earthly things." Nevertheless we need not deem this simple egotism. In the high Roman tradition, Constantine was sincerely devoted to the public weal. The main point is that in this same tradition he regarded Christianity as a State cult, and was primarily concerned with the City of Earth, not with Augustine's City of God.

As I have written elsewhere, the clearest certainty about the epoch-making policy of Constantine is that he foresaw neither its immediate nor its long-range consequences, and builded at once far better and far worse than he knew. Immediately, his policy restored neither material prosperity nor spiritual unity to the empire; it alienated and demoralized the pagan majority, while the liberated Christians devoted their energy and zeal to fierce controversy over dogma. In the long run, the Church that this Latin from the West elected as a means to victory was to survive the Empire he was above all trying to save; a century later St. Augustine would stigmatize his Earthly City as the City of Satan. In the meantime Constantine's specific policies followed naturally from his conception of God and his own divine mission, and again had some unexpected consequences.

His relatively slight interest in the ethical teachings of Jesus is reflected in his legislation. Only a few of his laws might be called Christian in inspiration—for instance, the repeal of disabilities on celibates, the restriction of grounds for divorce, the denial of all rights of inheritance to bastards, and the prohibition of gladiatorial shows (though this soon became a dead letter). The thinness of Constantine's humanitarianism is illustrated by a law on the flogging of slaves: the master was not guilty of homicide if the slave died of it unless he had deliberately killed him or tortured him to death. Another law decreed that slaves who married free women should be burned to death. In general, Constantine made no serious effort to Christianize the social structure of his empire. Neither did any Christian monarchs for fifteen hundred years after him. Like him, the more humane were content to protect the helpless or unfortunate against the more brutal abuses of privilege, while accepting slavery, serfdom, and the natural rights of privilege.

An incidental but more positive influence was the mission he entrusted to his mother Helena. She went to Jerusalem to find the site of Calvary, and not only found it—helped by the usual dream—but dug up, with a speed and sureness that archaeologists must envy, the True Cross and the attendant relics of the Passion, including the Lance, the Sponge, and the Crown of Thorns. Thrilled by this blessed discovery, Constantine proceeded to build a monument worthy of it—the Church of the Holy Sepulchre. It was to remain a shrine for pilgrims through the ages, and an incentive for the Crusaders.[3] The discovery also led to the extraordinary popularity of the cult of relics, which swamped Eastern Christendom and later spread to medieval Europe. The True Cross engendered tons of fragments, and with them a stupendous variety of inspired fabrications, from heads of John the Baptist (I have myself seen two) to the authentic relic of the Lord's circumcision. Paganism had never hit upon such a cheap and wondrous means of awing the multitude.

Paganism suffered much more, however, from the official suppression that began with Constantine. His famous (if possibly legendary) Edict of Milan was scarcely the declaration of "spiritual freedom" that Christian historians like to call it. It freed Christians from State interference; but as they won power, other religions ceased to enjoy their freedom. Constantine himself was slow to learn the intolerant ways of a jealous God, and no doubt felt his way out of caution too, even a decent respect for the rights of the pagan majority. He suppressed only a few temples famous for their cures; he allowed the free expression of pagan opinion and the private worship of pagan gods. Yet he thoroughly looted the temples, appointing commissioners to tour the provinces and confiscate

[3] Some bases of its columns still show in front of the present church, built by the Crusaders. Unfortunately, the holiest spot in Christendom is an architectural horror and a religious scandal: a murky maze of altars, chapels, and grottoes on different levels, owned by different sects, alike chiefly in the gaudiness of their ornamentation, the phoniness of their legends, and the attendance of panhandling clerics. Only a Christian of exceptionally firm and simple faith could visit this shrine—and others in the Holy Land, such as the site of the Nativity and the Virgin's Milk Grotto in Bethlehem—without having his faith shaken.

all their gold. If his main object was to replenish the imperial treasury, he was probably doing his best as well to discourage the veneration of the old gods. Toward the end of his reign, when he was in firm control, he possibly prohibited the celebration of sacrifices, as a law issued by his son Constantius implies. In any case, Constantius decreed that "superstition shall cease and the madness of sacrifice shall be abolished," under penalty of death. Superstition did not cease, in spite of repeated decrees; but paganism was sufficiently undermined by the work of Constantine and his Christian-educated sons in their rule of half a century. Julian the Apostate could not undo their work in his brief reign of eighteen months. Thereafter persecution of pagans became more rigorous and systematic than any that Christians had ever suffered from, except briefly under Diocletian.

The spiritual cause of Christianity was not aided comparably. A host of pagans, especially in high places, became converts merely out of expediency; even Bishop Eusebius saw through the hypocrisy of many who flattered the gullible emperor by adopting his God. Enforced conversion did still less to regenerate the pagan world. Constantine himself was embarrassed when he exempted the clergy from the costly service on town councils, for so many wealthy men swarmed into holy orders that it became impossible to fill the councils, and necessary to restrict the number and qualifications of the ordained. Even so, the Church triumphant grew worldlier. Constantine's characteristic way of promoting his success religion was by increasing its material wealth and political power. A bishopric became a means to a princely life; the higher clergy felt at ease in an Earthly City that was as corrupt as ever. One by-product of Constantine's donation was the rapid growth of monasticism and extreme forms of asceticism, as the purer spirits fled to cell, desert, or pillar. "Wonderful irony of history!" wrote Theodore Zahn. "So long as the world was honestly heathen the earnest Christian could live in it. The practice of other-worldliness was then all-too-possible in the world. But in Constantine's New Jerusalem, this kingdom of God so happily realized upon earth, the real Christian was not at home."

Ardent Christians suffered in other ways that were to grow much more painful. Within a year after the conversion of Constantine, bishops forced on him their controversy with the Donatists. Zealots rejecting the ministry of bishops who had been backsliders during the persecution by Diocletian, the Donatists insisted that sacraments could be administered only by spiritual leaders who were in fact superior to their flock; their principle was lofty but fatal to the authority of bishops and the efficacy of sacraments. Constantine duly ruled against them, and when they continued to defy his decrees, ordered the shutting down of their churches and imprisonment of their leaders. Thus began the persecution of Christians by a Christian state. Constantine wearied of it, but under the constant goading of high churchmen his successors grew accustomed to it. By the end of the century Theodosius the Great, the last emperor to rule over a politically united empire, deprived heretics of civil rights; for the first time in history, literal orthodoxy became a requirement of citizenship. In the following century Pope Leo the Great endorsed the death penalty for erroneous opinions. For the next twelve hundred years Christians suffered a more savage persecution by fellow Christians than they had ever suffered from pagans, producing unnumbered millions of unsung martyrs.

Involved in this persecution was a fundamental problem, of the relation of Church and State, that was also to plague Christianity ever after. The bishops had appealed to the authority of Constantine to settle the Donatist controversy, and though he was ignorant of the particular issue at stake, he saw nothing strange in their appeal. He was head of a State in which religion had always been a department, the protection of the gods being essential to its welfare; the only novelty was that the new State God would not tolerate other gods, and had come to demand nicety in opinions about his divine nature. Constantine was properly concerned about any dissension that might displease God and reflect on himself. And presently he was faced by the much more serious controversy over Arianism. Arius preached the common-sense, scripturally sound, but theologically unsatisfying view that the Son was lesser than the Father who sent him. To settle this issue, Constantine took the momentous step of summoning a representative congress of bishops from all over the empire—the First Ecumenical Council, which met at Nicaea in the year 325. If it was not strictly representative, since only a few Westerners bothered to participate in discussions of a theological subtlety they were not yet much interested in, more than three hundred bishops gathered, including the most eminent scholars of the East, to give it a sufficiently ecumenical flavor. Constantine himself presided over the Council, arrayed in purple and gold, and played a decisive role in its proceedings. In the interests of the unity that seemed all-important to God and his own welfare, he forced through an agreement on a creed declaring that Jesus was "of one essence with the Father," and anathematizing all who declared otherwise.

Constantine stated proudly the lofty theory embodied in the Council of Nicaea: "The decision of three hundred bishops must be considered no other than the judgment of God, especially since the Holy Spirit, dwelling in the minds of so many men of such character, brought to light the

Divine will." The actuality was rather different. What the Council had most clearly brought to light was not the Divine will but the will of Constantine and certain of the bishops; many other bishops (including Eusebius) signed only under duress, remaining Arians at heart; and the aftermath, to the anger and dismay of the emperor, was more violent disunity. It took almost a century of ecclesiastical brawl and intrigue before Arianism was finally condemned. By this time other heresies had sprung up, to provoke still more furious and often indecent controversy. In the next centuries six more Ecumenical Councils were to meet, all in the East: at Chalcedon, at Ephesus, again at Chalcedon, twice at Constantinople, and finally again at Nicaea.[4] Their decisions were remarkable, Archbishop Benson observed, for being almost uniformly "uncharitable, unscriptural, uncatholic, and unanimous." Each anathematized more millions of Christians.

Now Constantine cannot be blamed for this disunity, which marked Christianity from the outset. It was bound to grow with the development of theology, more especially with the need of reinterpretation as the Second Coming failed to materialize. It was further intensified by the rise of an authoritarian Church, which in order to protect simple believers, or to strengthen its authority, felt the need of insisting on absolute right and wrong in all matters of dogma, and also on a very literal kind of truth—rejecting, for example, Origen's idea that the "wrath of God" was merely symbolical, like his "hand." In every controversy differences were aggravated by the earnestness of both sides, and by the impossibility of drawing a line between earnestness and spiritual pride or self-righteousness; after Clement and Origen, who still had the speculative spirit of the Greeks, few of the greater theologians and bishops seem to have considered seriously the possibility that they might be mistaken. Christianity might have harbored peaceable differences of opinion had it not become the imperial religion, but with the power it got from Constantine schism became virtually inevitable. We owe some pity to the unhappy emperor, to whom unity meant so much. "Give me back peaceful nights and days without care," he wrote the leaders in the Arian controversy, "that I too may keep some pleasure in the pure light and the joy of a tranquil life henceforth"; but he was rarely to know such pleasure. His later letters express his exasperation and dread as, in spite of all his efforts, the bishops refused to live in peace, doing "nothing but what tends to strife and hatred, and to speak plainly, the destruction of the human race."

Yet in these efforts Constantine had asserted the principle of "Caesaro-papism," the supremacy of the State over the Church, which would be-

4 See the Appendix, Section 9, for the history of this city.

come still another source of strife and hatred. "I am going to make plain to them," he declared of the Donatists, "what kind of worship is to be offered to the Divinity." Although he failed either to convince or to quell them, he had effectually claimed the right to settle disputes among bishops and to punish recalcitrant bishops. Wielding the power of an Oriental despot, he might in any case have resisted the claims of any higher power on earth; but he evidently believed in all sincerity that God had by special commission made him at least the equal of the bishops, given him the governance of all earthly kings, and that he had no higher duty than to "dissipate errors" and enforce "true religion." "You others are Bishops within the Church," he told them, "whereas I am divinely appointed Bishop-General outside the Church." So he summoned and presided over councils of bishops, removed bishops on his own authority, penalized dissenters by his own laws.

And the Church bowed to the Peer of the Apostles. Churchmen not only were grateful to Constantine but had need of his authority. As they themselves had appealed to it in their difficulties with the Donatists, so they acquiesced in his decisions; none openly rebuked him. Rule by the emperor was now regarded as the equivalent of monotheism. Eusebius pictured an ideal marriage between the single sovereign and the one true Church, while in effect recognizing the sovereign as the male, the supreme authority. Dissenters naturally had doubts about the consummation of this marriage, and by the end of Constantine's reign even some orthodox churchmen showed signs of uneasiness over the secular power. In the West they came to resist it, as Bishop Ambrose proclaimed that "the Emperor is within the Church, not over it," and succeeded in humbling the great Theodosius. The increasing feebleness of the Western emperors enabled the bishops of Rome to develop the tradition of papal supremacy, which in the Middle Ages resulted in the fatal struggle between the popes and the Holy Roman emperors. In the East, however, the tradition of Caesaropapism established by Constantine held sway to the end of the Byzantine Empire. The Emperor appointed and removed patriarchs; only the Emperor could call an Ecumenical Council. Although strong-minded patriarchs often resisted particular decrees, none successfully challenged the basic principle of imperial supremacy.

Altogether, historians have good reason to speak of Constantine's work as a "fatal gift." The ethical and spiritual standards of Christianity were lowered by its triumph as the imperial religion. The consecration of the State to the service of God meant that God had to serve the State (as in this century he has to be on both sides of wars between Christian nations), and it was still an unregenerate empire. Yet Constantine's donation was by no means simply fatal. He established Christianity in the nick of time. By identifying it with Roman civilization, he facilitated the conversion of the German barbarians, who were growing fascinated by the splendors of the world they were overrunning. He established it firmly enough to enable it in time to make its major contributions to Western civilization. And in the East, more particularly, he laid the foundations of the Byzantine Empire. Another of his momentous decisions was the foundation of Constantinople: the "New Rome" that was to become the heart of the Empire in a fuller sense than Rome had ever been, or than almost any other capital has been, and that for centuries was to remain the citadel of Christendom.

2. THE NEW ROME

Constantinople, wrote the Byzantine historian Procopius, is the city where Europe stretches out to embrace Asia. He recalls the artificiality of this persistent geographical distinction. Here the two "continents" are separated only by the Bosphorus, a channel about a mile wide. As today one may ferry across the Bosphorus with no sense of entering a different continent, so throughout history men could cross it without entering a different culture. Nevertheless Constantinople was indeed a historic gateway, and a lodestar for men who did feel that they came from different worlds. Historians have described it as by nature the imperial city par excellence. The people on the site were slow to realize their historic destiny; but under Constantine the Great they at last began to.

A few years before Greek colonists founded the city of Byzantium, in 657 B.C., other Greeks had founded the city of Chalcedon on the Asiatic side of the entrance to the Bosphorus. They accordingly became proverbial among Greeks for blindness: Byzantium was a far better site for both defensive and commercial purposes. It lay on a promontory jutting out between the Sea of Marmora and the Golden Horn, which curves back inland to provide a superb harbor; it commanded the entrance to the Bosphorus, up and down which went the Black Sea trade. Above all, Procopius wrote truly, its glory was the sea, "nobly set about it, winding its way in, narrowing into straits and expanding into a great open sea." Even so, Byzantium did not become a great or brilliant city. It was almost always prosperous, through trade and the fish that still teem in the Bosphorus; it was never a center of art and learning, and contributed no more to Greek culture than Chalcedon. Its shrewd citizens were perhaps as shortsighted as the settlers across the bay. Its history for a thousand years gave no hint of the greatness it would know as Constantinople.

Little is known about early Byzantium except that it was an inseparable part of the Greek world. Legends associated the region with Jason and the Argonauts, who reputedly built temples on both the European and Asiatic sides of the Bosphorus, including an altar to Cybele. The city appears on the historic scene as a free *polis*, but one that was usually under foreign domination—Persian, Athenian, and Spartan. It was vitally important to Athens during the Peloponnesian War because of its command of the entrance to the Black Sea, from which Athens got most of its corn. Later it achieved some glory by its heroic resistance when besieged by Philip of Macedon, father of Alexander. During the Hellenistic Age it enjoyed a somewhat inglorious prosperity; other Greek cities, led by Rhodes, united against it because of its excessive levies on the Black Sea trade—the same reason, possibly, why the Homeric Greeks had united against Troy. In its prudence it was among the early Greek cities to choose the Roman side in the wars with the Seleucids. Under Roman rule it throve as usual, without distinction. It was important enough to be visited by Apollonius of Tyana and favored by one of his miracles, but not to attract St. Paul. At the time of Constantine it was still not a major city, ranking as a local bishopric under the Metropolitan of Heraclea, on the Black Sea.

Meanwhile, however, the strategic importance of Byzantium had become clearer. During the civil wars of the third century it again put up a valiant resistance when besieged by Septimius Severus, holding out for two years; he razed its walls to the ground. Later in the century they were razed again by another emperor. But each time they were soon rebuilt, the last time by Diocletian; the absence of a fortress here had made it easy for Gothic pirates to sail down and ravage the coasts. Licinius then made the city his headquarters and European bridgehead in his final struggle with Constantine. He held it against a vigorous siege, abandoning it only when the fleet that had been supplying him was destroyed in the Dardanelles at Callipolis (Gallipoli). Its natural strength must have influenced Constantine's decision to build his capital here. In 326, at any rate, he ceremonially laid the foundation of the western wall, and in 330 solemnly dedicated his new city, named after himself.

As this was Constantine's most enduring political achievement, it has inspired further debate over his motives. Jacob Burckhardt, who described it as "the most conscious and purposeful act of his entire reign," also remarked our uncertainty about his "deepest political plans." Probably they were not so deep as they may seem in retrospect. Emperors had long since been given to living away from Rome, building themselves palaces in some provincial city; Diocletian had reigned from Nicomedia. Contemporaries expressed no wonder over Constantine's decision. Doubtless vanity had something to do with it, and the passion for building that he shared with Hadrian and most Roman emperors. It is not certain that he himself called his city the "New Rome." At least he did not make it a formal rival of Rome or seek to displace the official capital.

Yet he did solemnly dedicate it, and gave it a privileged status to go with some "eternal name" he also gave it. He had something deeper in mind than a new residence or a monument to his victories. His own word is that he acted "on the command of God"—received in another of the dreams through which divinities were wont to communicate with the ancients. He had started to build his capital at Troy, suggesting some pious idea of rebirth or regeneration. Now he made a fresh start, to symbolize more positively his new state. Rome was too steeped in ancient tradition for such purposes; its churches were lost in the crowd of temples, forums, baths, theaters; and according to later Christian writers, even its Christian community was degenerate.[5] The New Rome was to be a genuinely Christian center. Here again Constantine's intentions were obscured by some conventional pagan accessories, such as his temples to Tyche and the Mother of the Gods, a colossal statue of Apollo on which he substituted his own head as the Sun God, and a Neoplatonist orator and magician who participated in the initial dedication. Christian writers added an aura of pagan superstition by fables of eagles that helped out by carrying measuring tape and building stones from Chalcedon to Byzantium. Nevertheless the New Rome was a Christian city. No more pagan temples were built in it, no more pagan rites publicly celebrated. Its most magnificent buildings were churches—the Holy Wisdom, the Holy Apostles, the Holy Peace. The legend that Constantine dedicated the city to the Virgin Mary is almost certainly untrue, but none the less appropriate. The Virgin soon became the patron of a city that had formerly worshiped Aphrodite and known Cybele since it had known of Jason.

At the same time, Constantine did not simply break with the classical past. His new capital incorporated a Greek-speaking populace, in an ancient Greek land, and he aspired to make it a center of Hellenism, if in somewhat dubious taste. To adorn it, he looted the cities of Greece and Asia Minor of their most famous art treasures; in front of the Church of the Holy Wisdom ("Saint Sophia") he heaped up more than four hundred statues. Constantinople remained a museum, whose main streets

[5] St. Jerome was shocked by the prevailing corruption, such as the clergy's habit of living in luxury with *agapetes*, or "spiritual sisters." He was then secretary to Bishop Damasus of Rome, who had won his exalted position by a struggle with a rival candidate that littered a basilica with 137 corpses.

and forums would daily remind its citizens of their Greek heritage. Likewise Constantine built libraries and stocked them with Greek manuscripts, to make it a center of learning. And his capital was to be a real
Roman city too. It had seven hills, like Rome itself. Constantine endowed
it with a Senate, though of a less distinguished grade than that of Rome,
and an elegant Senate House. He induced some Roman aristocrats to
move to the city, supposedly by building them facsimiles of their palaces
and villas at home. From other cities he attracted the necessary common
people by free bread and circuses, distributing 80,000 loaves a day. To
the end the official title of the city remained the "New Rome which is
Constantinople."

Hence Constantine inaugurated the cosmopolitan city of the future: a
city populated largely by assorted Asiatics who alike professed Christianity, spoke Greek, and called themselves Roman. If one may doubt
that he foresaw its future, at least he chose its site wisely for both immediate and long-range purposes. Other sites that he apparently contemplated—his birthplace Nish in Serbia, Sardica (modern Sofia), and
Thessalonica—were too remote from the wealthy East and the critical
Eastern frontier; other great Eastern cities, such as Alexandria and
Antioch, were too remote from the critical Danube frontier, or too great
or Oriental to become really new foundations; Diocletian's Nicomedia
was a natural provincial city, off the main military and commercial highways. Constantinople was a natural stronghold at the crossroads. It could
draw readily on the wealth and culture of the East, especially Asia Minor,
and also on the man power of the Balkans, from which the empire had
been recruiting its sturdiest soldiers and generals, including Diocletian
and Constantine himself. It vindicated his choice by a rapid growth. In
the next century it had a population greater than Rome's, rising to a million. Early in this century (413) were built the famous walls that held the
city until its fall to the Turks in 1453.

The West suffered from Constantine's momentous decision. Deprived
of the wealth and man power that supported Constantinople, its emperors succumbed more quickly to the growing pressure of the barbarians. The East suffered too, apart from the loss of many of its art
treasures. It had to pay for the prodigality of Constantine, who spared
no costs in building his capital, and then it had to feed the capital. Later
it suffered from the religious domination of Constantinople. Unlike Rome,
however, the new capital was not a parasitic city. It promoted trade and
industry, became the commercial, artistic, and religious as well as political
center of the empire. It kept vigorous enough to hold off invading hordes
of Huns, Avars, Persians, Bulgars, Russians. Above all, it withstood the

all-conquering Arabs in the great siege of 717–18. The New Rome founded by Constantine, a Christian citadel for a thousand years, was never betrayed or surrendered to foreign enemies until it was taken by the barbarians of the Fourth Crusade in 1204.

3. THE FUSION OF EAST AND WEST

Although the Byzantine Empire is conventionally dated from the foundation of Constantinople, its beginning is not much clearer to historians than it was to Constantine. Nobody consciously planned or created it. Some historians date its beginning from the end of the fourth century, when Theodosius divided the Roman Empire and made the final separation of East and West; others from the reign of Justinian the Great (527–65), when the empire achieved its characteristic art and architecture; still others from the beginning of the eighth century, when a new start was made under Leo III after the successful defense of Constantinople against the Arabs. Any selection is to some extent arbitrary, since the Byzantine Empire was a continuation and gradual transformation of the Eastern Roman Empire. Essentially it was a Christian state that maintained Greek and Roman traditions but also became more Orientalized, developing a profoundly conservative but distinctive culture. The founding of Constantinople may still be regarded as the decisive event initiating this process. In any case, the important thing is to keep an eye on the process, to make out what was conserved and what changed or created.

In *The Uses of the Past* I began with the question forced by the mysterious vitality of the Byzantine Empire. What kept it going for a thousand years after the fall of Rome? I can still find no definite answer, or at least none really satisfying to the moralist, the philosopher, or the scientist. Perhaps the best explanation is simply that the eastern half of the Roman Empire was older and richer than the western half, having a more highly developed economy and a more deeply rooted culture. Otherwise it apparently had as good reason to fall as Rome did, and often enough was on the verge of fall; in its periodic crises it was saved by the unpredictable emergence of great emperors, or more particularly by its possession of the terrible secret weapon of "Greek fire"—a vulgar matter of technology that may have been more decisive than its whole Greek heritage. One reason why it has so often been disparaged by Western historians, when not simply ignored, is that its ups and downs obey none of the fashionable laws and fit into none of the fashionable patterns of history, such as those of Marx, Spengler, and Toynbee. It has been most conspicuously ignored by many who have explained why Rome fell— usually why its fall was "inevitable"—for their theories would logically require the fall of Byzantium too. C. N. Cochrane, for example, argued that the fatal error of Constantine and Theodosius was their effort to bend Christianity to the service of a decadent Roman State; it was impossible to reconcile the claims of Classicism and Christianity, hence "inevitable that *Romanitas*, despite her pretension to eternity, should perish from the earth"; and he neglects to mention that although the Byzantine Empire persisted in this fatal error, it successfully defied the inevitable for another millennium.

In my previous study I also sought conscientiously to do justice to an empire that is naturally unattractive to Westerners, especially those devoted to the Greek ideal of the life of reason, in freedom; and on this score I have ever since felt uneasy. It is still unattractive, finally. I do not believe that we can really admire its basic institutions. Only a romantic like Yeats can see in it an ideal unity, and only through ignorance of its history. Yet it has suffered from the cultural prejudice of the West, and it deserves better than a merely professional sympathy. Following Gibbon, European historians generally represented its history as a prolonged decadence, giving currency to the vague popular notion of an empire full of Greek scholars, but rotten and corrupt. In this century historians have treated it with increasing respect.[6] Its story has more intrinsic dignity, and more historic importance, than lovers of freedom are disposed to recognize.

From the outset the Byzantine Empire had a consciousness of a high mission, primarily religious but also cultural, as the defender of civilization; and this gives its drama something of the quality of high tragedy. It was never an easy mission, nor a mere excuse for imperialism. The almost incessant wars fought by the emperors were often aggressive but more often defensive or retaliatory, and in either case they were usually fought against forces superior in numbers. War was a grim, carefully studied business in which valor was properly honored, but without the

---

[6] Among the best studies for the general reader—critical but sympathetic studies—are *Byzantine Civilization* by Steven Runciman and *Byzantium*, a collection of essays edited by Norman H. Baynes and H. St. L. B. Moss. More provocative is Jack Lindsay's *Byzantium into Europe*, a Marxist interpretation indebted to Soviet historians. (Russians have naturally been much more sympathetic to the civilization from which their own directly sprang.) Lindsay makes the history of the empire respectable by seeing its essence as the transformation of the ancient world into the feudal world, which would then inevitably create capitalism, which in turn must end in communism; he also manages to trace socialism to it. Byzantium accordingly "kept alive both the forward movement of history and the rebellious dream of a valid harmony." In this view Lindsay has some strange things to say about Byzantine art as a product of the "new mass-forces" and "forms of revolt." But readers who can discount his too insistent thesis, and sometimes ludicrous corollaries, may find his study illuminating.

boyish heroics inspired by Western chivalry. The most obviously un-attractive aspects of the history of the Byzantines—the unscrupulous diplomacy, the intrigue and treachery, the superstition, the frequent cruelty, in general the shockingly un-Christian behavior—may be in part explained and condoned by the high tension in which they habitually lived. For the Byzantines did not believe that their New Rome was an Eternal City—it would go the way of all earthly things; their Greek ancestors had taught them this sad wisdom, and their Christian prophets often reminded them of it. Nevertheless they carried on, through alternate dark periods and brilliant periods, until the turning point in their history—the victory of the Seljuk Turks at Manzikert, in 1071, which cost them most of Asia Minor. Then set in the long decline. It was painfully slow and long because they still hung on tenaciously, for almost four centuries, until their once great empire was reduced to little more than Constantinople and its suburbs. Their last emperor died heroically in the defense of the city, as no Roman emperor had in the defense of the Eternal City.

Today we are likely to be struck chiefly by the stubborn, unenlightened conservatism of the Byzantines. But they also exemplified the dignity and the value of conservatism in their defense of a precious heritage. They successfully resisted the barbarization to which the West succumbed; to the end they kept their form. In so doing they not only defended but spread civilization, directly converting and educating the Slavic peoples, indirectly helping to civilize the Arabs, and contributing much to western Europe, where throughout the Dark Ages they maintained outposts of civilization, as at Ravenna. They made an incalculable contribution simply by serving as a bulwark against the Eastern hordes. The West has seen a savior in Charles Martel, who in France turned back a plundering expedition of Moors from Spain, on the distant border of the Moslem world. It owes much more to the defenders of Constantinople, who turned back the main drive of the Arabs, aimed at the heart of Christendom. "Under the shelter of that defense of the Eastern gateway," concluded Norman Baynes, "western Europe could refashion its own life: it is hardly an exaggeration to say that the civilization of western Europe is a by-product of the Byzantine Empire's will to survive."

Even so, this empire was never so static as it aspired to be—no civilization ever can be, until it is reduced to immobile ruins. The ancient heritage that it was bent on conserving was itself a fluid, unstable amalgam of Greek, Roman, and diverse Oriental traditions. In the course of its development the Oriental elements became most prominent, if only because the chief influences to which it was subject came from the East.

Nevertheless, the underlying Greco-Roman tradition always tempered them, and gave the Byzantines some right to feel superior to the "barbarians" around them. To illustrate, I shall take up their political life, their religion, and their art and learning—all centered in Constantinople.

Now we cannot at every point clearly separate these traditions, of course, and must be wary of simple or simply invidious distinctions. Let us first consider, for instance, the controversy over Iconoclasm that shook the empire for over a century. Beginning with Leo III, the savior of Constantinople from the Arabs, the Iconoclast emperors tried to ban the popular worship of images. Historians regularly describe them as leaders of an Oriental reaction, who like the Hebrews and the Moslems were outraged by Greek idolatry. They were in fact of Eastern origin; Leo was contemptuously called "the Phrygian." The impassioned resistance they met looks humanistic and independent in spirit. On this vital issue the Church was not subservient to the emperors, and it was aided by the Roman Popes. Its theologians used Platonic arguments, pointing out that images made visible the invisible realities just as God himself had in the creation and in the living image of Jesus. In a sense they were defending both the value of the material world and the dignity of Christian art, which had grown out of Greek art.

Still, the issues were ambiguous. The "Oriental" Iconoclasts seem more rational than their opponents, who in effect were also defending Oriental pomp and superstition; image worship unquestionably encouraged gross idolatry. The motives of the emperors were political as well as religious, and would make good sense to patriotic Greeks and Romans of the old school: they were attacking the excessive wealth and power of the monasteries, which throve on a superstitious reverence for their icons and were weakening the beleaguered empire by draining off much of its material and human resources. The Church was hardly a St. George in the struggle; the Council of Nicaea that eventually anathematized all who did not worship images had to reverse a previous Council, in which 348 bishops had unanimously pronounced images to be inventions of the Devil. The victory of the image worshipers was sealed by two women, the empresses Irene and Theodora. Irene was rewarded by canonization, even though she had become empress by dethroning and blinding her son, whom she had carefully brought up in utter dissipation so as to unfit him for the throne. Other consequences of the victory were as ambiguous. It was followed by a revival of Greek humanism in art and learning; the Church became more submissive to the throne, which had made possible its triumph; and the theological growth of Byzantium ended—this was the last major controversy. Humanists who applaud the defeat of

Iconoclasm may do so for impious reasons. It meant a richer art, but a less spiritual religion.

With this tangle in mind, let us look at the Byzantine State. Essentially it was the Oriental sacred autocracy passed on by Constantine the Great. The emperor was an absolute monarch, in complete control of administration, legislation, finances, the making of war and peace. As the successor of Constantine he was "Equal of the Apostles"; his court was the "Sacred Palace," his edicts were "celestial commands," his annual taxation was "the Divine Delegation." His majesty and holiness were attested by prostration and Oriental pageantry (much of it later borrowed by the Vatican). His holiness did not protect him from palace intrigue, conspiracy, and assassination—only about a third of the Byzantine emperors died in the royal bed—but his successful rival or assassin automatically became the elect of God and wore a halo in his portraits. Normally he himself chose his successor, and would choose to keep the throne in the family. The history of the Byzantine Empire falls naturally into the history of dynasties.

After the brilliant but costly age of Justinian, the last of the great "Roman-minded" emperors, the empire in its prime was ruled, appropriately, by three Asiatic dynasties: the Isaurian, founded by Leo III; the short-lived Amorian or Phrygian; and the so-called Macedonian, founded by Basil I, an Armenian born in Macedonia. The varying fortunes of the empire caused some changes in procedure and inspired some emperors to introduce administrative and fiscal reforms. One major development was the growth of a feudal nobility, which was likely to conspire against the emperor, and which provided the dynasties that ruled the empire in its last centuries. But from first to last the basic structure and theory of the Byzantine State remained the same. Several popular "revolutions" were merely riots against unpopular or illegitimate emperors. The people never tried to change the structure of their society in the name of justice or freedom; the only real class struggle was within the ruling class. Byzantium produced no political theory. Runciman explains kindly that theory was not needed because its constitution worked so well, but in fact this often worked very badly. The most apparent explanation is the unreasoned conservatism that stamped Byzantine culture as a whole.

Few Westerners today, I take it, can admire the Byzantine State or regard it as the secret of the vitality of the empire. Those who regard a businesslike administration as the ultimate in government might pay some tribute to an Oriental custom that otherwise seems barbarous—the extensive employment of eunuchs in high positions, and deliberate castration of boys for this purpose. Eunuchs could be entrusted with high responsibilities because they could not sire ambitious sons, and by unwritten law were debarred from the throne. They in fact provided Byzantium with some of its ablest generals, statesmen, and patriarchs. Until toward the end they served as a generally capable administrative class, a bulwark against the rising feudal nobility, and a means of keeping society fluid. Castration was possibly as good a qualification for responsible states- manship as success in manufacturing automobiles.

Most of us must prefer to believe, however, that Byzantium owed more to the survival of the forms and especially the ideals of the Roman State. In theory the emperor was always elected by the Senate, the army, and the people of Constantinople. Their power was actually nominal; almost invariably they acclaimed whomever the emperor appointed, or whoever successfully deposed him or his son. Nevertheless the forms persisted to the end, and they helped to keep alive the idea that the people was ultimately sovereign, the emperor the servant of the commonwealth. In this Roman tradition the emperors were mostly patriotic, seldom as ir- responsible and self-indulgent as the contemporary caliphs of Baghdad. They knew, moreover, that their subjects still had some of the in- subordinate spirit of the ancient Greeks. Whatever the Byzantines thought, they did not really believe in the sacredness of their haloed emperors. The historian Michael Psellus remarked as a matter of course that emperors "inherited from God supreme power" and in the same breath noted that none of them were blameless, not even one of his own favorites. "Divine soul, forgive me," he added piously as he proceeded to detail with manifest pleasure the ungodly behavior of his divinity. Even the common people of Constantinople felt free to revile the em- peror, or if possible to defy him.

Another Roman legacy was the reverence for law. The power of absolute monarchs is always limited to some extent by law and custom, and Byzantine monarchs in this respect too were especially conservative. Although officially above the law, because its source, they were somehow beneath it as well; typically they proclaimed their devotion to it, not their superiority over it. One of the major achievements of the empire was the Code of the Emperor Justinian. It was a characteristically con- servative achievement—a pure digest of the law accumulated over cen- turies, with no effort at reinterpretation, much less innovation. It was also characteristically anomalous: except for a preoccupation with sexual behavior, the law of the Christian state was Roman, not Christian. But as such it retained an aura of sanctity.

Still more anomalous was the religion of the Byzantines. In spite of their scandalously un-Christian behavior, they were intensely religious—

as much so as the reckless sinners of medieval Europe. Christianity governed all their major interests outside of law, economic life, and amusement. It provided the inspiration and matter of their art, the basis and frame of their most serious thought. Commoners and intellectuals took a fervent interest in theology, the proper way of comprehending the incomprehensible Godhead.[7] No type—not even the great soldier—was more of a national idol than the ascetic who lived only for God. Christianity was indeed the deepest source of the national pride in a racially heterogeneous empire, and the most apparent source of its mysterious vitality. The Cathedral of Hagia Sophia in Constantinople, over which the Patriarch presided and in which the Emperor was crowned and consecrated to the service of God, might be called the soul of Byzantium.

As a State Church, however, the Holy Orthodox Church could not be purely soulful. The New Rome of Constantine introduced political complications into the controversies over the Godhead. Its Bishop sought equal rank with the Bishops of Alexandria, Antioch, and Rome, who claimed pre-eminence because their churches had traditionally been founded by Apostles; and while Constantinople dreamed up the legend that St. Andrew had been its founder, and brought his alleged remains to town, its claims were patently political. The Council of Constantinople that finally settled the Arian controversy cleared the way for a more fatal one by decreeing that the New Rome ranked second only to Rome. After the fall of Rome a patriarch of Constantinople assumed the title of Ecumenical. Pope Gregory the Great protested indignantly that no see had jurisdiction over another, all were equal under God, but later popes were less modest. There ensued a prolonged, unseemly struggle, exasperated by ambition as well as fervent difference over minute distinctions, which in the eleventh century culminated in the final separation of the Roman Catholic and Holy Orthodox churches. The official cause of the break was disagreement over the filioque—a matter of creed that probably not one out of a thousand Catholics today would be able to define.[8] Meanwhile Eastern Christendom had itself suffered from the pretensions of the New Rome. The fifth-century church historian Socrates observed that the

[7] St. Gregory of Nyssa is one witness: "People swarm everywhere talking of incomprehensible matters, in hovels, streets, squares, market places, crossroads. When I ask how many coppers I must pay, they reply with minute distinctions on the Born and the Unborn. If I ask the price of bread, I'm told the Father's greater than the Son. I call to ask the servant if my bath's ready, and he replies that the Son was created from Nothing."

[8] The issue is whether the Holy Ghost proceeds from the Father or from both the Father and the Son. The Orthodox Church held for the former view, sticking by Scripture and the oldest Creeds. The Roman Church preferred to depart from Scripture for the sake of the logic of the Trinity.

atrocities inspired by the Arian controversy, such as the scourging, burning, and ravishing of virgins, "were committed in all the cities of the East, but especially at Byzantium." Imperial persecution of the Nestorians and Monophysites so effectually alienated Syria and Egypt that these provinces succumbed to the Arabs with hardly a struggle, and were lost to Christendom forever.

The Byzantine Church also displayed some concern for social security, supporting charitable institutions to an extent that the pagan world never had. It produced one saint, John Chrysostom of Antioch, who was an incipient social reformer; he spoke out eloquently against the extremes of wealth and poverty, even calling for the abolition of slavery. But a State Church is unlikely to endorse such radicalism. In Byzantium it comforted the poor chiefly by a lavish provision of mystery and miracle, above all by the "Mystery of mysteries, the Sacrifice above all other sacrifices"—the Resurrection. On Easter these words were repeated one thousand times. For daily purposes, or special emergencies, the Church provided innumerable saints and holy relics. Among the most popular shrines in Constantinople was that of St. Artemius, who specialized in curing sexual complaints. The city accumulated a prodigious quantity of relics, beginning with all the relics of the Passion found by the sainted Helena, and then featuring holy corpses, from Samuel, Isaiah, and Daniel to Mary Magdalene, Timothy, and Luke. Even Apollonius of Tyana was called upon for a contribution. Although he had died about three centuries earlier, the great wonder-worker of antiquity showed up for the foundation of Constantinople, and in the Column of Constantine (under which were kept the loaves of Jesus' miracle) buried a list of all the emperors to come.

Sympathetic historians describe this superstition as a generous concession to the masses by a Church whose special virtue it was to keep close to the people and their State. It is perhaps fairer to say simply that popular religion has always involved such indignities. Visitors to Rome today may contemplate many products of a similar piety. (Among its wonders is another finding of Helena's, the stairs of Pilate's palace, made holy by the blood of Christ; women still climb it on their knees, praying for indulgence—earning the remission of a hundred days' punishment in Purgatory for each step.) And the miraculous presence of Apollonius in Constantinople was fitting, as a reminder that much of the superstition was a Greek legacy. The cult of saints and martyrs replaced the cults of the gods and heroes, some of whom—such as Bacchus and Hippolytus—were themselves canonized. The Virgin Mary, beloved patroness of Constantinople, replaced the Mother Goddess, to save the city by many a miracle. The Mother Goddess also merged somehow with the Holy Wisdom, which therefore became another person, "Saint" Sophia.

On the other hand, the Byzantine Church retained the Greek intellectual tradition as well. Most of the early Christian theologians came from the East, and all the basic dogmas of orthodox Christianity were hammered out in councils there. Even Anatolia helped by contributing the Cappadocian Fathers, St. Basil and the Gregories of Nazianzus and Nyssa. If the doctrines that emerged from the great controversies were not notable for Greek clarity, and indeed made the Godhead ever more incomprehensible, they at least followed out the logic of the Trinity, and at worst resulted from reason run wild. Moreover, something of Greek tolerance and freedom of thought survived the rigorous orthodoxy of the Holy Orthodox Church. It left room for speculation on important matters, such as the existence of Purgatory; it was lenient with intellectuals who dabbled in dangerous inquiries, so long as they professed Christianity; it permitted one of its bishops to write a poem asking Christ to include the noble Plato and Plutarch among the Christians. Its patriarchs were never so arrogant as to claim infallibility, or so inhuman as to set up an Inquisition.

It was un-Greek, however, in its characteristically Byzantine conservatism. The Holy Orthodox Church was strictly more orthodox than the Roman Catholic Church, whose theological development carried it ever farther from Scripture. Its own development ended with the seven Ecumenical Councils; today it still stands essentially where it did in the eighth century. And its essence looks more Oriental than Greek. Its main appeal was not to reason but to the "Mystery of mysteries," through a sensuous liturgy. Its main concern was not the good life on earth but the life to come. It discountenanced the old pagan joy in life. While accumulating more material than spiritual wealth, out of the sweat and superstition of the poor, it idolized the type of the monk, the hermit, the ascetic saint, in particular the stylite who passed his life in squalor on the top of a column. The pervasive odor of sanctity in Byzantium helps to explain the pervasive corruption and crime in the degraded natural world occupied by the transitory and despised flesh. Thus the routine punishment of mutilation—the countless noses cut off and eyes put out on every page of Byzantine history—was justified by the injunction of Christ to pluck out the offending eyes and cut off the offending limbs.

At best, the otherworldliness of Orthodox Christianity was mystical. Among its most popular and influential authors was Dionysius the Areopagite, who endeavored to combine Christian faith with Neoplatonism. Later mystics provided some oases in the long arid stretches of Eastern theology. But at best this Church has little to say to moderns in search of a soul. They might learn much from the philosophy and religion of India, as some have. It is difficult to imagine anyone but a scholar turning to the saints and theologians of Byzantium.

Its art, however, is a very different matter. If art is not clearly a reliable index to the quality or the health of a society, the art of the Byzantines was unquestionably their major creative achievement, and at its best a glorious statement of their religious faith, their living ideal. It accordingly reflected the basic anomalies of their culture. It was pre-eminently an otherworldly art, representing the supramundane world rather than the natural world of appearances, appealing to the "inner eye"; and it was an ultrasensuous, worldly art, directed from Constantinople as a means of mass propaganda, representing the imperial ideal in its predilection for the costliest, most dazzling materials. But that it too strikes Westerners as more Oriental than Greek is no reason for disparagement. Classical art was unmistakably played out by the time of Constantine the Great. A fresh impulse was imperative, and it came from the East. Scholars are still debating its precise origins, which they locate variously in Armenia, Syria, Persia, Mesopotamia, Egypt, and even Turkestan; so it would seem likely that all these lands contributed something. At the same time, classical art remained a vital influence, periodically revived. Christianity continued to provide the major inspiration and content. All in all, Byzantine art is the shining example of the fusion that characterizes Byzantine civilization.

In architecture, Rome continued to provide the models for secular buildings, such as baths and palaces. The major innovation of Byzantium was its church. Early Christians had adopted the simple rectangular basilica with aisles divided by columns—a classical, functionally sound type of structure, but limited in possibilities of development. They had also experimented with round buildings, of which Hadrian's Pantheon was a classical example. Byzantine architects created a landmark in the history of architecture by mastering the problem of setting a dome over a square, by means of pendentives. Their greatest triumph was the cathedral of Hagia Sophia in Constantinople (better known or misknown as "Saint" Sophia), completed by the Emperor Justinian in A.D. 537.[9] The remarkable architectural enterprise of this supposedly decadent society is emphasized by different types of churches, also still standing, that were

[9] Toynbee's preordained scheme requires the age of Justinian to be a late phase in a dying "universal state," which by definition can do nothing really creative; so he describes Hagia Sophia as a "new-fangled" work, expressing the disgust of its builders with "a dead and rotting past." But it is unlikely that he will ruin the reputation of this superb monument, or that he really wants to.

built in Constantinople about the same time. The vast dome of Hagia Sophia crowns a square interior in which colonnades preserve something of the effect of the early basilica. In the church of St. Irene two domes are set end to end on a rectangular basilica, while in the church of Saints Sergius and Bacchus, known as "Little Hagia Sophia," the dome is set on an octagon. Justinian's once famous cathedral of the Holy Apostles (destroyed by the Turks to make way for a mosque) was in the form of a cross, with a dome at the crossing and one on each of the four arms. It was widely copied, most notably by the builders of St. Mark's in Venice.

All these buildings were classical in spirit in that their design was balanced and structurally adequate; they required no Gothic buttresses. They differ from both the classical temple and the Gothic cathedral in that their exterior is relatively unadorned and unimposing. It was the interior that engrossed the Byzantines.[10] The dome, symbolizing the heavens, added splendor to this interior. In Hagia Sophia the splendor was enhanced by columns of porphyry and verd antique, walls of polished and varicolored marble slabs, and a profusion of gold-leaf mosaic—some four acres of it. Set cunningly to reflect the sunlight streaming in from the dome, the mosaic made heavenly the house of God. These richly decorated, gleaming interiors were still mysterious, as befitted the mystery of the Mass performed in them, but it was the mystery of light, not gloom. "You would imagine," wrote Procopius of Hagia Sophia, "that it was not merely illuminated from without by the sun, but that radiance springs also from within it." David Rice has added that like all Byzantine art this cathedral has something indefinite and unrealizable about it which sharply distinguishes it from the finite perfection of classical Greek art: "it seeks for the infinite"—the infinity of the Christian God. Westerners may feel that this search is expressed still more eloquently by the soaring Gothic cathedral, but there is no denying that Byzantine builders did gloriously by their God.

Later Byzantine architects never sought to surpass this masterwork, or to build on so mighty a scale, but they clung to the basic design of dome over square. They contented themselves with some variations, such as higher domes set on tall drums and decorative brickwork on exteriors.

---

[10] Robert Van Nice, who has spent many years on a close study of the structure of Hagia Sophia, has informed me of a curious qualification. Art historians have uniformly marveled at the large semidomes thought to buttress the great central dome, while scholars have argued over the source of this wonderful system of support. It turns out that the semidomes apparently do not support anything. Van Nice discovered that their shells are only one or two bricks thick—not so thick as the central dome, whose thrust they were supposedly designed to counter. Their purpose seems to have been primarily aesthetic.

Their smaller churches seem more classical in their appeal to the outer eye, as well as in their grace and lightness. (A lovely example in Constantinople is the Church of the Virgin Pammakaristos.) The trend toward the naturalistic and humanistic was more pronounced, however, in the wall mosaics adorning their interiors. As sculpture declined—a victim, one might say, of the Orient, which in this region had never taken to three-dimensional statuary—the Byzantines had turned to the mosaic; and this was their most distinctive contribution to art.

Since the Iconoclasts destroyed the early mosaic paintings in Constantinople, one must go to Ravenna to appreciate the evolution of the Byzantine style. A mausoleum behind Justinian's Church of San Vitale is covered with late Roman mosaics, purely decorative and predominantly blue and green; in the apse of the church itself is an idealized classical figure of Christ, resembling a youthful Apollo. But on the side walls, against a background of gold, stand Justinian, his empress Theodora, and their retinues: stiff and solemn figures, all in frontal attitudes, the women arrayed in rich Oriental costumes. This mosaic painter was less interested in his drawing than in his color—a daring use of color that was to make vibrant this seemingly static, ultraformal art. Later artists would combine an intense emotional realism with a more pronounced indifference to the world of appearances, in ethereal, elongated, sometimes emaciated figures that inspired the art of El Greco; Christ would become a Semitic figure, bearded, hollow-cheeked, somber, awesome. The mosaics remained glittering symphonies in color, glittering the more as artists learned to take full advantage of the curved surfaces in apse or dome, to achieve ever-changing effects by reflected light.

Because a primary object of the mosaics was to instruct the simple worshipers, their position and style were as conventionalized as the ritual Mass they illustrated. In the heavenly dome was Christ, the Pantocrator; in the apse the Virgin, usually dressed in blue; on the pendentives often the four Evangelists; on the lower walls and vaults saints, prophets, and haloed emperors, and later on scenes from the earthly lives of Christ and the Virgin. The background for all scenes was gold. Yet this sacred propaganda did not become stereotyped. While imperial Constantinople set the style, local schools in the provinces developed somewhat different styles of their own. Within the fixed conventions the typically anonymous artists managed to add some individual detail—now an impressionistic landscape, now a lively background figure. And in the centuries following the defeat of the Iconoclasts the art moved toward an ideal fusion of the Hellenistic and Semitic. The mosaics became more lifelike and took on more plasticity, grace, and refinement, reflecting an aim to delight as well as to awe or edify. In the beautiful panel of the Deesis in the south gallery of Hagia Sophia, for example, the portraits are so delicately shaded that from a short distance they look like paintings; but while less intense and austere than earlier portraits, they are still idealized, and are strong in Christian feeling of a gentler kind. It is hard to understand how so many men in the Western world, until this century, could have been blind to so gorgeous an art as this.

Byzantium also produced religious music that Westerners are beginning to appreciate. Otherwise, however, its creativity virtually ends with its visual arts. Its literature is a sorry contrast. Although the empire had enough civilized writers to maintain its pride, it produced no major writer in either poetry or prose. None of its works have entered the stream of world literature; very few have been translated or are read by anyone except scholars. Neither did Byzantium contribute anything of consequence to philosophy or science. We are brought up against the severely limited range of this civilization, the more marked by contrast with the ancient world before it and with the rising Western world. In ten centuries it produced no man comparable to Homer, Thales, Aeschylus, Plato, Euclid, or Archimedes; to Lucretius, Virgil, Horace, Cicero, or Marcus Aurelius; to Dante, Aquinas, Montaigne, Cervantes, Newton, Locke, or innumerable others. The best that can be said of it in this respect is that it piously preserved its Greek classics, together with the skills of antiquity, and enjoyed several revivals of learning.

Early Christians had generally been hostile to pagan culture, except its rhetoric. St. Augustine had to struggle with his guilty love of the classics. In the early centuries of the Byzantine Empire "Hellenism" was still a term of reproach, a symbol of pagan idolatry. The Emperor Justinian issued a law forbidding anyone "infected with the madness of the unholy Hellenes" to teach any subject, and his closing down of the schools in Athens may be said to mark the end of antiquity. By this time, however, the self-called Romans were losing the use of Latin. As Greek became the official language of the mongrel empire, Greek literature and learning were the natural core of education. Following the defeat of the Iconoclasts, a humanistic revival stirred a positive enthusiasm for the classics. Later humanists made "Hellenism" a proud word synonymous with the glory of Athens. And all along the Byzantines were at least good Greeks in their passion for education. Ignorance was a favorite subject of ridicule, learning a means of rising in the world.

But on the whole the priceless heritage that the Byzantines became proud of was of doubtful value to them. It was a positive hindrance to the growth of a vital literature. The classical Greek that they so carefully learned, and had to use if they made any pretensions to learning or culture, was not their spoken vernacular; no Dante or Chaucer rose to make their living language a literary one. At best, they never understood their heritage well enough to appreciate the saying that the only way to imitate the great Greeks is never to imitate them, since they imitated no one. What the Byzantines acquired was not the tradition of Ionia and Periclean Athens, but the academic tradition of the Hellenistic Age. What liberties they took with it were mostly unfortunate, as in their fondness for abridging and amending, or their perfection of an abysmal grammatical science they called schedography. They were not stimulated by it to fresh adventures in thought. Few caught anything of the essential Greek spirit of free critical inquiry.

In the last days of the empire, as we shall see later, there were stirrings of a genuine renaissance. Meanwhile we might let their own historians speak the last word about Byzantium in its prime. Their interest in history was part of their Greek legacy. From Procopius to Anna Comnena, the first woman historian and still perhaps the greatest, their secular historians were about their most notable writers. All prided themselves on telling truth; and they told even more than they knew.

Procopius, the greatest of them, is the most damaging witness. A contemporary of the Emperor Justinian, he wrote an objective account of the age in his *Wars*, consciously modeled on Herodotus and Thucydides, and a panegyric in his *Buildings;* but he also left his *Secret History,* a work of extraordinary virulence in which Justinian and the empress Theodora are presented as literally "devils incarnate," bent on destroying the human race. How much factual truth it contains is impossible to say. What it reveals most plainly is a pathological hatred in Procopius himself, and indirectly the blight of despotism, in an age when some men still had some memories of freedom of thought but were denied the right of open criticism. So Procopius had dutifully prostrated himself before the royal couple who styled themselves "our divine and pious despots," while his grievances festered into impotent rage; and so Justinian earned this epitaph from the one distinguished writer of his time. Unconsciously Procopius also wrote the epitaph of Byzantium. His chief complaint was of the radical "innovations" of Justinian, who except for his tastes in architecture was an ultraconservative.

A much fairer witness is Michael Psellus of the eleventh century, whose *Chronographia* records the history of this century. Psellus was not only a scholar but a philosopher, courtier, politician, diplomat—Byzantine man of the world. As such he was lively, shrewd, and sophisticated enough to be congenial to moderns. He also exemplifies an attractive democratic quality of Byzantine life. He was no aristocrat but a bourgeois, whose mother had made sacrifices to get him a good education, and who by his own abilities rose to be the adviser of emperors. There is a portrait of one emperor listening to a lecture by him.

His aim in the *Chronographia,* Psellus insisted, was to be neither a eulogist nor a scandalmonger but a strictly truthful historian. Although he insisted too much, he was generally inquisitive and critical, at least until he approached his own day and his imperial patrons. He could even be fair to an emperor he described as "entirely void of Hellenic culture" —the culture he himself had no false modesty about. He had a more acute insight into character than most ancient historians, who like classical writers in general had little conception of growth, change, or basic inconsistency; Psellus took for granted the irrelevancies and incongruities of human behavior. He had some insight as well into his own time of troubles. Writing shortly after the victory of the Seljuks at Manzikert, he could hardly be expected to realize the fatefulness of this event, but he did see that the main trouble was not simply "these wild unexpected inroads" of barbarians. It was internal corruption.

Psellus exposes more clearly than he knew, however, the basic anomalies of the Byzantine State. While remarking more than once that emperors derived their power from God, he observes that "really, of course, their power rests on three factors: the people, the Senate, and the army." The Senate he describes as a gang of "rascally vagabonds of the market" who had been elevated by compliant emperors. After a vivid, sympathetic account of a popular revolution, as the city spontaneously rose against a tyrannical usurper and set on the throne the Empress Theodora, he notes casually the ironic sequel: she was quite unfit to rule. So was her sister, the Empress Zoë: an aging virgin who ascended the throne to run through three husbands, and whom he describes as "absolutely ignorant of public affairs." (She is immortalized in a mosaic adorning Hagia Sophia.) Psellus dwells with relish on her various oddities but without remarking another oddity, that a great empire should be content to be ruled by such as these through accidents of birth. He mentions disapprovingly but calmly the quirks of another divine emperor, who punished the Romans wholesale by blinding them on the spot, and then was apt to be "terribly downcast at what he had done."

As unwittingly Psellus exposes the anomalies of Byzantine piety. Devoted to Greek philosophy, and admittedly fascinated by the forbidden subject of astrology, he declares with manifest sincerity that Christian theology is the base and crown of his thought; it was "no scientific reason" but "some divine force" that made him give up his belief in astrology.

He seems touched by the piety of the Empress Zoë, who had made a little figure of Jesus; by changes of color it answered questions and made prophecies. He knows that Divine Providence governs history, which he proceeds to explain in terms of human causation. In particular he reveals the otherworldliness of Byzantium. His closest friends retired to monasteries, many of the characters in his narrative ended their lives there, and he himself was once tonsured because of the inconstancy of an emperor (the last of Zoë's husbands). Page after page reflects the profound Byzantine conviction of the vanity of this life. Nothing is clearer—except the worldly ambition of Psellus, his avid desire for all the goods of this life. Page after page reveals the habitually un-Christian behavior that is the most apparent reason why life seemed vain to the Byzantines. A repeated example is the solemn oath sworn by emperors or their underlings, and then broken, presumably ensuring their eternal damnation—were it not for the power of their icons, or the convenience of the many monasteries.

Since Psellus never mentions the historic break of the Orthodox Church with Rome that occurred in this century, one must suppose that he did not think it worth mentioning. In this insularity he also gives away the limitations of Byzantine culture. There is no questioning his ardor for the cause of true learning and culture, and apparently he assumed that his readers shared it; his pages are strewn with quotations from Homer, identified only as "the poet." But one may wonder what poetry meant to Michael Psellus. He writes that literature has two branches—oratory and philosophy. While professing humility before the great orators and philosophers of antiquity, he is sufficiently complacent about his ability to unite the two branches, even though "many persons have reproached me for this and dislike the way I brighten a philosophic discourse with the graceful arts of rhetoric." His way may seem less graceful than affected, as in the frequent quotation merely for the sake of quotation. (As "the poet" said, he "stretched forth his hands to the food that was ready.") He is proud to state that he drew his "small measure of wisdom from no living fount"—proud because he had opened and cleansed the sources, and plumbed their depths; though he adds sadly that no city in his time, not even the New Rome, "glories any longer in literary achievement." And the last chapter of his book, celebrating his own most glorious pedagogic achievement, is by all odds the worst. It is a fulsome eulogy of Michael VII, "a human nature of such divinity" that he "far surpasses all others that we have ever known before." Psellus, his tutor and intimate, had trained him to be a philosopher-king. Other historians agree that he was among the feeblest, most contemptible of Byzantine emperors. After he was forced to abdicate, in 1078, nothing more is heard of

Michael Psellus. The *Chronographia* breaks off abruptly; it was never completed.

Even had it been, Psellus could not be ranked among the greater historians. He lacked not only a great theme but the ability to handle such a theme. Constantly insisting that a historian must be objective and "methodical," he is forever obtruding himself, digressing, returning, repeating, with no clear guiding purpose or consistent point of view; all that holds his book together is the thread of chronology. A shrewd observer and often lively recorder, he is never profound or masterly. His limitations become more pronounced when he is set beside Herodotus, who had nothing like his advantages in learning, and whom he mentions only once, disparagingly. He is much more insular, displaying no curiosity about other peoples in East or West; one would never guess from his work that in his time existed the great city of Baghdad, which did glory in literary achievement, or that Europe was a growing power, whose Crusaders would in a few years cause further trouble for Byzantium. He is less critical than Herodotus, and less trustworthy. Despite his sophistication, he seems more naïve as he perpetually preens himself on his rhetoric, his encyclopedic knowledge, his true piety, his "brilliant reputation," his indispensable counsel to the emperors. He intimates that the ultimate cause of the ruinous state of affairs in Byzantium was "the babblers who make a habit of contradicting all I say."

The personality that Psellus obtrudes on almost every page is not a very attractive one. Although loyal to a few close friends, he seems generally uncharitable, calculating, disingenuous; one can never wholly trust his account of affairs in which he himself was involved. He shows little concern for justice in any broad or deep sense. With his devout faith went little Christian feeling for his fellow men. Likewise Procopius, Anna Comnena, and other Byzantine writers who reveal themselves typically reveal a more or less unpleasant self. Almost all tend to be cold or bitter; almost none have a warm, engaging personality. Even the saints of Byzantium are rarely lovable; most of them belonged in the caves or on the tops of pillars where so many spent their lives. With a better understanding of the Byzantines one may still have to strain to extend them the sympathy they so seldom displayed themselves. There is much to admire in their valorous achievement, much to be grateful for. But it is hard to love them, or even to like them very much.

4. THE DEATH OF THE POLIS

Constantinople! It was long a magic word for Europeans. For hundreds of years this was indeed the greatest city in the world. Its early rivals gave way as Rome entered the Dark Ages, as Alexandria and Antioch fell to the Arabs. Although it had its ups and downs, its growing trade enabled it to recover; wealth poured in on it from China, the Indies, Persia, Arabia, Egypt, Russia, Spain. In the ninth century it entered a Golden Age that lasted until its fall to the Fourth Crusade in 1204.

Villehardouin, the chronicler of this Crusade, left the best-known description of the city, with its majestic palaces and churches rising behind its great walls and towers. Centuries before him a Chinese traveler reporting on the wonders of "Fu Lin" had mentioned not only its imperial buildings, decorated with gold, crystal, ivory, and rare woods, but its mechanical marvels, such as water-power machines that made fountains to cool the city in summer, and a human figure of gold that marked the hours by striking bells. In the imperial palace envoys from other lands were awed by golden lions that roared and golden birds that sang. Gold was everywhere—and nowhere more dazzling than in the interiors of the incredibly numerous churches and monasteries. For all its wharves and bazaars and workshops, the turbulent life of its Hippodrome, the squalid life of its tenements, the luxurious life of its palaces, Constantinople remained the "holy ark" of the Byzantine Empire, enclosed by triple walls. It was Jerusalem, Rome, Paris, and New York rolled into one.

The provinces, however, naturally suffered from its domination of the national life. A major casualty of the fame of Constantinople was the *polis*. The old cities had retained sufficient vigor to help the Roman Empire survive in the East, and they long continued to manifest some independence of spirit, especially in religious controversy. At the "Robber Council" of Ephesus, for example, the Patriarch of Constantinople was kicked so hard in the belly by another bishop that he died three days later. An annual fair at Ephesus on St. John's day indicated that the cities were still enterprising in commerce as well. Some remained known for their specialties, as Sardis for its carpets, Laodicea for its linens; and a new market was opened up by the traffic in holy relics. But the rich civic life of the Greco-Roman world was a fading memory. The cities were no longer providing a good education for their sons, or sufficient opportunity for the most gifted. Constantinople was the Mecca for talent and ambition.

The reign of Justinian the Great marked the turning point. Asia Minor profited by the building enterprises he carried out all over the empire, in the Roman imperial tradition, and on a scale that makes him perhaps the greatest builder in all history. Ephesus got its great Church of St. John. Tarsus was freed from its fear of recurrent disastrous floods by the diversion of its Cydnus River into a new channel constructed outside the city. The island of Tenedos off Troy had its transport business improved by the addition of a huge granary. Nicaea had its palace and baths restored, and was endowed with new monasteries. Antioch, destroyed by an earthquake, was completely replanned and rebuilt. Everywhere the cities were benefited by new construction, religious, commercial, and recreational, while communication between them was improved by the building or repair of roads and bridges. On the surface, Asia Minor was regaining its former splendor.

But the cities paid more than their share for these benefits, directly and indirectly. A contemporary reports that the tax collectors of Justinian were more dreaded than enemy invaders—and the cities could do even less about them. They had no constitution, no real rights against the imperial government. Justinian proclaimed that the emperor alone had the right to make and interpret the laws. While municipal liberties largely disappeared under Diocletian and Constantine, some tradition of self-government had survived to this time; city councils were still organizing their food supply, staging games and festivals, and doing odd jobs for the imperial government. Under the centralized bureaucracy of Justinian local government became worse than nominal. Service on the city council was a fearful responsibility, enforced by imperial law and entailing no opportunity for independent action. Freedom of movement—the freedom most prized under the Roman Empire—was virtually gone for good; there was no escaping to Constantinople except by official permission, for the capital had to be fed. The freedoms that Pericles had boasted of in his Funeral Oration were simply unthinkable. With the reign of Justinian the history of the *polis,* and of the Greek as a political animal, may be said to end.

No doubt there was more bustle in the cities, and more local pride, than we hear of; but the significant thing is that we hear almost nothing. Very little is known of Byzantine town life. The departed glory is most evident in western Asia Minor, particularly Ionia. Smyrna remained a fairly important port, though it suffered from the competition of Constantinople. All the other once great cities—Ephesus, Miletus, Pergamum, Sardis—dwindled and crumbled. Now and then we hear of an eminent son, such as Saint Nicephorus of Miletus or Mark of Ephesus, a learned theologian. Otherwise about the only mention of them in Byzantine annals is of their capture by the Arabs, or later by the Seljuks. Their inhabitants might have got some comfort from the dictum of St. Augustine, that the *polis* was the greatest of heresies and Athens as shameless as Nineveh; but one doubts that they had a live memory of the days when they had been free cities.

Asia Minor was also transformed by Arab inroads. The northern part now became the most prosperous and important; among its still notable cities were Nicaea, hallowed by its Councils, and Trebizond, the port for the northern trade route to the East. The southwest and the western coast were exposed to attack by the Arabs. In Cilicia, which the Arabs sought to hold permanently, they might rebuild or refortify cities, as they did Tarsus. Regions that they were unable to hold they were content to raid and ravage. Such great ports as Alexandria Troas and Side were deserted because they suffered so heavily from raids by pirates. In the interior other once wealthy cities were gradually deserted for the same reason. The Hellenistic kings, and the Romans after them, had founded or refounded cities primarily for purposes of trade and with an eye to comfort, not defense; now their inhabitants looked for stronger sites. Laodicea took to the hill above, in the region of modern Denizli. Celaenae-Apamea gave way to the nearby fortress town of Choma. Colossae, which gave way to another one, best symbolizes the disenchanting fate of the enchanted cities. Once an important Phrygian city that had decayed as nearby Laodicea prospered, it had grown again under the Byzantine Empire as a religious center; its great church of the Archangel Michael was famous for the miracles it worked. In time the city was so completely forgotten that St. Paul's Epistle to the Colossians was thought to be addressed to the Rhodians, because of their Colossus.

Although the new strongholds eventually went the way of all others in history, some had enduring importance and added to the glamour as well as the melancholy of the historic landscape of Asia Minor. Most enduring were the works of the Emperor Justinian, though not under the royal name he was so proud of. In the course of building an excellent system of roads and fortresses as a defense against Persian invasions, he founded a number of Justinianopolises that have disappeared as such, but he chose routes and sites that remain on the map of Turkey today. One Justinianopolis, for example, was some ten miles from Pessinus, the ancient seat of Cybele; it has survived as the city of Sivrihisar, while Pessinus disappeared from sight and memory. On the Mesopotamian frontier Justinian rebuilt the city of Edessa (Urfa), which became not only a key Byzantine fortress but a major Christian center; in the tenth century it had as many as three hundred churches, including a cathedral rated among the wonders of the world.[11] Another city that rose to importance was Dorylaeum, a station on the main road from Constantinople to the East, through which passed many a Byzantine army, Crusader, and

---

[11] None of them remain today. About all that remains is the citadel, held by Crusaders as well as Byzantines, which failed to save the churches.

pilgrim to Jerusalem. As Eskishehir ("Old City") it is still a main station on the railway from Istanbul to Ankara and Baghdad, though unfortunately a city of little interest or charm. Perhaps the most spectacular Byzantine landmark is the fortress of Acroïnum or Nicopolis, at the modern railway center of Afyonkarahisar, on a rock that rises abruptly out of a broad plain to a height of almost a thousand feet. Here, about 740, the Arabs were decisively defeated as their celebrated hero Seid Batal Ghazi met his death.

The Byzantine era also worked some change in the peasantry, beyond the substitution of Christian for pagan deities and the admixture of some Slavic blood in their indefinable race. A number of free farmers and village communes had survived the feudalizing drive in the late Roman Empire, and their number was greatly increased by the disorder resulting from Persian and Arab invasions, as landlords took to flight. Peasants bore the brunt of the resistance, often fighting as guerrillas in the hills. A sturdy peasantry seems to have contributed much to the resurgence of the Byzantine Empire. So did rude mountain peoples previously given to banditry. Those in the mountains behind Cilicia Aspera, who centuries before had taken to piracy, became known as Isaurians and gave their name to the dynasty of Leo III, the savior of Constantinople. With the return of order and security, however, the peasants largely lost their freedom. By the tenth century vast estates had arisen, some belonging to monasteries, others to a feudal nobility. Peasants were bought out as they were unable to compete or to pay taxes in hard times, and became tenants or virtual serfs. As always, very little is heard of them, but it is safe to assume that they now bore the brunt of taxation, and accepted basically the same life as their ancestors had under all their masters since Hittite times.

Meanwhile Anatolia had made some contributions to Byzantine art and architecture which historians only recently have begun to trace. It was not so deeply influenced by Constantinople as were the more highly civilized regions of the empire, just as it had never been by Hellenism. The main current of influence seems rather to have flowed from or through it toward Constantinople, where it was deflected into Greece and the Balkans. Among the signs of activity are the reappearance of ancient Anatolian animal motifs and the ruins of Bin bir Kilisse, the "Thousand and One Churches." Most striking are the weird rock churches of Cappadocia, in the region of Kayseri. These give a vivid idea of the Oriental religiosity that was always close to the heart of Byzantium.

"That race," wrote the Byzantine chronicler Leo Diaconus of the Cappadocians, "was formerly called Troglodytes, because they burrowed

in holes and clefts and labyrinths, as it were in dens and lurking places."
Monks and hermits in fact made labyrinths of the cliffs of Cappadocia.
Near modern Ürgüp they holed up in a fantastic surrealist landscape—a
valley sprouting hundreds of tall rock cones, many crowned by caps resulting from erosion. They burrowed into the cliffs bordering the valley
and into the taller cones, which look like tenement houses drawn by a
demented child. They also cut out rock chapels, some large enough to be
called churches. Between the ninth and the eleventh centuries they
decorated these chapels and churches with wall paintings, most of which
have been preserved in fairly good condition because of the remoteness
and aridity of the region. These portray brooding Christs, Old Testament
figures, Constantine and Helena, Biblical and apocryphal cycles, St.
George killing dragons, and other such legends—all with a crude but
vigorous, often intense, realism. Apparently they were inspired by no
aim of Hellenic beauty, ceremonial pomp, or theological instruction, but
served simply to mirror the broodings of the monks. Their style seems to
have carried into southern Italy and the Balkans.

Just who these holy troglodytes were, when they came, why they left,
and where they went is not certainly known. It appears that Christians
moved in as early as the third century, enlarging caves that had previously been occupied. At some time their example grew popular, for
there are thousands of such tenements in the vicinity, many of considerable size. For some centuries they maintained in isolation their forbidding
ideal, free from both the best and the worst in Byzantine civilization.
Their eventual disappearance no doubt had some connection with the
Seljuk conquest of the region, even though the Seljuks were not given to
religious persecution.

It accordingly brings us back to the main story of the empire, the fatal
loss of most of Asia Minor to the Seljuks. While Constantinople was the
heart and soul of the empire, Asia Minor had always been its backbone.
It had served as the bulwark against Eastern invaders. It had provided
the major dynasties, much of the food and the material resources, and
the bulk of the army, especially the celebrated heavy cavalry. After its
loss the Byzantine army was never the same, as the emperors depended
increasingly on foreign mercenaries. Constantinople was defended against
the Crusaders chiefly by Anglo-Saxons.

Yet in the long view the death of the *polis* seems more significant. As
the empire went into its decline, the free town was emerging in the
West, spurring a new development. Byzantium had no such spur. It had
only Constantinople, which had created a rich culture, but had administered the empire through an ultraconservative bureaucracy that always

discouraged local initiative. Its Church-State was incapable of inspiring new ideals, or generating a new social effort. The contrast with the rising West was accentuated in the fourteenth century by an embryonic popular revolution, led by reformers known as the Zealots. It broke out in Balkan cities—not in Asia Minor. The Zealots confiscated the wealth of the rich and attempted to establish free cities, seemingly on the model of Italian cities. In Thessalonica they held out for two years against the imperial authorities, refusing admission to a high ecclesiastical envoy. Then they were crushed. Imperial Byzantium was too far gone to be rejuvenated.

5. THE LAST DAYS OF BYZANTIUM

The long decline after the disaster of Manzikert was again not the simple decadence that Western historians used to picture. The ever-harassed Byzantines continued to display courage and vigor, in culture even a surprising creativity. They were at their best as well as their worst in their last days. But the political drama is mostly depressing. It may be exemplified by the reign of Alexius Comnenus (1081–1118), an emperor who was installed in desperation by the feudal nobility, and whose life was recorded by his daughter Anna Comnena.

Alexius doubtless had something of the exalted sense of duty to the dead and to posterity avowed by Anna in the Preface of her history. He succeeded in more than holding his own, against not only the Seljuks but the Normans in the west and barbarians from the north. He succeeded chiefly by diplomatic guile, however, and at a heavy cost. Short of both money and man power, he enlisted the aid of Venice by commercial concessions that hurt the trade of Constantinople, he imposed taxes that made Seljuk rule seem mild, and he began to tamper with an imperial currency that had maintained its standard value since the time of Constantine the Great. His exertions are at once more admirable and more depressing because he could never count on the loyalty of his generals, his court, or even his family. Anna worshiped her father, but otherwise she had little faith in human nature, and makes clear why Byzantine tradition gave little reason for faith or hope. She was proud of her father because he took nobody at his word, nothing at its face value. For her, wisdom was chiefly cunning, deceit was ordinary intelligence. Her history is full of the idea of *noblesse oblige*, with no obligations to honor or simple honesty. The routine duplicity seems worse because of her Byzantine arrogance and contempt for all other peoples.

This contempt was most marked for her fellow Christians—the Crusaders. First arriving in Constantinople in 1096, they were a further source of trouble for the emperors. Many were filled with a crusading zeal that Byzantium was no longer capable of, and Anna could understand only as simple-mindedness. Their leaders also had political designs on Constantinople and a natural dislike for the heretical Greeks, which was heartily reciprocated. Alexius managed the troublesome invaders skilfully, using them to recover some territory from the Seljuks, then sending them on their way to the Holy Land. But their success against the Moslems weakened Byzantium. They set up independent kingdoms at formerly Byzantine cities, such as Antioch and Edessa, and presently made alliances with the Seljuks. Much of the Eastern trade now went directly from Syria to the West on Italian ships, instead of through the customs of Constantinople. The decline in trade accelerated the debasement of the imperial coinage.

A century after Manzikert, in the vicinity of Antioch-in-Pisidia, Manuel Comnenus fought a great battle to recover Asia Minor from the Seljuks, and met as decisive a defeat. Meanwhile the Second Crusade had come and gone, plundering on its way, to no good end; it was a complete failure. The next generation saw the last of the Comneni, Andronicus I, a compound of all the qualities that typified the Byzantine monarch: gallant, energetic, shrewd, refined, unscrupulous, despotic, and cruel. The chief event of his brief reign (1183–85) was a massacre of the Italian merchants in Constantinople. Feeling between Eastern and Western Christendom was not improved by a similar massacre of Greeks as the Normans captured Thessalonica. A frightened emperor managed to make peace with the Third Crusade, ferrying it across the Dardanelles, and was relieved when it petered out, as Frederick Barbarossa was accidentally drowned in the Calycadnus River on the border of Cilicia. But then the Fourth Crusade arrived.

Though blessed by Pope Innocent III, its leaders were more inspired by Venetian greed. They began their crusade by destroying the Christian city of Zara in Europe, and ended it by conquering the Christian city of Constantinople. For three days they permitted their army to pillage and slaughter. "Since the world was created," exclaimed Villehardouin, "never had so much booty been won in any city!" Much of the booty, in particular the stupendous collection of holy relics, was carried back to Europe. (It included at least two heads of John the Baptist, consigned to Soissons and Amiens.) Most of the priceless art treasures accumulated over nine centuries were simply destroyed as the Crusaders burned, smashed, or melted them down into coinage. Goths and Huns had never done such irreparable damage. And the long-range consequences to Christendom were even more disastrous. The Latins who ruled Constantinople from 1204 to 1261 were too rude and incompetent to learn from their more civilized subjects, or to reconcile them to the Roman Church. The city and the Byzantine Empire never recovered from the blow. Whatever chance there might have been of uniting Christendom, or of preserving Eastern Christendom from the Turks, was killed for good by the Fourth Crusade.

Immediately, the Byzantines again exhibited their astonishing vitality. Preventing the Crusaders from taking over the whole empire, they set up three local "empires," at Epirus, Trebizond, and Nicaea.[12] The emperors of Nicaea reconquered much of Greece and at length won back Constantinople; the last of them, Michael Palaeologus, founded in 1258 the last Byzantine dynasty, which ruled the empire for almost two hundred years. But it was a shrunken empire, ruled from a largely ruined, depopulated city. Michael lacked the means to rebuild the capital, even to restore the Great Palace. To recover it he had depended on the aid of the Genoese, and in return he had to grant them trading privileges, including the possession of the town of Galata across the Golden Horn; they took over much of the remaining trade of Constantinople, which grew still poorer as Galata flourished. Its inhabitants must have taken a melancholy pride, if any, in the knowledge that even as a decaying shell their city still awed visitors. Ibn-Batuta, the Moslem world traveler, dwelt on "its marvelous and rare sights," especially the magnificent churches and monasteries, "not to be counted for multitude." Later travelers commented on the splendor of the ancient ceremonies maintained by the emperor, but stressed more the poverty and shabbiness of the people.

In the meantime the doomed empire had suffered further losses. Michael Palaeologus had been granted a respite by the collapse of the Seljuk Empire, following the Mongol invasion, but his successors soon had to contend with the Ottoman Turks, who took Nicaea as early as 1329. Although Tamerlane provided another respite by defeating the Turks in Asia Minor, they quickly recovered and kept carving slices off the empire. At the end it huddled about Constantinople, protected only by its great walls. A city that once numbered over a million people now held fewer than a hundred thousand.

In their desperation, the last Byzantine emperors sought a reconciliation with Rome, hoping to get military aid against the heathen; but this was an even sorrier story. A number of "unions" were signed between the Roman and the Orthodox Church, all ineffectual. Most of the Greek clergy and the common people violently opposed any submission to Rome, while one pope, Clement V, announced that all who joined a

[12] See the Appendix, Section 10, for the history of Trebizond.

crusade against Constantinople would be eligible for the same indulgences that crusaders to the Holy Land got. The final Act of Union was signed at the Council of Florence in 1439. For the price of a crusade against the Turks, the Byzantine emperor pressured a majority of his ecclesiastical delegation into compromising on a hairline restatement of the filioque, and recognizing the universal supremacy of Rome.[13] Instead of the promised crusade the emperor got only a Roman cardinal, who infuriated his subjects by solemnly celebrating the union in Hagia Sophia, just five months before Constantinople fell to the Turks. A Greek dignitary gave immortal expression to the fervor of Eastern Christendom: "It is better to see in the city the power of the Turkish turban than that of the Latin tiara!" It proved better for the Holy Orthodox Church, which repudiated the union, retained its freedom, and increased its power under the Turks. It was also better for the unholy cause of Islam.

Nevertheless the Church had displayed considerable intellectual energy in the bitter struggle. The energy appeared too in a controversy within it over a movement known as Hesychasm, a form of mystical quietism that produced some of the finest religious writing of Byzantium. And if the quietism was symptomatic of a dying empire, the creativity may be associated with the final and most remarkable proof of the vitality underlying its rigid forms. This was the renaissance that lent both splendor and pathos to the last days of Byzantium.

The classical revival that marked the age of Michael Psellus, and continued under the Comneni, might well have been ended by the fall of Constantinople to the Fourth Crusade. Libraries had been burned, precious manuscripts destroyed, scholars scattered and impoverished, and the whole system of learning disorganized. But now, at the court of Nicaea, began the most brilliant period of Byzantine learning. Nicaea became known as a second Athens. Upon the recapture of Constantinople cultural activity grew still more intense, and more markedly humanistic. Even emperors and their ministers were steeped in the classics. A typical figure was the humanist Theodore Metochites, a statesman who wrote poetical, philosophical, historical, astronomical, and other works; who restored the Church of the Chora, embellishing it with its now famous mosaics; and who spent his last days in this church, after losing his home and fortune in a palace revolution. As the city grew poorer and shabbier, its schools attracted students from all over, even from Italy. At

---

[13] Among those who refused to assent was Mark, Bishop of Ephesus. It would be pleasant to see in him a resurgence of the old independent Greek spirit, but he seems rather to have been a rigid Greek sectarian.

the very end Byzantium produced two of its most important writers in the Patriarch Gennadius and the philosopher Plethon.

Much of this work has a pathetic aspect, betokened by the pride of Anna Comnena in the purity of her "Attic" prose. It was artificial in style, academic in content, remote from the realities of Byzantine life. It represented a futile effort to revive ancient glories, or to obscure an inglorious present. Yet the revival as a whole was a heroic defense of a way of life, a cultural heritage that Constantinople had preserved for ten centuries. It sprang from deep reverence, and it was not merely futile—it passed on this heritage, in a somewhat richer form. And in this afterglow there was at least a glimmer of the true Greek spirit, some sparks that might have ignited a renaissance comparable to that in Europe, had the empire survived. Plethon, the last of the Byzantine philosophers, was the most nearly original. He was a freethinker, bolder than any in Europe at the time; he regarded Christianity as a menace to thought, and hoped that with further enlightenment it would disappear. Although his last book was accordingly banned by the Orthodox Church, he had been allowed to teach freely, and the Patriarch Gennadius was unhappy at having to kill so brilliant a work. Gennadius himself was more attractive than the saints of Byzantium. "I would never say that I was a Hellene," he wrote, "for I do not believe as the Hellenes believed." He preferred to call himself a Christian and a Byzantine. Still, his statement reveals his awareness of a great heritage, and there was much of the Hellene in him.

More available, and more transparently humanistic, is the art of the last centuries of Byzantium. As the impoverished empire could rarely afford costly materials now, the chief example of the final phase in mosaics is the series in the Church of the Chora (or Karieh Jami) in Istanbul, representing the complete cycles of the lives of the Virgin and Christ. These are the lightest and brightest of Byzantine mosaics, not only gorgeous in color but warm, intimate, tender. For some critics, indeed, they are not spiritual enough, too Hellenistic or too tender. The piety that made them so warm and bright conveys more pathos than sense of joy in life and the natural world, and it may seem more pathetic because the life of the Virgin as recorded here with such loving care is wholly mythical, lacking any basis in Scripture. Yet most will agree that these are glorious mosaics. So far from being decadent, they bewildered art historians by their freshness when they were first uncovered. Some scholars thought that they must have been executed by a pupil of Giotto.

Frescoes that have more recently been uncovered in the Church of the Chora gave the same impression. When no longer able to afford mosaics the Byzantines turned to painting, and their paintings most plainly reflect the growing naturalism and humanism, the new interest in personality and stress on personal feeling. This development was at first attributed to Western influence, but in fact it started earlier in Byzantium. And so we are led to a further irony. An early theory of historians had it that the main cause of the Renaissance in Europe was the flight of Byzantine scholars from Constantinople. Now that this theory has been properly discredited, the actual indebtedness to Byzantium grows clearer. Its scholars—notably Plethon—did stir considerable enthusiasm and excitement in Italy; in particular they contributed Platonism to European thought. Although "influences" are always easy to exaggerate, it appears that Giotto owed much to Byzantine art, at least more than it owed to him. In El Greco the Byzantine tradition is unmistakable.

All along Byzantium had been a civilizing influence on Western Europe. Its art was planted in Italy from the beginning—at Rome and Ravenna, later at Venice, the major intermediary between East and West, and still later in Norman Sicily. Through the Dark Ages it helped to keep Rome literate and semicivilized, while traders and pilgrims in search of holy relics kept the rest of Europe aware of the existence of civilization. It educated Irish and Anglo-Saxon monks, and strongly influenced Anglo-Saxon art. (Its ceremonial still persists in the English coronation service.) It provided the model for the imperial court and art of Charlemagne. It influenced the early Romanesque style in architecture. What it meant at the dawn of civilization in the West is perhaps best shown by a trivial example. When Otto II married a Byzantine princess, in the tenth century, she shocked the Germans by her un-Christian habits of wearing silk and taking baths, just as her cousin shocked a saint by introducing forks to Venice. Europeans were slow to take up the habit of baths, since ages of piety are not given to personal cleanliness; but they soon learned to wear silk and use forks.

Most important, once more, was the service rendered by Byzantium simply as a bulwark behind which the new civilization of the West could grow up in safety, and learn to despise its savior. Although the proud Byzantines would not have relished the idea that this was their main claim to respect, we owe it to them to review in sympathy the last scene in their history, the fall of Constantinople to the infidels. It was an appropriately dramatic, incongruous scene, in keeping with the whole history of the empire. For seven weeks the defenders of the city had fought valiantly in their hopeless cause. As the later historians had dwelt on the past glories of the empire, so the Emperor Constantine Palaeologus heartened his people by reminding them of the feats of their Greek and Roman ancestors. On the eve of the city's fall the accent was on the distinctive piety of Byzantium. The Emperor received communion at the last Christian service held in Hagia Sophia, presided over by the learned Patriarch Gennadius. Then multitudes joined in religious processions through the streets, singing "O Lord, have mercy on us." They prayed more particularly to the Virgin and to St. Theodosia, a martyr manufactured in the struggle against the Iconoclasts, whose relics had worked many miracles and whose saint's day fell on the morrow. On this day, May 29, 1453, the last of the Constantines returned to the thousand-year-old city walls, to fight and die like an old Roman.

CHAPTER VIII

Konya: The Triumph of Islam

---

1. THE PROPHET MOHAMMED

ALTHOUGH THE Seljuk Turks are more interesting in their own right than one would gather from most histories by Westerners, their historic importance is still due primarily to one simple fact: they established Islam in Anatolia. They prepared the way for the Ottoman Turks, who brought all Asia Minor under Moslem rule and proceeded to build an empire that for centuries threatened the Christian West. To understand the success of both, we must go back to the most remarkable success story in religious history—the work of the Prophet Mohammed.

In his name, within a generation or so after his death, the previously obscure Arabs had come out of their desert to conquer Persia, Mesopotamia, Syria, Palestine, and Egypt, overrun North Africa, penetrate Asia Minor, and attack Constantinople itself. Their astonishingly rapid surge is not, it is true, simply astonishing. They were aided by the weakness of the two contemporary empires, the Sassanian and the Byzantine, which had largely exhausted themselves by their wars on one another. They profited as well from the Christian habit of persecution, which had alienated the predominantly Monophysite inhabitants of Syria and Egypt; these provinces put up only token resistance to the more tolerant Arabs, even welcoming them as liberators. Nor were these Arabs simply zealots fired by the ideal of a Holy War. They were by long tradition tough fighters, accustomed to raiding out of hunger and want; many or perhaps even most of them were not ardent followers of Mohammed. Yet there can be little question that what got the Arabs started, and kept them going, was mainly the personality and the teaching of the Prophet. He enabled a small nation to impose his religion and his language on most of the Near East. Other men may have made as epochal a difference in history, but none has made a plainer or more direct one.

Immediately, the historical foundations of Mohammedanism are a great deal firmer than those of Christianity. We know far more about the man Mohammed than we do about the man Jesus. There is no question whatever about his historical existence and very little about the major events in his life, which raise no such problems as the Christian claims of a virgin birth and a resurrection. The Koran, much of which was written down before his death and the rest within a few years later, much more certainly represents his own gospel than the New Testament, with its four Gospels and other accretions, represents the teaching of Jesus. We know far more, too, about the early history of Mohammedanism than we do about the slow, obscure growth of Christianity. If its triumph was more "miraculous," it is easier to follow in the light of recorded history.

Nevertheless there has been endless disagreement over the man Mohammed, his teaching, and its consequences; and there is ample reason for confusion and uncertainty. By his own word, the Koran was revealed in installments to "the Prophet who can neither read nor write." As taken down and put together, in an uncertain but chronologically different order, the revelation is sometimes obscure as well as ungrammatical, and is full of apparent contradictions. The contradictions were multiplied and intensified by the growth of tradition, sprung from the hadith or further sayings of the Prophet to his companions. Later theologians would sift hundreds of thousands of hadith in a necessarily uncertain effort to determine the authentic ones, and a more hopeless effort to reconcile them with the Koran and with one another.[1] "Whoever shall repeat of me that which I have not said," runs one credited by many companions, "his resting place shall be in hell"; and if so, a great many pious theologians are in hell. Much of the tradition reflects the ignorance and credulity of the early Arabs. In the Koran the Prophet said repeatedly that he was no angel or worker of miracles, but a mere mortal: "Miracles rest with God alone—I am only a man, warning you." Presently, to compete with Jesus, he was equipped with the usual miracles. For such reasons modern scholars no longer repeat the saying of their predecessors, that Islam grew up in the full light of history. And always there remains the problem, as H. A. R. Gibb observed, of accounting for "the gap between the bare facts and the tremendous results."

---

[1] The sifting was begun by al-Bukhari, more than two centuries after the Prophet's death. He worked honestly as well as piously for sixteen years, traveling all over Islam to question sheiks, and according to his biographer considered some 600,000 hadith. He testified to his critical conscience, and to the gullibility of his fellow Moslems, by accepting only 7,000. One hadith had Mohammed flatly condemning the whole business: "A book other than the book of God! Do you not know that nothing but the writing of books beside the book of God led astray the peoples that were before you?"

As always, one cannot simply stick to the facts, which do not speak for themselves. Neither can any but the arrogant or the innocent pretend to offer an utterly objective account of the work of Mohammed. If outsiders can be more objective than Moslems, they cannot have the intimate knowledge and natural sympathy necessary to full understanding and full justice. But one can at least begin with factual statements, and again hope to attain a clearer understanding and a more impartial judgment through an awareness of the sources of confusion and bias.

As an avowed mortal, Mohammed was naturally influenced by his time and place. The religion of the Arabs before him was a very primitive one. Their holy of holies was the Kaaba—the Black Stone of Mecca. This was of a piece with the black stone "to which of yore the Amazons all used to pray," according to Apollonius of Rhodes, and in which Cybele was wont to reside. Together with nature spirits, the Arabs worshiped various goddesses. One was Allat, mentioned by Herodotus; she was their version of the Mother Goddess, akin to Astarte and Cybele. Allah himself was ancient—a thousand years before Mohammed the Persians wrote that "Allah is exalted"—but he was only one of many deities. All this refutes the seductive and popular idea of Renan that monotheism is the "natural religion of the desert." Mohammed himself was not a man of the desert. He was a man of Mecca: a busy, prosperous city on a caravan route (like Petra and Palmyra before it), which largely controlled the overland trade between the Indian and the Mediterranean oceans, and which confronted the Prophet with the familiar problem of the rich and the poor. He shared in the chief spiritual possession of the Arabs aside from the Kaaba—their poetry. In their passion for poetry and their common illiteracy, the Arabs developed a prodigious capacity for memorizing that enabled them to preserve the Koran. The scattered verses of the Prophet had been inscribed not only on date leaves and shreds of leather but on "the hearts of men."

On his own heart had been inscribed more than Arab tradition. There were large numbers of Jews and Christians in Arabia, including many converted Arabs; the Monophysites, preaching the One Nature of Christ, had been especially active missionaries. Mohammed had direct relations with colonies of Jews in and about Medina. In the Koran he displayed an acquaintance with their Scriptures, if an imperfect one (he declared that the Jews worshiped Ezra as the son of God); often he used Biblical characters to preach his doctrines. Of Christian Scriptures he had a more limited, garbled knowledge, or at least he felt freer to reinterpret them, in an original and somewhat incongruous fashion. Thus he denied the divinity of Christ and rejected the Crucifixion as a Jewish falsehood, while for some reason he accepted the miraculous birth (perhaps because there were paintings of Jesus and Mary on the inner walls of the Kaaba). But he identified Allah with the God of Judaism and Christianity. He borrowed other ideas foreign to Arab tradition, notably the Last Judgment and the resurrection of the flesh, which the Arabs of Mecca thought ridiculous and revolting. We cannot know to what extent he consciously borrowed, and may assume that he was more deeply indebted than he realized. When he threw out Allat, for example, blaming Satan for a previous admission that she might have real powers of intercession, we may suspect that he did not appreciate the uniqueness of Israel in rejecting the Mother Goddess, or know the ancestry of Satan. In any case, his basic teaching is unmistakably in the line of Judaism and Christianity.

The key events of Mohammed's career are also beyond dispute. After some forty years of respectable but obscure life, during which his abilities in business won him the confidence and the hand of a rich widow, he felt his calling as a prophet. In his belief, the Angel Gabriel appeared to him and dictated this calling; but whatever his experience—call it mystical, visionary, or epileptic—it was as compulsive as that of St. Paul en route to Damascus, or those of the great prophets of Israel. His subsequent career supports the tradition that he was at first appalled by God's orders, knowing that there would be no more sleep or rest for him. Like Jesus, he was from the beginning opposed by the most powerful, respectable, God-fearing members of his community. "Men said: Shall we forsake our gods for a mad poet?" Although he won over a few influential men, most of his early converts came from among the poor people and the slaves of Mecca. The mockery of the respectable turned to violent hostility when his preaching threatened the profitable business of Mecca as the sanctuary of all Arabia, the hostelry for the annual pilgrimage. The persecution of Mohammed was so effective that conceivably his mission might have failed had not a few men come from Medina one year to hear his message, and returned home as missionaries. Finally, in A.D. 622, after thirteen years of generally disheartening and increasingly dangerous obedience to God's orders, he fled in the night and sought refuge in Medina—the hegira that marks the beginning of the Mohammedan era with a certainty that cannot be claimed for the beginning of the Christian era.

At Medina the Prophet entered the triumphant phase of his career, and the most dubious for a man of God. He became the political as well as spiritual leader of a community. He waged war against the Meccans, initiating hostilities by raiding one of their caravans in the holy month of pilgrimage, when war was banned in Arabia; to justify his aggression, he preached war against idolaters as a sacred duty (jihad). With a force of only three hundred, he routed some thousand Meccans in the piddling but momentous battle of Badr, and later proved his generalship by holding off much larger forces sent against him. He also attacked several wealthy Jewish communities, which had refused to recognize him as a prophet. When one of them surrendered after a short siege, he had all its men put to death and its women and children sold into slavery. By these campaigns he won much booty as well as prestige; one may suspect that it was not so much his spiritual message as his worldly success that now drew the Arabs to Allah. At length the Meccans gave in: eight years after the hegira, Mohammed returned to his native city in triumph. As he then proved his wisdom and clemency by putting only four people to death, the Meccans accepted him as the apostle of Allah and joined his army. In the short time left to him he sent an expeditionary force to attack a Byzantine outpost in Syria. In the year 632 Mohammed shocked and confused his followers by dying. Most had refused to take his own word that he was a mortal.

Now Mohammed had certainly not lived like an angel. While often preaching an otherworldly gospel, he was a worldly man, with a shrewd eye to both political and economic interests. He enjoyed the company of a number of concubines in addition to his eleven wives. Most troublesome is his addiction to war. One may argue that in the Arabia of his time he could not have succeeded except by war, and that he was at least above the hypocrisy of Christendom in its alleged devotion to the author of the Sermon on the Mount; but the fact remains that his was no gospel of love, no message of peace and good will on earth. In preaching the holy war he could sound very naïve: the special rewards in Paradise he promised to martyrs who fell in battle included marriage to "seventy dark-eyed virgins." His preaching involved some bloody texts as well: "It is not for a Prophet to hold captives till he hath dealt slaughter through the earth." To all but pious Moslems Mohammed is bound to seem a distinctly fallible mortal, limited by his time and place. If his is indeed God's final revelation to man, the Lord have mercy on us.

Yet as certainly Mohammed was a great man, superior to his time and place. He not only preached but practiced a morality that was lofty for his society. If he could be ruthless, he was more often gentle, kind, generous, magnanimous. He could be Christlike in his sympathy for the weak and poor. Through the pious fog of tradition one catches many glimpses of an attractive humanity, as in his unfailing courtesy touched by shyness, his fondness for jokes and fun, his humble sharing of the household chores, his wry indulgence of the frailties of his womenfolk, his tolerance of the foibles of the companions. One can understand why he was so deeply loved by those around him. As one reads of his death and of the quiet, unaffected way in which he met it, one may almost share the grief of the companions, if not their bewilderment. Say the worst about his human limitations, and there remain a heroic and inspired life, a complete dedication to the service of his God, and a power of personality that made as deep an impression on his followers as Jesus made on his, in some ways a more lasting impression. The man Jesus was soon obscured by the resurrected Christ. The man Mohammed ibn-Abdallah survived the long effort of tradition to transform him into a miracle man and a saint. Jesus might seem more real, even more inspiring, if we knew of him, as we know of Mohammed, that he liked honey and fresh butter and was especially fond of milk.

The Koran is much harder for Westerners to admire. In Arabic, one gathers, it makes a magnificent music that still moves its readers to tears and ecstasy. In translation it strikes most Westerners as an uninspired work, occasionally eloquent but more often dully didactic, and on the whole loose, incoherent, and insufferably repetitious. The Angel Gabriel who dictated it to Mohammed seems most prosaic when he retells Biblical stories, as in the whole sura (chapter) on Joseph and his brethren. There are dull enough passages in the Old Testament, but few—even among unbelievers—would call it a mediocre book, as many do the Koran.

Our major concern, however, is the teaching of the Koran. Here the difficulty is that Mohammed was hardly a clear, consistent thinker, if a thinker at all. He did not reason—he merely preached or revealed, as the spirit dictated. The difficulty is aggravated by the lack of logical or chronological order in the suras of the Koran. Although Moslems make out a subtle sequence, to outsiders the only apparent principle is the arbitrary one of putting first the longer suras, which are generally the later ones chronologically. We must remember, at any rate, that Mohammed at first spoke as the prophet of a weak minority sect in Mecca, unable to enforce his will, given to calling himself the "Warner"; then as leader of an independent, increasingly strong community in Medina, and in this capacity both as prophet and statesman; and finally as the triumphant ruler of a temporal kingdom—the one great religious leader whose career ended in worldly success, rather than sacrifice or renunciation. Mohammed himself seemingly provided for possible inconsistencies in at least one text: "If we abrogate or cause any verse to be forgotten, we will replace it by a better one or one similar." Theologians would therefore embark on an endless hunt for abrogated verses. But the ruling tendency has been to stick to the sacred text, which reflected all the diverse moods and shifting fortunes of the Prophet.

Even so, his basic teaching is clearer and more nearly uniform than that attributed to Jesus by the diverse authors of the New Testament. The theme of more than half of the Koran is an insistence on an absolutely pure monotheism, a denunciation of all forms of polytheism and idolatry. "There is no god but God." Allah is the God preached by the prophets, from Abraham and Ishmael through Moses to Jesus, and revealed in the Scriptures of the Jews and the Christians; Abraham was the true founder of the faith, Mohammed the last prophet, and the Koran the final, complete, perfect revelation, correcting the false beliefs that had corrupted Judaism and Christianity. In particular Mohammed repudiated the ideas that Allah had a Son and a Mother, or was part of a Trinity, and with them all the elaborate theology that Christianity had spun around its Godhead. While admitting angels and the old Arabian jinn, the bad ones of whom were led by "the Satan" or Eblis, he rejected all human intermediaries between Allah and man—the priests and monks whom men "have taken as lords beside Allah." Like Yahweh, Allah strictly banned all images, which might also become objects of worship.

Another uniform, almost obsessive teaching was the Christian doctrine of the Last Judgment and Day of Resurrection. Good Moslems—"Whosoever believeth in Allah and the Last Day and doeth right"—went to the Garden; all others were consigned to the Fire. The Garden was a masculine paradise with Arabian accessories, which Mohammed described in vivid detail. It was on a cool, well-watered mountaintop, far from the desert, where men lying on couches enjoyed such pleasures as silk raiment, silver goblets, ever-ripe fruit, streams of honey, "boys of everlasting youth," and virgins as eternally young and lovely; women enjoyed a less sensual but sufficient bliss. The Fire was a place of torture familiar to Christians, though not to all Jews. Like the later Puritans, Mohammed constantly reminded his followers that Allah was "severe in judgment."

His accounts of the afterlife are so literal that to unbelievers they inevitably seem naïve, but essentially his Garden is no more incredible than the Christian Heaven of pearly gates, his Fire no more atrocious than Hell. The most troublesome thing about these fabulous rewards and punishments is that they are predestined by Allah, not really earned by men. Allah is infinite in power and knowledge, responsible for literally everything in his creation; so the logic is inescapable that he had willed that some men should believe in him, more should not believe. Naturally Mohammed did seek to escape this appalling logic. He constantly described Allah as "Compassionate and Merciful," he preached a gospel of hope, and his whole missionary activity implied that men can save themselves. During the period of free thought in Islam theologians found

texts to support the belief that men are free and responsible agents. But
the plainest texts support the doctrine of predestination, which has remained the official doctrine of Islam. "Whom Allah will He sendeth astray,
and whom He will He placeth on a straight path." Like St. Paul, Mohammed could understand only as the will of God the refusal of men to
recognize him as the Prophet. In his humility he likewise did not claim
credit for the conversions he made; all credit went to Allah alone. The
very essence of Islam is the absolute dependence of man on Allah, the
necessity of a complete surrender of his own will and purpose. The Koran
declares that to be "a slave of Allah" is the proudest rank a man can
aspire to. That logically men cannot be anything else but his slaves is
only the inescapable contradiction of predestination.

In practice this led to some serious uncertainties or inconsistencies.
Christians justified their practice of persecution and holy war by a single
text: "Compel them to come in." In the Koran we read: "Let there be no
compulsion in religion." During the early years at Mecca, when the
Prophet lacked the power of compulsion, he was likely to preach in a
gentle spirit, calling on his followers to "reason with them in the better
way." Allah did not require man's help, after all, and his Prophet respected the Jews and Christians, "the people of the Book." At Medina,
however, the warring Prophet preached in a different spirit. Allah now
commanded the faithful to "slay the idolaters wherever ye find them"—a
verse said to have abrogated 124 others commanding tolerance—and at
least to humble the people of the Book who persisted in rejecting his
Prophet. The official policy of Islam became pretty much the actual policy
of Mohammed, who had subjugated Jewish colonies, sent out an expedition against the Byzantines, and denounced the halfhearted "hypocrites"
among the Arabs who had refused to join this expedition. Jews and
Christians were never to be compelled to embrace Islam, which remained
different from Christianity in that it did not try to drive all other religions
off the field; but they were properly to be conquered and taxed to help
support Islam. Later, both the more tolerant and the more fanatical
Moslems could find appropriate texts to justify their conciliatory or
militant policies.

For the rest, Mohammed spelled out in minute detail the ceremonial
and ethical requirements of Allah, many of them drawn from Arab
custom. The major ceremonial duties were the daily prayers, fasting during the holy month of Ramadan (in which the Koran had been revealed),
and the pilgrimage to Mecca. The latter involved a major concession to
pagan idolatry—the retention of the sacred Black Stone. Possibly Mohammed felt obliged to make this concession, or shrewdly calculated it

as a means of uniting the Arabs behind him and making Islam a national crusade; just as possibly he had a sincere reverence for the ancient shrine of his people, in the belief that it had been set up by Abraham. He was not free from superstition. He also retained the jinn, and his prescriptions included some primitive taboos, such as those on the eating of pork and strangled animals.

About ethical duties Mohammed was no less explicit. Like St. Paul, he always coupled the necessity of faith with a demand for good works and never permitted the faithful to conclude from the idea of predestination that they could coast to salvation. His essential teaching is summed up in Sura II (177): "It is not righteousness that ye turn your faces to the East and the West; but righteous is he who believeth in Allah and the Last Day and the angels and the Scripture and the Prophets; and giveth his wealth, for love of Him, to kinsfolk and to orphans and the needy and the wayfarer and to those who ask, and to set slaves free; and observeth proper worship and payeth the poor-due." Almsgiving was a primary duty of the Moslem. Mohammed retained, however, the ancient penal code, which befitted a God who punished by torture. The next verse in this sura reads: "O ye who believe! Retaliation is prescribed for you in the matter of the murdered; the freeman for the freeman, the slave for the slave, and the female for the female." In a later sura Mohammed echoed the old Biblical code more literally: "The life for the life, and the eye for the eye, and the nose for the nose, and the ear for the ear, and the tooth for the tooth, and for wounds retaliation." He never called upon the faithful to love their enemies or turn the other cheek. While requiring of them a loftier morality than they had been accustomed to, he set up no ideals beyond their reach. At best his ethics may be called reasonable: "God does not charge a soul with more than it can bear." Thus he asserted that Allah permitted trade but forbade usury, and he made detailed provision for the use and bequest of property without implying that wealth and acquisitiveness are sinful.

Otherwise both the strength and the weakness of Mohammedan ethics derive from the definiteness of the Prophet. A practical, literal-minded man, addressing a relatively rude, lawless people, he was more specific than Jesus in condemning current evils, such as idolatry and infanticide, and in defining humane conduct, as in the treatment of women and slaves. Moslems could not so easily distort his teachings, rationalize their violation of them, as Christians could take liberties with the Gospels. But in his definiteness he tied his ethical system to the peculiar customs and limited ideals of his age. He positively legalized slavery, for instance, as he did polygamy and war. His prescriptions were likely to be unsuited to the needs of a developed civilization, while the more general teaching of Jesus could always remain a guide and inspiration. And both the strength and the weakness were more pronounced because Mohammed was laying down the law for a kingdom of this world, laying the foundations of a theocratic state.

Christianity grew up under a highly developed political state with a complete system of law. When it triumphed, the Church had to adjust itself to this state; later Christian nations would continue to operate on the basis of a secular law. In Mohammed's Arabia there was no state—there were only scattered independent tribes and towns. The Prophet formed his own state, and he gave it a sacred law prescribed by Allah. Moslem nations would continue to base their law on their religion; in theory there was no confusion between the things that are Caesar's and the things that are God's. Still, a system designed for the small cities of Mecca and Medina was scarcely adequate for great nations and empires, and there would in fact be considerable confusion.

In practice, the most marked difference between the Christian and the Moslem worlds has been in the status of women. In the Koran the Angel Gabriel had more to say about this than any other social question. One reason, to be fair, was that Mohammed was striving to elevate their state, giving them legal rights they had not enjoyed before. In granting men the right to four wives he was not instituting but regulating polygamy, which had been unrestricted in Arabia. (Allah made an exception with the Prophet himself, who in his old age took more wives.) While recognizing that "it is not in your power to deal equally between wives," he commanded that all be treated kindly and as impartially as possible. He did not specifically prescribe the veil and segregation. Yet he prepared the way for this practice, and by more than his habit of segregating his own womenfolk. He had some harsh texts on women, perhaps drawn from the Christian ascetic tradition: "Thy worst enemies are the wife at thy side and thy concubine. . . . The least in Paradise are the women. . . . Women are the faggots of hell." He stated that Allah had put men in charge of women because he made men superior, and he spelled out other God-given privileges. A husband could divorce a wife at any time (the Prophet's own grandson al-Hassan ran through a hundred of them in his forty-one years of life), whereas a wife could not sue for divorce on any grounds. Besides his four legal wives, a man could have women slaves as concubines—a further incentive for the Arab hosts that burst out on the Old World. And Mohammed recommended severe as well as kind treatment of wives: "As for women from whom ye apprehend disobedience, admonish them, banish them to beds apart, use the whip on them." His later followers chose to take most seriously his warnings. Under Islam, women became more degraded than under any other of the higher religions.

This is also to say that like all the other religions, and for similar reasons, Islam was not completely loyal to the teaching of its founder. Many of its followers chose to disregard some of the Prophet's plainest commandments, such as the prohibition of wine. (Today they are happy that he did not mention whisky.) Mohammedanism took on the customary cargo of superstition as it was popularized, and it became more profoundly altered as it entered a greater, more civilized world. Nevertheless it remained much truer to the spirit of Mohammed than did Buddhism and Christianity to their founders. The historic Jesus would be simply bewildered by a mass in a Holy Orthodox or Roman Catholic church; Mohammed might feel quite at home in a modern mosque. For he had been very thorough and specific in his teaching. Above all, it had a basic simplicity that evidently made it more congenial to Eastern peoples than Christianity, which it triumphed over without compulsion or serious persecution. This is the story we are approaching. But first we might look more closely into the "tremendous results"—the reasons why even Christian historians, such as Christopher Dawson, have declared that the Koran has had more influence on world history than any other single book.

In one view, Mohammed unquestionably purified Judaism and in particular Christianity. Allah was a truly universal God, with no chosen people, no feelings about race, and he shared the Godhead with no one; there was no metaphysical nonsense about him. Likewise Mohammed purified the worship of the One God. He abolished the hierarchical priesthood, the monkery, the sacraments, and the elaborate ceremonials that had got between the simple worshiper and God. He made the daily prayers a pure act of adoration, not a petition for special favors or a bribe. Even in the most splendid mosques the worshipers of Allah perform their individual devotions with a modest piety and decorum that might justify Byron's saying, that the calls of the muezzin were preferable to all the bells of Christendom. The mosque is neither a place of mystery nor a social center for the Sabbath. "Islam set the terms of a new experiment in human religion," concluded Professor Gibb, "an experiment in pure monotheism, unsupported by any of the symbolism or other forms of appeal to the emotions of the common man, which had remained embedded in the earlier monotheistic religions."

But "purity" is not quite the word for the religion of Mohammed, nor clearly the secret of its success—the masses of men are not won by purity.

The Prophet encumbered Islam with a great deal of indiscriminate legalism. He prescribed ablutions before prayer and regulations for women suckling their children in much the same spirit as he laid down the moral law; the bulk of his prescriptions hardly tend to elevate the spiritual life. At the same time he retained some obvious "forms of appeal to the emotions of the common man," such as his ludicrous Garden Paradise. With this he reverted to primitive religion by stressing much more than Jesus the fear of God and the Fire. And as the Prophet's conception of Allah grew clearer it grew more crassly anthropomorphic, and more exclusive. An ostensibly universal God, Allah had no apparent interest in the vast majority of the human race except to feed them to the Fire because of the unbelief with which he had cursed them. In general, Mohammed tended to take most literally the most questionable tenets of Judaism and Christianity. To unbelievers, his "purification" of them often looks more like a crude simplification or reduction. The idea that the Angel Gabriel dictated to an illiterate native of an obscure small town the whole truth about God is at bottom, perhaps, no more preposterous or blasphemous than the idea that God made a special covenant with another obscure people, or that he revealed himself by sending his Son to them while leaving whole civilizations in darkness; but naïve is the kindest word for it.

Hence one must qualify Toynbee's description of Islam as the "most rational" of the Judaic religions because of its severe monotheism. As preached by Mohammed, it was essentially irrational, or at best non-rational. It was radically different from the deism to which it has often been compared, for it was based wholly on revelation. As the mouth-piece of Gabriel, Mohammed did not reason, demonstrate, or speculate. He was naturally hostile to speculation about fundamentals, and tried to close the door to it by insisting that the Koran was the final, complete revelation. His triumph is often described as a vicarious triumph for Nestorian and Monophysite Christianity, in their revulsion against the abstruse doctrines evolved by Greek theologians. More profoundly, Mohammed represents a repudiation of the whole Greek spirit. With him the ancient East came into its own again.

Beneath all the appearances of "a new experiment in human religion," Allah was a familiar type of Oriental deity. He was not strictly incomprehensible or ineffable—Mohammed knew and could say a great deal about him. He seemed inscrutable chiefly because he was arbitrary and gave no reasons for willing that some men go straight, more go astray. He was comprehensible enough to men familiar with Oriental gods and despots. They were grateful that he could be Compassionate and Merciful

—to whomsoever he willed his favors. So they prostrated themselves in prayer, as they had long been wont to do in the royal presence. They were proud to be his slaves, the more so because he was so lavish in his rewards. They were not too unhappy about his scheme of predestination. In bad times they could fall back on their long tradition of fatalistic resignation. In good times, especially when Islam was on the rise, his scheme was a form of assurance. Like the later Calvinists, the faithful were naturally disposed to assume that they were the Elect.

All this is by no means the whole truth about Islam. It is an important part of the truth, however, and historically the most enduring part. It must be kept in mind as we consider the actual influence of the Koran on history. Islam inspired new peoples, such as the Seljuk Turks, and embarked on new adventures, especially when it discovered the thought and learning of the Greeks. But the outcome of the drama was that the whole Near East reverted to the ways of the ancient East—the ways of "miracle, mystery, and authority."

2. THE COMING OF THE TURKS

When ibn-Batuta came to Asia Minor, early in the fourteenth century, he was at once filled with enthusiasm. "This country is one of the best in the world," he wrote; "in it God has united the good features dispersed throughout other lands." Arriving at Alanya, down the Pamphylian coast from Antalya, he was struck by its magnificent citadel, built by the Sultan Alaeddin on the heights above the city, and by the handsomeness, cleanliness, and kindness of its men. Leaving here for Antalya, he must have passed en route the still imposing remains of the ancient cities of Side, Perge, and Aspendus; but he made no mention of them. Later he went to Denizli or Ladhiq—ancient Laodicea—which he found a most important town, with seven "cathedral mosques"; but again he was silent on its former glories. He visited many a fine city, with pleasure, and passed many an old city in ruins, without comment. "Greek" to him was chiefly a synonym for infidel. At Smyrna, which he found mostly in ruins, he was impressed only by its governor, "a generous and pious prince and constantly engaged in war with the Christians."

Although as a Moslem ibn-Batuta was accustomed to lavish hospitality, he commented most enthusiastically on the exceptional courtesy and generosity of the people of Asia Minor. At Antalya he met the first of the Young Brotherhoods that entertained him everywhere. Apparently the leader of these brotherhoods would build and furnish a hospice; the brethren worked during the day and brought him their earnings, with which he purchased supplies to entertain travelers. If no traveler appeared they would eat, and then sing and dance, but they were happiest when entertaining. Batuta marveled repeatedly at the joy with which they greeted him. "What an excellent body of men these are!" he exclaimed when he came to Bolu, "—how noble-minded, how unselfish and full of compassion for the stranger, how kindly and affectionate they are to him, how warm their welcome to him!" Again he did not know that Bolu had once been Bithynium, the hometown of the Emperor Hadrian's Antinoüs, nor did he comment on all the Roman forts, bridges, and aqueducts in the vicinity, remains of which have lasted to this day.

The gracious people described by ibn-Batuta were the Seljuks—Turks whom Anna Comnena of Byzantium had described as "Ishmaelite barbarians." With their coming the old world of Asia Minor had vanished so rapidly that he may be forgiven his apparent ignorance of it. Later Western historians were accordingly disposed to regard the Seljuks as destructive barbarians, and even today they are seldom treated with much sympathy. For they were interlopers. Within two centuries after they defeated the Byzantines at Manzikert, their kingdom in Asia Minor was overthrown, and presently they were swallowed up by the Ottoman Turks. They represent one of the "transitions" that are dear to historians, but fatal to the dignity of the people who provide them.

Still, the Seljuks are worth knowing. They not only represent a major transition but by their own works attained to a real dignity. They were not simply destructive or barbarous. The magnificent citadel of Alaeddin at Alanya still stands; so do many of the "cathedral mosques" mentioned by ibn-Batuta. With him, they testify to the gracious, promising culture that the Seljuks developed during their brief ascendancy in Asia Minor. Even Anna Comnena had some praise for them as brave soldiers who fought like gentlemen and treated their prisoners chivalrously, while unwittingly she revealed that their occasional cruelty was likely to be in reprisal for the atrocities committed by Christians. She at least did not think it beneath the dignity of her history to mention Turkish names, as she did the names of the barbarian Frankish Crusaders. She points to another reason why the "Ishmaelite barbarians" are worth knowing: it was they who brought on these Crusaders.

The origins of the Turks are obscure. Although they are often referred to in books about ancient history, particularly in association with the Huns, they did not actually enter history until the sixth century A.D. They were one of the nomadic peoples who periodically swarmed out of central Eurasia—or nowhere—to threaten or destroy civilized nations, and to stir conjecture that comes to pass for fact.[2] Turkish inscriptions found near

[2] Among the uncertainties is the traditional identification of the Huns with the

the Orkhon River, dating from the eighth century, tell a simple but moving success story: "The poor I made rich; the few I made many." The only other major source of firsthand information about central Eurasia, an inscription in Mongol, records a later chapter by a presumably related people. Batuta called Turks the Mongols or "Tartars" he met in Russia, and Turkish-speaking descendants of Tamerlane later founded the Mogul Empire in India. But there is little point of dwelling on such racial affinities. As the Turks entered the Near East, they mingled with other peoples and lost whatever clear racial identity they might have had. The modern Turk looks not at all Mongolian.

Like most of the nomads, the advancing Turks were good horsemen and warriors who were disciplined on the battlefield and restless off it. They might incidentally have worshiped Alexander the Great, who was known in Eurasia as the god Iskander. (Chiefs in Turkestan still claim descent from him.) It was their early conversion to Islam, however, that made them potential empire builders. By the ninth century Turkish "slaves" were serving as guardians of the Caliph in Baghdad, anticipating the Janissaries of the Ottomans, and soon they became the real masters of the state. Finally, in 1055, a Turkish horde known as the Seljuks, after a famous chief, overthrew the feeble dynasty in Baghdad and officially took over the rule of Persia. Their leader Tugrul Beg assumed the title of Sultan, meaning the holder of temporal power, to distinguish himself from the Caliph, who ostensibly held the spiritual power. It was his son Alp Arslan who crushed the Byzantines at Manzikert. Malik Shah, the next Sultan, built an empire that reached from Transoxiana to Egypt.

Now the Seljuks who swarmed over Asia Minor were still mostly a rude people, and no doubt destroyed a great deal that they were unable to restore. They and their Ottoman successors never would learn to build and maintain such roads, aqueducts, and irrigation systems as the Romans had built. Most destructive were the hordes of nomads who followed in the wake of the armies, spreading over the land, isolating the cities, disrupting trade, discouraging agriculture—reducing the country to a more primitive economy than it had known for well over a thousand years. Yet the Seljuks did not come merely to plunder and wander, or to find better pasturage for their herds. They fought under the banner of the Prophet,

---

Hiung-nu mentioned by the Chinese. Nobody knows who these Huns were or what language they spoke. As an example of the inspired conjecture, Denis Sinor cites a distinguished historian of religion who made a careful analysis of a Eurasian god named in a Turkish inscription, and ingeniously fitted him into religious history; only the god happened to be a misreading that an obscure specialist had corrected fifty years before. Even so, Sinor adds, this god will probably haunt manuals of religious history for years to come.

with more fervor than sophisticated Arabs and Persians now had. They had already learned much from the Persians, many of whom followed them into Asia Minor. Soon they demonstrated their own potentialities by producing Nizam al-Mulk, the vizier of Malik Shah. A friend of Omar Khayyam, he won fame as not only a statesman but a patron of literature and learning, who founded the first university in Baghdad and schools in other cities. He himself wrote a book on the science of government.

Most important immediately was the religious zeal of the Seljuks. As warriors and recent converts, they were naturally champions of orthodoxy; Nizam al-Mulk founded his university in Baghdad to promote orthodox learning and combat heresy. When the Seljuks conquered Palestine they were less hospitable to Christian pilgrims than the Arabs had been. The threat of their power brought on the first of the Crusades (1096–99). Christendom and Islam now came into full conflict—and chronic misunderstanding began. "One of the essential differences between Christianity and Islam," observed Sir Harry Luke, rather surprisingly for a student of Turkey, "is that, while the former is one of the religions that provide martyrs, the latter is one that creates them." In fact, Christianity both provided and created many more martyrs, by its more systematic and prolonged persecutions. The persistent notion that the early Moslems were fierce fanatics is a Christian fiction stemming from the Crusades, which embittered relations that had been friendly and peaceful enough except for the wars that all neighbors are prone to fight.

As conquerors, the Arabs naturally made subjects of the defeated Christian peoples, but they never sought to suppress or destroy the religion of the "people of the Book." At the outset of their conquests they took Damascus with the help of its bishop, on a promise of generous terms that they fulfilled. They were as generous when they took Jerusalem. The later Crusaders celebrated their capture of the Holy City by massacring Moslems and Jews, boasting that they rode in blood up to their horses' bridles "by the just and marvelous Judgment of God"; the Arabs guaranteed its Christian defenders safety for their persons, possessions, churches, and crosses, and probably as another favor to them compelled its few Jewish inhabitants to quit Palestine. In general, the Christians of Syria and Palestine had reason to welcome the Arabs as liberators, since most were "heretics" and many had recently had their noses and ears cut off by order of their holy Emperor Heraclius. The Byzantines in turn displayed a more surprising tolerance of the Moslems. Leo the Isaurian, the savior of Constantinople, allowed them to build a mosque there. St. John of Damascus, greatest of Orthodox theologians, lived at the court of the caliphs, where he had amicable discussions over their religious differences. A tenth-century Patriarch addressed the Emir of Crete as "most illustrious and most honorable and beloved," writing that as the "two powers of the whole universe" they should "live in common as brothers, although we differ in customs, manners, and religion." [3]

The Crusades that destroyed such hopes had fateful consequences for Asia Minor, hastening the fall of Byzantium to the Turks. Otherwise they made more romance than momentous history, and represent an incidental ironic complication of the theme of East and West. While they deepened the feeling of European unity and at best gave western Europe a vision, their leaders were scarcely champions of freedom, rationality, enlightenment, civility, or any high civilized ideal. On military and religious grounds they were a dismal failure after the initial success in conquering the Holy Land. They began with the Turks camped at Nicaea and ended with the Turks on the Danube; the later Crusades were fought everywhere except the Holy Land, which the Moslems had recovered in less than a century. Their consequences for the West were chiefly secular. They increased the power of kings and nobles, and of the lay spirit; they led to modern forms of taxation, on personal property as well as land; they promoted trade with the East, and banking to finance this trade; they brought in new fashions in food and dress, new motives in art, new skills, new modes of fortification and war. Perhaps the most important consequence is the least calculable. The Crusades gave the West a wider view of the world, an acquaintance with civilizations higher than its own, making it less fervent in its Christian idealism but also less provincial and bigoted.

For the Moslem East the Crusades were a minor episode. They called out a countercrusade that produced Saladin, one of the noblest of Moslem leaders, and they naturally led to more hatred of Christians, and less tolerance. But Islam had little to learn from the rude Franks. The Seljuks, who were most directly affected by them, were not seriously affected. While they lost some cities to the Crusaders, they went on consolidating their dominion over most of Asia Minor. They did not grow fanatical, neither massacring nor systematically persecuting their Christian subjects. Instead, they won over the masses of peasants by promising them freedom in return for a light head tax and by giving them a relatively mild rule. Some Greeks fled to Constantinople and western regions, others remained

---

[3] At first the Byzantines failed to recognize a new religion in Islam, considering it a heretical Christian sect—a kind of Arianism—but viewing it with less horror than the heresies closer to home. This was the opinion of St. John of Damascus, among others. In his *Inferno* Dante still placed Mohammed among the heretics—considerably above the arch-traitor Marcus Brutus.

and clung to their faith, but the majority in Anatolia evidently became converts to Islam. In time they disappeared as Greeks and Christians, as they did at Celaenae-Apamea.

During this assimilation, and through their associations with the Byzantines, the Seljuks came under Christian influence. It appears that some even dreamed of reconciling or fusing Islam and Christianity. They did not succeed, of course. But their effort brings up the fascinating ifs and might-have-beens of history, it was another example of the promise of Seljuk culture, and it left some mark in the influential dervish orders. It lends an added interest and charm to the Seljuk capital of Konya. When they made this their capital, at the beginning of the twelfth century, they chose a site richer in appropriate association than they knew.

3. THE BRIEF GLORY OF THE SELJUKS

Konya is a garden city on a broad, treeless Anatolian plain, an oasis much like Damascus. Ibn-Batuta, who found it a large town with fine buildings, exceptionally broad streets, admirably planned bazaars, and many streams and fruit gardens, added that it was said to have been built by Alexander—presumably the oldest and mightiest man in antiquity known to the Seljuks. Because of its abundant water it was actually a much older city, known to the Hittites as Kuwanna, to the Phrygians as Kawania, and to the Greeks as Iconium. Like Damascus, Iconium was very proud of its antiquity, if as ignorant of the prehistoric settlements buried in the many *hüyüks* on the plain about it. It had a legend of a King Nannakos (or Annakos) who reigned before the Flood: when he learned of the imminent catastrophe from an oracle, he wept so vehemently with his Phrygian subjects that "the weeping in the time of Nannakos" became proverbial among the Greeks. He has been identified with the Biblical Enoch, and possibly harks back to the Sumerian flood myth. When Iconium got around to inventing its inevitable Greek founders, it clung to the tradition that it was the first city to emerge after the Flood. One story was that Athena and Prometheus, on instructions from Zeus, made "icons" of mud into which the winds breathed life. Twin peaks on its horizon also made it hoary, for such conspicuous landmarks invariably attracted deities.

Little is known of the early history of Iconium, beyond the passage through it of Cyrus and Xenophon and its recapture from the Persians by Alexander. In the Christian era it emerges as a Greek *polis*, with a Jewish colony. The author of Acts called its inhabitants Hellenes, as he did not those of other Galatian cities visited by St. Paul. Hadrian blessed it with another fiction, making it a Roman *colonia*. But its common people evidently clung to their Phrygian-Anatolian ways. It was devoted to Cybele, here known as the Zizimene Mother from her home at Zizima in the mountains some miles away. Although she had to make way for Athena when the city was Hellenized, she remained popular. The Good Fortune on the later coins of Iconium is seated on a throne in the manner of Cybele; other coins bear a statue of Marsyas. Its Phrygian tradition helps to explain why Iconium became one of the more influential Christian centers in Asia Minor, and also why it made little of St. Paul, even though he and Barnabas had spent considerable time in it.

Cybele was transformed into Thecla, the earliest saint of the city, who then gave her name to one of its twin peaks. To St. Paul Iconium preferred St. Philip, seemingly the Apostle, who somehow got identified with the other peak. Among the other local cults was that of St. Amphilochius, an archbishop of Iconium who had stood out against the Arians; the church dedicated to him remained a popular shrine throughout the Byzantine era. The Turks then enriched the religious associations of the city by discovering that his tomb, which worked miraculous cures by exuding a holy oil, was the tomb of "Plato the Divine." It accordingly attracted both Moslem and Christian pilgrims. The Turks also discovered the "Spring of Plato" some fifty miles from Konya, at the site of a remarkable Hittite monument. They revered him as a magician who had made disappear the sea that once covered the whole region—redeeming the calamity that had caused such grief to King Nannakos.

Iconium suffered repeatedly from the Arab raids that began in the seventh century, and it was not a major city when it was captured by the Seljuks, soon after their victory at Manzikert. Neither was it a great capital when it fell briefly to Frederick Barbarossa and his Crusaders. But a few years later, in the reign of the Sultan Alaeddin (1219–36), there began the most brilliant period in the history of the city, now called Konya. Alaeddin had such a passion for building that he has been called the Seljuk Justinian. He made his capital one of the great cities of the age, inspiring an old Turkish saying: "See all the world—but see Konya." The city also became still holier through the work of mystics and religious teachers attracted to the court of Alaeddin. It was the jewel of an empire that had taken more than a century to become really civilized, and that was now to enjoy a tragically brief golden age, arrested when it met defeat by the Mongols in 1243.

The art of the Seljuks was essentially Persian, or broadly Islamic. Although they introduced some Anatolian animal motifs, such as the twin-headed eagle of the Hittites, they contributed little that was original. Under their patronage, however, all the major characteristics of Islamic art were fully developed and perfected. Seljuk architects made superb use of color and abstract ornament. They covered their graceful minarets and interior walls with tiles of rich blue and green, or blue and white, in which rhythmical patterns were worked. Most distinctive are their gateways and portals, beautifully carved with arabesque designs. Lord Kinross has aptly described these arabesques: "Geometric and bold, contrapuntal in rhythm, combining intricacy of conception with clarity of effect, they are like Bach fugues in stone." Among the best-known exhibits of the delicacy and calm purity of aspiration that mark Seljuk art is the Inje Minare of Konya, or mosque with the "star-reaching" minaret. It is today a misnomer, since the top half of the minaret has tumbled down or been lopped off; but for this reason it suggests more strongly that these builders might have come still closer to the stars had their empire remained strong and prosperous. Even as it was, the many Seljuk mosques and khans in Anatolia remain about its loveliest monuments, superior to almost all the monuments of the mightier Ottomans outside their capitals of Bursa and Constantinople.

The literature and learning of the Seljuks were also primarily Persian. Poets, philosophers, scholars, and holy men found refuge in Konya, fleeing the Mongols. The Seljuk monarchs built for them beautiful *medressehs,* or colleges—reputedly as many as Baghdad had had. They also welcomed Byzantine scholars at their court, and sent some of their princes to Constantinople to finish their education. Possibly Phrygian-Anatolian tradition contributed something to this fusion of culture, for the Young Brotherhoods described by ibn-Batuta closely resemble ancient societies—of Hymnodoi, Theologoi, etc.—that had been connected with the mystery religions and taken on such related functions as hospitality. It was fitting, at any rate, that among the most famous newcomers to Konya was Jelaleddin, a Persian mystical poet who had apparently been born in Asia Minor. He became the founder and patron saint of a liberal brotherhood, the Mevlevi order of whirling dervishes. They whirled to the music of cymbals and flutes, the instruments of Cybele; but they sought heavenly bliss, not frenzy.

It appears that Sultan Alaeddin was not only tolerant of Christianity but sympathetic to it, and Jelaleddin was certainly more so. As a saint he inspired the usual legends—for example, of how as a youngster he amazed his playmates by disappearing into the sky, explaining that a "legion of beings clothed in green mantles" had conveyed him there to show him "strange things of a celestial character." Nevertheless he was without question a saintly man, of a gentle, lovable type. Only heavenly music, it was said, kept him on earth; and for him this music was a means of communion with man as well as with God, a message of brotherly love. The veneration of Plato in Konya may have been due to his effort to form a cult in which both Moslems and Christians could participate, as may also a legend that a Christian cleric was buried beside him. More concrete evidence is a haunting old Turkish folk song composed or inspired by his order—a prayer for universal brotherhood. In the last century and this the whirling dervishes were still known for their liberality; they openly drank the forbidden wine and graciously entertained Christians in their sanctuary. The particular jewel of Konya today is the tomb of Jelaleddin, containing the treasures of his order, and testifying eloquently to its piety, civility, and high culture.

As an aristocratic, intellectual brotherhood, the Mevlevi naturally had a limited influence. At about the same time, however, there grew up among the common people another order of dervishes, the Bektashi, which likewise reflected the mingling of Moslem and Christian in the Seljuk era. It grew in the name of a more or less mythical saint and miracle worker, Haji Bektash, who was possibly used as a shield or figurehead by another Persian mystic. Although its teaching was far from uniform or clear, it was a missionary, semiheretical order, with Neoplatonic tendencies toward pantheism and mysticism, and also tendencies toward good-humored irreverence, witty criticism of orthodoxy. The Bektashi used wine frankly as a means to spiritual intoxication. They gave women a unique equality with men, allowing them to participate as equals in their rituals. In keeping with this possibly Anatolian or pre-Islamic heritage, they were an essentially Turkish sect that held to the Turkish language instead of the sacred Arabic of the Koran. For all such reasons they carried out their initiations and rituals in a strict secrecy that made them more suspect to the authorities, but more popular among the common people. Their shrines, such as the alleged tomb of Haji Bektash, attracted both Moslems and Christians. They made many converts among Christians.

The secrecy of the Bektashi, and their known indulgence of wine and women in their rituals, laid them open to charges of immorality, which no doubt had some truth. But on the whole they won a reputation for superior morality, and at least their proclaimed ideals were lofty. An obscure Albanian summed them up in a truly catholic spirit:

The faith of the Bektashi is a broad Way lighted by wisdom, brotherhood, friendship, love, humanity, and all the virtues. . . . The Way of the Bektashi is open and broad: it is the Way of Wisdom and of goodness to all who have intelligence. Man is not bound, but free in all respects, and he is answerable for all his acts. But he has a mind which reasons, knowledge by which to choose, a soul which recognizes, a heart which discerns, and a conscience which weighs all his deeds. Thus he has all that is necessary and needs no help from without. . . . The Bektashi reject no religion, but respect all. Nor do they reject the books of any religion.

One could wish that they had succeeded in imparting this spirit to the leaders of Islam, and to the Holy Orthodox and the Roman Catholic churches.

Unfortunately, the idealism of the Bektashi was mixed with a good deal of hocus-pocus. They attracted followers less by their liberal doctrine than by their popular magic, their cult of saints and relics. They stressed as well the magic of numbers and of taboos, the horror of touching rabbits or stepping on thresholds. Their initiates were taught by official leaders who had absolute spiritual authority over them, and who were as likely to be ignorant as learned. Their martyrs included fanatics, whose tombs became especially noted for miracles. Such vulgar superstition is hardly fatal to the growth and spread of a religion, but it weakened the appeal of the Bektashi to the cultivated. It lessened whatever chance there may have been of an official reconciliation or a higher synthesis of the Judaic religions, and with it of a Byzantine Empire revitalized by Islam, or a Seljuk Empire revitalized by Christianity. This was a very slight chance at best. For the popularity of the Bektashi was itself an unhealthy sign—a symptom of the basic insecurity of the Seljuks, due to the collapse of their empire.

The immediate and perhaps sufficient cause of their failure was the Mongol invasion. It may be viewed as a tragic accident. Looking for logical causes, trying to make good sense of history, with the advantage of hindsight, we are always apt to be unfair to defeated peoples; so let us grant that the collapse of the Seljuks was not clearly inevitable, and that except for the unforeseeable coming of the Mongols they might have fulfilled the bright promise they were displaying at Konya. Nevertheless their empire was disintegrating before the Mongols appeared on the scene. They were losing Persia and Mesopotamia by poor administration; Saladin, a Kurdish officer, drove the Crusaders out of the Holy Land and took over the rule of Syria and Egypt. Nizam al-Mulk, the great Seljuk vizier, had warned the Sultan of a basic weakness in his political system— the influence of irresponsible friends. It was likely to be a fatal weakness because there was no constitutional defence against the personal short-comings of the sultan, no means of assuring responsibility. The plainest reason for the failure of the Seljuks was their want of a sound political system. An inscription on a Seljuk building in Akshehir, on the Konya plain, points to the old story of Oriental monarchy: "The great Sultan, the mighty King of Kings, the shadow of God in the universe."

This was part of their legacy from Islam. Islam stamped much more plainly and indelibly the societies that took to it than Christianity has stamped Western civilization; it had much to do with both the rise and the fall of the Turks. It had itself proved a complete political failure by the time the Seljuks appeared on the scene, and in its heartland the brilliant period of its cultural achievement was nearing the end. The Seljuks might have revitalized it, as the Moors did for a time in Spain; but to succeed they would have had to contend against the main forces of orthodoxy, which they began by strengthening. To understand more fully their story—and that of the Ottomans to come—we need to review the greater story of Islam itself, which is still a live issue today.

4. THE HISTORIC RECORD OF ISLAM

Modern apologists for Islam find in it basic principles that are especially relevant and congenial to the modern Western world. In "Science, Democracy and Islam," Humayun Kabir asserts that it provided the basis of the scientific outlook by its emphasis on the unity of God, which broke down the distinction between the phenomenal and the transcendent and led to a reverence for the empirical fact. Likewise it provided the basis of democracy by its concept of equality and its reverence for the individual, as well as by its practical checks on the accumulation of wealth and consequent economic inequality. Abdul Qayyum also stresses its democratic principle, in that "the people are the political sovereign in an Islamic state"; he quotes Maude Royden's observation that Islam "proclaimed the first real democracy ever conceived in the mind of man," since Allah was of such transcendental greatness that all differences between men were nought before him. In the introduction to *The Glorious Koran,* a recent translation, appears the still more sweeping claim that Mohammed "for the first time in history made universal human brotherhood a fact and principle of common law."

Now with a religion or a society as with an individual, it is humane to stress its ideal principles instead of its common failings, or to regard its best as its essence. But especially with religion this honorable impulse is a constant source of confusion, of obscurantism, even of hostility to humane endeavor to improve men's lot on earth. The many who are now equating spirituality with religion, or proclaiming that we can be saved only by a return to God, are especially apt to ignore the historical actualities of religion: what it becomes under established churches, and how it works out in the thought, feeling, and social behavior of the great mass of its adherents. For the sake of understanding—for the sake, too, of the many millions of poor Moslems today—I should say flatly that these high-minded apologists for Islam are talking about a fiction or a dream. The religion preached by Mohammed, and thereafter practiced in his name, is quite different from the Islam they describe. The Prophet had nothing of the scientific outlook, and demanded absolute obedience to the law that he alone laid down. Islam never produced a democracy or a state in which the people were actually sovereign. In all its states, past and present, economic inequality has been glaring. Its holy wars fought on principle, its degradation of women, and its formal acceptance of slavery make nonsense of its theoretical principle of equality, or any profession of universal human brotherhood. It had a brilliant period, during which it made major contributions to the world's culture; but it ended as it began, in a complete rejection of the free Greek spirit. And almost from the outset it was corrupted by its worldly success in the temporal kingdom where Mohammed had squarely set it.

As orthodox Moslems see it, their Golden Age came under the first two caliphs who ruled after Mohammed's death, Abu-Bakr and Omar. (Caliph means successor or vicegerent.) These were fighting puritans, able and devoted, who kept their eyes on the other world while they conquered large provinces in this one, and started piling up the booty that would enrich and enslave their successors. This Golden Age lasted less than a score of years, however. The third Caliph was assassinated, by a party led by the son of the first Caliph. His successor, Ali, was also murdered as he was calling his people to prayer, even though he was the Prophet's son-in-law. Already Moslems were warring on one another. The martyr's death of Ali and his son Husayn led to a schism that permanently destroyed the unity of Islam. Two major sects, the Sunnites and the Shiites, still quarrel over the rightful succession, the Shiites being devoted to Ali.

The political development of Islam was understandable, but uninspired. "By God!" said Omar, according to tradition, "I know not whether I am a Caliph or a king. And if I am a king, it is a fearful thing." His successor knew he was a king and did not think it fearful; he began appointing his relatives to high posts, while heeding the advice to keep the people content by keeping them busy in outland wars. But the decisive change followed the murder of Ali, when the Umayyad caliphs moved the capital from Medina to Damascus. By now the Arabs were ruling an empire, with no previous experience and no guide except the simple order set up by Mohammed. The Umayyads naturally took over the imperial forms of the Persians and the Byzantines, together with the services of many of their officials. They established a dynasty, set up a worldly court, introduced eunuchs into their harems, and in general ruled like Oriental kings, no longer associating with their fellows in the manner of Arab chieftains. Church and State, theoretically one, became in fact separate. Islam retained a misty devotion to the theory, but had no real political doctrine.

The Umayyad dynasty (661–750) did much for Islam, expanding its dominion from India to Spain and beginning to adorn it with an appropriate art and architecture. Nevertheless Moslem tradition has been hard on these caliphs, describing them as usurpers, tyrants, and enemies of the True Believers. They in fact displayed little religious fervor, much more of the worldly ambition behind the now not so holy wars. They were especially resented, however, because they represented a small Arab aristocracy living off millions of subjects who included many converts to Islam, underprivileged fellow Moslems. The Abbasid caliphs who succeeded them succeeded in destroying their reputation.

The new dynasty proclaimed itself truly Moslem, ruling in the interests of all Islam. The caliphs were no longer pure Arabs; most were born of slave women—Persian, Armenian, Abyssinian, Slav, Turk. The Abbasids built a new capital at Baghdad, a cosmopolitan city that became the site of the *Arabian Nights,* and of a civilization much richer than Arabian. They brought Islam to the summit of its material wealth and power and its cultural creativity, producing the famous symbol of its splendor in the reign of Harun al-Rashid (786–809). Yet in this reign the basic rottenness of the Abbasid regime was already apparent. Harun had ascended the throne more easily because his brother had been murdered in the harem; he had to contend with many revolts in his empire; and his death was followed by civil war between his sons. The Islamic world shortly began to fall apart, as Persia, Spain, Egypt, and other provinces became independent kingdoms. The empire built in the name of Mohammed and Allah had nothing of the staying power of the secular Roman Empire.

Strictly it had never been a real empire with a uniform government. The spiritual unity of Islam failed to inspire political unity; its rulers displayed little political intelligence and less idealism. While the Abbasid caliphs made a show of orthodox piety, most of them were recklessly impious and still more recklessly extravagant, squandering the wealth of Islam in luxurious living. They consciously modeled themselves upon the Persian kings before them. They had themselves crowned with the diadem, became increasingly autocratic and remote from their subjects, and made the army their personal property, recruiting it from among foreign slaves. Another innovation was the executioner who always accompanied them. The founder of the dynasty, Abu Abbas, had taken the name of Bloodspiller; his successors often had their own blood spilled, in assassinations resulting from court intrigue. By the tenth century the caliphs of Baghdad were puppets of their "slave" army, lacking any real political or spiritual authority over their dwindling domains. The sorry pretense of their rule was ended in 1031. More caliphs popped up elsewhere in Islam, as in Egypt and Spain, but they too had only nominal authority. Other Islamic states repeated the Baghdad story of imperial splendor, intrigue, and civil war. An Arabian poet summed up the moral for their subjects:

> Get sons—for Death! Build high—for Ruination!
> March on—this road goes to Annihilation!

The corresponding development in Moslem law illustrates both the value and the danger of a law based on religion. In theory, its basic principle was political and civil equality, and it explicitly affirmed the racial equality that remains perhaps the strongest claim of Islam to the ideals of universality and brotherhood. "The white man is not above the black nor the black above the yellow; all men are equal before the Maker," said Mohammed, according to tradition. Moslem jurists also affirmed that "the fundamental rule of law is liberty." They always had the advantage of speaking with spiritual authority, since they professed to judge human relationships from an ethical and religious, not a merely legal, point of view. But they always suffered from the embarrassment of having to accommodate themselves to a State that had taken over a great deal of nonreligious law from its subject peoples, and that was headed by autocratic caliphs ruling by the sword. They managed to rationalize the political *fait accompli,* with the help of a text in the Koran: "Were there more than one God, the universe would go to ruin." It followed that the sovereign on earth must be a prince, for authority cannot be shared. Thus religion again gave its sanction to absolute monarchy. Moslem jurists could do this more readily because in spite of their assertions about liberty their conception of law was authoritarian, in the spirit of Mohammed himself. They did not conceive it as a human product serving human needs, subject to reason or the approval of the people. Law was the will of Allah, revealed in the Koran, and therefore inalterable. In practice, of course, the jurists had to reason, and the sacred law did change; they displayed both catholicity and casuistry as they got around the Koran. Nevertheless the system that was gradually built up was still considered inalterable, and became essentially rigid and scholastic. It strikes outsiders as neither practical enough nor idealistic enough.

There remains, however, the rich cultural achievement of Islam. The followers of Mohammed went on to create a new civilization, acting sometimes under his inspiration, sometimes in defiance of his teaching, but almost always in his name. Their achievement is obviously important because they handed on this culture to the Turks and other peoples, and also contributed to the growth of the West; but it is a fascinating story in its own right.

Immediately, the illiterate Arabs had the advantage of association with the high culture of the Sassanian and Byzantine empires.[4] They began by borrowing most of their culture, as Mohammed had borrowed most of his religion from Judaism and Christianity. Nevertheless their growth was as amazing as their military expansion. Coming from a land poor both intellectually and materially, the Arabs within a century had set up in Damascus a civilized court far in advance of contemporary Rome. In the next century Baghdad was thronged with poets, scholars, and wits while Charlemagne and his court, as Professor Hitti remarked, were "still dabbling in the art of writing their names." Moslems later created other centers of civilization, as at Cairo and Córdoba, that rank among the great cities of history.

The sophistication of Baghdad owed little to the Prophet. The court of Harun al-Rashid in particular rejoiced in wine, women, dance, and song, and in irreverent wit. During the Golden Age of Islamic culture, down to the eleventh century, many Moslems took to the Epicureanism and skepticism known to the West chiefly through the *Rubaiyat* of Omar Khayyam. "We are all sorted into two great kinds," wrote one poet: "Clever godless and stupid godly minds." One of the clever godless declared that all religions were myths, "nothing but the means which men of power use to make other men their slaves." Short of such irreverence, imaginative literature was essentially romantic and sensuous. Poetry dwelt on the old pagan Arabian themes of wine, love, and hunting; tales were exotic or bawdy. Even mystical poetry was full of erotic imagery, while scholars and theologians contributed to the innumerable Arts of Love. Mohammed himself was no puritan in matters of sex ("The game of a man with a woman is one of the games the angels like to watch, as the Prophet said"), but he was hardly the inspiration of this literature.

He was a more positive influence, however, in the development of art

---

[4] I should acknowledge that Arnold Toynbee gives a very different account of them. To prove his thesis that higher religions are the product of dying societies, he is forced to describe the Arabs as the "internal proletariat" of the "Syriac society." But all other historians, to my knowledge, recognize them as newcomers who belonged to no civilization. Toynbee's Syriac society—a hodgepodge of Philistines, Phoenicians, Hebrews, etc.—is one of his most arbitrary fictions.

and architecture, the most distinctive, original creation of Islam (as previously of Byzantium). Painting and sculpture were naturally discouraged by the Prophet's ban on images or any representation of the human form, even though the ban came to be disregarded in Persia and the Mogul Empire of India. But at Baghdad, under Persian influence, Islam found compensation in the ornamental arts. Here it developed its genius for abstract design, as in the arabesque and the decorative use of Arabic script—the one Arabic contribution to its art.[5] Moslem artists did superb work, unrivaled in medieval Europe, in metal, glass, pottery, leather, and textiles. Later they took over the luxury trade of declining Byzantium, to the corruption of both Islam and Western Christendom.

Still more impressive was the achievement of Islam in architecture, under the direct inspiration of religion. As early as the end of the seventh century the Umayyads built the first grand mosque, the Dome of the Rock in Jerusalem. They had to employ Greek artists and artisans, who in the Byzantine style crowned the building with a dome, supported it with columns, and adorned it with mosaics; yet it already has the feel of a mosque, not a Christian cathedral, and is a much nobler structure than the Church of the Holy Sepulchre that centuries later was built to rival it. The mosque soon acquired its essential elements of mimbar, mihrab, and minaret (the last seemingly a relic of the ancient ziggurat), and in time it took on such other characteristic elements as the stalactite capital, the pointed arch, the cusped or multifoil arches, and the arabesque in low relief. Whether Moslems invented or borrowed all these elements is uncertain, but together they mark a style of unmistakable individuality, recognizable throughout the diverse regions of Islam, and beautifully suited to its relatively chaste, austere worship. It is one of the great styles in architecture. And though Mohammed himself was no builder, it nevertheless bears his signature. W. G. Palgrave observed that a Moslem workman who could not be trusted to do the simplest job competently would still do work of unerring precision on the mosque. "What love is to the world at large, that is Islam to the Eastern; it renders him architect, poet, metaphysician, carver, decorator, soldier, anything."

It was not clearly Islam that made him a metaphysician; this was rather the work of Byzantium, ultimately of ancient Greece. But it is no less remarkable that the illiterate Arabs soon developed a thirst for knowledge much more avid than their Prophet had manifested, or than contemporary Byzantium was showing. Under the Umayyads they began

[5] This was innocently borrowed by later medieval painters, such as Fra Angelico and Fra Lippo Lippi. The Virgin may have heresies about Mohammed and Allah decorating the sleeves or borders of her gown.

sporadically to translate Greek works. The Abbasids at Baghdad systematized the activity under official patronage; the Caliph al-Mamun, son of Harun, set up a school and library for translators, a "House of Wisdom," and sent scholars as far as Constantinople in search of manuscripts. Later scholars put out carefully annotated editions of the works of Greek thinkers, preserving some (such as Galen's on anatomy) that have been lost in the original Greek. Islam did more than Byzantium to transmit this Greek heritage to western Europe. The story is a strange one, somewhat unwholesome for the orthodox. The Arabs were put on to the Hellenistic tradition chiefly by the Nestorian and Monophysite heretics, who were keen Aristotelians; the thought of the ancient pagans reached Europe by translation from Greek through Syriac to Arabic, then, like as not, by a Jew into Latin via Hebrew; and in Moorish Spain the precious manuscripts were copied surreptitiously and brought to the libraries of European monasteries, where eager scholars pored over them, and unwittingly started undermining the foundations of medieval thought.

Meanwhile Islam was for several centuries the center of progress in philosophy and science. In the politically disastrous ninth century appeared its greatest thinker, al-Kindi, "Philosopher of the Arabs": a master of Aristotle and of natural science. More influential was the later ibn-Rushd, misknown to medieval Europe as Averroës, a physician, mathematician, and philosopher who anticipated the effort of St. Thomas Aquinas to reconcile Aristotle and the revealed faith, only to become a symbol of heresy. Ibn-Sina, or Avicenna, had a still greater influence on Europe by his immense compendium of Arabian medicine. Other Moslems made advances in mathematics and the sciences, especially geography, chemistry, physics, and astronomy. Their discoveries played some part in the scientific revolution that began with Copernicus, as earlier they had in the discovery of America by keeping alive the heretical Greek idea that the earth was a sphere. With all this they passed along to the West such key inventions as Chinese paper and the so-called Arabic numerals, including the all-important zero devised by Indians.

Most original by far, however, was the work of ibn-Khaldun (1332–1406)—a Moslem historian who had no influence to speak of, and who was unknown to Europe until the last century. He was incidentally a more objective, broad-minded historian than any that Byzantium had produced, or that Europe would produce until recent centuries; but he stands out as a scientific philosopher of history, the first to offer a closely reasoned, factually based theory of universal history. While interested primarily in political phenomena, he realized that the familiar cycles of rise and fall could not be understood merely in terms of the purposes and capacities of ambitious individuals. He defined history as the science that deals with all social phenomena, and perceived that all must be considered organically in relation to the society as a whole. His critical inquiry into the natural laws governing social action made him the first sociologist as well; he had many penetrating things to say about the processes of imitation and adaptation. Arnold Toynbee has called his *Prolegomena* "undoubtedly the greatest work of its kind that has ever yet been created by any mind in any time or place." At that, Toynbee might not sufficiently admire the remarkable empiricism of ibn-Khaldun. Though ostensibly a pious Moslem, he neither explained nor justified history by the will of Allah. Sticking to observed fact, seeking only natural causes, he did not pretend to make out any divine purpose or grand universal plan. Had Europeans known and appreciated him, they might not have been taken in by such as Hegel.

Ibn-Khaldun also left an autobiography, *The Journey*, a record of the events of his time and of his own achievements as a diplomat. It may have been suggested by the travel book of the much more cheerful ibn-Batuta, like him a native of North Africa, who a generation before had exhibited a similar curiosity about the great world. But unhappily it brings us back to the historic failures of Islam. Ibn-Khaldun was a solitary figure who had no followers. His masterpiece was soon forgotten; it fell victim to the law of growth and decay that he had made out. The decay is all too apparent in his record of intrigue, corruption, assassination, and civil war. Toward the end of his life, he took part in an unsuccessful expedition to stem the invasion of Tamerlane, the latest episode in the long struggle he had pictured between the Arabs and the Turks. And his own role in this dismal history was not too honorable. He was also a master of the arts of fulsome flattery and shrewd shifting of allegiance. As disheartening is the conventional, even perfunctory piety expressed in his work, which in view of his theory of history suggests that he did not dare speak out his real convictions. Free thought had become increasingly dangerous; a friend of Khaldun's had been lynched by a mob as a heretic. Islam was to produce no more philosophy or science of consequence. Long before his time a blight had settled on the thought of the heartland in the Near East. Now, just as the West was entering its Renaissance, the whole Moslem world was succumbing to an intellectual torpor that lasted until this century.

Within the limits defined in the Koran, writes Abdul Qayyum, Islam "gives the human spirit the fullest freedom to find new methods of fulfillment in creative effort." If so, Moslems never fully availed themselves of this freedom. In their enthusiastic discovery of Greek philosophy and science, they ignored Greek poetry, drama, art, and history; their culture was never so many-sided as the Greek, or the modern Western. For philosophers in particular the limits defined in the Koran are pretty narrow and rigid. Although Islam produced some original thinkers, it added little to the Greek philosophy it handed on, except for a hopeless effort to reconcile Aristotle and Neoplatonism, and both with orthodox faith. Philosophers were always handicapped by Allah, a very personal God who ruled the world in an arbitrary, despotic fashion; and the orthodox finally denied them the freedom to make Allah rational. Scientists too were denied freedom; their inquiries threatened proper belief. Most of the 265 works attributed to al-Kindi, the greatest scientific thinker of Islam, have been lost. The less subversive medical work of ibn-Sina was preserved, but progress in medicine ceased as magic and superstition crept back. That his compendium was still used in this century was only another sign of the long intellectual stagnation of Islam.

With the magic and the superstition the saints came back, and they recall us to the corruption of the Prophet's teaching. Much of the superstition entered official tradition. The learned ibn-Batuta tells of his raptures when he visited Jerusalem and saw the blessed rock to which the Prophet, one night during his lifetime, had been miraculously transported from Mecca by the Angel Gabriel, and from which he was then whisked up into the seven heavens, to meet Jesus and others, and to be granted an edifying view of the sinners in hell. This myth, which is still celebrated by an annual feast in the Moslem world, was based on a single verse in the Koran: "Glorified be He Who carried His servant from the Inviolable Place of Worship to the Far Distant Place of Worship, the neighborhood whereof We have blessed, that We might show him of Our tokens." [6] Batuta also tells of the many dervishes and fakirs, Moslem equivalents of the monks denounced by Mohammed, who often preyed on the gullible. And even in his own purer piety, which led him everywhere to seek out the religious judges and teachers—the ulema, or learned men of Islam— he points to another source of impurity. It is commonly said that Islam has no priesthood, no Papacy, no Church; and formally it does not. But the ulema were an aristocratic clerical class that controlled education,

[6] What Mohammed meant by this, as many other sayings, is not too clear, but the legend that grew out of it gave Dante the idea for his *Divine Comedy*. The blessed rock in Jerusalem is enclosed in the Dome of the Rock, and is still holier because it is the very place where Abraham offered Isaac to God. Hence Jerusalem is a holy city alike for Jews, Christians, and Moslems—a circumstance that might have made for better understanding and fellowship among them, but unfortunately has tended rather to aggravate their differences.

laid down the religious law, and in effect constituted a religious dictator-ship.

In particular it determined the theological development of Islam, which takes us to the heart of the issues raised by Mohammed's religion. Moslem theology perforce departed from the teachings of the Prophet, who was no more of a metaphysician than Jesus, and it bred a great deal of thought as incomprehensible and unknown to ordinary Moslems today as the Nestorian and Monophysite heresies are to ordinary Christians. At the end, however, it returned to the spirit of the Koran; and the end was fateful for all Islam.

Under the early Abbasids there grew up a school known as the Mutazilites, rationalists or freethinkers. They ridiculed the hadith, the traditional sayings and doings of the Prophet that included contradictory sayings on every subject, and that were tested not for their content but for an oral chain supposedly going back to some companion. (They pointed out, for example, that on the authority of one companion the Prophet never urinated while standing, on the authority of another he did.) While accepting the Koran as divine revelation, they insisted on the necessity of reason in interpreting it, and proceeded to interpret it in a Hellenic fashion. They declared its descriptions of Allah as seated on a throne, seeing and hearing, were merely symbolical. Allah was Infinite Justice, a purely spiritual being, and as such he could be known by reason even without revelation. In particular the Mutazilites insisted on human freedom and responsibility for good and evil: a just God would never will folly and evil, predestine his creatures to damnation. Their rational-ism was influential enough to drive the orthodox into philosophy in order to combat it. A conservative reaction, led by al-Ashari in the tenth cen-tury, culminated in the work of al-Ghazzali ("Algazel," d. 1111), the Aquinas of Islam.

The conservatives insisted on the literal meanings of the Koran, which seems clearly to have been the Prophet's own intention. Allah *is* seated on a throne and *does* have a face and two hands, just as the Koran says. The Garden is a Garden and the Fire is Fire; Allah will raise the dead from their graves, and where they will go was absolutely predestined. Nothing can happen that Allah has not willed. The only Creator, he created everything, including unbelief, folly, and evil. His creatures had no right to intrude their own notions of right and wrong: "The Lord of the Worlds is not under a Law." The faithful do not inquire "In what sense?" or "Why?" because "such inquiry is Innovation in Islam." The great al-Ghazzali exposed the contradictions that result from inquiry in *The Incoherence of the Philosophers,* in which he explained the decay of faith in Islam by the respect shown for such as Plato, Aristotle, and Hippocrates. Although his own contradictions were in turn exposed by Averroës in *The Incoherence of the Incoherence,* his book had a tremendous success. The upshot was that on every issue the rationalists were defeated and driven off the field. Al-Ghazzali led Islam back to a simple faith, based on tradition and the living Word instead of the vanity of reason, and again stressing fear. He couched it in terms that could be readily understood, if as readily debased, giving the theology of Islam essentially its final form.

Al-Ghazzali had the backing of the Seljuks, working under the patronage of their vizier Nizam al-Mulk. Long before him the loose-living Abbasids had won their reputation for piety by their persecution of the rationalists, executing large numbers of them. "Tolerance is laudable," their founder the Bloodspiller had said, "except in matters dangerous to religious belief, or to the Sovereign's dignity." A caliph who won a legendary fame by sleeping with every one of his four thousand concubines issued an order prohibiting research and philosophical discussion. The discussion went on, under caliphs too feeble to enforce such orders and denied the right to act as popes; but it is therefore more significant that Mohammed's community voluntarily grew together in the agreement summed up by a conservative: "Belief is a duty. Inquiry is heresy." The spirit of inquiry was killed as all intellectual activity was made subject to religious authority. So the research and the discussion stopped, and the long night set in.

Al-Ghazzali himself had come by his orthodox faith after a period of doubt and confusion, which taught him that certainty could be found only in religious experience. This experience, however, led to his association with the great mystical movement known as Sufism—a movement that was always liable to heresy, and constitutes a striking paradox. The mysticism of Islam was bolder, more richly varied, and much more popular and influential than Christian mysticism. It accordingly produced some dubious types of holy men—morbid ascetics, fakirs, fanatics—who often came to be worshiped as saints. But on the whole Sufism gave Islam its most attractive figures—at least to unbelievers—and inspired its most eloquent religious writings.

One reason for its popularity was that it usually taught a gospel of love. The God known ecstatically by mystics is not a stern judge or a creator of unbelief and evil. Sufism also rose above the Prophet's own stress on eternal rewards and punishments. "Whoever worships God for the sake of anything," wrote one holy man, "is worshiping himself, not God." If the purest mystics were prone to confuse themselves with God, or to love him at the expense of their fellow men, they could produce such Christlike martyrs as Hallaj, who in 922 was crucified for blasphemy. "I am the truth," he had said, and one may hope he was right; for at the cross he uttered the most beautiful prayer recorded in Islam:

And these Thy servants who are gathered to slay me in zeal for Thy religion and in desire to win Thy favor, forgive them, O Lord, and have mercy upon them; for verily if Thou hadst revealed to them that which Thou hast revealed to me, they would not have done what they have done; and if Thou hadst hidden from me that which Thou hast hidden from them, I should not have suffered this tribulation. Glory unto Thee in whatsoever Thou doest, and glory unto Thee in whatsoever Thou willest.

Thereafter the Sufis were more discreet, veiling their intimate knowledge of Allah by metaphors of love and wine, but the movement remained so popular that the orthodox were unable to suppress it.[7] As we have seen in Jelaleddin, Islam and Christianity drew close together in their mystics.

The sources of this mysticism, and of its popularity, are less flattering to Islam. Although the Sufis could twist many texts in the Koran to their purposes, since the Prophet had spoken more out of feeling than out of reflection, his Allah was plainly different from their God and did not encourage such intimacies; they seem to have drawn heavily on Neoplatonic and Christian sources. Their immediate impulse was a revulsion against the worldliness of the Abbasids. But the deepest reason for the widespread and continuous popularity of Sufism, one must suspect, was the worldly failure of Islam. Hence it did not invigorate Mohammed's people. While some Sufis retained his practical, militant spirit, most tended to quietism or an unworldly holiness. Among common people they confirmed the traditional fatalism and habit of submission. The poor invested their hope in sheik-saints and shared their little with many an idle dervish. A conscientious dervish summed up the historic record of Islam in explaining why he wore mourning: "God's Apostle left three legacies behind him: poverty, knowledge, and the sword. Men of power took the sword and put it to bad use. Scholars took the knowledge; all they did with it was to make teaching a profession. Dervishes took the poverty and made it into a way of getting an idle living."

The question remains whether God's Apostle did not have something to do with this outcome. Moslem reformers today acknowledge the legacy of ignorance, poverty, lethargy, political corruption, and social injustice

---

[7] One exception was a sheik reported by ibn-Batuta. "The Prophet—may God bless him and give him peace!—could not do without women," announced this heretic, "but I can do without them." Thereupon he was duly sentenced and executed.

from the centuries of stagnation, but they almost uniformly deny that the religion of Islam is at all responsible for this legacy. They trace the social evils to the failure of Islam to live up to its principles. Outsiders might agree that these evils were not Mohammed's doing—he hardly foresaw the civilization that grew out of his revelations, and he clearly tried to assure social justice. Yet the corruption has marked Islam throughout its history, and if its spiritual leaders often deplored it they made no concerted effort at social and political reform, led no movement to emancipate or educate the masses. For their mentality the Prophet does appear to have some responsibility. Although his teaching had little evident connection with the remarkable intellectual growth of the Arabs, it had much more to do with the cessation of inquiry and research, for he had given the finality of revelation to the limited conceptions of his age. His authoritarian spirit was not conducive to ideals of intellectual or religious freedom, or of an open society. The modern reformers themselves have not yet faced up to the crux of the problem—the fallibility of the Prophet. Few Moslems, and almost none who seek a career in public service, dare to say openly that the Koran is a human document, the word not of God but of Mohammed.

One may add that no Christian society has ever lived up to Christian principles, and that the Bible is no manifesto of intellectual freedom either; but this raises further questions. The obvious resemblances between medieval Islam and medieval Christendom accentuate the profoundly different outcomes in the two societies. Christendom too might well have ossified had it clung to its authoritarian religious mentality. One reason why it did not ossify is that Westerners caught and hung on to the most important thing the Greeks had to teach them—not their works, but the spirit that produced them. Such "explanations," however, only force the question why Moslems failed to do likewise. It is not enough, either, to say that Mohammed made a deeper impress on his people than Christ on his followers; for Islam did go on to build a new civilization, it followed the Greek gleam, it developed its rationalists and its Sufis—it seemed vigorous and adventurous enough to keep responding to fresh impulses and likewise to outgrow the authoritarian mentality bequeathed by Mohammed. And a final difficulty is that we cannot speak simply of its failure, for it remained a religious success. It lost very few of its adherents to rising Christendom; it continued to convert new peoples, sometimes in open competition with Christian missionaries; today it retains the allegiance of some 300,000,000 people, in a world long dominated by the West. Islam is still a force, and a problem, to be reckoned with.

If neither its prolonged stagnation nor its stubborn persistence can be wholly explained, they may be illumined in the long perspective suggested by Alfred Kroeber in "The Ancient Oikoumene as a Historic Culture Aggregate." From the Near East, the heartland of civilization, the major creative impulses had moved out and spread gradually to the Far East and to the West, which became the front of advancing civilization. The long-worked heartland was apparently no longer capable of real creativity. It was occupied by worn, tired societies overlaid with uncongenial Hellenistic and Iranian elements, capable only of a reduced, simplified culture. Islam succeeded because it offered such a culture in a welcome anti-Hellenistic, anti-Iranian, anti-Christian form. It gave the old heartland a chance, Kroeber writes, "to throw off the foreign cultural yoke and to establish its own free society—without art, without much intellectual curiosity or profundity, without many of the aspirations customary in civilizations—but fervid over its new autonomy and well satisfied at being at last able to impose its culture on others once more— no matter at what level—instead of having their culture and influence imposed upon it." Mohammed had an advantage in that he was not a member of a "Syriac" or any other ancient civilization, but one of Toynbee's "external proletariat." The civilization he founded "was new precisely in its proletarianism: its appeal to the common denominators and therefore to the commonnesses of men; its discarding of much of the heritage of the past; its simplification of ideas; its leveling and denunciations; its long list of prohibitions." Hence its appeal outside the heartland was chiefly to primitive peoples, such as the Turks, Africans, and Malayans.

This seems to me somewhat unfair to Islam, which for a time enjoyed a richer civilization than Kroeber suggests. His whole thesis is based on a metaphor, and is at most suggestive. The worn, tired societies of the heartland were not racially old, but were made up of mixed, shifting peoples, and there is no apparent reason why they should have been incapable of a new creative effort. But Kroeber's account at least corresponds to the historic record of Islam, especially in the heartland. Here its creativity was exhausted within a few centuries. Thereafter it went on blooming for some time in its outlying provinces, most brilliantly in remote Spain, where Islam never took such deep root as elsewhere. At home Mohammed's people did discard much of the heritage of the past, which for a time had dazzled them. They lost all curiosity; gave up all but commercial and military adventure. They disregarded whatever implications of the Prophet's teaching might have promoted democracy and the scientific outlook. They clung to his simplest, crudest teachings, as they clung to their Black Stone, and to their grotesquely inaccurate calendar based on the lunar year. In this deeper, wider sense Islam does look like the product of a "dying" civilization, or an exhausted one. It showed no capacity for renewal—until it felt the impact of the West in the last century.

Meanwhile it had provided the key to our next chapter, the rise and fall of the Ottoman Turks. The basic simplicity of Islam and the thoroughness of its discipline make it an attractive and effective religion for primitive peoples. More quickly than any other, the record suggests, it can inspire them with zeal, elevate their moral code, promote their self-respect, make them a disciplined community. It made the nomadic Turks a great power—such as Christianity failed to make of the Goths or any other barbarians before the rise of western Europe. But it quickens chiefly the military virtues of courage, fortitude, loyalty, and obedience, not so much the qualities that make for sophistication, enlightenment, and creativity. It impedes the continued growth of its converts by the rigidity of its doctrine and discipline. The Ottoman Turks restored an empire to Islam and adorned it with a suitable art; but they proved unable to extend or renew its culture, or to create a high civilization of their own.

CHAPTER IX

Bursa to Stamboul: The Ottoman Empire

---

1. THE RISE OF THE OTTOMANS

THE CITY OF Bursa was founded about 200 B.C. as Prusa, named after the Bithynian King Prusias, on the slopes of one of the most imposing Mount Olympuses in the Greek world. The story goes that it was founded on the advice of Hannibal, the lifelong enemy of Rome, who spent his last years in Bithynia lending his military genius to the service of its kings until driven to his death by the relentless Romans, then killing himself to avoid surrender to them. The story ought to be true if there is poetic justice. For in 1326 Bursa was taken from the Byzantines by a Turkish tribal chief named Othman, or Osman. It became the capital of the House of Osman, which finally overthrew an empire that still called itself Roman, and which went on to build the Ottoman Empire, the mightiest of its time, and again a terror to Rome. The long, ignominious decline of this empire, the prejudice of Western commentators, and the legends about the "terrible Turk" have obscured an amazing story. It is not an altogether edifying story, and its ignominious end was implicit in its beginnings; but it involved a display of energy, courage, disciplined zeal, and military genius worthy of Hannibal himself.

Ertugrul, the father of Osman, had led a tribe of only a few hundred families out of central Asia. His house then produced about as long a series of vigorous, able rulers as can be found in history—a series stretching over about two hundred years—under whom a small tribe grew into a great empire with a rapidity recalling the Arabs before them. Osman himself became master of one of the ten provinces in Asia Minor into which the Seljuk Empire had broken up. Under his son Orhan, in 1357, the Ottomans (or Osmanli) crossed the Dardanelles to plant their standard in Europe at a Byzantine castle inappropriately named "Pig's Castle," and to initiate European campaigns in which for two centuries they

299

would meet temporary reversals but no major setback. Murad I, son of Orhan, advanced into the Balkans, crushing both the Bulgars and the Serbs. In Asia Minor the Ottomans were halted when their mighty Bayazid I, who had subdued the remainder of the Seljuk principalities, was defeated and captured by the mightier Tamerlane in a battle near the site of modern Ankara; but they proved their vitality by their speedy recovery from this disaster. After a brief period of civil war Mohammed I restored order, and Murad II resumed the advance on all fronts. It was his son, Mohammed (or Mehmed) the Conqueror, who realized the Ottoman dream, and completed the resurgence of the East, by taking Constantinople.

The Ottomans had had an advantage over the Seljuk principalities, including Konya, in their proximity to Constantinople. They bordered on the undermanned Byzantine Empire, which both enriched and educated them. Nevertheless they triumphed on their merits. In giving them a fighting faith, Islam had strengthened their primary virtues. By their energy and their valor they attracted the service of wandering bands of Ghazis, or Warriors for the Faith. They built up a nation noteworthy especially for its discipline. In war its armies did not carry with them the wine flasks and whores that regularly accompanied the Christian armies of Europe. At home, the Turks to the end remained loyal to the House of Osman—a dynasty that ruled for some six centuries, or more than twice as long as the longest Greek or Roman dynasty.

From the beginning, moreover, they were by no means simply "terrible." In their fervor for Islam they retained its tradition of racial and religious tolerance. Orhan, son of Osman, married a Byzantine princess. With this "Greek blood" the Ottoman warrior-sultans acquired a taste for culture. At Bursa they soon demonstrated that they were not rude barbarians.

In antiquity Bursa had been a small inland city outranked by nearby Nicaea and Nicomedia, known chiefly (as it is again today) for its hot springs. These made it the home of a famous physician, Asclepiades, and a shrine of the healing god Asclepius. About the only other well-known native of the city was Dio Chrysostom, a wandering orator and philosopher who left it to perform in the greater cities. In the third century A.D. it shared the fate of Nicaea and Nicomedia, being sacked by the Goths, but unlike them it did not revive to become a major Byzantine city. Apparently no saint of account blessed its hot springs with miraculous curative powers. Not until the Empire of Nicaea did Bursa begin to prepare for its historic destiny. One of the Nicaean emperors rebuilt its walls (sections of which still stand), and the city became strong enough to hold out for almost ten years against siege by Osman.

The father of the Ottomans quickly repaired whatever damage he had done. As the capital of his son Orhan, Bursa was already flourishing enough to impress ibn-Batuta as "a great city with fine bazaars and broad streets," worthy of "the greatest of the Turkmen kings." (This is one of the very few contemporary references to the early Ottomans.) The successors of Orhan beautified and sanctified the city by building mosques and tombs, the earliest Ottoman shrines. The exquisite tomb and "Green Mosque" of Mohammed I would alone belie their unholy reputation. The architect who designed this mosque, Toynbee commented, would have had a low opinion of the contemporary dome of Brunelleschi in Florence, which excited all Europe. Bursa might have become another Konya had not the sultans kept building an empire and moving into a greater world. They shifted their capital to Adrianople.

Constantinople profited still more from its fall to the Ottomans. In European tradition this fall marked the end of its glory, a passage into the shades. In fact Mohammed the Conqueror entered a crumbling city whose shabby buildings held fewer than a hundred thousand people. Although it was pillaged for a few days, with the customary atrocities, this was the routine of the age, and the Conqueror put a stop to it before his men could rival the destruction accomplished by the Fourth Crusade. A contemporary Greek, Kritovoulos, reported that Mohammed wept in compassion at the ruin of so lovely a city. At any rate, he resolved to make it lovely again. Immediately he set about repairing and repeopling it, moving in new inhabitants from all over Asia Minor and Greece. To provide for their needs he built new residences, bazaars, inns, baths, kitchens for the poor, fountains, and gardens. For himself he built a palace on the site of the acropolis of ancient Byzantium, and commissioned a Greek architect to build a great mosque. In a short time he had made Constantinople a capital worthy of his empire.

"Verily Constantinople shall be conquered," Mohammed the Prophet was reputed to have said; "and excellent is the commander, excellent the army, who shall take it from the opposing people!" There is some question of the excellence of Mohammed the Conqueror. By Greeks and Westerners he has generally been described as a despot, debauched and cruel; by Turks as an emancipator, enlightened and magnanimous. He seems to have been something of both. Like so many men of the Renaissance, he could be as callous and ruthless as sensitive and gracious. But there is no question that he was a great leader. The seventh of the Ottoman sultans, the Conqueror had all the qualities that had made them empire builders, and other qualities that held unusual promise for their empire.

Impoverished though it was, Constantinople was still a rich prize and its conquest a notable feat. Its great walls had withstood sieges by earlier sultans. A young man of only twenty-two when he resolved to take it, the Conqueror proved himself a resourceful and imaginative as well as bold soldier. He had first cut the city off from its Black Sea supplies by building a massive castle at the narrowest part of the Bosphorus, on the site now known as Rumeli Hisar, arming it with stone-throwing cannon that could control the strait. When the defenders of the city threw back his assaults, he dismayed them by hauling his fleet overland into the Golden Horn, outflanking the chains across its mouth. In the final assault he depended on his Janissaries, "New Troops," an elite corps the organization of which he had perfected, and which was to defeat many a Christian army. Following the victory, he not only proceeded to consolidate and extend his empire by almost continuous campaigns but built up a strong navy, foreseeing the importance of sea power. On the Dardanelles he built forts with more stone-throwing cannon that for the first time in history could effectively prevent all ships from passing through the straits. Thereafter Turkish control of the Bosphorus and the Dardanelles would be a major factor in history to this day, if a mostly deplorable history.

As a statesman Mohammed was no less imaginative, and for a conqueror surprisingly broad-minded. One of his first acts after capturing Constantinople was to invest the Patriarch Gennadius with civil authority over all Orthodox Christians in his realm, assuring them religious freedom. In restoring the city he made it still more cosmopolitan. He moved in not only Turks but Jews, Armenians, and especially Greeks. As he conquered more Greek cities or reconquered rebellious ones, he kept transferring their inhabitants to his capital—from Phocaea in Ionia, from the islands of Lesbos and Samothrace, from the Peloponnesus. He brought back artisans, scholars, and artists who had scattered or fled from the doomed capital of Byzantium, building homes for them. Himself a poet, he sought to restore Constantinople as not only a fortress and administrative center but a center of learning and culture. By the breadth and catholicity of his interests he raised fascinating possibilities, as the Seljuks had at Konya.

More than tolerant of Christianity, Mohammed apparently toyed with the idea of adopting it. According to Kritovoulos, he honored the Patriarch Gennadius by visiting him in his home, encouraging him to hold forth freely on the Christian faith and doctrine. He took a heretical interest in the Italian Renaissance, defying Moslem custom by commissioning the Venetian Bellini to paint his portrait. (Marcel Proust chose it as a model for his character Bloch.) He was particularly interested in Greek culture. To his court he appointed George Amiroukis of Trebizond, whom Kritovoulos describes as "a great philosopher, learned both in the studies of physics and dogmatics and mathematics and geometry and the analogy of numbers, and also in the philosophy of the Peripatetics and Stoics." He was so charmed by the Acropolis of Athens that he granted the city autonomy. In recent times some Turks have dreamed over the possibility that the Conqueror might have led his people into the Renaissance, and the main stream of Western history.

But again this is only a haunting might-have-been. Kritovoulos has Mohammed paying a suggestive visit to Troy, like the conquerors before him. He inquired about the tombs of the heroes and remarked their good fortune in having so great a poet as Homer to preserve their memory. He added, however, that God had reserved for him the privilege of avenging the Trojans, and after all these years punishing the Greeks "for their injustice to us Asiatics at that time and so often in subsequent times." Us Asiatics! The story may be a fiction, as may have been that of Herodotus about the Persians and their desire to avenge the Trojans; but it too ought to be true. Mohammed remained loyal to Asiatic tradition. His first official act as sultan had been to order the death of his brother, to prevent conflict. Although he had been anticipated in this old Persian custom by Bayazid, he made the custom legal by a decree authorizing the execution of all brothers when a sultan ascended the throne. In Constantinople, where he took to the study of Aristotle and the Stoics, he took more avidly to the Oriental ways of the Byzantine emperors, giving up the relatively simple ways of his ancestors in Bursa. Many of his decrees had to do with matters of rank and ceremony. One flatly repudiated Ottoman tradition: "It is not my will that any one should eat with my Imperial Majesty; my ancestors used to eat with their ministers, but I have abolished this custom." With his successors the ceremonies grew more elaborate, the costumes more ornate, the titles more grandiloquent, the Sultan more inaccessible. The history of the Ottoman Empire was to be that of another Oriental monarchy.

2. SULEIMAN THE MAGNIFICENT: THE PEAK AND THE PRICE OF OTTOMAN GLORY

The Sultan Suleiman, who reigned from 1520 to 1566, announced himself in this fashion:

I, who am Sultan of the Sultans of East and West, fortunate lord of the domains of the Romans, Persians, and Arabs, Hero of creation, Neriman of the earth and time, Padishah and Sultan of the Mediterranean and the Black Sea, of the extolled Kaaba and Medina the illustrious and Jerusalem the noble, of the throne of Egypt and the province of Yemen, Aden, and San'a, of Baghdad and Basra and Lahsa and Ctesiphon, of the lands of Algiers and Azerbaijan, of the region of the Kipchaks and the lands of the Tartars, of Kurdistan and Luristan and all Rumelia, Anatolia, and Karaman, of Wallachia and Moldavia and Hungary and many kingdoms and lands besides; the Sultan Suleiman Khan, son of the Sultan Selim Khan.

The Oriental fanfare of the government known to Europe as the Sublime Porte, and to itself as the Glorious Government, grew more fatuous as its power declined. A later sultan would issue an ordinary decree "under the Sublime and lofty Signet, which imparts sublimity to every place, and under the imperial and noble Cypher, whose glory is renowned throughout all the world, by the Emperor and Conqueror of the Earth, achieved with the assistance of the Omnipotent, and the especial grace of God." Everything official was couched in terms of the glorious, the magnanimous, the sublime, with an ineffable disregard for sense or fact.

But there was nothing fatuous about the Sultan Suleiman. He was the mightiest monarch in an age of great monarchs—Henry VIII of England, Francis I of France, Charles V of Spain—and at least the equal of any in character and ability. He was indeed the lord of all the lands he named. His father, Selim the Grim, had considerably extended the Ottoman Empire, conquering Syria, Palestine, Egypt, and Mecca. Suleiman added Rhodes, Hungary, and part of North Africa, while his admiral Barbarossa made him master of the Mediterranean. In 1529 he launched his campaign against Vienna, the most serious threat to Christendom since Constantinople held off the Arabs. He might well have won the heart of Europe, and changed the course of history, had it not been for torrential rains that prevented him from bringing up the bulk of his heavy artillery. As it was, he aroused such awe of the Ottoman power that his feeble successors could long continue to deal haughtily with European ambassadors, freely humiliating them. (The Sultan whose asinine decree I quoted had a Russian envoy literally kicked out of the royal presence.) And unlike his father, who had won fame only as a warrior and by his ferocity had thoroughly earned as well his surname of the Grim or Terrible, Suleiman was much more than a conqueror. He was rightly known to all Europe as the Magnificent, and to his countrymen as the Lawgiver. As he brought the Ottoman Empire to the peak of its worldly power he most nearly realized its ideal potentialities.

The many campaigns of Suleiman were inspired by the normal ambition of monarchs of the period, but also by Moslem piety. He had a lofty conception of his inherited role as Commander of the Faithful. It was a dignified conception, not fanatical, that permitted enlightened statesmanship. Thus Suleiman shocked Europe by concluding an alliance with the French, granting them the first "Capitulations," which made their merchants subject only to French instead of Turkish law. At the time this concession was no surrender of "national sovereignty" but a gracious act of good will, and also a sensible way of at once encouraging trade and avoiding the nuisance of administering the affairs of infidels. (In time the other European powers recovered from their shock and applied for similar favors, Queen Elizabeth even appealing to a Sultan for aid "against that idolater the King of Spain.") Selim the Grim, who once ordered a wholesale massacre of Sufi heretics, would have ordered as well the forcible conversion of Christians had he not been prohibited by his mufti. Suleiman exemplified the wise liberality that until well into the seventeenth century steadily won converts among the Christian subjects of the Ottoman Empire, and that contrasted sharply with the engrained religious intolerance of contemporary Europe. It was fitting that the Commander of the Faithful made a contribution to Protestantism; for in fear of another campaign against Vienna the Holy Roman Emperor Charles arranged a truce with the troublesome Lutherans, to avoid distraction.

With the spoils won in the West, Suleiman not only maintained the magnificent court that awed European envoys but became the greatest builder among the sultans after the Conqueror. Among his many enduring works are the walls that still enclose the old city of Jerusalem. In Constantinople his Suleimaniye mosque is a superb example of the architecture that was the major Ottoman contribution to culture. Its architect, Sinan—an extraordinary genius who built hundreds of edifices of all kinds—had studied Hagia Sophia closely and owed much to Byzantine architecture, particularly the dome; but there is no mistaking his originality, or the distinctiveness of Ottoman architecture, of which the pencil-type minaret is only the most obvious sign. The Suleimaniye mosque is very different from Hagia Sophia, seeming at once vaster, grander, more imperial, and more modest and decorous. It has a majestic simplicity perfectly adapted to the service of Islam, with little to dazzle but nothing to distract the humble worshiper in his devotions to Allah.

Although Turks today bridle at the suggestion, Sinan was probably an Armenian. Suleiman's great sea warrior Barbarossa was a Greek. So was one of his grand viziers; another was a Slav. We are brought to the most remarkable institution developed by the Ottomans. Their empire was administered by a huge imperial family, numbering up to 80,000, which was made up almost entirely of Christian-born slaves, and from which Turks were excluded on principle.

The members of this royal family were boys selected between the ages of eight and twenty, most of them probably in their teens. Some were got by capture, purchase, or gift; most were recruited by teams sent out for this purpose. They were recruited from the provinces, not the sophisticated cities, and were carefully selected for physical and mental aptitude. Required to embrace Islam, they were then as carefully educated, primarily for war and government. Some would become Janissaries, the elite corps. Others took over administrative offices, including the highest in the state. All were rewarded on the basis of merit, by higher pay and especially by greater prestige. All were liable to punishment for failure in duty, the more severe as they rose in rank; the grand viziers in particular were eligible for death. All remained officially the slaves of the Sultan, who had unlimited power over their person, property, and life. The Janissaries were not supposed to marry (though this rule was not strictly enforced), and the ministers of state who might accumulate a fortune had no assurance of retaining it and passing it on to their children.

Just when, how, and why this institution was developed is uncertain. It was not wholly original with the Ottomans; the caliphs of Baghdad had employed slaves in state office, including Turks, and Byzantine eunuchs may also have suggested the idea. But the Ottomans were far more systematic and thoroughgoing than their predecessors, especially in the exclusion of their own people, and their purposes became clear enough. In part they were missionary; this was so effective a way of making good Moslems out of Christians that Christians believed the Devil himself had invented it. Mainly the purpose was to secure loyal, disinterested, efficient service of the Sultan. Although there is no evidence that the Ottomans got the idea from Plato, their system was the closest historical approximation of his *Republic,* most strikingly the education of the "guardians" and their subsequent separation into soldiers and rulers. For no stigma was attached to the royal slaves. The sultans had none of Aristotle's belief that some men are born slaves, none of the modern mystique of racial superiority. They were themselves sons of "slaves," for their harems were likewise made up chiefly of daughters of Christians. Long before Suleiman they virtually abandoned the practice of getting themselves royal brides, usually drawing their consorts from the harem.

Even so their system is naturally repugnant to a modern Westerner. Its "recruits" were in fact torn from their families, given no free choice; they and their parents must often have felt wretched. Conservatives will also be scandalized by this systematic defiance of "human nature." Yet it was a remarkable experiment, for long a successful defiance, and by no means simply inhuman. So many of the recruits considered their selection a special privilege that Suleiman had to take strict measures to keep out undesirables who tried to worm their way in, such as Russians, Persians, Gypsies, and the Turks themselves. Most of the recruits evidently became sincere Moslems, proud to call themselves the slaves of their sultan. There was something grand in this idea of taking the sons of peasants and deliberately fashioning them into not only soldiers but courtiers and ministers of state. Busbecq, a European envoy at the court of Suleiman, was inspired to make comparisons unflattering to Christian Europe.

The Turks, he commented, selected and bred men with a care that Europeans reserved only for dogs, hawks, and horses, and they showed the same delight in a fine specimen. At an audience with Suleiman he was awed by much more than the imperial magnificence: "There was not in all that great assembly a single man who owed his position to aught save his valor and his merit." Busbecq also testified to the pride of the royal slaves: "Those who receive the highest offices from the sultan are for the most part the sons of shepherds or herdsmen, and so far from being ashamed of their parentage, they actually glory in it, and consider it a matter of boasting that they owe nothing to the accident of birth; for they do not believe that high qualities are either natural or hereditary, nor do they think that they can be handed down from father to son, but that they are partly the gift of God, and partly the result of good training, great industry, and unwearied zeal." In Europe, on the contrary, "birth is the standard for everything; the prestige of birth is the sole key to advancement in the public service." Today we might add that the system provided more opportunity for the gifted individual than free private enterprise provides. Reward for merit was swifter and surer, and incentives were higher than the profit motive.

Suleiman was a stern parent of his slave-family. He accepted no excuses, showed little mercy; he put to death his best friend, the grand vizier Ibrahim, for displaying personal ambitions that threatened the system. But usually he was just and generous. To the end he commanded the loyalty of his slaves. "History may have known as large a slave-family," remarked Albert H. Lybyer in his study of Suleiman's regime, "but certainly none that was more powerful and honorable, better provided for and rewarded, more obedient and more contented."

Yet everything depended on Suleiman—and the sultan himself was not carefully selected and bred. The Ottoman system too finally depended on "the accident of birth," and the vagaries of intrigue. The intrigue was not discouraged by the drastic Ottoman way of ascending the throne. Suleiman had ascended it without bloodshed or trouble because he was an only son, and Selim the Grim had made a clean sweep of his relatives, slaughtering eight nephews as well as two older brothers. During his reign intrigue obliged him to put to death his two ablest sons, Mustafa and Bayazid. He also felt the need of changing his bedroom daily as a precaution against foul play. And the end of Suleiman's reign was not magnificent.

"So self-contained was the heart of that grand old man," wrote Busbecq of Suleiman after a victory he had won, "so schooled to meet each change of fortune, however great, that all the applause and triumph of that day wrung from him no sign of satisfaction." He was indeed a great man, but as an old one he had little cause for showing satisfaction. He had had to school himself to execute his best friend and his sons, one of the latter strangled in his presence. Although he grew more pious, or superstitious, abstaining somewhat from his accustomed magnificence, the Commander of the Faithful was not rewarded by the grand victory he wished to close out his career with. An all-out campaign to capture Malta was a failure. In 1566 he took the field again, though unable to sit on a horse, and died before the victory was won. The grand old man died, appropriately, on his feet; but it was a piddling victory, and one of the last the Ottomans would win. With his death the decline of the Ottoman Empire set in—a decline almost as rapid as its rise, and much less amazing. The chief threat to Europe became the "Sick Man of Europe."

It would be unprofitable to follow this story chapter by chapter. The entire history of the Ottoman Empire accommodates itself to the old-fashioned kind of political and military history, featuring kings and battles. Until Suleiman the names and dates are mostly glorious, after him mostly inglorious. A temporary revival a century later, under the leadership of a family of Albanian grand viziers, ended with another unsuccessful siege of Vienna. Thereafter the empire went wholly on the defensive. It kept shrinking under humiliating defeats, especially by the Russians. The repeated blows to the national pride caused some sultans to try to learn something from the despised infidels of the West, beginning with military techniques and even approaching political reform; such words as equality and liberty blossomed out among lofty, sublime, magnanimous, etc., in the meaningless pronouncements of the Sublime Porte. But what kept the empire going was not primarily its own efforts. In part it lived off its past—off the achievements of Suleiman—which led Europeans to overrate its military power. Chiefly it was preserved by

European diplomacy, which feared the growth of Russian power and opposed Russian designs on Constantinople.

The moral of this story is also old-fashioned and familiar, but it is worth looking into somewhat more closely. It illustrates a favorite Turkish proverb, that fish begin to stink from the head. Conquest had been the main objective of Suleiman, as of the greater sultans before him. When the conquests ceased, the basic weaknesses of the Ottoman imperial system became apparent. We can now see clearly both the symptoms and the causes of the oncoming sickness in the reign of Suleiman the Magnificent.

The stink came immediately from harem intrigue. Suleiman provided a central stage for the intrigue, being the first sultan to move his harem and its eunuch guards into the royal palace. One reason he felt obliged to do away with his ablest sons was love of his favorite wife, Roxelana, who unfortunately was not the mother of the eldest; she apparently conspired with the Janissaries on behalf of her own favorite son, Selim. Europe had more reason to be grateful to Roxelana than the popular romances she inspired, for Suleiman the Magnificent was succeeded by her favorite—Selim the Sot. After him came Murad III, a harem puppet known chiefly for his 112 children. In the next century such pleasures induced one Sultan to drown his whole harem, for the sake of a change. Meanwhile the sultans had given up the traditional custom of leading their troops in battle. In time they also gave up the custom of killing their brothers, but brought them up as prisoners, even forbidding the publication of the list of royal princes. Hence a palace revolution might set on the throne an elderly recluse, unknown to his people, and with no practical experience whatsoever.

Meanwhile the system on which the stay-at-home sultans had to depend still more had been fatally corrupted. The Janissaries, who had been influential in forcing the execution of Suleiman's sons, became ever more powerful. They succeeded in getting the right not only to marry but to enroll their sons in the corps—a practice that Suleiman began tolerating toward the end of his reign. Thus a carefully selected, tightly disciplined elite of some 15,000 troops grew into a self-perpetuating praetorian guard of over 50,000, pampered, unruly, and lawless. Early in the seventeenth century they murdered Osman II—the first open regicide in Ottoman history. (There were rumors that Selim the Grim poisoned his father.) They continued to dethrone or murder sultans until 1826, when one had the wit to blow up the whole corps in their barracks.

More directly traceable to Suleiman was the growth of corruption in government. He began admitting born Moslems into high office, a practice that naturally encouraged favoritism. One of his grand viziers introduced the policy that made venality and extortion almost obligatory: he put a tax on the higher offices, which were a means to great wealth. As the sultan took pay for the privilege of serving him, so presently did all the officials under him, and their underlings from those lower down. By the middle of the seventeenth century the imperial service was thrown open to freeborn Turks, and nepotism and graft were routine. The Ottoman bureaucracy, with its hordes of paper scribblers, was so fantastically inefficient and corrupt that three centuries ago ambassadors began predicting the imminent collapse of the government. At the beginning of this century Sir Charles Eliot could explain its failure to do so only on the grounds that the Sublime Porte completely ignored principles of political economy—theories of wages, supply and demand, and everything else. Its subjects could carry on because they were born and bred to chaos, surprised only by any appearance of economy or dispatch.

With the breakdown of their one major contribution to the art of government, the Ottomans had nothing more to offer. Their helplessness was a logical result of their imperial system. At its most admirable, the whole slave-family of Suleiman worked loyally to serve the Sultan—not the people. It was not responsible for many ordinary functions of government, such as the building and maintenance of roads, the promotion of agriculture and industry, postal service, public education, or the public welfare in general. Its main concerns were fighting wars and collecting taxes. And though no European state of the time was much concerned about the common people, the Sultan was farther removed from them than most other monarchs, by a system in which his own people could not participate. Suleiman's remoteness severely limited his efforts at justice or reform; he conferred only with a few high officials and could not follow up his orders. As a lawgiver he was neither a bold innovator nor a great codifier. Nor was his magnificence a simple boon to the nation. The people of Stamboul could occasionally enjoy it in imperial processions and entertainments, such as the most lavish one in which he celebrated the circumcision of his sons. The rest of the nation might take pride in it. But ultimately they paid its costs; and most of them lived in poverty, accentuated by contrast with the affluence of Suleiman's 80,000 "slaves."

His magnificence comes down to the old story. The relatively modest palace built by the Conqueror in Constantinople had developed into the glittering Seraglio, a vast establishment walled off from the rest of the city and staffed by such officials as the Keeper of the Turban, the Keeper of the Ewer, the Chief Keeper of the Parrots, the Custodian of the Heron's Plume. While the sultans incidentally treasured some of the Byzantine absurdities before them, such as a hand and part of the skull of John the Baptist, they specialized in gold and precious stones on throne and turban. The turban of the Conqueror is a majestic one, bearing a single huge emerald. Most of the rest are simply a blaze of precious stones, in barbaric taste. A golden throne studded with rows of emeralds was a fitting frame for these sultans, symbolizing a splendor that defeated its purpose by gaudy excess; for all this unvarying gold might as well be brass, the emeralds come to look merely like green glass. (The treasures may be viewed in the Seraglio—today a national museum.) And millions toiled in poverty that one man might live in such preposterous splendor—after Suleiman, a man who like as not was a weakling or a fool, not even master of his own harem, and quite unconcerned about the lot of the millions. So the Sick Man of Europe rotted away in a gilded, bejeweled, be-eunuched palace.

A library in the Seraglio suggests still another qualification of the magnificence of Suleiman. It includes books that had belonged to him, and others that had belonged to the Conqueror: books with beautifully tooled covers, and as beautifully executed illumination and calligraphy, which prove the Turks' mastery of the art of bookmaking. They prove as well that the early sultans were genuinely cultivated men; even Selim the Grim delighted in the company of scholars, and himself wrote poetry in three languages. But this library—according to its present curator the first real library in Turkey—was in the harem precincts. It was not freely available to scholars or at all available to general readers. Like the sultans' crown jewels, it was another sign of royal splendor and privilege, to be admired by their subjects from a distance, not to be communally shared or used. It did not help to inspire a notable art of book writing. No books were printed until the eighteenth century, when a Hungarian renegade set up the first printing press in Constantinople.

The enduring glory of the reign of Suleiman was the work of Sinan, supplemented by much exquisite work in the decorative arts. No other great names come down from his age—no names of poet, philosopher, scientist, historian, or theologian. Although we hear of such men at his court, as of that of sultans before him, none did creative work of note. Stamboul never became so brilliant a cultural center as Baghdad and Cairo or even Konya had been. Apart from architecture and the decorative arts, the Ottomans added nothing to Islamic culture. They piously preserved it, in the largely academic form in which they had received it, but in effect they narrowed and reduced it. Off the battlefield they were a docile, unspeculative, uncritical, unimaginative people. Even in architecture they proved unable to create a rich, living tradition. By the eighteenth century they were importing Italian architects to paint and restore their mosques, usually in poor taste, and thereafter they built few mosques of distinction.

Turkish literature most clearly illustrates the sharp limitations of Ottoman culture. Its language was a hybrid of Arabic, Persian, and Turkish, languages having nothing in common; its script was Arabic, which in its peculiar lack of vowels was about the worst imaginable script for a language especially rich in vowel sounds; and its form and content were borrowed from the Persians, whom the Turks despised as cowards. Consisting almost entirely of poetry, it was the last word in artificiality. The rules that bound it from the fourteenth to the nineteenth century were so rigid, observes its historian E. J. W. Gibb, that they suggest "a deliberate conspiracy to block every avenue against spontaneity and individuality." Among its victims was the national folklore. Aside from the common theme of homosexual love, it was as unrelated to the realities of Turkish life as were the official pronouncements of the Sublime Porte. "No Turk is in the least astonished if he does not understand a composition written in Turkish," wrote Charles Eliot. "He merely respects the author as having a command of choice expressions. He hardly regards literature or writing as a normal part of his life."

A conspicuous exception to these generalizations is Evliya Efendi, a lively seventeenth-century traveler; but he finally proves them. A man of grace and humor as well as learning, he was one of the few Ottomans to display curiosity about the world they had won, and in this respect might be counted a follower of Herodotus. His editors emphasize his "constant fidelity" in likewise reporting everything he saw and heard in his travels. He was much more uncritical than Herodotus, however; he could swallow without a gulp the most whopping tales. His book is full of blunders, woefully unreliable even on Arab and Turkish history. It is a delightful curiosity, but far from a great work. And his century was in Europe Whitehead's "Century of Genius": of Kepler, Galileo, Harvey, Boyle, and Newton; of Descartes, Hobbes, Locke, Spinoza, and Leibniz; in the arts, of Milton, Pascal, Molière, Rembrandt, Velázquez, and many others. That Evliya is about the best that the still great Ottoman Empire had to offer in this century is sufficient comment on its intellectual contribution. To the West that so long stood in awe of it it passed on only some incidental amenities, such as coffee and tulips.[1]

[1] The first coffeehouse in Stamboul was opened by an Arab during the reign of Suleiman. Coffee was at once denounced by religious authorities as one of the Four Ministers of the Devil, Four Pillars of the Tent of Lubricity, Four Cushions of the

Evliya also brings us back to the decisive influence of Islam. His avowed motive in his travels was to visit the tombs of saints; Mohammed had appeared to him in the invariable dream, to recommend travel as his calling. The Prophet did not put such heretical ideas into the head of other Turks—tradition had him say, "A Journey is a Fragment of Hell." In the beginning his religion had been almost a pure blessing to the Ottomans, bringing out the best in them. If it discouraged critical, independent thought, they had little disposition for such thought. But Islam became a serious hindrance once their conquests had ceased and they had to deal with the progressive, revolutionary West.

Beside the Ottoman State—strictly apart from the State—stood the independent institution of the ulema, the whole body of men holding religious office, headed by the mufti. It represented a check, often salutary, on the despotic power of the Sultan—as when Selim the Grim bowed to the decree of his mufti prohibiting the enforced conversion of Christians. It also represented a constant drag on the State. As in effect a privileged aristocracy, exempt from taxation, it included many indolent hangers-on. In administering the rigid Sacred Law, which governed civil law, it was impervious to independent reason. In controlling education it permitted no change in subject or method, no free inquiry. The education of Suleiman's slave-family, though primarily for war and government, included some Arabic and Turkish literature but little history and no geography, physics, logic, or mathematics. Thereafter the curriculum of the ulema gave an ever more hopelessly inadequate idea of the world. Toward 1800 a high dignitary would ask, "What's this place Prussia they're talking about?" and learn that it was "Brandabork." By this time, too, the ulema had gained power at the expense of the enfeebled State; it got deposed a reforming sultan who tried to limit its power of veto. It remained the most powerful, inveterate enemy of all efforts at enlightenment or reform.

Islam had one final, ironic contribution to make to the Ottoman Empire—the ghost of the Caliphate. Selim the Grim had assumed the title of Caliph when he conquered Egypt, deposing a shadow puppet there,

---

Couch of Voluptuousness (the others being tobacco, opium, and wine). It was at once relished, however, apart from such seductive labels; so coffee drinkers persisted in their vice through a century of persecution, even to the death penalty decreed by the drunken Murad IV. Another reason for their persistence was that Moslem severity tended to encourage excess. When one drop of wine would entail the same punishment after death as a gallon, the winebibber might as well toss off a gallon. Busbecq tells of one old fellow in his cups who kept shouting to his soul to get off in some odd corner of his body, or leave it entirely, to avoid defilement by the wine he was about to drink.

and his successors continued to use the title, but none made much of it.
Suleiman did not even bother to include it in the fanfare I quoted at the
outset. For all practical purposes the institution had been dead for seven
hundred years when it was revived, late in the nineteenth century, by
the wily despot Abdul-Hamid II, for purely political reasons. He invoked
its ancient magic to rally the Moslem world around the Ottoman Empire,
and to impress the European powers. He met with some success, especially in the West; it was still provincial enough to believe that the Caliph
was a kind of Pope, with genuine spiritual authority. No ghost could
revive the Ottoman Empire, however, and the fiction served chiefly to
show up the unsavory game that all the major European powers were
playing. The German Kaiser was only more blatantly hypocritical when
he paid a state visit to the unspeakable Abdul-Hamid in 1898 to assure
the Sultan, "and the 300,000,000 Mohammedans scattered over the world
who revere him as their Caliph," of the undying friendship of Germany.

3. THE FATE OF THE OLD CITIES

By the middle of the seventeenth century, the capital restored by
Mohammed the Conqueror again had a population of close to a million.
It had been ornamented with countless mosques, baths, caravansaries,
bazaars, fountains, kiosks. It had acquired its hauntingly beautiful skyline, made as enchanting as any in the world by its slender minarets. It
had become still more cosmopolitan. Later a local almanac would be
printed in six languages—Turkish, French, Bulgarian, Greek, Armenian,
and Spanish in Jewish script—and would record time according to five
different calendars. Even so, Constantinople was still something of a
"holy ark." It was the seat of the Orthodox Patriarch, the "Second Rome"
for millions of Christians, and a lodestar for the "Third Rome" in Moscow.
In transforming Hagia Sophia into a mosque, the Turks had made it one
of their major shrines; they moved in their Saint Khidr among others,
with a legend that he had aided Justinian's architect. At St. Andrew's
tomb they miraculously discovered the graves of Fatima and Zeinab,
Moslem saints who thereupon continued to work the traditional cures.
And at Eyup, at the end of the Golden Horn, they created an important
new shrine, where each sultan was ceremoniously girded with the Sword
of Osman, first known as the Sword of the Prophet. Here was the tomb of
Eyup (Job, according to the local Greeks), a companion of the Prophet
who had fallen a martyr in an early siege of Constantinople; during the
final siege by the Conqueror its site had been revealed in a dream—the
age-old way of the gods, known to Greeks and Romans, and to the

mother of Constantine the Great. Allah was maintaining the traditions of the great city.

Evliya Efendi is a vivid witness to its spell. He knew that Constantinople had first been built by Solomon, and then by the two-horned Alexander. Constantine (whose birth he placed in Jerusalem) was the ninth builder of the holy city, and had been guided by his astrological foreknowledge of the rise of the Prophet. Mohammed also contributed the dome of Hagia Sophia, which had been thrown down by an earthquake on the night of his birth; it was restored by his advice. Hagia Sophia contained, indeed, "some thousands of holy places of pilgrimage." Among the many Evliya mentions were a gate made of planks from Noah's Ark and the stone trough in which Mary had washed Lord Jesus immediately after his birth. Similarly he described the many talismans that protected Constantinople, such as the figure of a gnat, placed on a column by "the divine Plato," which kept all gnats out of the city, and another column on which "Pythagoras the Unitarian" had placed a bronze wolf to scare off wolves.

With this wondrous collection of lore, drawn from all the peoples and the gods who had contributed to the history of the city, Evliya offers many glimpses of its pageantry and its daily life. He devotes almost a volume to a detailed catalogue, based on an imperial census, of the "thousand and one" guilds that served the capital. Evliya lists at least seven hundred of these guilds. They were so highly specialized that the Musical Men, for example, included 55 types of Drum Makers, as well as a single Brass-Flute Maker—" an obstinate Greek." (The Prophet knew the drum but not the flute.) The most numerous were the 43,000 Gardeners and 30,000 Torchbearers. Among the more exotic specialists were 500 Nightingale Merchants, 70 Merchants of Rose Water, 400 Barbers of Circumcision, 30 Cooks of Saffron Pilaf, 70 Fire-Eaters, and 80 Orators or storytellers in coffeehouses. Hundreds of Confectioners of different kinds worked under the blessing of the Prophet, who had said, "The love of sweetmeats comes from the faith." The possibly less faithful were served by 5,000 Goldsmiths, while 500 Dung Searchers paid for an annual concession to search the dunghills for lost jewelry and other valuables. Each guild had its holy patron, its official costume, and its fixed rank in the procession of the imperial camp, ending with 200 Jewish tavernkeepers. At Constantinople this procession took up a whole day and led to three days of holiday, which no doubt helped to reconcile the 200 to their lowly status.

"Such is the crowd and population of that great capital Constantinople," Evliya concluded, "which may God guard from all celestial and

earthly mischief, and let her be inhabited till the end of the world. Amen!
By the Lord of all the Prophets." His catalogue suggests, however, that
in this as all other great capitals the Lord had to put up with a good
deal of earthly mischief. The guilds included 104 Opium Merchants,
2,000 Slave Merchants, and 1,005 Speculators in corn and barley—"a bad
set of usurers." The city had a thousand taverns, which did a flourishing
business even though the Prophet had banned their stock in trade, and
though they were not allowed to "put any sign to their hellish shops." It
also had thousands of Fools and Mimics, mostly boys "who have exhausted seventy cups of the poison of life and misrule"; one troupe of
200 boys was especially famous for "stripping their admirers by their
charms and caresses." Life in the great capital was not calculated to
maintain the vigorous, sturdy, disciplined Turkish character that had
won the empire. Constantinople was not really a national capital, indeed,
or at least never the heart of the Ottoman Empire as it had been for the
Byzantine. It had had little to do with the winning of the empire, but
had much more to do with its decline. Essentially it was a costly ornament.

Among those to pay its costs were the provincial cities. Asia Minor
played little part in the history of the Ottomans after Bursa, beyond
providing its share of money and troops. It was not the home of the leading figures or the scene of the historic events, glorious or inglorious. For
a lover of the ancient cities, its history under the Ottomans is almost
wholly depressing.

One still hears of some of these cities at the collapse of the Seljuk
Empire. The capitals of the principalities into which it broke up included
Bergama (Pergamum), Ayasoluk (Ephesus), and Cassaba (Sardis). The
famous names continue to crop up during the rise of the Ottomans. They
minted some of their early coins at Bergama and Smyrna, while Philadelphia, founded by the Attalids of Pergamum, lived up to the good
reputation it got from John of Revelation by putting up a vigorous resistance to the Ottomans, holding out until about 1400. One might have expected the cities to revive, now that a strong empire again ruled the land
and they were at last secure against ravage; but most of them continued
to decay, especially in the western coastal region. Nature, wrote one
historian, had ordained Ionia to be a land of rich and powerful cities because of its many excellent harbors and its river highways. In fact it
became such a land only because of the nature of the Greeks, as a seafaring people given to commerce. The Turks were not a commercial or
seafaring people. Most of the many ports along the coast disappeared, or

survived only as fishing villages. The main centers were now inland, where they had been before the coming of the Greeks.

Here some of the old cities prospered, or even entered history after a fashion. The sultans after the Conqueror maintained a palace at Manisa, ancient Magnesia-ad-Sipylum and the scene of the fatal defeat of Antiochus the Great; it was the governor's seat of Selim, the favored son of Suleiman the Magnificant, and took on something of his magnificence. Amasya was a headquarters of Suleiman himself, visited by many envoys, and for a while ruled by his unfortunate son Mustafa. Ancient Cotaeium in Phrygia flourished as Kütahya, a major center of ceramics, known for the beautiful blue in its pottery. Bursa, a shrine of the Ottomans, became famous for its silks as well. Other cities were known for their tiles, textiles, or carpets. Akshehir, a city up the Konya plain that had once been Philomelium, was hallowed by the tomb of Nasreddin Hoja, the beloved folk philosopher of the Turks. A delightful blend of sage and buffoon—now shrewd and now naïve, now the teacher and now the butt —Nasreddin became the repository of all the wisdom and the humor of the folk.[2]

In general, however, Asia Minor suffered from the maladministration of the Ottomans. Although it provided many recruits for the slave-family of the Sultan, this in return did little but collect taxes. The revenues of the sultans went chiefly into the maintenance of their army, their court, and their capital. Here and there they built a mosque, a khan, a bridge; one runs across some works of Sinan. But there is little imposing Ottoman construction in the interior. Asia Minor was the more neglected because the Ottomans never regarded it as their homeland. As nomadic invaders, they had no real ancestral homeland to which they were deeply attached or would devote loving care. Observers often remarked that the Turks were still nomads at heart, quick to change their residence; they did not build their homes for permanence and were careless of maintenance and repair. Even in Stamboul most homes were flimsy wooden structures, feeding the fires that periodically swept through the city, requiring it virtually to be rebuilt about three times each century.

[2] A typical anecdote among the hundreds attributed to him may have helped the people to put up with their sultans during the centuries of misrule. While serving as court jester for Tamerlane, Nasreddin joined his royal master in weeping for two hours when Tamerlane looked in a mirror and saw how ugly he was. The monarch was finally comforted by his courtiers, but Nasreddin continued to weep, more loudly. At length he explained: "If you, my Lord, wept for two hours after seeing yourself in the mirror for but an instant, is it not natural that I, who see you all day long, should weep longer?" His tomb is a gate with a huge, elaborate lock—and nothing behind it. Life is not to be taken too seriously, taught this philosopher.

In the last century the old cities, outside of Constantinople and Bursa, were the dreariest tidemarks of a receding civilization. Thus Kayseri (Caesarea), on a main caravan highway, was reputed to be the second greatest town in the eastern part of the empire; and travelers reported a filthy, ramshackle town, entered by an abominable road. Most depressing was Konya, the most purely Turkish of the larger towns. European visitors to the lovely Seljuk monuments approached this ancient garden spot by the usual wretched road. They found the walls of Iconium enclosing a space twice as large as that occupied by the Ottoman town. Within the walls they picked their way amid crumble and mud. The beautiful blue tiles were falling off the Seljuk mosques and colleges; some of the graceful minarets were leaning dangerously, though still used by the fatalistic muezzins. The little oasis maintained by the whirling dervishes only accentuated the squalor of the city about them.

A people who showed so little reverence for the monuments of its ancestors naturally took still less interest in Greek and Roman antiquities, except as stone quarries and possible mines of superstition. But here natural piety calls for a measure of forgiveness. In using ancient monuments as quarries the Turks were only doing what the Christians and the later Romans had done before them. In destroying they also preserved some sculptures and inscriptions that might otherwise have become buried. It is not simply depressing to find Corinthian capitals in village walls, or the memorial stone of an ancient dignitary marking the grave of a peasant. The marble is at least serving a humane use. Scholars were sometimes confused because the peasants had hauled the stones long distances from their original site, so valuable was the material, or so magical the writing on it; but they had reason to forgive this too. By their superstition the peasants maintained the deepest continuity in human history, that of religious tradition. Some of the famous old cities lived on as holy places.

Because of the more violent upheaval, the continuity from Christian to Moslem tradition was more irregular than that from pagan to Christian. Some of the most popular sanctuaries, such as the Asclepium of Pergamum, lost all their holiness and power—even though Pergamum had also been one of the Seven Churches of Asia. Superstition could work against their survival too, for the black magic exerted by Christian saints was occasionally too strong for the Turks. Thus at Pergamum they had to give up the effort to transform the great Church of St. John into a mosque—the saint kept making the minarets fall; it is today a huge ruin. They abandoned another church in Antalya because all Moslems who entered it died. Usually, however, the holy guardians were not so jealous.

More often the Christian saint co-operated with the Moslem, or when there was a struggle, it ended in a draw. Often as not, Greeks and Turks worshiped at the same wonderworking shrine. In Kayseri both went to the Church of St. John the Baptist, famous for its cures of animals. And both were drawn to the oldest holy places in Asia Minor—mountains, cairns, groves, springs. Among the official ones were the hot springs at Yalova, near Constantinople. The ancient Greeks had dedicated them to Apollo, Christians installed the Archangel Michael, and the Turks sanctified them by having a dervish buried on the spot.

In this pursuit of miracle the Turks had several advantages. They had no fixed calendar of saints, and did not need the official authority of a Church. Whereas the Christians often had to resort to farfetched legends in order to move an appropriate saint into a pagan shrine of proved efficacy, the Turks could freely choose patrons and build tombs or invent graves for them. Their saint did not even have to have a name—he could be known only as the Baba or the Dede. When a Christian saint was unmistakably good at curing, they could draw on a convenient Moslem legend: Allah had recognized as his elect some Christians who died before Mohammed, and had transported them from Christian to Moslem graves by 72,000 camels. In any event, they did not hesitate to invoke the saints of the infidels when their own fell down on their job. In Alashehir (Philadelphia) they frequented an abandoned church even though it was known to be haunted by dangerous Christian ghosts: it cured toothaches. Nor were they troubled by the usual duplications and confusions. On a mountain looking down on the Bosphorus, Turkish piety located the tomb of Joshua, who was venerated at many other tombs over the Moslem world because of an obscure reference to him in the Koran.

Greek Orthodox piety remained as active under the Ottomans. It was not helpless when a Moslem saint proved his powers; at Constantinople it identified St. Eyub with Job, or sometimes Samuel. It produced new martyr-healers, usually Christians who had turned Moslem, repented, and then died rather than renounce their faith. These included at least one known impostor (Auxentios of Bithynia) who was denounced by ecclesiastical authorities, but was retained because his bones continued to induce miracles. As late as the last century the Greeks at Ürgüp concocted St. John the Russian, with such success that the Russian monks at Athos bought his right hand.[3]

[3] Even the despised, clannish Jews got involved in these activities and contributed to some hybrid sects. The strangest of these sprang from one Shabbetai Zevi of Smyrna, who in 1648 stirred new hopes by proclaiming himself the Messiah. Many Jews sold their trade to follow him. Although he was briefly embarrassed when called upon to perform some miracles, a devout follower luckily saw a pillar of fire between

Of the famous cities, Ephesus lost most of its holiness until the recent discovery of the house of the Virgin, but it retained some vogue because of its Cave of the Seven Sleepers. In Moslem folklore the Seven acquired a dog Katmir, who is one of the animals admitted to Paradise. They also became patrons of shipping, especially on the stormy Black Sea, and their names were powerful charms, for example, on buildings to prevent fire. Their popularity naturally led to claims on behalf of many other caves, though without serious harm to the reputation of Ephesus. Of these others one at Cyprus failed to make good, but one at Tarsus became an important shrine and acquired a special reputation for curing barrenness in women, Christian or Moslem. Tarsus profited as well by the Moslem veneration of the prophet Daniel, whose grave at Susa had long been a place of pilgrimage; in the eighteenth century another tomb of Daniel's began to show up in an old Tarsian church converted into a mosque. It is regrettable that St. Paul himself apparently did not profit from these discoveries.

An incidental means to continuity, lastly, was medieval romance, which gave the name of Kiz, "maiden," to many a castle or tower. They were associated with popular tales of maidens who had fallen in love with a hero of the opposed religion, or for some reason had been imprisoned and had died unhappily. One striking "Kiz Kalesi" rises out of the sea off the coast of Cilicia Aspera. A small Byzantine one in the mouth of the Bosphorus has acquired the name of Leander's Tower, and with it a rival legend about a beautiful daughter of Constantine the Great. (He placed her in the tower to forestall a prophecy that she would die of snakebite, and though a snake did get in among some flowers sent her, a handsome prince saved her life.) Out of the Kiz legends grew others involving Belkis, the Queen of Sheba and wife of Solomon. Especially grand ruins could then be hallowed by association with Solomon, the arch-magician and builder of Constantinople. The village near the great Roman theater of Aspendus is now known as Belkis.

---

him and a Turkish follower; so his flock grew. At God's call Shabbetai went to Constantinople, where the Turks imprisoned him because of the disorders he was causing, but this misfortune only confirmed the belief of the faithful. When he was transferred to the prison in the castle of Abydus on the Dardanelles, Jews began to flock there from all over Europe. At length a prudent one requested the Turks to try him. The Turks obliged by testing his powers as a miracle man, proposing to strip him and shoot arrows at him, to see whether they would enter his body. Shabbetai preferred to stop playing Messiah. He acknowledged his imposture and made amends by cheerfully turning Moslem, apparently remaining a contented one until his death in 1676. Some of his followers, however, continued to believe in him, declaring that it was not he but a demon that had recanted. They formed a sect known as the Dönme, a Jewish heresy with Moslem trappings, centered in the Greek city of Salonika.

All this activity has contributed more to the romance than to the spiritual growth of Asia Minor. The spirituality of the Turkish peasantry was not appreciably deepened or heightened by association with their Christian neighbors, or by the common heritage of much older religious tradition. Still, these continuities are part of our story. They are too generally neglected by the many who equate spirituality with religion, and the many others who read history as pageantry or politics. If they reveal a depressing mentality, we might be more depressed by the thought of the ignorance, poverty, and pain that have been the lot of the masses of men throughout history, and that made them pathetically dependent on miracles. We can hardly begrudge them their healing gods and synthetic saints.

4. THE REDISCOVERY OF ASIA MINOR

A Western scholar who wrote a Moslem friend, requesting information about his city, got this answer:

My Illustrious Friend and Joy of my liver! The thing you ask of me is both difficult and useless. Although I have passed all my days in this place, I have neither counted the houses nor inquired into the number of the inhabitants; and as to what one person loads on his mules and the other stows away in the bottom of his boat, that is no business of mine. But above all, as to the previous history of this city, God only knows the amount of dirt and confusion that the infidels may have eaten before the coming of the sword of Islam. It were unprofitable for us to inquire into it. O my soul! O my lamb! seek not after the things which concern thee not. Thou camest unto us and we welcomed thee. Go in peace. . . . Listen, O my son! There is no wisdom equal unto the belief in God! He created the world; and shall we liken ourselves unto Him in seeking to penetrate into the mysteries of His creation? . . . I praise God that I seek not that which I require not. Thou art learned in the things I care not for; and for that which thou hast seen, I pour confusion on it. Will such knowledge create thee a double belly, or wilt thou seek Paradise with thine eyes?

This gentle soul may help us to appreciate an obscure traveler named W. M. Leake. In 1800 Leake found Asia Minor "still in that state in which a disguised dress, an assumption of the medical character, great patience and perseverance, the sacrifice of all European comforts, and the concealment of pecuniary means, are necessary to enable the traveler thoroughly to investigate the country, when otherwise qualified for the task by literary and scientific attainments, and by an intimate knowledge of the language and manners of the people." He was one of a line of unsung, unread heroes—from Pococke, Chandler, Arundell, Texier, Hamilton, Fellows, and Ainsworth to Radet, Hogarth, and Ramsay—who investigated

Asia Minor thoroughly, to uncover the dirt and confusion eaten by the ancient infidels. They traveled on horse, with much less comfort and ease than St. Paul had taken for granted. Roads were generally wretched or nonexistent, food and accommodations as bad; they put up in many a village room or hovel infested with vermin, running the constant hazard of disease. Most had a breadth of interest, knowledge, and skill that would shame a modern traveler. They knew geography, geology, history, the classics; they could sketch, map, and write. Often they took amazing pains. "Thursday, May 25, 1836. 7:20 A.M., S.S.E., Start through Moudaniah; 7:25 S.W. Ascending through Turkish town; 7:26 W.; 7:28 W.S.W. Clear of town. 7:31 S.S.W. Ascending ridge, ground slopes r. and l.; olives and vines. 7:33 Winding up steep road." So begins a page of the diary of William J. Hamilton, included in his two-volume *Researches in Asia Minor, Pontus, and Armenia,* "with Some Account of Their Antiquities and Geology." This sample of his thoroughness helps to explain why he is unread. But the point is that he was mapping a once famous land that in his time was largely unmapped and unknown. The Ottomans who owned Asia Minor were as incurious about it as our gentle Moslem friend.

Some of these travelers had an orthodox piety that gives their books as quaint an antique flavor. The painstaking Hamilton concluded his two volumes with a prayer that God, in His good time, might somehow turn the hearts of these Turks to Himself, and "the countries which first saw the effects of the Word will no longer be behind the Gentiles in adoring His holy Name!" The primary motive of them all, however, was a disinterested curiosity about the past, or a natural piety. Their dusty volumes are memorials of a precious spirit—a spirit that makes for solidarity, and may bind us more intimately to the generations before us and the generations to come. Ramsay may speak for all these explorers. On one expedition into Phrygia, he wrote, he found a long-sought inscription, identifying a high priestess of the imperial cult, Julia Severa, as a leader and benefactor of the Jews, and thus indicating their assimilation. While searching for a "black stone" reported by a peasant, he also ran across the finest specimen of Roman road he had found, cut into a hillside. But in leaving it to find the stone he ran into rain, lost the Roman road for good, and did not find the stone either. He added that his conscience had tormented him ever since because in his irritation he refused to pay the poor peasant who had promised to guide him to it. After sixteen days of hard work he returned to Smyrna, greatly disappointed as usual—"but consoled for all by the Jewish inscription."

So they were all repeatedly disappointed in their search for antiquities, and finally consoled. Peasants often misled them deliberately, because of the common belief that "written stones" had gold hidden in them. They were mystified by some of their finds, such as the Hittite monuments. They had to conjecture a great deal, and some of their conjectures now seem wild or naïve. (The pious Hamilton, for example, tried to demonstrate that the god Men or Manes of the Lydians, and also of the Egyptians, "was no other than their common ancestor Noah.") In time the more scholarly would be exasperated by the stubborn perversity of other scholars.[4] But always they were sustained by the exhilaration of the chase. They could at least count on running across many inscriptions and coins, which might identify the site of a long-forgotten city. And now and then they made exciting discoveries. In 1833 Arundell found the site of Antioch-in-Pisidia, where St. Paul became the Apostle of the Gentiles. Fellows opened up the whole glorious region of Lycia. Hamilton was rewarded for his infinite pains by the discovery of the fairy-pirate city of Isaura well up in the Cilician mountains: "an ancient city of great extent, strength, and magnificence," with massive walls and towers of beautiful workmanship, all untouched and well preserved because its original robber-builders had perched it on a lofty peak, where through the centuries it stood in solitude.

Today the much more comfortable traveler in Turkey might envy these early travelers for another reason. They told of many striking ruins that have since crumbled or disappeared, succumbing to the ravages of time—and of the Turkish peasant. All had their say about this peasant and the Ottoman regime of which he was the dumb, long-suffering victim. They throw considerable light on the next chapter that was to be written by Ataturk.

Generally the peasants were mystified by the foreign visitors. They could not understand trips that were not for business or religious purposes —trips taken out of mere curiosity or desire to learn. Hence they tended to regard the travelers either as freaks or as gold seekers, and to respect them chiefly for their occult knowledge of buried treasures. They also tended to be suspicious of them as possible government agents; anything that came from the government was bad. Even so they were loyal to their Sultan, as

[4] From his explorations Ramsay discovered serious errors in Kiepert's standard map of Asia Minor, due to Kiepert's dependence on "the notes of careless travelers"; but he got nowhere with the authorities. "I have utterly failed," he complained, "to make the professional geographers in England believe that there are faults in Kiepert, or to induce them to vary from the published maps. You may spend weeks or months drawing a better map; you put it into the professional geographer's hands, and out comes the old Kiepert unchanged, and the draftsman is quite hurt at your ingratitude, after he has taken so much care to correct all your vagaries and variations from the standard map."

to their Prophet. As good Moslems they had other admirable qualities, of honesty, integrity, and hospitality. They were seldom as miserable as they might look, for their wants were few, their demands fewer. Ramsay reported that there was no coined money in the villages because there were no shops, no circulation of money, no possibility of exchanging it. A Goldsmith or a Rousseau might accordingly have glorified these uncorrupted villagers, pictured their simple state as idyllic. A truer word for it was brute inertia. Their acceptance of their wretched lot, like their submission to arbitrary authority, was due to simple ignorance of better possibilities, or simple incapacity for enterprise and initiative.

The travelers were mostly sympathetic toward these peasants. For the Ottoman government they had scarcely a good word. Almost uniformly they stressed the corruption, the backwardness, the hopeless decay. The more honest officials they met were likely to feel helpless, the more enlightened ones despondent. Ramsay handed down the most sweeping indictment of the Ottoman regime. "The action of the Turks in every department of life," he concluded in his *Impressions of Turkey During Twelve Years' Wanderings* (1897), "has simply been to ruin, never to rebuild. . . . They destroyed the intellectual and moral institutions of a nation; they broke up and dissolved almost the entire social fabric; they annihilated every educative and humanizing influence in the land; and they brought back a great part of the country to the primitive simplicity of nomadic life. . . . In general, there is hardly a social institution in Asia Minor showing any degree of legal or social constructiveness that is not an older Anatolian creation, Moslemized in outward form, and usually degraded in the process."

This is too harsh an indictment—especially of the early Ottomans who rebuilt Bursa and Constantinople. It brings up a quality of arrogance in many of the travelers, who could be pretty lordly toward the "natives." One night, we will read, the guide lost his way, "for which he was well flogged"; or a poor village headman was called down sharply because he had slighted his duty of hospitality. These Westerners could also be provincial in their conceit. Hamilton was especially indignant about the Turks, "whose existence in Europe in the nineteenth century is a disgrace to all Christian countries." The geographical fiction of "Europe" was now a source of moral indignation, whereas the Turks had in fact preserved the medley of peoples and cultures that occupied southeastern Europe, with traditions differing widely from those of western Europe—just as they had preserved the Holy Orthodox Church, which under the rule of Western Christendom would most likely have become extinct. Hamilton proposed to end the disgrace by dividing up Asia Minor between the Greeks and

Armenians and exiling the Turks to the East. "The Turks, reduced to their native wilds in Tartary, might perhaps recover from the moral degradation in which they are now steeped," he added charitably; "and, with a more healthy state of feeling, a way might be prepared for their admission in the fullness of time to the pale of Christianity."

The more judicious Ramsay laid himself open more specifically to ironic contemplation. "It is difficult, perhaps impossible, to educate the Turk," he observed in his *Impressions;* "but there are so many sterling qualities in him that I have a profound conviction that he can be amalgamated with other elements to form a good mixed race." As he was at least an excellent follower and fighter, improvement was "quite possible" in Turkey, though "not under Turkish rule." Meanwhile Ramsay made out the wave of the future. "At the present day the central movement in Asia Minor is, what it has always been, a conflict between the Eastern and the Western spirit." The Greeks had grown much stronger on the coasts, and were moving inland with the railways. "The steady, inexorable, irresistible spread of European, and mainly of Greek, influence in the western parts of Asia Minor, is by far the most striking fact in modern Turkey. That progress is so patent that the Turks make practically no attempt to resist it: it is accepted as inevitable. The Asiatic Greeks have the future in their hands; and no man or no policy will be successful, which does not recognize that fact and build upon it as foundation."

Ataturk built upon a quite different foundation, with considerable immediate success, at the expense of the Greeks. None of the nineteenth-century travelers anticipated his accomplishment. Yet we can hardly blame them. This was an extraordinary accomplishment, which no one could have predicted. And Ramsay at least had his eye on the major issue. There was in fact a basic conflict between the Eastern and the Western spirit—as Ataturk also recognized. The rise of the Greeks was a key factor in the history of modern Turkey.

5. THE RETURN OF THE GREEKS

The relations of Greeks and Turks have provided one of the ugliest chapters of modern history; but it is not the simple story of Asiatic tyranny and cruelty, with the Turks cast in the villain's role, which until recently most Westerners saw in it. It began on a high enough note immediately after the fall of Constantinople, when Mohammed the Conqueror invested the Patriarch Gennadius with full jurisdiction over his Orthodox subjects. His act was not one of pure magnanimity, to be sure. It was a matter of political convenience, relieving the Ottomans of the fuss and expense of administration. They set up the same *millet* system for their

other subject peoples, classifying them all on the religious basis dear to
Eastern peoples; each *millet* or community (including the Armenian) was
put under a religious head who was given civil jurisdiction over it, but
was also held responsible for its allotted taxes and its good behavior.
Nevertheless this gave the Greeks religious freedom. With it they had
freedom to go about their business—the commerce on which they would
later thrive, just as they had risen on it in their glorious past.

As a subject people, they of course had grievances. They had to pay
taxes to support their masters, and their children were liable to enforced
recruitment in the slave-family of the Sultan. Except for this ignominy,
however, their condition was basically much the same as it had been. In
Constantinople they might feel at home under absolute monarchs who
took over the trappings of the Byzantine sacred monarchy; in the provinces they were ruled by Turkish beys instead of Byzantine nobles.
Generally they had little serious reason for complaint during the first centuries of Ottoman rule. Religious persecution was rare. As late as 1798 the
Patriarch of Jerusalem thanked God for the heavenly gift of the Ottomans
as champions of the Orthodox Church and guardians against Western
heretics. The sultans had in fact responded to appeals to banish Roman
Catholic missionaries who were trying to subvert the common people. At
times they even interceded to protect the *millets* from oppression by their
own heads. It was the Patriarchate, indeed, that struck the first really
sordid note.

Now the Patriarchate unquestionably did a great deal for the Greeks,
more than anything else helping them to maintain their identity and their
culture. In fairness one should note that as a spiritual institution it was
handicapped by the worldly powers and responsibilities the Turks gave
it; its leaders had more need of diplomatic and executive abilities than of
saintliness. At any rate, it was quicker to rise to its worldly than its spiritual possibilities—the profits to be made through tax collecting. When
Gennadius resigned after five years, his despairing successor threw himself down a well. (Fortunately he was rescued; so as George Finlay observed, the Greeks "were spared the scandal of hearing that their Patriarch
had voluntarily plunged into the pains of hell to escape the torment of
ruling the Orthodox Church on earth.") With his successor appeared the
scandal of simony. Noble families from the fallen Empire of Trebizond
competed for the prize by offering the Sultan an annual tribute of a thousand ducats if he would select their candidate, suitably named Simeon.
Soon the price of the office jumped to 3,000 ducats, then to 12,000; in the
seventeenth century one candidate was asked to pay 100,000. The competition did not make for harmony in an institution that from the outset

had had a stormy history. In the Byzantine era many Patriarchs had been deposed, some murdered; now still fewer died a natural death in office. It is surprising, commented Harry Luke, to read that in 1726 one Patriarch, Kallinikos III, died of joy on hearing of his election. It would be more surprising were it not for his opportunities of fleecing his flock. The Greeks—and especially the non-Greeks who belonged to the Orthodox Church—had reason to dread the pastoral visitations of their bishops, which were often raids on their purses.

The rise of a Greek plutocracy was likewise no boon to the common people. As the royal slave-family system broke down, the grand viziers began drawing officials from this plutocracy in the Phanar quarter of Constantinople, the headquarters of the Patriarchate; and these officials too were likely to prey on their fellow Christians. But the Greeks as a whole kept rising in the world. Toward the end of the eighteenth century, when the sultans decided to set up permanent diplomatic missions in the European capitals, they could find no Moslem Turks well enough educated to serve as ambassadors; so again they turned to the *millets*. Greeks and Armenians took over much of the administrative and foreign service of the empire, together with most of its business.

By this time, however, the uglier drama was under way. As Ottoman rule grew increasingly incompetent and corrupt, the spirit of nationalism was growing in Europe. The Greeks in mainland Greece began their struggle for independence. In western Europe their cause was viewed as a crusade to drive the infidel Turks out of "Europe," and it also enlisted the generous sympathy of liberals. The by now conspicuous evils of nationalism may obscure its ideal aspects—its connections with the cause of freedom and self-determination, and the selfless patriotism it may inspire. At any rate, the usual complications ensued. Patriotic fervor intensified by religious fervor produced heroism, and hatred. The War of Independence involved atrocities by both sides; Greek and Turkish civilians in Greece were alike massacred. At the outbreak of the war, the Patriarch in Constantinople anathematized its leaders, appealing to all Greeks in whom "every spark of piety and good sense was not extinct" to submit to the "world-renowned clemency of the Ottoman Government"; but even so he was hanged, together with six other bishops. In 1830 Greece became an independent kingdom.

The bad feeling between the peoples did not prevent a steady growth in the number and the wealth of the Greeks in Turkey during the nineteenth century. Many came in from the islands. Like their ancestors, they concentrated in cities along the coasts, dominating the import-export business. Smyrna became in effect their capital, and the symbol of the new type of the "Levantine": a Greco-Oriental city, French in its fashions, whose culture, like its bazaars, was a potpourri. Greeks made up half or more of the population in other busy ports, from Mersin, near Tarsus, to Samsun and Trebizond on the Black Sea. In Constantinople they remained a large, busy minority. And they dominated the professions as well as the commerce of Turkey. Unlike their ancestors, they contributed little to its art and architecture, exhibiting a bourgeois taste for the ornate and over-stuffed; but they were much more devoted to education than the Turks. By this century they largely represented the trained intelligence of the country.

About the character of the Asiatic Greeks, and their treatment by the Turks, there has been much controversy. The nineteenth-century travelers gave mixed reports of them. Some found them cultivated, generous hosts, and contrasted their lively intelligence with the ignorance and incom-petence of Turkish officialdom. Others complained that they were grasp-ing, and contrasted their mercenary spirit with the honesty and the hospitality of the well-bred Turk. It is always hard to draw a line between enterprise and greed, shrewdness and unscrupulousness; so it seems fair to say that the Greeks had both the virtues and the defects that make for success in business. As fairly one might add that their position as second-class citizens, forced to live by their wits, was not calculated to purify or ennoble their character. Those in high positions were Christians serving Turks, and short of revolutionary conspiracy were debarred from the service of an ideal cause, or from any ambition loftier than making a for-tune and trying to hang on to it. On moral and religious grounds, in any case, the Greeks were not clearly superior to the Turks. Their superiority lay rather in such qualities as intelligence, initiative, resourcefulness, and imaginativeness. These may be directed to evil as well as good ends, but they are none the less essential to the maintenance of a high civilization, and in particular of an open society.

As for the status of the Greeks in Turkey, they were indisputably treated as second-class subjects. Like all Christians, they had legal handicaps; their evidence in court was not given equal weight with that of Moslems, and might be ignored entirely. They had to pay a tax in lieu of military service, from which they were debarred. They were generally regarded with contempt when not with hatred by the Turks, who thought of them-selves as a ruling race even though—or because—they employed their sub-jects to rule for them. Sultans who attempted reform, or who bowed under European pressure, issued some admirable decrees about the equality of all their subjects, but these remained on paper. In 1840 Fellows remarked how mystified the Turks were when they heard the news that they were supposed to treat the Greeks as fellow citizens instead of conquered enemies. When the so-called Young Turks forced through positive reforms in this century, in the name of "Liberty, Justice, Fraternity," the Greeks did not profit. The Young Turks had left out "Equality." By now they too were becoming more and more nationalistic.

How much the Greeks suffered from this treatment is more debatable. They were at least not massacred as the unhappy Armenians were. It is doubtful that many resented their exclusion from the Turkish army, for which they had to pay only a small tax. Their legal hardships might be overcome by their smartness and superior education. European consuls who reported the abuses of Turkish justice added that they were partly due to the Christians, who were quick to exploit the corruption of Ottoman officialdom and had more money to bribe with. But this much seems certain. The Greeks enjoyed less prestige than the Turks, and resented the indignities to which they were subject. They also enjoyed considerably more prosperity than the great mass of Anatolian peasants, who continued patiently, dumbly, to go their rounds in the poor village, except when they were needed as cannon fodder. Harry Luke tells of the neglected fields and the wailing women he saw in Anatolia in 1913, immediately after the Balkan War, when the Young Turks began preparing for another war and so conscripted the sons of the peasants—while the despised Greeks went about their business in the towns. With Ataturk, this Anatolian peasant was at last to come into his own.

CHAPTER X

Ankara: The New Turkey of Ataturk

---

1. THE BACKGROUND OF THE REVOLUTION

"THE TURK changes not," wrote Sir Charles Eliot in 1908; "his neighbors, his frontiers, his statute-books change, but his ideas and his practice remain the same." Ten years later Mustafa Kemal set about revolutionizing the ideas and the practice of this changeless Turk. He started just as the Ottoman Empire had suffered a humiliating defeat in a war that the American Relief Committee estimated had cost it about a quarter of its population, through disease, starvation, and massacre as well as death in battle. Refusing to accept the terms dictated by the victorious Allies, he set up a new government in Ankara, gathered an ill-equipped army, and after three more years of war, costing untold blood, sweat, and tears, drove out of Turkey the Greek armies that had invaded it. Without pause he then tackled the staggering job of making a modern Western nation out of the impoverished remnant of the Ottoman Empire. He ousted the Sultan, the thirty-sixth of the House of Osman, which had ruled for six centuries; he horrified Islam by abolishing the Caliphate; he scrapped the whole Sacred Law, replacing it with the Swiss civil code; he started a school system to provide his mostly illiterate countrymen with a purely secular education; he took away their Arabic script and made over their alphabet and their language; he put them into Western clothes; he freed women from their age-old bondage, giving them complete equality; he made the men learn how to manage the commerce and industry that had been largely controlled by Greeks and Armenians. He met every crisis, in Toynbee's words, "by the 'kill-or-cure' expedient of teaching the child to swim by throwing it into water where it was out of its depth." The child sometimes drowned, needless to add; his countrymen are still thrashing in water over their heads. Nevertheless Mustafa Kemal was successful enough to justify the name he took—Ataturk, "Father Turk."

His extraordinary achievement was not a wholly unprecedented one. In the eighteenth century Peter the Great made as deliberate, in some ways as drastic, an effort to Westernize Russia, and even some Ottoman sultans prepared the way for Ataturk. Today it is a familiar kind of story: all over the Eastern world nations are taking to Western ways. Communist China is another revolutionary experiment, likely to be of much more historic consequence. Yet no revolutionary leader has gone faster and farther than Ataturk went, on so many different fronts. None has had to contend with a more massive, hostile tradition. Eliot was by no means foolish in his judgment, nor were the many others—like Ramsay—who thought it impossible that Turkey could ever be straightened out by Turks; they had centuries of history to back them up. And that this is now a familiar kind of story makes it all the more significant. It forces the basic issues of modern civilization.

The beginnings of the story were hardly inspiring. Military triumph had given the Ottomans a contempt for the West, but after a century of defeat they began to realize its military superiority and to suspect that they might learn something from it. They were rather slow to learn. An eighteenth-century sultan who introduced some military reforms thought that the secret of Frederick the Great's success was the efficient staff work of his astrologers. More mortifying defeats finally taught the Ottomans to study and copy more closely the techniques of the West, though not well enough to prevent further defeats. The most important result was that military officers were the first to receive the rudiments of a Western education; so it was mainly from their ranks—not from the intellectuals of Islam—that the future reformers were to come.

The first major break with tradition was made by Mahmud II (1808–39), the Sultan who wiped out the Janissaries. His extensive reforms included the establishment of primary education and a postal service, but symbolically more significant was his introduction of semi-European dress and manners in his court and army. He met fierce opposition when he ordered his troops to wear suspenders with their trousers (the suspenders formed a cross on the back, the badge of the infidels) and again when he imposed the fez, a despised Greek headgear. Nevertheless he was generally obeyed. The "Infidel Sultan" anticipated Ataturk by demonstrating what might be done with the stubbornly conservative Turks, who yet were habituated to following orders from on high.

The successors of Mahmud inaugurated the *Tanzimat*, a program of legal reform featuring equality for Moslems and non-Moslems. Turkish literature began to reflect Western influence, treating realistically the actual life of the country. But most educated Turks were still religious conservatives. The *Tanzimat* took its place with the other meaningless documents in the flatulent style of the Sublime Porte. Concessions to the infidels were more bitterly resented as the defeats continued and the empire shrank; Mahmud himself had lost Egypt, Greece, and the Caucasus. The reaction culminated in the long reign of his grandson, the notorious Abdul-Hamid (1876–1909). This sultan turned to Islam instead of the West, dusted off the Caliphate, and ruled as an Asiatic despot. His pathological fears for his safety made him the most oppressive of the Ottoman sultans. He set up a vast network of spies and informers, to breed distrust throughout the empire. He stopped the teaching of literature and history, as possibly subversive, replacing them with safe-and-sound Moslem theology. As a distraction his officials encouraged periodic massacres of Armenians.

This sordid chapter was ended by the Young Turks, a movement centered in the army. In 1908 their Society for Union and Progress sent an ultimatum to Abdul-Hamid, forced him to proclaim a republican Constitution, and the next year dethroned him in favor of his elderly brother. The country rang with such new words as "freedom" and "the will of the nation." Although it also rang with the indignation of upholders of the Sacred Law, who denounced these "ignoramuses" and "Devils" who "blindly imitate the West," the Young Turks were strong enough to set up a parliamentary government. Eventually they turned to the new ideal of Pan-Turkism, a union of all the Turks of Asia. Besides the nationalism of the West, this reflected the influence of the French writer Léon Cahun; his romantic novels glorifying the Mongol conquerors became immensely popular among the Turks, enlarging their ideas of their past. For the Ottoman Empire had not called itself Turkish. "Turk," indeed, had been almost a term of contempt, commonly applied to the slow-witted Anatolian peasant by city people who called themselves Osmanli.

But the new slogan of Pan-Turkism was a cover for the failure of the Young Turks to modernize and strengthen the Ottoman Empire. They soon betrayed their liberal Constitution, maintaining Union and Progress by the old method of silencing the opposition. After a dismal showing in the Balkan War, it did them no good to invoke the Caliphate and proclaim a "holy war" when they made the mistake of entering World War I on the side of Germany, for the Arabs turned against them. Their leaders were completely discredited by the disasters that followed. All that Turkish pride could salvage from the war was the feats of Mustafa Kemal, the hero of Gallipoli—a soldier who had worked with the Society for Union and Progress, but had fallen out with its leaders and devoted himself to soldiering instead of politics.

The selfishness and shortsightedness of European diplomacy now gave him his chance. The victorious Allies took over control of not only the Near-Eastern provinces of the Ottoman Empire but much of Turkey itself, in fulfillment of their secret treaties. French troops disembarked in Constantinople, to the cheers of the local Greeks. (Russia would have been given the city had it not turned Bolshevist and dropped out of the war.) More French troops invaded southeastern Turkey, while the Italians set themselves up in the region of Antalya. A Greek division landed at Smyrna under British auspices, ostensibly to maintain order, actually to begin massacring Turks. The last of the sultans, Mohammed VI, acceded to the Treaty of Sèvres, which permanently ceded most of western Turkey to the Allies who were occupying it, and divided up its eastern provinces between the Kurds and the Armenians. This ignominy fortified the resistance that had been organized by Mustafa Kemal. In 1919 he had summoned a national congress to replace the Sultan's government as the defender of Turkey. At this congress he expressed his indifference to the loss of the disloyal Arab provinces, but insisted on the absolute independence of Turkey itself, and prepared to fight for it. He then moved his headquarters to Ankara, where, on April 23, 1920, the Grand National Assembly of the new Turkey held its first session.

The Sultan's government proclaimed that the Nationalists were rebels. A mufti obediently affirmed that it was not only permissible but a duty to kill them, and all over Anatolia irregulars known as the "Army of the Caliphate" tried to do so. In the south there were also battles with the French. But the major war was with the Greeks. It was an especially nasty, bloody affair, beginning and ending with wholesale atrocities committed by both sides. The Greeks had a long record of grievances to avenge and believed that they were fighting to regain their ancient homeland; they fought fiercely enough. The Turks were defending their land against infidel invaders. They appear more heroic because they rose out of defeat, with no hope of outside support, to battle a much better equipped army. Patriots fled Constantinople by night to join the underdogs, often escorting munitions daringly stolen from the Allies.[1] Peasants and their womenfolk hauled the precious munitions over snow-covered mountains on their backs. Kemal met one crisis by confiscating 40 per cent of all available food, clothing, and other supplies, and issuing an order of the day that there were to be no more retreats—every unit was to keep facing the enemy and resist to the end, whatever the fate of neighboring units. The order was obeyed.

[1] A firsthand account of this epic of Turkish history is contained in the memoirs of Halide Edib, one of Turkey's first modern women, who served as a corporal in Mustafa Kemal's army. She does not idolize him, later having gone into exile because of disagreement with his dictatorial policies.

In 1920, when the Greek army had occupied an area running a little beyond Bursa, a communiqué announced that operations in Asia Minor were concluded, adding, with the peculiar fatuousness of diplomats and publicity experts, that the Turks were displaying "absolute confidence and sincere gratitude toward the Greeks, whom they consider their friends and protectors." Two years later the pulverized remnant of this army fled to its ships in Smyrna. The decisive battle had been fought in the region of Gordium, not far from Ankara. England, France, and Italy had by now washed their hands of the whole affair, declaring their neutrality. Following an armistice with the Nationalists, the Allies in 1923 signed the Treaty of Lausanne, which met almost all of Kemal's demands. Among its provisions was a wholesale exchange of the Turkish inhabitants of Greece and the Greek inhabitants of Turkey. The Greeks were allowed to remain only in Constantinople.

Mustafa Kemal was not attached to the great capital of the Ottomans, and for good reason. Although Stamboul was beloved by its residents, and still is, travelers reported that the Ottomans talked easily of leaving it and finding another capital in Asia. There was a legend that they would not be a great nation until they did so. Perhaps this was a sentimental relic of their nomadic past, perhaps a feeling that they were not really at home in Constantinople, perhaps an obscure realization that the great city had always been an incubus. It was a cosmopolitan, imperial city, now less than half Moslem, which had not only brought on many wars because of its control of a major commercial highway, but from the beginning had tended to subject the Ottomans to Byzantine influence and to denationalize the Turks. The new Turkey of Ataturk was designed for the Turks—"the last of the subject races of the Ottoman Empire," wrote Harry Luke, "to achieve their national emancipation." In 1923, accordingly, they signaled their break with the past by reducing Constantinople to a provincial city and making Ankara their permanent capital. This was a truly national capital, located in the heart of Anatolia, the homeland of the fighters who had won the war of emancipation. The modern city that Ataturk started building there symbolizes completely the aspirations, the achievements, and the contradictions of the new Turkey, which began facing West by shifting its center of gravity to the East.

2. THE NEW CAPITAL

According to Pausanias, ancient Ancyra was a Phrygian city founded by King Midas. The belief that its name meant "anchor" inspired a suitable explanatory legend. Another theory, which derives its name from a Lydian word meaning "way station," is better suited to its historic past. Although it became a Phrygian city, Hittites had been there much earlier. It has been identified with their Ankuwash and placed on the main road leading from their capital to the western coast—possibly the later Royal Road of the Persians to Sardis. In any case it was in Hittite country; so it recalls that now, for the first time in over three thousand years, Asia Minor is again being ruled from the interior.

The region about Ancyra, later known as Galatia, was much like Pontus to the north and Cappadocia to the south.[2] A land of ancient peoples, ruled successively by Hittites, Phrygians, Lydians, Persians, and other overlords, it never became deeply Hellenized. The marauding Gauls who settled down in it in the third century B.C. made little difference. Apparently they left its few old cities—Gordium, Pessinus, Ancyra—pretty much to themselves, as homes of powerful ancient gods, while they ruled the peasantry from fortified castles. Although at length they dropped their Celtic names, they developed no rich urban culture and disappeared from view soon after the Romans crushed them; the few cities remained small islands in a sea of mixed peasantry. Modern Ankara is by far the greatest city that Galatia has ever known. It is still surrounded, however, by a sea of peasants of ancient lineage. One memento of its heterogeneous past is the remains of the Temple of Augustus, adjoining the Seljuk mosque of Haji Bayram, the local saint. It was probably made over from a temple first built by the Attalids of Pergamum; later it became the site of a Byzantine church; and beneath lie the foundations of a Phrygian sanctuary. Worshipers of Allah in the mosque may still contain traces of the blood of the various peoples who worshiped all the other gods on this site.

In its early history Ancyra was not so important as Gordium and Pessinus. It rose with the Romans, who made it the capital of their province of Galatia. In gratitude Ancyra established the new cult of Augustus and Rome, in the extant temple, during the emperor's lifetime. It owed as much to the work of Constantine the Great, surviving its rivals as a station on the main highway from Constantinople to the East. It shifted its allegiance to the Christian God quickly enough to attract a council of bishops, met here to decide what to do about backsliders during the persecution of Diocletian, and then to be Constantine's first choice for the Ecumenical Council that eventually met at Nicaea. Thereafter little is heard of it until it was sacked by the Arabs in 838. Later in the ninth century it was recaptured and refortified by the Byzantines, to serve as a base of operations against the Arabs; holy stones from Palestine were

[2] See the Appendix, Section 11, for the history of Caesarea and Cappadocia.

built into its walls to make it stronger. The stones failed to keep out the Seljuks.

Under the Ottomans, Ancyra ranked among the lesser provincial towns. Now called Angora, it was known chiefly for its goats. When Ataturk made it his headquarters, it had no palatial residences to distract or corrupt the leaders of the new republic, and no such conveniences as hotels and electricity. The typically Turkish old town that survives today on a hilltop, within the walls of the ancient citadel, suggests the austerity and the backwardness in which the republic was born. The citadel walls are a hodgepodge of Byzantine and Turkish construction, on Roman or older foundations, and contain many ancient stones, probably including the holy ones from Palestine; some houses are perched on top of them. The town within is a maze of crooked alleys, picturesque, but lacking any buildings of distinction.

Travelers are nevertheless likely to find it more interesting and charming than the modern city in the plain below. Ataturk imported architects and sculptors, chiefly German, to build and adorn the capital; they laid the groundwork for a fairly handsome but unmemorable city. Still growing, Ankara still has no style of its own. It is a bourgeois city dressed in stucco and chrome, the home of a newly risen middle class that imports its fashions with its modern appliances. It may impress the foreigner as "cosmopolitan" in the Turkish sense of the word, which is now a disparaging sense; a recent dictionary defines a cosmopolitan as one "having no national and local color but assuming the outward form that suits his purpose." An incidental example of its form is a popular restaurant that has an ultra-Bohemian décor out of Greenwich Village, and is patronized chiefly by stolid Turks intent on their food, with no Bohemian spirit whatever. Ankara is a reminder that since the times of the Hittites and the Phrygians Anatolia has contributed little to the world's culture.

Yet the modern city represents a remarkable national effort. It is really up-to-date: airy, clean, spacious, well lit, equipped with the comforts and conveniences that travelers in Turkey learn to appreciate. It is a civilized capital, with sidewalk cafes and better shops and avenues than Istanbul; its public buildings include a brand-new university, an opera, an excellent museum. If somewhat garish, it has an air of vigor and potential permanence. Even its ragged edges may lend it an added dignity. A few blocks from a modern boulevard, one may climb a dirty, congested cobblestone street that straggles up to the old citadel, and from here look down on another hill that is littered with shacks of the many poor who might barely afford the cost of a bus ride down the boulevard; but with the inevitable reflections comes a sharper realization of the energy, pride, and fervor that built Ankara, in a poor, backward land.

Everywhere in Turkey, and most often in Istanbul, a foreign visitor is asked the same eager question: Has he seen Ankara yet? I came to appreciate its meaning one nightfall, when I entered the city on an overland bus crowded with passengers, some coming home, others visiting the city for the first time. The bus sang with their excitement. Ankara at last! For these modern Galatians it was not merely a Washington; it was also a Monticello, a New York, a Hollywood—a national shrine and a wonder city, the metropolis of the future. However imitative or secondhand, Ankara is a genuine national creation. All the new Turkey is in it—the best and the worst, and the average.

So it is well that the old town still stands in the citadel, and that scattered about in the sprawling city below it are ancient remains, of more than one culture. They mark significant continuities as well as contrasts. At the hour of prayer I have seen men prostrating themselves on a business street in Ankara. Turkey has not, after all, made a clean break with its past—no nation can. To understand it, one must keep an eye on the traditions that it has repudiated, and retained.

3. THE REFORMS OF ATATURK

In the process of making the new Turkey, Mustafa Kemal made many enemies, and on both counts inspired extreme judgments of his character that have confused or distorted judgments of his work. He has been pictured as a god, and as a schizophrenic monster. By now, however, there is little question of his main traits. He was certainly not a godly man, nor a humble, gentle, sweetly reasonable one. He was notoriously hard-drinking and hard-living, fond of gambling and women. Although not simply cruel, he was ruthless in disposing of those he regarded as dangerous opponents, exiling some, hanging others. He had terrific energy and determination, a celebrated example of which was his marathon speech in 1927 reviewing his achievements to date—a speech that went on for five days, seven hours a day. Call him a fanatic or call him an idealist, he was indisputably not only a great leader but a sincere patriot, with a blazing faith in his people as well as himself. No merely selfish, ambitious, or unprincipled man would have carried out his program of reform. And this program makes as plain his sincere belief—call it enlightened or call it naïve—in what he described as the "sublime dictates of civilization," represented by the modern West. "We're going to be civilized and proud of it," he told his people. "Look at the state of the rest of the Turks and Moslems!"

Ottoman history had taught him that it was not enough to modernize the army. It was necessary to go whole hog, to modernize government, economy, technology, education, dress—the whole mentality of his people. The major obstacle was clearly Islam: a religion woven through and through the political, intellectual, and social life of its followers, regulating their daily behavior even to the trimming of their beards. Most of the reforms that Ataturk forced through the Grand National Assembly were designed to weaken its hold on the people and remove every trace of theocracy.

In one session in 1924 the Caliphate was abolished, the imperial family deported, public education put under state control, and religious courts abolished. The next year a law still more shocking to pious Moslems compelled all men to wear hats instead of fezzes—hats that they had always felt were an infidel abomination. "We are going to adopt the civilized international mode of dress . . . including a headdress with a brim," Ataturk said in a speech; but an unspoken motive was to discourage prayer, as brims made it difficult to bow the head on the floor. At the same time he preached against the veiling of women and their custom of turning their heads or sitting huddled on the ground when a man passed by. "Gentlemen, do the mothers and daughters of a civilized nation assume this curious attitude, this barbarous posture?" So Ataturk went on: dissolving the powerful dervish orders and closing the magical tombs of their holy men; replacing the ludicrous Islamic calendar by the Gregorian one; ruling out Islam as the state religion and decreeing that any use of religion as a political tool was high treason; giving women the right to vote and to divorce; requiring all Turks to adopt a family name, which most had not had under the Arab system of nomenclature (at this time he himself became Kemal Ataturk); prohibiting the wear of clerical dress in public; converting the holy mosque of Hagia Sophia into a museum; making Sunday an official day of rest.[3]

Probably the most effective of Ataturk's attacks on Islam were his replacement of the Arabic by the Latin script and his reform of the Turkish language. A special commission appointed by him devised a phonetic Turkish alphabet, whereupon the Grand National Assembly dutifully passed a law requiring all books to be printed in it. Schools no longer taught the script and the language in which the Archangel Gabriel had dictated the Koran to Mohammed and in which the classics of Islam were written. The Turkish Linguistic Society founded by Ataturk then set about purifying the language, substituting old Turkish words or new

[3] Friday, the Moslem Sabbath, is not a day of rest. Moslems are revolted by the idea that God needed a rest after creating the world.

coinages for the many Arabic words in the Turkish lexicon. As a result, the young generation was at one stroke cut off from its whole religious and literary heritage—which was precisely his intention. While the literate among the older generation of Turks continued to use Arabic script for their daily purposes (as they still do), they had to learn the new Turkish if they wanted to keep up with the news, or in particular to retain their positions in public life. By the same stroke Ataturk had made them all officially illiterate.

Needless to add, the wisdom of his measures is debatable, and still more so the question of their lasting success. But before surveying the state of Turkey today, let us first consider some basic implications of Ataturk's achievement. We have grown all too aware of the impersonal, unconscious forces that make history, and are likely to feel impotent, at their mercy, in the vast world drama today. Ataturk showed that greatness still counts for something. If the new Turkey was made possible by the fortitude and heroism, and later the docility, of the Anatolian peasant, it was primarily his creation. More broadly, he showed that men can still make their history by conscious thought and will. There was nothing inevitable about his feat, seen even in retrospect; it would be hard to find any decisive event in history less predictable. It follows, moreover, that men can change as well as "the times." Within limits they can and do consciously readapt themselves to new conditions—as in a revolutionary world they are forced to. In the name of realism the "new conservatives" are now harping on the old refrain that you can't change human nature, human nature is everywhere the same, and its essence is Original Sin. Granted that you can't make angels of men (even by religion), Ataturk forces the realistic questions of the means and ends of social change, and the specific cultural obstacles.

In *New Lives for Old* Margaret Mead analyzed the astonishing achievement of the Manus of New Guinea, who in one generation have leaped over thousands of years of history, deliberately transforming their primitive culture into an essentially modern one complete with democracy, suffrage, schools, money, medicine, church, and individual responsibility. The implication, she suggests, is that rapid change is not only possible but more desirable than the partial, gradual change of traditional wisdom. Instead of here and there patching, grafting, clipping, and altering, and like as not creating new discrepancies and discordances, a purposeful group might better seek to transform the whole pattern at once, eliminate constant reminders of the past, and develop a complete, consistent set of new habits. Miss Mead believes that this is the lesson and the glory of America: a "new land" in which millions of immigrants at once began adapting themselves to a radically new life. The measure of their success developed the most precious gift of America to the world, the faith that "men can learn and change—quickly, happily, without violence, without madness, without coercion, and of their own free will." In this view, Ataturk faced a rather different problem: he had to remake an old land, at first through violence, always with a measure of coercion. But he had the essential faith of America, and he adopted the essential policy of the Manus, trying to open up his society on every front and to make it uniformly Western.

Now it is unthinkable that Turkey could become thoroughly Westernized in one generation. As Miss Mead herself points out, the "modern" culture of the Manus is still slight in content, and at that not wholly consistent. Their experience is hardly a reliable guide for a large nation with a much older tradition, a much more complex culture, much greater material and intellectual needs. Still, by this approach we might better understand the whole program of Ataturk, the basic problems of the new Turkey, and the basic reasons for its shortcomings, beyond Original Sin. We are led, finally, to the comparable issues in our own life.

"If in the last few years we have been able to save ourselves," Ataturk told his fellow countrymen, "it has been because of the change in our mentality. We can never stop again. We're going on, whatever happens; we can't go back. We must go on; we have no choice." So it is with all of us today: there is no going back to a simpler society, no sitting tight. No more can those of us who know and cherish a free society voluntarily surrender its values or ever be content with a life of bondage, really believe that ignorance is bliss. And as we know too well that we may lose our freedoms, we might reconsider what Ataturk, in a possibly naïve exaltation, called the "sublime dictates of civilization"—*our* civilization. It is now fashionable to despise Western civilization, or to despair of it. Arnold Toynbee has won a halo by proclaiming that all its distinctive achievements are only "vain repetitions of the heathen." We might come to appreciate more the values it has created as we survey both the successes and the failures of the new Turkey.

4. TURKEY TODAY: WEST AND EAST

Toynbee has displayed a somewhat odd sympathy for Turkey, considering that its major aspiration comes down to a secondhand repetition of the heathen. The evident reason for his sympathy is that he was on the scene during the early days of the adventure, and in its exhilaration could forget his religious thesis. Today a visitor from the West is more likely to be depressed by the poverty and backwardness of Turkey, and if he stays long enough he is sure to be exasperated by its officialdom. But to appreciate the impressive advance it has made, he has only to read the accounts of travelers to Ottoman Turkey. Ataturk had to start almost from scratch.

The immediate legacy of the Ottomans was an illiterate peasantry, which for centuries had been farming by primitive methods. Most aspired to little more than the possession of an ox or an extra wife. They had no incentive to produce more than their generally self-sufficient village required. There were no really good roads in the country, and only a few thousand miles of passable ones. There was one railroad that set out from Constantinople, split into two main branches, and threw out a few smaller branches. Peasants who did have access to a larger market had no canning industry to take their surplus. There were no technicians to teach them improved methods in a country ignorant of science and indifferent to all but military technology. They were prey to such diseases as trachoma, malaria, and typhoid, in a country as ignorant of hygiene and indifferent to public sanitation. They were the more lethargic because their religion disposed them to fatalism and hostility to change.

Urban Turkey was more literate and cultured, but by modern standards almost as backward. The Ottomans had developed no industry to speak of except textiles. Foreigners controlled the mines, as they owned the railroad they had built; Turks had learned to resent them, but had learned little else. Brought up to regard business as degrading, they had slight experience in organizing and managing. A few entered professional life, with the help of a few schools that provided some elements of a Western education, but education was still dominated by the ultraconservative ulema. The main field of opportunity, beyond the military and clerical professions, was the Ottoman bureaucracy. Aside from its ingrained corruption, the administrative system was a model of waste and inefficiency, as unco-ordinated as highly centralized, almost perfectly designed to bungle its only policy—expediency. Its object was not to plan, initiate, or manage but simply to collect and control, and its methods promoted the universal distrust that it premised, effectively discouraging co-operation. It left almost no scope for individual initiative or positive action. It held up chiefly because of the often-noted tendency of the mass of Turks to regard an act of government much as an act of God. They expected both to be arbitrary, and had no more voice in one than in the other.

All in all, Ottoman Turkey was distinctly inferior in government, in culture, in technology, and in material well-being to the Roman province of Asia. Only Constantinople, and perhaps Greek Smyrna, could compare with the great cities of antiquity. While Ataturk could draw on the knowledge and skills of the West, he had to work with a people the over-whelming majority of whom were inexperienced, untrained, unprepared for his demands on them.

I shall not cite statistics (never quite reliable or up-to-date in Turkey) on the material progress the nation has made: the mineral resources developed; the industries, railway system, and merchant marine built up; the irrigation and reclamation projects; the mileage of new and improved roads; the number of tractors, trucks, and busses; etc. For my purposes I should remark only that a periodic visitor to Turkey may cease belittling the material goods provided by Western civilization. He may now move around the country in relative comfort by bus or car, on roads that only a few years ago were fit only for oxcarts. He may travel by airplane, with some thought of how dazzled the ancient seafaring Greeks would have been by such wonders. He may understand the pride of many a town in its new electricity or refrigerating plant. He may realize the blessings of medicine and public health services. Malaria, for one thing, has been largely eliminated from regions that were once hellholes. Malaria weakens the despised flesh without making for a purer or loftier spirituality.

The social progress of Turkey has been spottier, but it too becomes more impressive after a look at the rest of the Moslem world. Islam has likewise begun to rouse itself from the intellectual torpor of five centuries. It is taking up Western science and technology; it is astir with ideas of independence, and some new political ideas; it has introduced some reforms, notably an improvement in the status of women. Yet Moslem countries have made only slight progress toward general well-being. The plainest reason for their backwardness is the moral and intellectual limitations of their ruling class; or to put it more plainly, the rottenness of their social and political structure. Edward Atiyah, a candid champion of the Arab world, spells out its root evils: "the poverty and ignorance of the vast majority . . . the little-cared-for health and well-being of the masses . . . the selfishness and cynicism of the big merchants and land-owners . . . the inefficiency and corruption of the governments that grew out of, and reflected, this unhealthy state of society." The reformers of Islam, who are mostly middle-class men with a Western education, still deny that its religion is at all responsible for the unhealthy state; but at least its religious ruling class has something to do with it. The ulema remain fundamentalists, typically allied with the wealthy and powerful, typically hostile to efforts at enlightenment and reform.

By contrast, secular Turkey has wrought wonders. Its government is relatively responsible and free from large-scale corruption. Although the success of its land reforms is debatable, there is little question that the peasants—still the great majority of the population—are on the whole better off than they were under the Ottomans, or than they are today in other Moslem countries. Turkey has fewer big landlords and many fewer fellahin; the gulf between rich and poor is not so wide and fixed. Peasants no longer regard as a natural enemy a government that subsidizes their wheat crop and exempts them from the income tax. In recent years many have become prosperous enough to buy radios, and so are less confined to their village world. Their children have a far better chance to become farmers instead of peasants. Illiteracy has been considerably reduced by an original experiment in rural education; in Village Institutes qualified students are trained at government expense and then sent back to the villages at teachers.

Most remarkable, in view of Moslem tradition, is the emancipation of women. In the larger cities they have become actually free; many are quite different from their mothers in mentality, or the Moslem idea of "human nature." If they do not enjoy full equality of opportunity, in a world still dominated by men, they enjoy a better opportunity in the professions than American women have yet won, and in commerce and industry receive the same pay as men. They contribute to the growth of a middle class. Such a class seems essential to Westernization and—Marx notwithstanding—to a healthy democracy.[4]

The new middle class is still small in Turkey, however, and naturally not sure of itself. It is given to naïve forms of conspicuous consumption; it is apt to put its first electric refrigerator in the parlor. Its dubious taste appears in the many pretentious public buildings and monuments in Ankara and provincial capitals. And these buildings bring up a more serious matter than taste. Their excessive cost may be justified as an expression of national pride or as a stimulus to self-confidence; yet it has meant the sacrifice of more urgent needs. An elegant hospital is likely to have an inadequate, poorly trained staff. An ambitious program of industrialization concentrated on heavy industries, including even an airplane engine factory, though the country still makes no airplanes; while such humbler, potentially much more helpful industries as food processing were slighted. In general, Turkey has been more concerned about forms and appearances than about substance. Hence the appearances suffer too.

Leaving Ankara, one immediately travels back thousands of years, into a primitive village culture. Most Anatolian peasants still make a bare living by tilling the soil with a wooden stick or plow, threshing with a

---

[4] Lacking a middle class, Toynbee observed, Russia and other countries seeking to modernize themselves have depended on an intelligentsia. Hence the current affinity of the Hindu, Chinese, and Islamic intelligentsia with the Russians.

sled, hauling their crops in oxcarts. They live in drab little villages, hud-
dles of mud brick. In Turkish towns a few fancy avenues may only call
attention to the shabbiness and dirtiness of the other streets. Sanitation is
still primitive, and like agriculture reflects the severe shortage of scientists, technicians, engineers, skilled workmen—the builders of the indispensable material foundations of modern civilization. Here too the Turks
have not concentrated on fundamentals.

Now the continued poverty and backwardness are not at all surprising.
Much more significant is the effort to overcome them, and the measure of
its success. The effort is still going on, as Ataturk said it must. It is going
on in spite of the large standing army that Turkey has felt obliged to
maintain in order to secure its independence against Russia. Yet as we
applaud this effort we are forced to consider the major obstacles to it,
apart from limited material resources. Ataturk himself provided the text.
The Turks had saved themselves, he said, by changing their mentality.
More important than the material changes and the new social forms—and
generally neglected in the mass of statistics—is the mentality of his people
today.

The Manus, observed Margaret Mead, belie the common assumption
that people merely submit to change—they completely wanted change.
So did Ataturk. One pertinent question is whether most of his fellow
Turks did, or now do. They clearly want the material goods of Western
civilization, they appear to want many of its cultural goods, they at least
like to think that they want its freedoms; but do they want to acquire the
habits necessary to produce the goods, the attitudes necessary to realize
the values and secure the freedoms? Do they really want to be like
Westerners? They need not, of course—they might work out their salvation in better ways. But sticking to the text of Ataturk, do they still want
to be different from "the rest of the Turks and Moslems"? Immediately,
this question leads to a basic paradox. The main drive behind the
program of Ataturk was an ideal that he adopted in all sincerity, for
understandable reasons, with Western sanction, and that contributed
greatly to his initial successes; but an ideal that also tended increasingly
to defeat his main purposes. This was nationalism.

Ataturk's crusade naturally aroused bitter opposition. Godly Turks
fought most fiercely to keep their fezzes (which a century before they
had as fiercely resented); a number of holy men had to be hanged for
their open resistance to the new law. In Bursa a "Revolutionary Committee for the Protection of the Moslem Religion" stirred up enough
trouble to cause more executions, while near Smyrna a dervish provided
the new Turkey with a martyr by decapitating a young officer who tried

to break up a demonstration against the "impious Republic." Probably Ataturk could not have pushed through his reforms had he not offered his countrymen the substitute religion of nationalism. "We Turks," he said, "are a people who throughout our history have been a byword for freedom and independence"; and he made them believe this whopper. He had an advantage over the rest of the Moslem world, indeed, in that the Turks had never been "natives" under foreign domination. Throughout the prolonged sickness of the Ottoman Empire they had at least retained their independence, and with it the notion that they were by nature a ruling race. At the same time, Ataturk made his cause simpler and clearer by rejecting Pan-Turkism with Pan-Islam, dismissing the dream of uniting the heterogeneous Turkish-speaking peoples of central Asia, warning against imperial ambitions. His slogan remained Turkey for the Turks.

This was a truly inspiring ideal during the Revolution and the early days of the Republic. But even then its price came high. The Kurds in the eastern provinces caught the contagion of nationalism; they sought their independence in an unsuccessful rebellion that left hard feeling in more than a million of these "Mountain Turks." The vaunted unity and strength of the Turkish nation were also belied by discrimination against the remaining Greeks and Armenians; the nation deprived itself of much-needed talent by debarring them from public service. The Turks themselves suffered from delusions of grandeur as their scholars, encouraged by Ataturk, began manufacturing a glorious past for them. They were taught that Turks were the authors of civilization, that the Turkish language was the mother of all languages. One proof was that both the Sumerians and the Hittites were Turks (a myth that survives in the names of two big national banks, the Sumer and the Eti). Another was that they originated the epic: although they had never bothered to write one, it was their heroic deeds that first inspired epics. This nonsense is no longer so fashionable, but it has left a large residue of complacence and conservatism in a people who are still far from the promised land of Ataturk.

While Turkey remains plastered with pictures of Ataturk, it has understandably lost much of the revolutionary ardor of the early days. With the cooling off, its nationalism has hardened into an exaggerated national pride that resents any criticism from within or without, that may readily be exploited by the self-seeking or cynical, and that generally represents as little clear understanding, firm faith, or lofty idealism as 100 per cent Americanism does. Turkism has proved costlier in a nation less able to afford such self-indulgence. It has discouraged searching criticism or revaluation by making "Turk-disparagement" a punishable offense. By closing such outlets for social tensions it has incidentally intensified the hatred of minorities, who serve as scapegoats; hence the ugly 1955 riots against the Greeks in Istanbul, in which well-organized mobs ran wild and destroyed millions of dollars worth of property. The national pride has levied a still heavier toll by constantly obstructing the Western aid that the nation seeks in order to realize its new purposes, for officials are always prone to regard as an insult any criticism of Turkish methods and to disregard suggestions of different methods. They are the despair of technicians who try to teach them how to use and maintain machinery.

The final paradox of Turkism is its glorification of the Ottoman Empire. Turks seem most sensitive about any disparagement of the past that in effect they have repudiated. A few years ago a major Istanbul newspaper ran scream headlines about another "fanatical" foreign professor who had insulted the Turkish nation in a book about Turkish art and architecture of the fifteenth and sixteenth centuries, which he praised as at least equal to the work of contemporary Europe; the insult was his common- place observation that Ottoman architecture was indebted to Byzantine architecture. Thus a proud people whose main effort is now to imitate Western civilization retains its pride by furiously resenting the idea that its ancestors ever imitated anybody or anything. And the Ottoman past is in fact very much alive—Ataturk did not succeed in cutting his people off from it. The major internal threats to the prospects of Turkey may be summed up as relics of its Ottoman heritage, and symbolized by the preposterous treasures of the sultans that it exhibits as objects of pride instead of an object lesson.

The plainest incubus remains the inherited mentality of the Turkish peasant. For all his sturdy virtues, he is something less than an en- lightened political animal. While he appreciates the uses of the tractor and the jeep—"the donkey of the infidels"—he has hardly learned these uses, even apart from his ignorance of machinery. Given the usually small holding that makes him too poor to buy a tractor, he might join his neighbors in some form of co-operative ownership and use, but he does not take to such co-operation. Moslem and Ottoman tradition never encouraged the free association of individuals for independent purposes, nor does the Turkish government encourage it today. And if the peasant remains an individualist of sorts, he still lacks energy and enterprise. Turkey's large standing army, all reporters say, is a drain on its man power as well as its finances. From my own observation, Turkish man power in the village spends most of the day sitting in the coffeehouse. The peasant is not really lazy or shiftless—he can stand up under brutal toil without complaint. He is merely sluggish, and accustomed to having his womenfolk do field as well as housework.[5]

The economy of Turkey naturally suffers from the limited output and buying power of most of its peasants, but as naturally from inexperience and pride. Economic missions from the West have offered a great deal of technical criticism (mostly ignored by Turkish officialdom) of national policies in operating and controlling industry and finance. A layman might say simply that in both State and private enterprises, managers and workers have yet to master the technical skills and acquire the basic co-operative habits of modern industry. He may realize the importance of the simple, familiar attitudes involved in the maintenance and repair of machinery. Turks rarely give the machine the loving care that comes naturally in lands where it has long been at home, and is viewed as a thing of beauty as well as use.

Political maladministration is a plainer legacy of the Ottomans. Although Ataturk early declared that the old bureaucracy was too hopelessly bad to be reformed and that the system would have to be built all over again, this feat was apparently beyond his powers. Government remains a fantastic system of red tape, laboriously unrolled by a host of underpaid, more or less incompetent underlings, in which the simplest operation—such as getting a package out of customs—involves the accumulation of a stack of papers, signed and countersigned by a chain of clerks, stamped with one or more of the ninety-eight varieties of tax stamps. The essence is still meticulous attention to form, for the sake of collection and control, with no regard for dispatch, economy, or the substance of efficiency. In keeping with the authoritarian tradition of the Ottomans, the chief executives are not disposed to delegate their authority, while lesser officials are typically subservient, fearful of doing anything that might displease their superiors; hence the men at the top are swamped by routine papers to sign and trifling decisions to make. The alleged free and independent spirit of the Turks is further discouraged because an avowed policy of decentralization has remained nominal. The national government appoints local officials, from the governors of

[5] Misled by peasants, I once hiked over a mountain to visit the "ruins" of an ancient Greek city. It turned out to be a gray, ghostly town of skeletal houses, roofless and eyeless, that had been deserted since the war won by Ataturk. It lay on the slope of a fertile bowl and had evidently been a lively, prosperous town, well built in stone; its Greek inhabitants had also built a cobblestone road over the mountain to the nearest port. Today the road is dilapidated, and below the town straggles a poor Turkish village. My local guide "explained" that its inhabitants had built a new village instead of occupying the deserted stone houses because they were so few and so poor. He could not recall the name of the Greek town.

provinces to the attorneys of towns. Although the provinces and towns also elect their own officials, these chiefly take care of routine matters, such as street cleaning. Local enterprise is controlled by the outsiders sent in by Ankara.

In all this many observers have seen chiefly the ogre of "socialism," which in Turkey has not been creeping. *Étatisme* was one of the explicit principles of Ataturk's Republic, later written into its Constitution. But a more fundamental issue is Turkish democracy. This has grown more acute in recent years, even though more private enterprise has been permitted. For the "Republic" that Ataturk was instrumental in setting up was actually a one-party totalitarian state. He himself, its President, was a dictator. Elected President by a bare majority of the Grand National Assembly, he was suspicious of opposition and soon began muzzling it, exiling liberals who wanted more democracy.

Most would grant, I assume, that Ataturk could not possibly have set up at once a full-fledged democracy in a nation 80 per cent peasant, 90 per cent illiterate, almost wholly inexperienced in democratic procedures. Only by dictatorship could he force through his liberal reforms. Free private enterprise was no more feasible in a nation that had few technicians, and that had long had its business run chiefly by Greeks and Armenians. (When the Greeks were eliminated from Smyrna, for instance, the managers of the railroads there found that they had lost 90 per cent of their personnel.) Ataturk's goal nevertheless seems to have been a Western type of state. While he got his way by coercion, he sought tirelessly to explain and persuade and did not impose his reforms by systematic violence, as Communists have done. He was probably sincere when he wrote, in 1930, "I have always been whole-heartedly in favor of the system of free discussion of national affairs, and the seeking of the nation's best interests by the efforts of all men and parties of good-will." At least he prepared the way for democracy at this time by allowing a liberal, Fethi, to form an opposition party and enter the municipal elections. Its program called for less state control and more freedom of speech and press.

This experiment collapsed, however. Although Fethi was greeted by enthusiastic crowds, the People's Party of Ataturk denounced his followers as Communists and reactionaries. Municipal authorities, mystified by the freedom granted such enemies of the State, or aghast at it, dutifully intimidated the voters and rigged the elections. Fethi dissolved his Liberal Republican Party in the year of its birth. In the same year the government dissolved another new party. It might be said that Ataturk's dictatorship was vindicated—Turkey was not yet ready for democracy.

Upon his death in 1938, at any rate, his immediate legacy was an authoritarian regime still run by one party.

So far history has written an uncertain verdict on his political handiwork. At the close of World War II his successor, Ismet Inönü, announced that he thought Turkey could now afford an opposition party, whereupon a group took him at his word and formed the Democratic Party. In the 1946 national election it won so large a number of votes—how large is unknown—that it was allowed to elect some members of the Grand National Assembly. Then, in 1950, an honest election was held under a new law providing for a secret ballot and the public counting of votes. As a result the Democrats elected an overwhelming majority in the Assembly. Democracy, it appeared, had at last triumphed in Turkey. In America, which had begun aiding Turkey a few years before, official rejoicing was louder because the victorious party favored the encouragement of private enterprise and foreign investment.

But its triumph was not due simply to a passion for democracy. Among its principal supporters were religious conservatives, who had been promised that Islam would be restored to its privileged position. The Democrats fulfilled their promises by various measures, such as introducing religious instruction in the schools. They have a habit of branding as "atheists" those who still wish to separate Church and State, as Ataturk himself obviously did. And once in power, the Democrats began oppressing the party of Ataturk and Inönü, another hero of the Revolution. Among other things, they shut down its many branch headquarters and took over the plant of its leading newspaper, which had been founded by Ataturk. They jailed newspapermen for criticizing the government; a new law prescribed severer penalties for spreading news "calculated to endanger the political and economic stability of the country." Another decisive victory in the election of 1954, which left the Republican People's Party with only a few seats in the Grand National Assembly, made the Democrats no more tolerant of this fractional opposition. Many wondered aloud whether the opposition party ought not to be suppressed. The government was given more arbitrary power over the universities and the press.

Even so, the voters can still throw out the Democrats too. Most important for the long run may be the sufficiently remarkable fact that a party in absolute power voluntarily gave up this power, and that Turkey has already progressed far enough to have really free elections. For the present, however, it appears that most Turks have yet to acquire the inbred attitudes essential to a free society. They have little idea of the usefulness of a loyal opposition; their politicians are apt to consider opposition at best a nuisance, always dangerous, even treasonable. On the subject of freedom they may recall the caliph who declared that tolerance was an excellent thing, except in matters of religion and government. Thus an Istanbul daily broke out in an indignant editorial attacking an opposition newspaper for giving an American reporter the impression that Turkey did not enjoy complete freedom of the press, and concluding that if this newspaper continued spreading such libels on the Turkish nation, it should be closed down for good. This logic makes more understandable why the proud Turks submit docilely to other restrictions on their independence. Workers are not allowed to strike, soldiers or police to vote, state employees to marry foreigners.

The cause of freedom is unlikely to be advanced by the resurgence of Islam, another token of the Ottoman mentality and the plainest threat to the reforms of Ataturk. For the masses of Turks the "return to religion" fostered by the Democrats was only a recognition of the status quo. All along they have regarded themselves as Moslems, and while they obediently took off their fez they remained attached to their mosques, their holy men, and their fetishes for warding off the evil eye; peasant women continued to shroud and avert their faces (as they still do in the old sections of Ankara itself). Educated Turks, like their counterparts in Christian countries, are disposed to a variety of religious attitudes—skeptical, lukewarm, liberal, earnest, worried—that makes it impossible to say how deep the revival goes or where it will lead.[6] Our own religious thinkers may rejoice in the thought that all this proves the inadequacy of any purely secular ideal such as Ataturk's. Meanwhile the most apparent results of the official encouragement of Islam have been outbursts of fanaticism, involving the desecration of statues of Ataturk and attacks upon the West. Although at the moment the fanatics are not numerous, nor conservatives yet disposed to ally Turkey with the rest of the Moslem world, they suggest that a continued religious revival might not promote the cause of world peace and good will. Most plainly they emphasize that Turkey still faces the basic problem of reconciling its new way of life with its traditional faith.

Such confusions, together with the cooling of revolutionary ardor and

[6] Toynbee, who specializes in long-range visions of still higher religions and a possible spiritual unification of the world, has written that Islam has "a mighty spiritual mission still to carry out"; but in an essay on its possible contribution to the West he dwelt only on its freedom from racial prejudice and its injunctions against the evils of alcohol. If Islam sticks to its orthodoxy, one may doubt that it will have much to offer the rest of the civilized world. If its modernists win control, it might carry out some kind of spiritual mission, but what this would be or how it would affect the world is anybody's guess.

the discouragement of independent thought and action, help to explain why the new Turkey has still to develop an art and culture of its own. Its young people have been taking with some enthusiasm to drama, poetry, painting, and music, using native materials, but treating them in imitative Western styles. The more sophisticated are prone to such fashions as surrealism, which give only the illusion of originality. Nationalism has not proved a vital inspiration to creative writers and thinkers, if only because neither the Ottoman tradition nor the synthetic past of Turkey provides them with much nourishment. On the other hand the folk, in their semi-Western dress, have been losing much of their tradition in art and handicraft. Chanakkale on the Dardanelles, once known for its pottery, now turns out a hideous ware, with blotches of ornament in gaudy color splashed on crudely executed designs. Modern Turkish rugs run to a similar gaudiness; their sellers boast that they are made with chemical instead of the old vegetable dyes. The many beautiful things still to be found in the bazaars of Turkey are almost wholly its antiquities, or the humble utensils and furnishings made in the traditional style by nameless craftsmen. The sentimental will say that here is another proof of the blight of the Machine. It is rather a sign that the Turks have not yet mastered the modern arts of industrial design, realized the possibilities of the machine.

Ultimately it points to the basic failing of the new Turkey, underlying all its specific shortcomings—its public education. Standards are pardonably low, given the limited resources of the country and the novelty of the whole effort. But at best it is a formalistic education, prescribed by Ankara, designed to stock the heads of the young rather than to teach the young idea how to shoot. Although its principles and methods were largely borrowed from France and Germany, the memory drill is less paralyzing in those countries because they have traditions of scientific inquiry, independent research, and free thought. Turkey has no such traditions. As a bold experiment, still on trial, it has the more need of a bold experimental spirit, or at least of men trained for the creative enterprise that it sorely lacks in all fields. Instead, it is in effect maintaining the Ottoman tradition of teaching the letter and the form, training docility and unimaginativeness, promoting orthodoxy—educating for the bureaucratic life.

The result is apparent in the two major universities, of Istanbul and Ankara. They contain their quota of eager, earnest students, and a few exceptional ones interested in reading and thinking for themselves. But the great majority do not wish to question or discuss, or many even to read. They wish only to memorize the professor's lectures. The most earnest memorize thoroughly, mechanically, indiscriminately. Foreign professors in all fields report the same experience: they can train the best of their Turkish students to follow instructions faithfully, but very few to do independent, sustained research. The students are not simply lazy—they have not been trained to think clearly, not been encouraged or even permitted to think for themselves. Especially in the controversial subjects of history and government (which no foreigner is allowed to teach), they are merely indoctrinated. Their professors are themselves members of a rigid hierarchy, built on military lines with something like military principles of authority and subservience, relieved only by the casualness and confusion that underlie all the elaborate Turkish appearances of system. They too have to be circumspect, for the nominally autonomous universities remain under the effective supervision of Ankara. They take for granted that among their students are government informers or spies.

I should now repeat that the shortcomings of Turkey are much less surprising than its achievements. No nation can make over its whole mentality in one generation, and none of the previous peoples in Asia Minor—including the Greeks and the early Christians—ever made such an effort. Americans have been having as hard a time in rooting out a single tradition, the prejudice against the Negro. That Turks are unable to understand this prejudice might remind us of our similar shortcomings, in spite of our much longer experience in democracy. American farmers are not conspicuously enlightened voters; the American military yield to none in their devotion to intricate precautions against economy and dispatch; American bureaucracy—in big business as well as government—is no model of flexibility and imaginativeness, and breeds its quota of yes men; many American students have little passion for reading or thinking, and their parents still less; most Americans are hostile to the critical spirit, except when it is directed at liberals, eggheads, and other such Communists in disguise; and so on. I should also repeat that it remains an open question whether men at large can acquire and maintain under stress the attitudes or habits of thought essential to the successful working of a free, open society in a revolutionary world. I have dwelt on the shortcomings of the new Turkey because they make clearer the fundamental importance of such attitudes, which Americans are apt to take for granted even though they may not be ingrained deeply enough in the national life, and which Turks are apt to overlook because of the new forms or appearances in their life.

5. THE NEGLECTED SIMPLICITIES

"Turkey is a lunatic asylum," a distinguished Turkish writer once confided to me. It may well seem so as one reads an article in a nationalistic newspaper, or spends a day wandering through a maze of "controls" and affixing tax stamps to a growing sheaf of papers in order to get some simple permit, or watches a friend go through the required farce of divorcing his American wife because he is about to do his two-year stint in the Turkish army, which America supplies with arms. Still, my informant was proud of having fought in the Revolution, deeply devoted to the Anatolian peasant, as deeply attached to the Turkish tradition of courtesy and hospitality. This asylum is full of exceptionally sturdy, friendly, gracious inmates.

"What is it to know man in particular?" wrote Voltaire. "It is to know fools and scoundrels. . . . The case is quite different with the study of man in general. Here he exhibits greatness and his divine origins." The human race is indeed much greater than the mostly mediocre individuals who compose it, its collective accomplishment infinitely beyond the capacity of its most gifted individuals. Yet the reverse of Voltaire's dictum is no less true. The ordinary man is often more decent than the great man, the individual often superior to the collective—in particular to the nation. Nations have an especial aptitude for behaving like fools and scoundrels. Perhaps the worst thing to be said about Turkey is that it exemplifies so conspicuously the contrast between the decent little man and the many stupid institutions that govern him. It is official Turkey that gets into the newspapers and the history books—as in my own chapter on the Ottoman Empire, and in most of this one so far. Neither chapter has done justice to the Turks. So I now propose to take up informally the simplicities of everyday life, the ways of the ordinary folk who play so minor a part in recorded history. In our own lives we know how important they are. The folk deserve more attention than they get or ever can get in studies of the distant past, because as the products of history they may give more concrete, human meaning to the sweeping generalizations about it; because we have come to realize that their habits, interests, attitudes, and beliefs, as well as their toil and blood, do play an important role in making history, even if they are not conscious agents of it; and because many of us have come to believe that among its major "meanings" is the effort to ease, enlighten, and enrich their lives.

These simplicities are still complex enough. They involve decencies and indecencies, confusions and contradictions, and they can be reported only through personal impressions, which may not be just. In Turkey they involve the inescapable continuities and contrasts of an ancient, many-peopled land. I accordingly begin with a party of happy, sentimental Greeks that steamed into Antalya a few years ago to revisit the homeland from which they had been removed in the exchange of populations thirty years before. Official Turkey had at last allowed them to return as tourists, but was still suspicious; their chartered buses were delayed an hour or so before the police gave the necessary permission for an expedition along the shore. The ordinary Turks who gathered about their buses to stare at them seemed friendly. There was no sign of the traditional hostility, except perhaps the condescending air of the Greeks. They were better dressed, more civilized in manner, and much more animated than the Turks. Even so they did not have all the better of the contrast. On the expedition they carried on like voluble youngsters, chattering and arguing excitedly; once the whole bus was in a sudden uproar, which as suddenly subsided. They made the staring Turks seem grave and dignified. The ancient Greeks, I imagine, may have made much the same impression on the natives they encountered; may have seemed by contrast as bright and juvenile.

But there is no idolizing the Turkish peasant. Even if one knew nothing of his mentality, his appearance and his manner resist all effort to see in him a simple, unspoiled child of nature. Usually he looks even poorer than he is in his tasteless Western clothes, which cannot be worn with dignity or style and give him little means of self-expression except the tilt of his ugly cap or the woolliness of his ugly vest. As he and his fellows gathered about the Greeks in Antalya, so they may gather in a circle about a stranger in the village and slowly press in, staring like cows. A foreigner can understand the open-mouthed curiosity, but can only wonder what goes on in the mind of this peasant as he sits for hours in the coffeehouse, sometimes playing backgammon or discussing politics, but as often simply sitting, silent. Although he smiles freely, and in time one learns that he relishes a simple, broad kind of humor, he still seems a somber, unimaginative type, partly because of the puritanical Moslem tradition, but also because of something in the Turkish or Anatolian tradition—the Arab is much livelier. There is little color in the Anatolian village, little gaiety, little dance and song.

I have commented on the solemn intentness of the village dancers in Antakya: men carefully going through the prescribed motions, which now and then entailed a leap or gambol, but which stirred little evident joy in either the performers or the onlookers. I should now stress that the dancers were all men. There were no women in the audience either. One never sees the peasant women in the coffeehouses, or as hostesses in the home. One sees them only at work in the fields or the barnyards, or come to town for market day; and there is no more depressing sight in Turkey. An occasional glimpse of a young face or a bright costume only accentuates the drabness of most of the women, ageless, shapeless, sexless creatures of toil, bundled up in garments that may display just enough color or design to suggest some pride in their appearance, and to make the pride more pathetic. They are no more seductive than farm animals, and not much more enlightened.[7] One may assume that the women meet affection and wield authority in the home, especially when old. One may try sympathetically to understand that Moslems are shocked by infidels who value their womenfolk so little as to expose them to other men. In the end one must declare that this Moslem tradition is a plain curse. It is a curse upon not only the women but the men, and particularly the young. It denies them the simple, natural pleasures of social life that almost all other peoples enjoy.

Nevertheless this unprepossessing peasant does have a genuine dignity. Lacking the liveliness and charm of the Greeks, he may impress one more because he is not eager to impress, or concerned about appearances. His simple, old-fashioned virtues might shame his betters. They are bound up with his limitations, but they also set off the costs of sophistication.

He has always been known for his fidelity, fortitude, and courage. No soldier is sturdier or braver. For me the platitudes came to life when an American officer told me of his visit to the Russian frontier, at a post where a Turkish squad faced two Russian companies. The Russians were entrenched behind the usual barbed wire, with guard towers looking down on the usual plowed strip. The Turks had only a machine gun and a guardhouse, and come war would be wiped out in a minute. Their pay was less than a dollar a month. And the officer reported that the morale of the squad was superb. All were proud and happy: eight Turks against two hundred Russians—it was just as it ought to be. The sophisticated may add, rightly, that this was not simply courage. It was also lack of imagination, fortified by ignorance; these peasant soldiers had no conception of communism, knew only that Russia had always been the enemy. They reflected a somewhat pathetic pride of the Turks, who in the confidence that their soldiers will die bravely, do not yet realize that they would die very quickly. Still, we cannot afford to disparage the spirit of this squad. Once upon a time it had made the Ottomans a great power; more recently it had won the Revolution; and so far it was preserving the independence of Turkey.

A purer virtue is the honesty of the peasant, ingrained by Moslem

---

[7] A schoolteacher told me that the women in his village were very much interested in birth control, but he dared not give out such knowledge. So they will go on bearing more men to sit in the coffeehouses.

tradition. In the cities and larger towns many Turks are going the way of commercial societies. Merchants and hotel men are learning to be smart, to recognize tourists as fair game; cab drivers are apt to be robbers, like their brethren over much of the world. Dishonesty is bred by routine petty bribery, since civil servants are paid so poorly that they are almost obliged to accept favors if they wish to live decently. But in rural Turkey one is very rarely cheated, almost never robbed. The villager has none of the smartness or cockiness of the half-educated man on the American street. And his honesty is warmed by the friendliness and hospitality that make the "terrible Turk" most likable. He is quick to offer the visitor his services as guide, porter, or custodian, with no thought of pay; he will refuse any offer of money. He still maintains the ancient tradition of hospitality to the passing stranger, which Mohammed specifically enjoined. The stranger—even the infidel—is lodged and fed without charge.

It can be a witless hospitality. The village elders may come to the guest room to sit and stare at the uncomfortable guest. "It is our duty, sir," the guide is always likely to say when one thanks him; and the duty is sometimes discharged in a perfunctory manner. None the less this old-world custom is a charming one, and might make us wistful. We cannot instantly welcome the stranger at the door—he is likely to be a salesman, trained to get his foot in. In our busy land we must expect to pay for all services. In Turkey itself the custom is doomed by modernization. With better roads and more traffic, villages will be unable to maintain it, and the stranger will be expected to go on to a hotel in the nearest town.

I felt most keenly the charm of the old world, and the strain of the new one, when I spent a night at Eski Antalya, on the site of ancient Side. My welcome was at first not at all warm, for it was a poor village and because of excavations on the site had had to entertain too many travelers of late. Nevertheless I was put up in the guesthouse, atop the old sea walls. It was bare, furnished only with a mat and mattress, but thoroughly scrubbed. Presently the headman of the village came in bearing a large tray on his head, apologizing for the simple fare of beans, tomatoes, cheese, and bread: it was the best that the village could afford. Later, in the coffeehouse, I listened to the villagers talking of their need of water to irrigate their fields. They expected the government to supply it in time, but *yavaş, yavaş*—slowly, slowly. "Haste comes from the Devil," runs an old Turkish proverb, "slowness from God." All about were the ruins of the once splendid city of Side, a mile of them—theater, gymnasia, baths, temples, tombs, houses with colonnaded patios. They included the remains of an aqueduct that had carried into the city an ample supply of

water, for lack of which a small village can now make only a bare
subsistence.

The plight of Eski Antalya was explained to me by a shy high-school
student, who typified the stirrings in Turkey. His shyness owed in part
to the respect for learning that makes the professor one of the most
honored types in Turkey, instead of a symbol of absent-mindedness, near-
sightedness, and impracticality. It also sprang from an ambition as vague
as it was intense. Some day, somehow, he hoped to go to America; and
the land of his dreams was the America of Hollywood, which most Turks
take straight. (An especially thoughtful university student told me that
while she greatly admired the freedom enjoyed by American women, she
thought they ought to spend *some* time in the home, give *some* attention
to their husbands and children.) That he was going to high school was
proof of his earnestness, for it meant exceptional sacrifice. His school was
in Antalya, about forty miles from Eski Antalya. Only the larger towns
offer more than a primary-school education.

As all commentators remark, there are two Turkeys—that of the village
and that of the big city. The gulf between them is so wide that the young
schoolteacher Mahmut Makal created a sensation by his book *Our
Village;* educated Turks had not realized how appalling the life of the
Anatolian village often is. (Official Turkey greeted Makal's simple truthfulness by jailing him as a Communist.) The towns, however, are closer
to the village. Outside the few large cities—Istanbul, Ankara, Izmir,
Bursa, Adana—one rarely sees men and women together in restaurants
or places of entertainment. There is little apparent gaiety in the towns
either, and as little to shock, dazzle, or awe the peasant come to market,
except perhaps the statue of Ataturk in the new square or the operations
of an ancient cement mixer. He meets his brother in the ragged, often
barefooted porters who do much of the hauling and the heavy work.
These throng the streets of Istanbul too, and the coffeehouses. Even here
the coffeehouse—the main center of Turkish social life—is patronized exclusively by men, and is somehow full of idlers throughout the working
day. The old world of Istanbul is different from the new world of Ankara,
and both from the world of the village; but all have in common certain
national characteristics.

Like official Turkey, the people are still wedded to the traditional
slackness of the Orient. They always seem somewhat startled by such
questions as when an academic year begins or ends, or how many weeks
it covers; then one learns that the question cannot be answered because
the year doesn't really end—it gradually peters out. A colleague calls up
to ask that his students be dismissed, because his cousin is going to

Ankara and he is helping her pack. The departmental librarian falls ill and is absent for a week before her absence is noted, although meanwhile the students have been unable to read any books. A faculty meeting gets under way an hour late and spends several hours in animated debate without reaching the agenda, finally appointing a committee to consider in detail what to do about a new government regulation, about which nothing whatever can be done. One leaves to join the confusion in a crooked main thoroughfare jammed by heedless pedestrians, porters, and stubborn cart drivers who prefer the middle of the street, and threaded by taxicab drivers who have learned a single principle of economy—to speed up to fifty miles an hour, turn off the ignition, and coast. Allah must be the true God, one concludes; else the university would long since have collapsed, and the city have been depopulated. Or perhaps the explanation is the careful attention to regulations. During a heavy rain a water wagon will keep sprinkling the streets and gardeners keep watering the public gardens. These people know an order when they see one.

But by the same tokens the Turks are warmer than the modern apartment dweller. In the large cities one meets the same friendliness and hospitality as in the villages, only in a more courteous form. Here too a perfect stranger may respond to an inquiry about directions by serving as a guide for hours. No one is more gracious than the cultivated Turk. I may now make some amends to the Ottoman tradition that produced him. One still encounters ugly relics of this tradition—for instance, a devoted old family servant who does not know who she is, or when or where she was born, because she had been sold as a baby and brought up as a slave in a rich man's harem. Nevertheless the tradition gives Istanbul much of its charm. It bred the love of flowers, vines, and fountains that offset the many congested streets. It built the *yali*, or summer houses, along the Bosphorus—unpainted, perishable wooden houses, but light, airy, many-windowed, high-ceilinged, graceful memorials of a cultivated life. It taught a beautiful courtesy. Its charm lingers after the passing of the exotic veil, fez, and turban, in the manners of the Turk in modern dress.

Granted the slackness, the last word belongs to the many earnest Turks who are struggling against the poverty and the backwardness of their country, and whose mentality has changed. The young schoolteachers who sprang up in the villages to act as my guide or my host were usually eager, conscientious, and thoughtful, in the spirit of Mahmut Makal. At first they seemed simply enthusiastic and proud of their schools; then the most thoughtful would reveal that they were troubled by the lethargy or hostility of the pious, superstitious peasants. In Istanbul a naval architect,

who once used to write surrealist poetry, spends nights poring over
American books on methods of increasing the efficiency and produc-
tivity of workers; only he can make little use of his hard-won knowledge
—the workmen in his shipyard are unskilled and not up to it. A prominent,
still optimistic journalist keeps printing independent editorials, even
though his newspaper has repeatedly been suspended by the government
for months at a time. In the university poorly paid young instructors labor
over poorly trained students from Anatolia and pampered ones from the
city schools, while taking on extra jobs in order to make a living. Once
they began to draw up a petition protesting against a government order
that they spend the whole day from nine to five in their offices, but they
learned that this was against the law; a petition signed by more than one
person amounted to insurrection. In general, there are a great many
intelligent, sensitive, liberal Turks, who are therefore liable to suspicion
as Communists or "Turk-disparagers." They are outnumbered—as their
type is in all countries. Still, they count for something; in time they may
take charge. In the Western democracies their type at any given moment
is likely to be on the defensive, but in the long run they have tended to
prevail.

6. THE OLD CITIES TODAY

The antiquities of Asia Minor, which for centuries were quarried when
not simply neglected, are now being treasured by the Turks. The destruction goes on, naturally. Peasants are still superstitious and still need
stone; statuary may suffer from their belief that the head contains the
hidden gold. They are now accustomed, however, to travelers interested
in ancient remains, no longer regarding them as freaks or dealers in the
occult. Many have listened to Turkish archaeologists, who are among the
most enthusiastic of the nation's scholars. The government is building
roads to some of the famous sites, such as Karatepe, and is providing
caretakers for them. Almost all the towns of any size or historical importance maintain a museum, commonly set up in an old mosque. Its
collection is likely to be something of a hodgepodge and to betray the
limitations of local learning. At Antakya the American tourist may read
notations carefully translated for his benefit: a "greeck inscription," a
"sleb on a tomb," a picture of a "nud famel." But he may then be touched
by the pains that are being taken by a poor country to preserve the relics
of an alien past.

The townspeople show little interest or pride in their museum, it is
true. In the oldest towns one is likely to feel that their inhabitants are
squatters who do not really belong on this ancient land, as the peasants

do. Except for the remains of classical antiquity, these towns have few if any houses or streets hallowed by association with famous names or deeds; almost no great men came out of them, beyond folk heroes and holy men. Most have not aged with the charm and dignity of medieval European cities. Instead of taking on ivy and moss, they crumble or sprout weeds. Generally they look more dingy and dilapidated than picturesque.

Yet there are some charming towns among them—Amasya, Afyonkarahisar, Manisa, Kütahya—the more pleasing because in true Turkish style they make no effort to be picturesque or quaint, have no Olde Shoppes. Kütahya, long one of the most purely Turkish, will do as a farewell example. Apart from its incidental antiquities, such as a Byzantine-Seljuk citadel and a Seljuk mosque, this does have the look and feel of a city that has been lived in for centuries. It still makes the pottery for which it was once celebrated, with much less art but handsomely enough, in the traditional patterns and colors. Through its unmodernized winding streets flows a slow stream of *arabas*, or horse-drawn cabs, and carts drawn by donkeys, oxen, and water buffaloes, driven by peasants often striking in feature. In spite of his nondescript Western clothes, the Turk in the old towns clings to his traditional love of color. He gets it in a sash, paints it on his cart, weaves it into coarse sacks and saddlebags— even sticks wads of colored paper into the rumps of slaughtered sheep. As genial are the characteristic sounds of old Turkish life in the streets of Kütahya: the cries of peddlers; the toot of *araba* horns and the clatter of wheels on cobblestones; during the night the loud whistles of the *bekji*, night watchmen proving that they are awake and on the job by keeping others awake; in the early morning the *"güle, güle"* of men greeting one another; and by day and night the most haunting of sounds, the muezzins calling to prayer from the minarets. In this still pious town the muezzins are uncommonly sonorous.

Probably few of its citizens know or care that Kütahya lies in a land once known as Phrygia, and that it was an early Christian center, of a heretical sort. Its name was then Cotaeium, which came from Kotys— another name for Cybele. The new Turkey has blurred such reminders of the distant past by changing some place names in an effort to erase the memory of the Greeks, and by officially designating its major cities Istanbul, Ankara, Edirne, and Izmir instead of Constantinople, Angora, Adrianople, and Smyrna. One must regret the passing of these storied names, though one should remember that the old Greek cities kept changing their names to flatter local pride or Roman emperors. But it is easy enough to see through most of the Turkish disguises and recover memories of the classical world. Ereğli on the Black Sea, for example, was Heraclea, one of the greater Greek cities and the scene of an exploit by Heracles. Another Ereğli-Heraclea not far from Konya takes one farther back; in its vicinity is a huge statue of the Hittite peasant god, in whom the Greeks recognized their Heracles. And for such antiquarian interests the national pride of the Turks has been something of a boon. The official nonsense about their kinship with the Hittites and the Sumerians at least called attention to real connections, in the form of unconscious survivals, with a past much older than their own.

We cannot isolate with assurance the specifically Anatolian elements in the Turkish heritage. We can make out resemblances that may or may not be direct legacies, but in any case point to the unquestionably ancient origin of much peasant practice and belief. Houses in the lower levels of Troy, dating from pre-Hittite times, were built of sun-dried brick on stone foundations, much like houses in Anatolia today. Ovens found in Troy V resemble the beehive ovens still used in the Troad and elsewhere. I have already noted the shoes with uptilted toes, worn alike by Hittites and Turkish peasants. Ramsay noted that Turks viewed with horror the eating of locusts, which are relished by their fellow Moslems, the Arabs; St. Jerome had observed that Arabs ate them, but Phrygians thought the custom unnatural. Even the vicissitudes sometimes fall into neat patterns. The beard in Asia Minor disappeared after Alexander the Great, inaugurator of a "modern" era; then it was restored by Hadrian, abolished by Constantine, restored again by Islam; and now it is disappearing again after Ataturk. In general, life is in many ways going on much as it has from time immemorial, in a land that outside the cities looks much the same, and in which men still cultivate the grape, the olive, the fig.

But my principal concern remains the old cities, with their memorials of a vanished life. I now take a lingering, sentimental leave of them, with some philosophical excuse. Immediately they recall us to fundamental changes rather than continuities: contrasts with Turkey both old and new, rural and urban; contrasts again of West and East. Ultimately they recall us to another deep continuity, in all that we owe to them.

Of Celaenae-Apamea, now Dinar, there is nothing more to say. It has not been excavated and probably is not worth excavating, except for the small Phrygian city of Celaenae and the obscure settlements beneath it. The great city of Apamea was never a really brilliant one. There is only to repeat that it is one of many such sites in Asia Minor, on which the ancients were able to maintain flourishing cities, and which today support only a village or a small town. But sometimes there is good reason for the mere village—as at Troy. Chanakkale on the Dardanelles is the logical location for the main town of the region. As Troy was primarily a fortress and became famous only because of a war fought over it, its pastoral setting today is right. One may rejoice that there is no tourist hotel in the adjoining village of Hisarlik, no pilgrim racket to disturb the storks on its thatched roofs or to ruffle its placid life of sheep, goats, camels, and oxen.

Not far from Troy, however, is the memorable site of Neandria, which over many centuries was unremembered. Situated on a mountain top, commanding a grand view of the Scamander valley and the Troad to Mt. Ida, the city has been deserted ever since the general Antigonus moved its inhabitants into his new city of Alexandria Troas on the coast. Neandria is therefore one of the very few sites in Asia Minor whose ruins are purely Greek, uncluttered by Roman construction. It must have been a considerable city, for its well-built walls make a circuit of five miles; so it may stir the usual melancholy reflections. A few years ago its very name was still unknown to the Turkish peasants living at the foot of the mountain in a village partly built of its stones. But a weird, mystifying sight near the village may stir thoughts more flattering to the ancients. Two polished monoliths about thirty-five feet long lie alone in a craggy wilderness with no sign of other ruins. Further on, the mystery is cleared up by six more monoliths lying at the foot of a cliff. This was a Roman quarry, probably for Alexandria Troas some ten miles away; the two columns must have been abandoned en route, for some bloody reason. Schliemann noticed them when he explored the vicinity of Troy. They have been left undisturbed because the inhabitants of the region still lack the equipment to move them, or a building worthy of them.

At Miletus too there is no city, for good reason: the Maeander River was remorselessly killing it in classical times. Julian the Apostate made a vain effort to restore the glories of the dying city, succeeding only in confirming its vanity; his reward was a complimentary pedestal by "the glorious Metropolis of the Milesian People and Nurse of Apollo of Didyma." The metropolis managed to outlive Apollo, surviving after a fashion through the Byzantine era. The Seljuks thought it worth dignifying with a mosque—a small but lovely one, built out of classical marble. The Maeander, however, went on removing it from the sea by silt, while also providing ideal breeding grounds for malarial mosquitoes. Today the site sustains only the poor little village of Balat, brightened chiefly by the many remnants of classical architecture built into its walls. The plain on which it lies is flooded in the spring, traversed by no good road, and served by no port. Where Greek ships once skimmed over a glistening gulf, trains of camels now plod, stately and stupid, led by the invariable donkey.

The extensive excavations at Miletus have penetrated to the Mycenaean level but mostly have stopped at the Hellenistic-Roman city—not the city that gave philosophy, science, and history to the Western world. The best-preserved of the remains is a massive theater, from the upper tiers of which one may gaze across the plain at the many coils of the Maeander River, and make out on the mountain beyond the ruins of Priene, which the river also killed. In a nearby palace is a statue of the river god in the conventional posture, serenely reclining on his side, as if contemplating his handiwork and finding it good. One may ponder the religious sense of man. Then one may have unwholesome thoughts even at the magnificent ruin of Apollo's temple at Didyma, a dozen miles away, for the temple was famous chiefly for its oracle. Apollo played rather shady politics at Didyma, as at Delphi.

I prefer to recall my host, the mayor of Balat. We walked a mile or so to his farm, following the remains of a Roman aqueduct through fields strewn with fragments of marble that gleamed in the light of a full moon. On his farm he still made use of a Roman cistern and several Roman wells—there are hundreds of these in the vicinity. In front of his summer house he had set up some columns, capitals, and assorted sculpture, all carefully whitewashed. The peasants, he explained, were annoyed because they were always turning up marble when they plowed or dug, but he liked the stuff, and tried to keep it clean. As we dined, I caught a glimpse of his wife hovering over an oven and was reminded of Herodotus, who told how the men and women of Miletus were accustomed to eating separately. The mayor knew nothing of this, of course. But he did have something like the old Milesian spirit—gay, worldly, shrewd, outspoken, irreverent. He loved the forbidden wine, which he made and drank in quantity. He indulged his contempt of the government and the People's Party, though he was himself a delegate. He talked cynically of the "feudal lord" who owned most of the plain, and whom he was careful to play up to. Among other things, he presented him with all the old coins, jewelry, and finer figurines that the villagers ran across; the feudal lord had no interest in such things but liked to give them to his business friends as curiosities. To this end the exquisite artists of antiquity had worked—whereas the shades of the homely well diggers might be happy. The moral is confused.

Although there is no city at Ephesus either, for similar reasons, it is a much more attractive and accessible site than its ancient rival, lying off a main highway and a railroad. Only an incorrigible moralist could resist the enchantment and the awe evoked by the relics of its long pageantry. By the railway station stand the tall pillars of an early Byzantine aqueduct, each capped by a nest of venerable storks. On the hill rising from the village and crowned by a medieval castle lie the remains of the Church of St. John, and beneath them his bones. Nearby is the shell of a Seljuk mosque, also built of the ancient marbles of Ephesus. Its superb façade looks down on the site of Diana's temple in the valley of the River Caÿster. Across the valley loom the city walls. Within them are many mementos of the magic that was once in the air: the Sacred Way, paved and lined with marble, that led to Diana's temple; the temples of Cybele and Serapis, the latter a sprawl of gigantic Corinthian columns; the "tomb of St. Luke," in reality another pagan temple; the great theater, seating 25,000, where the mob howled against St. Paul; the "double church" of the Virgin Mary, a composite of four successive churches; the Cave of the Seven Sleepers, in which were found hundreds of graves and little shrines, both Christian and Moslem. And on the mountain above stands the enduring testimonial to the magic of ancient Ephesus, whose people had the wit to play nurse to the immortal Diana instead of Apollo. Large crowds now come to the Virgin Mary's home on August 15, the day of her Assumption and of Diana before her.

In newspaper photographs some of the pilgrims look more like curiosity seekers or tourists, and the great theater might suggest other thoughts to a different kind of pilgrim. Pictures taken of it when it was excavated about thirty years ago show a well-preserved theater, with rows of seats reaching to the top of a high semicircle. A few years ago all but several rows at the bottom had disappeared, covered over with soil in which not only weeds but bushes and young trees had taken root. Now one realizes how great cities become buried—and how quickly nature can swallow them up. Most of Ephesus would soon disappear again were it not for the caretakers provided by the Turkish government. Only the endless care of man can preserve the great works of man.

In Tarsus, once more, there is little to stir piety in any but professional archaeologists. This overgrown village of mud brick may be reminiscent of St. Paul's ancestral Palestine, but it is quite unworthy of the Greco-Roman world he grew up in and traveled over. Like most of the old cities that have survived to this day in Turkey—Trabzon, Eskishehir, Adana, Kayseri, Izmit, Samsun—it may be more saddening than the deserted sites of other great cities, which can more readily summon up the magic of the past.

Or than the sites of obscure cities. Near Kütahya, at the village of Chavdihisar, are the ruins of Aezani. Who knows of Aezani? I had never heard of it until I read Hamilton's account of its ruins, among which he said was one of the most nearly perfect Ionic temples in Asia Minor. A few scraps of information about its history may be dug up. It was an ancient temple estate, Phrygian or pre-Phrygian, of a god who merged with Zeus and later was assigned land by the kings of both Pergamum and Bithynia. A Byzantine historian states that Euphorbus, its first priestly dynast, was appointed because he taught the proper method of sacrifice, which involved the hedgehog as well as the fox, and thus gave the city its name. The temple that so impressed Hamilton is late Ionic, with tall columns, built in the first or second century A.D. Less imposing than the temple of Olympian Zeus at Athens, it is more graceful and dignified, much better preserved, and much more of a credit to the little city. It is still a lovely thing, standing alone in a field against a distant mountain backdrop. In a nearby field are other remains of the familiar sort—a theater, a stadium, etc. Hundreds of such towns in Asia Minor, not great or famous, had proudly maintained classical standards.[8]

Among them, and probably less splendid than most, was Iconium. It was a city of some size but no historical importance or distinction until St. Paul singled it out, for reasons not too clear. In Konya today there is as little trace of the city he preached in as there is at Tarsus. The old walls that were still standing in the last century are now gone; the citadel in the center of the town has been made over into a public garden. But Konya is much brighter than Tarsus. The city that the Ottomans allowed to decay has had its face lifted. Quite properly the Turks have concentrated on preserving and restoring its Seljuk monuments, for these—not its classical remains—were its real glory. Nor were they simply impious in making over its ancient citadel into a public garden, for the walls were only picturesque. The local museum contains exhibits, ranging from Hittite to Roman times, that were unearthed in the course of clearing the garden and the approaches to it. Many are crude works, suggesting the relative backwardness of the region, and almost all are inferior to Seljuk art.

Unfortunately, modern Konya suffers as much by comparison with the Seljuk city. Attractive in panorama, it does not bear close inspection. Its bazaars offer little of interest, nothing so beautiful as the rugs it once produced; its old districts remain dingy. Still busy scrubbing its face, it is too much concerned with shiny appearances—tearing up good cobblestone streets to replace them with proud asphalt, while side streets remain wretched. When called on to admire the asphalt, one may hear the whisper of a wry ghost: "See all the world—but see Konya."

As the shrine of the Ottomans, Bursa had less need of rebuilding, and

---

[8] I refer to a few more of the many I have perforce neglected in the Appendix, Section 12, Some Suggestions for Tourists.

has in this view suffered more from it. Now a fashionable resort, its style is set by the *Palas*—new hotels and apartments catering to the tastes of the *nouveau riche*. Nevertheless Bursa retains a character of its own that resists all efforts to make it up-to-date. Old streets with old-style houses wander up and down the mountain, in spite of the apologies of the new-comers. A deep ravine that cuts through the city cannot be filled up or fancied up. Mountain air and water keep Bursa fresh and clean; there is little squalor. And the inviolable mosques and tombs of the early sultans still dignify the first capital of the Ottomans, built when Islam was still an inspiration and a discipline, a love that could make of the Moslem "architect, poet, metaphysician, carver, decorator, soldier, anything."

Yet Bursa—and Konya, Kütahya, and all the rest—cannot for a moment compare in interest with Istanbul. This is by far the most fascinating city in Turkey, the only one that remains among the great cities of the world. It is the richest museum of Ottoman culture. Its Seraglio, its innumerable mosques, *medressehs,* and tombs, its cemeteries with turbaned grave-stones, its fountains and kiosks, its bazaars and flower and spice markets, even its flimsy old houses and many shabby streets, with here and there a grapevine arbor, a splash of wisteria, a glimpse of garden or shaded courtyard—these give the most vivid impression of the magnificence of the Ottomans in the days of their glory, and of the color and charm of Turkish life down to their inglorious end. Istanbul then suffered from the rule of Ankara, losing much of its wealth and trade to State industries, but it has been compensated by some material improvements—avenues paved and broadened, squares cleared and brightened. The city was dressed up for the celebration of 1953, the five hundredth anniversary of its fall to the Conqueror. Since the destructive riots of 1955 an ambitious program of modernization has got under way.

As with the other cities, its new dress is undistinguished in style and not very becoming. A visitor welcomes the new avenues chiefly as more convenient means of access to the old buildings. Except for the abiding Bosphorus, the fascination of Istanbul derives almost wholly from its past and is confined to Stamboul, the city within the ancient walls. Galata, the old Genoese quarter across the Golden Horn, is simply squalid; Pera, the modern European section on the hill above it, is oppressively dull. Old Stamboul itself has a patchy, tumble-down appearance, due immediately to the many fires that have laid it waste, which recalls the failings of the Ottomans. They restored the great city they conquered, they adorned it with many monuments, they gave it its enchanting skyline, they made it their own by more than squatter's right; but even so Istanbul is a great and magical city primarily because of the peoples before them. One must deplore the loss of its storied name, Constantinople.

A simple tourist who wants to know the name and date of everything he sees may at first be troubled as he wanders about the old city. Everywhere he runs into crumbling walls or piles, unidentified by his guidebook, which may be a hundred or fifteen hundred years old, the remains of a Turkish bath or of a Byzantine palace. (Such a palace was recently discovered in a warehouse, the ornate capitals of its half-buried columns almost hidden by bales of paper.) But all about are the guidebook wonders, beginning with Hagia Sophia—still the greatest building in the city —and running through other Byzantine churches, colonnaded cisterns, and columns in the Hippodrome to the fabulous city walls.[9] While only sections remain of the sea walls, the city is still almost entirely enclosed by the fifth-century land walls, a triple row with towers. At their gates one may brood over "the boredom, and the horror, and the glory" of all the history made by Constantinople—always an imperial city, and never a really joyous one. Near the Golden Gate through which the Byzantine emperors returned in triumph peasants come in with their donkeys and vegetables, no doubt as they did a thousand years ago, with as little sense of history. Near the Edirne Gate, where the Turks first breached the walls, youngsters play soccer in the depression left by the old moat. Elsewhere the moat is filled with vegetable gardens, which grow a delicious variety of lettuce. Apparently blood-drenched soil is good for lettuce.

Of Byzantium, the Greek city before Constantine, nothing remains except some stone built into later foundations. Its own foundations lie beneath the Seraglio, on the site of its acropolis. Here one can only admire the beauty of its situation and the wit of its early colonists. Across the bay lies the ordinary town of Kadiköy on the ordinary site of ancient Chalcedon, chosen by the uninspired Greeks who first settled in the region. But from here one can also look up the Bosphorus, the "cow ford" of Greek legend; and then the past may come back.

It is difficult to define the peculiar charm of the Bosphorus that so

[9] One of the most exciting of the cisterns is the Yerebatan Saray ("Underground Palace"), a work of Justinian, in which a gloomy but wondrous perspective is afforded by 336 columns in ranks. It is typical of the Ottoman mentality that the discovery of this cistern was left to an obscure traveler, Petrus Gyllius, in the time of Suleiman the Magnificent. "Through the Carelessness and Contempt of everything that is curious in the Inhabitants," wrote Gyllius, "it was never discover'd but by me, who was a stranger among them, after a long and diligent search after it. The whole Ground was built upon, which made it less suspected there was a *Cistern* there. The People had not the least Suspicion of it, although they daily drew their Water out of the wells which were sunk into it."

many have felt. Although it is an obviously beautiful piece of water, winding between hills, its natural beauty is not spectacular or incomparable. It has a pleasant life of its own: dolphins playing in it, gulls and ducks bobbing on it, other birds often sweeping up and down in a straight line a foot or so above its surface—lost souls, according to Turkish legend. Man has contributed more to it by the becoming minarets, *yalis*, and medieval castles along its shores. The villages that line it give it endless variety, each having its own character, even a different climate (depending upon the degree of exposure to the north winds from the Black Sea), and all having picturesque nooks and corners. Perhaps most fascinating, however, is the indefinable—an aura of antiquity emanating from all the legend and historic event associated with it. The geographical fiction of Asia and Europe, the continents it separates, has something to do with this; and here it is no longer pure fiction. The Ottoman Turks, appropriately, favored the Asiatic shore, settling in such villages as Vaniköy ("the weary man's village") and Kanlija ("the bloody village"). The Greeks concentrated on the European shore, with which most of the ancient legends are associated.[10]

The legends begin within the city proper, in the district known as Beshiktash. Its name comes from "five stones," a row of pillars to which Barbarossa moored his galleys in the time of Suleiman the Magnificent; but long before this Jason had landed here, to give it the name of Jasonium. A celebrated laurel grove in the valley behind it was sacred to Apollo. Several miles up the Bosphorus Jason's witch-savior Medea planted a laurel tree at Kuruchesme, now a coaling station. In Byzantine times this district became known for its stylites, including Simeon; he steadily increased the height of the pillar on which he lived, from six to thirty-six yards. "I conclude," wrote the Byzantine historian Cedrenus, "that this mode of life could not have been possible without Divine direction for the advantage of the idle." Today some might conclude that Kuruchesme serves a better purpose as a coal dump. The next village, Arnautköy ("Albanian village"), had a great church to St. Michael, the Byzantine favorite, which ended more ignominiously. Pulled down by

[10] As studied by scientists, the very strong currents of the Bosphorus also fit into this picture. They run down from the Black Sea, which is less salty than the Mediterranean and all other seas because of the big Russian rivers emptying into it. Well beneath them a Mediterranean current goes up the Bosphorus; the sailing ships of the ancients managed to navigate upstream by letting big baskets down into it. But the Mediterranean current never gets into the Black Sea, what is left of it being turned back by a ledge at the entrance. When the north winds from Russia are strong and prolonged, the Mediterranean is driven clean out of the Bosphorus—and all Istanbul shivers from the cold. On the other hand, its citizens complain of the enervating winds from the south.

Mohammed the Conqueror, it survives in the walls of Rumeli Hisar, the castle he built to cut off aid to beleaguered Constantinople.

At Rumeli ("Roman" or European) Hisar one is outside Istanbul proper, and in the thick of ancient history. At this narrowest point of the Bosphorus, an Ionian architect built a bridge for the Persian Emperor Darius. On the site of Rumeli Hisar, Darius sat in a rock-cut throne, to watch his army cross over and set foot in Europe for the first time. Beneath the castle may lie the columns on which the passage was described in both Greek and Assyrian inscriptions. At this point Goths, Crusaders, and many another host later crossed into Asia.

The European villages farther up the Bosphorus also saw their share of history. Istinye, on a bay in which many sea battles have been fought, got its name from the temple of Sosthenia, "Safety," built by Jason and the Argonauts in gratitude for their safe return. Later it had another church to the Archangel Michael, dedicated by Constantine the Great. Tarabya, likewise the scene of many sea battles, comes from Therapia, "Healing." The superstitious Greeks so christened it, euphemistically, because Medea threw poison on its shore when she returned with Jason. And at the entrance to the stormy Black Sea, euphemistically called the Euxine, "Hospitable," the gods did double duty. On the European side Jason erected an altar to the Asiatic Cybele, later to be joined by Serapis in another temple. On the Asiatic side he dedicated altars to the Olympian gods, of whom Zeus and Poseidon were subsequently singled out and honored by a temple. From the ruins of this temple Justinian built still another church to the Archangel Michael, who had taken over the job of guarding the entrance to the Bosphorus. The more realistic Sultan Murad IV built fortresses on either side to keep out the Cossacks—a purpose served today by submarine nets as well.

Needless to say, we cannot believe all these Greek fables. Nevertheless they symbolized a major historic event—the coming of the Greeks into the region. Whether or not they captured gold on the Black Sea coast and carried off a princess, they settled at the entrance to the Bosphorus and began the history that has made the region so important. In a similar spirit they established a frontier in Ionia, and prepared the way for Homer. They bring me back to the major theme of the history of Asia Minor as I read it.

7. EPILOGUE

All along I have kept repeating that a historian cannot rightly pretend to complete impersonality or impartiality. Our final goal in the study of history is self-knowledge. To attain it, we must have sympathy for other

peoples, must try to see them as they saw themselves; as we look back on
the decisive clashes of ideas and ideals we must try to understand both
sides, particularly the side we disapprove of, which more often than not
proved to be the winning side; but our aim, in the words of Ernst Cas-
sirer, is not to efface the self but to enlarge and enrich it. This obliges
us finally to judge—it does not permit us to forgive all. More specifically,
it obliges most of us to acknowledge that our heart is naturally with the
Greeks. They were the pioneers in the free society that we cherish. They
won through to the intellectual and imaginative freedom that made
possible the very effort at understanding we are now engaged in. They
established our ideal of self-knowledge, and of the enlargement and enrichment of the self. With all due respect to the gods, they put foremost
the values of the true, the beautiful, and the good that man could
realize by his own powers, and maintain in defiance of death or even of
the gods.

Today we are more keenly aware that the Greeks "failed." I have
followed the long story of how they gradually succumbed to the ways
of the ancient East, the imperious need of "miracle, mystery, and
authority." For most of us it is a sad story; few openly rejoice at their
failure. But many do seem pleased to proclaim the failure of science, of
rationalism, of liberalism, of humanism—of the essential Greek faith at
the heart of modern Western civilization. Many are reverting to the
traditional Christian judgment—maintained from St. Paul and St. Augustine to Luther and Calvin—that this faith is sinful pride. They are saying
again that man can learn nothing and achieve nothing save by the grace
of God. They are too sophisticated to offer miracle, except in the guise of
salvation through prayer; but in effect they are calling us back to mystery
and authority. The magic word is Original Sin.

So I repeat: in the long view everything has failed. No faith of any
kind has worked for good, or simply for good. Christianity itself is a
failure by its own standards; it has neither won the world nor ever produced a truly Christian society. Arnold Toynbee has come to its rescue
by flourishing the Time Scale of Science, which indicates that the human
race has lived on earth for hundreds of thousands of years and the earth
has existed for many millions, whereas Christianity has had only a brief
moment to prove itself. But he makes no such allowance for the Greeks:
they simply failed, and by their failure proved the vanity of their faith. I
prefer to believe otherwise, even by a modest time scale. Their failure
was not at all surprising, once more: they were the first people to embark
on the adventure in freedom, and they had nothing like our material and
intellectual resources. They therefore challenge us, and might still hearten

us. For we remain their heirs. Their faith did not perish, but became the living faith of our civilization. Through us it has now become a far more vital force in the East than it was in their own day. The story of Asia Minor, or Turkey, is essentially the story of Asia today.

Until this century the vast communities of Asia were communities of want and ignorance. The great majority of its people were illiterate, lived in poverty, never saw a doctor. Throughout their history they had never known democracy or dreamed of civil liberties.The masses knew government only as taxes and police. Even the educated had no word for "liberty" in Chinese, none for "rights" in Sanskrit. Except for China, all cultures were based on religion, which for the masses meant a welter of gross superstition. Hence the peculiar difficulties of Eastern peoples today. What they are seeking to change, or are being forced to change, is not merely a form of government but a whole way of life.

As in Turkey, the effort has everywhere bred confusion and contradiction, and hostility from conservatives. It is by no means a uniform drama, to be sure. China, Japan, India, Turkey, Islam—all are going different ways. But there remain common themes, due to the common Western impact. Everywhere Eastern peoples are beginning to reject the fatalistic notion that poverty is the law of life or the will of God. They are studying science and technology in the belief that man by his own efforts can improve his lot on earth, and need not stake all his hopes on a life to come or an escape from the wheel of life. They are learning to read and write, and to question. However limited their freedom, their strong men at least pretend to offer them either democracy or a "truer" freedom. At the same time, Western impact has made them all more conscious of their own traditional culture. In this self-consciousness they are disposed, like the Turks, to be hypersensitive, to glorify an unserviceable or dubious tradition, to cling to methods, beliefs, and institutions that tend to defeat their new purposes. They may also hope to preserve much of value, maintain their identity, and enrich the commonwealth of culture.

No one can be sure of the outcome of this drama—the first actual world drama in history. Meanwhile the East is making greater demands on the West, immediately for economic and technical aid, ultimately for sympathetic understanding. The West in turn is forced to make greater demands on itself, in self-sacrifice and ultimately in self-knowledge. The most general and urgent need, no doubt, is a fuller awareness of its own sins: of imperialism, materialism, commercialism; of national, racial, cultural, and religious prejudice; or let us say simply, with the moralists, of pride, selfishness, and greed. Yet in the prevailing atmosphere of disillusionment and despair, at least among its intellectuals, it also needs sanity, resolution, and courage, in particular a faith in the values of a free society, which at heart most of its intellectuals really cherish and wish to preserve. I do not think that it helps to harp on the theme of Original Sin. This has flourished under all creeds, including Christianity. Pride, greed, and selfishness have sat on many a Christian throne, even the papal throne; they are as conspicuous in Orthodox Greece today as in ancient pagan Greece, in devout Spain as in secular America. Much rarer in history than such unoriginal folly and evil is the life of freedom, in reason, as conceived by the Greeks.

The historic East might therefore teach us something more than its traditional wisdom of tranquillity through resignation, renunciation, or nonattachment. By now we have come to realize the costs and risks of a free society, the abuses of technology and science, the depressing by-products of democratic education, political equality, and the privileges of common men. The ancient societies of the East are not the only alternative to our kind of society; but they force the question of alternatives, which might make us more aware of the elementary goods we take for granted. Is a society healthier when it rests on the manual labor of peasants living in poverty? Is a tractor really more inhuman than a wooden stick or plow? Is it better for the masses of men to be illiterate? To pray to saints in the absence of doctors? To believe in demons and witches? To have no voice in their government? To be wholly subservient to Church and State? To be discouraged against hopes of improving their material lot or their social status? We may still enjoy the distinctive goods of Western civilization "under God," even if they were not clearly God-given. We may very well lose them, under God or no, beginning with our freedoms. I am simply saying that they are precious goods.

Among the most precious is the simple hope of progress—life lived in a hopeful spirit. The history of Asia Minor does not for a moment suggest that progress is the law of human history. It does suggest that life is richer for this hope, that the human race has made a positive gain when ordinary men have been enabled to live in this spirit, and that it is inhuman to brand this faith as sinful pride.

Appendix

---

1. AMASIA: THE KINGDOM OF PONTUS

THE LUSH Black Sea coast, on which the kings of Pontus established their capital, was as rich in Greek fable as in timber and minerals; and they were not unrelated. The legend of Jason and the Argonauts may have been based on an actual Greek expedition, come to explore or plunder the mineral wealth that the Hittites and Assyrians had early discovered. Even the Golden Fleece might reflect historical fact: until recent times the natives of the region moored fleeces in the streams to catch gold dust. At any rate, the Argonauts were very real to Xenophon, who had much the same spirit as they, and who gave the first historical account of the region. After a year of marching and fighting, he and the Ten Thousand caught their first glimpse of the Black Sea from the mountains above the Greek port of Trapezus, later to become famous as Trebizond. After further adventures the Ten Thousand reached the city of Sinope, from which they sailed to Heraclea (modern Ereğli) and finally reached Byzantium. En route they saw Jason's beach, where the *Argo* had been moored, and the Acherusian Peninsula, where Heracles descended into the underworld to fetch Cerberus. Earlier they had passed the plains that had been the home of the Amazons, and that are backed up by mountains still known as Mason Dagh.

Sinope, which was to be the capital of another bold adventurer, Mithridates the Great, was the oldest and greatest of the cities along the coast. Although its reputed founder was Autolycus, an Argonaut who had fought with Heracles against the Amazons, it had served as a port for the Hittites, under the name of Sinuwa, and was sometimes referred to as a "Phrygian city" by the Greeks. The Greeks were quick to exploit its natural advantages as the best harbor on the coast and the terminus of a road leading into the interior. By 756 B.C. it was prosperous enough to found a colony at Trapezus. Its wealth and its location on the frontier invited the usual ups and downs, and prepared its cosmopolitan citizens for the new era in its history that began in 183 B.C., when King Pharnaces of Pontus conquered it and presently made it his capital. A century later it reached the height of its political power and its splendor under Mithridates the Great. Here he was born, here he mobilized his great armada against the Romans, and here he was buried by Pompey, his conqueror. Another famous son of Sinope, Diogenes the Cynic, would have been pleased to write his epitaph. Or that of Sinope itself: now a minor Turkish port (Sinop), with no trace of its splendid palaces and temples. It is ignored by little steamers that put in at a dozen other small towns along the Black Sea coast, including the sites of its former colonies.

But I am not disposed to give Diogenes the last word—else men would never make history, good or bad. A better key to the history made by Mithridates is the city of Amasia, which still thrives. Probably it too went back to Hittite times, for it is a natural stronghold on one of the best passes to the coast, and Strabo reported many ruined fortresses in the vicinity. In any case, Amasia was the original capital of Pontus. It was the only real city in the interior of the kingdom, where the Black Sea mountains give way to the Anatolian plains; and though the ambitious kings had the wit to move their capital to the Greek coast, their heart and soul belonged to the Asiatic interior. The rock tombs of the early kings, who claimed royal Persian descent, still look down on Amasia.

The rise of Pontus began when an adventurer named Mithridates, nephew of a Greek tyrant, assumed the royal title and made good his declaration of independence from the Seleucids. Amasia became the royal stronghold. By 200 B.C. Pontus was a real power, which began raiding Cappadocia to the south and the Greek cities on the coast. It was a mongrel kingdom that made Greek its official language but had no Greek *polis;* it retained the Asiatic system of domain land belonging to the king, nobles, and priests. Its first coins were characteristic, representing the enthroned Zeus of Alexander the Great on the reverse, and in the field a star and crescent (which still appear on the flag of Turkey) to symbolize the sun and moon, the emblems of Persian royalty. It signaled its eminence, and sealed its destiny, by forming an alliance with Rome. As a reward for its aid in the third war against Carthage, the Romans made Mithridates V a present of Phrygia. When he was assassinated they found an excuse to revoke the gift, thereby arousing the hatred of the young prince who was to become Mithridates the Great. He took the throne before he was twenty years old by murdering his mother and younger brother. Within ten years, through war, intrigue, and assassination, he made himself the most powerful king of Asia Minor.

Mithridates was not simply a barbarian. Legendary for his huge physique and powers of endurance, he was as well a man of exceptional mental vigor who had a genuine appreciation of Greek culture. He

adorned Sinope and Amisus (modern Samsun) with magnificent buildings, and invited poets and philosophers to his court. His coins—among
the handsomest of the period—display his proud claim of descent from
Perseus; on the reverse a winged Pegasus is lowering its head to drink of
the Pierian spring. He conquered southern Russia in the role of champion
of the Greeks against the barbarians. And he may well have been quite
sincere when, about 90 B.C., he assembled an immense armada to play
the same role against the Romans. His conquest of western Asia Minor
amounted to a triumphal procession. Most of the Greek cities opened
their gates to him, hailing him as an emancipator; the Romans had made
themselves hated by their greed. He championed the cause of democracy,
proclaiming the abolition of debts and liberation of slaves. Even the
brutal massacre he ordered—a slaughter of some eighty thousand Roman
men, women, and children on the appointed day—was not an act of blind
or frenzied brutality: the Romans were too numerous to be deported or
easily disposed of. At least the Greeks had shown often enough that they
could be ruthless, and on this occasion they co-operated enthusiastically.
In the great cities of Ephesus and Pergamum it was they who seemed
frenzied, massacring even Romans who had sought sanctuary in the
temples.

Yet Mithridates was at heart an Oriental despot, with a lust for power
and pomp that made him increasingly tyrannical. The Greek cities soon
began to rebel against him. His armada was as showy and flabby as that
of King Xerxes, a mixed multitude of barbarians encumbered by a huge
train of gilded luxuries; and when it went on to invade Greece it too was
defeated and largely destroyed by a much smaller Roman army under
Sulla. Mithridates had to relinguish all his conquests. When he returned
with another huge armada twelve years later, he was resisted by most of
the Greek cities and again outmaneuvered and outfought by a smaller
Roman army, this time under Lucullus, while his fleet was largely
destroyed by a storm on the Black Sea. Thereafter he was magnificent
only for his inexhaustible energy and indomitable courage. Lucullus defeated still another army he raised and drove him out of his own kingdom.
When the enemies of Lucullus in Rome succeeded in getting him deposed
and recalled (to retire in disillusionment to the life of luxury for which
he became celebrated), Mithridates managed to recover most of his
kingdom, but this feat only brought upon him the great Pompey, with an
army now outnumbering his own. Driven out of the mountain fortresses
where he had piled up his vast treasure hoards, he escaped to southern
Russia. Here he made himself master of another kingdom, raised another
army and fleet, and prepared to invade Europe—only to be betrayed by

his son Pharnaces, who persuaded the troops to make him king and prepared to sue for peace. Mithridates met his end in the Roman manner, with Oriental overtones. According to Plutarch, he had ordered his chief eunuch to arrange for the death of his sisters and his wives, to avoid the shame of their falling into the hands of the Romans. Now he himself committed suicide rather than surrender.

The aftermath was ignominious. As a peace token, Pharnaces offered the poorly embalmed body of his father to Pompey. The Roman conqueror could afford the decency of refusing to look at it: his immense booty included a colossal solid-gold statue of Mithridates. When Pharnaces in turn began to make trouble, in the delusion that he was his father's son, Julius Caesar came out to rout his army with ridiculous ease. It was this victory, won not far from Amasia, that Caesar announced in the laconic words once known to all schoolboys—"I came, I saw, I conquered." Pontus made no more serious trouble. If its people missed the colossal gold statue of Mithridates, they were apparently content under Roman rule, and certainly had reason to prefer it. They might have reflected that the vast treasures hoarded by their great king had done them no good. The citizens of Amasia in particular must have rejoiced, for Pompey made it a free city.

As such, it produced its best-known son—Strabo (63 B.C.?–A.D. 24?). For us Strabo's work is the chief treasure to come out of Pontus. Although his *Geography* has been called the swan song of Hellenism, he himself took an exalted view of it and did not write as one conscious of a fading tradition, a dying race, or a lost kingdom. A geographer, he declared, must know astronomy, meteorology, geometry, natural history, human history, fable, philosophy—the "whole world" of nature and of man; and he was confident that his work would be especially useful for statesmen. There is some question whether statesmen read it, since later writers make almost no references to it. Modern scholars who have found it especially useful point out that Strabo knew less than he believed, and much that wasn't so. Yet he wrote in the rational, critical, inquiring spirit of the early Greeks. While showing a natural pride in his native city, he shows none in Mithridates or the "Persian" kings. He marks the gulf between the high Greek and the ancient Anatolian tradition, the more plainly because he noted the popular bridges between them. Of Comana in Pontus, a temple city devoted to the Goddess Ma, he remarked that it was "almost a little Corinth" because of the multitude of harlots dedicated to the goddess. Strabo took a calm view of such customs. "The great mass of women and common people," he observed, "cannot be induced by mere force of reason to devote themselves to piety, virtue, and honesty.

Superstition must therefore be employed, and even this is insufficient without the aid of the marvelous and the terrible."

With such aid, which its later rulers employed unconsciously, his native city remained a considerable one through the vicissitudes of the ages. In the eleventh century the Byzantine historian Michael Psellus described a battle fought at "the famous city of Amasia, the place that everyone is talking about." It soon fell to the Seljuk Turks, but as another inland people they favored it over the old Greek cities on the Black Sea coast; so men kept talking about it while Sinope slowly decayed. Its Seljuk conquerors adorned it and restored its citadel, which was able to withstand a seven-month siege by Tamerlane. The early Ottoman sultans also honored it, Bayazid II by building its most imposing mosque, Selim the Grim by being born in it, Suleiman the Magnificent by holding court and signing a peace treaty with Persia in it. Today, still called Amasya, it is one of the brightest towns in Turkey, famous for its apples, but more memorable for its natural beauty and its antiquities.

The town lies on a river (the ancient Iris) in a deep gorge. Houses along the river rest on ancient foundations, and one of the arched bridges crossing it is Roman. Fortress walls run up a cliff that rises steeply out of the river to a height of some hundreds of feet; the ruins of the citadel on top are mostly medieval but contain some Hellenistic foundations. The tombs of the early Pontic kings are cut into the face of this cliff. Rough-hewn and bare, with façades from ten to forty feet high crowned by an arch, they have little artistic distinction. They must have been more impressive, however, when they were covered or decorated with marble, as holes in their façades suggest, and they command a majestic view of the river, the jagged hills across, and a lush valley below. They are among the very few monumental relics of Persian rule in Asia Minor. It is a pity that Mithridates the Great, the magnificent barbarian, was not buried here instead of in alien Sinope.

2. THE ARMENIANS

The rugged tableland of Armenia in eastern Asia Minor is not a barrier but a bridge between East and West. Shut off by mountain ranges from the Black Sea on the north and Mesopotamia on the south, it includes a broad plain that stretches into modern Russia and has always been a natural route for commerce or invasion. In this century it was still being traversed by camel caravans, which from Trebizond carried the bulk of the trade between Europe and northern Persia. It was invaded by Russian armies in World War I. At that time it was still occupied by Armenians, another "Aryan" people who had enacted the familiar story of invading Asia and eventually founding an Asiatic kingdom, but who unlike almost all the others had succeeded in retaining their identity.

Greek legend traced the name of their land to Armenus of Thessaly, an Argonaut who had penetrated it with Jason. Herodotus described the Armenians as Phrygian colonists. Their language was in fact akin to the Phrygian—and their profile like that of the Hittites. They seem to have come in later, however, following on the heels of the marauding Cimmerians and Scythians, and settling down in what had been the Kingdom of Urartu about Lake Van. They then came under the sway of the Medes and the Persians, but after the death of Alexander they declared and made good their independence. By the first century B.C. they had established a kingdom powerful enough to have imperial delusions.

Little is known of their early history because none of their cities have been excavated, and the Greek accounts of them were chiefly fabulous. Strabo was surprisingly ill-informed about them, considering that he was a neighbor; he thought they were akin to the Syrians, Arabians, and Aramaeans. But the fables and delusions at least reflected the historic fact that they had taken to Oriental culture. Thus the Assyrian Queen Semiramis, builder of a legendary summer palace at Lake Van, was made to fall in love with an Armenian king, who died resisting her passion but was brought back to life; it was the old story of Ishtar-Astarte and Tammuz-Adonis. (Plato's story of Er, son of Armenios, also derived from the story of Tammuz.) The Armenians actually worshiped Anaitis, a Persian manifestation of the Mother Goddess, who like Cybele was served by temple prostitutes coming from the highest families. And the Armenian kingdom that emerged into the light of history was unmistakably Asiatic, on the Persian model.

Almost as soon as it emerged it reached its summit, under Tigranes the Great, who extended his dominions from the Caspian to the Mediterranean and built a new capital in Mesopotamia. Having married a daughter of Mithridates the Great (another Cleopatra), Tigranes was an ally of the Pontic king and shared in his early conquests. He was at first prudent enough to keep clear of the war with Rome, but became wrathful when Lucullus sent him a message addressed to the King, instead of the King of Kings. His eventual decision to aid Mithridates led Lucullus to invade Armenia. After beheading the first messenger who brought him news of the invasion, Tigranes collected a typically huge, flamboyant Oriental army. Strabo's report that some Romans were embarrassed to put on armor against such slaves is given some weight by the ease with which Lucullus routed his host and destroyed his new capital. Pompey had still less trouble when he invaded Armenia; the kingdom submitted completely and gave up all its conquests. For a few centuries thereafter it was a buffer state between the Romans and the Parthians, then between the Romans and the Sassanian Empire of Persia. It retained just enough independence to ensure a troubled history, now being courted by the rival powers, now raided and partitioned.

The turning point in the history of Armenia was its conversion to Christianity, by order of King Tiridates, about A.D. 300. It became the first Christian state, anticipating by some twenty years the Roman Emperor Constantine's official adoption of the new religion. Primarily it was the Armenian Church that made a semibarbarous people a nation, gave them a culture, and enabled them to preserve their identity. This conversion, however, was managed in an Oriental style. Only a despot could have so promptly imposed a new religion on his subjects. Oriental imagination contributed the fabulous accessories to the event, as the Armenians discovered that no less than four of the Apostles—Thaddeus, Bartholomew, Simon, and Jude—had preached the gospel and earned martyrdom in their land. They also boasted that Christ himself had established their church: he had appeared in a vision to St. Gregory the Illuminator, who converted King Tiridates, and had given specific orders for the construction of a church in the royal city of Vagarshapat (now Echmiadzin in Soviet Armenia). Even Hebrew tradition assisted, for Jewish colonists had long ago fixed the belief that the majestic mountain dominating this region was Mt. Ararat.[1] And once established, the Armenian Church rejected the metaphysical nonsense of the Greeks. Although it had approved the decisions of the Council of Nicaea, it eventually alienated both the Roman and the Greek Church by settling on the Monophysite heresy dear to the Orient. It asserted that Christ was one nature and one person, who became man in the fullest sense.

Like Rome, Armenia enjoyed no earthly reward for its conversion to the true faith. Within a century the Persian Emperor Shapur inaugurated its tragic history by destroying its great cities, massacring thousands of its people, and carrying more thousands off into captivity. For the next five centuries it maintained at best a kind of feudal order, or disorder, never quite subdued by the greater powers it separated, never really independent. Religious animosity prevented any lasting alliance or peace with the Byzantine Empire. The Armenian and Greek Orthodox Churches

[1] Scholars generally prefer some mountain nearer Mesopotamia, or even the mound of Sumerian Ur, as a more probable harbor for Noah's Ark; but the Armenian tradition persists. Only a few years ago another of many expeditions sought permission to search for remnants of the Ark on this mountain. If they had found some pieces of old timber, one wonders whether they expected them to be identified by some such sign as S.S. *Ark*.

were unable to settle their differences, which bred the characteristically Christian hatred of fellow Christians who had incorrect opinions about the incomprehensible Godhead; the Armenians preferred slavery or death to any compromise on dogma, and kept getting their preference. When the decline of the Baghdad Caliphate allowed them to regain their independence in the tenth century, two feudal kingdoms emerged, one in the north with a capital at Ani (on the present border between Turkey and Russia), another in the south with a capital at Van. They failed to unite, or even to consolidate their own domains. Internal strife, fanned by the Byzantine emperors, produced as many as six petty kingdoms. Hence the Armenians fell easy prey to the Seljuk Turks, who in the eleventh century overwhelmed their entire nation. They might have taken some comfort in the thought that an Armenian prophecy had been fulfilled: catastrophe was to come at the hands of barbarians a thousand years after the death of Christ. Probably they got more comfort from the catastrophe that befell the Greek heretics shortly afterward. In 1071, at the battle of Manzikert, the Seljuks crushed the Byzantine army, captured the Emperor himself, and proceeded to overrun most of Asia Minor—a disaster from which the Byzantine Empire never recovered. A united Christendom might have averted these catastrophes.

The Byzantines suffered further losses from the collapse of Armenia and the dispersion of its people. Armenians willing to change or conceal their religious opinions had long furnished the Empire with many of its ablest generals, statesmen, and even emperors, beginning with the great general Narses of the Emperor Justinian. They had lent their talents in all spheres of activity except the Church. In particular they had contributed to Byzantine architecture. Some scholars believe that they were the first to solve the problem of setting a dome on a square chamber, the central feature of Hagia Sophia in Constantinople. It is more likely that they originated the architectural form of the Greek cross, which became the basic form in Byzantine churches, and almost certain that they brought in the tall drums on which the domes of later churches rest. In any case, Armenian architects were extensively employed. One who was called in to repair Hagia Sophia when an earthquake caused part of its dome to collapse, in the tenth century, recalls the most tragic aspect of the fall of Armenia. In this century the northern kingdom had enjoyed an extraordinarily brilliant renaissance in art and architecture.

It was ruled from Ani by the Bagratids, a dynasty that traced its descent to David and Bathsheba—wife of Uriah the Hittite. Under these appropriate auspices the Armenians realized their ideal role as intermediaries between the Byzantine and Islamic civilizations, developing a style that was clearly influenced by both, but as clearly distinctive. At Ani they built the churches that still stand after centuries of complete neglect.[2] The most conspicuous feature of Armenian architecture is the cone that serves as a dome, crowning a circular or polygonal drum. It is also distinguished by exceptional refinement in detail, notably the delicacy of its stone filigrees, and by its superb masonry. But its historically most important elements are the pointed arches, vaults, and coupled piers that anticipated, and quite possibly influenced, the Gothic style that developed in Europe some generations later. After the fall of Ani to the Seljuks, some Armenians found refuge in Cilicia, in southwest Asia Minor, where they established a kingdom that held out for three more centuries. Here the early Crusaders became acquainted with Armenian architecture.

In the region of Lake Van there are no signs of a comparable brilliance, despite an old Armenian saying, "Van in this world and paradise in the next." It is a spectacularly beautiful region, favored as well by fertile lands, but under all its successive rulers—Armenians, Persians, Romans, Seljuks, Ottoman Turks—it failed to attain the splendor it had known under the Kingdom of Urartu; and today it is poorer than ever. Had the rich development of Armenian culture not been arrested by the Seljuk conquest, it might have recaptured its ancient glories. As it was, most Armenians could only hope for paradise in the next world.

"Who can foretell our future?" wrote John Katholikos, one of their historians, as he contemplated the monotonous wars and massacres even before the fall of Ani to the Seljuks. "Spare me the attempt. We are like a harvest reaped by bad husbandmen amidst encircling gloom and cloud." The Seljuk conquest was followed by a Diaspora; many Armenians emigrated to various regions in Europe. The many who remained in their native land faced an uncertain harvest. Because their Church still held them together, they were separated from the rest of the community. Some prospered in the cities as merchants and craftsmen doing business for the Turks. (Sinan, the greatest of Ottoman architects, seems to have been an Armenian—though it is almost a criminal offense in Turkey today to mention this probability.) Most remained on the soil as an unschooled peasantry. Although seldom persecuted, all were second-class citizens, or more strictly subjects. Having to live on sufferance or by

[2] The ruins of Ani, long deserted except for occasional nomads, are among the most impressive in Turkey, but only a favored traveler can be impressed by them. The site is a military defense zone, and the special permission needed to visit it is harder to get because of an official disposition to discourage interest in the unhappy past of Armenia. One who fortunately succeeded is Lord Kinross, whose book *Within the Taurus* (1954) gives an excellent account of Armenia past and present.

their wits, the Armenians at length acquired their reputation for being servile or grasping.

In the nineteenth century the harvest grew bloody. Roused by the nationalism that had enabled Greece to win its independence from the Ottoman Empire, the Armenians started a movement to recover their homeland. It was a hopeless cause. While there were more than a million of them in Turkey, they were scattered all over the country, a minority even in Armenia proper; and the Christian powers of Europe that gave some encouragement to their national aspirations gave no effective support. The outcome was the notorious massacres, sometimes led by religious fanatics, but generally organized by the Sultan's officials. The Turks had some excuse in that the Armenians aided the Russian armies that periodically invaded Turkey. In any case, the Armenians paid a terrible price; countless thousands of them were massacred in the 1890's. With the outbreak of World War I and another invasion by Russian armies came another wholesale butchery. An incidental episode was the utter destruction of Van by a Turkish general who boasted that "there will be either nothing but Turks or nothing but Armenians left in this city." No Armenians were left in it, or in other of their towns. Those who had not been exterminated fled to Russia or were dispersed. After the war the Armenians in Russia proclaimed the independence of their homeland, which the Allies then recognized in the Treaty of Sèvres; but nothing was done about it. Today only a few Armenians remain in Turkey, chiefly in Istanbul. Most live in the Soviet Socialist Republic of Armenia. If they are contented there, it is with something other than independence.

The marvel of their endurance is somewhat qualified by a still more ancient people who maintained their identity in the highlands of Armenia, without benefit of a Church. These were the wild Kurds—known to the Assyrians as Kurtie, to Xenophon as the Karduchi, and to the ancient Hebrews as a race descended from four hundred virgins who were raped by devils when en route to King Solomon's court. Nomads or mountain bandits, they were never really subdued. In the nineteenth century they preyed on the Armenians with little interference; local authorities were likely to feel helpless against them, and unlikely to consider robbing Armenians a criminal offense. When they rebelled against the new order of Ataturk, however, they finally were subdued. Many have been dispersed to other regions, as a means of absorbing or at least disarming them. Others still remain in their highlands, to give color to the landscape and some embarrassment to Turkish officials, but presumably to fight a losing battle to maintain their ancient way of life.

3. SARDIS: THE LYDIANS

"Do you take me for a Lydian or a Phrygian," remarks a character in Aristophanes, "and think to frighten me with your big words?" By this time the Lydians had acquired their reputation as an effeminate race of shopkeepers and harp players. It was hardly a worse reputation, however, than the Ionians had on the Greek mainland, and it was acquired only after their defeat by the mighty Persians. Before that the Lydians were known as brave warriors who fought on horseback; it was they who had driven the dreaded Cimmerians out of Asia Minor. They made, in fact, a quite creditable historic record during their brief ascendancy, even apart from their invention of coinage. They are among the most interesting examples of both the varieties and the continuities of culture in ancient Asia Minor.

In Homer the Lydians appear as the "Maeonians," Trojan allies who came from "beside the Gygaean lake" under Mt. Tmolus in the Hermus River valley. Aside from this broad, lush valley the chief source of their proverbial wealth was the gold dust washed down from Mt. Tmolus in the stream Pactolus, which flowed through their capital of Sardis. (King Midas had been cured of his golden touch by washing in the source of the Pactolus.) Sardis was a very old city, known to the Egyptians as Shardana as early as the fifteenth century B.C. Although the origins of the Lydians are typically obscure, they enter history as a mixed people speaking a hybrid language. Their kings were buried in Thracian tumuli similar to those of the Phrygians and the Etruscans, but had Asiatic names; their language included both Indo-European and Semitic elements. It seems almost certain that they were a non-Aryan people who had been in Asia Minor for centuries before the Greeks came. Greek tradition was unanimous that they did not come from Europe or the Aegean area, and their own tradition indicated connections with Anatolia. They traced their descent to "Atys, son of Manes." Manes was probably a form of the Phrygian Men, one of the supreme gods of Anatolia (whose name survives in the Turkish village of Menemen, near the mouth of the Hermus River); Atys was akin to Attis, the son of Cybele, and appears in the name of such historic kings as Alyattes and Sadyattes. The Lydians were especially devoted to the Mother Goddess, whom they knew as Kubebe and served as eunuch priests, and whose lion was also the sacred beast of their sun god. Their emblem of sovereignty was the Hittite double ax. The Greek story that the Lydians lost it to the Carians, who set up a statue to Zeus of the Double Ax (Labrandeus), illustrates the continuities that the Greeks could understand only in terms of divine marriages, rapes, or thefts.

The first clearly historic Lydian King was Gyges, known to the Assyrians as Guggu of Luddu. In 652 B.C. he was killed by the Cimmerians, who took all of Sardis except its citadel and moved on to ravage Ionia. Gyges himself had started attacks on the Ionian cities, which were continued by his successors Ardys, Sadyattes, and Alyattes. They subdued most of the cities but failed to take Miletus, their main objective. Alyattes, the king who finally crushed the Cimmerians, also waged war with the Medes to the east. Under his son Croesus the Lydian kingdom reached its peak. Near "Pteria," the former Hittite capital, Croesus fought an indecisive battle with the Medes, broken off when both sides were frightened by the eclipse that had been predicted by Thales; a peace treaty then divided Asia Minor between them. Through the Medes Croesus made his fatal acquaintance with the Persians.

In the meantime the Lydians had been making their more fruitful acquaintance with the Greeks. While warring on them, Gyges began paying tribute by making an offering to Delphi—the first "barbarian" after King Midas to do so. Alyattes drew much closer to them. He took himself an Ionian wife, among others; he presented two temples to Miletus, which had successfully defied him in a twelve-year war; he gave to the Delphic Apollo a great silver bowl that Herodotus thought was of all the offerings at Delphi the work most worth looking at; and he had extensive relations with Athens and Corinth as well. Periander of Corinth presented him with three hundred noble youths to serve as eunuchs. (En route to Sardis they were fortunately rescued by the Ionians of Samos.) But the warmest admirer of the Greeks was Croesus, their conqueror. He made rich gifts to all their well-known oracles, whom he seems to have consulted whenever he had to make an important decision. In gratitude the Delphians made the extravagant gesture of exempting Lydians from all charges, also granting them the perpetual right of becoming citizens. Ephesus too was especially grateful to Croesus for help in rebuilding its temple of Artemis, destroyed by the Cimmerians; the Lydian columns he contributed were possibly the prototypes of the Ionic order. At Sardis he maintained a brilliant cosmopolitan court, where he entertained not only the wise men of Hellas but noble Phrygians and envoys from other peoples. Himself the son of a Carian mother, he married one of his sisters to the ruler of Ephesus, another to the king of the Medes; he made a treaty of alliance with the Pharaoh of Egypt; he used the services of the kings of Babylon and Cilicia as arbitrators in drawing up his peace treaty with the Medes; and he sought the aid of the Spartans in his war with the Persians.

Of the original culture of the Lydians little is known. Archaeologists have yet to excavate systematically in their homeland, and what artifacts have been found date from the period after they came under Greek influence. Greek tradition, the chief source of information about them, stresses their love of pleasure. They were credited with the invention of games, balls, dice, knucklebones, and pitchers for drinking toasts; among their other delights were rich cookery, fine carpets, and parks and gardens. The cultural fusion between the Lydians and the Greeks became so complete that Herodotus noted only one important difference in their customs: all the daughters of the common people of Lydia took to prostitution as a means of raising their dowry. Inscriptions cut in stone pillars on the tomb of Alyattes, recording the contributions to it by the various classes of workpeople, indicated that the courtesans had contributed the largest share. This tomb—a great mound built up on a base of immense blocks of stone—Herodotus thought was inferior only to the monuments of Egypt and Babylon.

It is a reminder, however, that the Lydian kings were Oriental monarchs, and that from the Lydian apparently came the word *tyrant*. It suggests the well-known story told by Herodotus about the visit of Solon to Croesus. (The visit was chronologically impossible, as he should have known and probably did know; he sometimes preferred poetic truth to historic accuracy.) After showing the wise man of Athens his immense treasures, Croesus asked him who was the happiest man he had ever seen. Solon named several Greeks who had lived and died well. When the monarch grew angry at this apparent indifference to his splendor, Solon replied with the characteristic wisdom of the Greeks: the gods are jealous of all human greatness; great wealth is no guarantee of happiness, but may serve only to attract ill fortune; and no man may call himself happy until he dies peaceably. Croesus remembered the words of Solon when he was taken prisoner by Cyrus, but even then he had not learned his whole lesson. He sent his fetters to Delphi with a message: Was not Apollo ashamed of having encouraged him to start the fatal war against the Persians, and was it the wont of Greek gods to be ungrateful? The oracle answered: "It is not possible even for a god to escape the decree of destiny."

Sardis survived its royal master, and in time became essentially a Greek *polis*. It remained a great city through the Persian, Hellenistic, and Roman periods, as a textile center known for its carpets and as a station on a main highway to the East—the Royal Road of the Hittites and the

Persians. Many a notable marched through it at the head of an army, from Xerxes until Tamerlane, who wrecked it. Under the Ottomans it became a poor village but still had a large khan, to put up the caravans traveling from Persia and Aleppo to Smyrna. Today it is simply a poor village called Sert, without khan or caravan. A mile or so behind it a few towering pillars mark the remains of a Hellenistic temple to Cybele, excavated in this century. Little else shows except some sections of tumbled Byzantine wall on the hillside behind it, rising to the citadel of the Lydian city. This citadel has been largely destroyed by erosion, and the city itself lies deeply buried. Nothing remains of the works and the wealth of King Croesus.

Nevertheless Sardis is a memorable site. The Mt. Tmolus range towering above it has a Gothic grandeur; the rich plain of the Hermus River offers a suitable pastoral contrast. In the plain lie the "Gygaean lake" and the royal necropolis of Lydia—a hundred tumuli, including the vast mound that represents the tomb of Alyattes. The railroad from Izmir (Smyrna) to Sert follows the route of the ancient royal road. A few stations farther up the valley is Alashehir, ancient Philadelphia: one of the Seven Churches of Asia immortalized by St. John in the Book of Revelation. Down the valley at the foot of Mt. Sipylus—the mountain of the Sipylene Mother on which was carved the Hittite statue that the Greeks mistook for Niobe—is a village station called Choban Isa, meaning "Shepherd of Jesus." I am unaware of the connection, if any; but at least the kind of fusion that produced Lydia still haunts the valley that had been its home.

4. XANTHUS: THE LYCIANS

The most important Trojan allies in the *Iliad* came "out of far-off Lycia, from the eddying Xanthus." The Lycians appear as full allies and the only ones to be led by their kings, Sarpedon and Glaucus; Sarpedon in particular was a great hero, "the mainstay of Troy although a foreigner." Their presence on the scene is mysterious, however, since Lycia was indeed far off to the south, isolated from all the other allies, shut in by mountains. No main highway ever led to it—and none does today. As mysterious is the identity of these Lycians. Although they got their name from the Athenian Lycus (who also gave it to Lyceum) and came to be accepted as good Greeks, they spoke a strange language that is not yet well known. Generally classed among the Indo-European languages, it differs strikingly from all the others, having a syntax resembling that of the Polynesians and such phonetic combinations as *kssbeze, wzza,* and *tdi.* In historic times the Lycians remained different by clinging to their ancient matriarchal tradition, calling themselves after their mothers instead of their fathers.

Possibly for such reasons, one of their cities, Telmessus, was long famous for its snake men—seers and prophets consulted by both Lydians and Greeks. Arrian told the story that Gordius, disturbed by an eagle that settled on the yoke of his oxen, consulted a Lycian girl, and was so impressed by her advice that he married her; their son Midas was the first Phrygian king, and the knot tying the yoke became the Gordian knot. Alexander the Great was as impressed by Aristander of Telmessus, taking him along as his seer. But the Greeks might better have consulted the leaders instead of the magicians of this people, and studied their exceptionally honorable history. The Lycians remained more faithful to the heroic tradition of Homer than did the more famous Ionians. Strabo praised their integrity and restraint, remarking that they were "never influenced by the desire of base gain." They distinguished themselves above all by their political genius, as the one Greek people to achieve a united nation. The Lycians deserve much better than a note in an appendix— were it not that their history unfortunately was parenthetical, a sideshow off the main stage.

It begins before the Trojan War. Probably the Lycians were the people who occupied the "Lukka" lands mentioned in the Hittite royal archives as lands over which the kings had trouble maintaining their dominion. Early Lycian art and masonry suggest Hittite influence; among other things, the lion was a common symbol on coins and in bas-reliefs on rock tombs. And in Lycia the legendary hero Bellerophon destroyed the ubiquitous Amazons, who keep cropping up where Hittites had been.

Bellerophon is one indication of friendly relations between the Achaeans and the Lycians, even though at Homer's Troy they had somehow got on opposite sides. Apparently they had united in the expedition against Egypt, whose scribes list the "Luku" among the Sea Peoples. Greek tradition made "Cyclopes from Lycia" the builder of the celebrated wall of Tiryns in Argos. King Sarpedon was variously represented as a son of Zeus and a brother of Minos, in either case suggesting Aegean origin. Homer himself suggests the kinship of the two peoples in the scene between the Lycian hero Glaucus and the Achaean hero Diomedes. It is here that Glaucus tells the story of his grandfather Bellerophon: how he was maligned and driven from Argos, carrying to Lycia a "folded tablet" with secret instructions that he be put to death (this is incidentally the only allusion to writing in Homer); how he escaped death by performing his famous exploits, including the slaying of the terrible Chimera, the fire-breathing monster; how he became a king in Lycia, honored by all, until he gave offense to the gods by trying to fly to heaven on his winged horse Pegasus; and how he therefore ended his days as a lonely wanderer eating out his heart. Diomedes is delighted by the discovery that they are friends from far back—one of his ancestors had entertained the incomparable Bellerophon and exchanged gifts of friendship with him. Instead of fighting, the two champions thereupon clasp hands and swear friendship. Zeus then added a characteristic touch by sending Glaucus "clean out of his wits," inducing him to exchange his golden armor for the brazen armor of Diomedes; though probably the father of the gods did not mean to warn mankind to beware of a Greek bearing gifts.

When the Lycians re-entered Greek history centuries later they were still centered in the valley of the "eddying Xanthus," near the mouth of which was situated their leading city of Xanthus. They must have had exceptional energy and enterprise, for they attained a high level of culture and material prosperity in their rugged, out-of-the-way land. Except for the fertile Xanthus River valley they had little but mountains, which provided them with spectacular scenery but little else except timber. To-day the region supports no city of any size or importance. Under the Lycians it was dotted with cities, mostly small, but splendidly built. One still conspicuous sign of their wealth is their innumerable rock tombs, many elaborately sculptured and cut deep into cliffs.

In spite of their prosperity, however, the Lycians maintained their reputation for valor. They were the only people in western Asia Minor who were not subject to King Croesus of Lydia, and although they came under Persian domination they were still ruled by their own princes. In one revolt against the Persians Xanthus made history by fighting and dying to the last man, preferring complete destruction by flames to surrender. After Salamis it joined the Athenian Confederacy, indicating that the Greek world by now accepted the Lycians as true Greeks, even though they retained their peculiar language and script down to the fourth century B.C. They accordingly submitted to Alexander, "the liberator of Hellas," but supported Antiochus the Great against the Romans. When the Romans punished them by handing them over to Rhodes, they resisted so stubbornly that they were soon declared free. They preserved their freedom throughout the stormy second and first centuries B.C., earning the favor of Rome by holding out against Mithridates the Great, and later against Brutus when he was requisitioning money and men for his war against Mark Antony and Octavius. The citizens of Xanthus again fired their city after a heroic resistance, destroying themselves in the flames even though Brutus (according to Plutarch) begged them to spare their lives and offered his soldiers a reward for every Xanthian they saved. Only a hundred and fifty were saved, all against their will. One woman was found hanged, a hanged child dangling from her neck, in her hand the torch with which she had fired her home.

Meanwhile Xanthus had taken a leading part in the political achievement of the Lycians. While they had the Greek passion for independence, they also had a strong sense of national unity and succeeded in establishing an actual union, as the thoroughbred Hellenes never did. Early in their history they formed the Lycian League, a loose federation of princes that managed to agree on a common foreign policy. This was broken up in the last century of Persian domination, but when restored it became a genuine federation of republican cities—more than twenty-odd, including Xanthus, Patara, Pinara, Tlos (an apparent variant of Troas), Myra, and the large originally non-Lycian cities of Telmessus and Phaselis. Other Greek leagues failed to establish the principle of representation and left major decisions to the assemblies of the members. The Lycian League had not only a federal treasury, army, and navy but a federal congress, with representatives proportioned according to the size or importance of the cities, and with power to regulate foreign policy. History might have been quite different if the rest of the Greek world had had the political sense of the Lycians.

After the destruction of Xanthus by Brutus, Antony helped the Lycians to rebuild the city, as did Octavius when he became the Emperor Augustus. Under the Principate, however, their freedom became meaningless. The independent history of Lycia came to an end in A.D. 43, when the Emperor Claudius incorporated it into a Roman province. Its little cities remained splendid and Xanthus became known for its schools, but their real glory was no more. One wonders how their people felt about all the rock tombs in and about the cities—constant reminders of their heroic ancestors, and of death. For us these tombs throw a melancholy light on Lycian culture. The inscriptions carved on them (in letters painted alternately vivid red and blue) commonly include the curses of the deceased upon anyone who should put somebody else's bones in his tomb. The monotonous regularity of these curses suggests that the Lycians too could never feel sure of their private heaven, whatever it was.

Nevertheless they had one more gift for posterity—Santa Claus. St. Nicholas was born at Patara, below Xanthus, and became Bishop of Myra, from which St. Paul had sailed on his last journey, to Rome and martyrdom. He first became famous as a martyr and a patron of fishermen. His fame grew as his bones proved to have exceptional curative powers, and at length made Roman Catholics jealous that the heretical

Greeks should possess such relics. In 1087 a ship from Bari, with forty "bourgeois and merchants," stole the body of St. Nicholas from his church in Myra and carried it off to Bari, where it still rests. (Some Venetians who also had designs on it arrived too late, and had to content themselves with the bones of his uncle.) In Europe St. Nicholas took on the functions that have given him his present fame.

The feat of the Italians had been made possible by the Arab conquest of Myra shortly before. As an outlying region, Lycia suffered early from Arab raids; the ruins of Byzantine, Crusader, and Genoese fortresses along its shores are witness to its stormy history during this period. Soon it sank into a deeper obscurity than more favored regions of Asia Minor. Europeans forgot that St. Nicholas had come from here, and forgot Lycia itself. When Sir Charles Fellows finally rediscovered it, in the last century, he went into rhapsodies over both its natural beauties and its antiquities.[3] "This mountain country was literally strewed with cities and stately towers, which stand uninjured and unoccupied two thousand years after their builders are removed." Sir Charles was given to inaccuracy in his excitement, remarking more than once that the province of Lycia "has never been corrupted by the Roman or Christian styles." Elsewhere he specifically described some Roman buildings, and sometimes he mistook Roman for Greek. But his excitement was justified. The cities of Lycia had been little disturbed over the centuries because the region was thinly populated and relatively inaccessible. Some of them are perched high up on mountainsides.

Today most are still undisturbed, and seldom visited. A coastal steamer puts in at several of the old ports, such as Antiphellus (Andifli or Kash) and the very beautiful Telmessus (Fethiye), but one cannot travel readily into the interior except by jeep or on foot. One who is willing to adventure—and climb—may be somewhat disappointed, for the cities have suffered considerably from the inroads of nature since Fellows wrote. Where he saw stately monuments there is now likely to be only a tumble of stone in a tangled undergrowth. Even the Chimera, in the coastal mountains near Phaselis, is at last failing. In 1818 Captain Beaufort found it still a brilliant fire, which still refused to roast stolen meat; today it is only a sooty little flame. Yet Lycia has lost none of its natural beauty, and in spite of nature retains a wealth of Greek antiquities. Its cities are among the most magical sites in Asia Minor.

[3] *An Account of Discoveries in Lycia, Being a Journal Kept During a Second Excursion in Asia Minor*, London, 1840. The book is handsomely illustrated with his own drawings, and also contains many copies of inscriptions in the ancient Lycian script.

Xanthus stands out on a promontory above the river, looking out on a magnificent view of mountains and valley running to the sea; excavations here have brought to light more of the heroic city that preferred destruction to surrender. On hills in the valley above, the extensive ruins of Pinara and Tlos convey a vivid impression of once thriving, well-built cities, which still defy the wilderness in a haunted solitude and silence. The almost too obvious beauty of Telmessus, on a brilliant blue bay encircled by mountains—a Riviera calendar scene—is softened by the same air of antiquity. Scattered about the modern Turkish town are houses of the Lycian dead, some cut into the cliff behind it, with columned entrances, others perched on high pedestals with gabled roofs. One must hope that their vanished occupants slept better than they feared.

5. PERGAMUM

The city that was to become "the Athens of Asia" did not enter upon the scene until long after the Ionian cities had developed their brilliant culture. Pergamum first appears as the last stopping place of Xenophon and the remnants of the Ten Thousand, who recouped their dwindling fortunes by carrying out a final raid on the castle of a Persian nobleman in the vicinity. It was then an unimportant town, with an obscure past. Although it made up a founder in Pergamus, an alleged grandson of Achilles, its principal legendary figure was Telephus, son of Heracles, who became king of the neighboring region of Teuthrania and showed the Achaeans how to reach Troy. Some scholars have seen in him the Hittite Telibinus, and the legends about him at least point to the usual pre-Hellenic settlements in the region. *Pergamos* seems to be a Phrygian word, meaning burg or citadel; it appears in the *Iliad* as a synonym for Troy or Ilios, and has led Rhys Carpenter to argue that Pergamum was the actual site of the Trojan War. Also from the Phrygian come the names of Teuthrania and Caïcus, the river flowing past the city. It seems clear that the Great Mother had long resided in the region, for among the early popular cults of Pergamum were those of Cybele and Demeter.

The town rose to importance for the same reason that it long remained obscure—the Caïcus valley was not a major commercial route. Off the main highways, Pergamum was able to build up its power with little attention from the Persians and the successors of Alexander. It had a further advantage as a natural stronghold, situated on an isolated hill that towered a thousand feet above a plain running to the sea. In this stronghold Alexander left Heracles, his son by a Persian princess, who lived here for twenty years. More to the point, Lysimachus deposited here a treasure of 9,000 talents, or about ten million dollars, entrusting it to the care of a Paphlagonian eunuch named Philaeterus. Philaeterus later rebelled against Lysimachus, but in offering aid to Seleucus he shrewdly hung on to his treasure and his independence. He founded the Attalid dynasty that within a century made Pergamum a second Athens—

On a tall mountain, citied to the top,
Crowded with culture!

Although his successor, Eumenes, maintained its independence in wars with the Seleucids, it was Attalus I who firmly established the power and prestige of Pergamum by defeating the Gauls, the scourge of Asia Minor. Upon this victory he assumed the title of king and the name of Savior, and was recognized as such by other grateful cities. The oracle at Delphi proclaimed him son of Dionysus; the Athenians sought his favors by showering him with their highest honors, even ranking him among their eponymous heroes and gods. As the Attalids expanded their kingdom they lost much of this good will. While respecting the local autonomy of the cities in their realm—as they granted a democratic constitution to Pergamum itself—they required the cities to pay tribute and controlled their foreign policy. Many Greeks came to regard them as tyrants, as their ancestors had regarded Athens, and some historians are inclined to agree. There is no question, however, that they were able, vigorous, enterprising rulers. They improved agriculture, promoted industry in royal factories, instituted large-scale programs of public works, laid down progressive laws concerning public hygiene, and founded or refounded such notable cities as Attaleia (Antalya) and Philadelphia (Alashehir). Above all, they took with entire seriousness their mission as champions of Hellenism, the heirs of Athens.

In enlarging and beautifying their capital, the kings took full advantage of both its setting and the Hellenistic art of town planning. They built their citadel and palaces on the summit of the hill, commanding a spectacular view of mountain ranges and deep valleys to the north and west, and of the plain and sea to the south and east, with the island of Lesbos in the distance. The hill drops precipitously on three sides, in one of which they cut out a great theater. To the south it falls away in a long, gradual slope, and on this they laid out a series of terraces, each with its retaining walls, its statuary, and its harmonious group of buildings. From the Great South Gate in the lower fortification walls, a road wound up through these successive platforms, at every bend offering a dazzling new prospect. No Hellenistic city was handsomer than Pergamum.

Among its most sumptuous establishments was the colonnaded Gym-

nasium, the largest known from antiquity, whose ruins spread over several
terraces. The kings donated large sums to provide oil for anointing the
athletes but provided as munificently for the social, intellectual, and
artistic interests of the youth of Pergamum. Besides race tracks, baths,
and the usual facilities, the Gymnasium contained such amenities as a
small theater for practice in oratory, a room for practice in painting and
sculpture, and a king's hall where diplomas were handed out. (From a
list of promotions of young boys, scholars have estimated that the city
had a population of over 100,000.) Girls also attended, though in separate
schoolrooms. The official responsible for the "good conduct of the girls"
was responsible as well for contests in epic, elegiac, and lyric poetry, and
in reading and calligraphy. From other sources we learn that the Hellenistic curriculum included arithmetic, singing, and playing the cithara.
Athens in its prime had never done so well by its youngsters.

The most famous monument of the Attalids, the Great Altar of Zeus,
made somewhat too apparent their ambition to make their capital a
bigger and better Athens. The frieze of the Gigantomachia, running to a
length of almost 450 feet, covered so much space that the Olympians and
Titans were no longer adequate for this traditional subject; many other
gods and giants (including Cybele) had to be pressed into service.
Nevertheless the Pergamene sculptors executed the frieze with unflagging
power and ingenuity, achieving both unity and variety. They did their
work too well, indeed, for most of the heads have disappeared—probably
because early Christians were zealous to destroy these demons in the most
famous seat of Satan. The subject was a fitting symbol of the Attalid
ideal—the triumph of civilization over barbarism. And a nearby monument that directly commemorated the victory of Attalus over the Gauls
exhibited an ideal humanity. Its sculptors portrayed the Gauls not only
realistically but sympathetically; instead of the glorious triumph of the
Greeks, they represented the heroism and the dignity of the defeated.
From this school, if not this monument, came one of the finest examples
of Hellenistic sculpture, the Dying Trumpeter.

The Attalids were also generous in their gifts of monuments to other
cities, including Miletus and especially Athens. They made large donations to the Athenian schools of philosophy, in which at least one of the
kings had spent some years studying, and they built two stoas for the
city. (One in the Athenian agora has recently been reconstructed.) At
home, the kings were liberal patrons of art and learning. They were the
first art collectors of antiquity, transporting to Pergamum some famous
works of the classical period. Like the Medici, they entertained poets and
scholars at court, and to attract them built up a library second only to

the Museum of Alexandria. For bookmaking their factories turned out skins known as *charta pergamena,* which gave us our word *parchment.*

Except for art, however, Pergamum inspired little creative work of note. It produced no such men as Athens had. The best-known philosopher from its territory, Arcesilaus of Pitane, was known especially for his habit of suspending judgment, and perhaps for this reason wrote no books. Among the most important scholars at court was Crates, who was one of the first proudly to style himself a "critic"; he proved himself by his allegorical exegesis of Homer, demonstrating that Homer was the source of all knowledge, among other things of the Stoic cosmology. The only complete works of any Pergamene author to survive are two long didactic poems of Nicander, one about "the forms and deadly bane of beasts of prey" and how to obtain relief from their attacks, the other about antidotes for poisonous drinks. They help to reconcile us to the loss of some epic poetry written by scholars at the court of the Attalids. They make somewhat less tragic the end of the brilliant kingdom.

Attalus I had made an alliance with Rome, which all his successors maintained. Although this was probably wise statesmanship, it made many Greeks regard the kings as traitors to Hellenism, and made the kings themselves dependent on the uncertain favor of Rome; sometimes Rome chose to favor the rival kings of Bithynia, or even the Gauls. The dynasty—and in effect the Hellenistic Age—ended with the bizarre, baffling figure of Attalus III. Giving up all military operations, this Attalus confined himself to his palace. Apparently his chief hobby was cultivating medicinal plants in the royal gardens, but he is also reported to have whiled away his time studying zoology, writing treatises on agriculture, modeling in wax, playing with brass and bronze, and in general acquiring such a reputation that medieval tradition made him the inventor of chess. Other stories make him out as a despot who in an insane jealousy or fear had many officials, friends, and relatives treacherously murdered. These stories are given some credibility by his haste in getting himself deified in his lifetime; he was the only Attalid to pose as a god incarnate. Historians have therefore suggested unflattering motives for his bequest of his kingdom to Rome, such as unrest among the proletariat, a vindictive hatred of his subjects, and jealousy of the pretender to his throne. But quite possibly he was trying to protect his people against further aggression by Rome, since he stipulated that Pergamum was to retain its democratic constitution and its control of the surrounding territory. In any case, his act was logical and probably the best thing he could have done for Pergamum. The future plainly belonged to Rome. The last of the Attalids at least had the decency not to postpone the inevitable. In

133 B.C., after a reign of only five years, he joined his deified ancestors in the hereafter.

At first Pergamum had little reason to be grateful for his foresight. Its throne was claimed by Aristonicus, an illegitimate Attalid born of an Ephesian mistress, who started a rebellion and for a time succeeded in occupying the city. The Ephesians helped to assure the ascendance of their city by aiding the Romans and defeating him. The Pergamenes soon came to know the rapacity of the Roman tax collectors, and they enjoyed only a temporary respite when they co-operated wholeheartedly in the massacre ordered by Mithridates, who then set up his court in their city for some years. He shortly made it clear that he was more despot than liberator. Following his defeat, the city was punished by heavy taxes, and it suffered still more during the Roman civil wars. When the library of Alexandria went up in a fire, Mark Antony made Cleopatra a present of the library of Pergamum.

Under Augustus, however, the city recovered its library and its wealth. He honored it by making it one of two main centers for the new cult of Roma and Augusta, a form of worship that embarrassed him but delighted the erstwhile Greeks. This was perhaps a concession to his good friend Apollodorus of Pergamum, author of an *Art of Rhetoric* and head of the Apollodorian sect of philosophers ("whatever that may be," added Strabo). Later emperors embellished the city with still more temples. Like the other cities in Asia Minor, Pergamum enjoyed a long period of prosperity that to us looks uneventful but to its citizens no doubt seemed exciting enough, if not resplendent enough. It competed unsuccessfully with Ephesus and Smyrna for the official title of First and Greatest Metropolis of Asia. The Pergamenes had to be content with simple Metropolis, or the only one to be Twice Temple Warden of the Augusti; though at that Smyrna declared itself Thrice Temple Warden. We can only hope that they felt partially compensated by the fame of their city's greatest and most influential son—the physician Galen, who remained the chief authority on medicine down to the Renaissance, and whose technique of anatomical research was learned by Harvey at the University of Padua.

Probably they rejoiced more in the fame of their Asclepium, a grand establishment built about a sacred spring, to which patients from all over the empire came to be healed by the priests of Asclepius. This ever-gentle god of healing, who came to Pergamum when it was still an obscure town, recalls us to the wondrous anomaly that was Greek religion. In Homer Asclepius appears as a man, a physician. As a god he evidently began life in the form of a fertility daemon, specifically a snake. His snake is the most conspicuous symbol on both sides of the cistophori, a standard coinage issued by Pergamum and its subject cities (including Celaenae-Apamea) in the days of the kingdom, and later graced by the heads of Mark Antony and his Roman wife. On one side the snake is crawling out of a cista, a symbol also common to Dionysus, the sire of Antony; so we may be reminded of the reptile that crawled off with the secret of immortal life in the Babylonian Epic of Gilgamesh. Meanwhile Greek mythology had transformed Asclepius into a son of Apollo, born of a mortal woman; it was from his father that he learned the art of healing. He became revered as the father of medicine—the science that Galen studied in the Asclepium, and first practiced as surgeon to the gladiators of Pergamum. He was still more revered because he began resurrecting dead men, until Hades complained of this unfair practice. Zeus thereupon put an end to it by killing Asclepius (though on what occasion the stories differ), but later restored him to life and set his image, holding a snake, among the stars. Hence this immortal always remained half-human, and in a way most human as the Holy Snake, the symbol of regeneration.

The ruins of the Asclepium, a short distance from the foot of the hill of Pergamum, are centered about the great Incubation Chamber, a complex of underground passages and rooms for the sacred sleep, during which the god prescribed cures in dreams. For waking hours the sanatorium provided such spiritual and material comforts as the sacred fountain, marbled bathing basins, elegant toilets, a temple, a colonnaded walk, a library, and a small theater (now restored). Modern sanatoria might envy still more the secret of its legendary success—nobody ever died in the establishment; though possibly the secret was that dying patients were hustled out of it.

More striking, however, are the ruins of the city itself, as spectacular a site as any in Asia Minor. From the summit of the hill one may follow the route of the main road that wound down through the terraces to the Great South Gate. The Altar of Zeus is a disappointment, as only the foundations remain; all the statuary and sculptured frieze were removed to Berlin to adorn a reconstruction of the Altar in the Pergamum museum there—and to disappear in the last war, in which the forces of barbarism again threatened civilization. But enough remains of the palace of the kings, the gymnasium, the great theater, the many temples, the homes on the lower terraces, and the city walls and towers to give a vivid impression of the "Athens of Asia." Among the best preserved buildings is the so-called House of the Consul Attalus, named after its owner in the second or third century A.D., but dating from the time of the kings. Built to take full advantage of the terrain and the view, it was adorned with mosaics, wall paintings, and statuary. Here one may best appreciate the comfort and culture enjoyed by the more fortunate citizens of Pergamum.

Below the Great South Gate, where presumably hoi polloi lived, lies the modern city of Bergama. It has nothing of the splendor of ancient Pergamum, and no aspiration to become another Athens; but at least it retains an air of the far away and long ago. Following the slow traffic of donkeys and camels in its winding streets, one passes here the shell of a huge Byzantine basilica, there a Seljuk mosque, and everywhere much ancient stone built into house walls. One comes out on the plain leading to the sea, on which several tumuli recall the legendary past of a land once known as Teuthrania.

6. SMYRNA

Of the Seven Churches of Asia, Smyrna was one of two to receive only praise from John in Revelation; so religious scholars have found "not altogether without genuine spiritual significance" the fact that it alone is still a great city. The moral would be plainer if Philadelphia, the other Church so praised, had likewise thrived. It is further confused because the Ionian city of Smyrna was devoted to the Goddess Nemesis. Nemesis was known to other Greeks chiefly as the enemy of those touched by *hubris,* that pride of which the citizens of Smyrna certainly had their full share; yet it is the only Ionian city to survive to this day. The impious may therefore see a simpler reason for its success—commerce again. The city was beautifully located at the head of a long gulf commanding the trade of the Hermus River valley. It survived Miletus and Ephesus because the lower course of the Hermus was diverted. This river, which had been silting up its harbor in the manner of Ionian rivers, now empties into the gulf some miles to the north; and Smyrna still has a fine harbor.

The city was originally settled by Aeolians, on the eastern side of the gulf, on what was then an island. Excavations on the site prove that they came as early as 1000 B.C. and suggest relations with Homer's Achaeans: a gateway and some tombs in the vicinity resemble the Mycenaean. Greek tradition held that Smyrna was another of the cities founded by the Amazons, and certainly Hittites had been in the region. Mt. Sipylus, on which they carved the goddess mistaken for Niobe, was a little to the north. The patron deity of the city was the Sipylene Mother, another guise of Cybele. Nemesis was probably her offspring. That Nemesis became two in Smyrna was perhaps due to the twin peaks that stand out on the horizon on the western side of the gulf, and in ancient times would have demanded divine residents; or perhaps it was due simply to an incomplete fusion of the local and the Greek deity. If so, Homer might have had his say, for Smyrna and Chios were the cities most frequently mentioned as his birthplace. In any case the city was truer to the Mother than to the spirit of Homer. Goddesses figure prominently in the pantheon of later Smyrna. Among the many to assist Nemesis and the Sipylene Mother were Atargatis or Astarte, Isis, Diana of Ephesus, Hera, Persephone, "Lady Moon," and Semele, the mother of Dionysus.

The Ionians, who early took the city away from the Aeolians, proved to be too enterprising for their own good. Smyrna was a threat to the trade of Sardis; so the Lydian kings singled it out for destruction. It dropped out of history for several centuries. But Nemesis was still loyal to her city, or possibly forlorn. She visited Alexander the Great in a dream when he marched through the region, advising him to rebuild the city on the slopes of Pagus, a steep hill on the other side of the gulf. His successors carried out his plan. On this new site, where it still stands, Smyrna soon became one of the greater cities of Asia Minor. Ancient writers often called it the fairest of all cities. The sea, they wrote, "floated beneath it like a pedestal."

Although Smyrna made no notable contributions to Hellenistic culture or political life, it had an eye for history as well as for business. It supported the kings of Pergamum in their struggle against the Seleucids, and it early anticipated the ascendancy of the Romans. In 195 B.C. it built the first temple in Asia to the deified City of Rome. Under Roman rule it reached its zenith, becoming great enough to overshadow Pergamum, and even to vie with Ephesus. Unfortunately, its zenith coincided with the deterioration of classical culture. One of its most famous residents was the orator Aristides, who settled there in the middle of the second century. He was so admired that the Emperor Marcus Aurelius asked him for a speech during a visit to Smyrna, and he remained immensely popular down into Byzantine times. Today he is commonly cited as a ludicrous example of the verbosity and complacence that then passed for eloquence and wisdom.

Style grew more ornate in the next century, when the Roman Empire was on the decline. Smyrna now called itself "the First of Asia in beauty and size, and most brilliant, and Metropolis of Asia, and thrice Temple Warden of the Augusti, according to the decrees of the most sacred Senate, and ornament of Ionia." Even so, it fared better than the other metropolises in the long pull. Although its Church was not a major bishopric or ever the meeting place of an ecumenical council, its commerce held up. By the Middle Ages it was the most important city in the region, well ahead of its ancient rivals, Ephesus and Pergamum. In place of Nemesis and the Sipylene Mother it now had St. Anne, the supposed mother of Mary, for whom a nearby valley was named. Even a less apocryphal deity, however, might not have saved Smyrna from a calamity visited by another personification of *hubris*. In 1402 the mighty Tamerlane laid siege to its citadel, then held by the Knights of Rhodes, took it, and sacked the city with his usual thoroughness; its history thereafter is a blank until the seventeenth century. About all we know of it is that it was still fabricating religious tradition, in keeping with its ancient rivalry with Ephesus. From this period emerged the apocryphal tomb of St. Polycarp, the early martyr-bishop of Smyrna, which was also known as the tomb of St. John (as were other tombs) despite the strong tradition of his burial in Ephesus. But the city again rose on commerce, while Ephesus dropped out of history for good.

In the nineteenth century Greeks began streaming back to Asia Minor, animated by the business motives of their forefathers. Smyrna became in effect their capital. It was now the only considerable port of Ionia, the major outlet for all the rich river valleys, exporting their figs, grapes, melons, and olives. It prospered in spite of the frequent rapacity of its Ottoman governors; by the end of the century its commerce surpassed even that of Constantinople. And so it again invited nemesis, without the protection of its ancient goddess. At Smyrna, in the spring of 1919, landed the Greek army that invaded Turkey to recover their ancient homeland. A little more than three years later the remnants of this army streamed back into the city, with the forces of Ataturk on their heels. As they made their last stand in the course of re-embarking for Greece, the city was largely destroyed by a conflagration that the Turks blame on the Greeks, the Greeks on the Turks.

Smyrna has risen again, to become the third city of Turkey, but in a strange guise. When predominantly Greek, it was an exotic "Oriental" city, known for its bazaars and its polyglot people. As rebuilt by the Turks under the Turkish name of Izmir, it is a modern Western city, traversed by boulevards, gleaming with chromium and plate glass. A large district near the old harbor has been made over into a handsome park and fairground, where an International Fair is held annually—a link with the commercial past. But Izmir has little charm, less character. It is at once garish and drab in its newness, and unlikely to mellow with age. Its most interesting section is a poor one that survived the fire, on the steep slope of Pagus. Here one may find chunks of ancient stone in the crooked houses lining the crooked streets. Hidden behind a wall are the fairly imposing remains of the Roman agora; in the silence of this secluded spot one may commune with the ghosts of ancient Smyrna. For the rest, the pilgrim to antique lands may look upon Izmir chiefly as a convenient center for expeditions to its ancient rivals, Pergamum and Ephesus, or to the sites of other Ionian cities, such as Clazomenae, Erythrae, and Teos.

Yet from the summit of Pagus, at sunset, one may still look down a vista to the once fairest of cities. Here stand the massive walls of the castle taken by Tamerlane, and on the slopes some remnants of the city walls built by Lysimachus. Izmir, far below, becomes softer in the sunset haze, girdling a harbor as lovely as ever. The shimmering sea still floats beneath it like a pedestal; the twin peaks of Nemesis still stand out on the horizon that entranced ancient travelers to Smyrna. From the farther side of Pagus one looks out on a rolling landscape, silvered by olive trees, which as twilight falls is no longer Turkey, but Ionia.

7. ANTIOCH

Strictly, Antioch does not belong in this study. Although modern Antakya is in Turkey, the ancient city was in the province of Syria, not Asia Minor, and Turkish possession of the region is still disputed by modern Syria. But I cannot forbear from adding a note on so fabulous a city, whose history was so intimately connected with that of Tarsus in the Roman era, and of all Asia Minor during the Hellenistic era.

In *A Short History of Antioch* (1921) E. S. Bouchier pictures it as a predominantly Western city, which for many centuries was a bulwark of Western civilization, and which was therefore hated by the people of the interior, who repeatedly tried to destroy it. This is an appropriate conception for the city that first gave Christians their name. The ancients, however, had a rather different idea of it. They dwelt on the Oriental sensuality and effeminacy of its citizens, wholly devoted to luxury, ease, and licentious pleasure. Apollonius of Tyana found it more incorrigible than Tarsus, "characteristically insolent, and quite indifferent to anything Greek." Hadrian was especially lavish in his gifts of public buildings to it, but also became exasperated by its insolent, irresponsible gaiety. Juvenal made its Orontes River a symbol of the Oriental scum that was making a sewer of Rome:

> Obscene Orontes, diving under ground,
> Conveys his wealth to Tiber's hungry shores,
> And fattens Italy with foreign whores.

The ancients, I fear, were more nearly right.

The city lies toward the end of a broad alluvial plain, approached from the north by another historic pass through the mountains behind Alexandria-ad-Issum (Iskenderun). The plain is littered with about two hundred *hüyüks* containing the usual layers of settlements, dating as far

back as the Stone Age. Leonard Woolley's excavation of one, the mound
of Atchana that had been Alalakh, capital of a forgotten kingdom, demonstrated the far-flung, continuous relations it had had with the surrounding empires, from the Sumerian and Egyptian to the Hittite and Assyrian.
In this hoary land Antioch was a parvenu. It was founded by Seleucus,
general of Alexander the Great, to serve as the capital of his kingdom.
He moved in Athenian and Macedonian colonists and made Apollo its
patron, lord of a splendid temple in the nearby groves of Daphne. Presently it also had a large Jewish colony, which Josephus said was granted
a privileged position, and its lower class no doubt included native Syrians
and floating workers from elsewhere. Like the forgotten cities of the
plain, Antioch became a meeting place of many cultures.

As the Seleucid capital, it flourished throughout the vicissitudes of the
Hellenistic era. It commanded a fertile plain and commercial highways
leading east and west, south and north; it was blessed by abundant water
from mountain springs and streams as well as from the Orontes River on
which it lay; in the summer it was cooled by winds blowing in from the
Taurus Mountains. Under Roman rule Antioch became one of the greatest
cities of the empire, "Third Metropolis" and "Queen of the East," with a
population up to half a million. Its extent is indicated by the remains of
Roman walls running up and around the mountain behind the present
city of Antakya. Its opulent life was pictured by Libanius, one of its
celebrated sons, in an oration delivered in A.D. 360 when it was still near
the height of its prosperity. He described its crowded streets and gates,
brilliantly lit all night so that work and play could go on by night and
day; its residential district with three-story houses, the roofs of which
were used for sleeping in the summer; its many fountains, baths, temples,
villas, houses of entertainment; its nearby groves of Daphne, a religious
resort famous for its splendor and gaiety. Chinese merchants later
recorded their awe of the vast and sumptuous city.

Yet from the outset Antioch had little of the old Greek spirit, of Ionia
or Periclean Athens. Its great pride was a monument to its vulgar taste—
a colossal statue of Apollo, which Seleucus had made by an imported
sculptor (from Athens, alas). Representing Apollo as the leader of the
Muses, playing a harp and singing, this was a barbarous composite of
shiny materials: vine wood covered with a golden peplos, the exposed
parts of the body in white marble, the hair of gold intertwined with a
golden laurel wreath, the eyes two huge jacinths, etc. The Muses never
made Antioch their home. It had schools of rhetoric and logic, and
eminent sophists who attracted disciples from all over, but it had no
creative writers or singers of note.

In fairness to Antioch, it was born too late. It never knew independence, never was a genuine Greek *polis*. It was just Greek enough to be sophisticated, satirical in its wit, notoriously critical in spirit, often hostile to its rulers, always turbulent. Having been denied real freedom, its citizens took to license. They exercised their lively wit in ridiculing the traditional virtues of manliness and womanliness, honoring the arts and the vices of luxury. They expressed their civic pride in the magnificence of their games, festivals, and spectacles.

By their irreverence, at any rate, they helped to earn the chief historic distinction of their city. Christianity took root not in the virtuous, humble countryside, but in the wicked, decadent city—and first of all in Antioch. Antioch had a Christian community even before Paul came here from Damascus, and it remained for some centuries a major center of Christianity. In Ignatius it produced one of the earliest martyrs and most popular saints of the East. Its church then took a leading part in the doctrinal struggles that developed Christian theology. This was not an ideal role, however. Antioch produced no theologians so original as Clement and Origen of Alexandria, its chief rival, or so heroic as Athanasius. It was naturally given to schism, and it tended to take a more Oriental than Greek view of the Godhead. Mainly it was concerned with preserving the real humanity of Jesus. Paul of Samosata, Bishop of Antioch when the city was the capital of Queen Zenobia of Palmyra, taught here the heresy of Adoptionism, that Jesus was a man who had been adopted by God as his son; he denied the *Logos* supported by Alexandria. Lucian the Martyr, head of a school at Antioch, had as disciple Arius, who gave his name to the notorious Arian heresy that the Son was lesser than the Father. (During the brawls over Arianism a certain Bishop Stephen tried to discredit a Western peacemaker who came to the city by turning a harlot loose on him.) With the condemnation of these and the later heresies of Nestorianism and Monophysitism, the influence of Antioch waned.

In the meantime the ethical teachings of Jesus—man or God—apparently had little effect on its citizens, who maintained their reputation for insolence and ingratitude. Among the striking scenes in its history was the coming, in A.D. 362, of the Emperor Julian the Apostate, who considered making Antioch his capital. Upon his entrance he was greeted by a bad omen—the annual wailing for Adonis, an Oriental god who had outlived the upstart Greek gods to whom Julian was devoted. He found the temple of Apollo decaying and deserted, on the altar a lone goose instead of the fat oxen he had expected. He was more distressed when he removed from the sacred precincts of Daphne the bones of St. Babylas, a local martyr, whose presence had disturbed Apollo; for that night the temple and statue of Apollo went up in flames—a sure-fire miracle, in the view of local Christians. And as a pagan puritan, devoted to high thinking, Julian antagonized all classes and sects in Antioch. During a Saturnalia the streets rang with bawdy ridicule of his religion, his person, even his beard. As punishment, the magnanimous emperor was content to compose and publish "Enemy of the Beard," a satire on the effeminacy and licentiousness of Antioch; but he quit the city, to pass his last winter at Tarsus.

The treatment accorded Julian might have passed for Christian zeal were it not that later in the century the citizens of Antioch visited similar indignities upon Theodosius the Great, the Christian emperor who closed down all pagan temples. Infuriated by some edicts of taxation that interfered with their pleasures, a mob threw down the statues of the emperor and his family and dragged them through the streets. Antioch then suffered the most dreadful of punishments: it was stripped of not only its lands and revenues but its rank of Metropolis, and its baths, theaters, and Circus were closed. Fortunately Theodosius also proved merciful, presently restoring the Queen of the East to its ancient honors and pleasures. It expressed its gratitude wholeheartedly, if in a somewhat pagan fashion, by erecting hundreds of new statues to the emperor.

But early in the sixth century the sins of Antioch finally caught up with it. Its pleasures had periodically been interrupted by destructive earthquakes, and now there occurred the most catastrophic of them all (unhappily at a time when the city was celebrating the festival of the Ascension). A quarter of a million people are said to have perished. The city was rebuilt by the Emperor Justinian, but only to fall to the Sassanian Emperor Chosroes, who burned down most of it. Soon it fell again, to Chosroes II. By this time the Arabs were on the march, fired by their more austere faith. They took Antioch in the year 638, or only 16 by the Moslem calendar, meeting little resistance here or elsewhere in Syria; its Christians were militant only over their doctrinal differences with their fellow Christians. Even so, the natives could not have rejoiced in the thought that after almost a thousand years Syria had reverted to native rule, for the Arabs humiliated Antioch by classifying it as a provincial town of second rank.

It remained a great city, however, and after three centuries of quiet it re-entered history as a major objective in a new series of holy wars. It fell to the Byzantines, then to the Seljuks, then to the Crusaders. The Crusaders indicated the greatness of Antioch by boasting that they killed a hundred thousand Moslems in it. It could still inspire miracles too.

When the Crusaders suffered from a terrible famine, their leaders buried a rusty lance in the cathedral of Antioch, to unearth it solemnly as the Holy Lance of the Crucifixion and thus raise the spirits of the army and the populace. But it was still torn by dissension, now between Orthodox Greeks and Catholic Latins. The city that gave Christians their name—apparently in mockery—finally passed out of Christian history in the thirteenth century, when it was captured and pillaged by the Mamelukes of Egypt. Under their rule and that of the later Ottomans, it dwindled into an insignificant town.

Today very little remains of ancient Antioch except sections of its city walls. In a nearby cliff is the so-called Cave of St. Peter, which the natives show off as the oldest Christian church—regrettably having Peter preach in it instead of the more suitable Paul. It is not an imposing monument. By now scholars have also discredited a chalice found near Antioch, which for a time passed as the chalice used by Jesus at the Last Supper; it was made some centuries after his time. More dignified than its alleged Christian antiquities is the oldest mosque of Antioch, made over from a Byzantine church and named after "Joseph the Carpenter." Still better is the local museum, newly built to exhibit many late Roman floor mosaics unearthed at Daphne. (Others found here may be seen in the Louvre in Paris.) The mosaics exhibit a lively, gay fancy, and are a credit to the vitality of ancient Antioch. Pagan in subject matter, they are to some extent Byzantine in style, and anticipate the vigorous new art that was developing here, as elsewhere in the East, at a time when the Roman Empire was in theory hopelessly degenerate and uncreative.

Modern Antakya has preserved some of this vitality. Almost the same size as Tarsus, it is a much more attractive town that seems at once older and livelier. It has a medieval-looking section, a maze of alleys with an air of having been lived in for centuries; its main street is colorful and gay. One reason for the difference is that Antakya is inhabited by Arabs as well as Turks, and Arabs are a much more vivacious people. Hence the famous groves of Daphne, a few miles from town, are again a pleasure resort. They lie in a glen made cool and lovely by many little waterfalls, and noisy by too many picnickers; but the noise might not disturb the shades of the ancient residents. They might be more dismayed, or mystified, by the annual contest between teams of dancers from the sur- rounding villages. I watched these teams perform in the local stadium in brilliant sunshine, against the backdrop of the gaunt mountain over which run the Roman city walls. They danced with self-conscious intentness, since the winning team was to get a cash award and a chance to perform at the national contest in Istanbul. All were men, mostly middle-aged;

they displayed little flair for dancing, and as little apparent delight in it. It was a typically solemn Turkish performance, a far cry from the gaiety of old Antioch. I was more disposed to forgive the ancient sinners that evening when a full moon rose behind the walls on the ridge of the mountain—the walls they so poorly defended, but that they built, as they lived, as if they were going to live forever.

8. CYPRUS

The island of Cyprus, some fifty miles off the coast of Cilicia, had a history similar to that of Cilicia but even more varied. It was important from early in the Bronze Age as one of the main sources of bronze; it gave its name to the metal copper. It entered the books about 1500 B.C., when Egyptian scribes noted its conquest by Thutmose III. The legendary founders of its cities had the usual connections with Homeric heroes, with somewhat better than the usual reason; Mycenaean settlement was much more extensive here than in Asia Minor. There were also colonies of Phoenician traders, whose Astarte was akin to Aphrodite, the principal deity of Cyprus. Throughout its recorded history the island was a meeting place of East and West. After submitting to the Assyrians, it was ruled successively by Persians, the Ptolemies of Egypt, Romans, Byzantines, Arabs, Crusaders, Venetians, and Ottoman Turks. Its later history differed from that of Cilicia, or of Asia Minor in general, in coming under more marked Western influence. The kingdom established by the Crusaders—the House of Lusignan—was the richest and strongest of the Crusader kingdoms, lasting three hundred years. It was then taken over by the Venetians, whose misrule anticipated that of the Turks but first provided the legend of Othello. In 1878 the Turks handed it over to Great Britain in return for guarantees of protection against the Russians. The British had a sentimental claim to it. En route to the Holy Land, Richard the Lionhearted had taken possession of the island, staying long enough to marry Berengaria and have her crowned Queen of England, then turning it over for a price to Guy de Lusignan.

In spite of this pageantry, however, the history of Cyprus is relatively undistinguished; and therein is the excuse for this parenthetical note on an island that technically was not part of Asia Minor. The Cypriots—now agitating for union with Greece—have rarely been independent, never in the last two thousand years of their history. More to the point, they were throughout antiquity culturally backward and insular, failing to keep pace with the rest of the Greek world. They clung to a clumsy syllabary apparently derived from the Minoans, and made no contributions to literature. Their art was unoriginal, their coinage inferior. They had no famous schools. They had a few famous sons, such as Zeno the Stoic and Barnabas the companion of Paul, but these went off to do their work elsewhere. Chiefly the Cypriots won a reputation for sensuality and love of luxury. It seems fitting that Mark Antony presented the island to Cleopatra.

Its backwardness cannot be attributed to geographical handicaps. Cyprus was richer in natural resources than Ionia or mainland Greece, and it lay in the main stream of commerce; the no more favorably situated island of Rhodes to the north took a leading role in the Hellenistic era. The most significant factor, I should say, was its political backwardness. While the rest of the Greek world was developing the *polis*, Cyprus clung to kingship. Its local princes included some able, patriotic rulers, notably Evagoras of Salamis, who finally won independence from the Persians; but his feats emphasize that as late as the fourth century the cities of Cyprus were still ruled by princes. A people who had never known the full, free life of the *polis* were unlikely to distinguish themselves under the rule of the Ptolemies and the Romans.

Thereafter the Cypriots maintained their identity with the help of a miracle. In the fifth century A.D. their Archbishop was blessed by a vision that led to the discovery of the body of St. Barnabas; on his breast was a copy of St. Matthew's Gospel that St. Mark had placed there when burying him. In return for the gift of this gospel, the Emperor Zeno of Byzantium granted the Archbishop of Cyprus extraordinary privileges that he enjoys to this day, such as wearing an imperial purple cope and carrying an imperial scepter instead of a pastoral staff. The grateful Cypriots clung to their Holy Orthodox faith through three centuries of Arab raids and invasions, and then through the four centuries of Roman Catholic rule that began with the coming of the Crusaders.

The vigorous House of Lusignan most fully realized the potentialities of Cyprus, aided by Christian refugees from the Holy Land, and by a disposition to ignore papal protests against commerce with the infidels. This period (1192–1489) was the most brilliant in its history. The island became celebrated for its wealth and luxury; Famagusta in particular was known as "the richest of all cities." The most impressive monuments in Cyprus are its medieval castles, abbeys, and churches, including the Gothic cathedrals of Nicosia and Famagusta. It also contributed to medieval letters, directly and indirectly; St. Thomas Aquinas and Boccaccio dedicated works to its kings. This brilliance, however, was wholly Latin, a foreign importation. The natives—of whom we hear almost nothing—contributed only hard work and taxes. Under the rule of Venetians and Turks, who came only to exploit, Cyprus relapsed into insignificance. The Venetians left chiefly their fortifications, such as the city walls that still enclose the heart of Nicosia, the capital. In their three centuries of occupation the Turks built nothing of consequence. To Great Britain they bequeathed a headache by restoring the authority of the Orthodox Church, which in recent years has led the belated struggle for union with Greece, and by leaving a Turkish minority that is bitterly opposed to Greek rule.

The mixed peoples and cultures of pre-Christian Cyprus have made it a happy hunting ground for archaeologists, who have excavated numerous sites. But the remains from the Greco-Roman period are not very memorable. The great city of Salamis is a sandy waste. At Paphos only the foundations remain of the temple of the Cyprian Aphrodite, who was born on the coast nearby. At the site of a later city of Paphos, the "Tombs of the Kings," a catacomb-necropolis, are a ghostly reminder that Cyprus was ruled by kings to the end. Excavations at Curium, superbly situated on a cliff above the Mediterranean, have uncovered surprisingly little fine marble; its celebrated temple of Apollo nearby is built of an ordinary yellowish stone. More memorable are the mosaic pavements of a late Roman villa, luxurious with hot and cold baths. Inscriptions in the pavement express the hope that Christ would protect the establishment as Phoebus Apollo once had, but both fell down on the job—Moslem Arabs destroyed it. The hope seems more pathetic because except for the mosaics the villa was a rather shoddy construction, built atop the messy remains of earlier buildings. Some solid, well-built wall from an earlier period emphasizes the decay in the later Roman world. On Cyprus men were no longer building with pride, for keeps.

The excellent museum of Nicosia may also stir some melancholy thoughts. Among its most striking exhibits is a reproduction of graves, from the Stone Age to the early Greek period, with bones, pots, and other objects placed exactly as they were found. On the later tombs inscriptions in both Greek and Phoenician express the sentiment so common among the ancients—curses on whoever might violate the tomb. The curses rarely worked. Poor men might sleep in peace in their common graves, and take with them their few possessions; those who could afford a resting place worthy of their higher station were always likely to be robbed, or denied the privacy that apparently meant so much to them. Just what did it mean? And why? The poor, on the other hand, were given to an unenviable kind of piety. A collection of rude terra cottas from a sixth-century sanctuary includes a popular bearded, horned god later identified with Zeus-Amon. He is an unlovely figure without the slightest air of majesty, or even anything fearsome. He is simply crude and ugly—as sorry an exhibit of the religious spirit of man as one can imagine. And he was worshiped all over the island that gave birth to the beauteous Aphrodite, and was the first destination of St. Paul when he set out on his missionary journeys.

9. NICAEA

The city that was to give its name to the Nicene Creed was a Hellenistic foundation, named by the general Lysimachus after his wife, and laid out as a city of the new age, in an exact square with a gate in each side. It lies at the end of a twenty-mile lake, the ancient Lake Ascania, on a site previously unoccupied by Greeks. The region, however, was long familiar to them, and is more or less hallowed by sacrilegious association. Homer mentions Lake Ascania; Ascanius was the legendary son of Aeneas. In Genesis, Askenaz, the grandson of Japheth, denotes the Phrygians, one of whose favorite gods was Men Askaenos. (There was another Lake Ascania not far from Celaenae-Apamea.) Following the Phrygians came the Bithynians, also from Thrace, who gave their name to the region. They too adored Cybele, later building a temple for her in Nicaea. One legend made Nicaea a nymph, her daughter.

A warlike people, the Bithynians were a constant nuisance to the Greeks and Persians alike. They never submitted to Alexander the Great, formed an independent kingdom during the Hellenistic era, and then caused the Greeks more grief by bringing the Gauls into Asia Minor. Nevertheless they became urbanized and Hellenized. Their first important king, Nicomedes I, gave his name to the city of Nicomedia, which was also a foundation of Lysimachus. He or another Nicomedes proved his Hellenism by offering to redeem the whole public debt of Cnidus in return for its statue of Aphrodite by Praxiteles. (The city declined the offer.) The last of the Bithynian kings cultivated chiefly the vices of the Greeks, maintaining so scandalous a court that Julius Caesar was reproached for having spent some time there as a youth. Upon dying, in 74 B.C., he followed the example of Pergamum and bequeathed his kingdom to the Roman people. From another city of the kingdom, Bithynium (Bolu), later came Antinoüs, the beloved of Hadrian.

Throughout the Hellenistic and Roman eras Nicaea was a prosperous but undistinguished city. It was overshadowed by Nicomedia, the capital of the Bithynian kings and later of Diocletian. Although it could boast of having entertained many celebrated men, such as Julius Caesar and Hadrian, it produced almost none of its own except the astronomer Hipparchus. In its rivalry with Nicomedia it could only make up more exalted founders, claiming Dionysus, Heracles, and Asclepius. It was never famous for the "Nicaean barks of yore" mentioned by Edgar Allan Poe. What made it famous, and led Poe to take its name in vain, was Constantine's belated decision to make it the seat of the congress of bishops he summoned to settle the Arian unpleasantness. First deciding on Ancyra (Ankara), he chose Nicaea instead because of its "pleasant climate" and its convenience to Constantinople. Otherwise the Trinity would have been composed in the capital of modern Turkey.

Historians lament that we do not have the minutes of the first Ecumenical Council of Nicaea, as we do of the much less famous councils of Ephesus and Chalcedon. Even the number of bishops who attended is uncertain, for the traditional 318 was picked because of the mythical 318 servants of Abraham. But we do have an eyewitness account of the scene by Bishop Eusebius, and though this is typically florid, the pageantry was undoubtedly up to the historic occasion. The Council was formally opened on May 20, 325, in the Imperial Palace of Nicaea. The bishops were all assembled and at attention when Constantine entered, in imperial purple and gold. According to Eusebius he was ablush with modesty but looked like an angel of the Lord. In an unblushing fashion he presided throughout the proceedings, at which all Nicaea must have been agog. At the end he celebrated the formulation of the Nicene Creed by inviting all the bishops to attend a great banquet in honor of the twentieth anniversary of his accession to the throne. They marched between lines of imperial bodyguards with drawn swords, into the inmost chamber of the palace, some of them to recline at Constantine's own table. "It felt as if we were imagining a picture of the Kingdom of Christ," wrote Eusebius, "and that what was happening was no reality, but a dream."

The violent aftermath of the Council was no dream, since many of the bishops, including Eusebius, did not really believe in the creed that Constantine had forced through. Another major matter that they unanimously settled, and left permanently unsettled, was the dating of Easter: while they agreed on a formula, the Eastern and Western churches used different dates for the spring equinox from which Easter was calculated. (They were to disagree too on the dating of Christmas.) Hence the famous Council inaugurated a series of ecumenical councils, to resolve the issues it had raised and the further disputes arising from the requirement of unanimity. The seventh and last of these also met at Nicaea, in 787, to condemn Iconoclasm. Although its decision was later reversed under imperial pressure, and had to be reaffirmed, it effectively settled the matter and so marks an important date in Byzantine history. The formal theological development of the Holy Orthodox Church ended, as it began, at Nicaea. Fittingly, a church in Nicaea was later adorned with some of the finest Byzantine mosaics; though unhappily this church was destroyed in the war between the Greeks and Turks that followed World War I.

Nicaea became an important city in its own right, as a station on the main road from Constantinople to the East, and accordingly was often the scene of conflict of a different kind. Falling to the Seljuks, it became the first capital of their Sultanate in Asia Minor. Shortly afterward, in 1097, it was retaken by the Crusaders. The Second Crusade passed through it, to make a splendid show before meeting disaster at Dorylaeum. The most brilliant period of its history followed the fall of Constantinople to the Fourth Crusade, when the able Lascarid dynasty built up the Nicaean Empire and attracted to its court the greatest scholars of the time. It maintained this proud tradition by holding out valiantly against the Ottoman Turks, withstanding long sieges before it fell to them in 1329. Ibn-Batuta, who found the city in ruins, reported that the final siege lasted twelve years.

Nicaea regained some importance early in the sixteenth century, when the Sultan Selim I moved in families of Persian potters to make the faïence that replaces Byzantine mosaics on the walls of Ottoman mosques. In the last half of the century the Nicene potters perfected their distinctive style, turning out tiles with flower designs in green, blue, and a striking tomato-red, against a white background. (Their tiles may be admired in a number of Istanbul mosques, particularly the lovely Rustem Pasha and the Sokullu Mehmed.) Thereafter, however, their artistry declined; their red became paler and rarer, soon giving way to blue and white; and by the eighteenth century Nicaea had virtually ceased making tiles. Like many another famous city under the Ottomans, it faded out of history.

Today it is the village of Iznik, again overshadowed by its ancient rival: Nicomedia is the considerable city of Izmit. In spite of its fame it has attracted few travelers, for it is no longer on the main road or convenient to Constantinople. Although it is only some fifty miles distant as the crow flies, the trip used to take most of a day, by steamer, rickety bus, wagon, and motor boat. Improved roads and buses now make it easier to reach, but it is still off the main-traveled roads. The site that once resounded with imperial speeches, theological debates, and battle-cries of Christians and infidels is today disturbed only by the creak of wagons on cobblestones and the early-morning clatter of storks.

For this reason, however, it is one of the most charming sites in Turkey. The village and its gardens and pastures lie within the ancient walls, with tree-lined avenues leading to the gateways. The gateways and large sections of the wall are in fairly good condition; they form a square plainly visible from the Istanbul-Ankara airplane, which passes directly overhead. Although the walls are mostly Byzantine and Seljuk construction, the gateways were the work of Roman emperors, including the ubiquitous Hadrian. Scattered about the village, which is a relatively bright and clean one, are other mementos of the long history of Nicaea, including a section of Roman amphitheater, the foundations and arches of a Byzantine church, and a Seljuk mosque with a handsomely carved marble portico and a green-and-red tile minaret. On the hill above the town are remains of ancient tombs. A local museum has the usual collection of odds and ends of Roman antiquities, none very striking, but a decent salvage from oblivion.

I first visited Nicaea on an Easter—as reckoned by the Western churches. Although not then aware of the appropriateness of my timing, I responded piously enough to the pastoral setting. The village drowsed and the lake gleamed under a bright sun, in a still pleasant climate. Now and then a peasant and cart passed through the Roman gate that faces the lake, where Nicaean barks had no doubt sailed. Local youngsters pressed on me their services as guides, as well as presents of flowers and bits of mosaic from the rubble of the destroyed church. They would accept no presents in return, explaining solemnly that if they did they could no longer be my friend and make me further presents. This age-old hospitality to the infidel stranger was a pleasant epilogue to all the strife that had made Nicaea famous. Peace and good will had come at last.

10. TREBIZOND

The glamour that once was Trebizond dates from the Empire of Trebizond, founded by the Comneni family after the fall of Constantinople to the Fourth Crusade. The dynasty lasted for 257 years, the longest in Greek history. While their empire was actually a feeble one, it made up in pomp for what it lacked in power, becoming famous for its court. In the fourteenth century a Pope was pleased to address "His Magnificence the Emperor of Trebizond." The empire was also famous for the beauty of its princesses, who were its most valuable export and instrument of diplomacy; they were given in marriage to potential enemies, including Moslems. Shortly before the end of Byzantium the historian and diplomat Phrantzes came to Trebizond in style, with a large retinue of soldiers, nobles, monks, and musicians, looking for a wife for the last Constantine. The empire survived the fall of Constantinople, holding out until 1461. Unfortunately the Pope and Western monarchs from whom its last rulers sought aid failed to respond to the usual offer of beautiful princesses. The glamorous name lived on, however, in many a literary allusion, or illusion. Don Quixote imagined himself crowned "at least Emperor of Trebizond." Among the legends that sprang up was one making Napoleon a descendant of the Comneni. As late as the nineteenth century there were still pretenders to the crown of Trebizond.

The city was born as Trapezus, a colony of Sinope said to have been founded in 756 B.C., a century before Byzantium. The first major event in its recorded history was the arrival of Xenophon and the Ten Thousand, who hailed "The sea! The sea!" from the hills above it—back in the Greek world at last. During the Greek period it was outranked by the Black Sea ports of Sinope, Heraclea, and Amisus, but it was apparently a free and prosperous city. It retained the privileges of a free city under the Roman Empire because it had sided with Rome against Mithridates the Great. Hadrian built it an artificial harbor, remains of which were still visible in the last century. Although destroyed by the Goths in the third century, the city made a good start in Christian history by producing some martyrs for Diocletian. It developed the legend that St. Andrew had spread the gospel in it, and also found a conscientious patron in St. Eugenius, who repeatedly performed the miracles necessary to save it. The Emperor Justinian helped by rebuilding its walls and public buildings after a severe earthquake. Its walls were strong enough to repel the Seljuks after their victory at Manzikert.

During the Byzantine era Trebizond profited from the adversities of the empire, in particular the rise of the Arabs. When they won control of the Indian Ocean trade, it became the main port for the overland trade with Armenia, Persia, and points east. "All merchants frequent it," wrote an Arab geographer. "All Greek textiles, all the brocades that we receive, pass through it." The Mongols likewise contributed to its great wealth by destroying Baghdad, diverting more trade to it. European envoys en route to the East commented on the splendor of its palaces, churches, and monasteries. Scholars who studied in Persia and brought back the lore of the Orient helped to make it an intellectual center as well, known especially for its astronomers and mathematicians.

Nevertheless the political history of the Empire of Trebizond makes dismal reading. It was the familiar Byzantine story of palace revolutions and civil wars, abetted by a slavish but turbulent populace and frequently attended by trouble with their fellow Greeks in Constantinople. A Spanish envoy, Clavijo, noted the interesting custom in Trebizond of making the son Emperor during his father's lifetime in order to prevent strife. The usual result was that the son headed the opposition party or assassinated his father. To offset these murderous tendencies, the emperors cultivated the typical Byzantine taste for theology. John IV, the last of the parricides, was eulogized by eminent churchmen for the excellence of his opinions. It was his son who closed out the history of the empire, on a note of romantic tragedy. He surrendered Trebizond to Mohammed the Conqueror on a promise of good treatment, but two years later was put to death with his sons on some pretext. The widowed Empress Helene went down in legend by burying them with her own hands and then putting on sackcloth, to live out her life in a hovel.

Although the Conqueror was properly impressed by Trebizond, especially its church of the "Golden-Headed" Virgin, the city likewise became a hovel. Its leading families either fled or were moved out into Constantinople, leaving only a rabble. Its natural advantages, however, enabled it to fare better under Ottoman rule than most of the old cities. Until the time of Suleiman the Magnificent it was ruled by princes of the royal family; so Selim the Grim sallied forth from it to win an empire, and Suleiman himself was born in it. Little is heard of it in these centuries because the Black Sea was closed to European ships from 1475 to 1829, but its trade went on. At the beginning of the twentieth century the bulk of the transit trade between Europe and northern Persia still went by camel out of Trebizond. It was then a predominantly Greek city, and a busy one.

During World War I the city fell to the Russians, who occupied it for two years. Following the war its Greek inhabitants were expelled, and the remnants of their monuments largely destroyed or left to crumble. Its trade fell off. The Turks have been much more interested in building up the port of Samsun (ancient Amisus), which is connected by rail with the interior. Today there is little bustle in Trebizond, and little trace of its ancient magnificence. Medieval walls along the deep ravines that cut through the city recall its citadel; old bridges and the crumble in crooked alleys add picturesqueness. But its Turkish inhabitants seem like transients or aliens on the venerable site. The city has lost even its glamorous name, which has been corrupted into the ugly name of Trabzon. It would now make a kingdom only for Sancho Panza.

11. CAESAREA AND CAPPADOCIA

The land that became known as Cappadocia, in south-central Anatolia below Ankara, was an ancient melting pot that long remained among the backward regions of the interior, and is still chiefly a land of primitive peasantry. As early as 2000 B.C. colonies of Assyrian merchants settled among its nameless natives, as at Alishar and Kültepe. The Hittites took over control of it, Phrygians spilled into it, Medes and Persians set up fortresses in it, some Greeks found their way in. Strabo commented on the mixture of races that lived side by side in villages distinct in language and custom. A typical center then was the town of Comana. Formerly the capital of a Hittite kingdom (Kummanni), it was famous for its temple of Enyo or Anaitis, another manifestation of the Goddess Ma. In Strabo's time the temple owned more than six thousand serfs and was served by many sacred prostitutes of both sexes.

During the Hellenistic era Cappadocia became a kingdom, with a feudal nobility. One of its kings, Ariarathes V, made an earnest effort to Hellenize it. Related through marriage to the Attalids of Pergamum, he studied philosophy in Athens and became an Athenian citizen; as king he invited scholars to his court. He made little lasting progress, however, for Strabo reckoned that Cappadocia had only two real cities—Tyana and Mazaca. Its history after the reign of Ariarathes had not encouraged the growth of civilization.

The next Ariarathes was married to a sister of Mithridates the Great of Pontus, but his imperial brother-in-law had him assassinated in favor of a puppet. To combat Mithridates, the Romans then offered Cappadocia its freedom. Fearful of republican government, its nobles requested the blessing of another king; whereupon the Roman Senate picked out one of them, named Ariobarzanes. He remained loyal to Rome, but was not blessed. Mithridates drove him out of his kingdom; Sulla put him back on his throne, but when the Roman army left, Mithridates booted him out again; and so he went on serving as a football, King Tigranes of Armenia also taking a turn in booting him and ravaging his kingdom. The coinage of the unfortunate Ariobarzanes, which reflects his royal career from a smooth young man to a wrinkled old one with a hawklike Roman nose, might illustrate a discourse on the vanity of kingship. Finally Pompey rewarded him by not only restoring but extending his dominion, and presently by putting his son on the throne. A Roman chronicler wrote touchingly of the joy of the old man as he placed the diadem on his son, and of the sadness of the son. The son was wiser. He was a vassal king, ruling without an army and without money. Cicero described the miserable poverty of the next Ariobarzanes, who was eventually put to death by Cassius for refusing aid. Better times came when Mark Antony set up an able young man named Archelaus, who kept the throne for fifty years by the grace of Augustus. But with the death of Augustus he too came to an unhappy end. As an old man of eighty Archelaus was summoned to Rome to face a charge of treason, probably

trumped up, and died there of humiliation and exhaustion. Thereupon
Rome acquired the new province of Cappadocia.

Of its major cities, we have already encountered Tyana as the birthplace of Apollonius. A very old city on the road leading through the
Cilician Gates, it was once the capital of a Hittite kingdom, had a
Mound of Semiramis, knew King Midas (one of whose inscriptions has
been found on the site), and was still prosperous in Persian times.
Mazaca entered history later. Although ancient etymologists derived its
name from Meschus or Mosoch, the legendary ancestor of the Cappadocians, modern ones prefer the more apposite hybrid of the Avestan
maza, meaning large, and the Sanskrit suffix *aka*. It began to outstrip
Tyana when the Cappadocians kings made it their capital. It suffered
from their misfortunes, once having its inhabitants moved by King
Tigranes into his new capital, but it prospered with Archelaus. In gratitude to the Romans he rechristened it Caesarea, a name it still retains
in the Turkish form of Kayseri. It prospered not only as a main station
on the Eastern highway but as an emporium for the products of Cappadocia—the horses and cattle for which it was famous since Persian
times, and its mineral wealth of red ocher, alabaster, crystal, onyx, talc,
and especially the silver and lead of the Taurus Mountains. Hence
Caesarea became one of the major imperial mints. Though not hallowed
by legend or heroic exploit, it took on some aura from snow-capped Mt.
Argaeus, the highest mountain this side of Armenia, which towers above
it and dominates the region because it stands alone. As the only active
volcano in Asia Minor, it became the abode of the fire-breathing monster
Typhon.

At the site of the ancient town of Garsaura, an oasis midway between
Caesarea and Iconium, Archelaus built a new foundation, named Archel-
ais, that was to become an important city and survive to this day, as
Aksaray. (From a plane it looks like a salad bowl on the vast dusty spread
of the Anatolian plain.) But it was not until Byzantine times that Cappadocia made any serious claim to historic importance. Caesarea anticipated it by incurring the wrath of Julian the Apostate: it had become so
thoroughly Christian, in the process destroying great temples to gods
identified with Zeus and Apollo, that he expunged it from the list of
imperial cities. Now, suddenly and strangely, Cappadocia produced
several great men, the most eminent in its history—St. Basil and the
Gregories of Nyssa and Nazianzus, the Fathers of the Orthodox Church.
As theologians, they were not a type one would expect to emerge from a
region that had only a veneer of Hellenism. More likely types were the

many "Troglodyte" Christians who presumably at this time began to hole up in the cliffs and cones of the arid land, as at Ürgüp.

Under the Byzantine Empire, Cappadocia was important for its strategic highways. Justinian refortified Caesarea and stationed a garrison in it. At the small town of Mocesus, between it and Ancyra, he built up a strongly fortified city, endowing it with many churches, baths, and other public buildings, and renaming it Justinianopolis; today it is Kirshehir. Cappadocia returned such favors by bearing a number of leaders for the empire. Caesarea unfortunately gave it John the Cappadocian: a man of humble birth who rose to become Justinian's praetorian prefect, financed his great building and military enterprises, but extorted money by such arbitrary, unprincipled, and brutal means that he almost ruined the empire, largely nullifying the works on which Justinian prided himself; he ended in disgrace, forced to become a priest. The nobler Phocas family provided some great soldiers, including the Emperor Nicephorus Phocas, who recovered Cilicia, Cyprus, and Antioch from the Arabs; though its ambition also produced some rebels, one of whom had himself crowned at Caesarea. Finally Cappadocia gave birth to Romanus IV, the brave but unblessed emperor who met disaster at Manzikert.

Following his defeat by the Seljuks the whole region fell to them, at once and for good. The Turks merged with its ancient population. That Christianity disappeared from the land of the Cappadocian Fathers is perhaps less surprising than at first appears, for the kind of religiosity that produced all its cave dwellers might be attracted by the austerity of Islam. Another possible reason is that Caesarea, Archelais-Aksaray, and Justinianopolis-Kirshehir flourished under Seljuk rule. On a tomb in Kirshehir, however, a bey left a prophetic inscription: "Know that the world is a vain place." Under the Ottomans the land of Cappadocia relapsed into obscurity. It was no longer famous for its livestock, or for anything else to speak of. Caesarea remained an important city but a dreary one; the other cities dwindled into provincial towns. Their fate was not too melancholy, for none had a really glamorous past. Cappadocia had never known the Greek *polis*, never developed a rich culture.

Kayseri today is scarcely a haunting city. But the many peoples who have lived in and about it, under the shadow of majestic Mt. Argaeus, left enough remains to give it a venerable air. Sections of Roman and Byzantine wall run along behind the main streets or cut across alleys. A well-preserved Seljuk fortress in the center of the town is occupied by a market. Nearby an unusually large, colonnaded Seljuk mosque, with the usual handsomely sculptured gateway, is worthy of the high religious tradition of Cappadocia. The local museum, in the garden of the adjoining mosque school, has a small but representative collection, including good Hittite lions. It has almost no Hellenistic objects. Among the statuary is a weird, crude goddess, post-Hittite in execution, but no doubt pre-Hittite in ancestry—a deplorable object of worship, and a reminder of the low religious tradition of Cappadocia.

In all this the townspeople show little interest. As Caesarea was never important except as a commercial center, it is fitting that Kayseri is proud chiefly of its modern textile works.

12. SOME SUGGESTIONS FOR TOURISTS

There is no up-to-date Baedeker for Turkey, or likelihood of one. The conditions of travel have greatly altered in recent years. A site inaccessible today might be easily reached in a year or so; a town that has only a primitive hotel may soon have a new one, even with plumbing. I am therefore appending only some general information, with a passing bow to a few of the many ancient cities that I have had to neglect.

Outside the few major cities, there are almost no first-class hotels or restaurants in Turkey, and no such amenities as bars or cafés. In the smaller cities and the towns the traveler will do well to ask for the *en yeni* hotel—the newest—but he must not then expect modern comforts or conveniences, or ever a private bath. Often he will put up in a bare, un- carpeted room furnished only with a bed, a chair, a few clothes hooks— and always a pair of slippers. His lodging will be very inexpensive, how- ever, and the service as friendly as simple. It is likely to be pleasanter than a really new hotel. In more elegant rooms he may be struck by a dirty, empty water pitcher or an electric light that doesn't work. The Turks are generally courteous but inefficient hotelkeepers. For the rest, the traveler may count on eating well, if in not-too-clean restaurants. He may be charmed by eager special attentions, such as the immediate provision of a dozen toothpicks on a large plate. Coming from the big cities, with their more European ways, he may appreciate an almost in- variable eagerness to please that is almost never motivated by a thought of tips. If he pines for such luxuries as a modern bathroom, he may con- sole himself by reading what travelers had to put up with under the Ottoman regime. He can always return to the really modern, expensive hotels in Istanbul, Ankara, and Bursa.

Most cities are now connected by buses, but in the provinces these are often ancient, crowded, and uncomfortable. One may travel much more rapidly and agreeably by an admirable Turkish invention, the *dolmush:* a taxicab with a fixed destination that waits until it is filled up (*dolmush*) with passengers, each of whom pays a fixed, modest rate. Still pleasanter is the Turkish train. It is the European compartment type, with passengers leaning out of windows every one of which bears the legend that leaning out is prohibited. Although it is learning to run on time, it remains an informal kind of conveyance that mostly crawls along, dawdles at stations, stops at small villages where no efficient railroad would permit it to, and so may irritate foreigners in a hurry to reach their destination, but delight those who wish to see the countryside. (A fast new motor train cut several hours from the Istanbul-Ankara trip and could cut another—except that the train stops at every village station for the stationmaster to sign the engineer's book, or vice versa. I guessed the reason at once: this was the "control" system, to make sure that the engineer kept on schedule.) And the passing scenery—unmodernized, unadorned by billboards, undefiled by industry—is always fascinating, often spectacular.

Best of all is the Turkish steamer. In Istanbul agile little ferries ply the Bosphorus with surprising speed and dependability. Relatively new ships make overnight trips to Izmir, fast trips up the Black Sea. But for the unhurried and the unfastidious the most enjoyable means of travel is the coastal steamers—old, slow boats, of the vintage of Joseph Conrad, far from elegant in their accommodations, but comfortable enough and staffed by the friendliest of officers. They have a lively, colorful steerage life on their lower decks, which are usually crowded with peasants and their boxes, sleeping rugs, and livestock. Stops at the many ports of call are animated by the primitive loading facilities and the absence of piers. The steamers take on cargo, cattle, and passengers from lighters and bobbing rowboats, in a noisy, cheerful, scrambling confusion. As the procedure usually takes several hours, one has time to go ashore and stroll around the town. This is almost always the site of an ancient city.

One popular trip is along the Black Sea coast from Istanbul to Hopa. Here the scenery is lush as well as spectacular because of heavy rainfall. The mountains falling steeply to the coast are thickly wooded and much softer in contour than the hills along the western coast; their forests and valleys make a rich study in green, ranging from the darkest to the most vivid shades. Although the ports of call vary on different trips, depending on cargo, they usually include Inebolu (Abonutichus), Samsun (Amisus), Ordu (Cotyora), Giresun (Cerasus-Kerasunt), Trabzon (Trapezus-Trebizond), and Rize. Inebolu, in former Paphlagonia, was the main inlet through which supplies were smuggled to Ataturk during the Revolution, from there being carried over the mountains on the backs of peasants. Samsun is now booming as the major Turkish port on the coast, and losing whatever character or sign of ancient splendor it may have had, but the

vicinity remains venerable. Large *hüyüks* standing out on the hills behind it go back to Hittite times, and on the rich plains extending up the
coast dwelt the legendary Amazons. One also has to bring back memories
in order to glamourize Giresun-Cerasus, another commonplace town in a
beautiful setting. Ancient foundations in the medieval walls on what was
once its acropolis may recall that this town entertained Xenophon and
the Ten Thousand, and that from here the Roman general Lucullus
brought the first cherries to Europe. After Trabzon, already described,
the Greek world fades out. Rize, in the land of the Colchians, is a prosperous tea-growing center with no antiquities. At the village of Hopa, the
end of the journey, there is nothing to contemplate but the smokestacks of
Batum, dimly visible in the distance. Here as elsewhere the tough Turk
seems quite unperturbed by the knowledge that Soviet Russia is in his
backyard.

A less spectacular but more enchanting voyage for lovers of antique
lands is by the slow boat to Izmir—an ancient little steamer that chugs
across the Sea of Marmora to Gelibolu (Callipolis-Gallipoli), down the
Dardanelles, around the Troad, along Sappho's island of Lesbos, and in
and out along the coast of Aeolia to the Gulf of Izmir, putting in at a
dozen small towns and villages. The Dardanelles is less beautiful than the
Bosphorus but as rich in historic association. Along it are the sites of
ancient Lampsacus, Abydus, and Sestus, near which Xerxes built his
bridge; beyond Chanakkale and its medieval castles is the mound of
Dardanus, and inland the mound of Troy. (The officer on duty on the
bridge is always pleased to help one spot these sites on the mariner's
chart.) The steamer makes a call at Bozjaada, formerly the island of Tenedos, where an old castle may remind one that the Achaeans hid here
when they sent the Wooden Horse to Troy. Assus (modern Behram), near
the westernmost tip of the Troad, has no Homeric associations but offers
some of the oldest Greek ruins in Asia Minor; here Aristotle first set up
school and found a wife. Along the southern coast of the Troad memories
of Homer return as Mt. Ida begins to loom up and the steamer calls at
villages on or near the site of ancient Gargara, Antandrus, and Adramyt-
tium, the last on a plain that may have been the plain of Thebe raided
by Achilles.

Mt. Ida is still visible as the steamer rounds the gulf and calls at
Ayvalik, an olive-oil center, but unhappily this arouses thoughts of a
much less romantic war. The crumbling walls, churches, and monasteries
in and about it belonged to a thriving city that in the last century was
wholly Greek. Today, as a wholly Turkish one, it is brightly painted but
forgettable. Upon leaving it the streamer passes by the much more

interesting-looking city of Mytilene on the island of Lesbos; it makes no stop because this still belongs to Greece. Turkish and Greek fishing boats are careful to stay on their own sides of the channel, to which the steamer as carefully keeps. Its very friendly officers may give signs of tension.

Such unpleasantness detracts somewhat from the most memorable of the coastal tours, from Istanbul to Iskenderun. The steamer sails close to the islands of Chios, Samos, and Cos, but again without stopping; these islands also belong to Greece. One can get only a passing binocular view of their old cities, with here and there a castle, a monastery, a suggestion of old temple; only stare at the twin hills through which the men of Samos astounded Herodotus and the Greek world by cutting a mile-long tunnel (still extant). From a greater distance one can make out Patmos, the asylum of St. John of Revelation, and the gleaming walls and towers of Rhodes. The last of the Greek islands, Megiste or Castellorizo, adds a dismal footnote. It looks forbidding, almost barren of vegetation; yet men fought over this poor bit of land in the last world war. It had nuisance value as a possible submarine base.

But this is only a footnote. Again one has steamed down the Sea of Marmora and the Dardanelles, past Troy; and now, on a calm blue sea, under a bright blue sky, one sails lazily along the entire western coast of Asia Minor—an enchantingly beautiful country, and an outline of ancient history. A day's stopover in Izmir makes it possible to explore old Smyrna, or to take a side trip to Ephesus or Pergamum. Leaving Izmir, the steamer skirts the coast of Ionia, sails through the narrow straits between Samos and Mt. Mycale, seat of the Pan-Ionium, and passes by the mouth of the Maeander. With this one leaves Ionia for the rugged coast of Caria, a land of less memorable cities until the steamer enters the harbor of Bodrum-Halicarnassus, the birthplace of Herodotus. And so it goes: along the mountainous Lycian coast, past the mouth of the Xanthus, to Antalya (Attaleia); along the Pamphylian plain, backed by mountains with majestic contours, to Alanya and its towering Seljuk citadel; around the rocky coast of Cilicia Aspera to the roadstead of Mersin, from which the rich Cilician plain begins to belly out toward the Taurus Mountains and the Cilician Gates; along the plain, past Tarsus and Adana, to Iskenderun (Alexandretta), near which Alexander won his momentous victory over the Emperor Darius. From here one may take a *dolmush* over the mountain, through another historic pass, to Antakya—Antioch.

Of the ports of call, Halicarnassus-Bodrum offers perhaps the most food for reflection, if not very wholesome food. A beautiful Doric temple with a long colonnade, described by travelers in the nineteenth century, is no more. The mausoleum that was one of the Seven Wonders of the World disappeared long ago. Most of it went into a castle in the harbor, built by the Knights of Rhodes in the early fourteenth century. A Renaissance chronicler told of how the Knights found it still standing: "which having admired closely, and after having considered in their imagination the singularity of the work, at last they pulled down, cracked, and broke up to use as they had done the rest"—the Doric and Roman stone they also worked into their castle. On many marbles they not only sculptured coats of arms but inscribed prayers, especially toward the year 1500, when the Ottomans were advancing. One would like to think that with God's help, behind battlements made of a Seventh Wonder, they put up a heroic resistance; but actually they offered none to Suleiman the Magnificent. Their castle was so strongly built that it served as a Turkish fortress until well into the last century, and survived bombardment by the French after World War I. (It incidentally provided an illustration of the Ottoman mentality: when a soldier drowned in one of its cisterns, the garrison stopped using the cistern rather than go to the trouble of fishing him out.) It is today still about as fine an old castle as one can hope to find.

It was from Marmaris, a port farther along, that Suleiman sailed to make his first real conquest, the island of Rhodes. In the Greek world Marmaris was Physcus, a small town famous for nothing; and its situation is so magnificent that one must wonder why. It lies at the end of a fiord, a mountain-shadowed basin large enough to hold a modern fleet—as it has. But this travelogue could go on indefinitely, and I shall stop off at Antalya, a final example of the historical riches of regions that a tourist may never have heard of. Lying on a low cliff lined with ancient walls, Antalya is a city of considerable interest whose antiquities include one of the countless works of the Emperor Hadrian, a triple-arched gateway; but chiefly it serves as a convenient center for expeditions to more interesting sites nearby: Side, a little-known city, but a great one in its day; Perge, better known because St. Paul preached in it; Silleum, which has extensive Hellenistic ruins; Aspendus, with its best-preserved of great Roman theaters; and most spectacular—if one is willing to climb a mountain—Termessus, a stronghold that was able to hold off Alexander the Great. Antalya is today the only town of any size in this region.

I conclude as informally with an anecdote that may sum up both the difficulties and the delights of travel in Turkey, and that also brings me back to Dinar, where—a long time ago—I started. My wife and I were on a train (an hour late) scheduled to reach in the evening a junction some ten miles from Dinar. The conductor looked in our compartment from time to time with a worried air, and presently brought a French-speaking schoolteacher to make clear his concern: there was no hotel at the junction, no village even, and no train or bus from there to Dinar that evening. Other passengers came in to discuss the problem. Upon arrival at the junction, they all went into consultation with the engineer and the stationmaster, who managed after considerable trouble and delay to put through a telephone call to Dinar, requesting a taxi to come for us. The train waited until the taxi arrived. The whole group then pleaded with the driver to reduce the very reasonable fare he proposed to charge, reminding him that we were American guests. He not only agreed but made further amends. After driving us to a hotel in Dinar, he waited to take us to a restaurant, and again waited here to drive us back, refusing to accept payment. The hotel was typically primitive, as typically called a *Palas*. Something about our plain room—no doubt something that didn't work—reminded me of the hotel in Alanya where we had arrived at night a week before. We had trouble getting into this one because no one was on duty. At length the sleepy proprietor showed up, and led us down a dim corridor adorned with an electric meter. The meter was crowned by a nest on which three baby swallows sat in a row, trying to look like Walt Disney birds.

For some reason those baby swallows have haunted me—I suppose as symbols of the Turkish lunatic asylum. But I think of them fondly, as I do of the Turks. They might almost do as symbols of the blessed aspect of the miracle and mystery of all life, the simplicities that help to reconcile us to the boredom and the horror of history, and to realize the glory.

Index

Set in Linotype Caledonia
Format by Robert Cheney
Manufactured by The Haddon Craftsmen, Inc.
Published by HARPER & BROTHERS, *New York.*